mylabschool™
Where the classroom comes to life!

D1398475

From watching actual classroom video footage of teachers ar[...] building standards-based lessons and web-based portfolios . . . from a robu[...] "What Every Teacher Should Know About" series to complete instruction on writing an effective research paper . . . **MyLabSchool** brings together an amazing collection of resources for future teachers. This website gives you a wealth of videos, print and simulated cases, career advice, and much more.

Use **MyLabSchool** with this Allyn and Bacon Education text, and you will have everything you need to succeed in your course. Assignment IDs have also been incorporated into many Allyn and Bacon Education texts to link to the online material in **MyLabSchool** . . . connecting the teachers of tomorrow to the information they need today.

VISIT www.mylabschool.com **to learn more about this invaluable resource and Take a Tour!**

Here's what you'll find in mylabschool™
Where the classroom comes to life!

VideoLab ▶

Access hundreds of video clips of actual classroom situations from a variety of grade levels and school settings. These 3- to 5-minute closed-captioned video clips illustrate real teacher–student interaction, and are organized both topically *and* by discipline. Students can test their knowledge of classroom concepts with integrated observation questions.

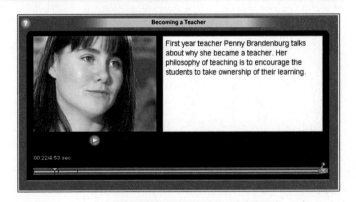

◀ Lesson & Portfolio Builder

This feature enables students to create, maintain, update, and share online portfolios and standards-based lesson plans. The Lesson Planner walks students, step-by-step, through the process of creating a complete lesson plan, including verifiable objectives, assessments, and related state standards. Upon completion, the lesson plan can be printed, saved, e-mailed, or uploaded to a website.

Here's what you'll find in (mylabschool™

Where the classroom comes to life!

Simulations ▶

This area of MyLabSchool contains interactive tools designed to better prepare future teachers to provide an appropriate education to students with special needs. To achieve this goal, the IRIS (IDEA and Research for Inclusive Settings) Center at Vanderbilt University has created course enhancement materials. These resources include online interactive modules, case study units, information briefs, student activities, an online dictionary, and a searchable directory of disability-related web sites.

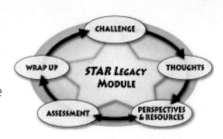

◀ Resource Library

MyLabSchool includes a collection of PDF files on crucial and timely topics within education. Each topic is applicable to any education class, and these documents are ideal resources to prepare students for the challenges they will face in the classroom. This resource can be used to reinforce a central topic of the course, or to enhance coverage of a topic you need to explore in more depth.

Research Navigator ▶

This comprehensive research tool gives users access to four exclusive databases of authoritative and reliable source material. It offers a comprehensive, step-by-step walk-through of the research process. In addition, students can view sample research papers and consult guidelines on how to prepare endnotes and bibliographies. The latest release also features a new bibliography-maker program—AutoCite.

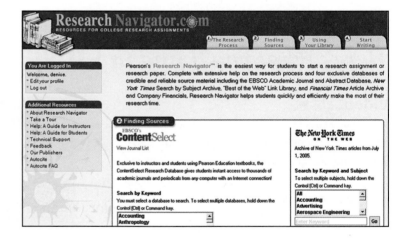

◀ Case Archive

This collection of print and simulated cases can be easily accessed by topic and subject area, and can be integrated into your course. The cases are drawn from Allyn & Bacon's best-selling books, and represent the complete range of disciplines and student ages. It's an ideal way to consider and react to real classroom scenarios. The possibilities for using these high-quality cases within the course are endless.

14TH EDITION

FOUNDATIONS OF AMERICAN EDUCATION

Perspectives on Education in a Changing World

James A. Johnson
Northern Illinois University

Diann Musial
Northern Illinois University

Gene E. Hall
University of Nevada, Las Vegas

Donna M. Gollnick
National Council for the Accreditation of Teacher Education

Victor L. Dupuis
Pennsylvania State University

PEARSON

Boston • New York • San Francisco
Mexico City • Montreal • Toronto • London • Madrid • Munich • Paris
Hong Kong • Singapore • Tokyo • Cape Town • Sydney

Executive Editor and Publisher: *Stephen D. Dragin*
Editorial Assistant: *Katie Heimsoth*
Development Editor: *Shannon Steed*
Marketing Manager: *Weslie Sellinger*
Production Editor: *Joe Sweeney*
Editorial-Production Service: *Omegatype Typography, Inc.*
Electronic Composition: *Omegatype Typography, Inc.*
Composition and Prepress Buyer: *Linda Cox*
Manufacturing Buyer: *Megan Cochran*
Interior Design: *Roy Neuhaus*
Photo Research: *Katie Cebile*
Cover Design: *Kristina Mose-Libon*

For related titles and support materials, visit our online catalog at www.ablongman.com.

Copyright © 2008, 2005, 2002, 1999, 1996, 1994, 1991, 1988, 1985, 1982, 1979, 1976, 1973, 1969 by Pearson Education, Inc.

All rights reserved. No part of the material protected by this copyright notice may be reproduced or utilized in any form or by any means, electronic or mechanical, including photocopying, recording, or by any information storage and retrieval system, without written permission from the copyright owner.

To obtain permission(s) to use material from this work, please submit a written request to Allyn and Bacon, Permissions Department, 75 Arlington Street, Boston, MA 02116 or fax your request to 617-848-7320.

Between the time Website information is gathered and then published, it is not unusual for some sites to have closed. Also, the transcription of URLs can result in typographical errors. The publisher would appreciate notification where these errors occur so that they may be corrected in subsequent editions.

Library of Congress Cataloging-in-Publication Data

Foundations of American education : perspectives on education in a changing world / James A. Johnson . . . [et al.].—
    14th ed.
      p. cm.
     ISBN 0-205-51469-3
      1. Education—Study and teaching—United States. 2. Education—United States.
   3. Educational sociology—United States. 4. Teaching—Vocational guidance—United States.
   I. Johnson, James Allen.

   LB17.I59 2008
   370.973—dc22

                          2006048765

Printed in the United States of America

10 9 8 7 6 5 4 3 2 1   VHP 11 10 09 08 07 06

Photo credits appear on page 514, which constitutes a continuation of the copyright page.

Contents

List of Features   xix

Preface   xxi

PART I
PROFESSIONAL PERSPECTIVES ON EDUCATION
IN A CHANGING WORLD   1

1   Teaching in a Changing World   2

Case Study: Heroes Every One   3

Learning Outcomes   4

Today's Teachers   5
The Importance of Teachers to Society   6
The Public View of Teachers and Schools   6
Who Teaches?   9
    Profile of U.S. Teachers 10   •   Remaining in the Profession 10
Teachers Needed   11
    Teacher Supply 11   •   Teacher Demand 12
GLOBAL PERSPECTIVES: Teaching Chinese to American Students   17

Teaching as a Profession   17
Perspectives on Professional Practice   17
    Professional Knowledge 17   •   Professional Skills 18   •   Standards 19   •
    No Child Left Behind 19
PROFESSIONAL DILEMMA: Who Is Cheating Now?   20
Quality Assurance   21
    Accreditation 21   •   Licensure 22   •   Advanced Certification 24   •   NBPTS 24
Professional Responsibilities   24
    Developing Professional Commitments and Dispositions 25   •   Educator Code of Ethics 25
Reflecting on One's Practice   25
    Systematic Observation and Journaling 26   •   Informal Note-Taking 26   •
    Analysis of Practice and Reflection 26   •   Reflective Journaling 26   •
    Folio/Portfolio Development   27

RELEVANT RESEARCH: Teachers' Perspectives on Most Rewarding Aspects of Their Work   29

Challenges Affecting Teachers   29
Salaries in a Changing World 29
    Salary Differences 31   •   Additional Benefits 31   •   Recruitment Incentives 32
Working Conditions 32
TEACHER PERSPECTIVES: Should Districts Offer Signing Bonuses to Attract New Teachers?   33

Beginning and Continuing a Teaching Career   35
Becoming Licensed 35
    Licensure Tests 35   •   Alternative Licensure 35
Searching for a Teaching Position 36
Remaining a Teacher 36
    Renewal of Licenses 37

Summary 37   •   Discussion Questions 38   •   School-Based Observations 38   •   Portfolio Development 38   •   Preparing for Certification: *The Praxis Series*™ **38   •   Websites 39   •   Further Reading 39**

PART II
SOCIOLOGICAL FOUNDATIONS OF EDUCATION   41

2 Diversity in Society   42

Case Study: Mother Tongue: Area Schools Find Themselves Teaching English to Thousands of Immigrant Children   43

Learning Outcomes   44

Culture and Society   45
Characteristics of Culture 46
Dominant Culture 47
Group Identity 47
Acceptance of Diverse Groups 48
    Assimilation 49   •   Pluralism 49   •   Cultural Choice 50

Socioeconomic Status   51
Social Stratification 51
Class Structure 52
Poverty 53

Race and Ethnicity   54
Race 55
Ethnicity 55
RELEVANT RESEARCH: ESL Programs in White Schools   56

Language   58
Language Diversity 58
Dialectal Diversity 59
TEACHER PERSPECTIVES: Should All Students Be Bilingual?   60

Gender   62
Differences between Females and Males 62
GLOBAL PERSPECTIVES: Women's Political Participation   63
Title IX 64

Sexual Orientation 64

Exceptionalities 65

Inclusion 66

Disproportionate Placements 67

PROFESSIONAL DILEMMA: Inclusion of Students with Disabilities 68

Religion 68

Summary 70 • Discussion Questions 72 • School-Based Observations 72 • Portfolio Development 72 • Preparing for Certification: The Praxis PLT Test and Diversity 72 • Websites 73 • Further Reading 73

3 Sociological Perspectives on Students and Families 74

Case Study: Culture Clash 75

Learning Outcomes 76

Today's Families 77

Parenting 77

PROFESSIONAL DILEMMA: What If He Has Two Mommies? 78

Children Alone 78

Where Students Live 80

Rural Communities 80

Suburban Communities 81

Urban Communities 81

RELEVANT RESEARCH: Race in a White School 82

Challenges of Childhood and Youth 83

Homelessness 84

Abuse 85

Harassment and Bullying 86

Sexuality 87

Teenage Pregnancy 88

TEACHER PERSPECTIVES: Is Retention Better Than Social Promotion for Students? 89

Dropping Out 90

Substance Use 92

Violence 93

Economic Realities 94

Power in Society 95

Ethnocentrism 96

Prejudice 96

Discrimination 97

Racism 97

GLOBAL PERSPECTIVES: Coming to Justice 99

Sexism and Other Isms 99

Resiliency 100

Summary 100 • Discussion Questions 102 • School-Based Observations 102 • Portfolio Development 102 • Preparing for Certification: Student Experiences and Democracy 102 • Websites 103 • Further Reading 103

4 Multicultural Perspectives in Education   104

Case Study: Anytown Fires Up Teens to Foster Acceptance   105

Learning Outcomes   106

Roles of Schools   107
Reproduction   108
Reconstructionism   108

Purposes of Schools   109
Citizenship   109
Workforce Readiness   110
Academic Achievement   110
Social Development   111
Cultural Transmission   111

Values in Schools   112
Whose Values?   112
GLOBAL PERSPECTIVES: Universal Values   113

Multicultural Education   114
Undergirding Tenets   114
    Diversity 115
TEACHER PERSPECTIVES: Is School the Best Place to Teach Tolerance?   116
    Social Justice 118   •   Equality 118
Culturally Relevant Teaching   120
    Building on Cultural Context 120   •   Centering the Cultures
    of Students 122   •   Validating Student Voices 122

Challenges in Multicultural Classrooms   123
Gender-Sensitive Education   124
RELEVANT RESEARCH: Boys and Girls in Performance-Based Science Classrooms   125
Education for Language Diversity   126
PROFESSIONAL DILEMMA: Communicating with Parents of English Language Learners   128

Teachers as Social Activists   129
Thinking Critically   129
Modeling Equity in the Classroom   129
Making Schools Democratic   130
Teaching for Social Justice   131
GLOBAL PERSPECTIVES: Social Justice in the Canadian Context   132

Summary 133   •   Discussion Questions 134   •   School-Based Observations 134   •   Portfolio Development 134   •   Preparing for Certification: Teaching for Equality 134   •   Websites 135   •   Further Reading 135

5 Organizing and Paying for American Education in a Changing World   138

Case Study: Push Is on for Magnet School at Jefferson to Attract Students   139

Learning Outcomes   140

The Structure of the American Education System   141

The Organization of Schools   142

School-Based Personnel   143

Principals 143   •   Assistant Principals 143   •   Department Heads and
Team Leaders 144   •   Teachers 144   •   School Support Staff 145

RELEVANT RESEARCH: Does Class Size Make a Difference?   145

The School Organization Chart 146   •   When to Talk to Whom 146

Organization of the School District   147

Local Board of Education 147   •   Powers and Duties of School Boards 147   •
Superintendent of Schools 148   •   The Critical Importance of Leadership 148   •
Central Office Staff 148

Organization of Education at the State Level   149

State Board of Education   150

State Board Membership 150   •   Chief State School Officer 150   •
State Department of Education 151   •   State Legislature 152

The Federal Government's Role in Education   152

Leadership 153   •   The U.S. Department of Education 154   •   Educational Programs
Operated by the Federal Government 154   •   No Child Left Behind (NCLB) 155   •
Impact of NCLB 156

Other Types of Education Agencies   157

Intermediate Units 157

School Choice: Increasing Options along with Uncertain Outcomes   157

Magnet Schools 157   •   Charter Schools 158   •   Year-Round Schools 158   •
Vouchers 159   •   Private, Parochial, and Independent Schools 159   •
Home Schooling 161

Politics in Education   161

TEACHER PERSPECTIVES: Should the School Year Be Longer?   162

Politics: Neither Positive nor Negative 164   •   Issue: Local Control versus Federalism 164

PROFESSIONAL DILEMMA: What Is the Appropriate Role for Teachers When
the Politics Get Rough?   165

**Financing Education: Sources of Funds and the Move
from Equity to Adequacy   166**

A System of Taxation and Support for Schools   166

Property Taxes and Local Revenue 167   •   State Sources of Revenue and Aid 169   •
Recent Challenges to School Finance within the States 169   •
Entrepreneurial Efforts to Fund Education 171

Education Spending   172

State Aid 172   •   General State Aid: Equality of Opportunity 173   •   Federal Aid 174

Accountability   175

Roots of Accountability 175   •   The Importance of Teacher Accountability 175   •
Rewards for Being Accountable 175   •   Rewarding Teachers and Principals 175   •
School and School District Report Cards 175

GLOBAL PERSPECTIVES: International Comparisons: Expenditures per Student as an Indicator   176
   Issue: Taxpayer Revolt   176

Summary 176 • Discussion Questions 178 • School-Based Observations 178 • Portfolio Development 178 • Preparing for Certification: School Organization and Choice 178 • Websites 179 • Further Reading 179

6 Legal Perspectives of Education   180

Case Study: The Forum: How One School District Found Religion   181

Learning Outcomes   182

Legal Aspects of Education   183
Legal Provisions for Education: The U.S. Constitution   184
   Tenth Amendment 184 • First Amendment 184 • Fourteenth Amendment 185
Church and State   185
   Public Funds and Religious Education 185 • Transportation for Students of Church Schools 186 • The *Lemon* Test: Excessive Entanglement 187 • Religious Activities in Public Schools 188
RELEVANT RESEARCH: Changing Strategies: Supporting/Challenging Vouchers   189
   Evolution versus Intelligent Design 190
Segregation and Desegregation   193
PROFESSIONAL DILEMMA: Should Science Teachers Be Required to Include Religion When Teaching about Evolution?   194
   "Separate but Equal": No Longer Equal 194 • Release from Court Orders 195 • Achieving Integration in Today's Diverse Society 196
Equal Opportunity   197
   Affirmative Action 198 • Opportunities for Students with Disabilities 198 • AIDS as a Disability 199

Teachers' Rights and Responsibilities   199
Conditions of Employment   200
   Teacher Certification and Licensure 201 • Teacher Employment Contracts 201 • Teacher Tenure 201 • Discrimination 205 • Right to Bargain Collectively 205
GLOBAL PERSPECTIVES: Legal Aspects of Education in Other Countries   206
   Right to Strike 206
Academic Freedom   207
   Academic Freedom for Elementary and Secondary Teachers 208 • Book Banning and Censorship 208 • Family Rights and Privacy Act 209
Teacher Responsibilities and Liabilities   210
   Educational Malpractice 210 • Negligent Chemistry Teacher 211 • Field Trip Negligence 211 • Governmental Immunity from Liability 211 • Liability Insurance 212

Students' Rights and Responsibilities   212
Students' Rights as Citizens   214
   Students' Right to an Education 214 • Students' Right to Sue 214 • Students' Right to Due Process 215
Students' Rights and Responsibilities in School   217
   Dress Codes and Grooming 217 • Corporal Punishment 217
TEACHER PERSPECTIVES: Would You Support the Use of Corporal Punishment in Your School?   218
   Sex Discrimination 218 • Marriage and Pregnancy 219 • Child Abuse and Neglect 220 • Student Publications 220 • Rights of Students with Disabilities 221 • Student and Locker Searches 222 • Peer Sexual Harassment 222

Summary 223 • Discussion Questions 224 • School-Based Observations 224 • Portfolio Development 224 • Preparing for Certification: Teachers' and Students' Rights 224 • Websites 225 • Further Reading 225

7 The Early History of Education in a Changing World   228

Case Study: Teaching Patriotism—With Conviction   229

Learning Outcomes   230

The Beginnings of Education (to 476 CE)   231
Non-Western Education   231
   Hindu Education 231   •   Hebrew Education 231
GLOBAL PERSPECTIVES: Educational Ideas Borrowed from around the World   232
   Chinese Education 232   •   Egyptian Education 233
Western Education   233
   Socrates 233   •   Plato 234   •   Aristotle 234   •   Roman Schools 234   •   Quintilian 234

Education in the Middle Ages (476–1300)   235
The Dark Ages (400–1000)   235
   Charlemagne 235   •   Alcuin 235
The Revival of Learning   236
   Thomas Aquinas 236   •   Medieval Universities 236

Education in Transition (1300–1700)   236
The Renaissance   237
   Vittorino da Feltre 237   •   Erasmus 237
The Reformation   237
   Luther 237   •   Ignatius of Loyola 238   •   Comenius 238   •   Locke 238

Educational Awakening (1700)   238
The Age of Reason   238
TEACHER PERSPECTIVES: Is "Abstinence-Only" the Best Sex Education Policy
for Schools to Implement?   239
   Descartes and Voltaire 240   •   Frederick the Great 241
The Emergence of Common Man   241
   Rousseau 241   •   Pestalozzi 241   •   Herbart 242   •   Froebel 242

Evolving Perspectives of Education in Our Developing Nation   242
Colonial Education   242
   Southern Colonies 242   •   Middle Colonies 243   •   Northern Colonies 243   •   Early School
   Laws 243   •   Types of Colonial Schools 244   •   Early American Colleges 244
The Struggle for Universal Elementary Education   244
   Monitorial Schools 244   •   Horace Mann 244   •   Henry Barnard 245   •
   Reflection on Early U.S. Elementary Education 245
The Need for Secondary Schools   245
   American Academy 245
GLOBAL PERSPECTIVES: Educational Transplantation from Europe   246
   High School 246   •   Junior High/Middle School 246
RELEVANT RESEARCH: Critiquing Historical Sources   247
The Evolution of Teaching Materials   247
   The Hornbook 247   •   The New England Primer 248   •   Blue-Backed Speller 250   •
   Teaching Materials in an Early School 251   •   Slates 251   •   McGuffey's Readers 251

Meager Early Education for Diverse Populations   251
Education of African Americans   252
   Early Church Efforts to Educate African Americans 252   •   Early Schools for African American
   Children 253   •   Frederick Douglass 253   •   John Chavis 253   •   Prudence Crandall 253   •
   Booker T. Washington 254   •   Early African American Colleges 254

Asian American Education 254
Hispanic American Education 255
Education of Women 255
    Emma Willard 255
GLOBAL PERSPECTIVES: Maria Montessori 256
    Ella Flagg Young 257 • Mary McLeod Bethune 257 • The Nineteenth Amendment 257
PROFESSIONAL DILEMMA: How Can the Busy Teacher Keep Up with Historical
and Contemporary Research? 258

Private Education in America 258
The Right of Private Schools to Exist 258
Parochial Schools 259
The Important Role of Private Education in America 259

**Summary 260 • Discussion Questions 262 • School-
Based Observations 262 • Portfolio Development 262 •
Preparing for Certification: The Evolution of U.S. Schools 262 •
Websites 263 • Further Reading 263**

8   Historical Perspectives of Education   264

Case Study: Casualties of Segregation Receive Honorary Diplomas 265

Learning Outcomes 266

More Students and Bigger Schools 266
Enrollment Growth 266
Need for More Schools 267
Need for More Teachers 267
School District Consolidation 267
Growth of Busing 267
Bigger School Budgets 268
Rapid Curricular Growth and Changes 268
Growth of Special Education Programs 268
RELEVANT RESEARCH: What Have We Learned about Homework and Students with Disabilities? 269

The Development of the Teaching Profession 270
Increasing Federal Involvement 270
    GI Bill 270 • National Science Foundation 271 • Categorical Federal Aid 271 •
    The Struggle for Equal Educational Opportunity 271 • No Child Left Behind (NCLB) 271
The Professionalization of Teaching 272
Continued Importance of Private Schools 272
Home Schooling 272
Continuing/Adult Education 273
Evolution of Educational Testing 274

Changing Aims of Education 274
Committee of Ten 275
Seven Cardinal Principles 275
The Eight-Year Study 275
"Purposes of Education in American Democracy" 276
"Education for All American Youth" 276
"Imperative Needs of Youth" 276
TEACHER PERSPECTIVES: Should High Schools Prepare All Students for College? 277

Preparation of Teachers 278
Colonial Teachers 278

GLOBAL PERSPECTIVES: European Beginnings of Teacher Training 279
Teachers as Indentured Servants 279
Teaching Apprenticeships 280
Teacher Training in Academies 280
Normal Schools 281
State Teachers' Colleges 281
Changes in Mid-Twentieth Century Teacher Education 282

Recent Trends in Education 283
New Emphases in Education 283
   Analysis of Teaching 283 • Teacher Effectiveness 284 • Study of the Learning Process 284
PROFESSIONAL DILEMMA: Can a Knowledge of History Help to Improve Multicultural Education? 285
GLOBAL PERSPECTIVES: Jean Piaget 286
   B. F. Skinner 286
Educational Critics 286
Changing Public Perspectives on Education 287
Major Educational Events of the Past Century 287

Summary 287 • Discussion Questions 289 • School-Based Observations 289 • Portfolio Development 289 • Preparing for Certification: Research and Theories of Learning 289 • Websites 290 • Further Reading 290

PART V
PHILOSOPHICAL FOUNDATIONS OF EDUCATION   291

9 Philosophy: Reflections on the Essence of Education   292

Case Study: Teacher Resigns over Plagiarism Fight   293

Learning Outcomes   294

Structure and Methodology of Philosophy   295
The Branches of Philosophy 295
   Metaphysics 295 • Epistemology 295 • Axiology 296
Thinking as a Philosopher 296
   Analytic Ways of Thinking in Philosophy 296 • Prophetic Ways of Thinking in Philosophy 299
PROFESSIONAL DILEMMA: Should Morals and Values Be Taught in Public Schools? 300

Schools of Philosophy and Their Influence on Education   302
Idealism 302
   Educational Implications of Idealism 302 • Plato and Socrates 302 • Immanuel Kant 303 •
   Jane Roland Martin 303
RELEVANT RESEARCH: Using Socratic Dialogue to Enhance Reflective Learning 304
Realism 304
   Educational Implications of Realism 304 • Aristotle 305 • John Locke 306 •
   Alfred North Whitehead 306
Pragmatism 306
   Educational Implications of Pragmatism 306 • Charles Sanders Pierce 307 •
   John Dewey 307 • Richard Rorty 307
Existentialism 308
   Educational Implications of Existentialism 308 • Jean-Paul Sartre 309 • Friedrich
   Nietzsche 309 • Maxine Greene 309
Eastern Ways of Knowing 309

TEACHER PERSPECTIVES: Does Prepping for High-Stakes Tests Interfere with Teaching? 310
Indian Thought 312 • Chinese Thought 312 • Japanese Thought 312
GLOBAL PERSPECTIVES: The Fabric of Eastern Ways of Knowing 313
Educational Implications of Eastern Ways of Knowing 313
Native North American Ways of Knowing 313
Navajo Thought 314 • Lakota Thought 314 • Hopi Thought 314 • Educational Implications
of Native North American Ways of Knowing 314

Summary 315 • Discussion Questions 316 • School-Based Observations 316 • Portfolio Development 316 • Preparing for Certification: Philosophical Thinking 316 • Websites 317 • Further Reading 317

10 Building an Educational Philosophy for a Changing World 318

Case Study: Scientists Explore the Molding of Children's Morals 319

Learning Outcomes 320

The Dynamic Relationship between Philosophy and Education 321

Teacher-Centered Locus-of-Control Educational Theories 322
Essentialism 323
Essentialist Focus of Learning 323 • Essentialist Curriculum 323
ESSENTIALIST CLASS ACTIVITY 323
Essentialist Schools Movement 324
Behaviorism 324
BEHAVIORIST CLASS ACTIVITY 325
Behaviorist Focus of Learning 325 • Reinforcement: A Behaviorist Practice 325
Positivism 325
Positivist Focus of Learning 326 • Objective Forced-Choice Testing:
A Positivist Requirement 326 • Direct Instruction: A Positivist Approach
to Teaching and Learning 326
POSITIVIST CLASS ACTIVITY 326

Student-Centered Locus-of-Control Educational Theories 327
Progressivism 327
Progressivism and Democracy 328
PROGRESSIVIST CLASS ACTIVITY 328
Critical Pedagogy: A Progressivist Curriculum 329
Humanism 329
HUMANIST CLASS ACTIVITY 330
Humanistic Curriculum 330 • Humanistic School Environments 330
Constructivism 331
Constructivist Curriculum 331
PROFESSIONAL DILEMMA: Should I Use Homogeneous or Heterogeneous Ability Grouping? 332
Problem-Based Learning: A Constructivist Pedagogy 332
CONSTRUCTIVIST CLASS ACTIVITY 333

Developing Your Own Philosophy of Education 333
Classroom Organization 335
Lesson Planning 335 • The Physical Setting 335 • Student Assessment and Evaluation 336
Motivation 336
RELEVANT RESEARCH: Can Children Philosophize? 337
Discipline 338
Control or Choice Theory 339 • Assertive Discipline 341 •
Discipline with Dignity 342 • Conflict Resolution 342 • Peer Mediation 342 •
Rules for Discipline 342

Classroom Climate 343
    Voice 343 • Space 344
Learning Focus 344

Using Philosophy of Education beyond the Classroom 345
Teachers as Change Agents 345
    Change as Adaptation 345 • Change as Rational Process 345 •
    Change as Reconstruction 345 • Change as Dialectic 346
Teachers as Leaders 346
TEACHER PERSPECTIVES: Should Teachers Express Their Views on Controversial Topics in Class? 347
    Vision 348 • Modeling 349 • Empowerment 349
GLOBAL PERSPECTIVES: The World as a Classroom 350

Summary 350 • Discussion Questions 352 • School-Based Observations 352 • Portfolio Development 352 • Preparing for Certification: Educational Theories and Learning Climates 352 • Websites 353 • Further Reading 354

PART VI
CURRICULAR FOUNDATIONS OF EDUCATION
355

11 Standards-Based Education and Assessment of Student Learning 356

Case Study: State's Kids Rate Low on Reading Test, National Exam Results Disappoint After Schools' Efforts to Improve 357

Learning Outcomes 358

Traditional versus Standards-Based Education 359

Standards-Based Education 360
Differing Conceptions of Standards 361
    World-Class Standards 361 • Real-World Standards 362 • Discipline-Based or Content Standards 362

TEACHER PERSPECTIVES: Should We Reward Good Grades with Money and Prizes? 363
Other Uses of Standards in Education 365
    Standards for Beginning Teachers (INTASC) 366 • Standards for Expert/Master Teacher Certification (NBPTS) 366 • Teacher Education Program Accreditation Standards (NCATE) 366 • Opportunity-to-Learn Standards 366
The Common Theme across Standards 367
    No Child Left Behind and Standards 367
Why Standards Differ 367
The Future of Standards-Based Education 368

Assessment: The Other Side of Standards 369
What Is Assessment? 369
Purposes for Assessment 370
    Evaluating Student Learning 370 • Diagnosing 370 • Gatekeeping 371
Traditional Assessments 371
    Norm-Referenced Assessments 371 • Criterion-Referenced Assessments 372 • Capstone/Summative Assessments 372
Performance Assessment 372
    Designing Authentic Performance Assessments 374 • Basing Assessment in Standards 374 • Selecting an Authentic Context 374 • Making the Assessment Reflective of the Instruction 375 • Rubrics 375 • Basing Assessment in the Discipline 375

Professional Aspects of Good Assessments 378
    Principles for High-Quality Assessments 379 • Fairness 379 • Reliability and Validity
    of Assessments 379

Accountability 380
Testing Ups and Downs 380
RELEVANT RESEARCH: Similar Students, Different Results: Why Do Some Schools Do Better? 381
PROFESSIONAL DILEMMA: What Is the Proper Way to Prepare for High-Stakes,
State-Mandated Tests? 382
    High-Stakes Testing 382 • Pressures to Cheat 383 • Teaching to the Test 383 •
    One-Size-Fits-All 384 • The Threat of a National Exam 384
GLOBAL PERSPECTIVES: Assessment of Student Learning across Nations 385
    Increased Teacher Burden 386
Equity within Accountability 386

**Summary 387 • Discussion Questions 388 • School-
Based Observations 388 • Portfolio Development 388 •
Preparing for Certification: Standards and Assessment 388 •
Websites 389 • Further Reading 389**

12 Designing Programs for Learners: Curriculum and Instruction 390

Case Study: Guidelines for Teaching English Are Adopted 391

Learning Outcomes 392

Curriculum: Relating Expectations for Learning to What Is Taught 393
Developing Curriculum Is a Process Involving Different Perspectives 394
    Steps in the Curriculum Development Process 394 • Perspective Matters 394 •
    Some Difficult Curriculum Development Questions 394 • Curriculum Designs 397 •
    Cocurriculum and Extra-Curriculum 397
Selecting Curriculum Is a Complex Business 398
    Different Levels of Influence 398
Curriculum Resources and Selection 400
    Curriculum Libraries and the Web 400 • Textbooks 400
GLOBAL PERSPECTIVES: German Education 401
    Curriculum Guides and Course Syllabi 402 • Standards Are the First Place to Look 402 •
    Tests 402
Managing Curriculum 403
    The State Role in Managing Curriculum 403 • The District's Role in Managing Curriculum 404
Evaluating Curricula 405
    Classroom-Based Curriculum Evaluation 405
RELEVANT RESEARCH: Some Achievement Gaps Are Narrowing 406
    International Curriculum Evaluation Studies 407

Instruction: Turning Curriculum into Classroom Activities 407
Instructional Objectives for Student Learning 408
    Aims, Goals, and Objectives 408 • The Hidden Curriculum 408
TEACHER PERSPECTIVES: Should Teachers Allow Students to Use Profanity in Their Writing? 409
    Objectives Are about Student Learning 410
Different Kinds of Instructional Objectives 411
    Behavioral Objectives 411 • Learning Objectives for the Cognitive Domain 412 •
    Learning Objectives for the Affective Domain 412 • Learning Objectives
    for the Psychomotor Domain 414
Teaching Strategies 415
    Direct Instruction 415 • Indirect Instruction 415 • Student Grouping 417
Teaching Strategies for Addressing Students with Exceptionalities 417
    Accommodating Students with Special Needs 418 • Classroom Management 421

PROFESSIONAL DILEMMA: Adjusting the Attitude of Learners 422
Models for School Reform 422
    School Improvement 423 • Accelerated Schools 424 • Success For All (SFA) 424 •
    Institute for Learning 424 • School Reform Models for High Schools 425 •
    Multiple Intelligences 425

Summary 426 • Discussion Questions 427 • School-Based Observations 427 • Portfolio Development 427 • Preparing for Certification: Curriculum and Instruction 427 • Websites 428 • Further Reading 428

13 Technology in a Changing World 430

Case Study: Technology: A Class Act 431
Learning Outcomes 432
Technology Basics 433
Standards 433
Fundamental Concepts 434
    Computer Hardware 434 • Computer Software 435
Networks 436
The Internet 436
Teachers' Use of Technology 437
Outside the Classroom 437
    Teacher–Family Communication 438 • Tracking Student Learning 438 •
    Lesson Planning 439
Inside the Classroom 439
RELEVANT RESEARCH: Social Context in the Use of Computers 441
    Information Resources 441
GLOBAL PERSPECTIVES: China's Filtering of the Internet 443
PROFESSIONAL DILEMMA: Assigning Homework That Uses Technology 444
    Project Development Tools 444 • Collaboration Tools 445
Distance Education 445
Issues Related to the Use of Technology 446
Equality in Access 446
TEACHER PERSPECTIVES: Should School Computer Labs Be Phased Out? 447
Stipulating Student Use 450
Plagiarism 451
Copyright 452
Globalization 453
A Look Ahead 453

Summary 454 • Discussion Questions 456 • School-Based Observations 456 • Portfolio Development 456 • Preparing for Certification: Teachers and Technology 456 • Websites 457 • Further Reading 457

14 Education in the Twenty-First Century 458

Case Study: Take a Hike 459
Learning Outcomes 460
The Nature of Change in the Twenty-First Century 461

Characteristics of Change   462
Size of Educational Change   462
PROFESSIONAL DILEMMA: How Do I Create an Authentic Learning Environment
in the Twenty-First Century Classroom?   464

Futurism and Transformational Trends in Twenty-First-Century Education   464
Increased Accountability and Testing Focused on Student Achievement   465
Providing Safe Schools   465
Schools as the Center for Delivery of Coordinated Service   466
Emphasis on Character Development   467
Increased Competition among Schools   467

The Changing Profession of Education   468
Career Development Continuum   468
Professional Collaboration   468
Participation in the Profession   469
   Teacher Unions 469   •   Professional Associations 471   •   Specialty Professional Associations 471
GLOBAL PERSPECTIVES: Education International   472

A Vision for Twenty-First-Century Schools   472
Professional Learning Communities   472
RELEVANT RESEARCH: Can Groups Learn?   473
Classrooms as Dynamic Centers of Learning   474
New Forms of Teacher Leadership   474
TEACHER PERSPECTIVES: Will Public Education Survive the Next Century?   475

**Summary 477   •   Discussion Questions 478   •   School-
Based Observations 478   •   Portfolio Development 478   •
Preparing for Certification: Professional Relationships and Standards 478   •
Websites 479   •   Further Reading 479**

APPENDIXES
**A. State Certification and Licensure Offices
   throughout the United States   481**
B. Code of Ethics of the Education Profession   483
C. Teaching Job Websites   485
D. Important Dates in the History of Western Education   487
E. Professional Education Associations: A Selected List   491

Notes   493

Name Index   499

Subject Index   502

Photo Credits   514

List of Features

CASE STUDY

Heroes Every One   3
Mother Tongue: Area Schools Find Themselves Teaching English
    to Thousands of Immigrant Children   43
Culture Clash   75
Anytown Fires Up Teens to Foster Acceptance   105
Push Is on for Magnet School at Jefferson to Attract Students   139
The Forum: How One School District Found Religion   181
Teaching Patriotism—With Conviction   229
Casualties of Segregation Receive Honorary Diplomas   265
Teacher Resigns over Plagiarism Fight   293
Scientists Explore the Molding of Children's Morals   319
State's Kids Rate Low on Reading Test, National Exam Results Disappoint
    After Schools' Efforts to Improve   357
Guidelines for Teaching English Are Adopted   391
Technology: A Class Act   431
Take a Hike   459

PROFESSIONAL DILEMMA

Who Is Cheating Now?   20
Inclusion of Students with Disabilities   68
What If He Has Two Mommies?   78
Communicating with Parents of English Language Learners   128
What Is the Appropriate Role for Teachers When the Politics
    Get Rough?   165
Should Science Teachers Be Required to Include Religion When Teaching
    about Evolution?   194
How Can the Busy Teacher Keep Up with Historical and
    Contemporary Research?   258
Can a Knowledge of History Help to Improve Multicultural Education?   285
Should Morals and Values Be Taught in Public Schools?   300
Should I Use Homogeneous or Heterogeneous Ability Grouping?   332
What Is the Proper Way to Prepare for High-Stakes, State-
    Mandated Tests?   382
Adjusting the Attitude of Learners   422
Assigning Homework That Uses Technology   444
How Do I Create an Authentic Learning Environment in the Twenty-First
    Century Classroom?   464

TEACHER PERSPECTIVES

Should Districts Offer Signing Bonuses to Attract New Teachers?   33
Should All Students Be Bilingual?   60
Is Retention Better Than Social Promotion for Students?   89
Is School the Best Place to Teach Tolerance?   116
Should the School Year Be Longer?   162
Would You Support the Use of Corporal Punishment
     in Your School?   218
Is "Abstinence-Only" the Best Sex Education Policy for Schools
     to Implement?   239
Should High Schools Prepare All Students for College?   277
Does Prepping for High-Stakes Tests Interfere with Teaching?   310
Should Teachers Express Their Views on Controversial Topics in Class?   347
Should We Reward Good Grades with Money and Prizes?   363
Should Teachers Allow Students to Use Profanity in Their Writing?   409
Should School Computer Labs Be Phased Out?   447
Will Public Education Survive the Next Century?   475

RELEVANT RESEARCH

Teachers' Perspectives on Most Rewarding Aspects of Their Work   29
ESL Programs in White Schools   56
Race in a White School   82
Boys and Girls in Performance-Based Science Classrooms   125
Does Class Size Make a Difference?   145
Changing Strategies: Supporting/Challenging Vouchers   189
Critiquing Historical Sources   247
What Have We Learned about Homework and Students
     with Disabilities?   269
Using Socratic Dialogue to Enhance Reflective Learning   304
Can Children Philosophize?   337
Similar Students, Different Results: Why Do Some Schools Do Better?   381
Some Achievement Gaps Are Narrowing   406
Social Context in the Use of Computers   441
Can Groups Learn?   473

GLOBAL PERSPECTIVES

Teaching Chinese to American Students   17
Women's Political Participation   63
Coming to Justice   99
Universal Values   113
Social Justice in the Canadian Context   132
International Comparisons: Expenditures per Student as
     an Indicator   176
Legal Aspects of Education in Other Countries   206
Educational Ideas Borrowed from around the World   232
Educational Transplantation from Europe   246
Maria Montessori   256
European Beginnings of Teacher Training   279
Jean Piaget   286
The Fabric of Eastern Ways of Knowing   313
The World as a Classroom   350
Assessment of Student Learning across Nations   385
German Education   401
China's Filtering of the Internet   443
Education International   472

Preface

In this fourteenth edition of our book we have chosen to emphasize what we consider the key challenge for educators in the twenty-first century—responding to multiple perspectives in a changing world. By *multiple perspectives* we mean that educators must consider, reflect, and respond to divergent ideas drawn from different disciplines of study, different points of view, different experiences, different contexts, and different voices. Readers come to this course of study with perspectives of their own based on unique personal experiences, cultures, and communities. During this course, you will be exposed to other perspectives, values, cultures, and points of view. This text helps you analyze these divergent perspectives through academic disciplines including history, philosophy, politics, sociology, and the law. These new perspectives will interact with your own views and ultimately influence your role as a teacher. This process of analyzing and responding to differences does not end when you enter the teaching profession; different perspectives continue to emerge and your response to them changes as your own unique career path evolves.

Multiple perspectives provide points of view that can enhance your own understanding of the changing world. For example, there is the political perspective or way of thinking about the world ranging from conservative to liberal—or independent. There are experiential perspectives that influence your thinking while working in an inner city, suburban, or rural setting, whether at home or traveling abroad.

By *change* we acknowledge the fast-paced world of information that influences you and your experiences. Your identity as a teacher emerges and evolves in response to this unending road of changes. The anchor that we provide in this sometimes chaotic and confusing world is the anchor of reflection and analysis. Throughout this edition, we provide numerous opportunities to make sense of the changes in the world, to determine a reflective response to the present, and to adjust your response as new changes emerge. This edition also presents a broad perspective of the changing world with a view to a global economy and global citizenship.

We believe that our theme of "Perspectives on Education in a Changing World" accurately describes a key component to the tenor and flavor of our developing twenty-first century. The theme directs our writing and provides a focused purpose; it allows us to bridge many related, important topics such as authentic case studies drawn from contemporary news articles, reflective thinking exercises, global perspectives for a changing world, relevant research, professional dilemmas, and opportunities to respond by developing a professional portfolio. We believe you will enjoy this challenging journey through the complex world of education and, with the help of the different perspectives and features, develop a clearer notion of the unique gift you have to offer the profession.

New to This Edition

- **New Theme!** This new edition is framed by the theme "Perspectives on Education in a Changing World." The new theme focuses on the diversity of perspectives within education and how these perspectives are affected by changes within U.S. society and the larger world community.
- **New Case Studies!** Each chapter begins with a real-life case study featuring current news in education and also a series of reflection questions to tie these cases to personal teaching experience.
- **New Chapter!** Chapter 13, on technology in a changing world, covers basic technology concepts to help new teachers better integrate technology into their classrooms.
- **MyLabSchool Activities!** Each chapter of the new edition contains a section correlated to MyLabSchool, a collection of online tools developed to help students transition from student to teacher.
- **Updated Emphasis!** In response to readers' feedback, this new edition has increased coverage on current events and legislation in U.S. classrooms. Coverage of teacher certification and certification testing is found in Chapters 1, 5, and 11. Expanded coverage of No Child Left Behind and its effects is found in Chapters 2, 3, 4, and 5.
- **Focus on Reflective Practice!** New Journals for Reflection are found throughout each chapter. These activities give students an opportunity to pause and reflect on chapter content and how it relates to their own experiences in the classroom.
- **Correlations to INTASC Standards!** The Learning Outcomes feature includes INTASC correlations that indicate how the chapter content reflects the INTASC standards. See the inside front cover for a complete correlation chart to INTASC.
- **Classroom Applications!** The School-Based Observations feature suggests activities students can do during field practice.
- **Content Cross-References!** This marginal annotation feature indicates where topics are discussed elsewhere in the book and helps build a complete understanding of the information presented in the chapters.
- **Annotated References!** The Further Reading feature and the Websites list at the end of each chapter are annotated to act as useful supplements to the information in the chapter.

Features of the Fourteenth Edition

- **Part openers** introduce and connect the specific chapter topics to the broader foundations of education—professional, sociological, organizational and financial, historical, philosophical, and curricular. They also provide a preview to the key concepts of the upcoming chapters and a connection to the theme "Perspectives on Education in a Changing World."

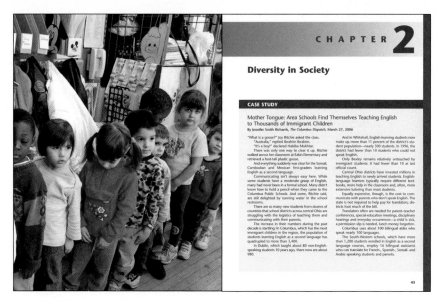

- **Chapter openers** provide two features. **Case Study** highlights and asks students to reflect on current education topics in the news. **Learning Outcomes,** which are correlated to the INTASC Standards, identify the big ideas of the chapter.

- **Professional Dilemma** features in each chapter provide opportunities to analyze real-life problems that teachers encounter in their classrooms. These features conclude with questions, which readers can answer on the companion website (www.ablongman.com/johnson14e) and e-mail to their professors.

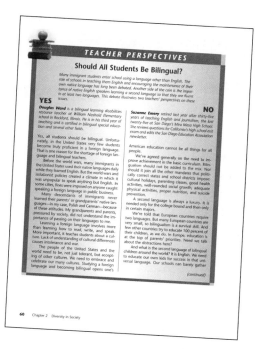

- Each chapter contains a **Teacher Perspectives** feature, in which two educators present opposing sides of an issue related to the chapter topic. Readers also have an opportunity to register their own opinions on each issue at the companion website (www. ablongman.com/johnson14e).

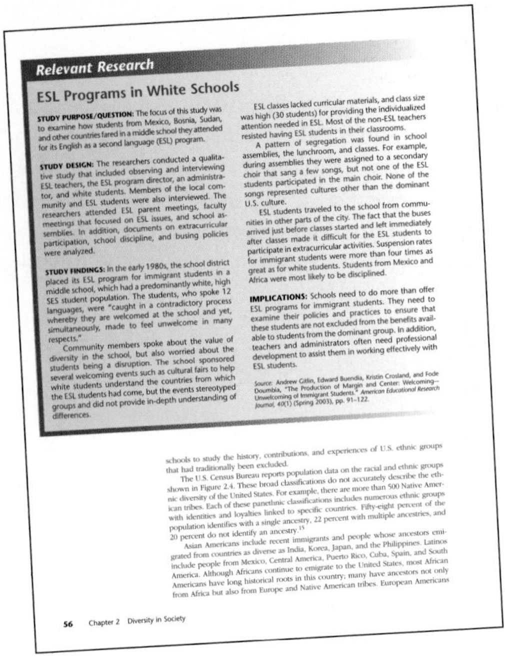

Relevant Research

ESL Programs in White Schools

STUDY PURPOSE/QUESTION: The focus of this study was to examine how students from Mexico, Bosnia, Sudan, and other countries fared in a middle school they attended for its English as a second language (ESL) program.

STUDY DESIGN: The researchers conducted a qualitative study that included observing and interviewing ESL teachers, the ESL program director, an administrator, and white students. Members of the local community and ESL students were also interviewed. The researchers attended ESL parent meetings, faculty meetings that focused on ESL issues, and school assemblies. In addition, documents on extracurricular participation, school discipline, and busing policies were analyzed.

STUDY FINDINGS: In the early 1980s, the school district placed its ESL program for immigrant students in a middle school, which had a predominantly white, high SES student population. The students, who spoke 12 languages, were "caught in a contradictory process whereby they are welcomed at the school and yet, simultaneously, made to feel unwelcome in many respects."

Community members spoke about the value of diversity in the school, but also worried about the students being a disruption. The school sponsored several welcoming events such as cultural fairs to help white students understand the countries from which the ESL students had come, but the events stereotyped groups and did not provide in-depth understanding of differences.

ESL classes lacked curricular materials, and class size was high (30 students) for providing the individualized attention needed in ESL. Most of the non-ESL teachers resisted having ESL students in their classrooms.

A pattern of segregation was found in school assemblies, the lunchroom, and classes. For example, during assemblies they were assigned to a secondary choir that sang a few songs, but not one of the ESL students participated in the main choir. None of the songs represented cultures other than the dominant U.S. culture.

ESL students traveled to the school from communities in other parts of the city. The fact that the buses arrived just before classes started and left immediately after classes made it difficult for the ESL students to participate in extracurricular activities. Suspension rates for immigrant students were more than four times as great as for white students. Students from Mexico and Africa were most likely to be disciplined.

IMPLICATIONS: Schools need to do more than offer ESL programs for immigrant students. They need to examine their policies and practices to ensure that these students are not excluded from the benefits available to students from the dominant group. In addition, teachers and administrators often need professional development to assist them in working effectively with ESL students.

Source: Andrew Gitlin, Edward Buendia, Kristin Crosland, and Fode Doumbia, "The Production of Margin and Center: Welcoming–Unwelcoming of Immigrant Students." *American Educational Research Journal*, 40(1) (Spring 2003), pp. 91–122.

schools to study the history, contributions, and experiences of U.S. ethnic groups that had traditionally been excluded.

The U.S. Census Bureau reports population data on the racial and ethnic groups shown in Figure 2.4. These broad classifications do not accurately describe the ethnic diversity of the United States. For example, there are more than 500 Native American tribes. Each of these panethnic classifications includes numerous ethnic groups with identities and loyalties linked to specific countries. Fifty-eight percent of the population identifies with a single ancestry, 22 percent with multiple ancestries, and 20 percent do not identify an ancestry.[15]

Asian Americans include recent immigrants and people whose ancestors emigrated from countries as diverse as India, Korea, Japan, and the Philippines. Latinos include people from Mexico, Central America, Puerto Rico, Cuba, Spain, and South America. Although Africans continue to emigrate to the United States, most African Americans have long historical roots in this country; many have ancestors not only from Africa but also from Europe and Native American tribes. European Americans

56 Chapter 2 Diversity in Society

- **Relevant Research** features in each chapter showcase published research studies about education.

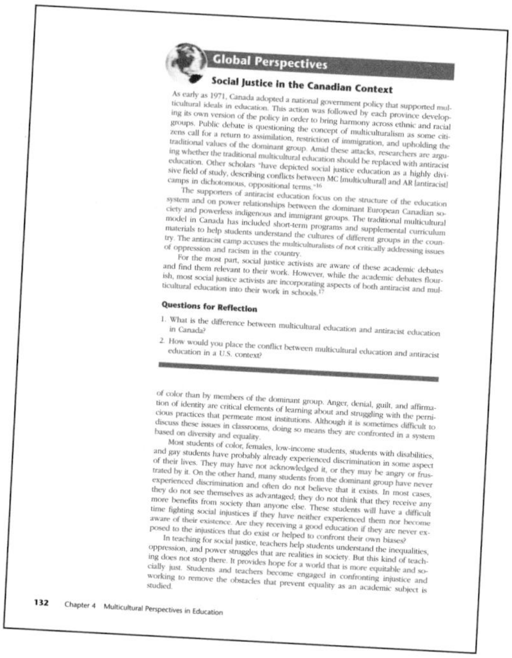

Global Perspectives

Social Justice in the Canadian Context

As early as 1971, Canada adopted a national government policy that supported multicultural ideals in education. This action was followed by each province developing its own version of the policy in order to bring harmony across ethnic and racial groups. Public debate is questioning the concept of multiculturalism as some citizens call for a return to assimilation, restriction of immigration, and upholding the traditional values of the dominant group. Amid these attacks, researchers are arguing whether the traditional multicultural education should be replaced with antiracist education. Other scholars "have depicted social justice education as a highly divisive field of study, describing conflicts between MC [multicultural] and AR [antiracist] camps in dichotomous, oppositional terms."[16]

The supporters of antiracist education focus on the structure of the education system and on power relationships between the dominant European Canadian society and powerless indigenous and immigrant groups. The traditional multicultural model in Canada has included short-term programs and supplemental curriculum materials to help students understand the cultures of different groups in the country. The antiracist camp accuses the multiculturalists of not critically addressing issues of oppression and racism in the country.

For the most part, social justice activists are aware of these academic debates and find them relevant to their work. However, while the academic debates flourish, most social justice activists are incorporating aspects of both antiracist and multicultural education into their work in schools.[17]

Questions for Reflection

1. What is the difference between multicultural education and antiracist education in Canada?
2. How would you place the conflict between multicultural education and antiracist education in a U.S. context?

of color than by members of the dominant group. Anger, denial, guilt, and affirmation of identity are critical elements of learning about and struggling with the pernicious practices that permeate most institutions. Although it is sometimes difficult to discuss these issues in classrooms, doing so means they are confronted in a system based on diversity and equality.

Most students of color, females, low-income students, students with disabilities, and gay students have probably already experienced discrimination in some aspect of their lives. They may have not acknowledged it, or they may be angry or frustrated by it. On the other hand, many students from the dominant group have never experienced discrimination and often do not believe that it exists. In most cases, they do not see themselves as advantaged; they do not think that they receive any more benefits from society than anyone else. These students will have a difficult time fighting social injustices if they have neither experienced them nor become aware of their existence. Are they receiving a good education if they are never exposed to the injustices that do exist or helped to confront their own biases?

In teaching for social justice, teachers help students understand the inequalities, oppression, and power struggles that are realities in society. But this kind of teaching does not stop there. It provides hope for a world that is more equitable and socially just. Students and teachers become engaged in confronting injustice and working to remove the obstacles that prevent equality as an academic subject is studied.

132 Chapter 4 Multicultural Perspectives in Education

- **Global Perspectives** sections in every chapter provide preservice teachers with a better understanding of educational practices in other countries and how they compare to practices in the United States. These sections include Questions for Reflection.

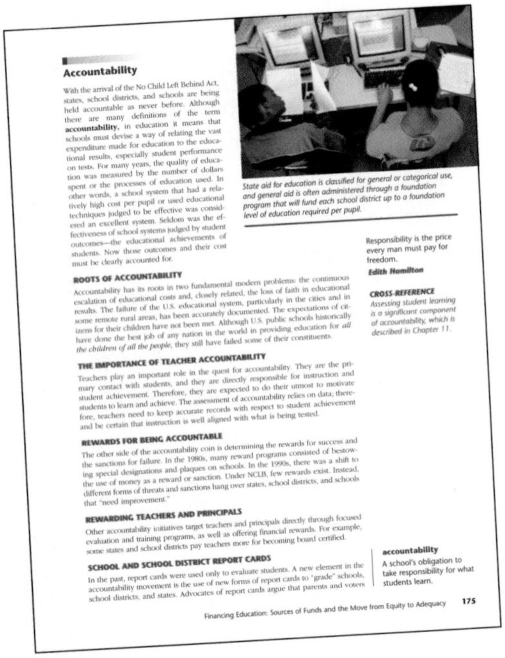

Accountability

With the arrival of the No Child Left Behind Act, states, school districts, and schools are being held accountable as never before. Although there are many definitions of the term **accountability**, in education it means that schools must devise a way of relating the vast expenditure made for education to the educational results, especially student performance on tests. For many years, the quality of education was measured by the number of dollars spent or the processes of education used. In other words, a school system that had a relatively high cost per pupil or used educational techniques judged to be effective was considered an excellent system. Seldom was the effectiveness of school systems judged by student outcomes—the educational achievements of students. Now those outcomes and their cost must be clearly accounted for.

State aid for education is classified for general or categorical use, and general aid is often administered through a foundation program that will fund each school district up to a foundation level of education required per pupil.

Responsibility is the price every man must pay for freedom.
Edith Hamilton

ROOTS OF ACCOUNTABILITY

Accountability has its roots in two fundamental modern problems: the continuous escalation of educational costs and, closely related, the loss of faith in educational results. The failure of the U.S. educational system, particularly in the cities and in some remote rural areas, has been accurately documented. The expectations of citizens for their children have not been met. Although U.S. public schools historically have done the best job of any nation in the world in providing education for *all the children of all the people*, they still have failed some of their constituents.

CROSS-REFERENCE
Assessing student learning is a significant component of accountability, which is described in Chapter 11.

THE IMPORTANCE OF TEACHER ACCOUNTABILITY

Teachers play an important role in the quest for accountability. They are the primary contact with students, and they are directly responsible for instruction and student achievement. Therefore, they are expected to do their utmost to motivate students to learn and achieve. The assessment of accountability relies on data; therefore, teachers need to keep accurate records with respect to student achievement and be certain that instruction is well aligned with what is being tested.

REWARDS FOR BEING ACCOUNTABLE

The other side of the accountability coin is determining the rewards for success and the sanctions for failure. In the 1980s, many reward programs consisted of bestowing special designations and plaques on schools. In the 1990s, there was a shift to the use of money as a reward or sanction. Under NCLB, few rewards exist. Instead, different forms of threats and sanctions hang over states, school districts, and schools that "need improvement."

REWARDING TEACHERS AND PRINCIPALS

Other accountability initiatives target teachers and principals directly through focused evaluation and training programs, as well as offering financial rewards. For example, some states and school districts pay teachers more for becoming board certified.

SCHOOL AND SCHOOL DISTRICT REPORT CARDS

In the past, report cards were used only to evaluate students. A new element in the accountability movement is the use of new forms of report cards to "grade" schools, school districts, and states. Advocates of report cards argue that parents and voters

accountability
A school's obligation to take responsibility for what students learn.

Financing Education: Sources of Funds and the Move from Equity to Adequacy 175

- The margins of the fourteenth edition feature three types of resources. **Definitions of key terms** correspond to terms that appear in bold on the page; **quotations** provide thought-provoking comments about education; and **cross-references** indicate where chapter topics are discussed elsewhere in the text.

- **Chapter-closing** material contains numerous resources as study aids, applications, and expansions of the chapter contents. **Summary** provides a chapter recap organized by major headings; **Discussion Questions** are thought-provoking suggestions for classroom discussion; **School-Based Observations** suggest chapter-appropriate activities that can be done during field practice; **Portfolio Development** suggests artifacts for portfolios based on chapter information; **Preparing for Certification** provides sample questions for state teacher certification exams such as *Praxis;* **Websites** and **Further Reading** provide annotated bibliographies for additional information; MyLabSchool information correlates chapter contents to additional Allyn and Bacon media resources.

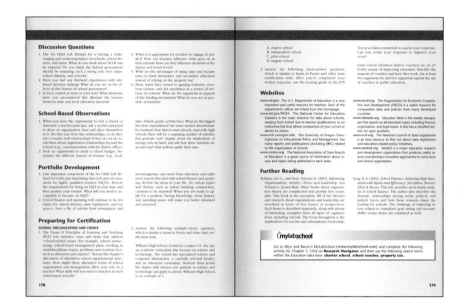

- Five **Appendixes** provide up-to-date resources for preservice teachers, including state certification websites, the NEA Code of Ethics, websites that list teaching positions, an educational history time line, and professional organization websites.

A Comprehensive Teaching and Learning Package

Allyn and Bacon is committed to preparing the best supplements for its textbooks, and the supplements for the fourteenth edition of *Foundations of American Education* reflect this commitment. The following supplements provide an outstanding array of resources that facilitate learning about the foundations of education. For more information about the instructor and student supplements that accompany and support the text, ask your local Allyn and Bacon representative, or contact the Allyn and Bacon Sales Support Department (1-800-852-8024).

Outstanding Media Resources

 The classroom comes to life at MyLabSchool, a collection of online tools designed to help prepare students for success in this course as well as in their teaching careers. Visit www.mylabschool.com to access the following:

- **Video footage** of real-life classrooms, with opportunities for students to reflect on the videos and offer their own thoughts and suggestions for applying theory to practice.
- Help with research papers using **Research Navigator,** which provides access to four exclusive databases of credible and reliable source material, including EBSCO's ContentSelect academic journal database, the *New York Times* On The Web subject archive, the "Best of the Web" Link Library, and FT.com business archive.
- An extensive archive of **text and multimedia cases** that provide valuable perspectives on real classrooms and real teaching challenges.
- **Help with lesson planning and building digital portfolios** of professional resources, including study guides for licensure preparation.

COMPANION WEBSITE

An exciting array of **tools and activities** will help students study more effectively and can take them beyond the book. It includes INTASC Learning Outcomes, web links, essay questions, practice tests, and flash cards. It provides an opportunity for students to respond to the Professional Dilemma and Teacher Perspectives features. The website also features an interactive time line and selected *New York Times* articles. Visit www.ablongman.com/johnson14e.

VIDEOWORKSHOP FOR FOUNDATIONS/INTRODUCTION TO TEACHING

An easy way to bring video into your course for maximized learning! This total teaching and learning system includes quality video footage on an easy-to-use CD-ROM plus a Student Learning Guide and an Instructor's Teaching Guide—both with questions and activity suggestions. The result? A program that brings textbook concepts to life with ease and that helps students understand, analyze, and apply the objectives of the course. VideoWorkshop is available for students as a value-pack option with this textbook.

Instructor Supplements:
A Complete Instructional Package

INSTRUCTOR'S RESOURCE MANUAL

The Instructor's Resource Manual includes a wealth of interesting ideas and activities designed to help instructors teach the course. Each chapter includes a chapter-at-a-glance grid, an extended outline, learning objectives, strategies for introducing the chapter, chapter overview and analysis, class activities, professional dilemmas, relevant research, diversity notes, journal reflection activity masters, websites, and recommended supplementary resources. (Please request this item from your local Allyn and Bacon sales representative; also available for download from the Instructor's Resource Center at www.ablongman.com/irc)

TEST BANK

The Test Bank includes hundreds of questions, including multiple-choice items, true/false items, short answer, essay questions, case studies, and alternative assessments, plus text page references and answer feedback. (Please request this item from your local Allyn and Bacon sales representative; also available for download from the Instructor's Resource Center at www.ablongman.com/irc)

COMPUTERIZED TEST BANK

The printed Test Bank is also available electronically through the Allyn and Bacon computerized testing system, TestGen EQ. Instructors can use TestGen EQ to create exams in just minutes by selecting from the existing database of questions, editing questions, and/or writing original questions. (Available for download from the Instructor's Resource Center at www.ablongman.com/irc)

POWERPOINT™ PRESENTATION

Ideal for lecture presentations or student handouts, the PowerPoint™ presentation created for this text provides dozens of ready-to-use graphic and text images including illustrations from the text. (Available for download from the Instructor's Resource Center at www.ablongman.com/irc)

ALLYN AND BACON TRANSPARENCIES FOR FOUNDATIONS OF EDUCATION AND INTRODUCTION TO TEACHING, 2008 EDITION

A set of 100 acetate transparencies related to topics in the text.

ALLYN AND BACON INTERACTIVE VIDEO: ISSUES IN EDUCATION

This video features news reports from around the country on topics covered in the text. The VHS video contains ten modules of news clips exploring issues and debates in education. Topics include teacher shortages, alternative schools, community–school partnerships, standardized testing, and bilingual classrooms. An accompanying instructor's guide outlines teaching strategies and discussion questions to use with the clips.

COURSE MANAGEMENT

Powered by Blackboard and hosted nationally, Allyn and Bacon's own course management system, CourseCompass, helps you manage all aspects of teaching your course. For colleges and universities with WebCT™ and Blackboard™ licenses, special course management packages are available in these formats as well. Allyn and Bacon is proud to offer both premium content for introduction to teaching and foundations of education courses as well as MyLabSchool in all three platforms. (Your sales representative can give you additional information.)

- Allyn and Bacon CourseCompass for introduction to teaching and foundations of education (Access code required)
- Allyn and Bacon WebCT for introduction to teaching and foundations of education, Version 3.0 (Access code required)
- Allyn and Bacon Blackboard for introduction to teaching and foundations of education (Access code required)

About the Authors

James A. Johnson, professor of education emeritus at Northern Illinois University, has been an educator for more than thirty-five years, serving as a public school teacher, teacher educator, and university administrator. He has been coauthor of fourteen editions of *Foundations of American Education,* as well as author or coauthor of a dozen other college textbooks.

Diann Musial, professor of foundations of education and Northern Illinois University Distinguished Teaching Professor, has taught middle school science and mathematics in Chicago, served as principal of an Individually Guided Education elementary school, and worked in industry as director of training. She has directed more than twenty state and federally funded staff development grants, developed countless performance assessments and test item banks, and coauthored *Classroom 2061: Activity Assessments in Science Integrated with Mathematics and Language Arts* (Skylight Professional Development, 1995).

Gene E. Hall, professor of educational leadership at the University of Nevada at Las Vegas (UNLV), has served for more than thirty years as a teacher educator, researcher, and university administrator. He is active in assisting teacher education institutions in their efforts to become nationally accredited. He is also internationally known for his research on the change process in schools and other types of organizations. He is the lead architect of the widely used concerns-based adoption model (CBAM), which organizational leaders and staff developers employ in studying and facilitating the change process. In addition to coauthoring the last five editions of this text, he is coauthor of *Implementing Change: Patterns, Principles and Potholes,* Second Edition (Allyn & Bacon, 2006).

Donna M. Gollnick is senior vice president of the National Council for the Accreditation of Teacher Education (NCATE), where she oversees accreditation activities. She is also past president of the National Association for Multicultural Education (NAME) and is a recognized authority in multicultural education. In addition to her work in teacher accreditation, she has taught in secondary schools and coauthored four editions of this text. She is also coauthor, with Philip C. Chinn, of *Multicultural Education in a Pluralistic Society,* Seventh Edition (Merrill, 2006).

Victor L. Dupuis, professor emeritus of curriculum and instruction and Waterbury professor of secondary education at Pennsylvania State University, continues a professional career that began forty-five years ago. Currently, he serves as a private consultant in areas of staff development, Native American education, and curriculum development and evaluation with Dupuis Associates. He has also taught social studies and English and served as a school district curriculum director and teacher educator. In addition to coauthoring fourteen editions of this text, he has published widely in the areas of curriculum and instruction and Native American literatures.

Acknowledgments

We are sincerely grateful to the many colleagues, reviewers, and editors who have helped us over the years to make this text the most popular and widely used book in the field. We thank our publisher, Allyn and Bacon, for its continued support over the years, and for enabling us to deliver the message that we, as professional educators, deem crucial for the preparation of teachers. In particular, we especially thank Shannon Steed for her outstanding work as our developmental editor, as well as Steve Dragin, our series editor and longtime good friend, for his support and assistance. We also thank our colleagues and other members of the academic community for their assistance: Leslie Sassone for her advice on the philosophy section; Michele Clarke for research assistance; Mary Ducharme for contributing the Preparing for Certification features; and Kendall Hartley, associate professor of educational technology at UNLV, for his contribution to the new chapter on technology.

We also sincerely thank our current and past reviewers for their help and guidance:

Gilda Benstead, *Methodist College*
Stephen Brand, *University of Rhode Island*
Barbara Burkhouse, *Marywood University*
G. Kathleen Chamberlain, *Lycoming College*
James L. Dawson, *Rochester College*
Rebecca L. Dye, *Culver-Stockton College*
Carole D. Errett, *Schreiner University*
Susan M. Ferguson, *University of Dayton*
Franklin B. Jones, *Tennessee State University*
M. Jerome Leavy, *University of South Florida*
Linda Maguire, *New Kensington Campus of Penn State University*
Darren Martin, *Concord College*
Thomas R. Oswald, *North Iowa Area Community College*
Mark Ryan, *National University*
Susan C. Scott, *University of Central Oklahoma*
Theresa M. Stahler, *Kutztown University of Pennsylvania*
Dale N. Titus, *Kutztown University of Pennsylvania*
Juan A. Toro, *Elizabethtown College*

In addition, we thank our families and friends for supporting us throughout the revision process and appreciate the comments and recommendations from the faculty and students who have used this book during the last edition. Their suggestions have led to a number of changes in the current edition. We encourage all of our readers to provide feedback for improving future books.

PROFESSIONAL PERSPECTIVES ON EDUCATION IN A CHANGING WORLD

We live in a world of rapid change in many aspects of life, and many people have become so accustomed to change that they hardly take notice of it. In this changing world, people have many different perspectives on, and opinions about, many things, including schools, teachers and education. Schools in general, and teachers in particular, are affected in many ways by this rapid change and by people's different perspectives on education. For instance, societal and parental expectations of schools constantly change; these expectations even change from parent to parent and from school to school.

These two realities—countless differing perspectives on education and a rapidly changing world—greatly affect the work and lives of educators and are therefore developed in various ways and used as themes throughout this book. Each chapter approaches these topics by sharing pertinent information and posing thought-provoking questions regarding perspectives on education in a changing world. Our goal is to help you learn more about these important realities and to enable you to make informed progress toward developing your own professional perspectives on education in our changing world.

Teaching in a Changing World

CASE STUDY

Heroes Every One

By Reg Weaver, NEA President, *NEA Today*, May 2005

We read about them every month in the pages of this magazine. We rub shoulders with them in our schools. We team up with them to make our communities better places.

Heroes.

The single mom who, after working hard all day as a high school custodian, trudges off to the local elementary school to meet with her child's teacher, instead of staying home and putting her feet up.

The retired music teacher who spends his mornings using music to teach language to preschool children with special needs. His students often learn to sing first and then to speak.

The middle school math teacher who stays late four days a week to tutor students in geometry and algebra so someday they will be able to attend college.

The cafeteria worker who, while dishing out the food she's cooked, keeps a vigilant eye on her diabetic students so they don't eat too much sugar and starch.

The elementary school teacher who goes to school at nights to learn Spanish so she can communicate with her students' parents.

The special education assistant who helps the special education teacher with children with the most severe disabilities—changing their diapers when they need changing.

The science teacher whose enthusiasm and preparation makes the subject come alive in her

students' minds, lighting a fire that will glow for a lifetime.

The high school teacher who starts a chess club as an outlet for his most restless, high energy students—and then hauls them off to every chess tournament in the state.

The school bus driver who every year organizes a skiing weekend for inner city kids who otherwise would never get to ski or play in the snow.

The community college instructor who teaches English as a second language to immigrants at four different campuses and spends so much time in her car that her colleagues have dubbed her "the road scholar."

Heroes every one.

It is easy to take these folks for granted, though, because they don't toot their own horn. They're everyday people, not celebrities. I like to call them "unsung heroes." In fact, they don't think of themselves as heroes at all, and when someone like me sings their praises, it kind of embarrasses them. But that doesn't stop me.

Our unsung heroes are the exception to the rule that when all is said and done, more is said than done. Their actions speak louder than words. And in a society that rewards getting rather than giving, they give of themselves for the good of others, and then they give some more.

Yes, it is easy to take our unsung heroes for granted, but we must not. For they are the heart and soul of our Association. These are the folks who, when you come to them with a problem, always say: "What are we going to do about it?" They think in terms of possibilities rather than impossibilities, solutions rather than setbacks, and dos rather than don'ts.

Of course I am aware that a hero is often defined as somebody who does something dangerous to help somebody else. The firefighter who rushes into a burning building to save a child is definitely a hero. For me, however, the burn unit nurse who tenderly and skillfully cares for that firefighter's wounds through his long and agonizing recovery also qualifies as a hero. And so, too, do the many public school and college employees and retired and student educators I have had the privilege of meeting and knowing as president of NEA.

As educators and Association members, we are in the hope business, and these unsung heroes of ours, above all else, give us hope even during the times when hope seems ready to freeze over.

Unsung heroes of NEA, I am your number one fan!

Questions for Reflection

1. What is your perspective on the ideas about heroes suggested in this news item?
2. What heroes would you add to those mentioned?
3. What are some of the heroes that parents might have? Students? The general public?

Reprinted by permission of the National Education Association.

INTASC

Learning Outcomes

After reading and studying this chapter, you should be able to:

1. Identify the characteristics of professions and develop arguments for or against declaring teaching a profession.
2. Articulate the role demographics play in determining teacher supply and demand and identify areas where teachers will be in high demand over the next decade.
3. Identify sources of evidence to show that you are developing the knowledge, skills, and dispositions outlined in the INTASC standards. (INTASC 1–10)
4. Outline the professional responsibilities of a teacher as viewed by the public, parents, and professional colleagues. (INTASC 1: Subject Matter)
5. Identify some of the challenges that affect teachers and not other professionals and clearly articulate why you plan to pursue a teaching career.
6. Identify the basic requirements for the initial teaching license in the state where you plan to teach, including the types of tests and other assessments that will be required.

As you read this book you will find many different perspectives on education as well as much information about our changing world, especially those aspects that affect the lives of educators and their schools. As an aspiring teacher, you are now hopefully in the process of developing your own tentative perspectives on what the job of teaching entails and what you need to know and be able to do to become an excellent and successful teacher. This chapter also will help you learn more about successfully completing your teacher education program and eventually finding a position as an educator and about the salary and benefits that you may receive. Answering these and related important questions about the profession of teaching are the topics of Chapter 1.

Although people hold many different perspectives on education, most agree that teaching is a profession that is critical to the well-being of youth and of society. Many students indicate that they have chosen teaching as a career because they care about children and youth. Teaching requires caring, but it also requires competence in the subject being taught and in the teaching of that subject. Teachers' knowledge and skills should lead to the ultimate goal of successful student learning.

Educators must undergo stringent assessments and meet high standards to ensure high quality in the teaching profession. The teaching profession includes at least three stages of quality assurance, beginning, most commonly, with college-level teacher preparation programs, such as the one in which you are likely now enrolled. Next, state teacher licensing systems give the public assurance that teachers are qualified and competent to do their work as educators The third stage of continuing professional development is tied to retaining the state license and seeking national certification. Each of these stages is accompanied by performance assessments to determine whether individuals are qualified for the important job of teaching.

Reflection is one of the important characteristics of successful teachers. Professionals who reflect on and analyze their own teaching are involved in a process that is critical to improving as an educator. Individuals who are making a commitment to teaching, whether lifelong or short-term, should consider the responsibilities and expectations of a teaching career. In this chapter, you will begin exploring the realities of what it means to be a teacher.

In addition to these concepts, Chapter 1 presents a number of big ideas about teaching. These include the facts that education is extremely important in our society, that educators are members of an established profession, that educators are generally well respected and valued by the public, and that the future job market for educators is complex but promising.

Today's Teachers

More than three million teachers provide the instructional leadership for public and private schools in the United States. Today's new teachers must meet rigorous national and state standards for entering the profession that did not exist a decade ago. Requirements for entering teacher education programs in colleges and universities are now more stringent than admission requirements for most other professions. Grade point averages of 3.0 and higher are becoming more common requirements for admission; tests and other assessments must be passed before admission, at the completion of a program, and for state licensure. Clearly, not everyone can teach. Teaching is becoming a profession that attracts the best and brightest college students into its ranks.

Teacher candidates today are diverse in age and work experience. Some of you are eighteen to twenty-two years old, the traditional age of college students, but still more of you are nontraditional students who are older and have worked for a number of years in other jobs or professions. Some of your classmates may have worked as teachers' aides in classrooms for years. Others may be switching careers from the armed forces, engineering, retail management, or public relations. Welcome to a profession in which new teachers represent such wonderfully diverse work experiences, as well as varying educational, cultural, and economic backgrounds.

Teaching is a challenging, complex, and demanding profession that draws from many diverse groups in the United States.

The Importance of Teachers to Society

Society has great expectations for its teachers. "Nine out of ten Americans believe the best way to lift student achievement is to ensure a qualified teacher in every classroom," according to a national survey.[1] In addition to guiding students' academic achievement, teachers have some responsibility for students' social and physical development. They are expected to prepare an educated citizenry that is informed about the many issues critical to maintaining a democracy. They help students learn to work together and try to instill the values that are critical to a just and caring society. Teachers are also asked to prepare children and youth with the knowledge and skills necessary to work in an **information age.**

Given these challenging responsibilities, teaching is one of the most important careers in a democratic society. Although critics of our education system sometimes give the impression that there is a lack of public support for schools and teachers, the public now ranks teaching as the profession that provides the most important benefit to society. Public perceptions of the importance of teaching have improved over the past years.[2] In fact, respondents to a survey ranked teachers first by more than a three-to-one margin over physicians, nurses, businesspeople, lawyers, journalists, politicians, and accountants, as shown in Figure 1.1.

Teachers were also given a vote of confidence in a recent Gallup Poll that asked people to indicate the most trusted group of people in the country. The results, as shown in Figure 1.2, indicate that teachers were ranked first as the most trusted group in the country. This public trust should be both encouraging and perhaps a bit frightening to you as a future educator—encouraging because you will be entering a highly regarded and trusted professional group and frightening because you will be responsible for helping to uphold this public trust.

information age

The current age in which information and its management are critical to education and societal advancement.

The Public View of Teachers and Schools

Teachers and the public agree that the quality of the teaching staff is of primary importance in selecting a school.[3] Parents, guardians, families, and students know who the effective teachers are in a school and will do everything possible to ensure that

FIGURE 1.1

Professions That Provide the Most Benefit to Society According to Survey Respondents

Source: Based on data from Recruiting New Teachers, Inc., *The Essential Profession: A National Survey of Public Attitudes toward Teaching, Educational Opportunity and School Reform.* Belmont, MA: Author, 1998.

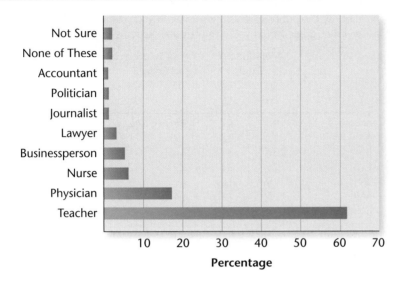

Percentage

FIGURE 1.2

Teachers Get America's Vote of Confidence

You may not make as much as a CEO or a pro baseball player, but your stock has a lot more currency than theirs in the eyes of the American public.

In a recent Gallup Poll, Americans ranked teachers as the most trusted group of people in the country.

Source: Phi Delta Kappa/Gallup Poll, July 2002, as reported in *NEA Today,* October 2002, p. 9.

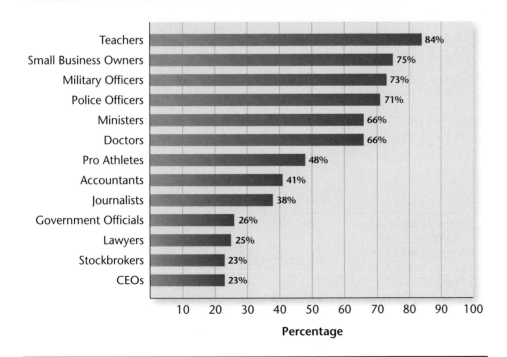

Percentage

FIGURE 1.3

The Public's Opinion of Public Schools

Source: Lowell C. Rose and Alec M. Gallup, "The 37th Annual Phi Delta Kappa/Gallup Poll of the Public's Attitude toward the Public Schools," *Phi Delta Kappan* (September 2005), p. 45. Reprinted by permission of Phi Delta Kappan.

Students are often given the grades of A, B, C, D, and FAIL to denote the quality of their work. Suppose the public schools themselves, in your community, were graded in the same way. What grade would you give the public schools here—A, B, C, D, or FAIL?

	National Totals		No Children in School		Public School Parents	
	'05 %	'04 %	'05 %	'04 %	'05 %	'04 %
A & B	48	47	45	42	57	61
A	12	13	9	11	20	17
B	36	34	36	31	37	44
C	29	33	29	37	29	24
D	9	10	9	9	8	10
FAIL	5	4	4	3	5	5
Don't know	9	6	13	9	1	*

*Less than one-half of 1%.

> No nation can remain free which does not recognize the importance of our education. Our public schools are the backbone of American life and character.
>
> **Samuel M. Lindsay**

their children are in those teachers' classes. At the same time, they know the teachers who are not as effective, and they steer their children into other classes if possible. They know the value of an effective teacher to the potential academic success of their children.

The annual Phi Delta Kappa/Gallup Poll survey on the public's attitudes toward public schools asks respondents to grade schools in both their local area and the nation as a whole. Figure 1.3 shows the results of this recent survey, which indicates that parents generally give high grades to schools, especially so for their local schools.

This same annual PDK/Gallup Poll asks citizens to indicate the most serious problems facing our schools. The results of the survey are shown in Figure 1.4.

FIGURE 1.4

The Public's View of Problems in Schools

Source: Lowell C. Rose and Alec M. Gallup, "The 37th Annual Phi Delta Kappa/Gallup Poll of the Public's Attitude toward the Public Schools," *Phi Delta Kappan* (September 2005), p. 44. Reprinted by permission of Phi Delta Kappan.

What do you think are the biggest problems the public schools of your community must deal with?

	National Totals			No Children in School			Public School Parents		
	'05 %	'04 %	'03 %	'05 %	'04 %	'03 %	'05 %	'04 %	'03 %
Lack of financial support/ funding/money	20	21	25	19	22	26	21	20	24
Overcrowded schools	11	10	14	9	9	12	15	13	16
Lack of discipline, more control	10	10	16	12	10	17	8	8	13
Use of drugs/dope	9	7	9	9	7	10	8	7	7

TABLE 1.1	What Would You Change to Improve the Public Schools in Your Community?		
		Public (percent)	Teachers (percent)
Discipline/more control/stricter rules		12	6
More teachers/smaller class size		10	12
Funding		5	8
Better/more qualified teachers		7	*
Higher pay for teachers		3	5
More parent involvement		3	18
Prayer/God back in schools		4	*
Security		4	*
Academic standards/better education		3	2
Dress code/uniforms		3	*
More/updated equipment/books/computers		2	3
Curriculum/more offered		2	*

* = Less than 1 percent.

Source: Adapted from Carol A. Langdon and Nick Vesper, "The Sixth Phi Delta Kappa Poll of Teachers' Attitudes toward the Public Schools," Phi Delta Kappan, 81(8) (April 2000), pp. 607–611.

Parents in their combined opinions view discipline, getting good teachers, and overcrowding as major school problems.

Curiously, the public and teachers do not agree on all of the changes necessary to improve schools, as shown in Table 1.1. Teachers would like to see more parental involvement, whereas the public sees discipline and stricter rules as most important. Both groups agree on the importance of having more teachers and/or reducing class size. Over half of the respondents in another survey were concerned about student drug use, school violence, student drinking, lack of parental involvement, teenage pregnancy, and students' lack of basic skills. They were less concerned about large classes and poor-quality teachers. Latino and African American respondents were more likely than others to find the lack of teacher quality a serious and widespread problem. Respondents also affirmed the desire to "keep the guarantee of a free public education for every child."[4] These differences between teacher and parent opinions on school problems again show that different groups hold differing perspectives on education.

Who Teaches?

Teachers should represent the diversity of the nation. However, white females are overrepresented in the teaching force, particularly in early childhood and elementary schools. Teachers come from varied backgrounds and hold a wide

The common teacher is not common at all. He (or she) is bulging with talent, with energy, and with understanding. What we human teachers have to give, ultimately, is ourselves—our own love for life, and for our subjects, and our ability to respond to the personal concerns of our students.

Terry Borton, Reach, Touch, Teach

In addition to being passionate about helping learners, teachers are good managers and take time to collaborate with their colleagues.

Parental involvement ranks right up there with smaller class size and improved student discipline at the top of the list of (NEA) members' professional wish list.

Reg Weaver, NEA President

Instead of asking why women lag behind men in mathematics, we might ask the following: Why do men lag behind women in elementary school teaching, early childhood education, nursing, full-time parenting, and like activities? Is there something wrong with men or with schools that this state of affairs persists?

Nel Noddings

variety of views. Some are Democrats, some Republicans, and some members of the Reform and other parties. Some belong to unions, but others don't. They hold a variety of religious views. Because of these many differences, it is difficult to generalize about educators in the United States. However, some of the similarities and differences among teachers may help you to understand the current teaching profession.

PROFILE OF U.S. TEACHERS

Although demographic data are elusive and constantly changing, the following snapshot of educators in the United States should help you get an idea of the profile of U.S. teachers. The United States has about 2.7 million public school teachers, about 400,000 private school teachers, and about 932,000 college and university faculty members. Over 60 percent of the teachers work at the elementary school level. In addition to teachers, our schools have about 411,000 administrative and education professionals. Approximately 1.25 million teachers' aides, clerks and secretaries, and service workers staff the nation's public schools. There are another roughly one million education-related jobs, including education specialists in industry, instructional technologists in the military, museum educators, and training consultants in the business world. Altogether, there are approximately five million educators in the United States, making education one of the largest professions in the country.

REMAINING IN THE PROFESSION

A relatively high percentage of classroom teachers eventually decide that teaching is not the profession they wish to pursue. It is estimated that approximately 20 percent of the new teachers hired annually are not teaching three years later. Teachers leave the classroom for a number of reasons. Some decide to return to school full time for an advanced degree. Others decide to pursue another career that might be more satisfying or pays a higher salary. Other reasons for leaving teaching are related to poor working conditions in schools, including lack of administrative support, perceived student problems, and little chance for upward mobility.

Like all other professionals, teachers become accomplished through experience. Most states do not grant a professional license to teachers until they have worked for at least three years. Teachers cannot seek national certification from the National Board for Professional Teaching Standards (NBPTS) until they have taught for three years. When teachers leave the profession in their first few years of practice, schools are losing an important developing resource. Induction and mentoring programs for new teachers increase the numbers of teachers who remain in the classroom. Good professional development programs for teachers such as **induction** programs also help to retain new teachers. When you search for your first teaching job, find out whether the school district provides induction, mentors, and professional development, especially for beginning teachers. These are services that help teachers improve their skills as well as their chances of being successful teachers who remain teachers over a longer period of time.

Many schools now have a system that provides **mentoring** among teachers. This peer mentoring system is designed to facilitate teachers helping one another. As part of a new teacher induction program, many of these schools assign an experienced master teacher to mentor beginning teachers.

Most teachers enter and remain in their profession because of a desire to work with young people.

Teachers Needed

Many factors influence the number of teachers that a school district needs each year. The number of students in schools, the ratio of teachers to students in classrooms, immigration patterns, and migration from one school district to another influence the demand for teachers. The supply of teachers depends on the numbers of new teachers licensed, teachers who retired or left the previous year, and teachers returning to the workforce.

Sometimes the supply is greater than the demand, but various estimates for the next decade indicate a demand for new teachers beyond the number being prepared in colleges and universities. The United States does not have a general teacher shortage. The problem is the distribution of teachers. School districts with good teaching conditions and high salaries do not face teacher shortages. However, inner cities and rural areas too often do not have adequate numbers of qualified and licensed teachers. There also are greater shortages of teachers in parts of the country with increasing populations, such as states in the Southwest.

TEACHER SUPPLY

The supply of new teachers in a given year consists primarily of two groups: new teacher graduates and former teacher graduates who were not employed as teachers during the previous year. Not all college graduates who prepared to teach actually teach. Generally, only about half the college graduates who have completed teacher education programs actually take teaching positions in the first few years after graduation.

It is estimated that nearly half the teachers hired by the typical school district are first-time teachers. A third are experienced teachers who have moved from other school districts or from other jobs within the district. Experienced teachers reentering the field make up the remainder of the new hires. Unfortunately, not all teachers who are hired have been even minimally prepared to teach before they take charge of a classroom. Over a fourth of newly hired teachers are not qualified for the beginning license to teach. Some new hires do not have a license; others have a temporary, provisional, or emergency license.

NEW TEACHERS   A number of new teachers are not recent college graduates. They are people who are changing careers or retirees from the military or business. These

induction
The first one to three years of full-time teaching.

mentoring
An experienced professional helping a less experienced colleague.

More than 200,000 new teachers graduate from colleges each year. Of them, about one-third never teach; about one-third teach for only a few years; and only the remaining one-third make teaching a career.

older new teachers with years of work experience often have completed alternative pathways into teaching through school-based graduate programs that build on their prior experiences. These teachers bring a different perspective on education to their teaching positions.

Still other new teachers have no preparation to teach; some do not even have a college degree. More often they have a degree in an academic area such as chemistry or history but have not studied teaching and learning or participated in clinical practices in schools. A number of states and school districts allow these individuals to teach with only a few weeks of training in the summer. Participants in these programs are more likely to be dissatisfied with their preparation than are teachers who have completed either regular or nontraditional programs for teacher preparation. They often have difficulty planning the curriculum, managing the classroom, and diagnosing students' learning needs, especially in their first years of teaching. Individuals who enter the profession through this path leave teaching at a higher rate than other teachers.

RETURNING TEACHERS   A number of licensed teachers drop out of the profession for a time but return later in life. These teachers constitute about 20 percent of the new hires each year. Therefore, when you finish your teacher education program, you will be competing for teaching positions not only with other new graduates but also with experienced teachers who are returning to the classroom or moving from one school district to another.

TEACHER DEMAND

The demand for teachers in the United States varies considerably from time to time, from place to place, from subject to subject, and from grade level to grade level. One of the major factors related to the demand for teachers is the number of school-age children, which can be projected into the future on the basis of birthrates.

The projected demand for K–12 teachers is shown in Figure 1.5. Many teachers will be retiring over the next decade, raising even further the number of new and reentering teachers needed to staff the nation's schools. As you plan your teaching career, you will want to consider a number of factors such as salary, benefits, cost of living, workload, and so forth, that influence the demand for teachers. They may

FIGURE 1.5

Relative Demand by Field

Source: "Relative Demand by Field," 2006 AAEE Job Search Handbook. Columbus, OH: American Association for Employment in Education, Inc., 2006, p. 15. Reprinted with permission.

Fields with Considerable Shortage (5.00–4.21)	
Emotional/Behavior Disorders	4.39
Severe/Profound Disabilities	4.37
Visually Impaired	4.33
Multicategorical	4.33
Mild/Moderate Disabilities	4.33
Learning Disability	4.29
Hearing Impaired	4.25
Mathematics Education	4.22

Fields with Some Shortage (4.20–3.41)	
Mental Retardation	4.18
Dual Certificate (Gen./Spec.)	4.17
Physics	4.16
Early Childhood Special Education	4.13
Chemistry	4.06
Bilingual Education	3.98
Languages—Spanish	3.95
Speech Pathologist	3.89
English as a Second Language	3.88
Earth/Physical	3.80
Physical Therapist	3.78
Biology	3.76
General Science	3.74
Audiologist	3.65
School Nurse	3.60
Technology Education	3.55
High School Principal	3.53
Middle School Principal	3.51
School Psychologist	3.45
Superintendent	3.44
Elementary Principal	3.43

Fields with Balanced Supply and Demand (3.40–2.61)	
Home Economics/Consumer Science	3.38
Agriculture	3.34
Reading	3.32
Computer Science Education	3.25
Library Science/Media Technology	3.24
Languages—French	3.20
Counselor	3.19
Music—Instrumental	3.16
Gifted/Talented Education	3.16
Occupational Therapist	3.13
Music—Vocal	3.13
Elementary—Middle	3.13
Languages—Classics	3.11
Speech Education	3.10
Business Manager	3.10
School Social Worker	3.09
Music—General	3.06
Languages—German	3.02
Driver Education/Traffic Safety	3.00
Languages—Japanese	3.00
Curriculum Director	3.00
English/Language Arts	2.97
Business Education	2.96
Human Resources Director	2.96
Elementary—Intermediate	2.84
Dance Education	2.80
Theatre/Drama	2.78
Journalism Education	2.76
Elementary—Pre-Kindergarten	2.74
Art/Visual Education	2.70
Elementary—Kindergarten	2.67

Fields with Some Surplus (2.60–1.81)	
Elementary—Primary	2.58
Health Education	2.46
Social Studies Education	2.43
Physical Education	2.42

Fields with Considerable Surplus (1.80–1.00)	
None	

From preliminary data supplied by survey respondents. In some instances, the averages are based on limited input and total reliability is not assured.
Demand codes: 5.00–4.21 = Considerable shortage; 4.20–3.41 = Some Shortage; 3.40–2.61 = Balanced; 2.60–1.81 = Some Surplus; 1.80–1.00 = Considerable Surplus

influence decisions you make about the subjects you will teach and the area of the country where you will teach.

STUDENT-TO-TEACHER RATIOS Obviously, one measure of a teacher's workload is class size. The number of students taught by a teacher varies considerably from school to school and from state to state. Elementary teachers generally have more students in a class than secondary teachers, but secondary teachers have five to seven classes each day. Figure 1.6 shows average student-to-teacher ratios in public and private schools in the United States.

The number of school-age children in the United States is expected to increase to 54.2 million by 2009.

The demand for teachers has increased, in part, because some states and school districts are limiting the student-to-teacher ratio, especially in the primary grades. In large school districts, lowering the student-to-teacher ratio by even one student creates a demand for many more teachers. Statewide initiatives to reduce the ratio have an even greater impact on the number of teachers needed.

LOCATION OF THE SCHOOL DISTRICT Even within a given metropolitan area, population shifts may be causing one school district to grow rapidly, build new schools, and hire new teachers because of new housing developments, while a neighboring school district is closing schools and reducing its number of teachers. Nevertheless, the greatest shortages are usually in urban schools with large proportions of low-income and culturally and linguistically diverse populations. Some teachers do not want to teach in large urban school districts because of poor working conditions in many schools and relatively low salaries as compared to schools in the wealthier suburbs. Many other teachers believe that teaching in a large city is challenging and fulfilling, with many advantages.

Urban schools are more likely than others to be staffed by unprepared teachers who have not met the qualifications for a state license. New, inexperienced teachers are disproportionately represented in the schools that need the best teachers. Attrition rates for new teachers in these districts are high in the first five years of teaching, leading to the constant need for replacements. To address this problem, some states have scholarships and loan-forgiveness programs to encourage teacher candidates to work in these high-demand areas.

Student enrollment also varies depending on the part of the country. By 2009, increases of more than 15 percent are expected in Arizona, Idaho, Nevada, and New Mexico; decreases are expected in most midwestern and northeastern states. Student enrollment in the District of Columbia, Maine, North Dakota, and West Virginia is projected to decrease by 7 to 12 percent.[5]

Almost all teachers can find a teaching position if they are willing to move to a place where jobs are available. One of the problems is that new teachers often want to remain close to home, which is more likely to be in small towns and suburban areas. To attract teachers to areas with teaching shortages, some school districts are offering signing bonuses and paying moving expenses. Others are exploring strategies to offer teachers housing and favorable mortgages.

FIGURE 1.6

Pupil/Teacher Ratio in Elementary and Secondary Schools, with Middle Alternative Projections: Selected Years

Source: U.S. Department of Education, National Center for Education Statistics (NCES): Common Core of Data surveys, various years.

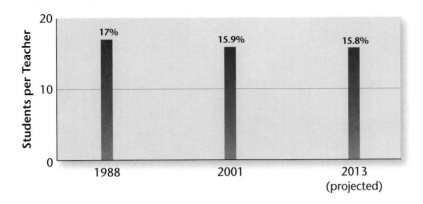

TEACHING FIELD SHORTAGES Teacher shortages are more severe in some fields than others. For instance, the number of students diagnosed with various disabilities has increased considerably over the last decade and now totals more than five million throughout the country. As a percentage of the total public school enrollment, the number of students requiring special education has risen considerably in recent years. Consequently, most school districts report the need for more special education teachers.

There is also a critical shortage of bilingual teachers. The need for bilingual teachers is no longer limited to large urban areas and the southwestern states. Immigrant families with children have now settled in cities and rural areas across the Midwest and Southeast. The projected demographics for the country indicate a growing number of students with limited-English skills, requiring more bilingual and English as a second language (ESL) teachers than are available today.

Licensed mathematics and science teachers are prime candidates for job openings in many school districts. One of the problems in secondary schools especially is that teachers may have a state license but too often not in the academic area they are assigned to teach. The National Commission on Teaching and America's Future reported that nearly one-fourth of all secondary teachers do not have even a college minor in their main teaching field. This is especially true for mathematics teachers. Among teachers who teach a second subject, about one-third are unlicensed in that field and about one-half lack a minor.

Teachers receive these out-of-field assignments when teachers with the appropriate academic credentials are not available. Sometimes the assignments are made to retain teachers whose jobs have been eliminated as enrollments shift and schools are closed. The tragedy is that students suffer as a result. It is difficult to teach what you do not know. The federal legislation commonly referred to as the No Child Left Behind Act (NCLB) is designed to significantly reduce this out-of-field teacher assignment problem in the near future.

TEACHERS FROM DIVERSE BACKGROUNDS Although the student population is rapidly changing and becoming more racially, ethnically, and linguistically diverse, the teaching pool is becoming less so. The number of Latino students is rapidly increasing, pulling almost even with the number of African American students in

CROSS-REFERENCE
Much more detail regarding multicultural education is present in Chapters 2 and 3.

Bilingual teachers are in short supply throughout the United States—especially in southern and western states. What employment opportunities does this need present?

the 2000 census. The racial and panethnic composition of the student population and teaching force is shown in Figure 1.7.

Having teachers from different ethnic and cultural backgrounds is extremely important to the majority of people in the United States.[6] Most school districts are seeking culturally diverse faculties, and districts with large culturally diverse populations

---

FIGURE 1.7

The Racial and Panethnic Composition of the Student Population and Teaching Force in Public Schools

Sources: Based on data from National Center for Education Statistics, U.S. Department of Education, *The Condition of Education 2000.* Washington, DC: Author, 2000; National Center for Education Statistics, U.S. Department of Education, *Digest of Education Statistics, 1999.* Washington, DC: Author, 1999.

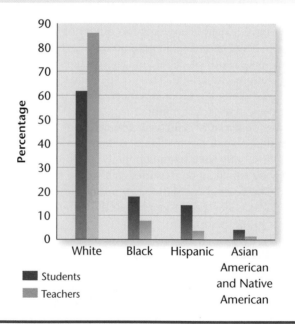

Global Perspectives

Teaching Chinese to American Students

Our schools recognize that we live in a rapidly changing world in which more people now speak Chinese than any other language. China has become a major market and supplier for American industry. With these facts in mind, the Portland, Oregon public school system instituted a K–12 Chinese-language instructional program for their approximately 50,000 students. Starting in kindergarden, students will study the Mandarin language and Chinese culture.

Questions for Reflection

1. What is your perspective on this idea?
2. What foreign language(s) are the most important for students to learn today?

are aggressively recruiting teachers from diverse backgrounds. The federal government and some states provide incentives to colleges and universities to support the recruitment of a more diverse teaching force. Another implication of the demographics of increasing student diversity is that all teachers need to become skilled at teaching in diverse schools and classrooms.

Teaching as a Profession

Historically, fields such as law, medicine, architecture, and accountancy have been considered professions, but teaching and nursing have sometimes been classified as semiprofessions. This distinction is based in part on the prestige of the different jobs as reflected in the remuneration received by members of the profession. Although teaching salaries remain lower than those of other professionals in most parts of the country, most educators consider themselves professionals. The good news is that over the past decade the prestige of teaching has risen. Most teachers have master's degrees and continue to participate in professional development activities throughout their careers. They manage their professional work, designing and delivering a curriculum during a school year. They develop their own unique teaching styles and methods for helping students learn. In this section, we will explore the factors that determine a profession and a professional and demonstrate that teaching itself is a full-fledged profession.

> Teaching is a profession laden with risk and responsibility that requires a great deal from those who enter it.
> *John I. Goodlad*

Perspectives on Professional Practice

Professionals provide services to their clients, and their work is based on unique knowledge and skills grounded in research and practice in the field. Professions require their members to have completed higher education, usually at the advanced level. The competence of most professionals is determined in training by **authentic assessments** in real settings. Traditionally, they have had control of their work with little direct supervision.

PROFESSIONAL KNOWLEDGE

One of the characteristics of a profession is that its members have some generally agreed-upon knowledge bases for their work. This professional knowledge has evolved from research and practice in the field. Teachers who have prepared to

authentic assessment

An assessment procedure that uses real-world situations to assess students' ability to encounter those situations successfully, using journals, drawings, artifacts, interviews, and so on.

teach are more successful in classrooms than those who only have a degree in an academic discipline. These competent and qualified teachers are key to student learning. They also remain in the classroom for longer periods.

First and foremost, teachers must know the subjects they will be teaching. Secondary teachers often major in an academic area that they later will teach so that they learn the structure, skills, core concepts, ideas, values, facts, and methods of inquiry that undergird the discipline. They must understand the discipline well enough to help young people learn it and apply it to the world in which they live. If students are not learning a concept or skill, teachers must be able to relate the content to the experiences of students in order to provide meaning and purpose.

Elementary and middle school teachers usually teach more than one subject. A growing number of states and some colleges are requiring these teacher candidates to major in an academic area or have a concentration in one or more areas. Middle school teachers may teach one or two subjects; sometimes they team teach with others whose academic preparation is in other subjects. Elementary teachers, by contrast, often teach reading, English language arts, social studies, mathematics, and science in a self-contained classroom with few or no outside professional resources to assist them. They are often also expected to help students develop healthy lifestyles and an appreciation for music and art. To begin to have the academic knowledge to teach requires more than four years of college for many teacher candidates.

PROFESSIONAL SKILLS

One of the cornerstones of the field of teaching is knowledge about teaching and learning and the development of skills and **dispositions** to help students learn. Therefore, teacher candidates study theories and research on how students learn at different ages. They must understand the influence of culture, language, and socioeconomic conditions on learning. They also have to know how to manage classrooms, motivate students, work with parents and colleagues, assess learning, and develop lesson plans built on the prior experiences of fifteen to thirty or more students in the classroom. Teaching is a complex field. There are seldom right answers that fit every situation. Teachers must make multiple decisions throughout a day, responding to individual student needs and events in the school and community, all while keeping in mind the professional ethics required by the education profession.

Qualified teachers have also had the opportunity to develop their knowledge, skills, and dispositions with students in schools. These field experiences and clinical

dispositions

The values, commitments, and professional ethics that influence beliefs, attitudes, and behaviors.

Each teaching discipline has unique requirements and knowledge bases needed for certification.

practices such as student teaching and internships should be accompanied by feedback and mentoring from experienced teachers who know the subject they teach and how to help students learn. Work in schools is becoming more extensive in many teacher education programs. Some teacher candidates participate in yearlong internships in schools, ending in a master's degree. Others work in professional development schools in which higher education faculty, teachers, and teacher candidates collaborate in teaching and inquiry. In both of these cases, most, if not all, of the program is offered in the school setting.

The knowledge about teaching and learning, translated into student learning in the classroom, makes up the professional knowledge for teaching. People who begin to teach without this professional knowledge and the accompanying experiences for honing their skills in classrooms have difficulty managing classrooms and teaching effectively.

STANDARDS

Yet another example of recent change that has occurred pertains to the establishment of standards created by states, professional associations, and various accrediting agencies. Standards are now a very important part of all professions, including the education profession. They define, in part, what professionals should know and be able to do. They indicate the core values of the profession and the essential, agreed-upon knowledge and skills that professionals should have. Members of the profession develop standards to guide training, entry into the profession, and continuing practice in the profession. States also develop standards that define the minimal expectations to practice the profession in a particular state. Standards represent the collective perspectives held by the group that created them. Teachers are now impacted by various sets of standards and must therefore become knowledgeable about those pertaining to the education profession.

CROSS-REFERENCE
Standards and assessments are discussed further in Chapter 11.

Standards and standards-based education are prevalent at all levels of education today. To finish your teacher education program, you will have to meet professional, state, and institutional standards that outline what you should know and be able to do as a novice teacher. When you begin teaching, you will be expected to prepare students to meet state or district standards. Assessments are designed to determine whether students meet the preschool–grade 12 standards at the levels expected. Most states require teacher candidates to pass standardized tests at a predetermined level before granting the first license to teach. Some states require beginning teachers to pass **performance assessments** based on standards in the first three years of practice in order to receive a professional license.

Standards developed by the profession can be levers for raising the quality of practice. When used appropriately, they can protect the least advantaged students from incompetent practice.[7] Some educators view standards as a threat, especially when a government agency or other group holds individuals or schools to the standards, making summative judgments about licensure or approval. Others see standards as powerful tools for positive change in a profession or in school practices.

NO CHILD LEFT BEHIND

The No Child Left Behind Act was signed into law by President George W. Bush on January 8, 2002. This act, which is actually a reauthorized version of the earlier Elementary and Secondary Education Act (ESEA), is built around four national education reform goals: stronger accountability for student learning results, increased educational flexibility and local control, expanded educational options for parents, and an emphasis on using teaching methods that have been proved to work. The act received overwhelming support from the U.S. Congress and the Administration and is likely to guide much of our public education for at least the next decade. This far-reaching law will require the tracking of all students' progress from grades 3 to 8 and will also require every student to pass the state proficiency test(s) by the end of the 2013–14 school year.

performance assessment

A comprehensive assessment system through which candidates demonstrate their proficiencies in the area being measured.

Professional Dilemma

Who Is Cheating Now?

Testing is pervasive in our educational system today. Many school districts and states require students to pass tests to move from one grade to another grade. They must pass tests to graduate from high school and to enter most colleges and universities. Teacher candidates must pass numerous standardized tests to be licensed.

Not only are students and teacher candidates tested regularly and often, but also their schools and universities are held accountable for their performance on these tests. The aggregated results are published in newspapers and on websites. Schools and colleges are ranked within a state. Some are classified as low performing and lose part of their public funding. In some schools, teachers' and principals' jobs depend on how well their students perform on these standardized tests.

The standardized tests that are being used in elementary and secondary education are supposed to test for evidence that students are meeting state standards. For the most part, they are paper-and-pencil tests of knowledge in a subject area. Although the state standards are advertised as being developed by teachers and experts, many educators argue that many of the standards expect knowledge and skills that are developmentally inappropriate at some grade levels. In areas such as social studies, recall of specific facts that cover spans of hundreds of years is not an uncommon requirement.

It probably comes as no surprise that some teachers are teaching to the test, talking weeks out of the curriculum to coach students for the test.

Questions for Reflection

1. What are your perspectives on student cheating at this point in your professional development?
2. What are some things that teachers can do to reduce student cheating?
3. What are some of the changes and factors that probably cause students to cheat?

To answer these questions on-line and e-mail your answers to your professor, go to Chapter 1 of the companion website (www.ablongman.com/johnson14e) and click on Professional Dilemma.

CROSS-REFERENCE
NCLB is discussed in a variety of places throughout the text. (Consult index for details.)

Most important to you as a future teacher, this new legislation requires that every classroom have a highly qualified, competent teacher who is fully certified and licensed in the areas being taught in every classroom. Like all sweeping pieces of legislation, the No Child Left Behind Act is controversial and has many critics. Because it will have a considerable impact on your future as an educator and citizen, we highly recommend that you review it more closely (see www.nochildleftbehind.gov).

The major goal of the No Child Left Behind legislation is to improve learning for all children.

Quality Assurance

One of the roles of professions and their standards is to provide quality control over who enters and remains in the profession. Most other professions, such as law, medicine, and dentistry, require candidates to graduate from an accredited professional school before they are even eligible to take a licensing examination to test the knowledge and skills necessary to practice responsibly. Some professions also offer examinations for certification of advanced skills, such as the CPA exam for public accountants, or for practice in specialized fields such as pediatrics, obstetrics, or surgery. The same quality assurance continuum now exists for teaching. Figure 1.8 depicts a comprehensive quality assurance system for teaching that includes complementary sets of standards and assessments for initial teacher preparation, state licensure, National Board certification, and continuing professional development.

ACCREDITATION

Both public schools and teacher education programs are subject to accreditation programs, some of which are mandated and some of which are voluntary.

REGIONAL ACCREDITATION The general concept of accreditation is related to an internal attempt on the part of a professional training system to examine and improve the quality of the profession that it serves. This is the case for the six regional accreditation bodies that offer accreditation to all K–12 schools and to colleges and universities. One of these six agencies, all of which are named by the general region in which they function, is functioning in your state right now. For instance, the North Central Association of Schools and Colleges (NCA) covers a large number of states in the upper central part of the nation. You might want to inquire whether your own institution is accredited by one of these six regional accrediting agencies. There is a good chance that the schools in which you will eventually teach will also be involved in some type of regional accreditation.

FIGURE 1.8

The Professional Continuum and Quality Assurance in Teaching

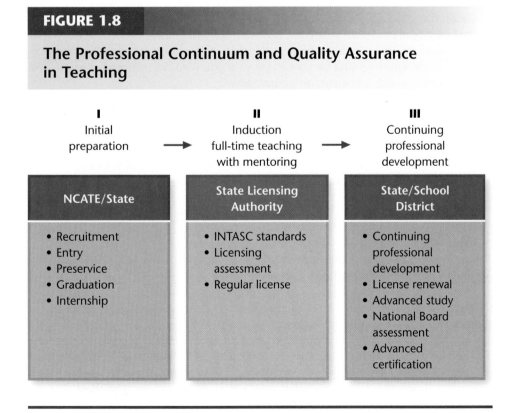

NCATE   Do you know whether the teacher education program you are in is part of an accredited institution? Your college or university is probably accredited by one of six regional accrediting bodies that apply standards to the university as a whole by reviewing its financial status, student services, and the general studies curriculum. However, professional accreditation in teacher education is granted to the school, college, or department of education that is responsible for preparing teachers and other educators. Fewer than half of the roughly 1,300 institutions that prepare teachers in the United States are accredited by the profession's accrediting agency, the National Council for Accreditation of Teacher Education (NCATE).

Accreditation also provides assurance to the public that graduates of programs are qualified and competent to practice. The proportion of accredited schools, colleges, and departments of education in a state has been found to be the best predictor of the proportion of well-qualified teachers in a state.[8] Because well-qualified teachers are the strongest predictor of student achievement on national achievement tests, accreditation is an important first step of a quality assurance system for the education field. To learn more about the accreditation status of institutions, visit NCATE's website at www.ncate.org.

LICENSURE

When you graduate, you will be required to obtain a teaching license for the state in which you wish to teach. The requirements for your license are determined by the state in which you teach.

STATE TEACHER CERTIFICATION   State licensure is a major component of a quality assurance system for professionals. To practice as a physician, nurse, lawyer, architect, or teacher, you must be granted a license from a state agency. A license to teach usually requires completion of a state-approved teacher education program and passing a standardized test of knowledge. A growing number of states require teacher candidates to major in an academic area rather than in education. In addition, student teaching or an internship must be completed successfully. Requirements for licensure differ from state to state. For this reason, if you plan to teach in a state different from the one in which you are going to school, you may want to contact that state directly for licensure information. Information on licensure requirements is available on the websites of state licensing agencies; for a list of agencies and contact information, see Appendix A at the end of this book. The certification officer at your institution should be able to provide you with licensure information and details about seeking a license in another state.

The initial license allows a new teacher to practice for a specified period, usually three to five years, or the induction period. On completion of successful teaching during that period and sometimes a master's degree, a professional license can be granted. Most states require continuing professional development throughout the teacher's career and periodic renewal of the license, typically every five years.

States traditionally required candidates to take specific college courses, complete student teaching, and successfully pass a licensure examination for a license. Most states are now in the process of developing **performance-based licensing** systems. These will not specify courses to be completed; instead, they will indicate the knowledge, skills, and sometimes dispositions that candidates should possess. Future decisions about granting a license will depend on the results of state assessments based primarily on licensure test scores.

INTASC   Concerned about the limitations of standardized tests and their ability to predict successful classroom practice, more than thirty states are participating in a consortium to develop performance-based licensure standards and assessments. The ten principles of the Interstate New Teacher Assessment and Support Consortium (INTASC) have been adopted or adapted for licensure by many states. Figure 1.9 shows these ten principles, which describe what teachers should know and be able to do in their first few years of practice. You should be developing

performance-based licensing

A system of professional licensing based on the use of multiple assessments that measure the candidate's knowledge, skills, and dispositions to determine whether he or she can perform effectively in the profession.

FIGURE 1.9

INTASC Principles: What Teachers Should Know and Be Able to Do

1. The teacher understands the central concepts, tools of inquiry, and structures of the discipline(s) he or she teaches and can create learning experiences that make these aspects of subject matter meaningful for students.
2. The teacher understands how children learn and develop, and can provide learning opportunities that support their intellectual, social, and personal development.
3. The teacher understands how students differ in their approaches to learning and creates instructional opportunities that are adapted to diverse learners.
4. The teacher understands and uses a variety of instructional strategies to encourage students' development of critical thinking, problem solving, and performance skills.
5. The teacher uses an understanding of individual and group motivation and behavior to create a learning environment that encourages positive social interaction, active engagement in learning, and self-motivation.
6. The teacher uses knowledge of effective verbal, nonverbal, and media communication techniques to foster active inquiry, collaboration, and supportive interaction in the classroom.
7. The teacher plans instruction based on knowledge of subject matter, students, the community, and curriculum goals.
8. The teacher understands and uses formal and informal assessment strategies to evaluate and ensure the continuous intellectual, social, and physical development of the learner.
9. The teacher is a reflective practitioner who continually evaluates the effects of his or her choices and actions on others (students, parents, and other professionals in the learning community) and who actively seeks out opportunities to grow professionally.
10. The teacher fosters relationships with school colleagues, parents, and agencies in the larger community to support students' learning and well-being.

Each of these ten principles is accompanied in the full INTASC document with knowledge, dispositions, and performance expectations for candidates. INTASC content standards also have been developed for teachers of the arts, English language arts, mathematics, science, social studies, elementary education, and special education. INTASC standards can be accessed from the web at www.ccsso.org.

---

this knowledge and skills in the college program in which you are currently enrolled. Before granting a professional license, some states are requiring teachers to submit **portfolios,** which are scored by experienced teachers, as evidence of teaching effectiveness. The portfolios that you begin to compile during your teacher education program could evolve into the documentation you will later need to submit for your first professional license.

PRAXIS   The Educational Testing Service (ETS) has developed a series of three examinations, commonly called the *Praxis Series*™, that are designed to assess the knowledge and skills required to be an effective educator at various stages of a beginning teacher's career. Praxis I assesses academic skills, Praxis II assesses the subjects to be taught, and Praxis III assesses classroom performance. Some teacher education programs and most states make use of these tests as part of their admission, retention, graduation, and certification requirements. Perhaps you are familiar with these Praxis tests; you may even have taken some of them. In any case, you should become familiar with them, including Praxis II, which illustrates the subject matter that you should know in your particular teaching field. You can learn more about the *Praxis Series* by visiting its website at www.ets.org/praxis.

portfolio

A compilation of works, records, and accomplishments that teacher candidates prepare for a specific purpose to demonstrate their learnings, performances, and contributions.

ADVANCED CERTIFICATION

Advanced certification has long been an option in many professions but is relatively new for teaching. Like all issues related to education, requiring advanced certification is not supported by everyone.

Many states now have an advanced certification option for educators. Some states actually require teachers to progress through a series of certification levels, whereas other states have either optional levels of certification that are made available to teachers or only one certification level. You should inquire about the certification levels required or available in your state. You should also eventually understand the certification requirements and options in any school district in which you might consider working.

NBPTS

The National Board for Professional Teaching Standards (NBPTS) was established in 1987 to develop a system for certifying accomplished teachers. The first teachers were certified in 1995, and the number of teachers seeking national certification continues to increase.

The National Board standards outline what teachers should know and be able to do as accomplished teachers. These standards state that nationally certified teachers:

1. Are committed to students and their learning.
2. Know the subjects they teach and how to teach those subjects to students.
3. Are responsible for managing and monitoring student learning.
4. Think systematically about their practice and learn from experience.
5. Are members of learning communities.

Why then do teachers seek national certification? For one thing, recognition of accomplishment by one's peers is fulfilling. Nationally certified teachers are also aggressively being recruited by some school districts. Some school districts and half the states pay an extra salary stipend that can be several thousand dollars annually to nationally certified teachers. Your current teacher education program should be providing the basic foundation for future national certification.

Teachers must have taught for at least three years before they are eligible for national certification. The process for becoming nationally certified requires at least a year. You can learn the details about this opportunity by visiting the National Board website at www.nbpts.org.

The certification process requires the submission of portfolios with samples of student work and videotapes of the applicant teaching. In addition, the teachers must complete a number of activities at an assessment center. Experienced teachers score the various assessment activities. Many teachers do not meet the national requirements on the first try but report that the process is the best professional development activity in which they have participated. Overwhelmingly, teachers report that they have become better teachers as a result. More and more parents in the future will likely request nationally certified teachers in their children's classrooms.

Professional Responsibilities

Being a professional carries many responsibilities. Professionals in most fields regulate licensure and practice through a professional standards board controlled by members of the profession rather than the government. Professional standards boards for teaching currently exist in about one-fourth of the states; other agencies have this responsibility in the remaining states. These boards have a variety of titles and typically include many practicing educators. Not only do these boards set standards for licensure, but they also have standards and processes for monitoring the practice of teachers. They usually have the authority to remove a teacher's license.

DEVELOPING PROFESSIONAL COMMITMENTS AND DISPOSITIONS

Successful teachers exhibit dispositions that facilitate their work with students and parents. Teachers' values, commitments, and professional ethics influence interactions with students, families, colleagues, and communities. They affect student learning, motivation, and development. They influence a teacher's own professional growth as well. Dispositions held by teachers who are able to help all students learn include:

1. Enthusiasm for the discipline(s) she or he teaches and the ability to see connections to everyday life.
2. A commitment to continuous learning and engagement in professional discourse about subject matter knowledge and children's learning of the disciplines.
3. The belief that all children can learn at high levels.
4. Valuing the many ways that people seek to communicate and encouraging many modes of communication in the classroom.
5. Development of respectful and productive relationships with parents and guardians from diverse home and community situations, seeking to develop cooperative partnerships in support of student learning and well-being.

EDUCATOR CODE OF ETHICS

One of the characteristics of a profession is the acceptance of a statement of ethics that professionals are expected to uphold. A number of professional associations have codes of ethics for individuals in a particular role, such as the special education teacher. Professional standards boards apply a code of ethics as they investigate complaints against teachers and other educators, sometimes removing an individual's license because of infractions. The code of ethics adopted by the largest organization of teachers, the National Education Association (NEA), outlines the critical values and behaviors expected of practicing teachers. This code of ethics can be found in Appendix B at the end of this book.

Given the trend to include students with disabilities in general education classrooms, it is likely that some of your students will have special needs, no matter what grade or subject you teach.

You are likely to have made some of these professional commitments when you decided to become a teacher. Your teacher education program should help you to further develop these dispositions and commitments and learn new ones. They are usually assessed as you work in classrooms with students and families.

Reflecting on One's Practice

It is interesting, and perhaps useful to educators, to note that physicians proudly claim to "practice" medicine throughout their careers. Many people have suggested that teachers should borrow this concept and also proudly undertake to "practice" teaching throughout their careers. This interpretation of the word *practice* implies that teachers, like physicians, should constantly strive to improve their performance—something that all good teachers do. This section provides you with a few practical suggestions as you prepare to "practice" your profession as a teacher.

SYSTEMATIC OBSERVATION AND JOURNALING

As you proceed through your teacher education program, you should seize every opportunity to observe a wide variety of activities related to the world of education. For instance, in addition to the observation and participation assignments you will have as part of the formal teacher education program, you should seek out opportunities to visit and observe a wide variety of classrooms. You should also attempt to find summer employment that allows you to work with young people.

INFORMAL NOTE-TAKING

One of the most common ways to collect information is by writing down your observations. This type of note-taking can be done in a variety of ways. For instance, when you go into a classroom you could start by writing a brief description of the setting, such as the physical appearance of the room, the number of students, the teaching devices available, and so on. You can then systematically describe each thing you observe. The more detail you can record, the more you will learn from your observations. Create a list of questions before you begin any given observation. If you are interested in how a teacher motivates students during a particular lesson, write down the question "What techniques does the teacher use to help motivate students?" Then record your observations under that question. The School-Based Observations feature, located with the end matter of each chapter of this book, will help you get an idea of the types of observations you can make.

ANALYSIS OF PRACTICE AND REFLECTION

Once you have collected observations of teaching, children, classrooms, and schools, take time to think about what you have seen. Several techniques exist for systematically analyzing your observations, but equally important is taking time to reflect on these analyses. In our rush to get everything done, we frequently fail to take time to examine our experiences and impressions. However, being serious about finding time for thoughtful reflection is an important part of becoming an excellent teacher, and some of the following processes can be helpful.

REFLECTIVE JOURNALING

Educators at all levels have come to realize that learners profit greatly from thinking reflectively about, and then writing down, what they learn in school. This process is called *reflective journaling*. If you are not now required to keep a journal in your teacher education program, we strongly recommend that you start doing so. If you are required to keep a journal, we urge you to take this assignment seriously because you will learn much in the process.

You can go about keeping a journal in many ways. All you need is something to write on and the will to write. A spiral notebook, a three-ring binder, or a computer works fine. Preferably at the end of each day (at the very least once each week), briefly summarize your thoughts about and reactions to the major events and concepts you have experienced and learned. Spend more time thinking and reflecting, and write down only a brief summary. We believe that your journal should be brief, reflective, candid, personal, and preferably private, something like a personal diary. Try to be perfectly honest in your journal and not worry about someone evaluating your opinions.

When you start to work in schools, you will discover (if you have not already done so) that teachers in elementary and secondary schools are using journaling more and more with their students. Something about thinking and then writing down our thoughts about what we have learned helps us internalize, better understand, and remember what we have learned.

Within each chapter in this book, we offer several suggestions for entries in your journal. We sincerely believe that reflective journaling throughout your teacher education program will enrich your learning.

FOLIO/PORTFOLIO DEVELOPMENT

As you move through your teacher education program and into your career as a teacher, you will find that you have been collecting stacks, boxes, and files of information and "stuff" related to you, your teaching, and the accomplishments of the students you have taught.

COLLECTING AND ORGANIZING MATERIAL   If you are like most teachers, you will not know for sure what to do with all of it, yet you will be reluctant to throw any of it away. Be very careful about discarding material until you have organized a folio and anticipated the needs of various portfolios that you might have to prepare. A *folio* is an organized compilation of all the products, records, accomplishments, and testimonies of a teacher and his or her students. Imagine the folio as a large file drawer with different compartments and file folders. Some of the material included is related directly to you and your background. Other items or artifacts reflect what others have said about you. And some are examples of projects that your students have completed.

A *portfolio* is a special compilation assembled from the folio for a specific occasion or purpose, such as a job interview or an application for an outstanding teacher award. The portfolio might also be used by you and your professors throughout your teacher education program to document your performance in meeting state, professional, and institutional standards. Portfolios are required in some states as evidence that you should be granted a professional teaching license after the first few years of actual work in classrooms. Portfolios will also be required for National Board certification later in your career. A folio and/or portfolio can be organized in any way you think will be most useful.

Many pieces of factual information about you belong in your folio. Demographic information, where you attended school, the states in which you are licensed to teach, and the record of your work experience are examples of these factual items. When organizing your folio, you should identify areas in which you should aim to add information. Now is the time to anticipate some of the material you might need in preparing a particular portfolio in the future. For example, when you apply for most teaching positions, a prospective employer will want to know the kinds of experiences you have had in schools and classrooms with diverse students. If you do not currently have any examples in your folio, plan to add some related experiences as your teacher education program unfolds. Your professors may expect to see evidence that you are meeting standards such as INTASC or those of a specialty professional association.

The occasions on which other people recognize your contributions and achievements are called *attestations*. Awards, letters of commendation, newspaper articles, elected positions, and committee memberships are examples of attestation items to keep in your folio.

Through your efforts as a teacher candidate and teacher, students complete assignments, assemble projects, achieve on examinations, and receive awards. In this part of the folio, compile the works and successes of the people you have worked with, along with photographs and video records of your classroom and student projects. You may want to include videotapes of your teaching with a description of your classroom context and analysis of your teaching. Also include copies of your best lesson plans, committee reports, grant proposals, and other products that have resulted from your leading the efforts of others.

PREPARING A PORTFOLIO   When the need arises to prepare a portfolio, such as for use in documenting that you meet standards or in your interview for a teaching position, you will be delighted that you did the advance work with your folio. Time always seems too short when a special portfolio needs to be developed. But when you do the folio work along the way, you will find it relatively easy to pull specific examples and documents to fit a particular job interview or to make a final application for a teaching award. Also, when you develop the folio with the broader

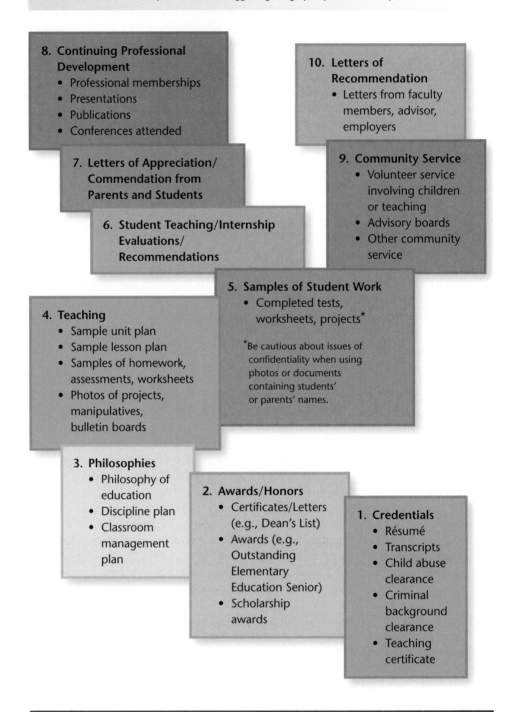

FIGURE 1.10

Sample Portfolio Contents

Source: Claude Netterville, "Sample Portfolio Contents," *2002 AAEE Job Search Handbook.* Columbus, OH: American Association for Employment in Education, Inc., p. 23. *Special thanks to Claude Netterville, University of Arizona, for suggesting the graphic presentation of portfolio contents.*

8. Continuing Professional Development
- Professional memberships
- Presentations
- Publications
- Conferences attended

10. Letters of Recommendation
- Letters from faculty members, advisor, employers

7. Letters of Appreciation/ Commendation from Parents and Students

9. Community Service
- Volunteer service involving children or teaching
- Advisory boards
- Other community service

6. Student Teaching/Internship Evaluations/ Recommendations

5. Samples of Student Work
- Completed tests, worksheets, projects*

*Be cautious about issues of confidentiality when using photos or documents containing students' or parents' names.

4. Teaching
- Sample unit plan
- Sample lesson plan
- Samples of homework, assessments, worksheets
- Photos of projects, manipulatives, bulletin boards

3. Philosophies
- Philosophy of education
- Discipline plan
- Classroom management plan

2. Awards/Honors
- Certificates/Letters (e.g., Dean's List)
- Awards (e.g., Outstanding Elementary Education Senior)
- Scholarship awards

1. Credentials
- Résumé
- Transcripts
- Child abuse clearance
- Criminal background clearance
- Teaching certificate

array of items suggested in Figure 1.10, you will be able to prepare a higher-quality presentation of your accomplishments.

PORTFOLIO DEVELOPMENT TASKS   To help you start your folio, we have included at the end of each chapter several suggestions under the Portfolio Development

Relevant Research

Teachers' Perspectives on Most Rewarding Aspects of Their Work

STUDY PURPOSE/QUESTION: What do newer teachers perceive to be the most rewarding parts of their work as educators?

STUDY DESIGN: Eight hundred public school teachers, all of whom were in their first five years of teaching, were surveyed on the telephone. One part of the survey attempted to determine the teachers' degree of satisfaction working with students, with other teachers, with the principal, with other school or staff administrators, and with parents.

STUDY FINDINGS: Sixty-eight percent of the teachers felt that working with students was "very satisfying," 57 percent felt working with other teachers was very satisfying, 53 percent felt working with their prin-

cipals was very satisfying, 39 percent indicated that working with other school or staff administrators was very satisfying, and only 25 percent felt that working with parents was very satisfying.

IMPLICATIONS: Future teachers, according to this study, will likely find it most satisfying to work with their students and may find it less satisfying and a bigger challenge working with other groups with whom they will be in contact. So it would behoove you to learn all you can at this point about ways to effectively work with other teachers, administrators, and parents.

Source: MetLife Survey of the American Teacher, 2004–2005, "Transitions and the Role of Supporting Relationships."

section. These suggestions anticipate some of the items you may need to include in future portfolio presentations; we have selected topics and tasks that are important to you at this early point in your teacher education program.

Journal for Reflection

Record your thoughts at this stage of your professional development about (1) the teaching profession, (2) its strengths and weaknesses, (3) your interest in teaching as a career, and (4) your excitement and doubts about working in the profession.

Challenges Affecting Teachers

The working conditions for teachers have improved measurably in recent years, and the following sections will show some of the ways these improvements are implemented. This information represents more good news for those who are preparing for careers in the education field.

Salaries in a Changing World

Salaries vary considerably from state to state and from school district to school district. Table 1.2 shows average and beginning teacher salaries in each state. As you can see, salaries in most northeastern states are higher than those in other parts of the country. One reason for the higher salaries is a difference in the cost of living from one area to another. It is more expensive to live in a number of the northeastern states, Alaska, Hawaii, and large urban areas. However, cost of living alone does not explain the differences. Connecticut and school districts such as Rochester, New York, view teachers as professionals, have high expectations for them, support them through mentoring and professional development, use multiple assessments to determine teacher effectiveness, and pay salaries commensurate with those of other professionals.

TABLE 1.2	Average and Beginning Teacher Salary in 2003–2004 Ranked by Average Salary within Region	
State	Average Salary	Beginning Salary
NEW ENGLAND		
Connecticut	$ 56,516	$ 34,462
Rhode Island	$ 54,809	$ 32,902
Massachusetts	$ 53,274	$ 34,041
Vermont	$ 43,009	$ 25,819
New Hampshire	$ 42,689	$ 27,367
Maine	$ 39,864	$ 25,901
MID-ATLANTIC		
New York	$ 55,181	$ 36,400
New Jersey	$ 53,663	$ 37,061
Pennsylvania	$ 52,640	$ 34,140
Delaware	$ 51,122	$ 34,566
Maryland	$ 50,303	$ 33,760
GREAT LAKES		
Michigan	$ 54,474	$ 34,377
Illinois	$ 53,820	$ 35,114
Ohio	$ 47,791	$ 28,692
Indiana	$ 45,791	$ 29,784
Minnesota	$ 45,010	$ 30,772
Wisconsin	$ 41,687	$ 23,952
PLAINS		
Nebraska	$ 39,635	$ 28,527
Kansas	$ 38,622	$ 28,530
Iowa	$ 38,381	$ 26,967
Missouri	$ 38,247	$ 28,938
North Dakota	$ 35,411	$ 24,108
South Dakota	$ 33,236	$ 25,504
SOUTHWEST		
Arizona	$ 42,324	$ 28,236
Texas	$ 40,476	$ 32,741
New Mexico	$ 38,469	$ 31,920
Oklahoma	$ 35,061	$ 29,473
SOUTHEAST		
Georgia	$ 45,848	$ 35,116
Virginia	$ 43,936	$ 32,437
North Carolina	$ 43,211	$ 27,572
South Carolina	$ 41,162	$ 27,883
Florida	$ 40,598	$ 30,969
Tennessee	$ 40,318	$ 30,449
Kentucky	$ 39,831	$ 28,416
Arkansas	$ 39,226	$ 26,129
West Virginia	$ 38,496	$ 26,692
Alabama	$ 38,282	$ 30,973
Louisiana	$ 37,123	$ 29,655
Mississippi	$ 36,217	$ 28,106

TABLE 1.2	(continued)		
ROCKY MOUNTAINS			
Colorado	$ 43,318	$ 31,296	
Idaho	$ 40,111	$ 25,908	
Wyoming	$ 39,537	$ 28,900	
Utah	$ 38,976	$ 26,130	
Montana	$ 37,184	$ 24,032	
FAR WEST			
California	$ 56,444	$ 35,135	
Alaska	$ 51,136	$ 40,027	
Oregon	$ 47,829	$ 33,396	
Hawaii	$ 45,456	$ 37,615	
Washington	$ 45,437	$ 30,159	
Nevada	$ 43,211	$ 27,942	
U.S. AVERAGE	**$ 46,597**	**$ 31,704**	

Source: E. Muir, F. Howard Nelson, and Aaron Baldaro, *Survey and Analysis of Teacher Salary Trends 2004*. Washington, DC: Research and Information Services, American Federation of Teachers, AFL-CIO, 2005. Reprinted with permission.

SALARY DIFFERENCES

Each board of education is an agent of the state and is therefore empowered to set salary levels for employees of the school district it governs. Each school system typically has a **salary schedule** that outlines the minimum and maximum salary for several levels of study beyond the bachelor's degree and for each year of teaching experience. For example, a beginning teacher with a bachelor's degree might be paid $35,000, and one with a master's degree might be paid $42,000. Teachers with twenty years of experience might be paid $50,000 to $76,000, depending on the school district in which they are employees. Although Table 1.2 shows 2003–2004 average and beginning state teacher salaries, remember that these figures change each year.

Some people might argue that teachers are paid less because they do not work year-round. However, they actually earn less than most other professionals even when the number of weeks worked during a year is taken into account.

The somewhat lower salaries of teachers can become a deterrent for those who would like to teach. Some people argue that raising teachers' salaries will make no difference in the quality of the teaching force. Experiences in states such as Connecticut are contradicting those arguments. Higher salaries are attracting teachers to the state even though candidates must meet performance assessments required for licenses at high levels. As a result, students in the state's classrooms are also performing at higher levels.

The organization Recruiting New Teachers found that more than 75 percent of the public supported raising teachers' salaries. Over half of the respondents in this survey indicated that they would choose teaching as a career if they were guaranteed an annual income of $60,000. Further, they would recommend teaching as a career for members of their family if the salary was at this level.[9] These findings suggest that the pool of available teachers would be much larger if teachers' salaries were higher.

ADDITIONAL BENEFITS

Almost all full-time teachers receive additional benefits that, when added to their basic salary, constitute their total compensation package. When you pursue your first teaching position, you will want to inquire about these benefits as well as the salary. Although the salary is usually of first concern to a teacher, additional benefits are equally important over the long term. Additional benefits vary from school to school but frequently include some type of insurance benefits—hospitalization insurance, medical/surgical coverage, and major medical insurance. Somewhat less

salary schedule

A printed and negotiated schedule that lists salary levels based on years of experience and education.

frequently, a teacher's medical insurance also includes dental care and prescription drugs; it may include coverage of eyeglasses and other types of less common medical services. Benefits often include a group life insurance policy as well.

Many school districts also provide some type of professional liability insurance for their teachers. In fact, some states require by law that school districts do so. The liability insurance covers teachers and other educators who may be sued for not providing appropriate services or other abuse of professional responsibilities.

Full-time public school teachers are usually eligible for retirement benefits as part of their total compensation package. These benefits vary from state to state. In some states, teachers receive a combination of state teacher retirement and social security retirement. In other states, a teacher's retirement may depend totally on a state program and be divorced entirely from the federal social security retirement system. It is sometimes possible for teachers who move from state to state to transfer their retirement benefits to the state in which they ultimately retire. A teacher's retirement package is an extremely important part of the total compensation package and needs to be well understood by everyone entering the profession.

School districts also usually provide special leave provisions for teachers. Leave policies should clearly indicate the number of days available with pay for personal illnesses, emergencies, and deaths. Some school systems allow a day or so of personal leave for special situations. Professional development leave may be available in some school districts to support the continuing education of teachers, but the availability of such leave varies greatly from district to district.

RECRUITMENT INCENTIVES

The increasing shortage of teachers is leading to a number of innovative strategies for recruiting teachers. Job fairs are held in areas where there is an apparent surplus of teachers so that school districts from areas of shortage can interview prospective applicants. Technology is being used in innovative ways too. For example, the Clark County School District in Las Vegas, Nevada, will ship overnight a video telephone to an applicant so that he or she can be interviewed without having to travel to Las Vegas. In March 2000, the federal government began offering teachers 50 percent discounts on vacant homes in economically distressed neighborhoods. This program, which has also been offered to police officers, gives teachers an economic incentive to live and teach in low- and middle-income school districts. At the time, Federal Housing Administration chief Andrew Cuomo stated, "A good teacher can make a great neighbor as a mentor, an inspiring role model, and as a living link between the classroom and the community."[10]

Working Conditions

Almost everyone feels better about his or her work when the environment is supportive and conducive to high-quality output. The same is true for teachers and students. Like other factors in education, working conditions differ greatly from school to school. Within a single school district, the conditions can change dramatically across neighborhoods. Some schools are beautiful sprawling campuses with the latest technology. In others, toilets are backed up, paint is peeling off the walls, classes are held in storage rooms, or administrators are repressive. Most teachers who begin their careers in the second type of setting either aggressively seek assignments in other schools as soon as possible or leave the profession.

Teachers do work under very different conditions from those of most other professionals. Secondary and middle school teachers usually work with students in forty-five- to fifty-five-minute time periods with brief breaks between classes. Elementary and early childhood teachers are usually in self-contained classrooms in which they have few breaks, and they even have to supervise students during recesses and lunch periods. They have little time during the school day to work with

Should Districts Offer Signing Bonuses to Attract New Teachers?

Difficulty recruiting a sufficient number of teachers has led some school districts to offer contract signing bonuses to new teachers. Needless to say, this is a controversial practice that is opposed by some experienced teachers.

YES

Virginia Hoover is a school social worker with 11 years in the Guilford, North Carolina, schools. She was the state's School Social Worker of the Year in 1997–98 and the Student Services Support of the Year in 1999.

Yes, I believe school systems should offer a sign-on bonus to staff. A bonus would definitely be an added attraction to new employees, whether they are graduating from college or just trying to get into education.

For new graduates, a bonus would help offset the expense of preparing their first classroom. Buying the materials and supplies needed to make classrooms inviting and exciting places for students can take a lot of money.

If a new teacher has to relocate to take the job, that's another expense. A bonus could relieve the stress of moving and help make the transition a more pleasant experience.

For the more seasoned staff person, a sign-on bonus would be a great help in meeting the expenses that come with taking a new job.

Many times, when a staff person accepts a new position in another system, the person ends up missing time from work. That time lost means less income. A bonus could help save a staff person from having to go deeper into debt after a job change.

What a relief it could be to have this extra money. I have a friend who recently accepted a position in another state. She and I discussed the burden that would have been lifted if the system had offered her a sign-on bonus. Moving expenses can be very taxing, especially if you're not in a superintendent's position.

The gesture of offering a bonus would also benefit the school system that makes the offer. It's a win–win situation. A bonus, once accepted by the new staff person, serves as a commitment to work for the school system—and helps prevent

NO

Bob Kaplan teaches eighth-grade social studies at Jane Addams Junior High in Schaumburg, Illinois. He has taught for 23 years and served four times on bargaining teams, once as chairman, and most recently last spring.

Signing bonuses. What a great idea! What's next, no-cut contracts? Free agency? The traditional teacher pay scale may not be ideal, but it's fairer than having a rookie make more than a three-year veteran because the rookie teaches bilingual classes and the other teaches a multi-age elementary class.

If we were to have signing bonuses, who's going to determine what's more important for a bonus? Who's going to figure out how much of a bonus is deserved? Whatever happened to collective bargaining?

I can easily see a personnel director paying the extra dollars to fill a position. I can also foresee the same personnel director using these extra dollars as a backdoor to merit pay.

Our Association needs to represent all members. These first-year teachers aren't even members yet. How, as a labor organization, can we explain to our members in their second or third year, "Gee, sorry you were too late for a bonus, but remember to keep paying your dues dollars!"

Instead of offering signing bonuses, let's try to solve the underlying problem. If there are positions that are tough to fill, let's build the supply. How? Through academic advising in colleges and government financial support for students going into high-demand fields.

These steps, along with increased teacher pay throughout the salary schedule, would help increase the supply of new teachers. If more money will get better *new* teachers, then more money throughout the scale will serve as a motivator for *all* teachers.

(continued)

(continued)

YES

a staff person from going out the backdoor to accept a position with another system.

With a bonus in the balance, a school system wouldn't have to worry about whether a newly hired staff person is going to show.

On the other side, a staff person is going to think long and hard about leaving a school system that helped when help was most needed. Bonuses would help retain good and experienced staff.

A sign-on bonus would keep school systems from having to scramble in August to fill vacant positions. Scrambling school systems often just accept whoever is available at the last minute. With the sign-on bonus as an attraction, a system could have the best upon finding the best.

Staff, meanwhile, are seeking systems that are willing to offer something extra. A sign-on bonus would be an added recruiting incentive.

We need that incentive. With so much competition for graduating college students, districts need some added attraction to help fill the positions being vacated by our retiring educators.

As for me personally, I have no problem with systems offering such a sign-on bonus perk to attract capable people to education. I'm concerned about who will fill my role as social worker when I retire.

I won't be offended if my system begins offering a sign-on bonus to new staff. Those of us who are working hard pulling the load until vacant positions are filled would welcome the sight of quality applicants swarming to get those vacant jobs.

NO

Collective bargaining has brought us dramatically increased salaries, and we should stand by it. Any measure that would give special treatment to any segment of our members ought to be analyzed very closely.

I realize signing bonuses have been around for a long time in business and sports. But products in these fields are more measurable. I'm a much better teacher now than I was 23 years ago. Why don't we give me a bonus for that?

New teachers who have yet to step into the classroom are a risky investment. What is their average length of employment? What if these new teachers have difficulty and are released?

I guess we shouldn't worry. We'll just sign up some other untested new teacher with a signing bonus.

One final point: We already have huge salary discrepancies between school districts. Signing bonuses would increase those discrepancies. Wealthy districts would have much more money to dole out for bonuses than less affluent districts.

If signing bonuses become the rule, the rich will get richer, the poor will be stuck with vacancies. This isn't what public education should be all about.

Signing bonuses, on the surface, sound good. Administrators would love to fill tough positions by throwing money to a few.

But before we should even consider signing bonuses, we need standards and an effort to increase the supply for hard-to-fill positions. Let's use all this bonus money to reward teachers who have made and will continue to make a positive difference.

Source: "Should Districts Offer Signing Bonuses to Attract New Teachers?" *NEA Today* (April 2000), p. 11. Reprinted by permission of the National Education Association.

WHAT IS YOUR PERSPECTIVE ON THIS ISSUE?
Should districts offer signing bonuses to attract new teachers?

To give your opinion, go to Chapter 1 of the companion website (www.ablongman.com/johnson14e) and click on Teacher Perspectives.

colleagues or to plan for the next lesson or the next day. In many schools, teachers still have limited access to telephones or computers for support in their work.

One cause of these problems is aging school facilities that desperately need to be replaced. Recent federal legislation is providing some support for replacement and renewal of schools. With the student population growing dramatically over the next decade, additional resources will be required to provide working conditions that facilitate the work of educators. Public support will be needed to use taxes for these purposes.

Beginning and Continuing a Teaching Career

It is never too early to begin thinking about becoming licensed and finding a job. You can start by taking the appropriate courses and participating in activities that provide experiences for becoming licensed and being successful in your early years of teaching. One of the steps will be to collect and organize the materials that may be required for performance assessments throughout your teacher education program, job applications, and future renewal of your license.

Becoming Licensed

Teachers must obtain a license before they can legally teach in public schools. Each state determines its own licensure requirements. Although requirements may be similar from state to state, unique requirements exist in many states. You will need to check the requirements for the state in which you plan to work to ensure that you have completed an appropriate program and to determine the assessments that will have to be completed. Appendix A, located at the end of this book, lists these state certification websites.

LICENSURE TESTS

Most states require teacher candidates to pass one or more standardized tests at a specified level to be eligible for their first license to teach. Written assessments are required in many states, and many states require basic skills tests; in fact, many institutions require candidates to pass these tests before they are admitted into teacher education programs. Over half the states require candidates to pass tests in both professional pedagogical and content or subject-area knowledge. The cutoff scores that determine passing are set by states and vary greatly. Teacher candidates who do not pass the test in one state may be able to pass in another state that has a lower cutoff score.

An increasing number of states are requiring future teachers to major in an academic area rather than in "education." Students complete courses in education, field experiences, and student teaching or an internship along with courses in the academic major to become eligible for a license when the program is completed. You should clearly understand the requirements for a license in the state in which you are attending school and in any states in which you may wish to teach.

ALTERNATIVE LICENSURE

As mentioned earlier in this chapter, some states have developed alternative licensure opportunities for people who wish to become teachers. In some states, due to severe teacher shortages, anyone with a bachelor's degree in just about any major can begin teaching with some type of provisional certificate. These teachers might be introduced to teaching and learning in intensive programs of a few weeks before they are responsible for a classroom. Some school districts do assign mentors to these teachers during their first year of practice, and the teachers are usually required to take education courses to retain their licenses over time. These alternative routes to licensure have come under considerable criticism from teachers and the teacher education establishment because they do not recognize the importance of learning about teaching and learning and practicing under the supervision of an experienced teacher before beginning to teach.

Alternative routes are often designed to facilitate midcareer changes from other professions, such as business or the military, into the teaching profession. Candidates in these programs often participate in yearlong internships in which they are mentored by experienced teachers and work collaboratively with both higher education and school faculty in taking courses and working with students. These alternative route programs are available at many colleges and universities.

Searching for a Teaching Position

Teacher education candidates should begin thinking about employment early in their college careers. A helpful annual resource is the *Job Search Handbook for Educators* from the American Association for Employment in Education (www.aaee.org); it may be available in your college's job placement office. This handbook contains suggestions for preparing your résumé, cover letters, and letters of inquiry; it also provides excellent practical suggestions for improving your interviewing techniques. Information on teacher supply and demand in different fields is included in the handbook as well. Appendix C found at the end of this book lists many teaching job websites that should be helpful to you.

School districts would like applicants to present evidence that responds to the following questions, along with portfolios containing illustrations of performance, which are very helpful in this process:

1. Can the candidate do the job? Does the candidate have the necessary academic background? Can the candidate provide evidence that his or her students learned something? Does he or she know how to assess learning? Is he or she sensitive to the needs of diverse children? Can the candidate respond well to individual differences? How strong is he or she in regard to community activities?
2. Will the candidate do the job? What interview evidence does the candidate provide that communicates a professional commitment to getting the job done?
3. Will the candidate fit in? Is this candidate a good match for the needs of the district and the student needs as identified? How will the candidate work with other teachers and staff?
4. Will the candidate express well what he or she wants in a professional assignment? Does the candidate have personal and professional standards of his or her own?
5. Does the district's vision match the candidate's vision? Understanding the expectations of both the district and the candidate is critical if the candidate is to be successful.

Many state agencies responsible for teacher licensing and school districts have job openings listed on their websites. If you have a specific state and school district in mind, these job listings should be helpful in determining the possibilities and narrowing your search.

Remaining a Teacher

Most educators feel that teaching improves dramatically during the first five years of practice. Often teachers hone their skills alone as they practice in their own classrooms and take advantage of available professional development activities. A more promising practice is the assignment of mentors to new teachers to assist them in developing their skills during the early years of practice. Teachers who do not participate in an induction program (such as mentoring), who are dissatisfied with student discipline, or who are unhappy with the school environment are much more likely to leave teaching than are their peers.[11]

Continuing professional development is one of the ongoing activities of career teachers. Often teachers return to college for a master's degree that may help to increase their knowledge and skills related to teaching and learning and the subjects they teach. They learn new skills such as the use of the Internet to help students learn. They learn more about the subjects they teach through formal courses, reading on their own, exploring the Internet, working in related businesses in the summers, or traveling. They ask colleagues to observe their teaching and provide feedback for improving their work. They seek advice from other teachers and professionals with whom they work.

Experienced teachers see teaching as a public endeavor. They welcome parents and others to the classroom. As cooperating teachers and mentors, they become actively engaged with higher education faculty in preparing new teachers. They become researchers as they critically examine their own practice, testing various strategies to help students learn and sharing their findings with colleagues in faculty and professional meetings.

RENEWAL OF LICENSES

Most states require teaching licenses to be renewed periodically. A professional license is usually not granted until after several years of successful practice. Some states require a master's degree; a few require the successful completion of a portfolio with videotapes of teaching that are judged by experienced teachers. To retain a license throughout one's career, continuing professional development activities may be required.

> You are free to rise as far as your dreams will take you. Your task is to build the future of this country and of our world. You are now a global citizen.
>
> *Geraldine A. Ferraro*

Journal for Reflection

Record in your journal information about, and your reaction to, each of your visits to the classrooms you observe.

Summary

TODAY'S TEACHERS. Total school enrollment is projected to increase throughout the next decade, resulting in a teacher shortage unless many more new teachers are trained and the large numbers of teachers who have been certified but are not teaching return to the classroom. Although teachers do not yet earn salaries comparable to those of other professionals, teaching is evolving into a full profession that sets its own standards and monitors the practice of its members.

TEACHING AS A PROFESSION. Successful teachers are reflective about their work, as shown in their ability to gather, analyze, and use data to improve their teaching. These teachers have a natural curiosity about their work and are continually searching for better answers to the challenges they face. Beginning in their teacher education programs, teachers should write in reflective journals, collect and organize information and data, and compile information from these folios into portfolios for specific purposes such as performance assessments and job applications. Teachers must continue to refine their professional skills throughout their entire careers to keep pace with our rapidly changing world.

BEGINNING AND CONTINUING A TEACHING CAREER. This chapter focuses on a variety of topics related to the professional aspects of the education profession. It makes the point that educators must constantly be attuned to the many different perspectives on education that are held by policymakers, parents, students, fellow educators, and society in general. Several big ideas about the teaching profession grow out of this chapter, including the fact that education is extremely important to the development of our society and that teachers play the key role in this important activity.

Discussion Questions

1. What are the characteristics of a profession? What are your arguments for or against recognizing teaching as a profession?
2. Why do shortages of teachers probably exist in some subjects and not in others?
3. What should national accreditation tell you about your teacher education program?
4. What is National Board certification and why is it important in a teacher's career?
5. Of what potential value are journals, folios, and portfolios in preparing to teach?
6. What support should school districts provide to teachers in the induction years to encourage retention in the profession beyond three years?

School-Based Observations

1. Begin a list of the teaching challenges that you observe in schools. Reflect on the challenges that you had not expected when you initially thought about teaching as a career and how those challenges may influence your decision to become a teacher. How much have the teaching challenges you have observed met your initial expectations?
2. Ask several teachers you are observing what they see as the major problems they face and about their greatest satisfactions as educators. Analyze their answers and think about the major challenges and satisfactions you may experience as an educator.

Portfolio Development

1. Your first folio development task is to find and organize the many materials, artifacts, and records that you currently have. If you are like most of us, the bits and pieces are stored in several different locations. Examples of term papers, transcripts, awards, letters of recognition, and journals of trips are scattered. Take some time now to find and begin organizing these materials. Organize them by categories that you think are logical. Keep in mind the ultimate purpose of developing this folio. At various points in the future, you will be drawing items out of the folio to develop a portfolio for completion of student teaching or to apply for a teaching position or national certification.
2. The U.S. Department of Education now annually publishes a national teacher education report card, which includes information about all teacher education institutions in your state. Review the performance of candidates on state licensure tests in your field at your institution and other institutions in your state. Reflect on why there are differences in performance across institutions and whether state licensure tests are an appropriate measure of teaching competence.

Preparing for Certification

THE PRAXIS SERIES™

1. As mentioned in this chapter, many states require that prospective teachers take one or more standardized tests as part of certification. Some states, such as California, Massachusetts, and Texas, require their own tests; many other states require one or more tests in *The Praxis Series™*, published by the Educational Testing Service (ETS). Learn more about certification requirements, including testing requirements, for the state in which you plan to teach by visiting that state's website (see Appendix A).
2. The best way to prepare for Praxis or any other standardized test for certification is to understand the concepts covered in the test and how they relate to the content in each of your courses and field experiences. ETS provides a wealth of information about the Praxis assessments on their website. Learn more about the Praxis II assessments, including the test format and topics covered, by visiting their website (www.ets.org/praxis).
3. As you read further in this book, note how issues covered in the chapters relate to the topics covered in the Praxis II tests, particularly those on principles of teaching and learning. Even if your state does not use Praxis, you will find the information useful; the topics covered on the test are important for Praxis-related documentation in your portfolio.

Websites

www.ablongman.com/johnson14e The companion website for this textbook contains a wealth of enrichment material to help you learn more about the foundations of education.

www.rnt.org The website of Recruiting New Teachers, Inc., includes information about becoming a new teacher and offers a number of handbooks for people who are considering teaching as a career, including *Take This Job and Love It! Making the Mid-Career Move to Teaching.*

www.ncate.org A list of institutions with teacher education programs accredited by NCATE and information about becoming a teacher are available on this website. It also includes links to state agencies and their licensure requirements.

www.nea.org A rich source of constantly updated information about the National Education Association, national educational issues, governmental activities related to education, and the teaching profession in general.

www.nbpts.org The website for the National Board for Professional Teaching Standards includes information on the process for seeking National Board certification as well as the board's standards, assessments, and publications.

www.theteacherspot.com A great resource for new teachers dealing with many topics (discipline, technology, teacher resources, etc.).

www.nasdtec.org Information on licensure requirements and state agencies that are responsible for teacher licensing are available on this website of the National Association of State Directors of Teacher Education and Certification.

Further Reading

American Association for Employment in Education. *The Job Search Handbook for Educators.* Evanston, IL: Author, published annually. An excellent source of practical information for anyone searching for a teaching position.

Jacobson, Linda. (June 22, 2005). "Survey Finds Teachers' Biggest Challenge Is Parents." *Education Week,* p. 5. An informative report of the difficulties facing teachers.

Langdon, Carol A., and Vesper, Nick. (April 2000). "The Sixth Phi Delta Kappa Poll of Teachers' Attitudes toward the Public Schools." *Phi Delta Kappan, 81*(8), pp. 607–611. Interesting information on what teachers think about major educational issues. This survey is repeated and published in *Phi Delta Kappan* periodically.

Rathbone, Charles H. (February 2005). "A Learner's Bill of Rights." *Phi Delta Kappan,* pp. 471–473. An excellent reminder to teachers and parents of the inherent learning rights of students.

Rose, Lowell C., and Gallup, Alec M. "The Annual Phi Delta Kappan/Gallup Poll of the Public's Attitude toward the Public Schools." Published each September in *Phi Delta Kappan.* A wonderful annual source of information on the public's opinion on a wide variety of educational issues.

---

mylabschool
Where the classroom comes to life!

Go to Allyn and Bacon's MyLabSchool (www.mylabschool.com) and complete the following activity for Chapter 1. Click on MyLabSchool **Case Archive,** then click on **Teaching as a Profession.**

PART II

Chapter 2
Diversity in Society

Chapter 3
Sociological
Perspectives on
Students and Families

Chapter 4
Multicultural
Perspectives in
Education

SOCIOLOGICAL FOUNDATIONS OF EDUCATION

Sociology provides a perspective on human social behavior and how people interact with each other and social institutions such as schools, government, and religion. It investigates how society has been organized to meet its needs and analyzes the components that are effective and those that are not effective in serving the needs of the population. Sociological thinking helps policymakers and professional educators make sense of practices that contribute to or make it difficult for us to meet the goals of society.

Sociological perspectives depend on the analysis of data about the population, groups in society, and institutions such as the government, businesses, and schools to help us understand who we are. It allows us to ask questions about critical issues that affect our lives and the lives of others. In the following three chapters, we explore the impact of sociology on education by examining issues that affect schools, families, and students. The filters through which we will examine sociology in education in this section include diversity, culture, family structures, challenges of childhood and youth, purposes of schools, democracy, equality, multicultural education, and social justice.

CHAPTER 2

Diversity in Society

Mother Tongue: Area Schools Find Themselves Teaching English to Thousands of Immigrant Children

By Jennifer Smith Richards, *The Columbus Dispatch*, March 27, 2006

"What is a goose?" Joy Ritchie asked the class.

"Australia," replied Ibrahim Ibrahim.

"It's a boy!" declared Habiba Mukhtar.

There was only one way to clear it up. Ritchie walked across her classroom at Eakin Elementary and retrieved a foot-tall plastic goose.

And everything suddenly was clear for the Somali, Cambodian and Mexican first-graders learning English as a second language.

Communicating isn't always easy here. While some students have a moderate grasp of English, many had never been in a formal school. Many didn't know how to hold a pencil when they came to the Columbus Public Schools. And some, Ritchie said, are still delighted by running water in the school restrooms.

There are so many new students from dozens of countries that school districts across central Ohio are struggling with the logistics of teaching them and communicating with their parents.

The increase in their numbers during the past decade is startling: In Columbus, which has the most immigrant children in the region, the population of students learning English as a second language has quadrupled to more than 3,400.

In Dublin, which taught about 80 non-English-speaking students 10 years ago, there now are about 980.

And in Whitehall, English-learning students now make up more than 11 percent of the district's student population—nearly 300 students. In 1996, the district had fewer than 10 students who could not speak English.

Only Bexley remains relatively untouched by immigrant students: It had fewer than 10 at last official count.

Central Ohio districts have invested millions in teaching English to newly arrived students. English-language learners typically require different textbooks, more help in the classroom and, often, more extensive tutoring than most students.

Equally expensive, though, is the cost to communicate with parents who don't speak English. The state is not required to help pay for translators; districts foot much of the bill.

Translators often are needed for parent–teacher conferences, special-education meetings, disciplinary hearings and everyday occurrences—a child is sick, a permission slip is needed, lunch money forgotten.

Columbus uses about 100 bilingual aides who speak nearly 100 languages.

The South-Western schools, which have more than 1,200 students enrolled in English as a second language courses, employ 16 bilingual assistants who can translate for French-, Spanish-, Somali- and Arabic-speaking students and parents.

Dublin has them, too: 11 full-time and five part-time aides who speak Japanese, Korean and Spanish. The district pays most of the $350,000 cost.

Some federal money is earmarked to help districts communicate with immigrant families, but districts say it's not enough. Columbus receives about $1 million for its new English speakers.

"Because the population has grown so, the demand for translation has also grown," said Ken Woodard, who oversees the Columbus Public Schools' English as a second language program. "It's gotten so involved."

Parent–teacher conferences are especially problematic, said Myra Singnysane, who helps coordinate the district's translation needs. Many schools have conferences on the same day and interpreters can't make them all, she said.

Teachers, such as Ritchie, shoulder some of the job translators can't take on.

"I have 68 children and I translate all of the report cards to Spanish," she said.

Columbus' 50 schools and three welcome centers—immigrant students' first stop if they know little or no English—are bulging, Woodard said.

Districts don't expect the flow of immigrant children to slow anytime soon. A good barometer might be Columbus' middle- and high-school welcome centers, which now teach 578 students the basics of going to school in America.

Elementary grades have shown the greatest growth, Woodard said. The district gained 450 non-English-speaking kindergartners during the past two years.

With them, teachers must start at the beginning.

"I still have children who cannot work the doors," Ritchie said.

Questions for Reflection

1. What kind of diversity exists in the elementary and middle schools of central Ohio?

2. If you were a teacher in Eakin Elementary, how would you help these young students learn English while introducing them to reading and mathematics?

3. What do you know about linguistics and learning a second language?

Source: Reprinted with permission.

INTASC

Learning Outcomes

After reading and studying this chapter, you should be able to:

1. Describe culture and some of its characteristics. (INTASC 3: Diverse Learners)

2. Identify the dominant culture in the United States and describe how it is influenced by and affects other cultures in the United States.

3. Understand some of the theories and ideologies that describe ways that schools respond to students from diverse groups. (INTASC 3: Diverse Learners)

4. Identify groups with which students and teachers identify and explain why some are more important to their cultural identity than others. (INTASC 3: Diverse Learners)

5. Understand that student learning is influenced by language, culture, and family and community values. (INTASC 3: Diverse Learners)

diversity

The wide range of differences among people, families, and communities based on their cultural and ethnic backgrounds as well as their physical and academic abilities.

More than a million new immigrants annually introduce different religions, languages, and ways of thinking and acting into schools and communities, including areas of the United States that previously lacked the rich **diversity** of urban areas. The diversity to which educators are exposed daily is much broader than the new immigrants themselves. It includes **socioeconomic status,** ethnicity, race, religion, language, gender, sexual orientation, academic and physical ability, age, and geography. Educators should incorporate the history, experiences, and perspectives of diverse groups into their teaching and draw on students' diversity to help them learn. The big ideas that will help you understand diversity include **culture** and group identity. These concepts and groups that are represented in many classrooms are introduced in this chapter.

The diverse groups in the United States share many characteristics, but their different histories and experiences may lead to the development of different perspectives on society and the education of their children. Many people in this country celebrate the differences among cultural groups and the contributions they have made to society. Others worry that these differences are leading to a divided society. These two perspectives sometimes lead to misunderstandings, **stereotypes,** and even conflicts about ourselves and the inclusion of diverse groups in society and schools. At the same time, diverse groups share many characteristics and can learn what they have in common, develop common interests, and appreciate and value their differences.

Representatives of diverse groups have challenged the monocultural, universalist view of the world and society that has guided the country's laws and practices. They question the curriculum taught in schools, colleges, and universities. They ask why so many Latinos drop out of school, why students in poverty attend dilapidated and filthy schools with few licensed teachers, why so many young African American men are in jail, why single mothers do not earn enough to stay out of poverty, and why so few students with disabilities are in general education courses.

Diversity raises concerns about equality in society and schools. Concerned educators are exploring the intersections of race, ethnicity, gender, and class as they relate to individual and group identity. They work to overcome stratification based on race, able-bodiedness, language, gender, and socioeconomic status that often tracks different students into special education, gifted programs, advanced placement courses, low-level courses, and uninteresting, academically unchallenging courses. Educators who believe that all students can learn understand that the cultural backgrounds and experiences of their students must be respected and reflected in all aspects of the education process.

The federal legislation that supports education, No Child Left Behind (NCLB), recognizes that students from some groups have different experiences in schools, which have resulted in white students from higher-income families performing at higher levels on achievement tests. NCLB expects schools to ensure that all students achieve standards and perform at grade level in reading, mathematics, and science regardless of their race, socioeconomic status, native language, and disability. It holds schools accountable for student learning across groups and publicly identifies the schools whose students are not making adequate yearly progress (AYP) on standardized tests. Test scores for students in a school must to be disaggregated by the groups identified above to show the differential (or lack thereof) in test scores across groups. The NCLB has had a great impact on school practices, especially in preparing students for annual achievement tests.

CROSS-REFERENCE
No Child Left Behind is discussed in greater detail in Chapters 1, 6, 8, and 11.

socioeconomic status

The economic condition of individuals based on their or their family's income, occupation, and educational attainment.

culture

Socially transmitted ways of thinking, believing, feeling, and acting within a group of people that are passed from one generation to the next.

stereotypes

The attribution of common traits, characteristics, and behavior to a group of people without acknowledgment of individual differences within the group.

Culture and Society

Society is composed of individuals and groups that share a common history, traditions, and experiences. Culture provides the blueprint for how people think, feel, and behave in society. A culture imposes rules and order on its members by providing patterns that help them know the meaning of their behavior. Members of the same cultural group understand the subtleties of their shared language, nonverbal communications, and ways of thinking and knowing. But they often misread the cultural cues of other groups, a problem that can lead to miscommunications and misunderstandings in society and the classroom.

All people around the world have the same biological and psychological needs, but the ways in which they meet these needs are culturally determined. For example, the location of the group, available resources, and traditions have a great influence on the foods eaten, grooming and clothing patterns, teaching and learning styles, and interactions of men and women and parents and children. The meaning and celebration of birth, marriage, old age, and death also depend on one's culture. In other words, culture affects all aspects of people's lives, from the simplest patterns of eating and bathing to the more complex patterns of teaching and learning.

Children learn how to think, feel, speak, and behave through the culture in which they are raised. Their parents, teachers, and other adults in the neighborhood and in the religious institutions they attend teach the culture and model the cultural norms. Furthermore, when schools use a different language or linguistic pattern from that used in the home, dissonance between schools and the home can occur. When students never see themselves in textbooks or stories, they learn that their own culture is inferior to the official culture of the school or dominant culture.

Each of us belongs to a number of different groups within our own culture. We have not only an ethnic identity such as African American, Navajo, German American, or Korean American, but we also identify ourselves as male or female, heterosexual or homosexual, Christian, Muslim, atheist, or member of another religious group. Who we are is influenced by our place on a continuum from poor to wealthy and young to elderly, as well as by the geographic location where we grew up and are living. Our behaviors in these groups are influenced by the culture in which we are raised and later live. However, our behaviors may differ based on the cultural expectations for men and women, which will be influenced by our ethnicity, religion, and socioeconomic status. Membership in these groups, the interaction across groups, and society's view of the group are critical factors in determining our cultural identity. When we meet new people, we usually identify them immediately by their gender and race and maybe their ethnicity. We will not know their religion and its importance to them unless they are wearing a garment or jewelry associated with a specific religion. We don't know the importance of their ethnicity, language, or socioeconomic status to their identity. Therefore, educators need to be very careful about stereotyping students and their families solely on the basis of factors that can be easily identified. Culture is far more complex, not allowing us to make assumptions based only on an individual's appearance.

Characteristics of Culture

Culture is learned, shared, and adapted. It is also dynamic. People learn their culture through **enculturation.** Parents and other caretakers teach children the culture and the acceptable norms of behavior within it. Individuals internalize cultural patterns so well and so early in life that they have difficulty accepting different, but just as appropriate, ways of behaving and thinking. But when people live and actively participate in a second culture, they begin to see more clearly their own unique cultural patterns. Understanding cultural differences and learning to recognize when students do not share your own cultural patterns are critical steps in the provision of an equitable learning environment. Therefore, it is important to learn about your own culture as well as others.

An important aspect of culture is that it is dynamic and continually adapts to serve the needs of the group. Individuals and families adapt their culture as they move from one section of the country to another or around the globe. The conditions of a geographic region may require adjustments to the culture. Technological changes in the world and society can also lead to changes in cultural patterns.

enculturation

The process of learning the characteristics and behaviors of the culture of the group to which one belongs.

Dominant Culture

The dominant culture in the United States is that of white, middle-class Protestants whose ancestors began immigrating from Western and Northern Europe five centuries ago. Today, the dominant culture is reflected primarily in the lives of business managers or owners and professionals who are college educated and represent a number of ethnic and religious groups. The dominant culture is the one most middle-class families have grown up in or adopted.

The legal system, democratic elections, and middle-class values have their underpinnings in institutions and traditions of Western and Northern Europe. Historically, men have dominated the country's political system and held the highest government positions. Policies and practices have been established both to maintain the advantages of the dominant culture and to limit the influence of other cultural groups.

Parents are primary transmitters of their culture, as they interact with their children on a daily basis.

What are some of the characteristics of the dominant culture today? Universal education and literacy for all citizens are valued. Mass communication, which has been enhanced by technology and electronic networks, influences people's view of themselves and the world. A job or career must be pursued for a person to be recognized as successful. Fun is usually sought as a relief from work. Achievement and success are highly valued and are demonstrated by the accumulation of material goods such as a house, car, boat, clothes, and vacations.

Individualism and freedom are core values that undergird the dominant culture in the United States. Members believe that individuals should be in charge of their own destiny and success. Freedom is defined as having control of one's own life with little or no interference by others, especially by government. Members of the dominant group rely on associations of common interest rather than strong kinship ties. Many people believe in absolute values of right and wrong rather than in degrees of rightness and wrongness.

Members of this group identify themselves as American. They often do not see themselves as primarily white, Christian, English-speaking, middle class, male, or heterosexual. Many middle-class Catholics, Jews, and members of other faiths share values and behaviors similar to those of the dominant group, as do a number of middle-class African Americans, Latinos, Native Americans, and Asian Americans. Many low-income families also hold the same values but do not have the income to support a similar lifestyle. The mass media and international communications systems such as the Internet are contributing to the development of a universal culture that mirrors the dominant U.S. culture. Some people worry that the positive aspects of other cultures are losing ground as television and movies teach a common culture.

Group Identity

Cultural identity is not determined by ethnicity and race alone. As shown in Figure 2.1, individuals are members of multiple groups. They are female or male and members of specific socioeconomic, religious, linguistic, geographic, and age groups. In addition, mental and physical abilities help define who we are. Membership in these groups determines our cultural identity.

Students in U.S. schools are among the most diverse in the world. At the beginning of this century, one-third of the students in the nation's schools were

FIGURE 2.1

Cultural Identity Is Based on Membership in Multiple Cultural Groups That Interact with One Another

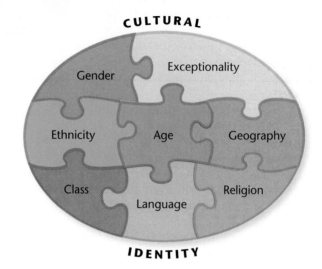

young people of color. They will make up 40 percent of the school population by 2020 and half of the population by 2050. They are already the majority in schools in California, Texas, and many of the nation's largest cities. In many schools, the native languages of students are other than English. Some school districts can identify more than 100 languages used in the homes of their students. Religious diversity is no longer limited to traditional Judeo-Christian roots as immigrants from Asia, Africa, and the Middle East bring their religious beliefs to the mix. In addition, a growing number of students with disabilities are active participants in schools and society.

The relationship of individuals' group memberships to the dominant culture may have a great influence on how individuals perceive themselves and are viewed by others. Because of the importance of power relationships between groups in discussions of diversity and equality, educators should understand how they themselves are positioned in this dialogue. Educators need to know which groups they belong to and what influence those memberships have on their own identity. A critical self-examination is helpful in the identification of otherness and difference that pervade a culturally diverse society. Later in this chapter, we will look in some detail at group memberships and their significance in U.S. education.

Acceptance of Diverse Groups

Over time the relationship of groups to society has been described differently by sociologists, politicians, philosophers, and educators. These differing perspectives have led to the development of policies and practices that range along a continuum from promotion to condemnation of group differences. Assimilation, pluralism, and cultural choice are three theories and ideologies that help clarify the integration of groups into society and schools.

ASSIMILATION

Assimilation is a process by which an immigrant group or culturally distinct group is incorporated into the dominant culture. The group either adopts the culture of the dominant group as its own or interacts with it in a way that forges a new or different culture that is shared by both groups. Members of a group experience a number of stages in this process.

The first step involves learning the cultural patterns of the dominant group. The speed at which group members become assimilated is usually enhanced by interactions in settings such as work, school, and worship. In many cases, previous cultural patterns are shed—either enthusiastically or grudgingly—as those of the dominant group are adopted. Native languages and traditions can be lost within a few generations. Society usually requires an individual to take these steps in order to attain some modicum of financial success or achievement of the "good life."

The final stage of assimilation is structural assimilation.[1] At this stage, members of the immigrant or culturally distinct group interact with the dominant group at all levels, including marriage. They no longer encounter prejudice or **discrimination** and share equally in the benefits of society.

At the beginning of the twentieth century, the melting pot theory emerged as a description of how immigrants contributed to the evolution of a new American culture. This theory described the egalitarian state that is one of the core values of a democracy. Many immigrants believed that the prejudices and inequities they had experienced in their native countries would not exist in the United States and that they would become valued members of society. Although many European immigrants did merge into the dominant society, people of color were prevented by the prevailing racist ideology from "melting" or becoming structurally assimilated. Racism has prevented Native, African, Latino, and Asian Americans from becoming structurally assimilated for generations.

Assimilation remains the guiding principle in most schools. **Acculturation,** or learning of the dominant culture through immersion, is the prevailing strategy. School success usually depends on how well students are able to adjust to the dominant culture that permeates the curriculum and school activities. Their own unique cultural experiences and patterns are often not officially recognized, valued, or used in the teaching and learning process.

PLURALISM

Pluralism exists in societies in which the maintenance of distinct cultural patterns, including languages, is valued and promoted. Groups may be segregated in pluralistic societies, but they participate somewhat equally in politics, economics, and education. In some cases, groups have established and maintained their own political, economic, and educational systems within the larger society.

Pluralism in its ideal form does not exist in the United States. Although diversity does exist, parity and equality among groups do not. For example, some Native American nations do have their own political and educational systems, but they do not share power and resources equally with the dominant group. Some groups choose to maintain their native culture, religion, and language. This goal is more likely to be attained if families live in communities where there is a fairly large

Today's classroom reflects the diversity in U.S. society. Students may look similar but come from different cultural backgrounds and life experiences.

assimilation

A process by which an immigrant or culturally distinct group is incorporated into the dominant culture.

discrimination

Individual or institutional practices that exclude members of a group from certain rights, opportunities, or benefits.

acculturation

The process of learning the cultural patterns of the dominant culture.

pluralism

The maintenance of cultures as parallel and equal to the dominant culture in society.

Ethnic and religious communities exist in many areas of the country. Group members in these neighborhoods are more likely to maintain the group's cultural traditions, language, and practices than members of the group who have moved into integrated communities.

concentration of others from a similar cultural background; Little Italy, Chinatown, Harlem, East Los Angeles, and Amish and Hutterite communities provide these settings. Sometimes culturally distinct groups have been forced into segregated communities because of discriminatory housing patterns.

The implementation of pluralism in schools requires the recognition of the multiple cultures that make up society. Rather than the dominant culture being centered in the classroom and school, the cultures of the particular group or groups served by the school are the predominant focus of the curriculum. Examples include the Afrocentric and Native-centric programs that exist today in some urban areas and tribally controlled schools. Also, some ethnic and religious groups have maintained their culture and history in private schools. The Amish and Hutterites, for example, operate their own schools to prevent the destruction of their cultures by the dominant group. Jewish and Islamic private schools promote religious study and practices; the rules of the religion guide student and teacher behavior.

Public schools generally reflect the dominant culture. The faculty might not represent the diversity of the students in the school and might have little, if any, knowledge about students' cultures or personal experiences with them. Students who are from low-income families or from ethnic, racial, religious, or language groups other than the dominant culture too often do not achieve well academically in these schools.

Schools in a pluralistic society are staffed by a diverse teaching force that at a minimum represents the cultures of students. Teachers who share the cultural backgrounds of students understand the students' language patterns. Teachers from different cultural backgrounds are expected to know multiple cultural patterns of communication and learning and be able to use them to help students learn.

CULTURAL CHOICE

cultural choice

The freedom to choose and adapt the characteristics from one's own and other cultures in developing one's own cultural identity.

Cultural choice is the freedom to choose and adapt the characteristics that determine our cultural identity. Some immigrants plan to assimilate into the dominant culture as soon as possible. They choose to adopt the new culture and shed the old. Others do not want to shed their unique cultural identity and patterns in order to be successful members of society. Many learn to be bicultural and bilingual, bridging two cultures and learning when it is appropriate to use the patterns of each. Others do not have a choice. Ideally, we could choose to assimilate, maintain our native culture, or become bicultural or multicultural and function effectively in more than one culture. Under cultural choice, society supports these choices and does not value one choice more than another or discriminate on the basis of group membership.

Unfortunately, this description does not match reality for large segments of the population. Many people of color are acculturated, but discrimination prevents them from being structurally assimilated even if they choose that route. Strong identity and affiliation with their cultural group has been necessary as a source of solidarity in the effort to combat inequities and obtain adequate housing and education. Although members of some cultural groups may be able to live almost solely within their distinct cultural milieu, most are forced to work within the dominant culture. Those who choose to assimilate might not be accepted by the dominant group and might also be rejected by the group into which they were born.

Schools that value cultural choice consciously avoid promoting the dominance of a single culture. Such schools integrate the contributions and histories of diverse groups, particularly those represented in the school, throughout the curriculum. Bilingualism and the use of dialects prevail in classrooms as well as school hallways. Students are the center of instruction, and teachers use students' cultural patterns to promote learning. Students learn to operate comfortably in both their own and other cultures, including the dominant culture. Equality is manifested in the equal participation of all groups in courses and extracurricular activities, as well as in comparable achievement on academic assessments.

Journal for Reflection

1. What experiences have you had with members of a culture different than your own?

2. What are some of the cultural differences between your culture and another one with which you are familiar?

3. What are your perceptions of the other culture?

4. How have your impressions of the group changed over time?

Socioeconomic Status

Most people want the "good life," which in the United States includes a decent job, affordable housing, good health, a good education for their family members, and periodic vacations. One way to estimate the good life is socioeconomic status (SES), which is the primary determinant of the standard of living families are able to maintain. It also has a great impact on one's chances of attending college and attaining a job that ensures material comfort throughout life.

Socioeconomic status serves as a criterion to measure the economic condition of individuals. It is determined by one's occupation, income, and educational attainment. Wealth and power are other important factors that affect the way one is able to live, but these data are difficult to measure. We often can guess a family's socioeconomic status if we know such things as where they live, their jobs, the type of car they drive, the schools attended by their children, and the types of vacations they take.

Social Stratification

Most societies are characterized by **social stratification,** in which individuals occupy different levels of the social structure. Wealth, income, occupation, and education help define these social positions. However, high or low rankings are not based solely on SES criteria. Race, age, gender, religion, and disability can contribute to higher rankings as well. Although members of most **ethnic groups** can be found at all levels of the socioeconomic status scale in the United States, those from northern and western European backgrounds historically have a higher representation at the highest levels.

Social mobility remains one of the core values of the dominant culture. We are told that hard work will lead to better jobs, higher income, and a better chance to participate in the good life. We read the Horatio Alger stories of individuals who were born in poverty but through hard work became wealthy as a corporate president, prestigious publisher, successful writer, athlete, or entertainer. Although upward mobility continues to occur, the chances of moving from poverty to riches, no matter how hard one works, are low without interventions such as a college

social stratification

Levels of social class ranking based on income, education, occupation, wealth, and power in society.

ethnic groups

Groups based on the national origin (that is, a country or area of the world) of one's family or ancestors in which members share a culture and sense of common destiny.

education and lots of good luck. Individuals who are born into wealthy families are likely to attend good schools, finish college, and find high-paying administrative jobs. They are raised with high expectations, have the economic resources to assist them in meeting these expectations, and usually end up meeting them.

Class Structure

Some researchers have divided the population into distinct classes to study inequities in society and the characteristics of individuals and families at different economic levels. One of the early categorization systems identified the population as lower, middle, and upper class, with finer distinctions in each of the three groups. The "underclass" is the label sometimes given to the portion of the population that lacks a stable income and is persistently in poverty.

Individuals who do manual work for a living are sometimes described as the "working class" or "blue collar" workers. When farm laborers and service workers are included in the working class, this group represents 40 percent of the employed population.[2] Most members of this class have little control over their work. Some of the jobs are routine, mechanical, and not challenging. Work sometimes is sporadic and affected by an economy in which employees face layoffs, replacement by computerized equipment and other advances in technology, part-time work, and unemployment as jobs move to locations with cheaper labor. Benefits such as vacation time and health plans are often limited. The education required for working-class jobs is usually less than that for many middle-class positions, except for skilled and crafts workers who have had specialized training and may have served apprenticeships. Even some of these skilled workers, however, work as long and hard as others, often working overtime and holding two jobs to make ends meet.

The middle class is large. Most people who don't perceive themselves as poor or rich identify themselves as middle class. Annual middle-class incomes range from $30,000 to $80,000, encompassing 38 percent of the population.[3] It includes both blue-collar and professional or managerial workers. For most of the middle class, $80,000 would be the top of their earning potential, and this is often possible only because both spouses work. Families in this class have very different lifestyles at opposite ends of the income continuum. Clerical workers, technicians, and salespeople in the group have less control over their jobs than the professionals, managers, and administrators who often supervise them. These workers tend to have somewhat better benefits than do members of the working class. The professionals in this group expect to move beyond $80,000 in their careers with the goal of becoming one of the 19 percent of U.S. families earning more than $100,000 annually.[4]

Many professionals, managers, and administrators receive incomes that are above $75,000, placing them in the upper middle class. They have become the affluent middle class, but they often believe that their condition is universal rather than unique. Many think that most of the U.S. population shares the same affluence, advantages, and comforts. An $80,000 salary in a neighborhood where most families earn over $200,000 seems low; in another neighborhood, a family making $80,000 would be considered well off. Professionals are men and women who have usually obtained professional or advanced degrees. They include teachers, lawyers, physicians, college professors, scientists, and psychologists. Excluding teachers, most of these families earn far above the median income of $52,680.[5] Successful executives and businesspeople are the managers and administrators in this group. These workers usually have more autonomy over their jobs and working conditions than working- and lower-middle-class workers.

The upper class consists of wealthy and socially prominent families. The income and wealth of members of this class are far higher than those of the other classes, and the gap is growing. For example, in 1980 corporate chief executive officers earned forty-two times as much as their employees; by 1990 they earned eighty-five times as much; and by 2004 the multiple had grown to 431.[6] These great differences

For years now a small fraction of American households have been garnering an extreme concentration of wealth and income while large corporations and financial institutions have obtained unprecedented power over who wins and who loses.

Bill Moyers

contribute to limited interactions with members of other classes. Children in this class rarely attend public schools, isolating them from peers of other social classes. Probably the greatest assimilation of lifestyles and values occurs among members of ethnically and culturally diverse groups who attain an upper-class status.

Poverty

The U.S. government has established a poverty index that sets a conservative ceiling on poverty. This threshold sets an annual income of $18,810 for a family of four, leaving 35.9 million persons in poverty—12.5 percent of the population.[7] These poverty thresholds are set at about half the income needed to make ends meet.[8] As a result, many families are above the poverty level, but still do not have an adequate income to purchase the basic needs of housing, clothing, and food. Many members of these low-income families work in full- or part-time jobs that pay such low wages they cannot pull their families out of poverty.

Although 68 percent of the population living below the poverty level is white, only 10.5 percent of all whites in the country live in poverty.[9] The percentage of other racial and ethnic groups in poverty is higher because of disparate incomes. The median income of Asian American families was $63,251 in 2003 as compared to whites' median income of $55,768. African American families earned 62 percent and Latino families 61 percent as much as whites.[10] Although this income disparity decreases when one compares two-income families with the same level of education, it does not disappear. Women who work full time year-round also encounter discriminatory practices that keep their incomes at 70 percent of those of men.[11]

Children, the elderly, and persons of color suffer disproportionately from poverty, as shown in Figure 2.2. Eighteen percent of U.S. children live in poverty,[12]

> Just because a child's parents are poor or uneducated is no reason to deprive the child of basic human rights to health care, education, proper nutrition.
>
> ***Marian Wright Edelman***

FIGURE 2.2

Persons in Poverty in the United States

Source: U.S. Census Bureau, "Persons below Poverty Level by Selected Characteristics: 2003" (Table 696), *Statistical Abstract of the United States: 2006,* 125th edition. Washington, DC: U.S. Government Printing Office, 2006.

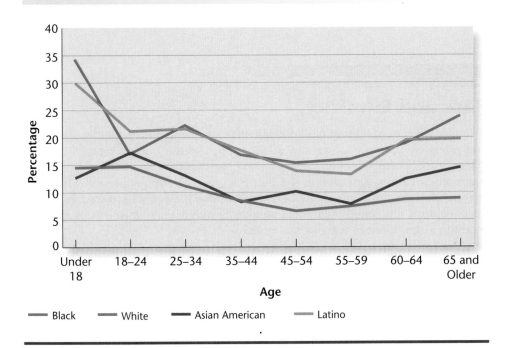

FIGURE 2.3

Children in Low-Income Families by Racial and Ethnic Group

Source: Based on data from National Center for Children in Poverty, "Basic Facts about Low-Income Children: Birth to Age 18." Retrieved on May 7, 2006, from www.nccp.org/pub_lic06.html.

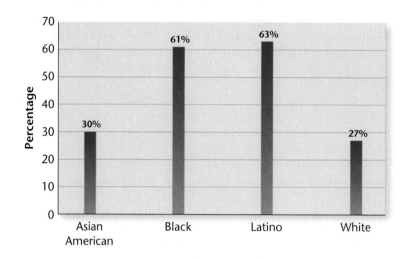

Journal for Reflection

1. How would you characterize the SES and social class of the family in which you grew up?

2. Why do you think some people live in poverty?

3. How might your perceptions of low-income people influence your interactions with their children in the classroom?

which is more than double that of most other major industrialized nations, even though the United States has the highest gross domestic product per capita. Many industrialized nations have reduced child poverty levels to below 5 percent.[13] Another 22 percent of the nation's children live in low-income families above the federal poverty level. Thus, 40 percent of our children live in low-income families, often making them eligible for free or reduced lunches in schools.[14] As with adults, Latino and African American children are more likely to live in low-income families as shown in Figure 2.3.

Race and Ethnicity

National origin is an important part of identity for many individuals. Native American tribes are the only indigenous ethnic groups in the United States; therefore, more than 99 percent of the U.S. population, or their ancestors, came from somewhere else at some time during the past 500 years. Many people can identify a country of origin, although the geographical boundaries may have changed since their ancestors emigrated. A growing number of people have mixed heritage, with ancestors from different parts of the world.

panethnic membership

Ethnic membership based on national origin from a large geographic region that includes numerous countries such as those in Africa or Asia.

Although many people now identify themselves by their **panethnic membership** (for example, as African American or Asian American), race remains a political reality in U.S. society. It has become integrally interwoven into the nation's policies, practices, and institutions, including the educational, economic, and judicial systems. As a result, whites have advantages that are reflected in higher achievement on tests and higher incomes as adults. The issue of race encompasses personal and national discussions of affirmative action, immigration, desegregation, and a color-blind society. Race and ethnicity may be linked, but they are not the same. Both influence one's cultural identity and status in society.

CROSS-REFERENCE
The legal ramifications of segregation and desegregation in education are presented in Chapter 6.

Race

Race and gender are among the first physical characteristics we notice when we meet another person. Although race is no longer accepted as a scientific concept for classifying people, it has become a social construction for identifying differences. We are asked to indicate our race or our panethnic identity on forms that we complete. Race is used inappropriately by many people to explain differences in behavior, language, socioeconomic standing, and academic achievement. Ideas about race are created from experiences in our own racial group and with other groups. They are also informed by reflections of racial differences in the media. Ideas about race are politicized and institutionalized in the policies and actions of judges, teachers, legislators, police, employers, and others who are in charge of institutions that affect people's lives. Stereotyped views of race usually bestow positive attributes and high status on one's own race and negative attributes and low status on others.

Skin color is a signifier of race but does not capture its meaning. Many people have mixed racial backgrounds that place them along a continuum of skin color; they might not be obviously white, black, brown, or otherwise easily identifiable as one race or another. Until recently, state laws declared a person's official race as nonwhite if a small percentage of his or her racial heritage was other than white. The official message was, and continues to be, that white is the ideal and that anything else, even small percentages of a race other than white, is less than ideal. This example is one of many ways that race affects our everyday lives and becomes an integral part of our identity. Whether we like it or not race continues to be used to sort people in society.

People of color usually identify themselves by their race or ethnic group and are usually identified as such by others. They are confronted with their race almost daily in encounters with employers, salespeople, and colleagues or as they watch the evening news. Whites, on the other hand, are seldom confronted with their race; in fact, many see themselves as raceless. White has become the norm against which persons of color are classified as *other*. As a result, many whites are unable to see that they have been privileged in society. Their silence contributes to the maintenance of a racist society.

> I have a dream my four little children will one day live in a nation where they will not be judged by the color of their skin but by the content of their character.
>
> **Martin Luther King, Jr.**

Ethnicity

National origin is the primary determinant of one's ethnicity. Ethnic group members share a common history, language, traditions, and experiences in the United States. Identification with an ethnic group helps sustain and enhance the culture of the group. Ethnicity is strongest when members have a high degree of interpersonal associations with other members and share common residential areas.

Ethnic cohesiveness and solidarity are strengthened as members organize to support and advance the group, fight discrimination, and influence political and economic decisions that affect the group as a whole. In the 1960s, these struggles with the dominant culture led to calls for changes in schools, colleges, government programs, and employment to support equality across ethnic groups. During this period, African, Latino, Asian, and Native Americans called for recognition of their ethnic roots in the school curriculum. By the 1970s, European ethnic groups, especially those of southern and eastern European origins, had also joined this movement. Ethnic studies programs were established in colleges and universities and some high

Relevant Research

ESL Programs in White Schools

STUDY PURPOSE/QUESTION: The focus of this study was to examine how students from Mexico, Bosnia, Sudan, and other countries fared in a middle school they attended for its English as a second language (ESL) program.

STUDY DESIGN: The researchers conducted a qualitative study that included observing and interviewing ESL teachers, the ESL program director, an administrator, and white students. Members of the local community and ESL students were also interviewed. The researchers attended ESL parent meetings, faculty meetings that focused on ESL issues, and school assemblies. In addition, documents on extracurricular participation, school discipline, and busing policies were analyzed.

STUDY FINDINGS: In the early 1980s, the school district placed its ESL program for immigrant students in a middle school, which had a predominantly white, high SES student population. The students, who spoke 12 languages, were "caught in a contradictory process whereby they are welcomed at the school and yet, simultaneously, made to feel unwelcome in many respects."

Community members spoke about the value of diversity in the school, but also worried about the students being a disruption. The school sponsored several welcoming events such as cultural fairs to help white students understand the countries from which the ESL students had come, but the events stereotyped groups and did not provide in-depth understanding of differences.

ESL classes lacked curricular materials, and class size was high (30 students) for providing the individualized attention needed in ESL. Most of the non-ESL teachers resisted having ESL students in their classrooms.

A pattern of segregation was found in school assemblies, the lunchroom, and classes. For example, during assemblies they were assigned to a secondary choir that sang a few songs, but not one of the ESL students participated in the main choir. None of the songs represented cultures other than the dominant U.S. culture.

ESL students traveled to the school from communities in other parts of the city. The fact that the buses arrived just before classes started and left immediately after classes made it difficult for the ESL students to participate in extracurricular activities. Suspension rates for immigrant students were more than four times as great as for white students. Students from Mexico and Africa were most likely to be disciplined.

IMPLICATIONS: Schools need to do more than offer ESL programs for immigrant students. They need to examine their policies and practices to ensure that these students are not excluded from the benefits available to students from the dominant group. In addition, teachers and administrators often need professional development to assist them in working effectively with ESL students.

Source: Andrew Gitlin, Edward Buendia, Kristin Crosland, and Fode Doumbia, "The Production of Margin and Center: Welcoming–Unwelcoming of Immigrant Students." *American Educational Research Journal, 40*(1) (Spring 2003), pp. 91–122.

---

schools to study the history, contributions, and experiences of U.S. ethnic groups that had traditionally been excluded.

The U.S. Census Bureau reports population data on the racial and ethnic groups shown in Figure 2.4. These broad classifications do not accurately describe the ethnic diversity of the United States. For example, there are more than 500 Native American tribes. Each of these panethnic classifications includes numerous ethnic groups with identities and loyalties linked to specific countries. Fifty-eight percent of the population identifies with a single ancestry, 22 percent with multiple ancestries, and 20 percent do not identify an ancestry.[15]

Asian Americans include recent immigrants and people whose ancestors emigrated from countries as diverse as India, Korea, Japan, and the Philippines. Latinos include people from Mexico, Central America, Puerto Rico, Cuba, Spain, and South America. Although Africans continue to emigrate to the United States, most African Americans have long historical roots in this country; many have ancestors not only from Africa but also from Europe and Native American tribes. European Americans

FIGURE 2.4

Panethnic and Racial Composition of the U.S. Population

Source: U.S. Census Bureau, "Resident Population by Race, Hispanic Origin, and Age: 2000 and 2004" (Table 14), *Statistical Abstract of the United States: 2006,* 125th edition. Washington, DC: U.S. Government Printing Office, 2006.

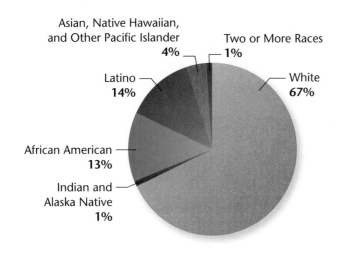

Asian, Native Hawaiian, and Other Pacific Islander 4%

Two or More Races 1%

Latino 14%

White 67%

African American 13%

Indian and Alaska Native 1%

range from western Europeans who may have lived in the United States for several hundred years, to those from eastern Europe who immigrated in large numbers at the beginning of the twentieth century, to recent immigrants from Russia and other former Soviet countries.

In describing the United States, many people proudly refer to it as a land of immigrants who left their original homelands because of economic hardship or political repression. However, this picture is only partially true. The groups that are most oppressed in this country are those who are indigenous or whose ancestors entered the country involuntarily. Native Americans were here long before Europeans and others appeared. They suffered greatly as the foreign intruders took over the land, almost annihilating the indigenous population. Not until the year 2000 did the U.S. government admit to the near genocide of native peoples, when the head of the Bureau of Indian Affairs apologized for "the agency's legacy of racism and inhumanity that included massacres, forced relocations of tribes and attempts to wipe out Indian languages and cultures."[16]

Additionally, the ancestors of most African Americans were brought by slave traders as a commodity to be sold. They were not treated as full humans until well into the nineteenth century. Not until late in the twentieth century did Africans begin to voluntarily immigrate to the United States in any significant numbers. Similarly, Mexican Americans in the Southwest were inhabitants of lands that were annexed as part of the spoils for winning the Mexican-American War; they did not immigrate. Today, many Mexicans would like to immigrate to this country but, prevented by immigration laws, cross the border illegally to obtain jobs and have a better chance for economic stability. However, illegal immigrants constantly face possible deportation, loss of everything they have gained in this country, and separation from their families.

Who can immigrate or be admitted as a refugee is determined by Congress. Immigration policies have prevented or severely limited the immigration of some groups while favoring others. For example, people with either Chinese or Japanese heritage have been excluded at different times. Individuals fleeing Communist regimes have often been granted refugee status, but others have found it difficult

Journal for Reflection

1. How do you characterize your ethnic and racial heritage?
2. With what other groups have you interacted?
3. What was the nature of your experiences with other groups?
4. How could you better get to know individuals from ethnic and racial groups different than your own?

to obtain such status when fleeing regimes supportive of the United States, even though those regimes may be dictatorships with numerous human rights violations. Immigration quotas historically were heavily weighted toward western Europeans; beginning in 1965, however, immigration became more open to people from other countries. As a result, the numbers of Latinos and Asians coming to the United States have grown dramatically.

Schools are early recipients of a growing number of new immigrants. Immigrants today are settling beyond the urban areas of California, Florida, Illinois, New Jersey, New York, and Texas. States that have had limited ethnic diversity in the past—among them Arkansas, Iowa, Montana, and Nebraska—are becoming home to students from other countries as immigrant families are sponsored by persons in these communities or settle in rural areas and small to medium-sized towns because of jobs. Many immigrants also believe that these rural communities have values more similar to their own.

Language

Language interacts with our ethnic and socioeconomic background to socialize us into linguistic and cultural communities. Children learn their native language by imitating adults and their peers. By age five, they have learned the syntax of language and know the meanings of thousands of words. When cultural similarities exist between speaker and listener, spoken messages are decoded accurately. But when the speaker and listener differ in ethnicity or class, miscommunication can occur. Even within English, a word, phrase, or nonverbal gesture takes on different meanings in different cultural groups and settings. Educators need to recognize that miscommunications between themselves and students may be due to inaccurate decoding rather than lack of linguistic ability.

Who does not know another language, does not know his own.

Goethe

Language Diversity

Nearly 50 million U.S. residents speak a language other than English at home. Spanish, Chinese, French (including Patois and Cajun), and Tagalog are the most common languages spoken other than English.[17] A number of new immigrant students enter U.S. schools with no or very limited school experiences in their home countries.

The length of time required to learn English varies. Most students become conversationally fluent within two or three years.[18] However, young people may require five to seven years to reach the proficiency necessary for success in academic subjects such as social studies and English. Students who are conversationally fluent may be immersed in English-only classrooms without appropriate support to ensure that they can function effectively in academic work. The result is that these students may fall further behind their classmates in conceptual understanding of the subjects being taught.

As immigrants assimilate into the dominant culture of the United States, their native language is often replaced by English within a few generations. The native language is more likely to be retained when schools and the community value bilingualism. As commerce and trade have become more global, professionals and administrators have realized the advantages of knowing a competitor's culture and language. They are encouraging their children to learn a second language at the same time that many of our educational policies are discouraging native speakers from maintaining their native language while learning English. The movement in some states for English-only usage in schools, in daily commerce, on street signs,

Bilingual education uses both the native languages of students and English in classrooms to ensure that students learn the academic concepts being taught.

and on official government documents highlights the dominance of English desired by some citizens.

American Sign Language (ASL) is officially recognized as a language with a complex grammar and well-regulated syntax. It is the natural language that has been developed and used for communication among individuals with hearing disabilities. As with oral languages, children learn ASL very early by imitating others who use the language. To communicate with people without hearing disabilities, many individuals with hearing disabilities also use signed English, in which the oral or written word is translated into a sign. ASL is a critical element in the identity of people with hearing disabilities. The language can be more important to their cultural identity than their membership in a particular ethnic, socioeconomic, or religious group.

Dialectal Diversity

Standard English is the dialect used by the majority of dominant group members for official and formal communications. However, numerous regional, local, ethnic, and class (or SES) dialects are identifiable across this country. Each has its own set of grammatical rules that are known to its users. Although each dialect serves its users well, standard English is usually viewed as more credible in schools and the work world. For example, most individuals involved in the media use standard English. Although teachers may be bidialectal, they are expected to use standard English as the example that should be emulated by students.

Many Americans are bidialectal or multidialectal in that they speak standard English at work but speak their native or local dialect at home or when they are socializing with friends. Social factors have an influence on which dialect is appropriate in a specific situation. At one time, students were not allowed to use a dialect other than standard English in the classroom. Some schools have proposed using the dialect of the community as a teaching tool, but such proposals usually have limited public support. Today, students are generally allowed to speak their dialects in schools but are encouraged to learn standard English to provide them an advantage when they seek employment in the dominant culture.

Journal for Reflection

1. What language and dialect did you learn in your family?

2. How effective do you think you will be in working with English language learners and parents when you teach? Why?

Should All Students Be Bilingual?

Many immigrant students enter school using a language other than English. The role of schools in teaching them English and encouraging the maintenance of their own native language has long been debated. Another side of the coin is the importance of native English speakers learning a second language so that they are fluent in at least two languages. This debate illustrates two teachers' perspectives on these issues.

YES

Douglas Ward is a bilingual learning disabilities resource teacher at William Nashold Elementary school in Rockford, Illinois. He is in his third year of teaching and is certified in bilingual special education and several other fields.

Yes, all students should be bilingual. Unfortunately, in the United States very few students become truly proficient in a foreign language. That is one reason for the shortage of foreign language and bilingual teachers.

Before the world wars, many immigrants in the United States used their native languages daily while they learned English. But the world wars and isolationist policies created a climate in which it was unpopular to speak anything but English. In some cities, fines were imposed on anyone caught speaking a foreign language in public business.

Many descendants of immigrants never learned their parents' or grandparents' native languages—in my case, Polish and German—because of these attitudes. My grandparents and parents, pressured by society, did not understand the importance of passing on their languages to me.

Learning a foreign language involves more than learning how to read, write, and speak. More important, it teaches students about a culture. Lack of understanding of cultural differences causes intolerance and war.

The people of the United States and the world need to be, not just tolerant, but accepting of other cultures. We need to embrace and celebrate our many cultures. Studying a foreign language and becoming bilingual opens one's

NO

Suzanne Emery retired last year after thirty-five years of teaching English and journalism, the last twenty-five at San Diego's Mira Mesa High School. She reviews questions for California's high school exit exam and edits the San Diego Education Association newsletter.

American education cannot be all things for all people.

We've agreed generally on the need to improve achievement in the basic curriculum. Bilingualism should not be added to the mix. Nor should it join all the other mandates that politically correct states and school districts impose: cultural holidays, parenting classes, good health activities, well-rounded social growth, adequate physical activities, proper nutrition, and suicide prevention.

A second language is always a luxury. It is needed only for the college bound and then only in certain majors.

We're told that European countries require two languages. But many European countries are very small, so bilingualism is a survival skill. And few other countries try to educate 100 percent of their children, as we do. In Europe, education is at the top of parents' priorities. Need we talk about the distractions here?

And what is the second language of bilingual children around the world? It is English. We need to educate our own kids for success in that universal language. Our schools can barely gather

(continued)

(continued)

YES

mind to new thinking and creates new opportunities to communicate with other people.

Language can be the key to a lasting peace between enemies. Learning another language is the best way to make friends.

Students in many other countries learn at least one foreign language in their public schools. In the United States, few schools even offer a foreign language in elementary school.

As global businesses and trade expand, the need to know a second language is growing tremendously. Many businesses in other countries want to do business with us. Their salespeople speak English and know our customs. We need people who know other languages and cultures so that our exports will increase and our economy will become stronger.

Learning another language may also spill over into other areas. Research shows that bilingualism leads to cognitive advantages that may raise scores on some intelligence tests.

Studies also show a correlation between knowing two languages and linguistic abilities that may facilitate early reading acquisition. That, in turn, could boost academic achievement.

NO

materials and teachers for the standard curriculum, let alone for another language.

If schools required a second language, what would it be? Spanish, Japanese, or French? How should we decide? What about all our students who speak Hmong, Farsi, or Tagalog? Would we mandate a third language for them?

Comfort in two languages is valuable in many venues and often desired for reasons of tradition. But families that want another language can do what they've always done: Saturday school, magnet schools, and temple classes.

If a district is so insular that it lacks the diverse quilt of contemporary America, its sterility and guilt should not be visited on the rest of the country.

So many American schools are like mine in San Diego where students regularly exchange videos with relatives in Vietnam, make the annual family pilgrimage to Mexico, edit the Islamic Center's youth newsletter, and produce pamphlets in graphic arts class for the Buddhist temple.

Here in California, with the nation's largest enrollment of newcomers, the challenge is to prepare all students for world-class competition, culminating with a high school exit exam in English, because English communication is key to success in academics and in adult life. That also applies to the rest of the country.

We cannot afford another diversion added to the overflowing plate of public education.

Source: "Should All Students Be Bilingual?" *NEA Today* (May 2002), p. 11. Reprinted by permission of the National Education Association.

WHAT IS YOUR PERSPECTIVE ON THIS ISSUE?
Should all students be bilingual?

To give your opinion, go to Chapter 2 of the companion
website (**www.ablongman.com/johnson14e**) and click on Teacher Perspectives.

Gender

Males and females are culturally different even when they are members of the same socioeconomic, ethnic, and religious group. The two groups are often segregated at social gatherings, employed in different types of jobs, and expected to take on different family roles. The ways they think and act are defined by both biology and the expectations of their culture and society.

Differences between Females and Males

Because of our social circumstances, male and female are really two cultures and their life experiences are utterly different.

Kate Millett

Learning the gender of a baby is one of the important rites of parenthood. However, the major difference between infant boys and girls is the way adults respond to them. There are few actual physical differences, particularly before puberty. The socialization process in child-rearing and schools are primary determinants of gender identity and related distinctive behaviors.

By age two, children realize that they are a girl or a boy; by five or six, they have learned their gender and stereotypical behavior. In most cultures, boys are generally socialized toward achievement and self-reliance, girls toward nurturance and responsibility. In the United States, differences in the expectations and behaviors of the two genders may be rooted in their groups' ethnicity, religion, and socioeconomic status.

In schools many girls and boys perform differently in academic subjects and behave differently in the classroom. Males outperform females in the highest levels of mathematics and physics, but the differences are declining as more high school girls take higher level math and science courses. Girls continue to be ahead of boys in reading and writing proficiencies. In the classroom "boys tend to be louder, more physically aggressive, and more prone to attention-getting devices . . . than are girls, resulting in more teacher attention going to boys."[19]

Some researchers attribute these gender differences to the development of specific hemispheres at the top of the brain. Females tend to have a well-developed left side of the brain, which is associated with verbal skills such as reading, speaking, and writing. The right side, which boys use more often, is associated with spatial skills of measuring and working with blocks or other objects.[20] Other researchers dispute this claim as they find female and male performance more alike than different, suggesting that previously observed gender differences are not solely determined by biology. They find that the variations in performance and behavior are greater within male and female groups than between them.[21]

A major difference between males and females is how they are treated in society. For example, women earn less than men throughout their life span, as shown in Figure 2.5. In addition, society generally places men in positions of superiority, as evidenced by their disproportionate employment in the highest status and highest-paying jobs. Many times this relationship extends into the home, where the father and husband may both protect the family and rule over it. Sometimes this relationship leads to physical and mental abuse of women and children.

Schools often reinforce behavior that is stereotypically gender specific. Girls are expected to be quiet, follow the rules, and help the teacher. Boys and young men are expected to be rowdier and less attentive. Many working-class males develop patterns of resistance to school and its authority figures because schooling is perceived as feminine and as emphasizing mental rather than manual work.

Many males are also not well served by current socialization patterns; some do not fit neatly in the dominant culture's stereotypical vision of maleness. Some men would feel more comfortable working as preschool teachers, nurses, or librarians—traditionally female careers—but may have learned that those jobs are inappropriate for "real men."

FIGURE 2.5

Income of Males and Females Working Full-Time Year-Round

Source: U.S. Census Bureau, "Average Earnings of Year-Round, Full-Time Workers by Educational Attainment: 2003" (Table 686), *Statistical Abstract of the United States: 2006,* 125th edition. Washington, DC: U.S. Government Printing Office, 2006.

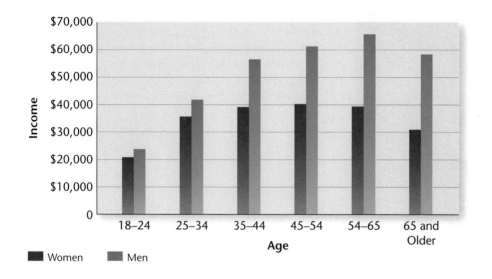

■ Women ■ Men

Global Perspectives

Women's Political Participation

Beginning in 1990, the global community agreed that gender equity was important in the development of a country. At the United Nation's World Education Forum in Dakar in 2002, gender equality became one of eight goals for eliminating poverty and hunger. The consensus among the world's leaders was that "no country's development can be judged satisfactory if women do not fully participate in community life, in society and in work."[22] Participants expected member countries to show women's progress in education, literacy, nonagricultural wage employment, and parliamentary representation.

A 2002 progress report by the United Nations Development Fund for Women (UNIFEM) shows limited progress in education, literacy, and employment. However, women's involvement in parliamentary bodies has made gains in a number of countries. Although women remain absent from these bodies in many countries, eleven have already reached the goal of 30 percent. They include Argentina, Costa Rica, Denmark, Finland, Germany, Iceland, Mozambique, the Netherlands, Norway, South Africa, and Sweden. The countries that met the benchmark did so by using quotas. The study also found that political participation is the only indicator in the gender equity goals that is not linked to poverty, which means that differences between wealthy and developing countries do not exist. For example, women's participation in legislative bodies in the United States, France, and Japan are 12 percent or less, which is behind thirteen of the countries in sub-Saharan Africa—countries suffering from great poverty.[23]

Questions for Reflection

1. Why has the United Nations determined that gender equity is important in a country's development?

2. In what ways could the increased political participation of women contribute to more girls and young women attaining an education?

Title IX prevents discrimination in education programs based on sex. Schools must make provisions for girls and young women to participate in intramural, club, and interscholastic sports.

Title IX

Title IX of the 1972 Higher Education Amendments is the major legislation that addresses the civil rights of girls and women in the education system. It requires federally funded colleges and schools to provide equal educational opportunity to girls and women. Title IX has been credited for increasing the number of girls and young women participating in college preparatory courses, completing professional degrees in college, and participating in sports. In the year that Title IX passed, only 7 percent of law degrees were earned by females as compared to 48 percent in 2002. Eight percent of medical degrees and 13 percent of doctorates were awarded to females in 1970, but by 2002, women received 44 percent of medical degrees and 48 percent of doctorates.[24]

The most controversial part of Title IX is the provision for equal opportunity in athletics. The courts have upheld the application of a three-part test by schools and colleges to determine equal opportunity:

1. The percentage of male and female athletes is substantially proportionate to the percentage of females and males in the student population.
2. The school has a history and continuing practice of expanding opportunities for the underrepresented sex to participate in sports.
3. Even if a school is not meeting the proportionate expectation in item 1 above, the school is fully and effectively meeting the interest and abilities of the underrepresented sex.[25]

The number of girls and women participating in sports has increased dramatically since 1972. When Title IX was passed, less than 300,000 girls participated in high school sports. That number has increased by 847 percent, with over 2.7 million girls now participating in high school sports. The number of women participating in college sports has increased from 32,000 to 150,000. Some groups argue that Title IX has led to the elimination of some men's sports as women's sports are expanded. However, the rate of male participation in high school sports over the past 30 years has remained at one of every two students. In the same period high school girls' participation has moved from one in 27 to one in 2.5.[26]

Journal for Reflection

1. Thinking back on your own education, what differences in classroom behavior between boys and girls do you recall?
2. What differences existed in academic achievement?
3. Why are some people particularly concerned about the education of boys today?

Sexual Orientation

Sexual orientation is established early in life. The majority of gay adults report feeling different from other children before they entered kindergarten.[27] The common understanding among the research community is that sexual orientation is not chosen.[28] However, some cultural groups place high value on heterosexuality and denigrate or outlaw homosexuality as part of their religious doctrine or community mores. Nevertheless, it is estimated that 5 to 10 percent of the population is lesbian, gay, bisexual, or transgender (LGBT). Gay men and lesbians are concentrated in some areas such as Vermont and San Francisco, but they live all over the country. The 2000 census found same sex couples living in 99.3 percent of all counties in the country.[29]

Gays and lesbians often face discrimination in housing, employment, and social institutions, as evidenced when schools and universities prohibit the establishment of gay student clubs. Homophobia, as expressed in harassment and violence against gays and lesbians, is tolerated in many areas of the country. Society's prejudices and discriminatory practices result in many gays and lesbians hiding their sexual orientation and establishing their own social clubs, networks, and communication systems to support one another.

Isolation and loneliness are the experiences of many gay and lesbian youth. If gays and lesbians openly acknowledge their sexual orientation or appear to be LGBT, they are likely to be harassed and face reprisals from peers and school officials. A 2005 study by the Gay, Lesbian and Straight Education Network (GLSEN) found that verbal, sexual, and physical harassment are common experiences for LGBT students in our schools. Sixty-four percent of LGBT students reported being verbally harassed (name calling, threats), about two-thirds sexually harassed (sexual comments, inappropriate touching), 38 percent physically harassed, and 18 percent physically assaulted. Females and youth of color report even higher incidences of abuse when homophobia interacts with racism and sexism.[30]

Journal for Reflection

1. What interactions have you had with gays or lesbians?

2. How will you feel about meeting with the same-sex parents of your students?

3. How will you respond if you hear a student making a homophobic comment?

Structures within the schools do not provide the same kind of support to LGBT students that is available to others. Sixty-four percent of LGBT students fear for their safety in schools. However, students feel more comfortable and safer in schools when faculty and staff are supportive, LGBT people are portrayed in the curriculum, gay–straight alliance or similar clubs exist, and a comprehensive policy on harassment is enforced.[31] Most educators often know little about this group and have had few or no contacts with LGBT people who are out, or open about their sexual orientation. They may not have taught students whose parents are gay or lesbian. Without a better understanding of homosexuality, teachers may find it difficult to work effectively with LGBT students or the children of gay and lesbian parents.

Exceptionalities

More than forty-nine million people, or 19 percent of the population over five years old, have a **disability.** About one-fourth of the persons with a disability indicate that their disability existed at birth or developed before they were age twenty. The number of people with disabilities increases with age; over 40 percent of the population over 65 have a disability.[32] Those with physical disabilities can be readily recognized by their use of supports such as a cane, braces, or wheelchair. Some individuals are labeled very early in their school careers as *mentally retarded, emotionally disabled,* or with some other disability. Figure 2.6 shows the number of students with different disabilities in today's schools. Critics of labeling declare this system to be demeaning and stigmatizing.

Some educators make a determination as early as kindergarten of the potential of students with disabilities, which can lead to low academic expectations for students who could perform at high levels with appropriate accommodations for their disability. Seventy-two percent of persons with disabilities hold a high school diploma and 11 percent have college degrees.[33] Dropout rates for this population are relatively high. Persons with disabilities are disproportionately underrepresented in the labor force, sometimes because they are unable to go to work, but more often because the workplace has not made the accommodations that would make it possible for them to work productively.

Persons without a disability often react with disdain toward individuals with disabilities and view them as inferior. But like all other individuals, people with

It doesn't matter who you are, there are some things you can do and some things you can't. It's about ability, not disability.

Christopher Reeve

disability

A long-standing physical, mental, or emotional condition that can make it difficult for a person to perform activities such as walking, climbing stairs, dressing, bathing, learning, or remembering.

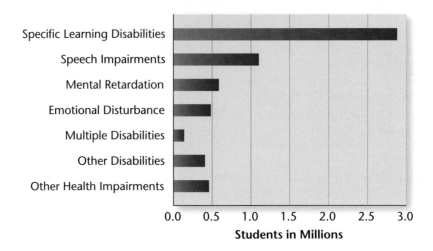

FIGURE 2.6

Students with Disabilities Served by Selected Programs

Source: U.S. Census Bureau, "Children and Youth with Disabilities Served by Selected Programs: 1995–2004" (Table 249), *Statistical Abstract of the United States: 2004–2005,* 125th edition. Washington, DC: U.S. Government Printing Office, 2006.

disabilities want to be recognized as persons in their own right. They have the same needs for love and the same desire to be successful as persons without disabilities. Instead, society has historically not accepted them as equals. Some individuals with severe disabilities are placed in institutions out of the sight of the public. Others are segregated in separate schools or classes. Too often they are rejected and made to feel inept and limited in their abilities.

Schools, which should be part of the solution, have often contributed to the problems of students with disabilities. Most classrooms are not physically designed to accommodate the special needs of all students. Chalkboards are too high for students in wheelchairs. Desks do not usually accommodate wheelchairs, and special ramps and elevators are often nonexistent. However, special equipment such as computers and amplification devices can make participation in learning possible for many students who were not provided that opportunity in the past.

Inclusion

Inclusion is the practice of fully integrating all students into the educational process, regardless of their race, ethnicity, gender, socioeconomic status, religion, physical or mental ability, or language. Students see themselves represented in the curriculum as well as in classes for the gifted. Historically, inclusion referred primarily to the integration of students with disabilities in general education classrooms and schools. Inclusion of all students requires collaboration among the adults, including parents, who work with students with disabilities. Teachers should not be expected to serve as both the teacher and specialist. Ideally, teachers of general education collaborate with a special educator, often accompanied by a teacher's aide and appropriate specialists, such as a speech/language pathologist, occupational therapist, physical therapist, vision specialist, adaptive physical education teacher, school psychologist, or school nurse. The team individualizes instruction for each student in an individualized educational plan (IEP). At times,

inclusion

The integration of all students, regardless of their background or abilities, in all aspects of the educational process.

students with disabilities may be pulled out of the classroom for special services, but these special sessions should be limited and should be used only to meet complex individual needs.

One of the goals of inclusion is to provide students with disabilities the same opportunities for learning academic content to which others are exposed. Most students with disabilities can achieve at the same levels as their peers without disabilities, but they require accommodations that allow them to access the content, the instruction, and the tools for learning. These accommodations may require physical changes in the classroom, such as increasing the height of a desk so that students in wheelchairs have a work space. It may require the provision of computers for students who cannot hold or control a pencil. It may require books in Braille, the use of sign language, and taped books.

Researchers are finding improved student outcomes for students with disabilities who are in inclusive classrooms. Students without disabilities also receive positive benefits. Inclusion helps them become more tolerant of others, appreciate diversity, and be more responsive to the needs of others.[34]

Many students with disabilities are included in classrooms and other school activities alongside students who do not have disabilities. All students benefit from this arrangement, with improved outcomes for students with disabilities and an enhanced appreciation for diversity among all students.

Disproportionate Placements

Twelve percent of all students are provided with special education services. However, students in special education classes are likely to be students of color, English language learners, or whites from low-income families. Three percent of Asian American and eight percent of white students are classified as having mental retardation, emotional disturbance, and specific learning disability as compared to 11 percent of African American and 10 percent of American Indian students. Males are also almost twice as likely as females to be identified as having these disabilities.[35] Students labeled *mentally retarded* or *emotionally disabled* disproportionately are from low-income families. Low-income children are also overrepresented in classes for seriously emotionally disturbed students. Middle-class students are more likely to be classified as *learning disabled*. This pattern is also found in the placement of males and students of color in special education and gifted classes. African American and Native American students are overrepresented in disability categories of learning disability, mental retardation, and emotionally disturbed, as are males in general. On the other hand, Latino, African American, and Native American students are underrepresented in gifted and talented programs. Educators need to monitor the reasons for their referrals of students to be tested for placement in these classes and provide equity in the delivery of education services.

Disproportionate placements of students in special education and gifted education programs may be due to a number of factors. Tests used for placement may be biased against low-income students, English language learners, and students who have not assimilated into the dominant culture. Some educators who recommend students for special programs are intolerant of cultural differences and do not want students in their classes who they believe will disrupt the classroom. Schools

CROSS-REFERENCE
Legal requirements for education of students with disabilities are discussed in Chapter 6.

Journal for Reflection

1. What experiences have you had with persons with disabilities?

2. What do you think of having several students with disabilities integrated into your future classroom?

3. How will you learn what accommodations are needed to best serve these students?

Inclusion of Students with Disabilities

Over time, classroom teachers have been given increased responsibility for making sure the needs of a child with an IEP are met in their classroom. Although a child may enter the classroom with an IEP requiring support from special educators, ultimately and legally it is the teacher's responsibility to make sure the IEP is implemented in the classroom. It is also the teacher's responsibility to handle any behavior or social difficulties that may occur in the classroom. Furthermore, the teacher must work with special educators to adapt lessons and assignments to the ability level of all of the students. Teachers must promote success for all learners rather than expecting failure.

Picture yourself as a teacher in an inner-city second-grade classroom. You have twenty-five students from low-income homes and several children for whom English is their second language. Among these students are three children with IEPs and four learners who are making limited academic progress but do not qualify for special education services.

The three children with IEPs have varied needs. One child is a girl in a wheelchair with physical needs requiring a nurse to accompany her in the classroom. Another child is an eight-year-old boy who was born with Down syndrome. He too has multiple needs, including speech/language therapy, occupational therapy to work on his fine-motor skills, and a behavior plan monitored by the school psychologist. The third child has attention deficit hyperactivity disorder (ADHD). His academic skills lag behind by a full year below grade level, and his attention span is minimal during periods of instruction.

In addition to these three children with IEPs, four children are reading at first-grade level. Although these children are obviously having difficulties with reading,

writing, and spelling, they do not currently qualify for special education services as their performance level is not two standard deviations below their intelligence quotient–derived ability level.

Unfortunately, there is no reading specialist in your school to help teach the learners performing below grade level. Furthermore, the special education teacher is only required to provide direct services to the students with IEPs for two hours a week. There is a special education assistant assigned to assist with the children with IEPs in your classroom, but her time is split between all twelve first- and second-grade classes, so you are lucky to have her assistance on a daily basis. If the special educator or assistant is out for any reason, a substitute is rarely provided.

Questions for Reflection

1. What would you do to include the student in the wheelchair in as many classroom activities as possible and to encourage social interactions with her peers?

2. What would you do to make sure the child with Down syndrome is accepted and included by his peers?

3. Where would you designate that the child with ADHD take his breaks in the classroom, and what would you provide to make him feel as though he were having a break?

4. What would you do to differentiate instruction to meet the needs of the children who aren't reading on grade level but do not receive special education services?

5. How will you meet the needs of all the other students in your classroom and teach them at each of their ability levels?

To answer these questions on-line and e-mail your answers to your professor, go to Chapter 2 of the companion website (**www.ablongman.com/johnson14e**) and click on Professional Dilemma.

should monitor recommendations and placements to find out if students from some groups are being disproportionately placed in these programs and take corrective action if needed.

Religion

Religion can have a great influence on the values and lifestyles of families and can play an important role in the socialization of children and young people. Religious doctrines and practices often guide beliefs about the roles of males and females.

They also provide guidance regarding birthrates, birth control, marriage, child-rearing, friendships, and political attitudes.

By age five, children are able to generally identify their family's religious affiliation. Although 84 percent of the population regard their religious beliefs as very or fairly important, less than half attend a religious service on a weekly basis.[36] However, strong religious perspectives are reflected in the daily lives of many families.

Religious pluralism flourishes in this country. Members of religions other than those with Judeo-Christian roots are increasing as more immigrants arrive from Asia and the Middle East. Other families declare themselves atheists or simply do not participate in an organized religion. Some individuals and families live in religious cults that are established to promote and maintain a religious calling. Some religious groups believe that their religion is the only correct and legitimate view of the world. Other groups recognize that

Public schools cannot advance a religion, but neither can religion be ignored in the curriculum. Diverse religious beliefs should be acknowledged and respected in classrooms and schools.

religious diversity has grown out of different historical experiences and accept the validity of diverse groups. At the same time, every major religion endorses justice, love, and compassion as virtues that most individuals and nations say they are trying to achieve.

Although they are not as dominant as earlier in U.S. history, Protestants are still in the majority with 52 percent of the adult population, followed by Catholics who comprise 25 percent of the population. Four percent of the population practice other religions with the largest being Jewish (1.4%), Muslim or Islamic (0.5%), and Buddhist (0.5%). Fourteen percent identify themselves as agnostic, atheist, humanist, or not practicing a religion.[37] Within each of the major religious groups, there are distinct denominations and sects that have the same general history but may differ greatly in their beliefs and perspectives on the correct way to live. Most Western religions are compatible with the values of the dominant culture; they usually promote patriotism and emphasize individual control of life.

With the influx of immigrants from Asia, Africa, and the Middle East over the past few decades, religious diversity among the population has increased further with the introduction of non-Western religions such as Islam, Hinduism, and Buddhism. The interaction of these faiths with Western religions and their impact on dominant society have yet to be determined. In the meantime, students from diverse religious backgrounds appear in classrooms. Teachers need to respect these differences if they are going to serve the students and community well.

For many people, religion is essential in determining their cultural identity. Some religious groups, such as the Amish and Hutterites, establish their own communities and schools to maintain the religion, foster mutual support, and develop group cohesiveness. Members of groups such as the Mormons promote primary relationships and interactions with other members of the same faith. Most

CROSS-REFERENCE
Issues and court cases related to religion in schools are presented in Chapter 6.

Journal for Reflection

1. How has your religious background had an influence on your perceptions of persons with other religious beliefs?

2. How does your religion influence your beliefs about evolution and sex education?

3. How will you respond if the school district in which you teach asks you to teach something against your religious beliefs?

social activities are linked to religion, and institutions have been developed to reflect and support religious beliefs. In many rural areas, the church is the center of social and community activities. Many religions expect their members to spend much of their nonworking hours in church and charity activities.

Families appear satisfied with schools when the schools reflect the values that are important in their religion. But they may attack schools when the curriculum, assigned readings, holidays, school convocations, and graduation exercises are perceived to be in conflict with their religious values. Many court cases over the past century have helped to sort out these issues.

Summary

CULTURE AND SOCIETY. Culture determines the way individuals behave and think, including their perspectives of the world and education. Although characteristics and contributions of diverse cultural groups are reflected in U.S. society, white, Protestant, heterosexual, middle-class European Americans have had the greatest impact on societal values and behavioral expectations. Three ideologies provide different perspectives on the acceptance of diversity in the United States: assimilation, pluralism, and cultural choice.

SOCIOECONOMIC STATUS. The way students and their families live is greatly affected by their socioeconomic status, which is determined by income, wealth, occupation, and educational attainment. The population is socially stratified, providing some groups more advantage and prestige in society than others.

RACE AND ETHNICITY. As a result of immigration from Asia, Mexico, Central America, and the Middle East over the past 40 years, the United States is becoming more ethnically diverse. Although race is not accepted as a scientific concept for classifying people, it is a social construct that continues to be used to sort people in the United States. Ethnicity is determined by the national origin of one's ancestors.

LANGUAGE. Nearly one in five residents of the United States speaks a language other than English at home. As a result, a growing number of English language learners are found in schools across the country. In addition, a number of students use a dialect that is not standard English in their home environments.

GENDER. Although few biological differences exist between females and males, differences in economic status, jobs, and educational attainment continue to exist. Theorists and researchers do not agree on the causes for these differences. Some credit biology and others culture or society.

SEXUAL ORIENTATION. More than half of LGBT students report verbal, physical, or sexual harassment by other students, and sometimes teachers, while they are in school. Many educators are not knowledgeable about homosexuality and do not know how to support LGBT students.

EXCEPTIONALITIES. Today's teachers are likely to have students with disabilities in their classrooms. Like members of other underserved groups in society, students with disabilities are often labeled and stereotyped in ways not conducive to learning.

RELIGION.   Religious diversity in the United States is expanding to include religions other than Christianity and Judaism. Families from other religious backgrounds seldom see their traditions and values reflected in the public schools and often feel discriminated against because of their religion.

Discussion Questions

1. Students and families bring their cultures into the classroom. Teachers also bring to school their cultures, which may be different than their students' cultures. Why shouldn't teachers establish their own culture as the norm that must be followed in the classroom? What cultural norms should guide a multicultural classroom?
2. Research shows that some students perform better academically and socially when they are segregated in single-sex classrooms. In which cases do you think such segregation is appropriate?
3. Which of the three ideologies (assimilation, pluralism, or cultural choice) related to the management of diversity in our society do you hope pervades the schools in which you will work in the future? Why?
4. How do you plan to manage your classroom to positively build on the racial, ethnic, gender, socioeconomic, and ability differences of students? What pedagogical strategies (e.g., cooperative learning) will you use? Why?
5. Most classrooms today include one or more students with disabilities. Where will you turn for assistance in providing the necessary accommodations to help those students learn at the levels they are capable of learning?

School-Based Observations

1. Identify the group memberships (e.g., race, ethnicity, language, gender, socioeconomic class, religion, physical and academic ability, and geographic background) of the students in a class that you are observing at the P–12 level. What are the differences within the ethnic groups represented in the class?
2. Examine the curriculum, textbooks, bulletin boards, and other materials used in the classroom to determine which groups studied in this chapter are included and which never appear.
3. In a school with English language learners, interview two or more teachers about the strategies they use to ensure that students do not fall behind academically because their native language is not English.

Portfolio Development

1. Identify one cultural group with which you have no or limited experience and write a paper on the group's historical and current experience in the United States. What other information will be helpful to you if students from this group are in your classroom when you begin teaching? How will you work effectively with the families from this group?
2. Contrast educational practices that have evolved to support different theories related to diversity and develop an argument for incorporating one or more of these practices into your own teaching.

Preparing for Certification

THE PRAXIS PLT TEST AND DIVERSITY

1. The Praxis II Principles of Learning and Teaching (PLT) test, which assesses a prospective teacher's knowledge about a variety of teaching-related skills, is required by many states. The test covers four broad categories: organizing content knowledge for student learning, creating an environment for student learning, teaching for student learning, and teacher professionalism. Learn more about the PLT test by reviewing the ETS *Test at a Glance* materials at www.ets.org/praxis.
2. Answer the following multiple-choice question, which is similar to items in Praxis and other state certification tests. If you are unsure of the answer, reread the "Acceptance of Diverse Groups" section in this chapter.

Seven of Ms. Bishop's third-grade students are recent immigrants, all from different countries and all speaking little English. Ms. Bishop says her goal is for all seven students to learn English and American customs as quickly as possible so they can rapidly become part of U.S. society. Which ideology about diversity most closely corresponds to Ms. Bishop's beliefs?

   A. cultural pluralism
   B. assimilation
   C. social stratification
   D. cultural choice

3. Answer the following short-answer question, which is similar to items in Praxis and other state certification tests. After you've completed your written response, use the scoring guide in the *Test at a Glance* materials to assess your response. Can you revise your response to improve your score?

Reread the chapter-opening case study. The students mentioned who attend the Columbus schools are members of several cultural groups. Identify at least three ethnic groups in these Ohio schools. How might membership in these groups affect the students' school experiences?

Websites

www.adl.org The Anti-Defamation League fights anti-Semitism, bigotry, and extremism. Its website includes information on religious freedom, civil rights, and the Holocaust as well as resources for teachers on fighting hate.

www.cec.sped.org The Council for Exceptional Children is dedicated to improving educational outcomes for individuals with exceptionalities, students with disabilities, and/or the gifted. The website identifies resources for educators.

www.feminist.org The website of the Feminist Majority provides information about women's issues, Title IX, and education, including links to additional resources.

www.glsen.org The website of the Gay, Lesbian, and Straight Education Network provides resources and updates for ending bias against LGBT persons in schools and society.

www.nabe.org The National Association for Bilingual Education (NABE) provides research and resources on bilingual education and multilingualism.

www.niea.org The website of the National Indian Education Association includes resources, facts, and history about American Indians, Alaska Natives, and Native Hawaiians.

Further Reading

Gollnick, Donna M., and Chinn, Philip C. (2006). *Multicultural Education in a Pluralistic Society,* 7th edition. Columbus, OH: Merrill. A fundamental text with expanded descriptions and information about the groups outlined in this chapter. This book also discusses the pedagogical implications and applications for ethnic, racial, socioeconomic, gender, linguistic, religious, age, and ability groups.

Hehir, Thomas. (Spring 2002). "Eliminating Ableism in Education," *Harvard Educational Review, 72*(1), pp. 1–32. An excellent discussion of ableism in schools that prevents students with disabilities from fully participating in the education system, having access to high levels of academic contact, and fully participating in society. Instead of accepting different ways of seeing, moving, and thinking, schools are guilty of ableism,

which results in devaluing persons with disabilities and treating them as inferior to others.

The Jossey-Bass Reader on Gender in Education. (2002). San Francisco: Jossey-Bass. A comprehensive anthology of differing perspectives on the nature/nurture debate, gender achievement gaps, testing and teaching bias, the cultural context of gender, gender equity in the curriculum, and sexual harassment.

Lardner, James, and Smith, David, Eds. (2005). *Inequality Matters: The Growing Economic Divide in America and Its Poisonous Consequences*. New York: The New Press. A series of essays that confront the growing concentration of wealth, income, and economic and political power in the United States and the resulting disparities in health, education, and political representation.

mylabschool

Where the classroom comes to life!

Go to Allyn and Bacon's MyLabSchool (www.mylabschool.com) and complete the following activity for Chapter 2. Click on MyLabSchool **Case Archive**, then click on **Is This Child Mislabeled?**

CHAPTER 3

Sociological Perspectives on Students and Families

CASE STUDY

Culture Clash

By Mary Ann Zehr, *Education Week,* February 5, 2003

HARRISONBURG, VA.—Leonard Yavny believes Darwin's theory of evolution contradicts biblical truths. He also thinks youths shouldn't be taught about sex; if they learn about it, they might try it, he reasons. He requires his own children to be chaperoned on dates until they are married. And he doesn't want his children to be exposed to Halloween, which he believes is a holiday originating from the devil. Yavny, the 42-year-old father of five children between the ages of 10 and 19, finds that these particular beliefs conflict with those of many of the teachers or students at the public schools his children attend here. But he has never complained to school personnel.

Instead, he counteracts what his children face at school by pointing out to them what he believes to be false teaching, holding them to specific expectations, and occasionally pulling them out of school activities.

Last Halloween, for example, he and his wife, Galina, kept their children home from school.

Yavny is a conservative Christian and an immigrant from Ukraine who shares with many immigrants a critical view of the prevailing attitudes and beliefs that his children encounter in school.

Having received the largest number of immigrants ever in a single decade during the 1990s, the United States has become home to an increasing number of parents such as Yavny whose traditional values don't mesh well with the more liberal values that tend to permeate public schools.

Harrisonburg, a city of 42,000 set in a farming region of Virginia, has received an immigrant wave of its own as jobs in the poultry industry have drawn newcomers here. In five years, the population of language-minority children in the Harrisonburg schools has swelled from about 400 students, most of whom spoke Spanish, to 1,180 students who speak 39 different languages.

And so, it's not hard to find immigrant parents here who share Yavny's perspective. They resist assimilation and expect their children to follow their lead. "We are raising our kids in the United States," says Benita Castro, a native of Mexico who along with her husband recently threw an elaborate church ceremony and reception, or *quinceañera,* to celebrate her daughter Nancy's 15th birthday, "but we'll stick to our morals."

Aisha Rostem, a Kurdish Muslim who sends her two teenage daughters to schools here, says through an interpreter, "I'm praying that they will be safe—that they don't fight, that they don't get involved in bad things."

How these parents help their children make sense of the two worlds they live in—the world of school and the more traditional world of home and community—can have a huge effect on their children's academic success and school life. So also can schools' handling of this cultural clash make a difference in immigrant children's lives.

Questions for Reflection

1. What is your general reaction to this article by Mary Ann Zehr?

2. What is your perspective on the subject of sex education for school students? Give the rationale for your response.

3. What are some of the advantages and disadvantages of having immigrant students in a classroom?

4. List several ways that you believe schools should serve immigrant students.

5. What legislation do you believe is needed to deal with the high number of illegal immigrants who have school age children?

6. What is your perspective on the subject of bilingual education?

Reprinted with permission.

INTASC

Learning Outcomes

After reading and studying this chapter, you should be able to:

1. Respect the differing family backgrounds from which students come and understand the importance of not stereotyping student behavior or academic potential on the basis of their family structure. (INTASC 3: Diverse Learners)

2. Identify some cultural differences based on where students and teachers live. (INTASC 3: Diverse Learners)

3. Understand that young people need caring adults to help them maneuver through the tribulations and challenges of childhood and the teenage years. (INTASC 5: Motivation and Behavior)

4. Identify the challenges that many students face as a result of being at risk because of societal factors, such as poverty, over which they have little or no control. (INTASC 2: Learning and Development and 10: Relationships)

5. Understand the role that prejudice and discrimination play in marginalizing many students. (INTASC 3: Diverse Learners and 10: Relationships)

A democratic society struggles with how to support individuality and yet develop a consciousness of shared concerns and actions that promote equity. This challenge is paramount in a society such as the United States, which includes many groups that affect and are affected by political, social, and economic systems. These societal influences have a great influence on young people and their teachers as they interact in school settings. The big ideas that help us understand the challenges of education for a society include the changing nature of families, differences as a result of where we live, the challenges of growing up, and prejudice and discrimination.

Families and their children face many challenges in today's society. Many children live in single-parent households with limited income. Children are sometimes left on their own, especially in the period after school. Teenagers struggle with figuring out who they are. Students from oppressed groups too often face **prejudice** from classmates and educators and overt discrimination in school policies and practices. They are usually assisted in this process by parents and other responsible and caring adults, but a number of them learn about sexuality, drugs, and violence from the media and their peers. Teachers and other educators play an important role in helping children and youth maneuver through these challenges toward the goal of becoming responsible adults.

prejudice

Preconceived negative attitude toward the members of a group.

Educators, families, and policymakers have varied perspectives on how schools and other institutions should support children and families as they deal with the challenges addressed in this chapter. Data about the population and how they are being served by institutions such as schools inform educational policies and practices. State and federal legislation sometimes reflects one perspective over another in the types of services and support that are available to students and their families.

Today's Families

Families in the United States have changed dramatically over the past fifty years. In the 1950s, the norm was a working father and a mother at home with two or more school-aged children. Today only 68 percent of children who are under eighteen years old live in families with two parents.[1] Seldom does a mother remain at home until her children finish high school. Families today include mothers working while fathers stay at home with the children, single-parent families, families with two working parents, remarried parents, childless marriages, families with adopted children, gay and lesbian parents, extended families, grandparents raising grandchildren, and unmarried couples with children.

Parents are older than in the past, in part, because they marry later. More than 85 percent of today's young people age eighteen to twenty-four years old have never been married.[2] Most men and women have worked for a number of years before marrying. Over one-third of first-time married couples have separated or divorced after ten years. Over half of divorced women remarry within five years and 75 percent of them by ten years.[3] The average age of people of color is younger than that of whites; thus, a larger percentage of women of color are of childbearing age, leading to higher birthrates than white families.

Most children live with two parents, even though one of them may be a stepmother or stepfather. One of three children in the United States lives with a single mother, a single father, grandparents, or another guardian.[4] Ideally, it would be an advantage for children to have two caring and loving parents to nurture children. However, children from all types of families are academically successful in school and become well-adjusted adults. It is not the type of family that disadvantages students or makes it difficult for them to adjust appropriately and achieve well in school. The factor that is most correlated to such disadvantage is the economic well-being of families. Those in poverty, who are more likely to be living with single mothers, are more likely than their better-off peers to have problems in school.

Educators should avoid labeling a child as dysfunctional because he or she does not live with both parents. Too often, teachers develop a self-fulfilling prophecy about students in nontraditional families not being able to achieve academically. Instead, they should have high expectations for their success in school, and do everything possible to help them learn.

Parenting

With the growing female influence in the family, the typical family structure is no longer as patriarchal as it once was. Many families are less autocratically controlled by adults and have become more egalitarian in the way they operate. In the past, nurturing children was the primary responsibility of mothers. Today many fathers are also actively involved in parenting.

Most parents want what's best for their children, but there is no simple guidebook for steering children through the complex terrain they will have to navigate as

What If He Has Two Mommies?

In the 1950s, most students came from families with both a mother and a father. In the subsequent fifty years, more and more students have been raised by single mothers and now by a growing number of single fathers. Some students do not live with either parent but stay instead with relatives or in a foster home. As society becomes more tolerant of a variety of family structures and as adults become more open about their sexual orientation, teachers will also be introduced to lesbian and gay parents who may be living with a partner or separated from a partner.

The curriculum in most schools, especially at the preprimary and elementary levels, is often developed around the family—a nuclear family with a mother, father, and siblings. But for decades now, schools have been populated with students whose families do not fit that model. The curriculum and instructional materials seldom mirror the diversity of families, which may include parents with special needs, interracial parents, single parents, gay and lesbian parents, and foster parents.

The dilemma for teachers extends beyond the curriculum. They must figure out how to value and respect the diversity of families. Otherwise, both students and parents will feel ignored and isolated from the school setting. Teachers may also have to help other students develop an understanding of this diversity. Sometimes students respond to such differences in negative and hurtful ways. Teachers will need to develop strategies for confronting homophobic behavior from the outset.

Questions for Reflection

1. How could a primary teacher introduce gay and lesbian parents into a reading lesson?

2. What are different ways that teachers are likely to learn some of their students have gay or lesbian parents?

3. How should a teacher with strong views against homosexual relationships approach the reality of having the children of gays and lesbians in the classroom?

4. How can a school develop a climate of acceptance of all students regardless of the structure and nature of the families in which they live?

To answer these questions on-line and e-mail your answers to your professor, go to Chapter 3 of the companion website (www.ablongman.com/johnson14e) and click on Professional Dilemma.

Thirty percent of children under eighteen years of age live in nontraditional families who provide the love and support necessary to raise children.

they grow up. Often parents draw from their own experiences as children and adults, but they did not encounter the same pressures from peers and the mass culture faced by today's students. To increase students' chances of making it safely through childhood and adolescence, teachers and parents need to work together, setting high standards and helping young people meet them.

Children Alone

Most single parents work outside the home; in many two-parent families, both parents work. Unless working parents have been lucky enough to arrange a flexible schedule that allows them to be home when their children are not in school, they are not available to care for their children during the period immediately after school. The result is children of all ages being left alone or in the care of others.

Parents provide supervision after school for over half of the students in grades K–5. Older students are more likely to care for themselves after school, as shown in Figure 3.1. Other children stay with adults other than their parents, attend center-

FIGURE 3.1

Before- and After-School Care Received by U.S. Children

Source: U.S. Department of Education, National Center for Education Statistics, *The Condition of Education 2004* (NCES 2004-077). Washington, DC: Author, 2004.

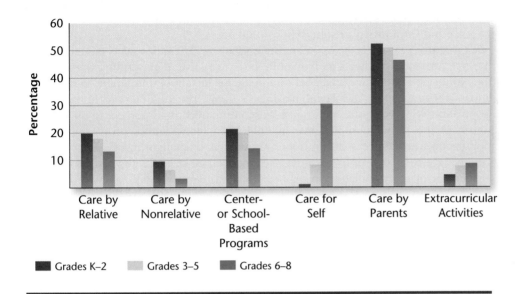

based programs, or participate in extracurricular activities such as sports, arts, or clubs. Children in poverty are slightly more likely to stay with relatives than other children.

Children who are responsible for their own care after school experience more accidents and injuries. They also are at risk of behavior problems, lower social competence, and poorer academic performance. Adolescents left on their own are more likely to engage in risk activities such as smoking, drinking alcohol, and using drugs. Self-care is more prevalent among children over ten than younger ones. It is also more prevalent among children in high-income families than low-income families. Families make these choices based, in part, on the safety of their neighborhoods and the health and maturity of their children.[5]

About half the students in kindergarten through eighth grade are under the care of their parents after school. Nearly one of five of them go to center- or school-based programs after school. Students in these programs are usually involved in specific activities such as sports, religion, and the arts. Some students are involved in the Scouts, academic activities, community services, and clubs. Parents of over 70 percent of these children pay a fee for their children's after-school care.[6] Unfortunately, some families cannot afford the cost of such care.

Educators should be sensitive to the realities faced by children left alone after school. Children sometimes are frightened to be at home alone, especially when they have no siblings. The process of traveling from school to home can be dangerous and scary in neighborhoods where drugs are being sold and peers are tempting one another to misbehave. Adolescents may be tempted to experiment with drugs and sex while adults are not around. Television often becomes the babysitter, providing children with the opportunity to learn from educational programs—or from inappropriate programs. In most cases, children are thankful for caring adults who can provide supervision and assistance.

Journal for Reflection

1. What was the most common family structure in the community in which you grew up?

2. What experience do you have with single-parent families or gay families?

3. How do you think children are influenced by having to care for themselves after school?

4. What recommendations about child care would you make to families who are unable to be at home immediately after school?

Where Students Live

Communities and their schools differ from one region of the United States to another. People in different parts of the country sometimes speak, behave, and dress differently even if they are from the same religious and ethnic backgrounds. As a result, children and families may suffer culture shock when they move from one region to another and from urban to suburban to rural areas.

Over the past thirty years, many individuals and families have migrated from the Northeast and Midwest to the South and West. The aging of the population in the Northeast and Midwest has led to a decrease in school enrollment, resulting in a loss of revenues for schools and closings of many. By 2010, 60 percent of the U.S. population will live in the South and West, compared to 48 percent in 1970. One-fourth of the population will live in California, Florida, and Texas alone.[7] The population in rural areas of the upper Midwest is older than in other parts of the country. By 2010, one of five Florida residents will be over sixty-five years old, and 15 percent of the population in Maine, Montana, Pennsylvania, and West Virginia will be retired.[8]

An examination of differences among rural, suburban, and urban communities captures some of the geographic variation. Differences also exist among communities in the Northwest, Southwest, Midwest, South, and Northeast. Within these regions, states have their own cultural uniqueness and differences. The geography of a state such as Colorado, for example, promotes the development of different cultural patterns among populations in the flat farmlands, urban centers, and mountains.

Rural Communities

Twenty-one percent of the population lives in the country or in communities with fewer than 2,500 residents.[9] **Values** tend to be conservative, and the immediate family is a cohesive unit. Children may travel long distances to school. By urban and suburban standards, families live long distances from one another. To the rural family, however, the distances are not great, and a feeling of neighborliness exists. The social structure is less stratified than in more populous geographical areas, and everyone may appear to know everyone else.

Workers in rural areas generally are poorly paid for their work, earning about three-fourths of the wages paid in urban areas. Although housing costs may be lower, other expenses are not much different. As a result, 14 percent of the rural population live in poverty, which is slightly higher than the total population.[10] Poverty is disproportionately high on Native American reservations but also exists on the midwestern plains, western ranches, and farms across the country. Some rural areas depend heavily on low-skilled immigrant labor, allowing large farm owners to prosper while workers earn such low wages they can hardly sustain themselves.

Employment in manufacturing is limited in rural areas. However, increasing numbers of urban and suburban dwellers are choosing to live in the country and commute to their employment in more populous metropolitan areas. These transplants are generally young and well educated. They are fleeing the complexities of city life to acquire self-reliance and self-confidence, to return to a physically healthier environment, or simply to be able to own an affordable home.

values

Principles, standards, or qualities that are considered worthwhile or desirable.

Children in farming communities experience aspects of life that are foreign to most city and suburban students.

In some instances, this exodus to the country has caused problems for schools because the newcomers' values have clashed with those of the more traditional rural community. Family living habits and expectations for school programs differ, and some newcomers demand increased social services. In many rural communities, it takes a considerable length of time for newcomers to be accepted into the social structure.

Eighteen percent of all U.S. students attend rural schools. These schools have a larger percentage of white and American Indian students than other ethnic and racial groups. The schools are smaller than ones in cities, and the student to teacher ratio is lower. Rural students perform better on national achievement tests than their central city peers but less well than students in most suburban schools.[11]

Despite the pivotal role of schools in rural life, these schools face real difficulties. Too often there are teacher shortages that result in the staffing of schools by teachers without a license or with limited academic background in the subjects they teach. Not all courses (for example, art and foreign languages) can be offered because of the limited number of teachers. Principals may be assigned to several schools and support services limited because of the lack of funds. Teachers in rural areas sometimes feel isolated, especially if they are not from the area. As ethnic diversity increases in these areas, teachers will be confronted with cultures and languages to which they may have had little or no exposure.

Rural communities cherish their small schools where all students know each other, all of the teachers, and most community members. They usually fight proposals for consolidating schools because of the long historical traditions associated with a school. In addition, they worry about consolidated schools being so far away that they cannot actively participate in their children's and grandchildren's education. Some students end up riding a bus for one or two hours daily to reach a new school.

Suburban Communities

Nearly half the U.S. population now lives in the suburbs. The suburban population has become more diverse as middle-class families of color have moved from cities. It is becoming even more ethnically and linguistically diverse as new immigrants settle in the suburbs. The most dramatic change in the suburbs, however, is that poverty now exists there as well as in cities and rural areas. The National Center for Children in Poverty reports that 30 percent of suburban children under age eighteen live in families with incomes below the poverty level.[12]

Suburbs are characterized by single-family homes, shopping centers, and space for parks and recreation activities. Funding for schools has traditionally been better in the suburbs than in other areas. As a result, most suburban schools are in good condition; some boast sprawling, beautiful, and technologically advanced campuses. Most teachers are licensed and generally teach the subjects they are qualified to teach. Students outperform their rural and urban counterparts on achievement tests, and more suburban students than students from other areas attend college. Safety is less of a concern for students, parents, and teachers. With changing demographics in the suburbs, however, these conditions are beginning to change—particularly in suburban areas close to major cities.

Urban Communities

Urban areas are usually rich in educational and entertainment resources such as libraries, museums, theaters, professional sports, colleges, and universities. The urban population is ethnically and racially diverse, but many residential areas remain

Race in a White School

STUDY PURPOSE/QUESTION: This study explored the characteristics of two successful African American schools in St. Louis and Atlanta where nearly all of the students were eligible for free or reduced-price meals.

STUDY DESIGN: The researcher collected ethnographic data over a period of several years through observations of faculty and staff interactions with students and families in Fairmont Elementary School in St. Louis and Lincoln Elementary School in Atlanta. He also observed and kept field notes of community observations and interviewed fourth- and fifth-grade parents. Documents that had been shared with parents were analyzed, and archival information provided the historical context for the two schools.

STUDY FINDINGS: Educators and parents in these two communities worked together to meet the social and educational needs of students. Both schools were advantaged by some teachers actually living in the school neighborhood so that they interacted with and knew some of the parents. In a number of the African American families at least three generations had attended the school. Because they thought they had received a good education, they were loyal to the school and continued to support it when their children and grandchildren attended. The teachers and administrators at these two schools "did not wait for parents to initiate parental participation; they reached out and welcomed these parents into the school" (p. 89).

The teachers in both schools wanted to teach African American children, and most of them had been teaching in the schools for many years. They affirmed the African American culture in their classrooms and the school. They enthusiastically celebrated African American historical and cultural celebrations. "The ambience in each school and the educators' pedagogical and interaction styles created an environment in which African American children could see themselves and their culture within the schooling process" (p. 93). In addition, educators sometimes wore African clothing or accented their clothes with Kente cloth, which is traditional ceremonial cloth that is about 4 inches wide of various colors and designs from the Asante people of Ghana.

Lessons were related to the everyday experiences of students (for example, using hip hop to help them understand a concept). The curriculum emphasized development of skills necessary to perform well on required achievement tests, resulting in their schools being among the best performing on state tests. Finally, the teachers in these schools were experienced (average of 19.4 and 14.8 years), and the senior teachers modeled expectations for high academic performance.

IMPLICATIONS: Because teachers in urban schools with high academic performance relate better with families and students when they understand their cultures, teacher candidates should consider taking a course on or studying cultures with which they have no experience. Another way to gain experience with other cultures is to participate in their community or church activities.

Source: Jerome E. Morris, "Can Anything Good Come From Nazareth? Race, Class, and African American Schooling and Community in the Urban South and Midwest," *American Educational Research Journal, 41*(1) (Spring 2004), pp. 69–112.

segregated. In many cities, people of color constitute the majority of the urban population. The majority of the foreign-born population live in cities. Those in which more than one in five of its residents are foreign-born include San Jose (41%), Los Angeles (40%), San Francisco (36%), New York City (36%), Boston (30%), Houston (27%), El Paso (27%), Dallas (26%), San Diego (25%), Chicago (22%), and Phoenix (22%). Twenty-two percent of elementary and high school students have at least one foreign-born parent.[13]

Class differences are evident across urban neighborhoods. Low-income families and families in poverty are often isolated in neighborhoods with few resources, inadequate police protection, and poorly maintained parks, schools, and public areas. Children who live in an underserved section of a city are often restricted by it, having few contacts outside the area. Their opportunities to participate in the educational and entertainment resources of the city are limited.

Although there are many single-family homes in a city, many children live in multifamily condominiums, apartments, and projects. Some city residents live comfortably by U.S. standards, but a disproportionate number of urban residents are economically oppressed. One of the reasons for high poverty rates among most groups in cities is the lack of academic credentials that qualify workers for better-paying jobs. Jobs that teenagers hold in other communities are filled in urban areas by adults for whom no other options are available. The result is high unemployment among youth from oppressed groups. Crime rates in many low-income neighborhoods exceed the national average. There are higher infant mortality rates, lower access to adequate health care, dangerous housing, and inadequate nutrition—all factors that are common when people have inadequate incomes to support themselves and their families.[14]

Public funding for city schools may be similar to that in other areas, but families in many urban neighborhoods are unable to contribute to schools at the same level as many suburban parents. Parents have less time to volunteer for school and community involvement or fund-raising projects. They often have more than one job. In some cases, they are caught in their own addictions and maladies exacerbated by the stress of poverty, violence, and lack of community support.

Many urban middle-class and upper-middle-class families opt for private schools over public schools. Children and youth in central cities of metropolitan areas experience poverty at higher rates than children in rural and suburban areas. African Americans make up 33 percent of central city school populations, and Latino students constitute 22 percent.[15] A disproportionately high percentage of students are foreign-born or first-generation immigrants with limited English proficiency. Bilingual education and federally funded programs such as Title I for students from low-income families help to meet the needs of urban schools.

Journal for Reflection

1. How would you describe the community in which you grew up?

2. How do your speech patterns and behavior differ from people who grew up in a different type of community?

3. In what community would you like to teach? Why?

Challenges of Childhood and Youth

Most U.S. teenagers are not the dangerous, drug-using, sexually promiscuous, nonproductive adolescents of the common stereotypes. Young people might not always agree with the adults with whom they interact, and sometimes they even break the rules, but they finish high school and attend college at higher rates than ever. And in many other respects, today's teens are more like their counterparts of past generations than different from them.

Young people face numerous challenges as they mature to adulthood. Increased pressures to grow up quickly, peer pressures, and the media provide conflicting messages that contribute to the difficulty of this period. Many students are able to draw on the support of friends, family, religion, and inner strength to resist being drawn into negative responses. Others find their own ways of countering circumstances over which they appear to have no control.

The love and care of adults help children and young people make a safe passage through childhood and adolescence. Teenagers are trying to figure out who they are and how they fit into the family, neighborhood, school, and larger world. They are searching for answers but in their own ways. One of the challenges for parents, caretakers, educators, and youth workers is to encourage young people to make sound choices among the unlimited possibilities while avoiding excessive interference.

The test of the morality of a society is what it does for its children.
Dietrich Bonhoeffer

The number one thing young people in America—indeed young people around the world—have going for them is their sense of honesty, morality, and ethics. Young people refuse to accept the lies and rationalizations of the established order.
Dick Gregory

Adults usually regard teenagers as too young to deserve the benefits of adulthood. They expect teenagers to enjoy youth, begin dating, develop friendships, plan their future, and learn how to behave like responsible adults. Other adults see adolescents as teenage mothers, gang members, drug abusers, and troublemakers. Young people are bombarded by messages about themselves in music, movies, books, and television. Other potent influences are the circumstances in which teenagers live, which may include drugs, violence, and the lack of adult support. Young people must sort through all these influences as well as the messages given by significant peers and adults in their lives. This section explores some of the challenges with which most teens struggle and about which they make decisions, whether alone or with help from others.

Many teens, especially inner-city youths, report that the messages they receive about themselves in the media and schools are usually negative. They feel that adults and communities do not care about them. This feeling is validated by cuts in funding of schools, parks, and community centers needed to assist youths in many communities.

Respect from adults is critical in helping youths to develop self-esteem. Teenagers don't always have appropriate adult support at home; their parents may be too tired or too busy or have too many problems themselves to care adequately for their children. For many teens, schools and neighborhood organizations are their primary sources of adult supervision and guidance. They need a caring adult who recognizes a young person as an individual and who serves as a mentor, as a gentle but firm critic, and as a coach or advocate. However, many youth, especially those in central cities, feel that schools have rejected them and do not expect much of them. In this section we will examine some of the societal challenges that our children and youth face on the way to adulthood.

Homelessness

> Increasing numbers of Americans are an illness, an accident, a natural disaster, or a paycheck away from becoming homeless.
>
> *Anonymous*

The National Law Center on Homelessness and Poverty estimates that up to three million people in the United States are without shelter at some point during a year.[16] Every night in the United States more than one million children have no home; many are staying with their families in shelters at night. The homeless include men and women, families, children, and persons with disabilities, as shown in Figure 3.2. One of every three homeless persons had run away from home. Just over one in four had lived in a foster care/group home. One of five had been homeless previously during childhood.[17] Like the adult homeless, homeless young people live in shelters, in abandoned buildings, and on the street.

One of the reasons for an increase in homelessness since the late 1970s is a shortage of affordable rental housing. Another is the large number of persons and families in poverty. Forty-four percent of the homeless population are working,[18] but employment is part-time or sporadic or they are earning wages too low to purchase necessary food, clothing, and housing. A full-time minimum-wage job often does not provide enough income for a family to rent a one-bedroom unit at fair market prices.

Homelessness is devastating to families. Only one of three homeless adults with minor children live with their child or children.[19] Most of their children are placed in foster care or left with relatives or friends. Children who live in shelters and on the streets often

Poverty and the lack of affordable housing are the major reasons for the growing number of homeless adults, children, and families in both rural and urban areas.

FIGURE 3.2

The U.S. Homeless Population

Source: Based on data from National Law Center on Homelessness and Poverty, "Homelessness and Poverty in America: Overview." Retrieved on May 11, 2006, from www.nlchp.org/FA%5FHAPIA.

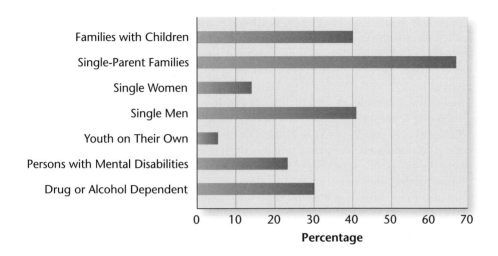

suffer from inadequate health care. They may be surrounded by diseases such as whooping cough and tuberculosis. They are not always inoculated against common childhood diseases, making them more susceptible to illness than most other children. They suffer from asthma and ear infections at disproportionately high rates. Children in homeless shelters also face hypothermia, hunger, and abuse by their parents or other adults.

Half of homeless students transfer from school each year; one of ten miss at least one month of school annually.[20] Although the McKinney-Vento Homeless Assistance Act, which was passed in 1987, eliminated the residency requirement for students, homeless children sometimes are not allowed to attend the school that would best serve their needs. Provision of transportation back to the student's school of origin is not always deemed feasible by school systems. Homeless students are sometimes forced to wait to enroll in a school while personal records are collected. However, access to schools is less of a problem than it was in the past. Today's advocates focus on students' classroom success. A high-quality education offers homeless children a chance for academic and economic success. To ignore them because they do not have a home or are not well-groomed deprives them of the opportunity to rise above their current circumstances. They need more, not less, of our attention as educators.

Abuse

Domestic violence is often hidden or ignored by society. About one-third of the females murdered in this country are killed by a spouse, ex-spouse, or boyfriend, as contrasted to less than four percent of male murder victims being killed by someone they know intimately.[21] Physical violence against women and girls is near epidemic levels in some countries. A report on domestic violence by UNICEF, the United Nation's Children's Fund, indicates that up to half the females in some countries have been abused by a family member or boyfriend. Over 60 million females in these countries have been killed by their own families either deliberately or through neglect.[22] Domestic violence has become the primary cause of homelessness for women with children. More than one in four homeless mothers in the United States are fleeing domestic violence.[23]

Most children have probably been faced with angry parents who raise their voices or even spank them. But each year nationally one of every hundred children is the victim of serious abuse or neglect by parents, caretakers, or relatives. Nearly three million children are the subjects of investigations for abuse annually.[24] Parents or caretakers are the murderers of over half the children under age five who are killed every year.[25] Neglect is the cause in 61 percent of the reported abuse cases, 19 percent are the result of physical abuse, and sexual abuse is reported in 10 percent of the cases.[26] Males are more likely to be the perpetrators of physical and sexual abuse. Twelve percent of high school girls and 6 percent of boys have been sexually abused.[27] Sensational news stories report sexual abuse of children by strangers, but these represent less than one-fourth of the cases. The abuser usually is a parent or friend.

Children and youths who are abused or neglected may arrive at school hungry, bruised, and depressed. They may arrive early at school and seem to have little desire to leave the safety of the school. These children, like all others, need teachers who are caring, retain high expectations for them, and can provide hope for the future. School and other social service professionals may be the only adults available to support abused youngsters.

Teachers and other professionals are required by law to report signs of child abuse to authorities. Not reporting could lead to fines and/or prison terms. Most school districts have procedures for reporting suspected abuse, including to whom the abuse should be reported. Even though a teacher has told his or her supervisor about possible abuse, the teacher should check to ensure that the appropriate agency was notified.[28]

When old enough, many abused youths run away from home, choosing to confront possible abuse on the streets rather than the known abuse at home. Abused children also make up a large proportion of the adults seeking psychological and mental health treatment. For many of these children, the negative experiences and conditions of their childhood become the foundation for mental health problems and delinquent behaviors. These young people have learned abuse from the adults who were closest to them.

Harassment and Bullying

Harassment by peers and teachers in schools is reported by students with disabilities and students who are female, LGBT, overweight, or different in ways that seem important to teenagers. Harassment is not rare in schools; it is a common occurrence for many students. Eighty percent of the students in a national survey indicated that they have been sexually harassed at school, with one in three experiencing it often. Sixteen percent of the students in this survey "said they avoided school or cut classes; 20 percent found it hard to pay attention; and 24 percent of students reported that they talked less in class."[29] The harassment of girls and young women in the hallways, classrooms, and cafeterias of schools ranges from name-calling to touching and, in some cases, rape. LGBT students report verbal, sexual, and physical harassment that sometimes ends in physical assault.

The most common harassment experienced by LGBT students is in the form of verbal abuse. Almost all of them report hearing homophobic remarks such as "that's so gay," "faggot," or "dyke" from other students. Nearly 20 percent indicated that faculty or school staff also sometimes make homophobic remarks. In many schools, these homophobic remarks are applied to both LGBT and non-LGBT students as derogatory terms meant to call into question a student's masculinity or femininity. Students most often make these remarks when faculty and staff are not around. However, faculty do not always intervene when they hear students making homophobic remarks; students intervene even less often.[30]

Another form of aggression in schools is bullying by bigger and stronger students to establish dominance over their victims. For younger students, the bully may be the student who pushes them out of the cafeteria line to get in front. The bully may be the student who forces others to turn over their money or do his or her homework. Such behavior cannot be excused as just "boys being boys." Bullying takes the form of belittling weaker students, calling them names, and harassing or threatening them. Sometimes the outcome of bullying is assault or murder. Bullies are 3.2 times more likely to carry weapons to school and be involved in fights in and out of school. In a survey of over 15,000 sixth to tenth graders, nearly a third of the males and 6 percent of the females reported that they had been bullies, victims, or both in the previous thirty days. The small group of children who begin bullying classmates early in elementary school are rated by their teachers as more aggressive than their peers as they progress through school.[31] Psychologists report that victims of bullies experience anxiety, stress, and depression. Some wonder whether the males responsible for multiple shootings in schools are reacting violently to the students who bullied them. Other studies have found a link between bullying and violence later in life.[32] Educators cannot afford to ignore the bullying that occurs in schools.

School should be a safe haven for children and youth. For many students, however, schools are not safe, and sometimes they are dangerous. Educators can assist in the elimination of harassment, bullying, and other youth violence. Among the strategies recommended by the Sexual Harassment Task Force of the American Association of University Women (AAUW) Foundation include modeling appropriate behavior with students by avoiding sexual references, innuendos, and jokes. Teachers should not be passive bystanders. Harassment that you witness directly or indirectly should be reported to the appropriate school official.[33]

Sexuality

The defining of one's sexuality—one's nature as a sexual being—begins in the early teens and continues throughout life. Coming to terms with one's sexuality often involves turmoil both within oneself and with parents and caretakers during the teen years. Even while trying to develop intimate relations with young men, young women may be confronted with the danger of sexual assault. The development of a healthy sexual self is a complicated process.

Many teenagers associate sex with the freedom and sophistication of adulthood. The decision to have sex is one that causes much consternation among youths. Their uncertainty is fueled by the mixed messages they receive from parents, teenage friends, religious doctrines, the media, and older friends. At the same time

Motivated by the AIDS epidemic, many schools now offer programs that promote awareness of sexually transmitted diseases.

that one medium glamorizes sex, other voices tell teenagers that sex is sinful and that abstinence before marriage is the only moral option.

Girls and women often connect sex with being accepted, being attractive, and being loved. Many boys and men, by contrast, link sex with status, power, domination, and violence—a far cry from the loving relationship that many females have envisioned. Thus, ideal sexuality for men and women may differ.

Teenage sex is not as rampant as some believe. The sexual activity of both teenage females and teenage males decreased during the 1990s. In 1991 over half of our high school students had had sexual intercourse at least once; by 2003 the percentage had dropped to 47 percent, with males being slightly more sexually active than females. One of three high schoolers was sexually active (that is, had had sex in the past three months). Most sexually active teens report using contraceptives more often than in the past.[34]

Teenage Pregnancy

Concurrently, the number of teenage pregnancies and births has declined, but they remain higher in the United States than any other industrialized nation. The data on all female teenagers show that one of twenty becomes pregnant, but of those nearly twice as many are older teens (eighteen- to nineteen-years-old). Only one of twenty-five female teenagers actually becomes a parent.[35] Eight of ten pregnant teenage girls indicate that they had not planned, nor intended, to become pregnant. Although 7 percent of students report having intercourse for the first time before they were thirteen,[36] 98 percent of middle-school girls reach the age of fifteen without becoming pregnant, and only about eight in 1,000 of ten- to fourteen-year-olds have a child.[37] Those who are more likely to become pregnant are young women who are sexually active and participate in other risk-taking behaviors such as smoking, drinking, and using drugs.[38] The fathers of the majority of these babies are not teenage males; they are in their twenties or older.[39]

Poverty appears to be the most important factor in determining teenage mothers. It is a key risk factor for teen pregnancy, but its damaging impact can be buffered through strong social networks and supportive institutions.[40] Most unmarried teenage mothers continue to live with their parents, but their families are disproportionately low income. To reduce teenage pregnancy, family poverty may need to be reduced. Many teenage parents, especially mothers, are forced to take on adult responsibilities much earlier than society expects of its youth. Teenage mothers are sometimes forced to fend for themselves in impoverished conditions. Their own parents can provide little or no support, and the fathers of their children are often absent and either not contributing or unable to contribute financially. Nevertheless, over 60 percent of these mothers are enrolled in school, have graduated, or have obtained a General Educational Development (GED) credential.[41] Staying involved in school is important. Otherwise, statistics show, "eight to twelve years after birth, a child born to an unmarried, teenage, high school dropout is ten times as likely to be living in poverty as a child born to a mother with none of these three characteristics."[42] Poverty also contributes to the births of babies with low birth weights, who are more likely than other children to experience health problems, developmental delays, abuse, neglect, and poor academic performance.[43]

Overall, teenagers are becoming more responsible about their sexual activity and are using contraception to reduce the risk of pregnancy and the transmission of AIDS and other sexually transmitted diseases. School programs such as sex education and health clinics are helpful, but they are not always supported by families and communities. Educators should be aware that the teen years are traumatic for many young people as they struggle with the development of their sexuality. Teenagers' apprehensions and activities related to sex may affect their school behavior and their ability to perform satisfactorily in school.

Is Retention Better Than Social Promotion for Students?

Today's emphasis on academic achievement may lead to students not meeting state standards as measured by standardized tests. As a result, they may not be able to graduate on time or even be pushed out of school because they fail the required tests, lowering the pass rates for a school district. What are the appropriate strategies for ensuring that students meet standards? These two educators debate the effectiveness of retention as an effective approach to help students learn at an acceptable level before being promoted to the next grade.

YES

John Mohl *teaches German and social studies at Cedarbrook Middle School in Wyncote, Pennsylvania.*

When I first called on "Brendan," a recent transfer to the district, to read, he refused. His homework was copied from a friend if done at all and he failed to comprehend a passage after fumbling over words when I finally got him to read aloud. Despite his third-grade reading level, Brendan was allowed into eighth grade. He was a product of social promotion.

Social promotion has three detrimental effects on the educational system. It taxes both teachers and students. Promoting a student into a higher level of English when he lacks basic reading skills, as was the case with Brendan, places undue burden on future teachers and students. Socially promoted students monopolize teacher attention, and other students' learning opportunities are limited as a result.

Second, it sends a message to students that they can move on to the next level even if they lack the required knowledge or effort. I once taught a summer school class with two particularly unruly students who were unfazed by the threat of being held back for failing. They knew they'd be eighth graders regardless of their performance. They were right, and became burdens to their new teachers (that oversight, fortunately, was later rectified).

Social promotion also distances schools from their goals of fulfilling No Child Left Behind standards. How can anybody expect a student with elementary math skills to perform proficiently on an eighth-grade standardized math exam?

NO

Jennifer Slifer *teaches sixth-grade language arts at Thomas Edison Magnet Middle School in Meriden, Connecticut.*

Each year, we all have a "Brendan" or two and we are frustrated and angry that he advances with such evident skill deficiencies. But would Brendan be helped by retention, the traditional solution for struggling students?

Social promotion by itself is not a good practice. Retention does not, however, solve the problems of low-achieving students. Research shows that retained students do not improve their academic performance compared with similar counterparts who were promoted, and retained students struggle with self-esteem.

Social promotion isn't the answer if it means we send students on to the next grade ill-prepared for the workload. "Brendan" is failing, but so are we as educators if we don't provide the help he needs to keep up with his peers. So let's provide that help.

Is it time to review our centuries-old system of grouping students by age? Perhaps all students should be placed in multi-age classrooms. This arrangement would assist students who struggle to learn as quickly as their peers of the same age and would eliminate self-esteem issues caused by retention.

Another approach: Instead of retaining a student, why don't we promote struggling students with an individualized education plan (as we do for our special education students) to help them catch up to their peers? Most struggling students who are promoted do not meet the requirements for

(continued)

(continued)

YES

Some argue that social promotion maintains the self-esteem of low-achieving students. I agree that humanism should be an important component in our teaching. But the "real world" has neither time nor regard for making sure every person feels worthwhile. Teachers have the responsibility to introduce, to some degree, the benefits of making the mark and the consequences of not doing so. Truth be told, I'd rather see Brendan held back in eighth than held back in life.

NO

special education but they do need assistance that, unfortunately, we are not mandated to provide.

Maybe it's time to get serious about early intervention and provide funding for programs for struggling students *before* they reach middle and high school.

Our choices should not be just promoting students versus retaining them.

Passing struggling students to the next grade is a failure of the system if we don't have a plan to help them catch up. But retention isn't the answer, either.

Source: "Is Retention Better Than Social Promotion for Students?" *NEA Today* (March 2005), p. 48. Reprinted by permission of the National Education Association.

WHAT IS YOUR PERSPECTIVE ON THIS ISSUE?
Is retention better than social promotion for students?

To give your opinion, go to Chapter 3 of the companion
website (www.ablongman.com/johnson14e) and click on Teacher Perspectives.

Dropping Out

Another challenge faced by some teenagers is the lack of engagement in school. Some do not see the value of finishing their education. Others do not see themselves as academically able students and find no reason to participate actively in their own learning. They are not meeting the minimal standards as determined on standardized tests, resulting in grade retention, which will prevent them from graduating with peers of the same age. They believe they can learn the lessons for survival more effectively outside school. As a result, they drop out of high school and college for different reasons, without realizing the harm it will cause them in the long term.

According to federal reports, 79 percent of eighteen- to twenty-one-year-olds had completed high school in 2003, the most recent year for which figures are available. However, by age twenty-four, 88 percent of the population had completed high school, the GED, or other alternative credentials.[44] A number of researchers are now questioning the federal statistics, indicating that they overstate graduation rates. The primary reason for the differences lies in the meaning of high school graduation. The federal legislation that supports elementary and secondary education, No Child Left Behind (NCLB), includes as graduates only students who receive regular standards-based diplomas on time with the class with which they began high school.

CROSS-REFERENCE
No Child Left Behind is discussed in greater detail in Chapters 1, 6, 8, and 10.

FIGURE 3.3

Graduation Rates by Sex and Racial or Ethnic Group

Source: Gary Orfield, Daniel Losen, Johanna Wald, and Christopher B. Swanson, *Losing Our Future: How Minority Youth Are Being Left Behind by the Graduation Rate Crisis.* Cambridge, MA: The Civil Rights Project at Harvard University with Contributions from Urban Institute, Advocates for Children of New York, and The Civil Society Institute, 2004.

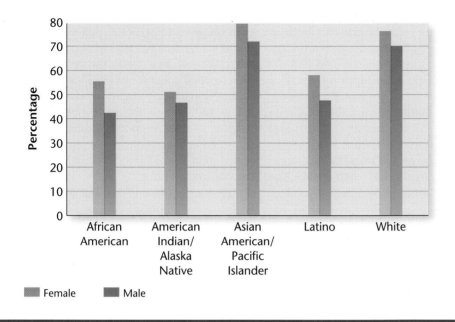

Both the Urban Institute and The Civil Rights Project at Harvard University have found that only 68 percent of the students who enter ninth grade graduate with a regular diploma at the end of the twelfth grade. The problem is particularly critical in large, urban, segregated schools. American Indians, African Americans, and Latinos have only a fifty-fifty chance of completing high school, placing them at great risk of not earning sustainable wages or being employed as adults. School districts with low graduation rates are more often in central cities. Rates are lowest in schools whose population is predominantly students of color (56%), includes a large percentage of English language learners (60%), comes from low-income families (58%), or has more students with disabilities than average (65%).[45]

Graduation rates vary across ethnic and racial groups, as shown in Figure 3.3. Latino students continue to have one of the highest dropout rates. The largest proportion of Latino dropouts were born outside the United States. They may have not attended U.S. schools nor have completed more than elementary school in their countries of birth. Although first- and later-generation Latinos graduate at higher rates than immigrants, they are still two to three times more likely to drop out of school than their white peers.[46]

Students from low-income families drop out of high school at a rate six times greater than that of students from middle- and high-income families.[47] A greater percentage of females finish high school than males, leading to concerns about fewer young men attending and completing college. Only two of three students with disabilities complete high school.[48] As one might expect, students who complete high school are more likely than dropouts to be employed. Sixty-three percent of high school graduates are in the labor force as compared to 45 percent of the population with less than a high-school diploma. More education does make a difference; 78 percent of college graduates are working.[49]

Substance Use

One of the questions with which many teenagers struggle is whether to experiment with cigarettes, alcohol, or drugs. Although not as glamorized in films and advertisements as in the past, drinking and smoking are still associated with independence and adult behavior. Teens use drugs for different reasons. Sometimes biological predispositions or psychological problems trigger drug use. In other cases, social pressures, family problems, or self-hate lead young people to drugs.

The public worries about drug use. In the 2005 Phi Delta Kappa/Gallup Poll of the Public's Attitudes Toward Public Schools, respondents ranked the use of drugs as the fourth greatest problem that public schools face. Drug use fell behind the lack of financial support for schools, overcrowded schools, and lack of discipline.[50] Parents worry particularly about drug usage that may lead to **chemical dependency** in the future. Chemical dependency, such as addiction to drugs, alcohol, or tobacco, is one of the causes of social and academic problems among youths. People are judged to be dependent when they find that their need for the chemical substance is constant and they can no longer control their use. Dependency can be difficult to overcome and often requires professional treatment.

A large percentage of teenagers do try one or more drugs, but alcohol is the favorite, being used more than twice as often as other drugs. Fifty percent of twelfth graders have used an illicit drug at some time, but less than one in four has used one or more drugs in the past month. Younger students also use drugs. Just over one in five eighth graders have tried drugs, with eight percent of them using in the past month. Nine percent of eighth graders also report smoking cigarettes in the past month. Although the rate of usage is higher than the public may find acceptable, current usage by all teenagers is down from what it was in the mid-1970s and throughout the rest of the twentieth century as shown in Figure 3.4. The bad news

chemical dependency

The habitual use, for either psychological or physical needs, of a substance such as drugs, alcohol, or tobacco.

FIGURE 3.4

U.S. High School Seniors Reporting Use of Selected Substances in the Past Month

Source: L. D. Johnston, P. M. O'Malley, J. G. Bachman, and J. E. Schulenberg, *Monitoring the Future—National Results on Adolescent Drug Use: Overview of Key Findings, 2005.* Bethesda, MD: National Institute on Drug Abuse, 2006.

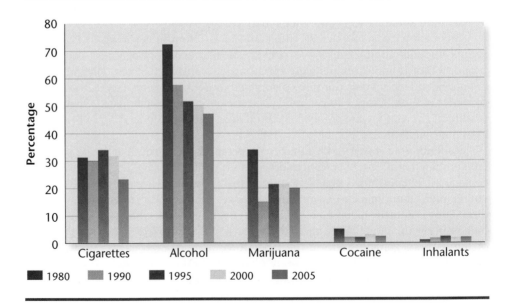

FIGURE 3.5

Current U.S. Drug Use by Type of Drug and Age Group

Sources: U.S. Census Bureau, *Statistical Abstract of the United States: 2006,* 125th edition, Washington, DC: U.S. Government Printing Office, 2006, Table 194; and U.S. Department of Health and Human Services, Substance Abuse and Mental Health Services Administration, *2003 National Survey on Drug Use and Health,* 2006, retrieved from www.oas.samhsa.gov/nhsda.htm#NHSDAinfo.

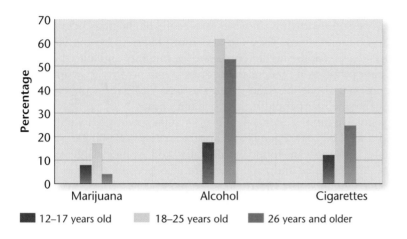

■ 12–17 years old   ■ 18–25 years old   ■ 26 years and older

is the high rates of nonmedical use of prescription pain killers such as Vicodin and Oxy Contin as well as sedatives/barbiturates.[51] Students who plan to attend college are less likely to use drugs. Male teenagers are more likely than females to use drugs other than cigarettes.[52] Drug use continues to be more prevalent among adults than teens as shown in Figure 3.5.

Violence

Many adults think that youths commit a larger proportion of violent crime than they actually do. Less than two of 1,000 juveniles were arrested for a violent crime in 2003. Eight percent of people arrested for murder are juveniles. The most serious charge in half the juvenile arrests is larceny/theft, simple assault, disorderly conduct, drug abuse, or liquor law violation.[53] Juvenile arrest rates for violent crimes are at the lowest level in two decades for all areas except aggravated assault. On the other hand, arrest rates for drug abuse violations have more than doubled since 1990.[54] Although most crimes are committed by males, juvenile arrest rates for females are increasing. African American youth are almost four times more likely to be incarcerated than their white peers. American Indian and Latino youth are 2.6 and 1.8 times as likely to be incarcerated.[55] Students with disabilities such as

Many schools are combating youth violence through conflict resolution and other programs that help students learn to respect others, stop harassment, and effectively handle interpersonal problems.

mental disorders, attention deficit hyperactivity disorder (ADHD), and learning disabilities are also overrepresented in the prison population.[56]

It is a myth that most murdered youths are killed by their peers in gang shootings and other conflicts. In fact, automobile accidents account for 77 percent of teen deaths.[57] Adults are most likely to be the perpetrators of other violence against teens. One of every four victims of violent crime is a juvenile, the majority being female; one of three juvenile victims are under twelve years old. However, murder victims are also more likely to be male; African American youth are four times more at risk of murder than white youth.[58]

Crime is related more directly to poverty than to the age of the criminal. At all age levels, persons with low incomes are more likely than persons with higher incomes to commit crimes. They are also more likely to be the victims of violent crimes. One reason for the higher crime rate for burglary and auto theft among teens is that a larger proportion of teens than adults live in poverty. Low-income teenagers commit crimes at about the same rate as adults who live in poverty. At the same time, most low-income people do not commit crimes.

Gangs involve more students than ever. A 2004 survey of law enforcement agencies found a total of 24,000 gangs and approximately 760,000 gang members in the United States.[59] Gangs are found in all states and in most large cities; a growing number of smaller cities and rural areas are also becoming home to gangs. There are some female gangs, but most gangs are made up of young men. For youths of both sexes, gangs can provide a sense of place and a feeling of importance as well as a strong identity structure. Gangs often provide a discipline that has been missing from the experiences of many young people.

Suicide is another form of violence that affects the student population. Seventeen percent of high schoolers report seriously considering suicide, and 9 percent actually attempt it. Latino and white teenagers are more likely to commit suicide than members of other groups. Adolescent and young adult males are more likely to commit suicide, but young women are more likely to think about it and make nonlethal attempts. Gay teens are at particular risk, being two to three times more likely to attempt suicide than their peers.[60] Suicide attempts are often calls for help. Teachers should be alert for signs that may suggest the need for a referral to other professionals. Providing support for gay students and recognizing signs of depression could lead to a reduction in teen suicide rates.

Many high schools students work after school and in the summer.

Economic Realities

Young people may be worried and somewhat pessimistic about their future economic conditions. However, they continue to seek out postsecondary education to improve their job and career opportunities. Sixty-four percent of high school graduates go to college immediately after high school. African American and Latino students attend at lower rates than whites. A larger number of females (57%) are attending college than males (43%).[61] Fifty-three percent of low-income students go to college as compared to 80 percent of high-income students.[62]

Many young people begin to work while they are in high school. Young people in low-income families have historically worked to help out the family. Although this pattern continues today, students from middle- and high-income families are more likely to work as teenagers. Their parents are also more likely to have finished college. Nearly half of white teens work as compared to one-fourth of African American and Latino teens. Over 40 percent of sixteen- and seventeen-year-olds have jobs, with males more likely to work than females. There is evidence of a strong positive link between working in high school and obtaining a job after graduation. However, teens working over 20 hours a week are more likely to have been suspended and neglect homework than their peers. At the same time, they are less likely to skip school or have serious behavioral or emotional problems.[63]

After-school jobs are particularly beneficial to students from low-income families who do not have family or school connections to help them find employment. Unfortunately, many students who could derive long-term benefits from working while in high school—those in inner-city areas—have limited access to jobs. The lack of employment opportunities contributes to low self-esteem and to pessimism about the future and the value of school. In addition, in communities experiencing high unemployment, many young people do not have opportunities to learn how to work either through their own experiences or through the modeling of working adults.

Journal for Reflection

1. Thinking back on your childhood and youth, which of the challenges discussed in this section did you face?

2. How were you able to manage the challenge in positive ways?

3. How did your family or educators provide support to you during this period?

Power in Society

A democratic society is built on the principles of social equality and respect for individuals within society. However, many persons of color, limited English speakers, women, persons with disabilities, gays and lesbians, people with low incomes, and people affiliated with religions other than Protestantism do not experience the equality to which most members of the dominant group appear to be entitled.

Schools provide an example of institutions in which power relationships have been developed and maintained. Students' work and class rules are determined by teachers. Teachers are evaluated and disciplined when necessary by principals who report to a superintendent of schools. The rules and procedures for managing schools traditionally have been established by authorities who are not directly involved with the school and who may not even live in the community served by the school. Parents, especially in economically disadvantaged areas, often feel powerless in the education of their children.

Power not only allows domination over the powerless, but it also allows access to societal benefits such as good housing, tax deductions, the best schools, and social services. A more equitable sharing of resources for schools would guarantee that all students, regardless of family income or ethnic background, would have qualified teachers, sufficient books

Teacher–student relationships, as with many other relationships in U.S. society, are defined by one person or group having power over others.

and other instructional resources, well-maintained buildings and playgrounds, and access to high-level academic knowledge. Such equality does not exist across schools that students attend today.

Ethnocentrism

Every American ought to have the right to be treated as he would wish to be treated, as one would wish his children to be treated.

John F. Kennedy

Most of the time, we are not aware of our own power or the lack thereof, as a result of our cultural upbringing. This phenomenon often leads to **ethnocentrism,** in which we view our culture as superior to all others. Ethnocentrism is sometimes promoted through patriotism, especially at times when a country is involved in a political conflict with another country. The other country is often denigrated through name-calling based on negative stereotypes of its citizens.

Ethnocentrism is not limited to relations with other nations; it often occurs between groups within the United States. For example, homosexuals are victims of abuse by some radio talk show hosts and some religious groups. Members of some religious groups believe that their cultural values and lifestyles are the only correct ones; they do not tolerate alternative beliefs. Many members of the dominant culture believe that their culture is superior to those with roots outside Europe.

One of the manifestations of ethnocentrism is the inability to accept differences among groups as natural and appropriate. The values and behaviors of the dominant group become the norms against which others are measured. The dominant group often treats the differences as deficits that must be overcome through education and special programs. For teachers to help all students learn, they must confront their own ethnocentrism. Many teachers do not recognize that they subtly, and sometimes overtly, transmit feelings of superiority over students and the groups to which they belong as they deliver curriculum and interact with students and their families. Teachers show their respect for diverse groups when they include them in the curriculum.

Prejudice

Power relationships among groups influence young people's perceptions of themselves and the members of other groups. One of the struggles of youth is the construction of self, including identification and affiliation with one's gender and a racial or ethnic group. This process appears to be integrally tied to identifying "otherness," which involves assigning characteristics and behaviors to members of other groups to distinguish them from oneself. The construction of "others" places them either in a dominating or submissive role relative to the individual. This construction is often dependent on stereotypes that are promoted among peers and reinforced by society.

Our perceptions of others not only affect how we see ourselves in relationship to them but also influence how society treats members of different groups. Prejudice is a preconceived negative attitude toward members of specific ethnic, racial, religious, or socioeconomic groups. This prejudice sometimes extends to people with disabilities or people of a different sexual orientation or gender. Such negative attitudes are based on numerous factors, including information about members of a specific group that is stereotypical and many times not true. The prejudiced individual may have had little or no direct social contact with members of the other group.

An individual's prejudice may have a limited negative impact on members of the other group. However, these attitudes are passed on to children through the **socialization** process. Also, prejudiced attitudes can be transformed into discriminatory

ethnocentrism
The belief that members of one's own group are superior to the members of other groups.

socialization
The process of learning the social norms of one's culture.

behavior that prevents members of a group from being interviewed for jobs, joining social clubs, or being treated like other professionals. Prejudices are often reinforced by schools in which a disproportionate number of students in low-achieving or special education tracks are males, English language learners, students of color, or students from low-income families. Observing that these students are not enrolled in academically challenging courses, some students form stereotypes of their low-income and foreign-born peers as academically inferior. Through this process, many students from low-income families and ethnic minority groups are prevented from gaining the skills and knowledge necessary to enter college or an apprentice trade.

Discrimination

Many members of groups other than the dominant culture have experienced discrimination through practices that exclude them from equal access to housing, jobs, and educational opportunities. They also sometimes experience unfair treatment by store clerks, police officers, and educators. Having experienced discrimination, members of excluded groups can describe differential power relations among groups. Members of groups who do not experience discrimination often have a difficult time acknowledging the differences in power and advantage. As a result, rights based on group membership versus those of individuals are debated on college campuses, in board meetings of corporations, by politicians, and in many formal and informal neighborhood meetings. These discussions focus on programs that are perceived to favor one group over another, such as affirmative action, bilingual education, or equal funding for male and female athletes. An honest examination of power relationships and experiences with differences highlights the struggles inherent in a democratic society.

In addition to supporting individual prejudice and discrimination, society has historically discriminated against members of powerless groups. Laws and systems that promote and support the dominant culture have been designed to help maintain its superiority and the power of its members. "English only" laws that prevent official documents and communications from being printed or spoken in any language other than English represent but one example of these efforts. Such practices have often become institutionalized in state and federal laws, the judicial system, schools, and other societal institutions. They have become so ingrained in the system that it is difficult to recognize them unless one is directly affected by the discriminatory policies.

CROSS-REFERENCE
Legal issues on discrimination are discussed in Chapter 6.

Racism

An assumption of superiority is at the center of **racism.** It is not a topic easily discussed in most classrooms. It is intertwined with the lived experiences of many people and evokes emotions of anger, guilt, shame, and despair. Most people have learned that the United States is a just and democratic society. They find it difficult to confront the societal contradictions that support racism. Educators must acknowledge the advantages, as well as the damage, caused by racism in order to overcome its negative impact on children and youth.

Students and adults go through stages of racial identity as they address issues of discrimination and their own racial identification. Teachers should recognize that students will be moving back and forth across the stages outlined in Table 3.1 in their struggle to know themselves. One of the first steps in this process is to begin to confront one's own racial identity. How close is one to an internalization or autonomy stage? If educators have not struggled with issues of racism, how it affects their lives, and how they may contribute to its perpetuation or elimination, it will be impossible for them to develop antiracist classrooms.

Racism is so universal in this country, so widespread and deep-seated, that it is invisible because it is so normal.
Shirley Chisolm

CROSS-REFERENCE
For information on the education of African American, Asian American, and Latino students, see Chapter 2.

racism
The conscious or unconscious belief that racial differences make one group superior to others.

TABLE 3.1   Development of Racial Identity

Black Racial Identity	White Racial Identity	Latino Identity
Preencounter: African American individuals have assimilated into the mainstream culture, accepting many of the beliefs and values of the dominant society, including negative stereotypes about blacks. *Encounter:* African Americans usually enter this stage when they are confronted directly by a racist act such as rejection by white peers or racial slurs or attacks. They are then forced to confront their own racial identity. *Immersion–Emersion:* One's identification as an African American becomes paramount. At first this identification is manifested in anger against whites, but it evolves into a growing knowledge base about African American history and culture. The result of this exploration is an emerging security in a newly defined and affirmed sense of self. *Internalization:* Individuals begin to build coalitions with members of other nonwhite or nondominant groups and to develop relationships with whites who respect and acknowledge them. *Internalization–Commitment:* Individuals are able both to maintain and to move beyond their personal racial identity—to be concerned with African Americans as a group.	*Contact:* White individuals are not aware of themselves as racial beings and are oblivious to acts of individual racism. They have a color-blind view of race and racism. *Disintegration:* Whites usually enter this stage as a result of some experiences with race that lead to the recognition that race does matter, that racism exists, and that they are white. They may show empathy when blacks experience racial discrimination but often fail to understand their anger. *Reintegration:* Individuals believe consciously or unconsciously that whites are superior to people of color. *Pseudoindependence:* One begins the intellectual process of learning about and fighting against racism. One begins to understand that whites have responsibility for maintaining or eliminating racism. *Immersion–Emersion:* Individuals begin to grasp the need to challenge racism. They often experience feelings of guilt and shame for the racist ideas that they believed in the past. *Autonomy:* White individuals have abandoned cultural, institutional, and personal racism. They have a more flexible view of the world, their own whiteness, and other racial groups. They value and seek out cross-racial/cultural experiences.	*White:* They identify themselves as white, not acknowledging their Latino culture. *Undifferentiated:* They accept the norms of the dominant culture without question. *Person of color:* They identify themselves as persons of color, but lack knowledge about their Latino culture. *Latino ethnic group:* They see themselves as members of one of many groups in the United States. They also can identify both the negative and positive aspects of their group. *Latino:* They place their Latino culture, history, and traditions at the center of their lives. *Latino-integrated:* They begin to identify themselves not just as Latino, but by their specific ethnic group (e.g., Mexican American).

Sources: "Black Racial Identity" column is based on the five stages of black racial identity developed by W. E. Cross, Jr. and described in Beverly Daniel Tatum, "Talking about Race, Learning about Racism: The Application of Racial Identity Development Theory in the Classroom," *Harvard Educational Review,* 62(1) (1992), pp. 1–24. "White Racial Identity" column is based on the six stages of white racial identity developed by J. F. Helms and described in Robert T. Carter, "Is White a Race? Expressions of White Racial Identity," in Michelle Fine, Lois Weis, Linda C. Powell, and L. Mun Wong, Eds., *Off White: Readings on Race, Power, and Society.* New York: Routledge, 1997. The "Latino Identity" column is based on B. M. Ferdman and P. I. Gallegos, "Racial identity development and Latinos in the United States," in C. L. Wijeyesinghe and B. W. Jackson, III, Eds., *New Perspectives on Racial Identity Development: A Theoretical and Practical Anthology* (pp. 32–66). New York: New York University Press, 2001.

Coming to Justice

The Anne Frank House was established in 1957 as a museum in Amsterdam in memory of Anne Frank and members of her family who were victims of the Holocaust during World War II. In addition to being a museum, the Anne Frank House is now a nonprofit organization with a goal of combating racism in all its forms around the globe. One of its guiding principles is the Universal Declaration of Human Rights, which is available on the Internet at www.unhchr.ch/udhr.

A new project of the Anne Frank House is a four-day program for older teenagers to introduce them to justice and injustice in an international context. The program, *Coming to Justice,* "is confrontational, challenging youth to think critically about their own views and assumptions, dispelling many myths regarding international conflicts and justice along the way."[64] During the first day of the program, students reflect on definitions of justice and injustice and are introduced to the experiences of Anne Frank and her family. Attention changes on the second day to the early-1990s conflict in the Balkans. On the third day students attend a trial at the International War Crimes Tribunal in The Hague, the Netherlands. On the final day students meet with people who have been eyewitnesses to these conflicts with a focus on justice and appropriate remedies for injustice. Participants report that they learn in this international context how complex the concepts of justice and injustice are as they relate them to their own local situations.

Questions for Reflection

1. What is the Universal Declaration of Human Rights?
2. Why is the study of justice in an international arena important?

Sexism and Other Isms

Women of all racial and ethnic groups, people with disabilities, gays, lesbians, persons with low incomes, the elderly, and the young also suffer from discrimination and their lack of power in society. Many individuals are members of more than one of these powerless groups. For example, a low-income Latina may be triply harmed as a result of racism, classism, and **sexism**—the cultural attitudes and practices that devalue women. This woman's chances of reaching a comfortable standard of living may be severely limited by her circumstances and group membership.

Some persons with disabilities and their advocates argue that **ableism** greatly disadvantages people with disabilities and their ability to live a full and productive life. Ableism not only leads to viewing persons with disabilities as inferior to others but also results in treatments and accommodations designed to help them become more like persons without disabilities. These efforts are not necessarily in the best interests of individuals with disabilities. For example, activists with a hearing disability may reject the view that they should become hearing through surgery and other aids. Being deaf is their normality, even though it does not seem normal to those who hear. In other instances, teachers and aides without disabilities sometimes provide assistance or do things for persons with disabilities rather than encouraging them to learn for themselves. For educators, the strategy of overhelpfulness may be easier and less time-consuming. Allowing individuals with disabilities to make the effort themselves may require a great deal of patience, but the long-term payoff for the student could be self-sufficiency.

sexism

The conscious or unconscious belief that men are superior to women and subsequent behavior and action that maintain the superior, powerful position of males.

ableism

The conscious or unconscious belief that persons with disabilities are inferior to persons without disabilities.

Journal for Reflection

1. What prejudice or discrimination have you experienced? How long ago? How often?
2. What discrimination might persons from a group other than your own experience that you don't?
3. Why do some sociologists find that whites are privileged in society?

Resiliency

Many young people have the **resiliency** to overcome disastrous childhood and adolescent experiences and go on to become successful workers, professionals, and community leaders. The challenges discussed earlier in this chapter along with growing up in poverty can place children and youth at risk for developmental delays, behavior problems, and poor academic performance. The students that are most at risk live in dangerous environments that lead to health risks and threats to their safety. They may be attending schools in which students are not expected to perform at high levels and are not being pushed to do so. Their own parents may be so busy coping with several jobs and their own problems that they cannot support their children.[65]

With all of these problems, some students are still able to perform well, even at high levels, in school. Their personal attributes give them strength and fortitude and help them confront overwhelming obstacles that seem designed to prevent them from reaching their potential. Children who are resilient are able to cope effectively with stress. They believe in their own **self-efficacy,** can handle change, and have good social skills. Higher family SES contributes positively to resiliency, but is not required. Other positive factors are family members who are involved with their children, provide caring environments, help their children with homework, attend to grades, and participate in school activities. Resilient students have positive relationships with teachers and lack exposure to violence or trauma. They are also helped by quality educational and recreational opportunities in school and their neighborhoods.[66] Regardless of the challenges they face, they are usually social, optimistic, energetic, cooperative, inquisitive, attentive, helpful, punctual, and on task.

Journal for Reflection

1. What characteristics do you have that make you resilient?

2. How did your parents or other adults help you develop resiliency?

3. How do you think a teacher could assist students at risk to develop skills that will assist them in facing the obstacles in their lives?

Summary

TODAY'S FAMILIES.   Students in schools today come from diverse family structures. Although a majority of children live with their mother and father, many live with single parents, grandparents, adoptive parents, foster parents, gay or lesbian parents, or relatives.

WHERE STUDENTS LIVE.   Poverty is greater in central city and urban areas, but it is growing in suburban areas. Schools in suburban areas, except those closest to urban areas, have greater financial support, and students perform at higher levels on achievement tests.

resiliency

The ability to overcome overwhelming obstacles to achieve and be successful in school and life.

self-efficacy

The belief that one can control one's life.

CHALLENGES OF CHILDHOOD AND YOUTH.   Teenagers struggle with economic and social realities that can prove dangerous when they make inappropriate decisions. The poverty suffered by young people contributes to some of them engaging in violent acts and sometimes dropping out of school. At the same time, many young people exhibit amazing resiliency, allowing them to overcome economic and social hardships to finish school and become productive adults.

POWER IN SOCIETY.   Members of groups that have controlled most of the country's institutions for centuries wield the most power in society. Being white, high-income, and English speakers provides benefits over people who are not white or speak a language other than English. The prejudice that young people learn at home and in school can lead to discriminatory practices that harm people who are different from themselves.

RESILIENCY. Although some children and youth face major obstacles because their families are low-income and/or they live in unsupportive homes or communities, some are able to overcome problems and become successful in school. Effective parents and supportive teachers and neighborhoods can contribute to the development of resiliency for at risk students.

Discussion Questions

1. Families face a number of social and economic challenges that affect the well-being of children in this country. Which factors do you think are most damaging to children? What should teachers and schools do to help students develop resiliency and be able to achieve academically under adverse circumstances?
2. The number of students in central cities and rural areas are nearly equal as is the income status of the populations. What are the obstacles to a good education that students face in these two different settings?
3. Children and teenagers need adult support as they cope with the challenges of adolescence. Who do you think should be providing this support? What should be the role of teachers in providing the support?

4. What signs might teachers see to make them wonder whether a child or adolescent is being abused? What steps should you take if you suspect abuse or other risk-taking behaviors?
5. Some researchers are suggesting that the testing requirements of No Child Left Behind (NCLB) are pushing students out of school. Some school districts have been accused of underrepresenting the number of dropouts. Why might a school system want to underreport the number of dropouts? Why would a sceptic suggest that the NCLB requirements are pushing some students out of school?

School-Based Observations

1. Visit schools in rural, urban, and suburban communities and systematically record characteristics such as the ethnic and racial composition of the students, the income levels of families, the size of the student population and teaching force, the student–teacher ratios, the general school climate, and other observable characteristics. What are the similarities and differences in the schools in different types of communities?

2. In your visits to a school, determine the types of programs available to assist students in handling issues of sexuality, drugs, or violence in their own lives. What approach is the school using to address these issues? Is there any parental involvement in the development of these programs?

Portfolio Development

1. At one of the schools with which you are working, identify the characteristics of students in gifted and special education classes. In a paper for your portfolio, describe the context of the school and present your data regarding the characteristics of students in these courses. Analyze the data for signs of discrimination against the members of a group of students and write your conclusions.
2. Prepare a paper on the educational opportunities for homeless students in your community or another area

of the state with larger numbers of homeless families. What services is the school district providing to these students? How are they being integrated into the schools they attend? Why are some schools more successful at serving homeless students than others? Conclude your paper by reflecting on how you will work with homeless children when you become a teacher.

Preparing for Certification

STUDENT EXPERIENCES AND DEMOCRACY

1. One of the topics covered in the Praxis II Principles of Learning and Teaching (PLT) test is "becoming familiar with relevant aspects of students' background knowledge and experiences." Effective teachers identify methods and procedures for gathering background information about their students. What types of information will you want to have about your students and their backgrounds? What methods will you use to gather background information that will help you teach more effectively and also respect the privacy of students and their families?

2. Answer the following multiple-choice question, which is similar to items in Praxis and other state certification tests.

Six-year-old Heather lives with her mother, who works as a waitress. Ms. Atwater, Heather's teacher, notes that Sara often arrives at school late and is inattentive in class. Heather says she frequently stays up past midnight if other people in the house are up. Ms. Atwater has observed bruises on Heather's arms and legs, suggesting that Heather may be being abused. What is the first action Ms. Atwater should take?

A. Visit the home to investigate
B. Arrange a conference with Heather's mother
C. Report the suspected abuse to the principal
D. Contact the county Office of Child Welfare

3. Answer the following short-answer question, which is similar to items in Praxis and other state certification tests. After you have completed your written response, use the scoring guide in the ETS *Test at a Glance* materials to assess your response. Can you revise your response to improve your score?

Identify two specific actions Ms. Atwater might take to connect school and Heather's home environment for the benefit of Heather's learning. For each action, explain how that action will benefit Heather's learning. Base your response on principles of fostering positive relationships with family to support student learning and well-being.

Websites

www.aauw.org The website of the American Association of University Women (AAUW) addresses the education and lifelong learning of girls and women, including many suggestions and resources for fighting sexual harassment.

www.childrensdefense.org The website of the Children's Defense Fund (CDF) includes data about the status of children in the United States. It also includes information on CDF's programs and activist work.

www.nationalhomeless.org The website for the National Coalition for the Homeless has information bulletins on homelessness in the United States.

www.calib.com/nccanch The National Clearinghouse on Child Abuse and Neglect Information's website serves as a national resource for professionals seeking information on the prevention, identification, and treatment of child abuse and neglect.

www.cgcs.org The Council of the Great City Schools is a coalition of the nation's largest urban public school systems. The website includes promising practices for serving students in urban schools.

www.nccj.org The National Conference of Community and Justice is a human relations organization dedicated to fighting bias, bigotry, and racism in the United States. It promotes understanding and respect among all races, religions, and cultures through advocacy, conflict resolution, and education.

Further Reading

Children's Defense Fund. (2005). *The State of America's Children in America's Union: 2005*. Washington, DC: Author. Information on the status of children today, including data on what happens to children daily in the United States. The report also includes a discussion of the No Child Left Behind Act and makes recommendations for families and others interested in the welfare of the nation's children.

Flores-Gonzalez, Nilda. (2002). *School Kids/Street Kids*. New York: Teachers College Press. Explores why Puerto Rican students in an urban high school stay, leave, and return to school. The implications of identification as a "school-kid" or "street-kid" are examined.

Kozol, Jonathan. (2000). *Ordinary Resurrections: Children in the Years of Hope*. New York: Crown. A description of living and being educated in the inner city through the experiences of inner-city children and the adults who try to assist them. The stories of individual children raise issues about recognizing the value and dignity of students as we teach.

Males, Mike A. (1999). *Framing Youth: 10 Myths about the Next Generation*. Monroe, ME: Common Courage Press. A debunking of myths about teenagers that have characterized them as the worst generation. Data about what teenagers are really like and what they need are a helpful resource for educators and parents.

ⓜmylabschool
Where the classroom comes to life!

Go to Allyn and Bacon's MyLabSchool (www.mylabschool.com) and complete the following activity for Chapter 3. Click on MyLabSchool **Case Archive**, then click on **On the Frontlines: Connecting with Families.**

CHAPTER 4

Multicultural Perspectives in Education

CASE STUDY

Anytown Fires Up Teens to Foster Acceptance

By Wendy Malloy, *The Tampa Tribune,* June 13, 2005

TAMPA—"Yo baby, yo baby, yo!"

The chant rises from the crowd of kids, growing louder as their traditional call to attention takes hold around the room. It's Culture Night at Anytown, and about 50 teenagers are gathered to perform what is part pep rally, part infomercial, part theater for the parents assembled to visit their kids, mid-week through the summer camp session.

But there are clues that Anytown isn't your typical summer camp.

Vivid banners tacked on the walls trumpet themes, past and present, of Anytown sessions. This year's message: "Keep the Flame Alive." As if in answer, the teens on this Wednesday evening occasionally break into fist-pumping choruses of "Fire it up! Fire it up!"

Among the banners, oversized charts provide details about participants, each name followed by spaces where the teens have filled in answers to a range of questions—nicknames, favorite foods, future goals.

Ethnicity? Turkish. African-American. Vietnamese. European-American. Guyanese.

Religion? Hindu. Catholic. Muslim. Earth-based nature-encompassing. Atheist.

Heroes? Martin Luther King. Mom. Mozart. Tyra Banks.

This is Anytown, a multicultural leadership program for teenagers sponsored by the National Conference for Community Justice. The umbrella organization has been around for more than six decades, working on the local level to rake through a broad range of "isms" and break down institutional barriers to create a more inclusive society. In 1950, NCCJ established the Anytown USA Residential Youth Program as the flagship opportunity for young people to get involved. Today there are Anytowns in more than 40 American cities.

Since the program took root locally in 1990, about 4,000 kids have experienced the weeklong set of workshops and dialogue aimed at opening them up to new cultures and fostering tolerance.

But the broader mission of Anytown, says Mike Trepper, NCCJ Tampa Bay director of education and community initiatives, is to help young people develop skills to go back into their schools and communities as strong voices for inclusiveness.

"Anytown builds connections," Trepper says. As co-director of the camp, he spends most summer days leading discussion groups and working with the kids. "This would not be Anytown if every kid came in believing in justice and peace and working things out. But that's what makes things special—when the kid with a rap sheet a mile long starts building a relationship with a kid who happens to be student body president. When those students start dialoguing and getting passionate about their conversation, they're finding a common place, and that's what Anytown is. Amazing things can happen."

One week at Anytown changed Steven Oudit's life.

Now 18 and on a pre-med track at the University of South Florida, Oudit was a student at Wesley Chapel High School in the fall of 2001.

During those uneasy days, Oudit, whose heritage is Indian and Pakistani, became a target in the school hallways.

"I was asked if my father was Osama bin Laden, whether I had a gun in my book bag, things like that," he recalls. "There were only four other Muslim students in a school of 1,500. Some hid by saying they were Puerto Rican, but it wasn't hard to pick us out. We'd hear, 'Sand [epithet], go back to your own country.' Another time my cousin and I were walking down the hall and somebody said, 'Watch out—we're going to tie you behind our truck and drag you down the street.' I was scared."

The end of the school year offered no relief. That summer, Oudit played defense on the New Tampa Comets soccer team, and tensions finally exploded. "A guy from the other team said, 'Sand [epithet], I'm going to burn you right now,' and he threw me to the ground. The ref had to break it up," Oudit says.

He spent the rest of the game on the bench, in tears.

"I just couldn't understand why people had to be this way," he says. "I kept thinking about what the world was going to turn into. After 9/11, a lot of people came together and showed their patriotism, which is great, but at the same time they viewed Muslim-Americans as stereotypes. It was tough."

Later that season, Oudit spent a week at Anytown. He had heard about the program from the principal at Wesley Chapel, who thought that by encouraging individual students to take leadership roles, the hostilities that had erupted after 9/11 might calm.

When he boarded the bus to Anytown, Oudit wasn't particularly looking forward to the week ahead. Spend six days talking? Any respectable teenage boy would sneer at the prospect.

"But the first night, we had this dialogue, and as soon as that opened up, it was amazing," he says. "It was, like, hey, you don't have to be scared to speak your mind."

By Culture Night on Wednesday, Oudit says the atmosphere was electric.

"We wanted to show our parents we're having a great time and learning so much. You realize that one voice can make a difference, but imagine what 55 can do!"

After that week, Oudit says, he was determined to step out of what he calls a stance of "quiet leader" and assume a more active role in his school and community.

"I no longer wanted to seclude myself from the rest of the world. I was ready to fight for what I believed in, to show people that not all Muslim-Americans are terrorists," he says. "Just going up to people and saying, 'What's going on?' or 'Did you go to the game Friday?'—just sparking up a conversation made a difference. I wanted to build that relationship with everyone and open up communication."

Questions for Reflection

1. Why are interventions such as Anytown sometimes necessary to change attitudes and stereotypes about people from cultural backgrounds different from our own?

2. What is the value of bringing together students with diverse voices and perspectives to seriously address issues of difference and inclusiveness?

3. Why is it important for students to develop leadership skills for promoting inclusiveness?

Reprinted with permission of *The Tampa Tribune.*

INTASC

Learning Outcomes

After reading and studying this chapter, you should be able to:

1. Discuss the importance of diversity, equality, and social justice in delivering high-quality education for *all* students. (INTASC 3: Diverse Learners)

2. Understand that students' learning is influenced by their language and culture and identify

teaching practices that are culturally relevant. (INTASC 3: Diverse Learners; INTASC 6: Communication Techniques)

3. Understand the importance of bringing diverse perspectives to the curriculum. (INTASC 1: Content; INTASC 3: Diverse Learners)

4. Describe the role that schools play in the education and socialization of today's children and youth.

5. Understand that educational equality requires that all students learn and are represented proportionately in advanced placement and special education classes.

Educators in a liberal democratic society face numerous tensions, in part because there is no one agreed-on way to educate students. In other words, people have numerous perspectives on how to teach, many based on their own experiences in schools. There is a strain between the public rights mandated by democratic principles and the private rights demanded by capitalist markets in our changing world. Democracy calls for equality, whereas capitalism adapts to inequality. A liberal education for all is the goal of democracy; preparation for work is the goal of capitalism. Public schools tend to heed both sides and simultaneously promote some of both. Teachers confront these tensions in their schools and in the communities that influence their work. Some of these issues are developed in this section.

Roles of Schools

Schools play many roles in society. They not only prepare students to be contributors to society, but they also reflect society's high ideals (universal education) and bad practices (racial and SES discrimination). One's philosophical and political perspectives determine how one views the roles of schools. For example, should schools:

1. Be a model of our best hopes for society and a mechanism for remaking society in the image of those hopes?
2. Adapt students to the needs of society by preparing them for specific roles and jobs?
3. Serve the individual hopes and ambitions of their students?[1]

In other words, should schools primarily support democratic equality, social efficiency, or social mobility? Advocates of democratic equality view education as a public good through which all students should be exposed to a liberal arts education and learn to be productive citizens in a democracy. Proponents of social efficiency believe that schools should serve the private sector by preparing students for future jobs; this goal has probably been the most dominant in the past. However, many people now see promoting social mobility as a more important role of schools. People with this perspective view education as an asset that can be accumulated and used for social competition. Credentials become more important than what is learned; the purpose is to gain a competitive advantage over others to secure a desirable position in society.

Reproduction

Historically, schools reproduced the cultural, political, social, and economic order of society. However, theorists differ in their views of how schools actually perform this role of reproduction. Functionalism, conflict theory, and resistance theory provide contradictory descriptions of how schools carry out this role for society.

CROSS-REFERENCE
Additional information about NCLB can be found in Chapters 1, 6, 8, and 11.

Functionalists view schools as important in supporting technological development, material well-being, and democracy. Since the release of the federal report *A Nation at Risk* in 1983, most reports calling for reform of schools have referred to the need for an educated workforce. The 2001 No Child Left Behind (NCLB) Act holds schools accountable for student learning regardless of race, native language, or disability. The goal is that all students will leave school with the knowledge and skills to work and be productive citizens. Schools are expected to provide equal educational opportunity for all students as a primary step in improving their social and economic status.

Conflict theorists also view schools as reproductive of society, but in ways less noble than those described by functionalists. Conflict theorists conclude that schools have been structured to maintain the power and dominance of individuals and groups that benefit most from the current system. Rather than being benevolent institutions that provide all students an equal chance to succeed, schools legitimize existing inequities. Advantages depend greatly on ascribed characteristics. Students whose parents graduated from college are much more likely to graduate from college; students whose parents never finished high school are themselves more likely not to finish high school. The academic tracking systems in many schools reinforce this unequal distribution. The number of middle-class students in college preparatory and advanced placement courses is disproportionately high relative to the total school population. The number of males and students of color in special education classes is disproportionately high; students of color and those from low-income families are underrepresented in gifted and talented programs. It appears to conflict theorists that one group is being groomed for management positions in the labor market while the second group is being prepared to labor under the direction of the first. Thus, schools provide neither equal educational opportunity nor a chance to improve one's status to any appreciable degree except in rare individual cases.

Over the past decade, researchers working on resistance theory have investigated the interactions of students and teachers as schools carry out their reproduction function. These researchers have found that reproduction is not an automatic process implemented with systematic precision. Students sometimes resist domination by school authorities, not readily accepting their inferior status. For example, they may resist following the rules or participating in some classes and activities. Resistance theory suggests much more interaction between students and teachers in the reproduction process than has been explained by the previous two theories. It also allows for the possibility that people can change the system of reproduction by encouraging the development of schools that are not based on domination and submission and that actually model democracy. Through the process of resistance, students can become active participants who help define and redefine schools.

Reconstructionism

CROSS-REFERENCE
Reconstructionism is also discussed in Chapter 10.

Some educators believe that schools are able to do more than just reproduce society. They believe that schools should not reflect the inequities that prevail in the broader society; rather, schools can reconstruct or transform society. Reconstructionist educators believe that all students can learn at a high level regardless of their

Citizenship education in public schools implicitly values patriotism and loyalty to one's country.

race, ethnicity, gender, or socioeconomic status, and they should not be tracked into courses based on these factors.

To implement a reconstructionist approach, classrooms and schools reflect democratic settings in which both students and teachers are active learners and participants. Students study problems confronting society and learn how to confront practices that are inequitable to some students. Teachers and other school personnel actively work with the community to overcome inequities and injustices to students and their families. Social justice, human rights, human dignity, and equity are critical values that guide the work of reconstructionism. In the reconstructionist process, the school itself becomes a model of democracy that leads, rather than follows, societal practices.

Journal for Reflection

1. As you reflect on your own education, would you characterize your schools as reproducing the status quo or as being reconstructionist? Why?

2. Why do you think Congress decided with the passage of NCLB in 2001 that schools needed to be accountable for the learning of all students?

3. What is the contribution of resistance theory in understanding how learning occurs in schools?

Purposes of Schools

School boards, educators, parents, and communities have their own beliefs and perspectives about the basic purposes of schools and the reasons for current problems in schools. These beliefs often draw on national reports calling for the reform of education. Through such reports and discussions and debates among individuals and groups, U.S. society continually refines and redefines ideas about the purposes of schools. The five purposes described in the following sections are only a sampling of those most often mentioned by educators and the public. Most schools address each of these purposes, but in any given school, one purpose may receive more prominence than others at a given time.

Citizenship

Educators, parents, and policymakers agree that schools should help students become good citizens. There is less agreement about the meaning of good citizens and how schools should go about preparing them. In some schools, especially elementary schools, students may receive a grade or rating on their citizenship within the classroom. Historically, students have taken a civics or government course or have studied citizenship issues in other social studies courses. The National Council for Social Studies includes a standard on civic ideals and practices. The focus in citizenship education or in civics and government courses is usually on the structure of the U.S. political system and on treasured documents such as the Constitution and Bill of Rights. Patriotism and loyalty to the United States are implicit values that often undergird both these courses and the school's **hidden curriculum.** A limitation of this approach is that students might not have the opportunity to grapple with the problems and issues that are inherent in a democratic society. Students might learn the civic values but never be encouraged to discuss why inequities remain in society.

Preparation for citizenship cannot be taught in a single course. Schools could work to develop democratic citizens who respect others, believe in human dignity, are concerned about and care for others, and fight for justice, fairness, and tolerance. Students could learn through practice in the classroom how to be active, involved citizens. What better place to model democratic practice and equitable participation than in our schools?

Workforce Readiness

A number of national reports on education over the past two decades have expressed concern about the quality of the workforce. Some employers report that schools do not provide students with the basic skills and behaviors necessary to participate effectively in today's economy. Business owners want graduates with dispositions for working such as punctuality and an ethic of hard work as well as vocational skills appropriate to the job. They report that many young people do not read, write, or compute at the level needed for the jobs available. In response, some employers have established their own programs to teach basic literacy.

A lack of agreement exists about the nature of these necessary skills, especially in an economy in which the greatest job growth will be in the service sector, where people of color and women have disproportionately high representation. Most high schools prepare students either to attend college or to get a job soon after graduation. Many areas of the country have vocational high schools to teach occupational skills. Many school districts also have established magnet schools with single purposes, including career preparation in the arts, health fields, computing, and service areas such as food, hotels, and tourism. The overrepresentation of low-income students, students of color, and females in nonacademic tracks is a serious dilemma.

Educators, policymakers, and the business community debate the "real" purpose of schools. Is it to ensure students have the knowledge and skills to keep the economy competitive in a changing world where new jobs continually emerge? Is it to help students learn a trade, learn how to learn, or learn how to take orders and follow the rules? This question is particularly important when conditions change as rapidly as they do in today's society. The vocation for which one is prepared initially may become obsolete within a few years. Perhaps students should be prepared to think, adjust to change, and be active participants in their life's work. They need to be able to handle change and adapt to new occupations and situations.

hidden curriculum

The informal curriculum that defines the behaviors and attitudes of students and teachers in classrooms and schools.

Many students begin preparing for a career by taking vocational courses in high school or at postsecondary vocational schools.

Academic Achievement

Media reports of student scores on achievement tests highlight a school's ability to offer students a strong academic background. Some school districts base their reputations on how well their students perform and how many are admitted to colleges. In some communities, parents camp out overnight to be first in line to enroll their children in a preschool that will provide the jump-start needed for success on future tests to ensure later admission to prestigious colleges and universities.

Countries and their education systems are compared through student scores on international tests. When the scores of U.S. students fall below those of students in other countries, parents and policymakers demand changes. Concern about performance in reading, writing, and mathematics periodically leads to a back-to-basics movement in which the traditional academic subjects are emphasized. "Frills" such as the development of self-esteem, leisure activities, and anything that takes time away from academic study are condemned as a misuse of public funds. In response, states and school districts have increased the length of the school day to provide more time to learn academic subjects.

Attention to academic achievement focuses on meeting standards in academic areas, the arts, health, and physical education. As a result, many schools have revised their curricula to be standards-based. Test publishers have revised standardized tests used by states and school districts to reflect these standards. The emphasis is on testing students annually to determine if they are at grade level. Low-income students, students of color, and females are expected to learn at the high levels historically expected of middle-class white males. School systems' reputations and their state funding are dependent on how well students perform on these tests.

CROSS-REFERENCE
For more information on standardized tests, see Chapter 11.

Social Development

Schooling also provides opportunities for students to develop their social skills by interacting with others. In this process, students should learn to respect others; they also learn a set of rules for working appropriately with peers and adults. Although schools usually do not provide a course that teaches skills in social development, appropriate behavior is constantly reinforced by teachers and other school professionals in the classroom and on the playground.

Teachers can give students opportunities to work with other students from diverse racial, gender, language, religious, and ability groups and to learn about those differences in the process. Teachers can encourage interactions across groups through cooperative learning activities in which students from different groups are placed together. Other team projects allow students who might not seek one another out otherwise to work together. A part of teaching is helping students learn to work together positively.

Today's technology also opens many possibilities for interactions with students and adults in cultures beyond school boundaries. Internet and two-way video connections allow students in rural New Mexico to talk directly with students in inner-city Chicago or Tokyo, Japan. Some teachers have developed these linkages themselves with the assistance of other knowledgeable teachers they have met in college classes or at professional meetings.

Cultural Transmission

Schools around the world are expected to transmit the culture of their nation to young people so they can both maintain it and pass it on to the next generation. Schools have often approached this task by teaching history with an emphasis on important events and heroes. This emphasis helps children learn the importance of patriotism and loyalty. Formal and hidden curricula reflect and reinforce the values of the national culture—the principles, standards, and qualities the culture endorses.

These national values and rules are so embedded in most aspects of schooling that most teachers and students do not realize they exist. The only exceptions may be students who do not belong to the dominant culture or whose families have recently immigrated. In these cases, students and families quickly learn that schools might not reflect or support aspects of their culture that differ from the dominant culture. This dissonance between schools and families is most noticeable when students are from backgrounds other than northern and western European. Students from religious backgrounds that have not evolved from Judeo-Christian roots are also likely to question the culture that is being transmitted at school. The challenge for educators is to transmit the national culture while including the richness and contributions of many who are not yet accepted as an integral part of that culture. In this way, schools begin to change and expand the national culture.

Journal for Reflection

1. What do you believe is the most important purpose of schools? Why?

2. Which purpose dominates in NCLB, the federal legislation for P–12 education?

3. What purpose(s) other than those discussed above do schools serve?

Values in Schools

Schools are microcosms of the societies that create them, and the dominant social values that prevail in a society will prevail in its schools.

Jing-Qui Liu

Although schools are expected to transmit the culture of the United States to the younger generation, educators do not agree on *whose* culture. Is there really a national or common culture that diverse racial, ethnic, language, and religious groups in the country accept? Dialects, behaviors, and values vary within the same cultural group as well as across groups whose members live in different regions of the country. Cultural differences are also experienced by people who move from rural areas to the city or vice versa.

How can schools begin to accommodate all of these differences? Some conservative politicians and popular talk show hosts argue that schools should ignore diversity. They believe that all students should learn the common heritage and adopt the national culture as their own. In this approach, students who are not members of the dominant group are expected to assimilate.

Multicultural theorists and educators present another perspective in a changing world that includes increased movement across countries. They argue that student diversity enriches the school community. They believe that cultural differences should be valued and integrated throughout the curriculum and all activities of the school. In this approach, teachers draw on the cultural backgrounds and experiences of students to teach academic knowledge and skills.

Whose Values?

Parents' choices of private schools, home schooling, or segregated schools have been based in part on the values that parents believe schooling can impart. Although schools usually do not offer a course in which values are explicitly presented and discussed, values implicitly influence the formal and hidden curriculum. Curricula usually support the current ideological, political, and economic order of society. For example, individualism is much more highly regarded than the rights of groups. The Protestant work ethic is evident in society's belief that someone who works hard will be successful in life. Although these values may

Competition in regional athletics and other extracurricular activities often reflects the traditions of a school's culture.

seem uncontroversial, they can be the cause of extensive debate and emotional pleas at school board meetings and community forums.

Some parents are concerned that the public school curriculum in the United States does not reflect their religious values; some think that their religion is purposefully denigrated in schools. These concerns are expressed most frequently by members of some fundamentalist Christian communities but also by Amish and Hutterite communities and by some Jewish, Muslim, and other non-Christian families and communities. On the other hand, atheists believe that religious values, especially Christian ones, pervade the school curriculum.

Additionally, the emphasis on individualism and competition prevalent in many schools is not compatible with the cooperative patterns practiced by Native American tribes and in many Latino and African American communities. These differences can lead to conflict between parents and schools and among groups within a community. Parents turn to the courts when they believe that schools have acted inappropriately. They may believe either that the schools do not have a democratic process in which they can be heard or that the majority of the community will not support their petitions. School prayer, creationism, the banning of books, sex education, and segregation are among the areas that have been tested in the courts.

Because parents and other groups in a community may vehemently disagree about the values to be reinforced in schools, teachers should be aware of their own values. Knowing their own values as well as those of the families represented in the school should help teachers prepare for potential conflicts. Expectations can vary greatly from one community or school to another.

CROSS-REFERENCE
Legal cases related to religion are presented in Chapter 6.

Journal for Reflection

1. Whose values do you think should be reflected in the school curriculum?

2. What argument could you make for and against multiple perspectives being incorporated into the school curriculum?

 ## Global Perspectives

Universal Values

One might wonder whether a diverse population can ever reach agreement on the values to be taught in schools. But one K–12 school in Lucknow, India, has been promoting diverse students' emotional and spiritual growth as well as academic excellence for over fifty years. The City Montessori School has 19,000 students in fifteen branches in a city with more than 1.5 million people and two very influential religious groups—Hindu and Muslim. Students learn and are expected to practice what the faculty and parents define as "universal values," which include "kindness, compassion, cooperation, responsibility, and other such values rooted in the world's religions."[2]

The school's approach integrates these universal values with excellence, global understanding, and service. In daily reflection times, students use texts and stories from many religions. They "visit India's holy places—Hindu, Sikh, Buddhist, Muslim, Christian, Jewish, Baha'i, and Jain—in order to learn tolerance for one another."[3] They also have exchange programs with schools in more than twenty countries. Students are expected to provide service to local communities and villages.

In developing this approach, those involved have drawn on effective practices from around the world. The school takes its teaching philosophy and its name from the Italian educator Maria Montessori. The mentoring aspect of teaching comes from Russia. The universal values are not those of one religious group but are basic to many religions. They also are the values of humanitarians around the globe, whether or not they are religious.

Questions for Reflection

1. Whose values are taught in the City Montessori School?

2. How does the Indian school incorporate religious diversity into its curriculum?

Multicultural Education

Equality is the heart and essence of democracy, freedom, and justice.

A. Philip Randolph

Diversity, equality, and social justice are the foundations for education that is multicultural. It holds educators morally and ethically responsible to help all students learn, regardless of their socioeconomic status, ethnicity, race, language, gender, religion, or ability. Multicultural education expects teachers and administrators to view all aspects of education—including the curriculum, teacher and student interactions, staffing patterns, discipline, and extracurricular activities—through a multicultural lens to ensure that the needs of diverse students are an integral part of the education process.

Education that is multicultural provides equity in the curriculum, relationships between teachers and students, the school climate, staffing patterns, and relationships with parents and communities. **Multicultural education,** on the other hand, usually refers to the curriculum content, which should include human relations; the study of ethnic, racial, gender, and other groups; the development of critical thinking skills; and the examination of issues such as racism, power, and discrimination.

Curriculum and instructional practices in multicultural education value diversity, drawing on the cultural experiences of students and including multiple ways of learning and viewing the world; they support democracy and **equity** in classrooms and schools. In culturally relevant teaching, teachers believe that all students can learn, and they place students at the center of teaching, drawing on their cultural backgrounds and experiences to develop meaningful learning experiences. Constant vigilance concerning the content and delivery of academic subjects is required. Many educators have mistakenly thought that multicultural education is for students of color. Rather, it is for all students regardless of their group memberships.

Many educators think they are offering multicultural education simply by including information about groups other than their own in a lesson. This additive approach is evident in black history and women's history months or in highlighted sections in textbooks that discuss, for example, Japanese Americans. If the only time students study these groups is during their special month then multicultural education is not being delivered. In some schools, attention to multiculturalism begins and ends with tasting ethnic foods and participating in ethnic festivals. Although these activities contribute to a superficial understanding of differences, they do not help students understand the history and experiences of diverse groups.

In multicultural education, all teaching is culturally relevant, and classrooms and schools are models of democracy and equity. This effort requires educators to:

1. Place the student at the center of the teaching and learning process.
2. Promote human rights and respect for cultural differences.
3. Believe that all students can learn.
4. Acknowledge and build on the life histories and experiences of students' group memberships.
5. Critically analyze oppression and power relationships to help students understand racism, sexism, classism, and discrimination against persons with disabilities, gays, lesbians, the young, and the aged.
6. Critique society in the interest of social justice and equality.
7. Participate in collective social action to ensure a democratic society.[4]

Although you should begin to struggle with these issues now, the process of learning about others and reflecting on one's attitudes and actions in these areas is a lifelong activity.

Undergirding Tenets

For centuries, women, people with low incomes, and members of oppressed ethnic and religious groups have fought for an education equal to that available to males

multicultural education

An educational strategy that incorporates the teaching of students from diverse backgrounds, human relations, and the study of ethnic and other cultural groups in a school environment that supports diversity and equity.

equity

The state of fairness and justice across individuals and groups; it does not mean the same educational strategies across groups but does expect equal results.

of the dominant group. In the nineteenth century, courageous educators established schools to serve some of these students, often encountering opposition from the community at the time. Eighty years ago educators at the Intercultural Service Bureau in New York City were fighting for the incorporation of intercultural education into the curriculum to increase knowledge about new immigrants, improve tolerance among groups, and reduce prejudice against them. In 1954 the Supreme Court declared illegal separate-but-equal education for black and white students in *Brown v. Board of Education*. The civil rights struggles of the 1960s laid the groundwork for new curriculum content about African Americans, Latinos, American Indians, and Asian Americans. Attention to equity for women, individuals with disabilities, and English language learners soon followed.

These events became the foundation of multicultural education. Three core beliefs about schooling and society guide the development of education that supports democracy for all. One is the belief that diversity is a national strength that should be valued and promoted. Social justice and equality are other viable goals for society that should be modeled in classrooms and schools.

DIVERSITY

There has been much public and academic discussion of multiculturalism over the past thirty years. Editorials, national news programs, radio talk shows, and debates among college students and faculty periodically focus on the importance of diversity in society and the school curriculum. Simply put, the perspective of one side is that the recognition and promotion of diversity will strengthen the nation. The other perspective views the promotion of diversity as dividing the nation and leading to greater conflict among groups. This second perspective also argues that the Western tradition is denigrated when diversity and multiple perspectives are highlighted.

Campaigns for members of Congress, governors, and mayors include debates about immigration, provision of services to undocumented workers and their children, English-only policies, as well as gay rights. Multiculturalists argue that multicultural education will help unify a nation comprised of numerous ethnic groups who have long faced discrimination. They believe that individuals should have the opportunity to learn more about one another and to interact on an equal basis in schools and society. They also believe that members of diverse groups can maintain their diverse history, traditions, and cultures while developing together a common civic culture. An outgrowth of these debates has been the establishment of general education requirements for ethnic, women's, and global studies in colleges and universities. Most states also expect teacher education candidates to study diversity and to be able to incorporate it into their teaching. Most of the developing state and national standards for preschool through college curricula include references to diversity.

The public believes not only that diversity should be incorporated in the curriculum but also that teachers in a school should represent different cultural groups.[5] A diverse student body and faculty make it possible for students not only to learn about others but also to interact in authentic settings with people from different backgrounds. The Internet has also created opportunities for students in schools with limited diversity to become acquainted with people from diverse backgrounds in other parts of the country and world.

Many schools sponsor cultural events to show their commitment to diversity. However, these efforts are not multicultural education, which requires a deeper understanding of diversity and equality.

Is School the Best Place to Teach Tolerance?

Children learn about their own and other children's families before they enter school. Many families teach their children to respect and value others. Others teach hate and intolerance toward groups that they believe are inferior to them. The role of schools in teaching students to be tolerant is an issue still debated by some educators.

YES

Bettie Sing Luke, *a multicultural trainer for the Eugene, Oregon, schools, works with teachers to help students develop tolerance and appreciation for each other's cultures. She has also worked in Seattle and, since 1973, has conducted diversity training in 30 states. E-mail: luke@4j.lane.edu.*

A resounding yes! on teaching tolerance in school! School is the only common institution, where *all* students can be touched and prepared to survive in our society's marvelous and sometimes maddeningly diverse mix.

We are less connected, as a society, than we were when travel and technology opportunities were more limited. Witness the recent instances of school violence, situations that cried out for tolerance.

Schools, I believe, can help redefine "family" and "belonging" and reinforce respect. They have to. It's unrealistic to depend on tolerance being taught at home.

Have you checked the percentages on single-parent and two-job families? Busy parents may have good ideals to pass on to their children, but we are no longer a society of "Dick and Jane" families sitting down for dinner and quality conversation each night.

Nor are all families models of tolerance. Some young people will reject the intolerant attitudes they might see at home, but what about children who are afraid to think beyond what they are told at home?

What if children never hear alternatives to intolerance at home—especially mainstream students, who can go through their entire lives and never be asked to reconsider their positions of privilege?

Religious or spiritual communities are a natural conduit for teaching tolerance, but in some localities there may be no religious leadership or opportunity to practice.

NO

Barbara Joan Grubman *is a speech specialist for the Los Angeles Unified School District at Grant High School in Van Nuys, California. She began teaching in New Jersey when Eisenhower was president and her salary was under $3,000. E-mail: bgrubman@lausd.k12.ca.us.*

It is how your father treats the neighbors. It is how your mother welcomes the world into your childhood home. It is the words they use to talk about others—the words that help or heal, that allow you as a child to develop a sense of tolerance.

Long before a child's historic first day of school, the home provides a foundation of values. Those early years are made up of precious opportunities for teaching children acceptance of others.

I believe children cannot learn this lesson in school. They have to see tolerance modeled by those nearest and dearest to them. They have to hear the words and read the body language of those who care for them and nurture them from infancy.

Toddlers are sensitive to our every look. They know that "funny" glance, the hidden disdain, the lowered eyes of parents that say "this person is different." Spend a few minutes with a young child, and you'll know they don't miss much. Babies take in attitudes with mother's milk.

My maternal grandmother, Rose, was a frightened and prejudiced woman. I grew up as a lower-middle-class kid in the East Bronx, New York. My father's mother, a loving and tolerant woman, also lived nearby. But my mother's mother lived right across the street from us and it was there that I went home for lunch and after school.

I can look back now with the perspective of time and see her fears, but then all I knew was that there were a lot of people out there she did

(continued)

(continued)

YES

Cultural beliefs about education can come into play as well.

In my culture, teachers have a highly elevated status. They are entrusted with children because their knowledge and wisdom are believed superior to those of parents.

Chinese heritage is imbued with the Confucian ethics of hierarchy. Parents do not sit and chitchat with their children—this just is not done in traditional families!

I observed, as a child, that my parents had to submit to bias and unfair treatment. If they didn't, they risked further harm to others who looked like us. Had I not had lessons from school, I might have acquiesced to the same fate.

Given these dynamics, schools are the prime choice for imparting tolerance. Dedicated teaching *can* overcome negative attitudes.

When I worked for the Seattle Public Schools, a rumble between Black and Asian students erupted in a middle school woodworking class. The conflict escalated and spilled out into the community.

I chose a Black male as an intervention partner and, together, we quelled the fears on both sides, letting the students know the school had adult advocates of their cultural group working on their behalf.

Young men of both groups were greeting each other in the halls within three weeks.

Schools can teach *all* children about tolerance and connectedness—through anti-bias programs and through *individual commitment* to tolerance, across the board, woven through all subjects.

Students, in turn, can then impact family and outside influences that may not be as tolerant.

NO

not like, who did not "measure up" to what we were. From her, I learned that blacks were not to be trusted, German Jews were the chosen ones, and many people had what she termed "shifty eyes."

Even as I sat at her oil cloth-covered kitchen table, as she prepared dinner, I knew that those people could not all be bad. Hating the way she treated her foreign-born husband—my beloved grandfather—and hearing her unkind words directed toward my unconventional father, I silently vowed never to be like her. I felt as if I needed to protect them from her barbs. So, ironically, I learned from a very intolerant woman what it meant to be tolerant.

How do we teach our children that those who are different should not be feared—that the kid next to them holds the same fears, loves, emotions as they do?

You have to open your ears to the words of an Orthodox Jewish grandmother who you see has an open heart and a hand for all who come in her path. You have to start to discern from another grandmother that the way she looks at others is not the way you wish to, even when you are too young to put a name to it.

If we wait until we send our children off that first day of school, proud in their shiny new clothes, it is too late. The window of opportunity for teaching tolerance, while it may not be shut and locked, is already lowered.

Being exposed to the lesson of tolerance at school is better than not hearing it at all, but without the foundations laid by family, educators face an uphill battle.

A lesson at school can reinforce what a child already feels, but home is where the heart is.

Source: "Is School the Best Place to Teach Tolerance?" *NEA Today* (May 2000), p. 11. Reprinted by permission of the National Education Association.

WHAT IS YOUR PERSPECTIVE ON THIS ISSUE?
Is school the best place to teach tolerance?

To give your opinion, go to Chapter 4 of the companion website (**www.ablongman.com/johnson14e**) and click on Teacher Perspectives.

Social justice calls for us to help those persons who have greater needs than we do.

SOCIAL JUSTICE

What is meant by *justice* in a society that places so much emphasis on individualism and the freedom to be left alone? Justice itself is related to fairness, moral rightness, and equity. Our judicial system is designed to guarantee legal justice for individuals and groups. Social justice, on the other hand, focuses on how we help others in the community who are less well off than we are. Most religions measure the quality of a society by the justice and care it gives to those in the greatest need—the homeless, the sick, the powerless, and the uneducated.

The ethic of social justice, especially as it relates to teacher–student relationships, is essential in the teaching profession, along with other moral commitments. Social justice in education requires schools to provide all students equal access to a high-quality education. Practices that perpetuate current inequities are confronted and strategies for eliminating them employed.

> Justice can never be done in the midst of injustice.
>
> **Simone de Beauvoir**

Schools reflect the inequities of the broader society. As you reflect on the inequitable conditions in schools, ask yourself the following questions:

- How fair is it for some students to attend school in dilapidated, foul-smelling, crowded buildings while others attend classes in beautiful buildings with future-oriented technology and well-groomed grounds?
- How fair is it for wealthier students to have the most experienced and best-qualified teachers, who also earn the highest teaching salaries?
- How fair is it that wealthier students are exposed to an intellectually challenging curriculum and experiences while many low-income students do not have advanced placement classes offered in their school?
- How fair is it that students of color, especially males, students with disabilities, and English language learners are pulled out of regular classes and isolated in segregated classes during much of the school day?
- How accurate are curricula and pedagogy that do not reflect the rich plurality of the people, histories, experiences, and perspectives of the groups that make up the United States and the world?

Educators ask themselves numerous questions about school practices if they are serious about providing social justice in schools. A theory of social justice suggests that school systems give those students with the fewest advantages the most advantages in their education and schooling to begin to ensure an equal and fair playing field. The goal might be to use the best-funded and most successful schools as the norm for all schools, with the least advantaged receiving the greatest resources for education. Practices today are usually the reverse with the most economically advantaged students attending attractive and safe schools with the greatest resources and most qualified teachers. Resources for education are not shared equally across groups.

meritocracy

A system based on the belief that individuals' achievements are based on their own personal merits and hard work and that the people who achieve at the highest levels deserve the greatest social and financial reward.

EQUALITY

Although equality is an espoused goal of democracy, its meaning differs from one person to another. Many believe that each individual has an equal chance at success, which is often measured by the dominant group in terms of wealth and accumulated material goods. This system of **meritocracy** is built on the idea that with hard work, diligence, and persistence, an individual should be able to finish school, attend college, and obtain a well-paying job. Poverty and discrimination are seen as obstacles to be overcome.

A problem with the meritocratic approach is that not all individuals begin the game of life from the same starting line. Whites from the middle class and above start with advantages such as membership in the dominant culture, sufficient family income to support a college education, decent housing, adequate health care, and good schools with qualified teachers. The children of the wealthy have a much greater chance of being wealthy in their adulthood than do the children of low-income families. The powerful are able to ensure that their children inherit their advantages. Therefore, equality of opportunity could begin to be realized only if children from powerless groups are provided the same or similar advantages.

Critics of the public rhetoric on equality charge that U.S. institutions and political and economic systems are rigged to support the privileged few rather than the pluralistic majority. Both the shrinking middle class and the widening gap between wealth and poverty contribute to this problem. Nevertheless, some people still think that a more equitable society is not only desirable but also possible to achieve. Resources could begin to be more fairly distributed if all workers received a decent wage or even equal opportunities. In a study of literacy in the United States and other nations, researchers found that U.S. workers with the highest literacy skills were ten times more likely to receive training from their employers than those with the lowest skills. These researchers found that "our nation concentrates on producing and rewarding first-class skills and, as a result, is world class at the top; however, it spends a great deal to achieve this result. It accepts in fact, if not in rhetoric, a basic skills underclass. It spends meagerly to help adults with limited or restricted skills or on the next generation that will join their ranks."[6]

The application of civil rights laws and a drastic reduction in discriminatory practices could contribute greatly to the provision of fairness and justice in the distribution of societal benefits, including education. Schools should question whether their policies and practices are equitable. One step in this investigation might be an examination of how accessible gifted, talented, and honors programs are to students from diverse groups. A truly egalitarian society ensures not only that their schools are safe, adequately staffed, and supportive of learning but also that the schools of other people's children have the same amenities. Such a society works toward the elimination of racism, sexism, and other forms of discrimination in education.

EQUAL EDUCATIONAL OPPORTUNITY   One way to address equality in the educational system is to offer **equal educational opportunity,** which should provide all students, regardless of their backgrounds, similar opportunities to learn and to benefit from schooling. Neither educators nor policymakers agree on what constitutes equal educational opportunity. On the surface, it would seem that all students should have access to high-quality teaching, small classes, up-to-date technology, college preparatory courses, buildings that support learning, and safe environments. In reality, most equal educational opportunity programs have been designed to overcome educational deficiencies of underserved students by providing compensatory or remedial programs to reduce the educational gaps that have given advantaged students a head start.

Even when a school has the latest technology, is clean and well maintained, and is staffed by qualified professionals, equal opportunity is not automatically guaranteed. Many other factors need to be considered. What percentages of students in advanced mathematics and science classes are female or students of color? Which students make up the college preparatory and advanced placement classes? Who is assigned to or chooses a general or vocational track? Who is referred to special education classes? Who has access to the best teachers? Who participates in which extracurricular activities? Who is suspended? If the percentages of students from diverse groups in these various school settings are somewhat proportional to their representation in the school population as a whole, equal educational opportunity may be approaching the goal of its supporters.

EQUALITY OF RESULTS   Schools today are expected to provide all students the opportunity to learn the skills outlined in national standards for mathematics, science, English, the arts, foreign languages, history, geography, civics, and economics. Policymakers not only expect U.S. students to meet minimal standards, they expect

equal educational opportunity

Access to similar education for all students regardless of their cultural background or family circumstances.

them to achieve higher scores on international tests than students in any other part of the world. If educators actually believed that all students could learn, they would ensure that all students have access to higher-level knowledge. Some students would not be tracked into low-ability and nonstimulating classes. They would promote critical thinking and the ability to view the world and academic subjects from multiple perspectives.

Some theorists and educators argue that we must not stop at merely providing the opportunity to learn. Opportunity to learn places the burden on individuals, in that they choose whether to take advantage of the opportunity. But if the goal is to ensure equality of results, teachers would be expected to develop strategies for helping all students learn at a high level. They would start their careers with the disposition or belief that all children, regardless of their group memberships or environmental circumstances, are capable of learning. Students who were not performing well academically or in other ways would become intellectual challenges for the teacher or a team of teachers and other support personnel. The goal would become to develop strategies to ensure learning rather than simply moving students from one grade to another. This is the goal of the federal legislation in the No Child Left Behind Act, which requires schools to show evidence that all students are performing academically at grade level.

CROSS-REFERENCE
No Child Left Behind is discussed from different perspectives in Chapters 1, 6, 8, and 11.

Culturally Relevant Teaching

All people have preferred learning and teaching styles that are embedded in their cultural backgrounds and experiences. Until teachers learn to recognize these differences and develop a repertoire of different strategies for teaching subject matter, some students will be deprived of appropriate support in the learning process. However, making generalizations about culturally diverse learners can be dangerous. Teachers need to be thoughtful about the role that culture—values, behaviors, and language—plays in learning; at the same time, teachers must avoid characterizing all students who appear to share the same ethnicity or class as being the same.

At first glance, it might seem that the guidelines for handling diversity in a classroom could be codified in a recipe book that clearly states what instruction is effective for students from a specific group. The problem with this approach is that not only are there differences across ethnic and cultural groups, but there are also many differences among members within the same group. The intragroup differences may be based on socioeconomic status, religion, language, and the degree of assimilation. Therefore, descriptions of a group usually do not apply to all members of that group. The generalizations in a recipe book would lead to stereotyping and prejudging students. Knowledge about groups different from one's own can be greatly expanded by taking courses in ethnic or women's studies, reading books by female authors and authors of color, and participating in the institutions and activities of communities different from your own.

Culturally relevant teaching is complex. A teacher cannot determine the learning styles, prior knowledge, or cultural experiences of students by simply knowing that they are from a specific ethnic group or SES. You will need to observe and listen to students and their parents as well as assess student performance to develop the most effective teaching strategy. Culturally relevant teaching validates the cultures of students and communities. As a result, students begin to feel that teachers care about them, which is a first step in building a foundation for trust between teachers and students who are from different groups.

BUILDING ON CULTURAL CONTEXT

To demonstrate respect for students' backgrounds and experiences, teachers should be able to help students see the relationship between subject matter and the world in which they live. Students should see themselves in the representations (that is,

Teachers must be able to transcend their own cultural backgrounds to develop learning experiences that build on the cultural backgrounds of all their students.

books, examples, word problems, and films) used by teachers. Use of students' prior knowledge and experiences with the subject matter is also critical. Students make sense of information in different ways. Therefore, an effective teacher teaches the same concept by explaining it in different ways, relating it to something meaningful in students' lives, and demonstrating it with multiple representations. For most beginning teachers, these various explanations may be limited; with experience, good teachers are able to draw on many different strategies to take advantage of each student's learning style and cultural patterns.

It is important to know what kind of knowledge, skills, and commitments are valued in the students' cultures. Some students rebel against academic study and school authority as a form of resistance against the values of the dominant society. For example, some white working-class families value common sense and working with one's hands. They place less value on academics than most middle-class families. Understanding these differences should help the teacher develop different strategies for making the subject matter meaningful to all students.

Some of the conflict in student–teacher interactions results from lack of information and understanding about cultural differences in oral and nonverbal communications. People usually think that the way they communicate with members of their own culture is normal. They don't realize that there are many other ways to communicate. As long as people interact only with members of the same culture, they use the same cultural cues about whose turn it is to speak, or the seriousness of a statement, or the meaning of a raised eyebrow, frown, or joke.

Often teachers do not realize that they and their students are reading cultural cues differently. Students may even be punished for responding inappropriately when they may have misinterpreted the teacher's intent because it was different from the norm in their own culture. Recognizing that miscommunications may be based on cultural differences is a first step in improving cross-cultural communications. A next step is to be able to admit that you may be part of the problem, followed by the development of alternate means for communicating and understanding messages from other cultures.

One approach is to systematically teach the communication patterns of the dominant culture to students who are not members of that culture. In this strategy, students' communication patterns are still valued, but they learn when it is to their advantage to use the communication patterns of the dominant group. In other words, they become bicultural, they are able to function in the different cultures of the school and their home. However, teachers who also learn to function effectively in more than one culture will gain respect from students and begin to genuinely model a multicultural pedagogy.

CENTERING THE CULTURES OF STUDENTS

Pluralism in the curriculum is not a matter of trivial pursuit, nor is it primarily about self-esteem. It's about truth.

Asa Hilliard

A major dimension of multicultural education is the integration of principles of diversity and equality throughout the curriculum. The curriculum for all academic areas should reflect these principles. Adding a course on ethnic studies or women's studies to the curriculum is an easy way to introduce students to the culture, history, and experiences of others, but it is not enough. Many students will be more willing to learn if their cultures are valued and integrated throughout the curriculum. As they learn within their own cultural context, they see themselves and their cultures valued by the teacher and school authorities.

An inclusive curriculum begins to reflect the reality of our multicultural world rather than only the piece of it that belongs to the dominant group. For example, learning science and mathematics would be enhanced for American Indian and other students if the knowledge and traditions of various tribes and nations were incorporated into the curriculum. Researchers Sharon Nelson-Barber and Elise Estrin report that

> Many American Indian students have extensive knowledge of mathematics and science knowledge that is rooted in naturalist traditions common to Native communities and arrived at through observation and direct experience. Because many Indian communities follow traditional subsistence lifestyles, parents routinely expose their offspring to survival routines, often immersing the children in decision-making situations in which they must interpret new experiences in light of previous ones. Unfortunately, a majority of teachers recognize neither Indian students' knowledge nor their considerable learning strategies. Thus, not only is potentially important content knowledge ignored but well-developed ways of knowing, learning, and problem solving also go unrecognized.[7]

Some parents and communities have become so upset at schools' unwillingness to respect and validate their own cultures that they have established charter or private schools grounded in their own, rather than the dominant, culture. Afrocentric schools exist in a number of urban areas. Some Latino and American Indian groups have set up schools in which their cultures are at the center of the curriculum. Jewish, Islamic, Black Muslim, Lutheran, Catholic, Amish, and other schools reinforce the values, beliefs, and behaviors of their religions in private schools across the country. Single-sex schools focus on developing the confidence, academic achievement, and leadership skills of young women or men by using the learning styles and cultural experiences central to their gender. Schools in some urban areas have been designed for African American young men to validate their culture and develop their self-esteem, academic achievement, and leadership capacities in order to confront the hostile environment they face in their interactions with the dominant society.

These schools are not multicultural in that they may exclude some groups. But the centering of their culture in the curriculum does not necessarily mean that the curriculum is not multicultural. No matter how great or how limited the ethnic diversity is in a school or whose culture is centered in the curriculum, the curriculum should be multicultural. Rural white students should have the same opportunities to view the world and subject matter from multicultural and global perspectives as students in diverse urban settings. Because students in some schools do not have opportunities to interact directly with members of diverse groups, the curriculum often becomes their only source for the exploration of diversity, social justice, and related issues.

VALIDATING STUDENT VOICES

In multicultural education, all participants have **voice.** Teachers do not dominate the dialogue. Students, especially low-income students and students of color, usually see teachers as representing the dominant cultural group and as not being open to hearing perspectives represented in the students' cultures.

voice

The right and opportunity to speak and be heard as an equal.

However, including student voices in the classroom dialogue is not always easy. Students usually have limited experience with active participation in their own learning. When the classroom climate begins to include student voices, students may express

Many educators must learn to relinquish their traditional role as the single voice of authority in order to allow student voices to be heard.

anger and be confrontational; they may test the limits of the language that can be used and the subjects that can be broached. Allowing student voices to be an integral part of classroom discourse often tests the patience of teachers as they and their students figure out how to listen and contribute to the learning process. At the same time, tolerance, patience with one another, and the willingness to listen will develop as student voices contribute to the exploration of the subject matter.

The wise person can see a question from all sides without bias. The foolish person can see a question only from one side.
Confucius

Respect for differences is key in affirming student voices. For many educators, this affirmation requires relinquishing the power they have traditionally had as the voice of authority with the right answers. Class time can no longer be monopolized by teacher talk. The meaningful incorporation of student voices requires the development of listening skills and the validation of multiple perspectives, languages, and dialects. It should allow students to participate in the dialogue through speaking, writing, and artistic expression. It should allow them to use the modes of communicating with which they feel most comfortable while teaching them other modes.

The affirmation of student voices requires that educators listen to the voices of *all* students. It is particularly important to hear the voices of students of color, low-income students, girls and young women, English language learners (ELLs), and students with disabilities. The formal and hidden curricula have always validated the voices of the dominant groups. One of the goals of multicultural education is to validate the voices and stories of others. Teachers must ensure that these voices are not drowned out again in their classrooms. The stories or narratives of others will increase student knowledge and tolerance of differences. Many students will learn to value both their own culture and those of others. In the process, teachers and students will also learn that they have much in common.

Journal for Reflection

1. How has your own education reflected diversity, social justice, and equality? What experiences will help you work effectively with students from groups different from your own?

2. What do you think are the advantages and disadvantages of centering the cultures of students in the curriculum?

3. Why (or why not) should student voices be validated in classrooms?

Challenges in Multicultural Classrooms

The challenges in delivering multicultural education are numerous. Because many teacher candidates have little or no experience with the ethnic and religious groups represented in their classrooms, they face the unknown. The ideals of diversity, equality, and social justice will require that these teachers engage in continuous learning about and with these communities.

In some schools, of course, teachers still face fairly homogeneous student populations and little exposure to racial, language, and religious diversity or the multicultural reality of the country as a whole. But even with limited ethnic and racial diversity, most schools have males and females from different religious and socioeconomic backgrounds. The ethic of social justice is just as important in these settings as in those with great ethnic and language diversity. To provide a well-rounded and balanced curriculum for these students, you will need to work harder at bringing different perspectives to presentations and discussions. You probably will need to develop innovative strategies for providing direct exposure to diversity and issues of equality.

Gender-Sensitive Education

In the past, most girls and young women were prepared for the traditional female roles of wife and mother rather than for the male roles of wage earner and head of household. They were prepared for lower-paying "women's jobs" such as teacher, nurse, child care worker, librarian, or health care worker. When they had to become the primary wage earner after the loss of a husband through divorce or death, women were at a significant disadvantage. They lacked the required skills or experiences necessary for jobs in which they could earn a wage high enough to maintain a comfortable living. However, over the past twenty-five years many women have broken those patterns.

Over 40 percent of the graduates from medical, dental, and law schools today are women.[8] Men, on the other hand, are still not as likely as women to work in jobs that were traditionally female. As in the past, society continues to need bright and committed males and females in the education profession.

The rigid definitions of gender roles that remain in some jobs, schools, religions, and ethnic groups limit the options and potential of both males and females. Men and women do not prepare for all professions at the same rate. Only 33 percent of the graduates in theology are women.[9] Fewer females earn computer science and engineering degrees. Even though more women are entering high-income professions that historically were dominated by men, women remain overrepresented at the other end of the income scale.

Schools have played an important role in helping young women realize their potential. Still, not all teachers or other school professionals are sensitive to gender differences that make a difference in learning. In some classrooms, students are separated and sorted by gender, reinforcing the stereotypical gender roles. Boys are expected to behave in one way, girls in another. Boys are expected to excel in sports competition, computer science, mathematics, and science. Girls are expected to perform better in English, reading, writing, and social studies.

If gender equity existed, females and males would be expected to participate at nearly the same rates in all courses, sports, and jobs. Let's look at some of today's realities:

- Girls and boys enroll in mathematics and science at about the same rate, but girls are more likely to stop with algebra II and less likely to take physics.
- Girls do not participate at the same rates as boys in computer courses; they are more likely to be in data entry and word-processing courses.
- Girls enroll in English at higher rates than boys; boys are more likely to be in remedial English courses.
- Both boys and girls from low-income families or ethnic backgrounds other than European are more likely to be in remedial classes than are affluent white students.
- Girls are more likely to be in gifted classes, but they drop out of them at higher rates than boys do.

Boys and Girls in Performance-Based Science Classrooms

STUDY PURPOSE/QUESTION: Do middle school girls and boys share equally in hands-on activities in science classes? Do performance behaviors account for changes in attitudes about science?

STUDY DESIGN: The researchers observed six middle school science classes in five schools twice a month, each month, for one academic year. Observers recorded students' behaviors as they worked with other students on hands-on activities. The number of male and female students was nearly equal and included European Americans, African Americans, Latino Americans, and Asian Americans.

STUDY FINDINGS: Both boys and girls exhibited leadership behaviors as shown in providing instructions to other members of the group or explaining a science concept. These leadership behaviors were generally predictors of positive science attitudes at the end of the year. However, girls who provided leadership at the same level as boys had lower perceptions about their science abilities at the end of the school year. Boys' perceptions of their abilities did not change. These perceptual differences did not have any real effect on grades or abilities. The involvement of girls in the hands-on activities did differ from the boys' involvement. Boys tended to manipulate the equipment more than girls did, relegating the girls to following the boys' directions. Possibly because they were not actively engaged in the science activity, girls sometimes became bored with the activity, not fully participating. Thus, the performance-based science classes did not guarantee equal participation in the science activity.

IMPLICATIONS: Developing science activities that are hands-on and performance-based helps to develop positive attitudes about science for both boys and girls. However, teachers need to figure out how to help boys learn to share the science activity more equitably with girls rather than controlling the equipment, shutting girls out of direct involvement in the activity. Otherwise, girls become bored and may develop a perception that they are not as capable in science as the boys. Since boys seem to shut girls out of these activities, teachers might sometimes group girls together to conduct the performance-based activities so they have opportunities to manipulate the equipment themselves.

Source: Jasna Jovanovic and Sally Steinbach King, "Boys and Girls in the Performance-Based Science Classroom: Who's Doing the Performing?" *American Educational Research Journal, 35*(3) (1998), pp. 477–496.

- Boys and girls are involved at about the same rate in advanced placement and honors courses except for physics.
- Girls earn equal or higher grades in all subjects.
- Males score higher on SAT and ACT tests used for college admission.[10]

To promote gender equity, females should be encouraged to be involved in mathematics, science, and computer science. Males should be encouraged to participate in areas in which they are underrepresented: the fine arts, foreign languages, advanced English, and the humanities.

A gender-sensitive education provides equity to boys and girls, young women and young men. It does not mean that males and females are always treated the same. Different instructional strategies may be needed for the two groups to ensure participation and learning. Understanding cultural differences among females and males is important in developing appropriate teaching strategies. Not all girls and young women respond to instruction in the same way. Their other group memberships intersect with their gender in determining their interactions with teachers and effective instructional strategies. Culturally relevant teaching will affirm students' gender and experiences in ways that promote learning for both males and females.

Teachers in gender-sensitive classrooms monitor interactions among girls and boys as well as their own interactions with the two genders. They intervene when necessary to equalize opportunities between them. If boys are not performing as well as girls in language arts or girls are not performing as well in mathematics, the challenge is to develop approaches that will improve their performance.

Different educational strategies that draw on students' cultural strengths may be needed to equalize performance in knowledge and skill development for girls and boys. Although competitive strategies are effective for many white boys, most girls and boys from other racial groups are more successful in collaborative settings. Instruction should include hands-on laboratory experiences, collaborative learning, practical applications, group work, and authentic learning to build on the learning styles of different students. The goal is to help both females and males learn the subject matter. Teachers will need to draw on multiple teaching strategies to reach this goal.

Education for Language Diversity

A growing number of immigrant students are populating schools in large cities. Even small cities and rural areas are now home to immigrant families and their children. In fact, nearly one in five students speak a language other than English at home. The rates are much higher for some groups. Sixty-five percent of Asian American children and 68 percent of Latino children are English language learners.[11]

The growing number of English language learners in U.S. schools calls for educators to understand language learning and how to help students learn English while they are learning math, science, and other subjects. Differences between the languages used at home and at school can lead to dissonance between students, their families, and school officials. Many students who enter school with limited English skills are not only trying to learn a second language but also adjusting to a new culture. This is particularly true for recent immigrants. Figures 4.1 and 4.2 show the percentage of students who speak a language other than English at home and have difficulty with English in school.

FIGURE 4.1

Students Who Speak a Language Other Than English at Home and Have Difficulty Speaking English

Source: U.S. Census Bureau, *Statistical Abstract of the United States: 2006.* Washington, DC: U.S. Government Printing Office, 2006, Table 222.

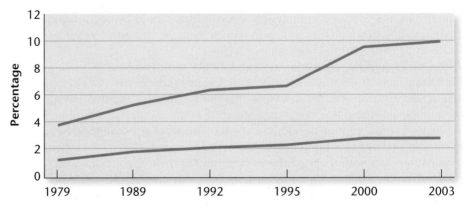

Speak a language other than English at home

Have difficulty speaking English

FIGURE 4.2

Students Who Have Difficulty Speaking English by Region of the Country

Source: U.S. Census Bureau, *Statistical Abstract of the United States: 2006.* Washington, DC: U.S. Government Printing Office, 2006, Table 222.

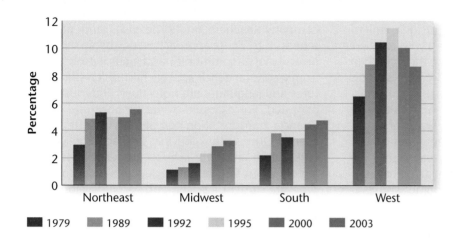

One perspective for teaching English language learners promotes **bilingual education.** Another perspective calls for total immersion of English language learners in English-only classrooms. Other educational strategies bridge these two perspectives as the best way to educate ELLs. Members of Congress, state legislators, and local school board members regularly debate strategies for teaching English language learners. The debate centers on whether to use students' native languages in instruction. Many school districts and some states require bilingual education if a specific number of students who speak the same native language are enrolled in a school. This approach requires teachers who are fluent in both English and the native language.

The No Child Left Behind legislation calls for ELLs to become English proficient and meet standards as measured by standardized tests. Some states have limited language assistance to one year through voter initiatives, known as the Unz Initiatives for its promoter, businessman Ron Unz. The problem is that research shows that one year of English instruction is generally not enough time to prepare ELLs to be proficient enough to succeed academically in classes taught only in English. The amount of time required for English proficiency "depends on multiple factors, including the child's age, level and quality of prior schooling of the child, parents' education level, type and quality of instruction provided, the child's exposure to English in his or her community, and quality of the teachers."[12] For most ELLs, at least five years is required to develop language skills and academic achievement equal to native English speakers.[13]

There are at least six different approaches to teaching academic content to English language learners.[14] Sheltered instruction, newcomer programs, and transitional bilingual education approaches are assimilationist in that they are designed to integrate students into the dominant or mainstream culture. Although the native language may be used for instruction early in the program, the goal is to move to English-only instruction as soon as possible, usually between one and four years. In sheltered instruction, teachers teach the academic subjects at the same time that they are teaching English to students. The newcomer programs are designed for new immigrants who have limited or no experience with English and often have

bilingual education

An education strategy that uses English and the native language of students in classroom instruction.

Communicating with Parents of English Language Learners

At least 13 percent of all people over five years old in the United States use a language other than English at home. Many parents who do not speak English fluently are reluctant to visit schools because of their limited English skills. The reasons for not meeting with teachers are not that parents do not care about their children and their education. This dissonance between schools and parents is exacerbated by the inability of most teachers to understand the language and culture of some parents. Parents often are embarrassed and misunderstood by school officials. They sometimes cannot attend school events or conferences because they are working, and employers will not give them the time off. Or they may have young children at home who cannot be left alone while the parent goes to school.

How then can teachers communicate with parents about their children and their social and academic development in school? Teachers might know only English and the parents only Spanish, Farsi, French, Japanese, Hmong, or Swahili. Even if the teacher visited the student's home, communications would be limited and possibly misinterpreted. Written notes or phone messages in English would have to be translated by parents, or for them by the child, placing the burden again on the family.

Some schools have hired bilingual teachers and aides who can help bridge the language differences. When the number of bilingual education professionals is limited, schools may hire community liaisons who work with parents and teachers to bridge language and cultural differences. These community liaisons may accompany teachers on home visits and parents on school visits. These approaches may begin to affirm the diversity of a community and help it to move away from a cultural deficit approach in which students' cultures and languages are not valued and must be compensated. For example, some schools have begun to arrange transportation for parents to attend school events. Others are using ESL to teach English to parents before and after school. Students are the benefactors when families and educators work together to promote student learning and social development.

Questions for Reflection

1. How will you communicate with parents who speak a language different from your own?

2. How will you learn about the resources available in your school district to assist you in working with families whose primary language is not English?

3. How can you ensure that you don't misunderstand parents when their language and culture are different from your own?

4. What responsibility do teachers have to understand and become comfortable in a culture other than their own?

To answer these questions on-line and e-mail your answers to your professor, go to Chapter 4 of the companion website (www.ablongman.com/johnson14e) and click on Professional Dilemma.

English as a second language (ESL)

An educational strategy for teaching English to speakers of other languages without the use of the native language for instruction.

limited literary skills in their native language. These programs are sometimes found within a school; some school districts have one or more schools specifically for new immigrants. The most successful programs are those which students attend for as many as four years.[15] Teachers using these two approaches—sheltered and newcomer—should have knowledge and skills in **English as a second language (ESL).**

In transitional bilingual education, academic subjects are taught in the native language as students learn English. Gradually, more and more of the instruction is conducted in English. After a few years, students in transitional bilingual education move into classes with instruction in English only. Developmental bilingual education, by contrast, supports bilingualism and literacy in both English and the native language. Both languages have equal status, and both are used for instructional purposes.

Two immersion language programs use a second language for instruction and help students understand and appreciate a second culture while maintaining their own native culture and language. Foreign/second language immersion is designed for English speakers who want to learn a second language in a classroom that uses

Spanish, French, Japanese, Farsi, or another language for instruction. Two-way immersion is used to develop bilingualism in all students as language training is integrated with academic instruction. Classes usually have an equal number of English speakers and speakers of another language.

As a school decides the appropriate approach for teaching English language learners, parents must be involved in the discussions and decisions. Together, educators and parents will have to decide whether they want to promote bilingualism among all students or only among the English language learners. Is the goal for English language learners to become competent in both English and their native language or to move into English-only instruction as soon as possible? Each approach has learning implications for students and cost implications for school systems.

Journal for Reflection

1. What gender differences have you observed in classrooms? What could the teacher have done to help boys and girls perform at the same levels?

2. Why do you or why do you not support bilingual education for ELLs?

3. Which of the six instructional strategies discussed in this section do you think would be most effective for ELLs? Why?

Teachers as Social Activists

Multicultural education requires educators to be active participants in the educational process. Social justice, democracy, power, and equity are more than concepts to be discussed in class; they are guides for action in the classroom, school, and community. Educators become advocates not only for their own empowerment but also for that of students and other powerless groups.

CROSS-REFERENCE
Teachers as change agents and leaders from a philosophical perspective are discussed in Chapter 10.

Never doubt that a small group of thoughtful, committed citizens can change the world. Indeed it is the only thing that ever has.

Margaret Mead

Thinking Critically

Educators who think critically ask questions about why inequities exist in their classrooms and schools. They wonder why girls are responding differently than boys to science lessons. But they don't stop with wondering; they explore and try alternatives to engage the girls in the subject matter. They realize that teaching equitably does not mean teaching everyone the same way. Nor, however, does it mean using thirty different lesson plans each tailored to the individual learning style and cultural background of each student. Teaching equitably may mean helping students function effectively across the multiple cultural styles used by students in the classroom. Teachers who think critically figure out ways to build on the diverse cultural backgrounds and experiences of students, acknowledge the value of that diversity, and help them all learn.

Critical thinkers are able to challenge the philosophy and practices of the dominant society that are not supportive of equity, democracy, and social justice. They are open to alternative views; they are not limited by narrow parochialism that is based on absolutes and the notion of one right way. They question content for accuracy and biases, and they value multiple perspectives. They seek explanations for the educational meanings and consequences of race, class, and gender.

Modeling Equity in the Classroom

Caring and fairness are two qualities that students praise when describing successful teachers. Students know whether teachers view them as special or as incompetent or worthless. Teacher perceptions may be based on a student's personal characteristics; sometimes they are based on group membership. A teacher may feel that homeless children who arrive in dirty clothes, smelling badly, have little chance of success. Teachers may pity children from one-parent homes and blame their lack

Teachers must model equity in the classroom if education that is multicultural is to become a reality.

of academic achievement on not having two parents. Teachers may ignore English language learners until they learn English. Are these fair practices?

A school that provides multicultural education will not tolerate such unjust practices by teachers. Both the classroom and the school will be models of democracy in which all students are treated equitably and fairly. In such a school, teachers and instructional leaders confront their own biases and develop strategies for overcoming them in their own interactions with students and colleagues. They learn to depend on one another for assistance, both in developing a culturally relevant curriculum and in ensuring that students are not subject to discrimination. As a result, students learn to respect differences and to interact within and across ethnic and cultural groups as they struggle for social justice in the school and the community.

Teachers sometimes give more help to some students than to others. They might praise some students while correcting and disciplining others. Their expectations for academic success may differ depending on students' family income or ethnic group. However, most teachers do not deliberately set out to discriminate against students, especially in any harmful way. The problem is that everyone has been raised in a racist, sexist, and classist society in which biases are so embedded that it is difficult for people to recognize anything other than the very overt signs. Teachers often need others to point out their discriminatory practices.

A good pattern to begin to develop even now, early in your teacher education program, is to reflect on your practice and the practice of teachers you observe. Among the questions that you might ask are these:

- Are students from different gender, economic, and ethnic groups treated differently? What are the differences?
- Are there fewer discipline and learning problems among the students who are from the same background as the teacher? What is contributing to the differences?
- Do the least advantaged students receive the most assistance from the teacher? What are the differences in the instruction given to students from different groups?
- How well are male and female students from different ethnic and racial groups performing on state standardized tests? How well are students with disabilities performing? How is the school making test-taking accommodations for English language learners and students with disabilities?

A key to ensuring that interactions with students are equitable is the ability to recognize one's own biases and make appropriate adjustments. Educators must be able to admit that they sometimes make mistakes. An ability to reflect on one's mistakes and why they occurred should lead to better teaching.

Making Schools Democratic

Democratic schools are ones in which students practice democracy by being active participants in their education. These schools encourage the exchange and exploration of ideas from multiple perspectives. They develop the individual and collective capacity of students to develop possibilities for resolving problems. Teachers in democratic classrooms teach students to analyze real-world ideas, problems, and policies. Students are involved in community issues, collecting and analyzing data, and often become involved in changes within the community. The goal is to understand that democracy is not so much an ideal to be pursued as an idealized set of values that we must live by and that must guide our life as a society.

Democratic schools reflect democratic structures and processes and include a curriculum that provides students with democratic experiences. These schools require students, teachers, parents, and community members to be active participants in the educational process. Equity undergirds the structure of democratic schools. All students have access to all programs. Tracking, biased testing, and other practices that deny access to some students are eliminated. The emphasis on grades, status, test scores, and winning is replaced with an emphasis on cooperation and concern for the common good. Those involved in this democratic project also work toward the elimination of inequities in the broader community as well as in the school.

A democratic curriculum encourages multiple perspectives and voices in the materials used and the discussions that ensue. It respects differences in viewpoints. It does not limit information and study to the areas chosen by members of the dominant group. It includes discussions of inequities in society and challenges students and teachers to engage actively in eliminating them. Establishing a democratic classroom or school is not an easy undertaking.

Sometimes colleagues and parents resist it; some people believe that teachers should be all-knowing authorities who exert control over their students. Those who want schools to prepare students for social efficiency are supportive of stratified systems using grades and test scores to sort students into tracks that prepare them for future jobs. Supporters of schooling as a route to social mobility expect competition to determine which students deserve the greatest rewards, such as acceptance into gifted programs or admission to prestigious colleges. Democratic schools, on the other hand, support equity, equal access, and equal opportunity for all students.

Teaching for Social Justice

Culturally relevant teaching helps students struggle in class with social problems and issues that many students face daily in their lives both within and outside of school. Racism, sexism, classism, prejudice, and discrimination are felt differently by students

Teaching for social justice helps students struggle through social problems and discrimination that many people face daily.

Global Perspectives

Social Justice in the Canadian Context

As early as 1971, Canada adopted a national government policy that supported multicultural ideals in education. This action was followed by each province developing its own version of the policy in order to bring harmony across ethnic and racial groups. Public debate is questioning the concept of multiculturalism as some citizens call for a return to assimilation, restriction of immigration, and upholding the traditional values of the dominant group. Amid these attacks, researchers are arguing whether the traditional multicultural education should be replaced with antiracist education. Other scholars "have depicted social justice education as a highly divisive field of study, describing conflicts between MC [multicultural] and AR [antiracist] camps in dichotomous, oppositional terms."[16]

The supporters of antiracist education focus on the structure of the education system and on power relationships between the dominant European Canadian society and powerless indigenous and immigrant groups. The traditional multicultural model in Canada has included short-term programs and supplemental curriculum materials to help students understand the cultures of different groups in the country. The antiracist camp accuses the multiculturalists of not critically addressing issues of oppression and racism in the country.

For the most part, social justice activists are aware of these academic debates and find them relevant to their work. However, while the academic debates flourish, most social justice activists are incorporating aspects of both antiracist and multicultural education into their work in schools.[17]

Questions for Reflection

1. What is the difference between multicultural education and antiracist education in Canada?

2. How would you place the conflict between multicultural education and antiracist education in a U.S. context?

of color than by members of the dominant group. Anger, denial, guilt, and affirmation of identity are critical elements of learning about and struggling with the pernicious practices that permeate most institutions. Although it is sometimes difficult to discuss these issues in classrooms, doing so means they are confronted in a system based on diversity and equality.

Most students of color, females, low-income students, students with disabilities, and gay students have probably already experienced discrimination in some aspect of their lives. They may have not acknowledged it, or they may be angry or frustrated by it. On the other hand, many students from the dominant group have never experienced discrimination and often do not believe that it exists. In most cases, they do not see themselves as advantaged; they do not think that they receive any more benefits from society than anyone else. These students will have a difficult time fighting social injustices if they have neither experienced them nor become aware of their existence. Are they receiving a good education if they are never exposed to the injustices that do exist or helped to confront their own biases?

In teaching for social justice, teachers help students understand the inequalities, oppression, and power struggles that are realities in society. But this kind of teaching does not stop there. It provides hope for a world that is more equitable and socially just. Students and teachers become engaged in confronting injustice and working to remove the obstacles that prevent equality as an academic subject is studied.

Students learn to apply the knowledge and skills they are learning to a local, regional, or global issue. The learning becomes authentic as it is related to the world that students care about. Students can take on community projects that examine pollution in their neighborhoods, political stances in their regional area, or the cost of food in their neighborhood versus another part of town. Students and teachers who tackle social justice as an integral part of their classroom work are providing multicultural education and reconstructionism. They are doing more than learning about the world; they are also working toward making it better for those who are least advantaged.

Journal for Reflection

1. Why is critical thinking important for teachers?

2. What does teaching for social justice mean to you?

3. How would you define a school that is democratic? What practices would you see in such a classroom?

Summary

ROLES OF SCHOOLS.   Theories of functionalism, conflict, and resistance provide different descriptions of the role of schools in reproducing culture and society. Reconstructionism suggests that schools can transform society by serving as model democratic and equitable institutions.

PURPOSES OF SCHOOLS.   Schools serve many purposes, including the development of citizenship, preparation for work, the development of academic and social competence, and the transmission of the culture to another generation.

VALUES IN SCHOOLS.   Not all parents and communities agree on the values and content to be taught in schools. These different perspectives can lead to conflicts among groups and school officials that sometimes have to be resolved in the courts.

MULTICULTURAL EDUCATION.   Multicultural education is based on the principles of democracy, social justice, and equality. The goal is to ensure that all students participate equally in the education system. Educators value the diversity of students as they strive to provide educational equality in which all students are provided challenging and stimulating learning experiences.

CHALLENGES IN MULTICULTURAL CLASSROOMS.   Boys and girls are often treated differently by teachers in ways that may advantage one group over the other. Gender-sensitive education helps teachers understand these differences and provide an equitable education to both. Schools work with English language learners along a continuum of instructional strategies that range from bilingual education to immersion in English-only classrooms.

TEACHERS AS SOCIAL ACTIVISTS.   Democratic schools and classrooms involve parents, students, teachers, administrators, and community members as partners in the design and delivery of education. The policies and practices of democratic schools promote equity for all students, abandoning practices that sort students and give privilege to those from advantaged backgrounds.

Discussion Questions

1. You may be assigned to a school in which the community monitors the curriculum to ensure that their values are reflected. What curriculum content could spark debates in the community? How important will it be to keep parents and other community members informed?
2. Diversity, equality, and social justice are the major tenets of multicultural education. What conditions and practices in schools suggest that these tenets are not the principles that undergird the educational system as you know it? What are signs that these tenets are being addressed in schools?
3. Democratic schools validate the voices of students as they actively participate in their education. How do you think student voices can be effectively included in the classroom? What are the potential benefits and perceived dangers of allowing student voices to be an integral part of instruction?
4. Reflect on your elementary and secondary education and identify ways that your teachers delivered a culturally relevant curriculum. Would students from cultural backgrounds other than your own agree with your assessment? Why or why not?
5. Policymakers and politicians disagree on the importance of helping English language learners maintain their native languages. What is your position on this issue? What programs would schools provide to ELLs if your position became policy in a school district? What results would you expect if your position became a policy?

School-Based Observations

1. Visit an inner-city school and a rural or suburban school to observe how student voices are incorporated in classes. Record the nature of the dialogue between students and teachers and among students; describe the degree of equality across the voices and whether any significant patterns of differences emerge.
2. Determine how multicultural education is being integrated in the classes you are observing. You can collect data from interviews with teachers and students in addition to reviewing the textbooks being used.

Portfolio Development

1. For the subject and level that you plan to teach, describe appropriate culturally relevant content that could be included in a selected curriculum unit. Write a lesson plan that incorporates culturally relevant content.
2. Identify a list of five to ten criteria for determining whether educators in a school have seriously and successfully attended to diversity, equality, and social justice. Include a statement of the things you would observe to know that each criterion is being met.
3. Write a summary of what democracy means to you. How do common good and equality fit into your perception of democracy and a democratic school?

Preparing for Certification

TEACHING FOR EQUALITY

1. One of the topics covered in the Praxis II Principles of Learning and Teaching (PLT) test is "structuring lessons based on the needs and characteristics of diverse populations." In this chapter, you were encouraged to develop culturally relevant teaching skills, including building on cultural context, centering on the cultures of students, and validating student voices. Think about the subject or grade level that you plan to teach. How might you incorporate these three principles into your future teaching?
2. Answer the following multiple-choice question, which is similar to items in Praxis and other state certification tests.

James Bryant describes the focus of his U.S. history course: "I want students to know more than facts about history; I want them to understand the strengths and weaknesses of our country and be prepared to tackle social issues and challenge inequities in our society. I want students to become active citizens, committed to issues of social justice, human dignity, and human rights." Mr. Bryant's philosophy most closely resembles

A. reproduction theory
B. conflict theory
C. reconstructionism
D. functionalism

3. Answer the following short-answer question, which is similar to items in Praxis and other state certification tests. After you've completed your written response, use the scoring guide in the ETS *Test at a Glance* materials to assess your response. Can you revise your response to improve your score?

The hidden curriculum is the informal curriculum that defines the behaviors and attitudes of students and teachers. Give two examples of the hidden curriculum. Describe how each example might affect students from varied backgrounds or cultures differently.

Websites

www.edchange.org/multicultural/index.html The Multicultural Pavilion links teachers with others who are dealing with issues related to multicultural education.

www.naeyc.org The website of the National Association for the Education of Young Children provides a number of resources on teaching preschoolers and primary students from diverse racial and language groups as well as students with disabilities.

www.nameorg.org The website of the National Association for Multicultural Education includes definitions and policies for educators working in the field of multicultural education.

www.rethinkingschools.org The Rethinking Schools website was designed by a group of teachers who wanted to improve education in their own classrooms and schools as well as to help shape school reform that is humane, caring, multiracial, and democratic.

www.splcenter.org The Southern Poverty Law Center combats hate, intolerance, and discrimination through education and litigation against hate groups. It publishes *Teaching Tolerance,* which is available at no cost to teachers, and numerous other teaching resources.

Further Reading

Anti-Defamation League. (2000). *Hate Hurts: How Children Learn and Unlearn Prejudice.* New York: Author. A guide for parents and educators on understanding and respecting differences and fighting hate against others. The booklet includes stories about children who have experienced hate and provides guidelines for challenging biased materials.

Grant, Carl A., and Sleeter, Christine E. (2006). *Turning on Learning: Five Approaches for Multicultural Teaching Plans for Race, Class, Gender, and Disability* (4th ed.). Columbus, OH: Merrill. A companion to *Making Choices for Multicultural Education: Five Approaches to Race, Class, and Gender* (2006), providing lesson plans and illustrations for incorporating multicultural education into the curriculum and classroom.

Multicultural Perspectives. The magazine of the National Association for Multicultural Education. A quarterly publication designed to advance the conversation about multicultural education. Each issue includes reviews of new resources for teachers.

Rethinking Schools. A news journal on teaching for equity and social justice published by Rethinking Schools. An activist publication written by teachers, parents, and students who care about equity and social justice in urban schools. Articles address current topics affecting students and schools and strategies for reforming classrooms and schools.

Teaching Tolerance. A magazine for teachers by the Southern Poverty Law Center. A publication for and by teachers for fighting hate and intolerance and fostering equity, respect, and understanding across diverse groups.

(mylabschool
Where the classroom comes to life!

Go to Allyn and Bacon's MyLabSchool (www.mylabschool.com) and complete the following activity for Chapter 4. Click on **MLS Stimulations,** then click on **Teaching and Learning in New Mexico.**

Chapter 5
Organizing and Paying
for American
Education in a
Changing World

Chapter 6
Legal Perspectives of
Education

GOVERNANCE, ORGANIZATION, AND SUPPORT OF AMERICAN EDUCATION

Today's schools are undergoing a surprising amount of change. Regardless of the perspective that is taken, teachers, students, families and communities are being impacted by these changes. As will be described in Chapter 5, from an organizational perspective schools and school districts are being structured in new ways. Another perspective that also is described in Chapter 5 concerns different ways schools are paid for and the changes that result. A completely different perspective for viewing schools is the law, which is the topic of Chapter 6. From the U.S. Constitution to the Congress to state legislatures to local school boards statutes, rules and regulations shape what schools can and cannot do. Often, when there is disagreement over the direction of education, opponents will turn to the courts to obtain a final determination. The legal perspective also addresses the rights and responsibilities of teachers and students. Each of these perspectives—organizational, financial, and legal—directly affect the lives and work of teachers.

CHAPTER 5

Organizing and Paying for American Education in a Changing World

Push Is on for Magnet School at Jefferson to Attract Students

By Sherry Saavedra, Staff Writer, *The San Diego Union Tribune*, May 4, 2006

CARLSBAD—A week after trustees approved the conversion of Jefferson Elementary into a magnet school, officials are well into an aggressive campaign to attract students, while educators at overcrowded campuses are hoping for relief.

School officials are distributing more than 2,000 brochures about the new school of choice to prospective parents, while volunteers have signed up to do public relations.

The first informational meeting for the public is scheduled for 7 p.m. Tuesday at the school, 3743 Jefferson St.

The magnet will feature an International Baccalaureate program, which exists in 120 countries and is most commonly associated with high schools.

At the high school level, students tackle an accelerated college preparatory curriculum with a global perspective to earn a prestigious IB diploma. In California, there are 66 IB high schools, but only four IB elementaries.

At Jefferson, lessons in each subject will be infused with a worldwide perspective, and students may begin learning Spanish as early as kindergarten.

Magnet schools use certain themes to enhance their program and draw students from other parts of a district.

In this case, every student at Jefferson would take part in IB, and school officials hope to lure more students to the campus. The school has suffered declining enrollment, from 850 students in 2000 to 500 today.

Principal Carol Van Vooren said that every summer, Jefferson loses more students. Parents with children move to less-expensive communities, and people without kids replace them, she said.

"There are some new developments in town that are just bursting with kids, but we don't have any new homes here," she said.

The hotbed of housing development in other parts of Carlsbad Unified School District has Calavera Hills, Aviara Oaks and Pacific Rim elementaries brimming with students.

Devin Vodicka, principal of Calavera Hills, said his school was built for 490 students, but is serving 615. And while the campus is undergoing construction that will add six classrooms, the school's growth will likely outpace the new classroom space, he said.

The crowding has forced the school to close computer labs, hold special education classes in offices, and conduct tutoring in hallways.

"Hopefully the program at Jefferson will reduce our high enrollment," he said.

The situation at Aviara Oaks is more dire. The school, built to accommodate about 675 students, has 930. To cope with the crowding, the school has instituted three different start times, and five recesses and lunch periods.

Principal Sheila Maddox said the magnet will give Jefferson a great program and bring schools like Aviara Oaks some enrollment relief.

Students from jampacked schools will get preference in admittance decisions to Jefferson.

The magnet's drawing card will be its kindergarten program, which will be extended to a full day and will have smaller class sizes capped at 20 students all day.

In Carlsbad Unified, the district has had to cope with budget constraints by curtailing its program to reduce kindergarten class sizes. Most kindergarten classes have low student–teacher ratios for only part of the day.

Van Vooren said Jefferson can accept up to 60 kindergartners and 350 students in all grades from other schools.

The principal plans to market the program at orientation meetings for prospective kindergarten parents at crowded schools. A Jefferson parent couple who own a marketing business created the brochures and are assisting with public relations efforts. Brochures are being distributed to local preschools.

Parents have until the last day of school, which is June 15, to apply.

"The goal for the first year is to attract 50 students (from other schools), and if we do that we will consider it a success," said Suzanne O'Connell, assistant superintendent of instructional services.

The program will cost $60,000 a year for three years to implement. The district is applying for a federal grant to help pay for it and to fund new magnets at other campuses.

Part of the implementation involves teacher training on how to help students think critically, ask questions and be compassionate.

The IB program weaves a global perspective into all subjects. Nancy Forster, administrator for the California International Baccalaureate Organization, said, "For math, a teacher might ask students, 'Where did we get these numbers from? What are these symbols? Did you know we got zero from India?'"

Forster said IB students are encouraged to develop a sense of compassion through community service and a worldwide perspective of human hardships.

Van Vooren said a teacher might expand a lesson on the Pilgrims to other countries where people have settled for religious and political reasons.

"A lot of kids think that we have the only pilgrims," she said. "But we don't. There are groups like this all over the world."

Van Vooren said the program is a good fit for Jefferson, where 42 percent of the students are non-native English speakers and 73 percent are Hispanic, according to state Education Department records for the 2004–05 school year. Most of the teachers are bilingual and well-traveled internationally.

Questions for Reflection

1. Before reading this article what did you know about magnet schools and IB programs?

2. Would you want to teach in Jefferson Elementary School? Why or why not?

3. Magnet schools are offered to provide parents and students with choices. What are some of the implications for parents, students, and other schools and teachers when a magnet school opens?

4. Do you think that an IB program can work in an elementary school? Why or why not?

Source: Reprinted with permission.

INTASC

Learning Outcomes

After reading and studying this chapter, you should be able to:

1. Describe the organizational structure of schools, school districts, and the authority relationships among schools, states, and the federal government. (INTASC 10: Collaboration)

2. Analyze pro and con arguments presented for increasing school choice. (INTASC 10: Collaboration)

3. Describe the relationship of teachers to their principal and how the responsibilities of the principal relate to those of the school district

superintendent and the school board. (INTASC 10: Collaboration)

4. Summarize the key sources of funding for public schools and issues related to overreliance on any one of these sources. (INTASC 9: Reflection; INTASC 10: Collaboration)

5. Describe the underlying theme related to the large number of states that have court cases

dealing with school finance. (INTASC 9: Reflection; INTASC 10: Collaboration)

6. Compare the spending for public schools in the United States with that of other developed countries. (INTASC 9: Reflection; INTASC 10: Collaboration)

This chapter addresses education in the United States from organizational and financial perspectives. Understanding schools from the point of view of teachers, the community, and students is common sense. So too is developing an understanding of schools in terms of how they are staffed and organized and how they are paid for. Although complex, school organization has an explainable pattern. On top of the local pattern is the organization of education within each state. Increasingly, the federal government is influencing the way schools operate. The combination of organizations and structures from local schools to the state and federal levels comprises the U.S. system of education. The second perspective developed in this chapter views schools in terms of how the education system is funded. The funds to finance schooling come from several different sources. Each of these sources brings with it certain advantages and particular problems.

The Structure of the American Education System

Descriptions of the U.S. education system generally start at the *top* of the organization chart, with the U.S. Department of Education; move *down* through the state structures; and ultimately arrive at the school district and school levels. This *top-down* approach reflects, in an organizational sense, the fact that it is easier to understand the pieces when you first have a view of the whole. Also, the top-down approach indicates that one has more authority and responsibility the further up one is in the structure. In many ways, this is true. However, in education, unlike many businesses, the "bottom" is composed of professionals (teachers and principals) who know as much or more about their business as those who are more removed from day-to-day life in classrooms. Therefore, teachers and principals correctly argue, they should have a great deal of say in determining what happens with their students on a day-to-day basis. Our decision to start this chapter with a description of schools, rather than at the federal level, is in some ways a symbolic statement that teachers can be viewed as being at the top.

To avoid many of the problems implied in a vertical (top-down) picture of the education system, some theorists have advocated a horizontal perspective, as represented in Table 5.1. One important emphasis of this horizontal **policy-to-practice continuum** is that for education to improve, the agencies and people at each point along the continuum have to do their job well. A second critical feature is that all have to trust people and agencies at other points along the continuum. This means,

policy-to-practice continuum

The range of roles and responsibilities for education, from the development of national policy to teaching in classrooms.

TABLE 5.1	The Policy-to-Practice Continuum in the U.S. Education System					
POLICY						PRACTICE
Federal	State	Intermediate	District	School	Classroom
President	Governor	Director	Superintendent	Principal	Teacher
Congress	Legislature	Board	Board	Site council	Students
Secretary	Chief state school officer			Teachers Staff	Parents
U.S. Department of Education	State department of education		District office staff	Community	

for example, that teachers have to develop an understanding of the functions and purposes of other parts of the education system. Teachers cannot stay isolated in their classrooms, unaware of the issues and expectations of the school, the school district, the state, and increasingly the federal government. At the other end of the continuum, it is important that policymakers learn more about the work of teachers and what goes on in schools.

Another important organizational concept to keep in mind is the difference between line and staff relationships. In any organization, some people will have the job of being supervisors, bosses, managers, or directors. Other people will report to these persons. The supervisor typically has the authority, at least to some degree, to direct, monitor, and evaluate the work of the subordinate. When one person has this type of authority over another, there is a **line relationship.** But when there is no formal supervisory authority of one person over the other, they have a **staff relationship.** This distinction becomes important in education because in many instances it is not clear or absolute who has the authority or responsibility to direct the work of others. For example, teachers, as professionals, can legitimately claim more independence than can employees of other organizations. But teachers are not completely free to do whatever they want. If they were, the system of education would break down, at least in the experience of the students who must move through it.

The Organization of Schools

The basic building block of the U.S. education system is the school. To an amazing extent, schools are organized in the same way in each state. In fact, schools are organized pretty much the same in other countries too.

Each school consists of a set of classrooms, with corridors for the movement of students, and a central office. It has one or more large spaces for a cafeteria and gymnasium/auditorium. The school has outside spaces for a playground, staff parking, and a driveway for dropping off and picking up students. Wherever you go, you will find this basic architecture.

This typical design of schools is frequently criticized for resembling an egg crate. If you viewed a school building with the roof off, you would see that it resembled an egg carton: a series of cells or pockets with routes running between them. Some educational critics see this architecture as interfering with the need to introduce new educational practices. For example, the walls restrict communication between teachers and channel the flow of student traffic.

line relationship

An organizational arrangement in which a subordinate is directly responsible to a supervisor.

staff relationship

An organizational arrangement in which one party is not under the direct control or authority of another.

Even when a school is built with modest attempts to change the interior space, teachers and students are able to preserve the egg-crate concept. For example, you may have visited an elementary school that had an open-space design. Instead of self-contained classrooms, there might be an open floor plan equivalent in size to three or four classrooms. However, if you observed the arrangement of furniture, bookshelves, and screens, you probably noted that teachers and students had constructed zones and areas that were equivalent to three or four self-contained classrooms.

This is not meant to criticize teachers for how they have adapted to new school architectures; rather, it is meant to point out how the organization of the space parallels the activities of the people who use it. There are many good reasons for organizing schools around self-contained classrooms. And in the case of the open-space concept, the noise from three or four teachers and 90 to 120 students can be so disruptive that little learning can occur. One key to the successful use of open-space plans, then, is to be sure the building is designed in ways that control and dampen noise.

The physical arrangement of a school into classrooms has organizational as well as instructional implications. For example, it is easy for teachers to be isolated in their classrooms. This geographic isolation contributes to their not knowing about or becoming engaged with issues that affect the whole school. Geographic isolation can affect the school as a whole too. The school staff might not be aware of community concerns or of what is going on in other schools across the district. Teachers and administrators must make deliberate efforts to learn about other parts of the education system.

> A school can create a "coherent" environment, a climate, more potent than any single influence—teacher, class, family, neighborhood—so potent for at least six hours a day it can override almost everything else in the lives of children.
>
> **Ron Edmonds**

School-Based Personnel

The most obvious adult role in schools is that of teachers. Once you stop and think about it, you will discover a number of other important adult roles, each of which is important for teacher (and teacher education candidate) success.

PRINCIPALS

The principal is in charge of the school. In law the principal is the final authority at the school. The principal is typically responsible for instructional leadership, community relationships, staff (including teachers, secretaries, and custodians), teacher selection and evaluation, pupil personnel, building and grounds, budgets, administration of personnel, provisions of contracts, administration of the attendance center office, and business management. The principal has a line relationship with the school district superintendent. In larger school districts, the principal may have an intermediate supervisor, such as an assistant superintendent or a director of elementary or secondary education.

Principals' tasks and responsibilities are expanding. For example, there has been a push to increase teacher and parent participation in making school decisions. This pressure has led to the creation of special committees of teachers and parents to work with the principal. This approach is called **site-based decision making (SBDM),** or school-based management (SBM). SBDM permits an individual school within a district to be more involved in decisions related to the educational operations of that school—for example, budgeting, personnel selection, and curriculum design.

ASSISTANT PRINCIPALS

Larger elementary schools and most junior high schools, middle schools, and high schools have one or more additional administrators. Normally, they are called assistant principals, although sometimes in high schools they are titled vice principals. Large high schools will have several assistant or vice principals and other administrators that have "director" or "dean" titles, such as director of athletics and dean of

site-based decision making (SBDM)

A school governance process that gives greater voice to teachers, parents, and community representatives in school policies.

The principal is responsible for the actions of all school personnel, and must work with committees of parents and teachers.

students. These administrators share the tasks of the principal and provide additional avenues of communication between teachers, students, staff, parents, community, and the district office. In elementary schools, the job differentiation between the assistant principal and the principal is less clear, and both administrators will be a part of most operations. In the high school setting, specific roles and tasks will frequently be assigned to the different administrator roles. For example, one assistant principal might handle discipline or the evaluation of some teachers. In most districts, each teacher must be observed formally. This activity takes more time than the principal has available, so the assistant principal(s) observes some teachers. Usually, the principal concentrates on observing the new teachers because he or she makes the recommendation on rehiring beginning teachers.

DEPARTMENT HEADS AND TEAM LEADERS

Elementary schools normally have another, less formal level of leadership: grade-level or team leaders. These are full-time teachers who assume a communication and coordination role for their grade level(s) or team. Junior high schools and high schools have department chairs. Normally, departments are organized around the major subject areas (mathematics, science, English, and social studies) and the cocurricula (athletics and music). Teachers are members of one of the departments, and regular meetings are held to plan curriculum and to facilitate communication. In middle schools, the leaders of interdisciplinary teams likely serve in the same way. In each case, these department heads or team leaders meet with the principal from time to time and meet regularly with their teachers.

TEACHERS

The single largest group of adults in the school is the teachers. A typical elementary school has from fifteen to thirty-five teachers, and a large high school may have more than one hundred. Teachers are busy in their classrooms working with their students, and this is where the egg-crate architecture of schools can be a problem. Unless special mechanisms are used, such as team leaders or department chairs, individual teachers easily become isolated from the school as a whole. The self-contained classroom architecture and the work of attending to twenty to forty students in the classroom give each teacher little time or opportunity to communicate with other adults. As a consequence, the principal and all the teachers need to work hard with the other members of the school staff to facilitate communication. All must make an effort to work together to continually improve the school.

SCHOOL SUPPORT STAFF

A school has other personnel who support the administrators and teachers. One of the most important of these supporting roles is filled by the school secretary. Every teacher and principal will advise you to be sure to develop a good working relationship with the school secretary, who is at the nerve center of the running of the school. When a student has a problem, when a teacher needs some materials, when the principal wants a piece of information from the files, or when a student teacher wants to know about parking a car, the first person to contact is the school secretary. Another useful education professional in most schools is the library media specialist. This person is a good instructional resource for teachers and certainly is key to students being able to access information and become skilled in using technology. A third important resource is the custodians. The cleanliness of your classroom and

Relevant Research

Does Class Size Make a Difference?

STUDY PURPOSE/QUESTION: Do students in the early grades who are assigned to smaller classes learn more each year and do better in their later years of schooling?

STUDY DESIGN: Beginning in the mid-1980s, the Tennessee legislature funded a multiyear study, which has become known as the Tennessee STAR (Student/Teacher Achievement Ratio) Project. This long-term, statewide study included 79 schools, 328 classrooms, and about 6,300 students. Student achievement was compared in three types of classrooms: *standard classes* (a certificated teacher and more than 20 students); *supplemented classes* (one teacher and a full-time, non-certified teacher's aide); and *small classes* (one teacher and about 15 students). Since that time this study has continued to develop and is now seen as the "largest, best-designed field experiment that has ever appeared for education" (p. 6). Initially, student achievement was assessed in each of their first years in school. The students were then followed into the higher grades and their academic records were monitored.

STUDY FINDINGS: Results from *standard classes* and *supplemented classes* were quite similar. This means that there were few advantages in terms of student achievement from simply having untrained aides in classrooms. Results in the *small classes* were noteworthy. There were substantially higher levels of student achievement. The gains were also higher for those students who were in small classes for more years. In addition, the small class advantages were found for all types of students, and they were quite similar for boys and girls. Students from poverty, African American students, and inner-city students had even greater gains.

The findings from the follow-up studies as the small-class students moved into secondary schools are more significant. The small-class students earned better grades, fewer dropped out of school, fewer were retained, and once they were in high school, more took foreign languages and advanced-level courses, more were found to be in the top 25% of their classes, and more graduated from high school.

IMPLICATIONS: The findings from this large-scale, long-term study are clear: students who have small classes during their first four years of schooling achieve more in each of those years and do significantly better in the rest of their years in school. However, small classes means having approximately 15 students; simply reducing class size from the high 20s, or 30s, to the lower 20s does not fit the definition of small classes observed in this research. The skill of the teacher could be a factor as well. Still, with this level of support from research, one would think that states would expect all primary grade classes to be small. However, an analysis completed by Harris and Plank (2000) suggests that it would cost from $200 to $435 per student to universally reduce class size. This study looked only at the teacher salary costs. There are other major costs in adding small classes, including the cost of constructing additional classrooms. As often is the case, there are trade-offs. Research tends to support that students learn more in small classes, but it will cost significantly more to have more small classes.

Sources: Bruce J. Biddle and David C. Berliner, "What Research Says about Small Classes and Their Effects," in *Policy Perspectives,* San Francisco: WestEd, 2002; D. Harris and D. Plank, *Making Policy Choices: Is Class Size Reduction the Best Alternative?* East Lansing, MI: Education Policy Center, Michigan State University, 2000, retrieved from www.epc.mus.edu.

FIGURE 5.1

A School Organization Chart

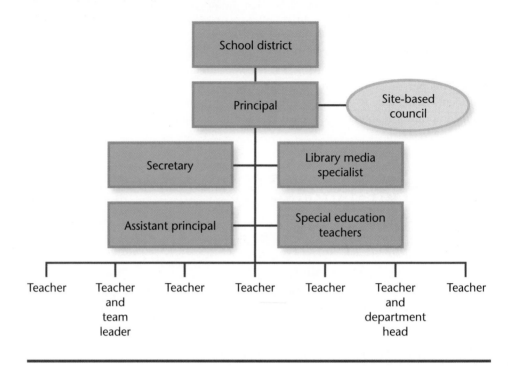

school depend on the efforts of the custodians, and they also can be helpful to teachers in locating supplies and moving furniture. Keep in mind that they observe and talk with students. Frequently, custodians and other support staff will know about something that is going on before the teachers do. Cafeteria workers are another group of adult workers in the school who can make a positive difference in how the school feels and functions.

THE SCHOOL ORGANIZATION CHART

All of the personnel described work in the school building. Their working relationships can be pictured in an **organization chart,** as shown in Figure 5.1. The principal is the single line authority for all of these adults *and* for all of the students! Most experts on organizations advocate that no more than five to seven people should be directly supervised by one administrator. Yet in nearly all schools, the principal is responsible for a minimum of thirty adults and several hundred students. In very large schools, the principal may have 200 to supervise. As you can see, the simple picture of top-down direction for education breaks apart when one considers the wide array of tasks and the sheer number of people at work in each school. A number of structures must exist for arranging the relationships among the varied role groups and facilitating coordination and communication.

organization chart

A graphic representation of the line and staff relationships of personnel in a school, school district, or other type of organization.

WHEN TO TALK TO WHOM

When teachers have an idea about the school or want to try something different, it is important for them to talk with their principal. If department heads or team leaders are in place, then the first discussions should be with them. In any organization, including schools, it is normal protocol to talk first with the person at the next level above. When there is a concern or problem, teachers should use the official administrative system and contact the principal. If this method fails and a serious problem exists, then a teacher may continue up the line by contacting the principal's supervisor: the assistant superintendent or the superintendent. If a serious disagreement occurs, then a teacher may file a grievance through procedures outlined in the negotiated contract. In any instance, a beginning teacher, or one who is new to the system, is wise to seek advice from experienced colleagues before taking action. In addition to knowing the system, one must know how the system works; colleagues and principals can be helpful in this regard.

Organization of the School District

Public schools in the United States are organized into school districts, which have similar purposes but widely different characteristics. Some districts provide only elementary education; others provide only high school education; still others provide both elementary and secondary education. For the 2003–04 school year, twenty-five school districts enrolled 100,000 or more students, whereas 2,994 districts enrolled fewer than 300 students. Only 1.8 percent of the districts have an enrollment in excess of 25,000 students, yet these districts enroll about 33 percent of the total student population. Thousands of school districts have only one school campus; in comparison, a few urban districts have as many as 500 schools.

The school district is governed by a school board, and its day-to-day operations are led by a superintendent. Each district has its own district office that houses an array of administrative, instructional, financial, and clerical support staff. As the state and federal levels of government have become active in setting educational agendas, a concomitant response has occurred at the district level in the form of an ever-increasing list of tasks that must be accomplished. These additional tasks have brought more functions and personnel to the district office.

LOCAL BOARD OF EDUCATION

Legal authority for operating local school systems is given to local boards of education through state statutes. The statutes prescribe specifically how school board members are to be chosen and what duties and responsibilities they have in office. The statutes also specify the terms of board members, procedures for selecting officers of the board, duties of the officers, and procedures for filling any vacancies. Local citizens serving as school board members, also called "trustees," are official agents of the state.

Most school boards in the United States are elected by popular vote in special nonpartisan elections. Some are appointed by city mayors. The percentage of appointed school boards is higher in school districts enrolling more than 25,000 pupils; yet even in three-fourths of these larger districts, the board members are elected.

Usually, teachers cannot be board members in the districts where they teach; however, they can be board members in districts where they live if they teach in different districts. The trend toward more teachers becoming board members most likely results from the goal of professional associations to secure seats on school boards.

POWERS AND DUTIES OF SCHOOL BOARDS

The powers and duties of school boards vary from state to state; the school codes of the respective states spell them out in detail. School boards' major function is the development of policy for the local school district—policy that must be in harmony with both federal and state law. Boards have only those powers granted or implied by statute that are necessary to carry out their responsibilities. These powers usually include the power to act as follows:

- Obtain revenue
- Maintain schools

- Purchase sites and build buildings
- Purchase materials and supplies
- Organize and provide programs of study
- Employ necessary workers and regulate their services
- Admit and assign pupils to schools and control their conduct

Some duties of school boards are **mandatory,** whereas others are **discretionary.** Some duties cannot be delegated. If, for example, the state has given boards the power to employ teachers, they must do this; the power cannot be delegated—even to a school superintendent. Boards can delegate much of the hiring process to administrators, however, and then act officially on administrative recommendations for employment. An illustration of a discretionary power left to the local board is the decision whether to participate in a nonrequired school program—for example, a program of competitive athletics. Another illustration of discretionary power is the decision to employ only teachers who exceed minimum state certification standards.

About 92 percent of the public school boards in the United States are elected by popular vote; about 7 percent are appointed.

SUPERINTENDENT OF SCHOOLS

One of the primary duties of the local board is to select its chief executive officer, the superintendent. There is one notable exception to the general practice of selection of the superintendent by school boards. In a few states, especially in the Southeast, school district superintendents are elected by the voters. In these situations, school superintendent selection is a political process just like that used for the election of mayors, county commissioners, some judges, and others. In either case, whether named by the board or elected by the people, the superintendent is responsible for the day-to-day operations of the school district, responding to school board members' interests, planning the district's budget, and defining the district's long-term aspirations. The superintendent is expected to be visible in the community and to provide overall leadership for the district.

THE CRITICAL IMPORTANCE OF LEADERSHIP

The importance of leadership by the superintendent and board members cannot be overemphasized. The quality of the educational program of a school district is influenced strongly by the leadership that the board of education and the superintendent provide. Without the communication and support of high expectations by boards and superintendents, high-quality education is not likely to be achieved. For example, offering curriculum programs over and above state-required minimums is discretionary. For a school district to excel, the local authorities, board members, and superintendent must convince their communities that specified school programs are needed and desirable.

CENTRAL OFFICE STAFF

The superintendent of schools works with a staff to carry out the program of education. Although the size of the staff varies with the school district, some kind of organization is necessary. Many school systems use a line and staff organization like that shown in Figure 5.2.

In this pattern, line officers hold the administrative power as it flows from the local board of education down to the pupils. Superintendents, assistant superintendents, and principals are line officers vested with authority over the people below them on the chart. Each person is directly responsible to the official above and must work through that person in dealing with a higher official. This arrangement is frequently referred to as the *chain of command.*

Administrative staff positions are shown in Figure 5.2 as branching out from the direct flow of authority. Staff includes librarians, instructional supervisors, guidance

mandatory

Duties and responsibilities that must be accomplished.

discretionary

Duties and responsibilities that may be done by the designated body or may be delegated to another.

FIGURE 5.2

Typical School District Line and Staff Organization

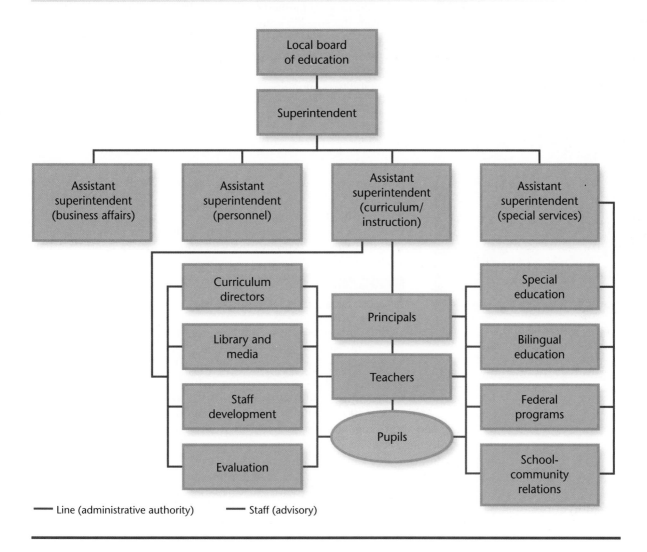

Line (administrative authority) ——— Staff (advisory)

officers, transportation officers, and others. They are responsible to their respective superiors but have no line authority over teachers. They assist and advise others from their special knowledge and abilities. Teachers are generally referred to as staff even though they are in the direct flow of authority. However, their authority in this arrangement prevails only over pupils.

Organization of Education at the State Level

In certain countries, such as Taiwan, the national constitution specifies responsibility for education; but the U.S. Constitution does not specifically provide for public education. The Tenth Amendment has been interpreted as granting this power to the states. As a consequence, the states are the governmental units in the United States charged with the responsibility for education. Local school districts, then, receive through state law their empowerment to administer and operate the school system for their communities. State legislatures, within the limits expressed by the

The states are the governmental units in the United States charged with the primary responsibility for education.

federal Constitution and by state constitutions, are the chief policymakers for education. State legislatures grant powers to state boards of education, state departments of education, chief state school officers, and local boards of education. These groups have only the powers granted to them by the legislature, implied powers from the specific grant of power, and the necessary powers to carry out the statutory purposes. The responsibilities and duties of intermediate units are also prescribed by the state legislatures. Figure 5.3 shows a typical state organization for education.

Stability, continuity, and leadership for education can come from the state board. However, as identified in Figure 5.3, many other individuals and groups are increasingly likely to engage in education issues. For example, many legislators have established records of heavy influence on the direction of education. Through their initiatives, new laws may affect any and all parts of the education system. There are "education governors" as well. Many state leaders have been very involved in supporting and attempting to shape education in their states. Suffice it to say, numerous participants and agencies and many kinds of influence have impacts on the shape and direction of the U.S. education system.

State Board of Education

State boards of education are both **regulatory** and **advisory.** Regulatory functions include the establishment of standards for issuing and revoking teaching licenses, the establishment of standards for approving and accrediting schools, and the development and enforcement of a uniform system for gathering and reporting educational data. Advisory functions include considering the educational needs of the state, both long and short range, and recommending to the governor and the legislature ways of meeting these needs. State boards of education, in studying school problems and in suggesting and analyzing proposals, can be invaluable to the legislature, especially because the legislature is under pressure to decide so many issues. A state board can provide continuity for an educational program that ordinary legislative procedures do not accommodate. A state board can also coordinate, supplement, and even replace study commissions appointed by a legislature for advising on educational matters. These commissions frequently include groups studying textbooks, finance, licensure, student learning standards, school building standards, and teacher education.

STATE BOARD MEMBERSHIP

regulatory

Functions for which the state board has the authority to establish rules and regulations that limit and permit action.

advisory

Functions and areas in which the state board can only offer suggestions and indicate preference for action.

Members of state boards of education get their positions in various ways. Usually, they are appointed by the governor, with confirmation by the senate, or they may be elected by the people, the legislature, or the local school board members in a regional convention—also with confirmation by the senate. The terms of members of state boards of education are usually staggered to avoid a complete changeover at any one time. Board members usually serve without pay but are reimbursed for expenses. The policies of nonpayment and staggered terms are considered safeguards against political patronage.

CHIEF STATE SCHOOL OFFICER

Every state has a chief state school officer, commissioner of education, or superintendent of public instruction. Some state superintendents are elected by the people, others are appointed either by the state board or by the governor.

Arguments advanced for electing the chief state school officer hold that, as an elected official, the person will be close to the people, responsible to them, and

FIGURE 5.3

Typical Structure of a State Education System

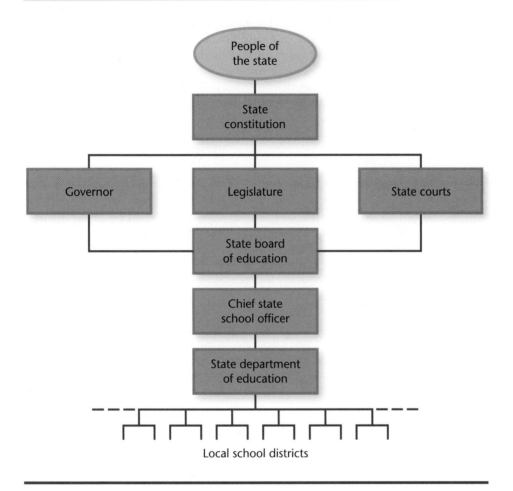

Local school districts

free from obligations to other state officials. An elected person will also be independent of the state board of education. Opponents of the election method argue that this method keeps the state department of education in partisan politics, that an elected official is obligated to other members of the same political party, and that many excellent candidates prefer not to engage in political contests. Those who advocate that the chief state school officer should be appointed by a state board of education claim that policymaking should be separated from policy execution, that educational leadership should not rest on the competence of one elected official, and that this method enhances the state's ability to recruit and retain qualified career workers in education.

Opponents of appointment by a state board of education claim mainly that an appointed chief school officer will not be responsible to the people. The principal objection to gubernatorial appointment is the inherent danger of the appointee's involvement in partisan politics. Another perspective on this issue is that an elected state school officer is legally an "official" of the state, whereas an officer appointed by a state board of education is generally an "employee," not a legal official.

STATE DEPARTMENT OF EDUCATION

The state government carries on its activities in education through the state department of education, which is directed by the chief state school officer. These activities have been classified in five categories: operational, regulatory, service, developmental, and public support and cooperation activities. Operational activities are those in which the state department directly administers schools and services, such as schools for the blind. Regulatory activities include making sure that teachers meet license standards, that school buses are safe, and that curricular requirements are fulfilled. Service activities include advising and consulting, disseminating research, and preparing materials (on state financial aid, for example). Developmental activities are directed to the improvement of the department itself and include planning, staffing, and research into better performance for the operational and regulatory as well as the service functions. Public support and cooperation activities involve public relations, political activities with the legislature and governor, and relations with various other governmental and nongovernmental agencies.

STATE LEGISLATURE

State legislatures are generally responsible for creating, operating, managing, and maintaining state school systems. The legislators are the state policymakers for education. State legislatures create state departments of education to serve as professional advisors and to execute state policy. State legislatures, though powerful, also operate under controls. The governors of many states can veto school legislation as they can other legislation, and the attorney general and the state judiciary system, when called on, will rule on the constitutionality of educational legislation.

State legislatures make decisions about how education is organized in the state; licensure standards and tenure rights of teachers; programs of study; standards of building construction for health and safety; financing of schools, including tax structure and distribution; and compulsory attendance laws.

State legislatures, in their legislative deliberations about the schools, are continually importuned by special-interest groups. These groups, realizing that the legislature is the focus of legal control of education, can exert considerable influence on individual legislators. Some of the representative influential groups are illustrated in Figure 5.4.

It is not uncommon for more than a thousand bills to be introduced each year in a state legislative session. Many of these bills originate with special-interest groups. In recent years, state legislatures have dealt with education bills on a wide range of topics, including accountability, finance, textbooks, adult basic education, length of the school year, legal holidays, lotteries, teacher and student testing, no-pass-no-play policies, and school standards of various sorts.

The Federal Government's Role in Education

Under the Tenth Amendment to the U.S. Constitution, education is a function of the states. In effect, states have the primary responsibility for education, although the schools are operated by local governmental units commonly called *school districts*. Although the states have the primary responsibility for education and the schools are operated at the local level, the federal government has assumed an ever-increasing involvement in education. In the 1960s and 1970s, the rationale for this interest and involvement was linked to national security and solving social problems. In the early 1990s, the rationale was based on economic competitiveness. In the late 1990s, the focus shifted to standards and testing, as well as concerns about funding of the infrastructure of schools.

The arrival of No Child Left Behind in 2002 accelerated the involvement of the federal government in education. This increasing centralization of power is called **federalism.** One consequence has been the establishment of more federal agencies, programs, and laws that address various aspects of the U.S. education system.

federalism

To centralize more power over education at the federal level.

FIGURE 5.4

Influences on Legislative Decision Making

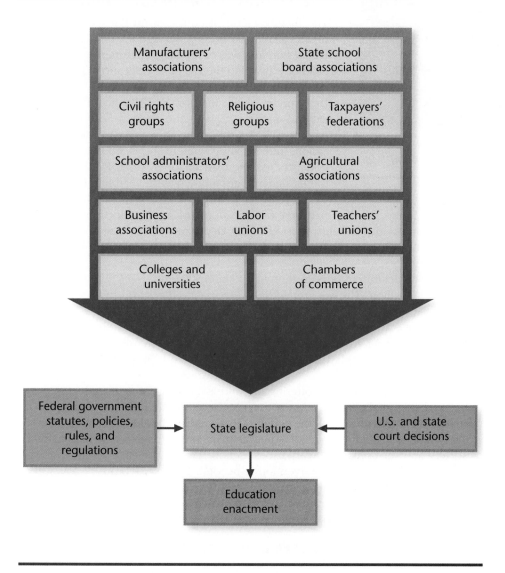

LEADERSHIP

The federal government has historically provided leadership in education in specific situations, usually in times of need or in crises that could not be fully addressed by the leadership in states or local school districts. In the 1980s, policymaker concerns over the quality of schools led to more active leadership on the part of the federal government, such as moves to establish national priorities in education and to raise major issues. For example, *A Nation at Risk,* the report prepared by the National Commission on Excellence in Education, was published in 1983.

That report was not a mandate, nor was funding recommended, but it did sound an alarm, as well as providing recommendations to be considered by states and local school districts. Identifying national educational issues and encouraging forums on these issues at the state and local levels, along with soliciting responses, are appropriate federal activities. Other activities include research on significant national educational issues and dissemination of exemplary practices. Over the last fifty years,

In the past sixty years, the federal government has increased its activity in and leadership of education.

the federal government has insinuated itself more and more by tying school district access to federal funds to education mandates.

THE U.S. DEPARTMENT OF EDUCATION

The first-ever unit of education in the federal government, established in 1867 through the diligent efforts of Henry Barnard, was called the Department of Education. Later, it was called the Office of Education (1869); at another time, it was the Bureau of Education within the Department of the Interior. In 1939 the Office of Education became a part of the Federal Security Agency, which in 1953 became the Department of Health, Education, and Welfare, wherein the U.S. Office of Education was assigned. In October 1979, President Jimmy Carter signed legislation creating a cabinet-level federal agency, the Department of Education. The new Department of Education took on the functions of the U.S. Office of Education. The latest version of the Department of Education, in contrast with the first (1867), has become a powerful agency, which is seen in its authority under NCLB.

The U.S. Department of Education has some 4,500 employees and its 2006 budget was $71.5 billion. The department includes many offices and resources, including the National Center for Education Statistics, which compiles a wide range of statistics about education, the Office of Special Education and Rehabilitative Services, and the Office of Civil Rights. Information about grants, teacher resources, and statistics is available through the various ED offices and programs or online at www.ed.gov.

There is no question that offering aid and awarding grants are effective ways to influence the goals of education nationally. However, there is continuing debate about whether the offices of the federal government should have a stronger or weaker influence on education. Some people maintain that the socioeconomic forces of society are not contained within local school districts or state boundaries and therefore that direct federal intervention is needed. Others advocate dissolution of the department, insisting that education is a state responsibility. As is easy to see with the No Child Left Behind legislation (NCLB), the clear trend in terms of acts of Congress and presidential leadership is toward a greater federal role in education.

EDUCATIONAL PROGRAMS OPERATED BY THE FEDERAL GOVERNMENT

The federal government directly operates some school programs. For example, the public school system of the District of Columbia depends on Congress for funds. The Department of the Interior has the educational responsibility for children of national park employees, for Samoa (classified as an outlying possession), and for the trust territories of the Pacific, such as the Caroline and Marshall Islands. Many of the schools on Native American reservations are financed and managed through the Bureau of Indian Affairs (BIA) of the Department of the Interior. Twenty-five of these schools have become what are called contract schools, in which the tribe determines the program and staff but the BIA supports the schools financially. The Department of Defense (DOD) is responsible for the Military Academy at West Point, the Naval Academy at Annapolis, the Coast Guard Academy at New London, and the Air Force Academy at Colorado Springs. The DOD also operates a school system (DOD Dependents Schools, or DoDDS) for the children of the military staff wherever members are stationed. The instruction supplied in the vocational and technical training programs of the military services has made a big contribution nationally to education as well.

The federal government also funds education research by individual university faculty and a set of ten Regional Education Laboratories, which provide curriculum development, technical assistance, and evaluation services to school districts and states. Another important resource for teachers has been the Education Resources Information Centers (ERIC). These centers are digital archives of research reports and curriculum materials. Teachers can request specific information and literature searches from the ERIC databases.

NO CHILD LEFT BEHIND (NCLB)

The widest-sweeping effort by the federal government to improve student learning and schools across the nation is the 2002 reauthorization of the Elementary and Secondary Education Act (ESEA). The first ESEA was passed by Congress in 1965 as one of President Lyndon Johnson's Great Society initiatives. Since then, the ESEA has been reauthorized every four or five years. Each time the scope of the bill has expanded. Unfortunately, although a major intent of the ESEA was to increase the success of poor and minority students, the results over the last fifty years have not been dramatic. With the leadership of President George W. Bush, the 2002 ESEA reauthorization represented a major rethinking based around the theme of No Child Left Behind (NCLB). Two major purposes of NCLB are to raise student achievement across the board and to eliminate the **achievement gap** among students from different backgrounds. The nearly 2,100 pages of this bill contain many directives and initiatives for states and school districts. Three of these are particularly important for future teachers to understand: HQT (highly qualified teachers), AYP (adequate yearly progress), and SINOI (school in need of improvement).

HIGHLY QUALIFIED TEACHERS (HQT)   The NCLB Act requires that school districts employ only teachers who are highly qualified. The law specifies what "highly qualified" means:

- Public elementary and secondary teachers must be fully licensed or certified by the state and must not have any certification or licensure requirements waived on an emergency, temporary, or provisional basis.
- New public elementary school teachers must have at least a bachelor's degree and pass a rigorous state test demonstrating subject knowledge and teaching skills in reading, writing, mathematics, and other areas of any basic elementary school curriculum.
- New middle or secondary school teachers must have at least a bachelor's degree and demonstrate competency by passing a rigorous state test in each subject they will teach, or successfully complete a major, or graduate degree, or advanced certification in each subject they will teach.

ADEQUATE YEARLY PROGRESS (AYP)   This is the basis for determining whether schools, districts, and states are in compliance with the law. The primary criterion is student performance on standardized tests. A key difference from the past is that under NCLB all students must be making progress, and there must be improvement each year so that by the school year 2013–14, all students in all schools will be "proficient." Student test scores are to be **disaggregated** by the subgroups of:

- Economically disadvantaged students
- Major racial or ethnic groups
- Students with disabilities
- English language learners (ELL)

An additional step in the NCLB mandate is that student performance in the 2001–02 school year is to serve as the baseline. States then have twelve years to have all students meet the 2013–14 proficient level, which means that students within each subgroup who had test scores in 2001–02 below the proficient level need to, on average, improve by one-twelfth each year. This is where the AYP concept comes from; states have to report to the federal government each year that test scores for students in all subgroups are moving toward being at least proficient.

Every time you stop a school, you will have to build a jail. What you gain at one end you lose at the other. It's like feeding a dog on his own tail. It won't fatten the dog.
Mark Twain

achievement gap
The systematic difference in learning between majority and minority, or rich and poor, students.

disaggregated
The process of separating test scores based on student characteristics such as gender, ethnicity, and socioeconomic status.

SCHOOLS IN NEED OF IMPROVEMENT (SINOI) NCLB sets timelines and establishes consequences for states, school districts, and schools in which student performance on test scores does not meet the AYP targets. One unfortunate consequence is that these schools will be labeled as "low performing" or "failing" schools. Another consequence of the way AYP is defined is that sooner or later most schools are likely to be labeled as SINOI schools. Corrective actions for schools in need of improvement include:

1. Schools that fail to meet AYP for two consecutive years must be identified as "needing improvement."
2. Schools that fail to meet the state AYP standard for three consecutive years must offer pupils from low-income families the opportunity to receive instruction from a supplemental services provider of the parents' choice.
3. Schools that fail to meet AYP for four consecutive years must take one or more of the following corrective actions: replace school staff, implement a new curriculum, decrease management authority, appoint an outside expert to advise the school, extend the school day or year, or change the school's internal organizational structure.
4. Schools that fail to meet AYP standards for five consecutive years must be restructured, which includes reopening as a charter school, replacing all or most school staff, state takeover of school operations, or other "major restructuring" of school governance.

IMPACT OF NCLB

The NCLB legislation has placed new demands on teachers, schools, school districts and states. There are many positive outcomes as well as many criticisms. One important outcome of the requirement to disaggregate test scores is that schools must strive to have increases in test scores for all students. No longer can expectations for achievement by minority, special needs, or ELL students be less. Another impact is the reality that more and more schools are failing to achieve AYP in all student categories and therefore are labeled as "needing improvement." A number of tactics are being used to increase test scores.

- "Bubble Kids" are those who scored a few points below the proficient level. By targeting them it is hoped that at the next testing they will score higher.
- "Safe Harbor" is the status of a school that was in need of improvement and has made progress in reducing the number of students scoring below proficient.
- "District in Need of Improvement" is the label applied when AYP is not maintained for all schools and categories of students.
- "Corrective Action" are the steps that must be taken if a school/district fails to achieve AYP over time.
- "Supplemental Services" are provided, such as consultants to analyze data and provide training, as well as the addition of after-school programs.

OTHER NCLB REQUIREMENTS Many more elements, mandates, and expectations are part of the 2002 version of the NCLB Act, such as annual testing of students in grades 3 through 8 in math and reading/language arts, as well as testing them three times in science by grade 12. Annual state report cards are required, and they must, among other things, name SINOI schools. Also, school districts must make available to parents, upon request, the following information about their child's classroom teacher:

- Whether the teacher has met state qualification and licensing criteria for the grade levels and subject areas taught
- Whether the teacher is teaching under emergency or other provisional status
- The baccalaureate degree of the teacher and any other graduate certification or degree held by the teacher and the subject area of the certification or degree
- Whether the child is provided service by paraprofessionals and, if so, the paraprofessional's qualifications.

In summary, the No Child Left Behind Act is a far-reaching, long-lasting federal statute intended to improve schooling, as defined in terms of student performance on standardized state testing in all states, all school districts, all schools, and all classrooms.

Other Types of Education Agencies

The organization of the U.S. education system described so far has been in a straight line from schools to the federal government. Obviously, the whole system is not this simple. Many related agencies and organizations are important as well. Some that will play a more direct role in your work as a teacher are highlighted here.

INTERMEDIATE UNITS

The **intermediate unit** of school organization, which may consist of one or more counties, functions between the state department of education and the local school districts. These units have different names in different states. For example, in some states, such as New York and Colorado, they are called BOCES (Boards of Cooperative Educational Services); in Texas they are called Regional Service Centers; and in California, County Education Offices.

A fundamental purpose of the intermediate unit is to provide two or more local districts with educational services that they cannot efficiently or economically provide individually; cooperative provisions for special education and vocational–technical education have been very successful. Other services that intermediate units can provide include audiovisual libraries, centralized purchasing, inservice training for teachers and principals as well as other school workers, health services, instructional materials, laboratories, legal services, and special consultant services. The inservice dimension of the intermediate units has escalated in some states in recent years, stimulated by educational reform.

School Choice: Increasing Options along with Uncertain Outcomes

The newspaper article in the Case Study feature at the beginning of this chapter foreshadows one of the hottest education topics across the United States: school choice. In the past, parents had no say in which public school their child would attend. Children were assigned to a school based on their home address. Now increasing numbers and types of alternatives to the traditional neighborhood public school are becoming available. Nearly one in four students is exercising some form of choice within public or private schools. The problem for many parents now is not whether they have a choice but which one of the alternatives is best. Many of these options are being installed within public school districts, whereas other alternatives are found in private schools. Most of these options allow for increased parent and student involvement in school decision making. All represent, in some way, a break with the traditional public school and classroom structures. The creation of choices also causes competition between the alternatives, which some people believe will lead to more efficiency and effectiveness. However, the research to date, though limited, does not provide clear evidence of a trend toward higher student achievement. The findings do indicate that upper-income and more educated families are more likely to exercise choice.[1,2]

MAGNET SCHOOLS

Many school districts have been pressured by citizens and ordered by the courts to equalize the proportions of different racial groups in each school. One response, especially by large urban school districts such as those in Houston and Kansas City,

intermediate unit

An education organization located between local districts and the state that delivers support services to one or more school districts.

has been to develop special academic programs and custom-designed facilities that will attract all students—hence the name *magnet* schools. Elementary, middle, and high school magnets exist. The program might emphasize the performing and visual arts, math and science, or the liberal arts. Whatever the theme, the faculty, curriculum, and all students in the magnet school are there because of their interest in the school's theme.

CHARTER SCHOOLS

CROSS-REFERENCE

School choice is a strategy for addressing the social challenges described in Chapter 2.

Charter schools are a relatively new approach to providing communities with alternative schools supported by public funds. These schools come into existence through a contract with either a state agency or a local school board. The school establishes a contract, or charter, that lays out how the school will operate in exchange for receiving public funding. Charter schools have greater autonomy than regular public schools and can be released from various district and state regulations. However, charter schools are still held accountable for student learning and, in most settings, having a diverse student body. Exponential growth in the number of charter schools has occurred since the first one was established in Minnesota in 1992. As of 1999, thirty-six states and the District of Columbia had passed legislation to permit the establishment of charter schools. For the 1999–2000 school year, 267,000 students were enrolled, representing 4 percent of all public school students.[3] However, as shown in Figure 5.5, charter schools tend to have significantly smaller enrollments than public schools.

YEAR-ROUND SCHOOLS

The normal school year of nine to ten months with the full summer off is often criticized. One concern is that students will forget too much over the summer. Critics

FIGURE 5.5

Estimated Distribution of School Size for Charter Schools and All Public Schools

Source: U.S. Department of Education, Office of Educational Research and Improvement, *The State of Charter Schools 2000.* Washington, DC: Author, 2000.

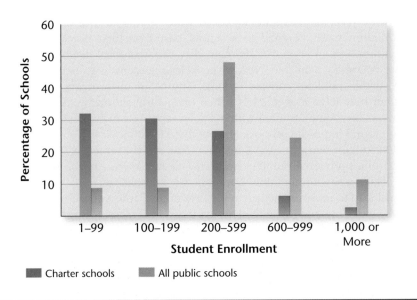

point out that the current school year was instituted back in the 1800s, when most people lived on farms and the children were counted on to perform summer chores. One interesting solution is the year-round school. This is not an extended school year in that students attend school for more days. Rather, year-round schools spread the time in school across twelve months. One way a school might do this is by having multiple "tracks" of six to eight weeks. During any one cycle, one-fourth to one-third of the students will be on vacation and the others will be attending classes. In this way, students have more frequent but shorter times away from school. An additional advantage is that the school site can handle more students on an annual basis. Curiously, much of the resistance to year-round schools comes from parents who are concerned about being able to schedule family vacations; however, once the schedule is implemented, they discover that being able to schedule vacations throughout the year has advantages.

VOUCHERS

Without a doubt, the most controversial choice alternative is school vouchers. At its simplest, a voucher program issues a check or a credit to parents that can be used to send their child to a private school. Most voucher programs are funded with state tax dollars. However, some voucher programs are funded by private foundations and occasionally individuals. For example, in the Edgewood Independent School District in San Antonio, Texas, a group of business executives offered $50 million over ten years for vouchers for low-income families to attend any private school or even public school in other school districts. The publicly financed programs have restrictions on who is eligible, as in Florida, where the state plan allowed vouchers to be used only after the state had designated the public school as a failing school. Typically, the amount of a voucher is equivalent to the amount the public school received for each student, in other words, $4,000 to $5,000. The debates about vouchers center on the use of public dollars to support private schools. The most serious point of contention is when the voucher funded with state education money is used to pay for a child to attend a religious school. This raises constitutional questions about the separation of church and state, which are discussed in detail in Chapter 6. The National Education Association has been active in opposition to voucher programs because it sees this choice as undermining public education. A useful summary of pros and cons about vouchers is presented in Table 5.2.

PRIVATE, PAROCHIAL, AND INDEPENDENT SCHOOLS

Alternative structures of schools exist outside the public school system too. These range from elite secondary schools (mainly in the Northeast), to dynamic alternative schools for high school dropouts, to church-supported schools, to schools that are operated for profit. As shown in Table 5.3 (p. 161), there has been a gradual increase in the number of private schools.

INDEPENDENT SCHOOLS   Private education, which preceded public education in the United States, continues to be available as an alternative to the public schools. Private schools are increasingly being referred to as independent schools.[4] One source of information on these schools is the Council for American Private Education (CAPE), a coalition of fourteen private school organizations. Another is the National Association of Independent Schools (NAIS). The following description of independent schools is based on an NAIS publication.[5]

An **independent school** is a nonprofit institution governed by a board of trustees that depends almost entirely on private funds—tuition, gifts, grants—for its financial support. Most independent schools are accredited by their regional accrediting group

independent school

A nonprofit, nonpublic school that is governed by a board of trustees.

TABLE 5.2	Voucher Pros and Cons
Critics' Arguments	**Supporters' Arguments**
Only the most motivated students will use vouchers, increasing the segregation of students by race, economic status, and parents' educational background.	Low-income parents should be able to choose private schools over poorly performing public schools.
Vouchers weaken the public schools by diverting resources from them.	Increased competition from voucher schools will force public schools to improve, or risk closure.
Lack of accountability and quality control at voucher schools is a misuse of public money.	Private schools are unburdened by bureaucracy and regulations that hamstring the public school system.
Spending public money on religious education is unconstitutional.	Private schools provide more tailored services at a lower cost.
Transportation problems and difficulties in providing adequate information to all parents will make voucher systems inequitable.	Voucher systems allow parents more influence over their children's education.
Property taxes will rise as state aid to local districts is lost.	Voucher programs emphasize educational choices, not requirements dictated by the government.
Vouchers will increase overall costs. Private schools, like any other government contractor, will become even more dependent on and demanding of public funds, causing more spending.	Vouchers expand options for low-income parents, enhancing their feelings of empowerment and inclusion in society.
Vouchers do not really equalize the playing field, since no voucher program so far provides enough money for poor children to be able to attend the most expensive private schools.	

Source: What We Know about Vouchers: The Facts behind the Rhetoric. San Francisco: WestEd, 1999.

and by state departments of education. All must meet state and local health and safety standards as well as mandatory school attendance laws. Unlike public schools, independent schools are not involved in or part of large, formal systems. They do, however, share many informal contracts among themselves and with public schools. The vast majority offer programs that prepare students for college.

Independent schools vary greatly in purpose, organization, and size, and they serve students from all racial, religious, economic, and cultural backgrounds. Some are progressive and innovative; some are conservative and traditional. They are both large and small, day and boarding, single-sex and coeducational. Independent schools have been an integral part of our nation's educational resources since colonial times.

Because each independent school is free to determine and practice its own philosophy of education, spirit and environment vary from school to school, even though schools may display similar organizational structures and educational programs.

TABLE 5.3	The Increase in the Number of Public and Private Schools over Time						
	Elementary and Secondary Schools in the United States						
Characteristics	1980–81	1987–88	1990–91	1995–96	1997–98	2001–02
All elementary and secondary schools	106,746	110,055	109,228	114,811	116,910	123,385
All public schools	85,982	83,248	84,538	87,125	89,508	94,112
All private schools	20,764	26,807	24,690	26,686	27,402	29,273

Source: U.S. Department of Education, National Center for Education Statistics, *Digest of Education Statistics 2004.* Washington, DC: Author, Chapter 2.

GOVERNANCE OF INDEPENDENT SCHOOLS Each independent school is incorporated as a nonprofit, tax-exempt corporation and governed by a board of trustees that selects its own members, determines the school's philosophy, selects the chief administrative officer, and bears ultimate responsibility for the school's resources and finances. The chief administrator responsible for the day-to-day operation of the school may be called the headmaster, headmistress, president, or principal. The head's duties are comparable to those of a public school superintendent.

HOME SCHOOLING

This rapidly growing form of schooling requires no public support; instead, children learn at home with one of their parents serving as the teacher. In Spring 2000, 1.1 million students were being schooled at home. They represent 2.2 percent of the K–12 population. Teaching a home-schooled student requires relearning subjects, organizing each day's instruction, and then teaching it. One of the advantages, as well as potential weaknesses, is that in most states the subjects taught are self-determined. This can work in favor of students' interests but may also contribute to gaps in their education. Still, the evidence is clear that for many students home schooling is a success. For example, home-schooled fourth graders watch less television and in high school they score on average eighty points higher on the SAT.

Politics in Education

So far this chapter has provided information about the formal structures of public education at the local, state, and federal levels. Although these organizational structures illustrate the line and staff relationships, another set of relationships is important to consider and understand. Each of these levels is involved in politics—the politics of education. For example, local school districts are likely to be interested in federal educational programs and grants, so they will contact members of Congress to express their opinions. The purpose is to influence representatives' understanding of local needs and their actions on relevant legislation. The same activities take place at the state level. Local school districts and professional associations follow closely what is happening in their state legislature. These groups do not hesitate to let members in the legislature know their opinions or to urge action. It is not unusual for local school superintendents and board members to lobby their senators and representatives in person. These contacts with federal and state agencies

Should the School Year Be Longer?

As the need for students to learn more increases one solution would be to lengthen the school year. Making this change would have implications for taxpayers, parents, students, and teachers. These two educators debate the consequences of an extended school year for students and teachers.

YES

Grace Leavitt teaches Spanish at Greely High School in Cumberland, Maine.

We are trying to fit the needs of today's students into a traditional calendar developed decades ago, and that doesn't work any better than my trying to fit into my outfits of 30 years ago!

Our students simply need to know more. The world they will enter demands much more than it used to. How often do you try to prioritize what to teach and then find that you never get to the "other" things that are also important?

And how many of us would like to see our schools have full programs in physical education, health, art, music, and world languages, but there's no time?

This is the age of accountability, and so far that means the age of assessment. We have added many hours of testing without lengthening the school year, so we have lost precious instructional time.

We don't even have time to reflect on the test results, give students feedback, and then encourage them to try again. We merely race on. Maybe with an extended calendar these assessments could truly be *for* learning, not just *of* learning!

NO

Dorothy Moody is a first-year math and science teacher at Jehue Middle School in Rialto, California.

As I write this in the middle of March, teachers are concentrating on how to maximize their students' test scores and how to ensure that they're prepared for the next grade, right? No, not really. The truth is that teachers are pondering two things this month: what to do for summer vacation and how to get through a month with no legal holidays.

Oh, the shock! Aren't teachers supposed to be altruistic examples of selflessness? Shouldn't teachers *want* to work year-round in order to better educate the students? The answer is an unequivocal *no*. Teachers are human. We suffer from burnout as much as any other occupation. But unlike many others, we are responsible for turning out well-educated students who can succeed in college and in life. That's why we need our summer break. It is a time to relax, recharge our batteries, and regain our patience, the latter of which is paramount to being an effective teacher.

One might think students would benefit from a longer school year. They would have more time

(continued)

are representative of political action. You also need to be aware of the many other types of education politics.

SCHOOL BOARD POLITICS Most school districts have "at-large" elections to select board members. In at-large elections every voter in a community is able to vote for a candidate for each seat on the board. The alternative is to have each board seat represent a particular region of the district. Either way there will be strong interest on the part of voters in having a board member that will represent his or her interests. Nearly every decision a board makes has a political component. Approving the superintendent's salary, changing the boundaries of a school, raising taxes, reducing staff or extracurricular programs, busing students, and tolerating a losing athletic season will bring out strong voices with often competing points of view.

TEACHER PERSPECTIVES

(continued)

YES

It is also the age of "all" kids. We are supposed to help all students achieve, and we know much more about how to meet their different learning styles. But there is precious little time for them to do hands-on projects, work collaboratively in groups, give presentations, or get engaged in service learning.

It may seem that our students already have as much school as they can stand, but with more time, we could be more creative, and they would learn more.

Then there is the long summer break and the struggle to resume school after it. Yes, many students are involved in summertime learning of all kinds. But these opportunities are not available to all, and so the inequities continue.

Many other countries have school years of 200 days or more. I am convinced that although tradition is a big hurdle, the main obstacle is that we have yet to make funding schools our priority.

NO

to learn the curriculum before standardized testing, and lessons could be taught in many ways to meet their diverse learning styles.

In a perfect world, maybe. Chances are that we would be required to cram more information into the curriculum. Students, like teachers, are only human. They can handle only so much education before suffering information overload.

Many other countries have a longer school year, but those countries treat their children like small adults. Our students need the summer to relax, play, and act like children before returning to school in the fall.

Yes, they may forget information in the meantime, but let's face it—they'll do the same thing over the weekend.

Extending the school year would result in irritable teachers, disinterested students, and even lower test scores. Taking a summer break is a necessary evil.

Source: "Should the School Year Be Longer?" *NEA Today* (May 2005), p. 44. Reprinted by permission of the National Education Association.

WHAT IS YOUR PERSPECTIVE ON THIS ISSUE?
Should the school year be longer?

To give your opinion, go to Chapter 5 of the companion website (www.ablongman.com/johnson14e) and click on Teacher Perspectives.

SUPERINTENDENT POLITICS As the chief executive officer the superintendent has to listen to the opinions of all board members and strive to maintain a majority of the board's support to be retained.[5] The superintendent also has to work with and listen to teachers, principals, central office staff, and various members of the community. All will have suggestions for the superintendent and for what the school district should be doing.

SCHOOL POLITICS Teachers often state that they do not wish to become involved in politics, as if they have a choice. Schools are not devoid of politics. Teachers will lobby the principal for a preferred teaching assignment, parents want particular teachers for their children, and teachers will join together to advocate for a particular instructional approach.

Special-interest groups organize to influence school board elections by using fund-raising, mass communication, and grassroots campaigning.

CLASSROOM POLITICS   Yes, there are politics in classrooms. When students approach the teacher to request clarification about an assignment or lobby to have test rescheduled, they are engaging in politics.

POLITICS: NEITHER POSITIVE NOR NEGATIVE

Although many of the examples presented here might appear to be negative, keep in mind that politics are neither good nor bad. Instead, politics are the way that all organizations work. Areas of disagreement will always exist in educational organizations. People have varying interests that must be discussed. In many cases, there are basic differences in point of view, but a decision has to be made for the organization to move ahead. This is where political skill becomes a special strength for teachers and school administrators. Those who are skillful in talking with all parties and negotiating areas of agreement make significant contributions. Rather than judging "politics" as bad, successful teachers learn to understand how politics work and develop the skills to contribute to and influence the political process. Closing the classroom door guarantees that your positions and ideas will not be considered. Learn more about organizations and political processes and you will see politics as fascinating and, yes, fun.

ISSUE: LOCAL CONTROL VERSUS FEDERALISM

In the past, an important and unique feature of education in the United States was **local control,** the belief that educational decisions should be made at the local level rather than at the state or national level. The rationale has been that people at the local level, including teachers and parents, know what is best for the students in their community. As has been described in this chapter, the trend over the last sixty years has been toward more federalism. The No Child Left Behind Act is the latest and heaviest centralization initiative by the federal government and includes many mandates to states, school districts, schools, and teachers.

Those who advocate for more federal and state involvement argue that education is a responsibility of all society. Some also argue that national survival requires centralized policies and programs. The underlying questions are not just about what is best for students and the nation; they are about power, authority, and who gets to decide.

local control

Educational decision making by citizens at the local level rather than at the state or national level.

What Is the Appropriate Role for Teachers When the Politics Get Rough?

The education accountability movement of the last decade has demanded that teachers and school administrators make serious efforts to change the way schools operate and to implement new approaches to help students learn. Policymakers, business leaders, and citizens at large have demanded that schools "reform" and "restructure." As is discussed in Chapter 11 and Chapter 12, schools are now expected to implement curriculum standards and to administer newly created tests of student learning. Yet major changes in the structure and operation of schools are difficult to accomplish. It is hard for teachers to give up or change what they have been doing. It takes a great deal of time to work through the process that is necessary to develop a consensus among teachers, administrators, and parents about how a school should be restructured and what it should become. It also takes several years to work out the kinks when trying something new.

Suppose that after you had spent three years discussing and then two years implementing a major restructuring of your school and saw that it was working with students, a newly elected majority on the school board demanded that you return to the old way. As a teacher, what would you do?

This is not a hypothetical question. In one recent example, after more than three years of broad-based discussions involving teachers, administrators, students, parents, and community members, one school district's school board approved new performance-based graduation requirements for one of its high schools. The new requirements were based on student accomplishments rather than on seat-time. In fact, the high school had received national recognition for its efforts.

In November of the second year of implementation, three conservative members were elected to the five-member school board. A major theme in their election campaign was an attack on the new graduation requirements, which they promised to remove. In January the new majority on the school board proceeded to implement its campaign promise. Although students from the school, parents, and school staff members asked that the board not do this, or that the board at least allow the new graduation requirements to be optional, the board voted three to two to return to the traditional requirements. Remember that there were now students in their second year of high school who had been told that they were expected to meet the new graduation requirements.

The school board did not stop there. In the same month, January, the board terminated the superintendent, who was viewed as a very able educator by most and was well known and respected nationally. By the end of the school year, several school principals and teachers had taken positions elsewhere, and the district was running advertisements nationwide for principals and teachers who held "traditional" educational values. This might sound like an extreme case, but similar events have happened in other school districts, and similar cases will happen in one form or another during your years as an educator.

If you were a teacher in a school district where something like this occurred, what would you do? Your colleagues, the school, your students, and the innovative program have been challenged. It is clear that there is the potential for casualties, including your job. Of course, your actions will depend partly on which side of the issue you are on. Either way, what will you do?

Questions for Reflection

1. Will you speak out or wait for others to do so?
2. What will you tell your students?
3. Will you support your principal publicly or leave the principal on his or her own?
4. How do you think you would feel the next time you were asked to invest four or five years in designing and implementing a major change in your school?

To answer these questions on-line and e-mail your answers to your professor, go to Chapter 5 of the companion website (www.ablongman.com/johnson14e) and click on Professional Dilemma.

Journal for Reflection

Develop an organizational chart for a school you are familiar with. Use solid lines to represent line relationships and dotted lines to signify staff relationships. Draw the arrangement of personnel in regard to each of the following decisions: (1) determining a child's grade on his or her report card, (2) expelling a student (hint—don't forget that the school is part of a school district), (3) deciding on the topic for a staff development day, and (4) determining whether a particular teaching activity will be used. After considering these different decisions, explain your thoughts and feelings about the authority and accountability of teachers within the school as an organization.

Thoughtful critics and historians have offered some interesting comparisons between the original 1965 ESEA and the 2002 reauthorization. Some critics of the original ESEA say that it failed because it provided money without accountability, and the NCLB Act will succeed because it requires strict accountability. The ESEA of 1965 may have offered money without much educational accountability, but the NCLB Act demands heavy accountability without much greater federal financial and technical assistance—an approach no more likely to succeed.

In 1965, extensive federal requirements like those of NCLB would never have made it through Congress. At that time, the federal role in education was marginal, and most state education agencies had limited authority and capabilities. Local people were extremely wary that more federal aid would bring federal control. Since then the federal and state roles in education have grown, and states and school districts recognize that accepting federal requirements goes along with receiving federal funding.

Financing Education: Sources of Funds and the Move from Equity to Adequacy

The whole people must take upon themselves the education of the whole people and must be willing to bear the expense of it.

John Adams

When the financing of education is considered, the first question asked by many is "How much? How much do I have to pay, and how much do schools receive?" In the last decade, two other questions have sharpened the discussions about education finance: "Does each school have the same amount of funding?" This is the **equity** question. "Is there sufficient funding so that all students can achieve?" This is the **adequacy** question. The equity question was at the center of many school funding lawsuits in the 1980s and 1990s. In 1989 a decision of the Kentucky Supreme Court brought the adequacy question to the front. That court decision held that every child in the state had the right to an "adequate" education. The direct consequence of that decision was the state legislature passing the Kentucky Education Reform Act (KERA). The significance of KERA is that it did not deal solely with equalizing spending by each school district—that is, equity. KERA went further by specifically connecting funding with implementation of school and curriculum reforms, specifying student outcomes and development of a statewide strategy for assessing academic achievement. Now questions related to the financing of education have to deal with all three questions: "How much?"; "Is there equity in the distribution?"; and "Are the resources adequate so that all students can achieve the identified outcomes?" We explore these finance questions in the remainder of this chapter.

A System of Taxation and Support for Schools

equity

Provision of the same amount of funding to all schools or students.

adequacy

Provision of sufficient funds so that all students can achieve.

Money to support education comes from a variety of taxes paid to local, state, and federal governments. These governments in turn distribute tax money to local school districts to operate the schools. The three principal kinds of taxes that provide revenue for schools are property taxes, sales or use taxes, and income taxes. The property tax is generally a local tax, whereas the sales tax generally is a state and local mix, and the income tax is collected at the state and federal levels. More than $388 billion in revenues were raised by local, state, and federal governments to fund public education in the 2002–03 school year.[7]

Each type of tax is a part of a system and has advantages and disadvantages, yet it is unlikely that any one of these taxes used by itself for education would be

FIGURE 5.6

Percent Distribution of Revenue for Public Elementary and Secondary Schools, by Source: School Year 2002–2003.

Note: Percentages may not sum to 100 due to rounding. Intermediate revenues were combined with local revenues.

Source: Data from U.S. Department of Education, National Center for Education Statistics, "National Public Education Financial Survey."

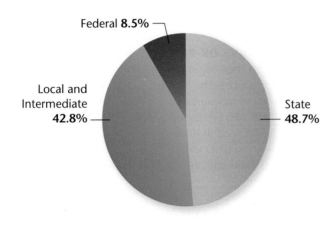

Federal **8.5%**

Local and Intermediate **42.8%**

State **48.7%**

sufficient. In evaluating a system of taxes, one should consider the varying ability of citizens to pay, the economic effects of the taxes on the taxpayer, the benefits that various taxpayers receive, the total yield of the tax, the economy of collection, the degree of acceptance, the convenience of paying, the problems of tax evasion, the stability of the tax, and the general adaptability of the system. Clearly, systems of taxation are complicated; each system is an intricately interdependent network.

Figure 5.6 diagrams the percentages of revenues that school systems nationwide receive from federal, state, and local sources. As you can see, public education is primarily funded by local and state sources of revenue.

PROPERTY TAXES AND LOCAL REVENUE

Until recently, the **property tax** has been the primary source of local revenue for schools. It is based on the value of property, both real estate and personal. Real estate includes land holdings and buildings such as homes, commercial buildings, and factories. Personal property consists of automobiles, machinery, furniture, livestock, and intangibles such as stocks and bonds. The property tax has both advantages and limitations.

PROPERTY TAXES: ADVANTAGES AND LIMITATIONS The main advantage of the property tax is its stability. Although the tax tends to lag behind changes in market values, it provides a steady, regular income for the taxing agency. Another advantage of taxing property is that it is fixed; it is not easily moved to escape taxation, as income might be. Also, because the owners of property pay the tax, it is easy to identify them.

The property tax has numerous limitations, however. It can have a negative impact on the value of housing: It tends to discourage rehabilitation and upkeep because both of these tend to raise the value of the property and therefore its taxes. The tax is often a deciding factor in locating a business or industry. And it is likely not to be applied equally on all properties.

DETERMINING THE VALUE OF PROPERTY One problem with the property tax lies in the potential unfairness of inconsistent property assessments. In some areas,

property tax
A tax based on the value of property, both real estate and personal.

assessors are local people, usually elected, with no special training in evaluating property. Their duty involves inspecting their neighbors' properties and placing values on them. In other areas, sophisticated techniques involving expertly trained personnel are used for property appraisal. In either circumstance, assessors are likely to be subject to political and informal pressures to keep values low in order to keep tax rates low.

The assessed value of property is usually only a percentage of its market value. This percentage varies from county to county and from state to state. Attempts are made within states to equalize assessments or to make certain that the same percentage of full cash value is used in assessing property throughout the state. In recent years, attempts have been made to institute full cash value for the assessed value. For the property tax to be a fair tax, equalized assessment is a necessity.

PROPERTY TAX: PROGRESSIVE OR REGRESSIVE   Property tax is most generally thought of as a **progressive tax**—that is, one that taxes according to ability to pay; the more wealth one has in property, the more one pays. But because assessments can be unequal and because frequently the greatest wealth is no longer related to real estate, the property tax can be regressive. **Regressive taxes,** such as sales and use taxes, are those that affect low-income groups disproportionately. Some evidence supports the contention that people in the lowest income groups pay a much higher proportion of their income in property taxes than persons in the highest income groups.

INEQUITIES OF THE PROPERTY TAX   Significant support for schools across the nation has been provided by the property tax. However, as has been described, because of schools' heavy dependence on property taxes for financing, enormous discrepancies in resources and quality have built up between schools located in rich and in poor communities.

To illustrate the school finance consequences of differences in local wealth, look at a simple example. A school district having assessed property valuations totaling $30 million and a responsibility for educating 1,000 pupils would have $30,000 of assessed valuation per pupil. Property taxes are calculated on the basis of assessed valuations, so a district with a high assessed valuation per pupil is in a better position to provide quality education than is one with a low assessed valuation per pupil. If school district A has an assessed valuation of $90 million and 1,000 pupils, for example, and school district B has an assessed valuation of $30 million and 1,000 pupils, a tax rate of $2 per $100 of assessed valuation would produce $1.8 million for education in district A and only $600,000 in district B. School district A could therefore spend $1,800 per pupil, compared with $600 per pupil in school district B, with the same local tax effort.

THE PERSPECTIVE OF THE COURTS ON TAXATION AND EDUCATION   Can the property tax continue to be the primary base for financing schools? This question was asked of the U.S. Supreme Court in *San Antonio (Texas) Independent School District v. Rodriguez* (1979). Keep in mind that the U.S. Constitution does not mention education, so any litigation has to be based on indirect connections. In the *Rodriguez* case, the challenge was initiated under the Equal Protection Clause of the Fourteenth Amendment. This clause prohibits state action that would deny citizens equal protection. The U.S. Supreme Court, in a five-to-four decision, reversed the lower court decision in *Rodriguez* and thus reaffirmed the local property tax as a basis for school financing. Justice Potter Stewart, voting with the majority, admitted that "the method of financing public schools . . . can be fairly described as chaotic and unjust." He did not, though, find it unconstitutional. The majority opinion, written by Justice Lewis F. Powell, Jr., stated, "We cannot say that such disparities are the product of a system that is so irrational as to be invidiously discriminatory." Justice Thurgood Marshall, in the dissenting opinion, charged that the ruling "is a retreat from our historic commitment to equality of education opportunity." Another part of the opinion in *Rodriguez* addressed the role of the states in supporting public education:

progressive tax

A tax that is scaled to the ability of the taxpayer to pay.

regressive tax

A tax that affects low-income groups disproportionately.

The consideration and initiation of fundamental reforms with respect to state taxation and education are matters reserved for legislative processes of the various States, and we do no violence to the values of federalism and separation of powers by staying our hand. We hardly need add that this Court's action today is not to be viewed as placing its judicial imprimatur on the status quo. The need is apparent for reform in tax systems which may well have relied too long and too heavily on the local property tax. And certainly innovative thinking as to public education, its methods, and its funding is necessary to assure both a higher level of quality and greater uniformity of opportunity. These matters merit the continued attention of the scholars who already have contributed much by their challenges. But the ultimate solutions must come from the lawmakers and from the democratic pressures of those who elect them.

These comments in *Rodriguez* foreshadowed the continuing string of school finance suits that have been filed in most states.

STATE SOURCES OF REVENUE AND AID

On the average in the United States, the states provide about 49.5 percent of the fiscal resources for local schools. This money is referred to as **state aid,** and within most states all or a major portion of this money is used to help achieve equality of opportunity.

The main sources of tax revenue for states have been classified by the Department of Commerce in four groups: sales and gross receipt taxes, income taxes, licenses, and miscellaneous. Sales and gross receipt taxes include taxes on general sales, motor fuels, alcohol, insurance, and amusements; income taxes include both individual and corporate; licenses include those on motor vehicles, corporations, occupations, vehicle operators, hunting, and fishing. The miscellaneous classification includes property taxes, taxes on severance or extraction of minerals, and death and gift taxes. The two largest sources of state revenues are sales and income taxes.

SALES AND INCOME TAXES   Sales and income taxes are lucrative sources of state revenue, and it is relatively easy to administer both. The sales tax is collected bit by bit, in a relatively painless way, by the vendor, who is responsible for keeping records. The state income tax can be withheld from wages; hence, collection is eased. Income taxes are considered progressive taxes because they frequently are scaled to the ability of the taxpayer to pay. Sales taxes are regressive; they affect low-income groups disproportionately. All people pay the sales tax at the same rate, so people in low income groups pay as much tax as people in high income groups. Part of the advantage of sales taxes and income taxes is that they can be regulated by the legislature that must raise the money.

GAMBLING: AN INCREASING SOURCE OF REVENUE   In 1964, New Hampshire implemented a lottery. By 2004, forty states and the District of Columbia were operating lotteries. Legalized gambling in its many forms, from casinos and riverboats to horse racing, has become the newest source of state and local revenues. Gambling is an indirect source of revenue in the sense that it is not seen as a direct tax on citizens; instead, the revenues come through taxes on the games. Commercial casinos (not including Native American casinos), operating in eleven states paid $4.9 billion in taxes in 2004. Income for states from lotteries grew from $978 million in 1980 to $14 billion in 2003. In fifteen states, part or all of the net proceeds from the lottery are allocated to education. In most states, such as California, the original intent was for these funds to be used for educational enhancements. But within three years of the California lottery's implementation, in a tight budget year, the California legislature incorporated the lottery funds into the base education budget. Other states have had similar experiences.

RECENT CHALLENGES TO SCHOOL FINANCE WITHIN THE STATES

The number of court cases related to school finance has increased in recent years. Some states have had new suits initiated, while others are continuing to struggle to

state aid
The money that states provide for the fiscal resources of local schools.

respond to earlier court decisions and directives. In all, nearly forty states have experienced or are experiencing court cases that deal with school finance.

THE STATE PERSPECTIVE ON TAXATION AND EDUCATION   Equal protection challenges have been or are currently being made at the state level. In some states, the plaintiffs have emphasized a claim of equal protection; in others the focus has been on specific language in the state's constitution. In all cases, the issue is whether the state has fulfilled its constitutional obligation to provide for education. The answer by the state supreme courts in some states has been that education is not a fundamental right, and that as long as there is provision for a minimally adequate education, the equal protection clause is met. In *Serrano v. Priest* (1971), the California Supreme Court was called on to determine whether the California public school financing system, with its substantial dependence on local property taxes, violated the Fourteenth Amendment. In its six-to-one decision, the California court held that heavy reliance on unequal local property taxes "makes the quality of a child's education a function of the wealth of his parents and neighbors." Furthermore, the court declared, "Districts with small tax bases simply cannot levy taxes at a rate sufficient to produce the revenue that more affluent districts produce with a minimum effort." Officially, the California Supreme Court ruled that the system of school financing in California was unconstitutional but did not forbid the use of property taxes as long as the system of finance was neutral in the distribution of resources. Within a year of *Serrano v. Priest,* five other courts—in Minnesota, Texas, New Jersey, Wyoming, and Arizona—ruled similarly.

STATES' RESPONSIBILITY TO GUARANTEE EQUAL EDUCATIONAL OPPORTUNITY
In 1989 and 1990, several state supreme courts made significant decisions about school finance. Since then, in a number of states, the education finance systems were knocked down by the courts, and the state legislatures were directed to remedy the wrongs.

In Montana, in *Helena Elementary School District v. State* (1989), the Montana Supreme Court ruled that the state's school finance system violated the state constitution's guarantee of equal educational opportunity. The state's constitution article mandates that the state establish an educational system that will develop the full educational potential of each person. In 1990 the court delayed the effects of its decision to allow the legislature time to enact a new finance system.[8]

The Kentucky Supreme Court also ruled that the entire system of school governance and finance violated the state constitution's mandate for the provision of an efficient system of common schools throughout the state (*Rose v. The Council for Better Education Inc.,* 1989). The Kentucky Supreme Court's opinion stated that

> The system of common schools must be adequately funded to achieve its goals. The system of common schools must be substantially uniform throughout the state. Each child, *every child,* in this commonwealth must be provided with an equal opportunity to have an adequate education. Equality is the key word here. The children of the poor and the children of the rich, the children who live in poor districts and the children who live in the rich districts must be given the same opportunity and access to an adequate education. This obligation cannot be shifted to local counties and local school districts.

The court directed the state legislature to develop a new educational system, which was adopted as the Kentucky Education Reform Act (KERA) in 1990.

Throughout the 1990s, there continued to be suits, court actions, and legislative initiatives regarding how best to address funding inequities for public schools. Further, earlier court decisions have been revisited. For example, in a turnaround of earlier decisions, in 1994 the State Supreme Court of Arizona ruled that the state's property tax–based school financing system was unconstitutional because it created wide disparities between rich and poor school districts. As has been true in other states, the court left it up to the legislature to rectify the problem.

Undoubtedly, changes are occurring in the state provisions for financial support for education. Equal expenditures per pupil might not, because of other factors, ensure equal opportunity, but equal expenditures per pupil do in fact enhance the likelihood of equal opportunity.

ENTREPRENEURIAL EFFORTS TO FUND EDUCATION

The combination of tight budgets, increasing enrollments, and demands for better educational services is pressuring schools, school districts, and state officials to search for new funding sources. Some sources that were highly controversial in the past, such as the lottery, have now become a regular part of the main revenue stream. Other potential new sources of funds are now being considered, debated, and utilized.

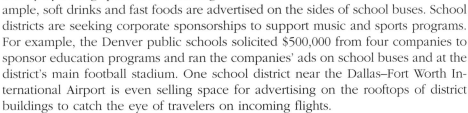

A rapidly expanding source of financial support for schools is advertising, although accepting this type of funding is a topic of intense debate.

ADVERTISING: A NEW SOURCE OF REVENUE

School districts have found that they can raise money by selling space for advertising. For example, soft drinks and fast foods are advertised on the sides of school buses. School districts are seeking corporate sponsorships to support music and sports programs. For example, the Denver public schools solicited $500,000 from four companies to sponsor education programs and ran the companies' ads on school buses and at the district's main football stadium. One school district near the Dallas–Fort Worth International Airport is even selling space for advertising on the rooftops of district buildings to catch the eye of travelers on incoming flights.

MORE STUDENT FEES Expanded use of student fees, especially for noncore subjects and extracurricular activities, is prevalent. Fees for enrollment, gym clothes, yearbooks, and lab equipment have become standard. Fees for student parking are becoming routine as well. For parents with more than one child in a secondary school, these fees can total more than $500 a year. Through various fees, a large high school can increase its revenues by $50,000 to $250,000 annually, which can add up to $1 million in four years. Participation in an athletic program means yet more fees.

MORE FUND-RAISING SCHEMES The entrepreneurial spirit seems to have no bounds once school and school district administrators jump on the capitalist bandwagon. Bake sales and parent booster groups are routine compared to some of the more innovative approaches being tried around the United States. For example, several school districts in California sent students home with forms their parents could sign to switch their long-distance telephone carrier. The school's parent–teacher association would receive 10 percent of the long-distance payment from each family. If the students signed up friends, neighbors, and relatives, the school would gain more revenue. Projections were that through this mechanism a large school could gain as much as half a million dollars a year.

Several years ago, Del Oro High School in Loomis, California, tested a novel way of raising money to support its sports teams. At one fall football game, three cows were turned loose on the football field for "cow-chip bingo." The field was marked off in one-yard squares and chances were sold. The owners of squares where the cows made a "deposit" were the winners.

QUESTIONS ABOUT FUND-RAISING EFFORTS Given the special place and role of schools in society, important questions are being raised about the appropriateness of many of these newer fund-raising efforts. Equity is one important issue. Schools in wealthy communities can raise more money than schools located in poor communities. If an important goal is to provide equal educational opportunity for all students, then the unequal distribution of funds and equipment is once again an issue. A second important question has to do with children being exposed to advertising

FIGURE 5.7

Percentage Distribution of Total Current Expenditures for Public Elementary and Secondary Schools, by Function: School Year 2002–2003

Note: Percentages may not sum to 100 due to rounding. Percentage distribution of total current expenditures reported here may differ from a previously published report of such expenditures due to rounding.

Source: Data from U.S. Department of Education, National Center for Education Statistics, "National Public Education Financial Survey."

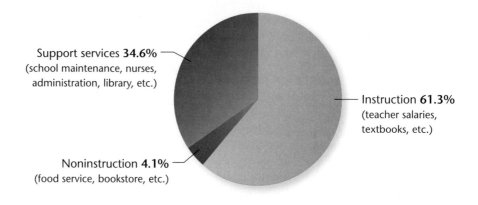

Support services **34.6%** (school maintenance, nurses, administration, library, etc.)

Instruction **61.3%** (teacher salaries, textbooks, etc.)

Noninstruction **4.1%** (food service, bookstore, etc.)

in schools. A report by Consumers Union points out how the underfunding of schools has led to students being a captive audience for marketers.[9] Many educators are concerned that students are impressionable, unsophisticated consumers and are easily influenced. In the school context, many students will have difficulty distinguishing advertising from lesson messages. Because of budget pressures, however, schools and school districts will likely continue to develop their commercial bent.

Education Spending

Once funds for education are collected at the local, state, and federal levels, they are distributed to schools and school districts. Some of the funds are targeted by state and federal governments for specific activities and programs, but most decisions about allocations of funds are determined by each school district. In general, teachers and principals have little say in how monies will be spent.

The overall pattern of distribution of the public education dollar is shown in Figure 5.7. By far the largest proportion of the expenditures (61.3 percent) is directly related to instruction, teacher salaries being the major expense. One-third of the education dollar goes to support services, including much of the amount needed for operating the school district office.

Another frequently used statistic for examining and comparing school districts and states is per-pupil expenditure. For the 2002–03 school year, the national average was $8,041 per pupil. However, as illustrated in Figure 5.8, per-pupil expenditures range from $4,838 in Utah to $12,568 in New Jersey.

STATE AID

State aid for education exists largely for three reasons: The state has the primary responsibility for educating its citizens; the financial ability of local school districts to support education varies widely; and personal wealth is now less related to real property than it once was. State aid can be classified as having general or categorical

FIGURE 5.8

Current Per-Pupil Expenditures in Membership for Public Elementary and Secondary Schools: School Year 2002–2003

Note: Current expenditures include salaries, employee benefits, purchased services, and supplies, but exclude capital outlay, debt service, facilities acquisition and construction, and equipment.

Source: U.S. Department of Education, National Center for Education Statistics, "National Public Education Financial Survey."

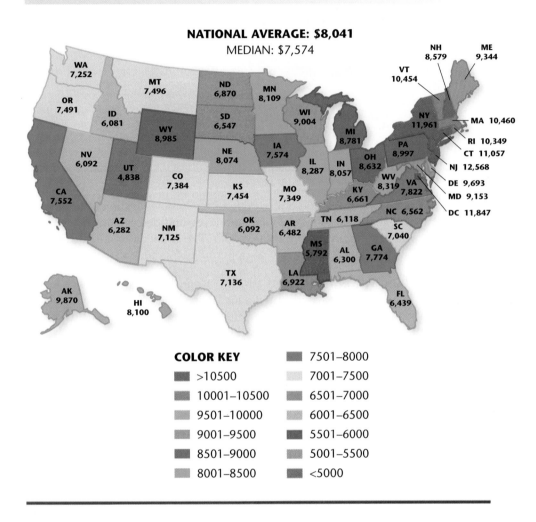

NATIONAL AVERAGE: $8,041

MEDIAN: $7,574

COLOR KEY	
>10500	7501–8000
10001–10500	7001–7500
9501–10000	6501–7000
9001–9500	6001–6500
8501–9000	5501–6000
8001–8500	5001–5500
	<5000

use. *General aid* can be used by the recipient school district as it desires; *categorical aid* is earmarked for specific purposes. Categorical aid may include, for example, money for transportation, vocational education, driver education, or programs for children with disabilities. Frequently, categorical aid is given to encourage specific education programs; in some states, these aid programs are referred to as *incentive programs*. Categorical aid funds may be granted on a matching basis; thus, for each dollar of local effort, the state contributes a specific amount. Categorical aid has undoubtedly encouraged development of needed educational programs.

GENERAL STATE AID: EQUALITY OF OPPORTUNITY

Historically, general aid was based on the idea that each child, regardless of place of residence or the wealth of the local district, is entitled to receive a basic education. General state aid was established on the principle of equality of opportunity and is usually administered through a foundation program. Creating a *foundation*

FIGURE 5.9

Equalization and the Foundation Principle

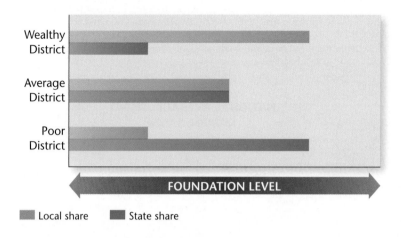

program involves determining the dollar value of the basic education opportunities desired in a state, referred to as the foundation level, and determining a minimum standard of local effort, considering local wealth. The foundation concept implies equity for taxpayers as well as equality of opportunity for students.

HOW STATE FOUNDATION PROGRAMS WORK   Figure 5.9 shows how a foundation program operates. The total length of each bar represents the foundation level of education required per pupil, expressed in dollars. Each school district must put forth the same minimum local effort to finance its schools; this effort could be, for example, a qualifying tax rate that produces the local share of the foundation level. This tax rate will produce more revenue in a wealthy district than it will in a poor district; therefore, the poor district will receive more state aid than the wealthy district. Local school districts do not receive general state aid beyond that amount established as the foundation but are permitted in most instances to exceed foundation levels at their own expense.

STATE FOUNDATION PROGRAMS: LIMITED EFFECTIVENESS   The effectiveness of using various state foundation programs to bring about fiscal equalization has been limited. A major limitation is that the foundation established is frequently far below the actual expenditure or far below the level needed to provide adequate educational opportunity. For example, if a state established a per-pupil foundation level of $1,500 and the average actual per-pupil expenditure was $3,000, equalization would not have occurred.

A second limitation is that most general state aid programs do not provide for different expenditure levels for different pupil needs. Special education and vocational education, for example, both require more money to operate than the usual per-pupil expenditure for the typical elementary or secondary school pupil.

FEDERAL AID

The United States has a history of federal aid to education, but it has been categorical and not general aid; it has been related to the needs of the nation at the time. Federal aid actually started before the U.S. Constitution was adopted, with the Northwest Ordinance of 1785, which provided land for public schools in "western territories." Such specialized federal aid has continued in a steady progression to the present. Almost 200 federal aid-to-education laws have been passed since the Northwest Ordinance.

Accountability

With the arrival of the No Child Left Behind Act, states, school districts, and schools are being held accountable as never before. Although there are many definitions of the term **accountability,** in education it means that schools must devise a way of relating the vast expenditure made for education to the educational results, especially student performance on tests. For many years, the quality of education was measured by the number of dollars spent or the processes of education used. In other words, a school system that had a relatively high cost per pupil or used educational techniques judged to be effective was considered an excellent system. Seldom was the effectiveness of school systems judged by student outcomes—the educational achievements of students. Now those outcomes and their cost must be clearly accounted for.

State aid for education is classified for general or categorical use, and general aid is often administered through a foundation program that will fund each school district up to a foundation level of education required per pupil.

ROOTS OF ACCOUNTABILITY

Accountability has its roots in two fundamental modern problems: the continuous escalation of educational costs and, closely related, the loss of faith in educational results. The failure of the U.S. educational system, particularly in the cities and in some remote rural areas, has been accurately documented. The expectations of citizens for their children have not been met. Although U.S. public schools historically have done the best job of any nation in the world in providing education for *all the children of all the people,* they still have failed some of their constituents.

THE IMPORTANCE OF TEACHER ACCOUNTABILITY

Teachers play an important role in the quest for accountability. They are the primary contact with students, and they are directly responsible for instruction and student achievement. Therefore, they are expected to do their utmost to motivate students to learn and achieve. The assessment of accountability relies on data; therefore, teachers need to keep accurate records with respect to student achievement and be certain that instruction is well aligned with what is being tested.

REWARDS FOR BEING ACCOUNTABLE

The other side of the accountability coin is determining the rewards for success and the sanctions for failure. In the 1980s, many reward programs consisted of bestowing special designations and plaques on schools. In the 1990s, there was a shift to the use of money as a reward or sanction. Under NCLB, few rewards exist. Instead, different forms of threats and sanctions hang over states, school districts, and schools that "need improvement."

REWARDING TEACHERS AND PRINCIPALS

Other accountability initiatives target teachers and principals directly through focused evaluation and training programs, as well as offering financial rewards. For example, some states and school districts pay teachers more for becoming board certified.

SCHOOL AND SCHOOL DISTRICT REPORT CARDS

In the past, report cards were used only to evaluate students. A new element in the accountability movement is the use of new forms of report cards to "grade" schools, school districts, and states. Advocates of report cards argue that parents and voters

> Responsibility is the price every man must pay for freedom.
>
> *Edith Hamilton*

CROSS-REFERENCE
Assessing student learning is a significant component of accountability, which is described in Chapter 11.

accountability
A school's obligation to take responsibility for what students learn.

International Comparisons: Expenditures per Student as an Indicator

Many indicators are used to demonstrate how the United States compares to other countries in education. Frequently the data are chosen to show that the United States is underperforming. One useful resource for international comparisons is the Organization for Economic Cooperation and Development (OECD) website at www. oecd.org. OECD is a partnership of the most developed nations, including those of Western Europe, the United States, Japan, Australia, and others.

One interesting set of financial data compiled by OECD is expenditures per student. The data for six countries are presented in Figure 5.10.

Questions for Reflection

1. Which country has the highest level of expenditure per student? Which is lowest?

2. How would you explain these findings, especially for higher education? Hint: "total expenditure" means funds from all sources.

3. How could you use these data to make a case for more/less spending for schools in the United States?

need to know how well their school or school district is doing in comparison to others. They also point out that evaluating schools is complex; many factors need to be considered. A report card can incorporate many factors and present a clear picture. Opponents express concern that report cards still are overly simplistic representations. They argue that report cards increase competition, which is not supposed to be a part of public education. Proponents argue back that competition will make low-performing schools improve and/or inform parents so that they can make the choice of sending their children to another school.

Journal for Reflection

Develop a list of the concerns and issues that came to mind as you read the school finance sections of this chapter. What topics have implications for you as a teacher? What topics have implications for you as a taxpayer? Then write a journal entry examining your ideas about how schools should be funded.

ISSUE: TAXPAYER REVOLT

In the last forty years, there have been a number of political initiatives by taxpayers to reduce their tax burden, especially the amount they pay in property taxes. This movement has been called the *taxpayer revolt*. A most dramatic instance of taxpayer revolt occurred in California in June 1978 with the passage of a citizens' ballot initiative called Proposition 13, which limited by constitutional amendment the property tax as a source of revenue. Subsequent and similar propositions have been added in other states. The trend is toward tax limitation, which reduces funds available for education. These efforts, along with a low success rate of local school bond referenda and the closing of school districts for periods of time because of insufficient operating funds, indicate problems ahead for the funding of public schools.

Summary

THE STRUCTURE OF THE AMERICAN EDUCATION SYSTEM. Teachers truly are part of large and complex system of education that includes all levels of government from the local, to the state, to the federal. Historically, since the U.S. Constitution does not address education, the primary authority and responsibility for schools has

FIGURE 5.10

Total Expenditures per Student in Public and Private Institutions in U.S. Dollars Converted Using Purchasing Power Parities (PPPs), by Level of Education and Country: 2000

Note: Education levels are defined according to the International Standard Classification of Education (ISCED). Higher education refers to ISCED level 5A (academic higher education-first stage) except where otherwise noted. For more information on ISCED levels, see the appendix. Educational expenditures are from public and private revenue sources. Within-country consumer price indices are used to adjust the PPP indices to account for inflation because the fiscal year has a different starting date in different countries. Includes all institutions, public and private.

Source: Sen, A., Partelow, L., and Miller, D. C. (2005). *Comparative Indicators of Education in the United States and other G8 Countries: 2004* (NCES 2005-021). Washington, DC: U.S. Department of Education, National Center for Education Statistics. Data from Organization for Economic Cooperation and Development. (2003). *Education at a Glance: OECD Indicators 2003.*

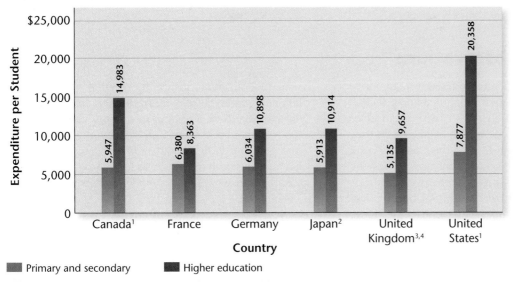

[1]Postsecondary nontertiary data included in higher education for Canada and the United States.
[2]Postsecondary nontertiary data included in both primary and secondary and higher education for Japan.
[3]Postsecondary nontertiary data included in primary and secondary education for the United Kingdom.
[4]The United Kingdom includes England, Northern Ireland, Scotland, and Wales.

been assigned to the states. In the last sixty years the federal government has become more directly involved. The No Child Left Behind statute is a clear example of this increasing federalism. The line authority for schools extends from the teacher in the classroom through the principal, to the school district superintendent, to the state, and on to the federal government. As was illustrated in Table 5.1, education covers a large and wide ranging policy-to-practice continuum.

FINANCING EDUCATION: SOURCES OF FUNDS AND THE MOVE FROM EQUITY TO ADEQUACY. Funding for schools is mainly from various forms of taxes collected at the local, state, and federal levels. On average 48.7 percent of the funding comes from the state level. Most of the expenditures (61.3%) directly support instruction. The challenge is to obtain sufficient funds from the various sources to support schools and teachers while at the same time not causing a taxpayer revolt. As one response, most states have turned to lotteries and other indirect sources of taxation to increase funding for schools. Still, the property tax is the main source of funding for schools in most states.

Discussion Questions

1. The No Child Left Behind Act is having a wide-ranging and continuing impact on schools, school districts, and states. What do you think about NCLB and its impacts? Do you think the federal government should be assuming such a strong role over states, school districts, and schools?
2. Have you had any firsthand experiences with site-based decision making? What do you see as the effects of this feature of school governance?
3. Is local control an issue in your state? What situations have you encountered that illustrate the tension between state and local education interests?

4. When is it appropriate for teachers to engage in politics? How can teachers influence what goes on in their schools? How can they influence decisions at the district and board levels?
5. What are the advantages of using sales and income taxes to fund elementary and secondary education instead of relying on the property tax?
6. Many states have turned to gaming (lotteries, riverboat casinos, and slot machines) as a source of revenue for schools. What are the arguments in support of this funding mechanism? What do you see as possible downsides?

School-Based Observations

1. When you have the opportunity to visit a school or interview a teacher/principal, ask a teacher/principal to draw an organization chart and place themselves in it. Do they just draw line relationships, or do they also consider staff relationships? If they do not do so, ask them about organization relationships beyond the school (e.g., communications with the district office).
2. Seek an opportunity to study a school budget. Determine the different sources of revenue (e.g., local,

state, federal, grants, activity fees). What are the biggest line-item expenditures? Are some monies discretionary for teachers? Note that in most schools, especially high schools, there will be a surprising number of activities that generate cash. Inquire about the implications of having cash on hand, and ask how these amounts are secured and what policies guide their uses.

Portfolio Development

1. One important component of the No Child Left Behind Act is the part mandating that each state set standards for highly qualified teachers (HQTs). Review the requirements for being an HQT in your state and then analyze your résumé. What will you need to accomplish to become an HQT?
2. School finance and spending will continue to be hot topics for school districts, state legislatures, and tax payers. Start a file of articles from newspapers and

newsmagazines and notes from television and radio news reports that deal with school finance and spending. Review the items in your file. Do certain topics and themes, such as school building construction, continue to be reported? When you are ready to apply for a position, having knowledge about finance and spending issues will make you better informed and prepared.

Preparing for Certification

SCHOOL ORGANIZATION AND CHOICE

1. The Praxis II Principles of Learning and Teaching (PLT) test includes cases and items that address "school-related issues (for example, school restructuring, school-based management plans, working in multidisciplinary teams, problems new teachers face, such as alienation and anxiety)." Reread this chapter's discussion of alternative school organizational structures. How might these alternative forms of school organization and management affect your role as a teacher? What skills will you need to function in such restructured schools?

2. Answer the following multiple-choice question, which is similar to items in Praxis and other state certification tests.

Williams High School, located in a major U.S. city, has an academic curriculum that focuses on science and technology. The school has specialized science and computer laboratories, a carefully selected faculty, and an advanced curriculum. Students from across the district with interest and aptitude in science and technology can apply to attend. Williams High School is an example of a

A. charter school
B. independent school
C. pilot school
D. magnet school

3. Answer the following short-answer question, which is similar to items in Praxis and other state certification tests. After you've completed your written response, use the scoring guide in the ETS

Test at a Glance materials to assess your response. Can you revise your response to improve your score?

Some school reformers believe vouchers are an effective means of improving education. Describe the purpose of vouchers and how they work. List at least two arguments for and two arguments against the use of vouchers in public education.

Websites

www.ed.gov The U.S. Department of Education is a very important and useful resource for teachers. Each of the department's offices are linked from this homepage.

www.ed.gov/NCES The National Center for Education Statistics is the main resource for data about schools, ranging from school size to teacher qualifications to an interactive link that allows comparison of your school or district to others.

www.eric.uoregon.edu The University of Oregon Clearinghouse on Educational Policy and Management has many reports and publications (including ERIC) related to the organization of schools.

www.nasbe.org The National Association of State Boards of Education is a good source of information about issues and topics being addressed in each state.

www.oecd.org The Organization for Economic Cooperation and Development (OECD) is a useful resource for comparative data and policies from many developed countries.

www.edweek.org *Education Week* is the weekly newspaper that reports on all education topics including finance, organization, and legal issues. It also has a classified section for open positions.

www.ncsl.org The National Council of State Legislatures is an easy resource to find out about state legislatures and education-related policy initiatives.

www.wested.org WestEd is a major education research and development organization that produces useful reports and develops innovative approaches to curriculum and school organization.

Further Reading

Bolman, Lee G., and Deal, Terrence E. (2003). *Reframing Organizations: Artistry, Choice and Leadership.* San Francisco: Jossey-Bass. Many books about organization theory are complicated and provide few examples. This book is the exception. All of the theories and research about organizations and leadership are described in terms of four frames or perspectives. Each frame is described separately, along with plenty of interesting examples from all types of organizations, including schools. The focus throughout is the implications for teacher and administrator leadership.

King, R. A. (2002). *School Finance: Achieving High Standards with Equity and Efficiency,* 3rd edition. Boston: Allyn & Bacon. This text provides an in-depth analysis of school finance. The author also describes the dynamic relationships among social, political, and judicial forces and how these tensions shape the funding for schools. The challenge of balancing issues related to centralized goal setting and accountability versus choice are examined as well.

mylabschool Where the classroom comes to life!

Go to Allyn and Bacon's MyLabSchool (www.mylabschool.com) and complete the following activity for Chapter 5. Click on **Research Navigator** and then use the following search terms within the Education data base: **charter school, school voucher, property tax.**

CHAPTER 6

Legal Perspectives of Education

CASE STUDY

The Forum: How One School District Found Religion

By Emile Lester and Patrick S. Roberts, *USA Today*, May 22, 2006

Modesto, Calif., wasn't looking for a controversy. Rather, the community was simply trying to create a safer learning environment. What it stumbled on was a successful experiment—one that led to the teaching of world religion in the classroom.

Americans have never been in greater need of understanding religious differences and cultivating respect for religious freedom. The events of 9/11 transformed America's relationship with Muslims at home and abroad, a surge in immigration from Asia and Africa has increased the nation's religious diversity, and cultural conflicts between secularists and religious conservatives occur like clockwork.

So you might think the last thing school districts would want is to bring religion into the classroom. Better to play it safe, and avoid lawsuits and angry parents by limiting any mention of faith to the private sphere. But school officials in Modesto, in Northern California, decided not to play it safe. In 2000, the religiously diverse community took a risk and, in an almost unheard-of undertaking for a public school district, offered a required course on world religions and religious liberty for ninth-graders.

As college professors and social scientists studying religious freedom in the USA, we wanted to know more. Could greater discussion of religious differences actually deepen cultural divides? From October 2003 to January '05, we surveyed more than 400 Modesto students and conducted in-depth interviews with students, teachers, administrators and community leaders. We granted anonymity to students so they could speak freely, but we recorded the interviews. No prior study on American teens' views on religious liberty has scientifically surveyed such a large number of students.

To our surprise, students' respect for rights and liberties increased measurably after taking the course. Perhaps more important, the community has embraced the course as a vehicle for fostering understanding, not indoctrination.

Questions for Reflection

1. What do you think about having a required course on world religions and religious liberty for ninth-graders?
2. How would having such a course be received in your community?
3. Do you think it is legal to offer such a course?

Source: Reprinted by permission of the authors. For the rest of the story, go to the archives at http://USAToday.com.

Learning Outcomes

After reading and studying this chapter, you should be able to:

1. Explain the relationships between the U.S. Constitution and the role and responsibilities of the states in ensuring the availability of public schools for all children. (INTASC 7: Planning)

2. Describe critical issues about the role of public schools for which the courts are being used to resolve points of debate. (INTASC 9: Reflection)

3. Identify and describe court-established guidelines related to the use of public funds for private schools. (INTASC 9: Reflection)

4. Identify and describe court-established guidelines related to religious activities in public schools. (INTASC 7: Planning)

5. Outline the role of statutes and court decisions related to civil rights and affirmative action as they relate to schools. (INTASC 9: Reflection)

6. Summarize key components of the rights and responsibilities of teachers as determined by key U.S. Supreme Court decisions. (INTASC 9: Reflection)

7. Be clear about a teacher's responsibilities and liabilities related to negligence. (INTASC 7: Planning)

8. Distinguish between students' rights and responsibilities as citizens and their rights and responsibilities as students. (INTASC 9: Reflection)

The legal perspective for learning about education in the United States begins with describing the importance of the U.S. Constitution and the Bill of Rights. All else evolves from interpretations of the Constitution. Another big idea has to do with the rights and responsibilities of teachers as employees. For example, teachers are protected from termination without cause. A related important big idea is teacher responsibility, including providing safe and well-supervised educational activities for students. Teachers also need to understand that children retain their rights as citizens while having related rights and responsibilities as students. Another big idea is that policymakers such as Congress, state legislatures, and local school boards also establish laws in the forms of statutes, policies, rules, and regulations. Teachers must know about and understand how these affect classroom practice as well.

Unlike the topics in other chapters it might be easy to assume that the legal perspective does not change, however that is not the case. To illustrate how dynamic the legal perspective is, this chapter presents an important set of social, political, and educational issues that have been debated within and addressed by the legal system. It examines topics such as the appropriateness of using public funds to support private education, desegregation, teachers' rights, and students' rights. The chapter draws on excerpts from the Constitution, state statutes, and court decisions to point out some of the important issues that have been addressed through the legal system. Each of the topics presented in this chapter, as well as the legal processes behind them, applies directly to what you can do and should not do as a teacher and a school district employee. The chapter is organized into three major sections: the legal basis and framing of the public education system, the legal rights and responsibilities of teachers, and the rights and responsibilities of students.

FIGURE 6.1

Sources of Legal Control in U.S. Education as They Affect the Classroom Teacher

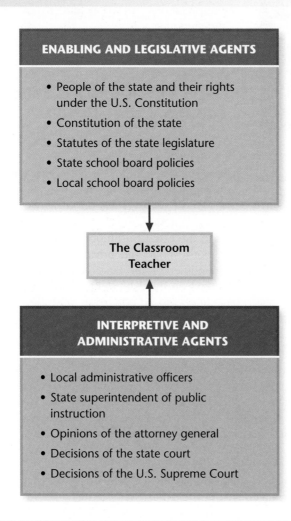

ENABLING AND LEGISLATIVE AGENTS

- People of the state and their rights under the U.S. Constitution
- Constitution of the state
- Statutes of the state legislature
- State school board policies
- Local school board policies

The Classroom Teacher

INTERPRETIVE AND ADMINISTRATIVE AGENTS

- Local administrative officers
- State superintendent of public instruction
- Opinions of the attorney general
- Decisions of the state court
- Decisions of the U.S. Supreme Court

Legal Aspects of Education

The legal foundation of the United States is the U.S. Constitution, and a pivotal part of the Constitution is the Bill of Rights. Within the boundaries of U.S. law, each state is guided by its own constitution. Several additional sources of laws exist at the federal, state, and local levels, and there are a number of processes for addressing disputes. As illustrated in Figure 6.1, in many ways the teacher is the implementer at the intersection between those who enact laws and those who interpret them. Some, but not all, laws are developed out of the legislative process. These are referred to as **enabling laws,** or those that provide opportunity or make it possible for educators to do certain things. Also, laws can impose mandates or prohibitions. Once legislation is enacted into law, if a question of interpretation is raised, then the **judicial interpretive process** is engaged. If an administrative interpretation is not accepted, then the judicial process can come into play. The judicial process also is used when

enabling laws

Laws that make it possible for educators to do certain things.

judicial interpretive process

The judicial process of drawing conclusions about the intent of the wording in the Constitution and statutes.

The U.S. Constitution laid the groundwork for the notion of equal access to education for all.

it appears that a law has been violated. The interpretations of the state and federal court systems form a body of case law. The sampling of legal topics presented in this chapter includes examples from constitutional law, state and federal statutes, and case law based on court interpretations. All apply directly to schools, teachers, and students.

Legal Provisions for Education: The U.S. Constitution

The educational systems of the United States, both public and nonpublic, are governed by law. The U.S. Constitution is the fundamental law for the nation, and a state legislature has no right to change the Constitution. When a state legislature makes laws that apply to education, these laws must be in accordance with both the U.S. Constitution and that state's constitution.

Three of the amendments to the U.S. Constitution are particularly significant to the governance of education, both public and private, in the United States. Interpretations of each of these amendments—the First, Tenth, and Fourteenth—by the courts have had profound impacts on the role and purpose of schools, the opportunities of all students to have access to an education, and the responsibilities and rights of teachers, students, and school administrators.

TENTH AMENDMENT

The U.S. Constitution does not specifically provide for public education; however, the Tenth Amendment has been interpreted as granting this power to the states. The amendment specifies that "The powers not delegated to the United States by the Constitution, nor prohibited by it to the States, are reserved to the States respectively, or to the people." Therefore, education is legally the responsibility and the function of each of the fifty states. Education in the United States is not nationalized as it is in many other nations of the world.

Each state, reflecting its responsibility for education in its state, has provided for education either in its constitution or in its basic statutory law. For example, Part 6, Section 2 of the Ohio Constitution reads:

> The General Assembly shall make such provisions, by taxation, or otherwise, as, with the income arising from the school trust fund, will secure a thorough and efficient system of common schools throughout the state; but no religious or other sect, or sects, shall ever have any exclusive right to, or control of, any part of the school funds of this state.

The Utah Constitution, Section 1, Article X reads:

> The Legislature shall provide for the establishment and maintenance of a uniform system of public schools, which shall be open to all children of the State, and be free from sectarian control.

Through such statements, the people of the various states commit themselves to a responsibility for education. The state legislatures are obliged to fulfill this commitment. While the interpretation of the Tenth Amendment places the responsibility for education on the states, the rights of citizens of the United States are protected by the Constitution and cannot be violated by any state.

FIRST AMENDMENT

The First Amendment ensures freedom of speech, of religion, and of the press, as well as the right to petition. It specifies:

To live under the American Constitution is the greatest political privilege that was ever accorded the human race.

Calvin Coolidge

The powers not delegated to the United States by the Constitution, nor prohibited by it to the States, are reserved to the States respectively, or to the people.

Tenth Amendment, U.S. Constitution

But of all the views of this law [universal education], none is more important, none more legitimate, than that of rendering the people the safe, as they are the ultimate, guardians of their own liberty.

Thomas Jefferson, Notes on the State of Virginia (1787)

Congress shall make no law respecting an establishment of religion, or prohibiting the free exercise thereof; or abridging the freedom of speech, or of the press; or the right of the people peaceably to assemble, and to petition the Government for redress of grievances.

As illustrated in the cases presented later in this chapter, two important clauses in the First Amendment have been applied repeatedly to issues confronting public education: (1) the *establishment clause*, "Congress shall make no law respecting an establishment of religion," and (2) the *free speech clause*, which has direct implications for teacher and student rights.

FOURTEENTH AMENDMENT

The Fourteenth Amendment protects specified privileges of citizens. It reads in part:

No state shall make or enforce any law which shall abridge the privileges or immunities of citizens of the United States; nor shall any State deprive any person of life, liberty, or property without due process of law; nor deny to any person within its jurisdiction the equal protection of the laws.

The application of the Fourteenth Amendment to public education as considered in this chapter deals primarily with the equal protection clause: "nor shall any State . . . deny to any person within its jurisdiction the equal protection of the laws." Equal educational opportunity is protected under the Fourteenth Amendment. In effect, the rights of citizens of the United States are ensured by the Constitution and cannot be violated by state laws or action.

Church and State

Our nation has a strong religious heritage. For example, in colonial times, education was primarily a religious matter; furthermore, much of this education was conducted in private religious schools. Many private schools today are under religious sponsorship. But debate about the rightful role of religion in public education continues. Should public funds be used to support students in religious schools? Can there be prayer at high school commencement services or in classrooms? Does the teaching of creationism amount to public support for religion, or is it merely the presentation of an alternative scientific view? Agreements have not been reached through the debate process, so proponents of differing viewpoints have turned to the courts.

Court cases concerned with separation of church and state most frequently involve both the First and Fourteenth Amendments of the U.S. Constitution. The First Amendment is interpreted as being applicable to the states by the Fourteenth Amendment. For example, a state law requiring a daily prayer to be read in classrooms throughout the state could be interpreted as "depriving persons of liberty" (see the Fourteenth Amendment due process clause) and as the state establishing a religion, or at least "prohibiting the free exercise thereof" (see the First Amendment establishment clause). States are not permitted to make laws that abridge the privileges of citizens, and the right to the free practice of religion must be ensured.

Court cases related to the separation of church and state can be classified in three categories: (1) those dealing with the use of public funds to support religious education, (2) those dealing with the practice of religion in public schools, and (3) those dealing with the rights of parents to provide private education for their children. Key cases related to each of these categories are presented next.

PUBLIC FUNDS AND RELIGIOUS EDUCATION

The use of public funds to support religious schools has been questioned on many occasions. Typically, state constitutions deny public funds to sectarian institutions or schools. However, public funds have been used to provide transportation for students to church schools and to provide textbooks for students in parochial schools.

> Religion, morality, and knowledge being necessary to good government and happiness of mankind, schools and the means of education shall forever be encouraged.
> **Northwest Ordinance, 1787**

Case	Issue	Decision
Everson v. Board of Education (1947)	Use of tax-raised funds to reimburse parents for transportation of students to church schools	Court ruled that reimbursement did not violate the First Amendment.
Lemon v. Kurtzman (1971)	Legislation to provide direct aid for secular services to nonpublic schools, including teacher salaries, textbooks, and instructional materials	Court ruled the legislation unconstitutional because of the excessive entanglement between government and religion.
Wolman v. Walter (1977)	Provision of books, standardized testing and scoring, diagnostic services, and therapeutic and remedial services to nonpublic school pupils	Court ruled that providing such materials and services to nonpublic school pupils was constitutional.
	Provision of instructional materials and field trips to nonpublic school pupils	Court ruled that providing such materials and services to nonpublic school pupils was unconstitutional.
Grand Rapids School District v. Ball (1985), and *Aguilar v. Felton* (1985)	Instruction of nonpublic school students in supplementary education by public school teachers	Court ruled that the action violated the establishment clause in that it promoted religion.
Zobrest v. Catalina Foothills School District (1993)	Provision of a school district interpreter for a deaf student attending a Catholic high school	Court ruled that government programs that neutrally provide benefits to a broad class of citizens without reference to religion are not readily subject to an establishment clause challenge.
Board of Education of Kiryas Joel Village School District v. Grumet (1994)	Creation and support of a public school district for Hasidic Jews by New York State	Court ruled that the district violated the establishment clause in that it was a form of "religious favoritism."
Agostini v. Felton (1997)	School districts' provision of Title I teachers to serve disadvantaged students in religious schools	Court overturned ban provided the district assigns teachers without regard to religious affiliation, all religious symbols are removed from classrooms, teachers have limited contact with religious personnel, and public school supervisors make monthly unannounced inspections.

Approximately 85 percent of the students who attend nonpublic schools are attending church-related schools. Of this number, some 70 percent are enrolled in parochial (Catholic) schools. In states with relatively large enrollments in parochial schools, there have been continuing efforts to obtain public financial assistance of one form or another for nonpublic school students. These attempts have often been challenged in the courts. We will present a sampling of these cases and issues here to illustrate the reasoning and to assess trends in this difficult area. A summary of cases related to the use of public funds for private education is presented in Table 6.1.

TRANSPORTATION FOR STUDENTS OF CHURCH SCHOOLS

The landmark case on the use of public funds to provide transportation for students to church schools was *Everson v. Board of Education,* ruled on by the U.S. Supreme Court in 1947. The Court held that in using tax-raised funds to reimburse parents for bus fares expended to transport their children to church schools, a New Jersey school district did not violate the establishment clause of the First Amendment. The majority of the members of the Court viewed the New Jersey statute permitting free bus transportation to parochial school children as "public welfare legislation" to help get the children to and from school safely and expeditiously. Since the *Everson* decision, the highest courts in several states, under provisions in their own constitutions, have struck down enactments authorizing expenditures of public funds to bus children attending denominational schools; others have upheld such enactments.

THE *LEMON* TEST: EXCESSIVE ENTANGLEMENT

A useful rubric emerged from the U.S. Supreme Court decision in *Lemon v. Kurtzman* (1971). This case dealt with an attempt by the Rhode Island legislature to provide a 15 percent salary supplement to teachers who taught secular subjects in nonpublic schools and a statute in Pennsylvania that provided reimbursement for the cost of teachers' salaries and instructional materials in relation to specified secular subjects in nonpublic schools. The Court concluded that the "cumulative impact of the entire relationship arising under the statutes in each state involves excessive entanglement between government and religion." The Court pointed out another defect of the Pennsylvania statute: It provided for the aid to be given directly to the school. In the *Everson* case, the aid was provided to the students' parents, not to the church-related school. The Court posed three questions that have since become known as the *Lemon* test: (1) Does the act have a secular purpose? (2) Does the primary effect of the act either advance or inhibit religion? (3) Does the act excessively entangle government and religion? Most subsequent cases dealing with the use of public funds in nonpublic school settings have referred to this test.

SPECIAL SITUATIONS   The U.S. Supreme Court seems to have wavered from a strict application of the *Lemon* test in two more cases: *Zobrest v. Catalina* and *Kiryas Joel v. Grumet.*

In a 1994 case, *Board of Education of Kiryas Joel Village School District v. Grumet,* the U.S. Supreme Court ruled that a New York State law that created a public school to serve children with disabilities in a village of Hasidic Jews was a form of "religious favoritism" that violated the First Amendment. Interestingly, in this case, as in some others recently, the justices ignored the *Lemon* test in making the decision. Instead, the focus was on the legislature's creation of a special school district;

In Zobrest v. Catalina *the Supreme Court ruled that no establishment clause was violated in the case of providing an interpreter for a student who was deaf attending a Catholic school.*

the justices noted the risk that "the next similarly situated group seeking a school district of its own will receive one." Another implication of this decision was the indication that the court was willing to revisit *Aquilar v. Felton* (1985) and *Grand Rapids v. Ball* (1985), which invalidated sending public school teachers to private religious schools to provide supplemental instruction.

Whether a public school district could provide an interpreter for a student who was deaf attending a Catholic high school was the central question in *Zobrest v. Catalina Foothills School District* (1993). Under a federal statute, the Individuals with Disabilities Education Act (IDEA), students who are deaf are entitled to have a sign language interpreter in all regular classes. In *Zobrest v. Catalina,* the Court concluded that no establishment clause violation occurred because the provision of the interpreter was a "private decision of individual parents." In terms of the federal statute, the Court determined that this was a situation in which "government programs that neutrally provide benefits to a broad class of citizens defined without reference to religion are not readily subject to an establishment clause challenge just because sectarian institutions may also receive an attenuated benefit."

CHILD BENEFIT THEORY The use of public funds to provide secular services has led to a concept referred to as **child benefit theory.** Child benefit theory supports the provision of benefits to children in nonpublic schools with no benefits to the schools or to a religion. More recent decisions supporting the use of public funds for transportation and textbooks for students in private schools have generally been based on the child benefit theory; this theory emerged out of commentary about the *Everson v. Board of Education* case. The reasoning was that transportation and books provide benefits to the children and not to the school or to a religion. Those opposed to the child benefit theory argue that aid to children receiving sectarian education instruction is effectively aiding the institution providing instruction.

The child benefit theory, as supported by the U.S. Supreme Court, has penetrated federal legislation. For example, the Elementary and Secondary Education Act of 1965 (ESEA) and its subsequent amendments, including No Child Left Behind, provide assistance to both public and nonpublic school children. Title I of ESEA, which deals with assistance for the education of children from low-income families, states that children from families attending private schools must be provided services in proportion to their numbers. When a school is demonstrated to be failing, the school district is required to provide transportation and access to other schools.

TITLE I TEACHERS IN RELIGIOUS SCHOOLS In a more recent decision, *Agostini v. Felton* (1997), the U.S. Supreme Court seemed to be providing increased flexibility and easing the tensions created by *Aguilar v. Felton* (1985). In *Aguilar* the court struck down the use of Title I funds to pay public school teachers who taught in programs to help low-income students in parochial schools. But in *Agostini,* the court decided that under specific safeguards Title I teachers can be sent to serve disadvantaged students in religious schools; refer to Table 6.1 (p. 186).

The issue of public aid to church-related schools is still in the process of being settled. Although it is clear that aid for certain secular services (such as transportation, textbooks, and—under prescribed circumstances—testing, diagnostic, therapeutic, and remedial services) can be provided, it is not yet absolutely clear what further aid will be approved. In fact, the whole body of law in this area continues to be somewhat confused and contradictory. As is presented in the Relevant Research box, some state legislatures are continuing to try to find new ways to provide aid to religious schools without violating the First Amendment. See Figure 6.2 (p. 190) for a summary of statements related to public funds and religious education.

RELIGIOUS ACTIVITIES IN PUBLIC SCHOOLS

The limits and boundaries of the First Amendment in relation to public schools have been and will continue to be tested in the courts, especially in relation to religion. Several cases have dealt with the teaching of creationism and evolution, the practice

child benefit theory

A criterion used by the U.S. Supreme Court to determine whether services provided to nonpublic school students benefit children and not a particular school or religion.

Changing Strategies: Supporting/Challenging Vouchers

STUDY PURPOSE/QUESTION: As was described in Chapter 5, choice has become an important area of innovation as well as controversy. One of the choice strategies is the use of vouchers. State legislatures in several states have passed laws legalizing vouchers for certain areas, usually urban, or in some cases statewide. An immediate question emerged about whether or not families could use vouchers to place their children in private church-affiliated schools. The U.S. Supreme Court ruled in *Zelman v. Simmons-Harris* 536 U.S. 639 (2002) that Ohio's tuition voucher program did not violate the Establishment Clause. Given this decision, opponents of vouchers have had to find an alternative basis for challenging the legality of vouchers.

STUDY DESIGN: Legal research has a different design than educators usually think of as research. Instead of making extensive observations in classrooms or administering a questionnaire to many teachers, legal researchers study case records, the reasoning in past decisions, and the patterns in cases over time. The analyses of these cases and decisions provide summaries and identify trends that can guide future decisions, as well as influence the directions of policy and practice. Obviously, education topics that are more controversial, such as vouchers, will have more related cases and decisions to analyze.

STUDY FINDINGS: An analysis of recent voucher cases by Wendy N. Davis has identified a shift in the bases for the court challenges. Instead of framing the cases singularly around separation of church and state, several recent cases have also been based in key phrases in state constitutions. Some fifteen states have a constitutional clause that requires "uniformity" in public education across the state. For example Florida's constitution states that there should be a "uniform, efficient, safe and high-quality system of free public schools." In *Holmes v. Bush,* 919 So. 2d 398 (2006) the state supreme court ruled that Florida's voucher program violated this clause. In 2004 Colorado's supreme court in *Owens v. Colorado Congress of Parents, Teachers and Students,* 92.3d 933 (2004) ruled that its voucher program violated the state constitution's local control requirements "because it directs the school districts to turn over a portion of their locally raised funds to nonpublic schools over whose instruction the districts have no control."

IMPLICATIONS: As this mix of court cases and reasoning makes clear, determining the legality of voucher programs is still being worked out. The U.S. Supreme Court has ruled that Ohio's program does not violate the Establishment Clause, while some state courts have ruled that their state's uniformity clause may be violated. At this point it is clear that under certain conditions voucher programs can be established, and in some states some families can use vouchers to send their children to church-affiliated schools. Still to be resolved, seemingly on a state-by-state basis, is the extent to which these programs need to be secular so they can be used in church-affiliated schools without being interpreted as state support of religion.

Source: W. N. Davis, "Vouchers Tested: School Vouchers Facing a Different Set of Legal Challenges in State Courts," *ABA Journal.com* (June 5, 2006).

of religion, and the religious use of public facilities. Each case has contributed to a gradual process of clarification of what can and what should not be done to ensure the separation of church and state. Table 6.2 (p. 191) is a summary of U.S. Supreme Court judgments in some of these cases.

PRAYER IN SCHOOL A number of attempts have been and continue to be initiated by school districts to incorporate some form of prayer into public school classrooms and activities. One such case began when the school district for Santa Fe High School, in Texas, adopted a series of policies that permitted prayer initiated and led by a student at all home athletic games. In June 2000, the U.S. Supreme Court ruled in *Santa Fe Independent School District, Petitioner v. Jane Doe* that the clear intent of the district policies was in violation of the establishment clause. The six-to-three majority observed, "the District, nevertheless, asks us to pretend that we do not recognize

Our examination of those circumstances above leads to the conclusion that this policy does not provide the District with the constitutional safe harbor it sought.

Santa Fe Independent School District, Petitioner v. Jane Doe

FIGURE 6.2

Summary Statements on Church and State Related to Public Funds and Religious Education

- Laws and policies that have the effect of establishing religion in the schools will not be upheld by the courts.
- Public tax funds to pay for secular textbooks for loan to students and transportation of religious school children have been upheld by the courts.
- Public tax funds to pay for salaries of teachers in religious schools have not been upheld by the courts.
- Using public funds to pay tuition of religious school children has not been upheld; in Minnesota, a tax deduction has been upheld for parents of children in public *and* private schools.
- Special support services such as speech and hearing teachers may be provided to students in religious schools.
- Religious schools may be reimbursed for administrative costs of standardized tests, test scoring, and record keeping required by the state.
- Public tax funds may not be used in support of public school teachers offering remedial or enriched instruction in religious schools.

The Louisiana Creationism Act advances a religious doctrine by requiring either the banishment of the theory of evolution from public school classrooms or the presentation of a religious viewpoint that rejects evolution in its entirety. The Act violates the Establishment Clause of the First Amendment because it seeks to employ the symbolic and financial support of government to achieve a religious purpose.

Edwards v. Aguillard

what every Santa Fe High School student understands clearly—that this policy is about prayer." Later in the decision, the Court noted, "This policy likewise does not survive a facial challenge because it impermissibly imposes upon the student body a majoritarian election on the issue of prayer." In other words, the district would be imposing a particular religious activity of the majority on all, a clear violation of the establishment clause. "It further empowers the student body majority with the authority to subject students of minority views to constitutionally improper messages. The award of that power alone, regardless of the students' ultimate use of it, is not acceptable." In concluding, the Court stated, "the policy is invalid on its face because it establishes an improper majoritarian election on religion, and unquestionably has the purpose and creates the perception of encouraging the delivery of prayer at a series of important school events."

In an attempt to clarify what is and is not permissible in relation to prayer and other religious activities in public schools, the U.S. Department of Education has published a set of guidelines for religious expression. Points from these guidelines are summarized in Figure 6.3 (p. 192).

EVOLUTION VERSUS INTELLIGENT DESIGN

Education has been placed at the center of what seems to be a never-ending debate between science and certain religious perspectives. The beginning of this debate is traced to the publication of *The Origin of the Species* by Charles Darwin in 1859. Following years of careful observation and documentation of the characteristics of plants and animals, Darwin

A continuing topic of debate and judicial action is the place of prayer in public schools as determined by the First Amendment.

TABLE 6.2 Selected U.S. Supreme Court Cases Related to the Practice of Religion in Public Schools

Case	Issue	Decision
Creationism		
Edwards v. Aguillard (1987)	Balanced treatment of biblical and scientific explanations of the development of life	A state cannot require that schools teach the biblical version of creation.
Practice of Religion		
Wallace v. Jaffree (1985)	Legislation authorizing prayer in public schools, led by teachers, and a period of silence for meditation or voluntary prayer	Court held that state legislation authorizing a minute of silence for prayer led by teachers was unconstitutional.
Mozert v. Hawkins County Public Schools (1987)	Request that fundamentalist children not be exposed to basal reading series in the public schools of Tennessee	Rejected by the Court of Appeals for the Sixth Court, which reasoned that the readers did not burden the students' exercise of their religious beliefs.
Board of Education of the Westside Community Schools v. Mergens (1990)	The right of a student religious club to hold meetings at a public school	Court ruled that based on Equal Access Act (EAA) of 1984, if only one non-curriculum-related student group meets, then the school may not deny other clubs.
Lee v. Weisman (1992)	Inclusion of a religious exercise in a graduation ceremony where young graduates who object are induced to conform	Prayers as an official part of graduation exercises are unconstitutional.
Use of Facilities		
Police Department of the City of Chicago v. Mosley (1972)	Government's refusal of use of a public forum to people whose views it finds unacceptable	"There is an equality of status in the field of ideas," and "government must afford all points of view an equal opportunity to be heard."
Lamb's Chapel v. Center Moriches Union Free School District (1993)	A church's screening of a family-oriented movie on public school premises after school hours	The district property had been used by a wide variety of audiences, so there was no danger of the district's being perceived as endorsing any given religion.
Santa Fe Independent School District, Petitioner v. Jane Doe (2000)	School district policy supporting student-led prayer before football games	"The policy is invalid on its face because it establishes an improper majoritarian election on religion, and unquestionably has the purpose and creates the perception of encouraging the delivery of prayer at a series of important school events."

theorized that today's animals and plants were the results of natural selection over thousands of years, in other words, evolution. In the approximately one-hundred-fifty years since that publication, the scientific base for evolution has become well established through study of the geologic record and more recently analysis of the genetic history of plants and animals.

Some religious perspectives, and a large proportion of the population, view evolution as an unproven "theory." The critics have used various strategies to challenge its teaching, or to require an alternative view based in religion to be taught as well.

FIGURE 6.3

Guiding Principles for the Association of Prayer and Religion in Public Schools

Source: U.S. Department of Education, *Guidance on Constitutionally Protected Prayer in Public Elementary and Secondary Schools.* Washington, DC: U.S. Education Department, 2003.

- Students may pray when not engaged in school activities or instruction, subject to the same rules designed to prevent material disruption of the educational program that are applied to other privately initiated expressive activities.
- Students may organize prayer groups, religious clubs, and "see you at the pole" gatherings before school to the same extent that students are permitted to organize other noncurricular student activities groups.
- Such groups must be given the same access to school facilities for assembling as is given to other noncurricular groups, without discrimination because of the religious content of their expression.
- When acting in their official capacities as representatives of the state, teachers, school administrators, and other school employees are prohibited by the establishment clause from encouraging or discouraging prayer and from actively participating in such activity with students.
- If a school has a "minute of silence" or other quiet periods during the school day, students are free to pray silently, or not to pray, during these periods. Teachers and other school employees may neither encourage nor discourage students from praying during such times.
- Schools have the discretion to dismiss students to off-premises religious instruction, provided that schools do not encourage or discourage participation in such instruction or penalize students for attending or not attending.
- Students may express their beliefs about religion in homework, artwork, and other written and oral assignments free from discrimination based on the religious content of their submissions. Such home and classroom work should be judged by ordinary academic standards of substance and relevance and against other legitimate pedagogical concerns identified by the school.
- School officials may not mandate or organize prayer at graduation or select speakers for such events in a manner that favors religious speech such as prayer.

One of the most famous trials involving religion and a teacher occurred in Tennessee in 1925, when a science teacher, John Scopes, was found guilty of teaching evolution. Although the decision was later reversed on a technicality, the Scopes "monkey trial" has been kept alive in the theater and through the more recent efforts of certain religious groups advocating for the teaching in science classes of alternative views based in the Bible. In the 1970s the alternative view was to advocate for a biblical account as scientific theory; this was called "creationism." As the courts failed to support this theory, a new one, called "intelligent design," has been advanced. Each of these views has argued that life is too complicated to have developed without there being a higher power involved. As summarized in Table 6.3 the courts have tended to view each of these efforts as attempts to advance religion.

Regardless of past Supreme Court decisions, some topics, such as the posting of the Ten Commandments in classrooms and Bible reading in public schools, continue to be challenged by legislatures, individuals, and various groups. One of the outcomes of these ongoing challenges is an accumulating series of judicial interpretations that can serve as guidelines about what can and cannot be done. The summary statements presented in Figure 6.4 outline the overall pattern of the many judicial decisions related to religion and the public schools.

TABLE 6.3	Selected Court Cases Related to the Teaching of Evolution in Science Classes	
Case	**Issue**	**Decision**
"Scopes Monkey Trial"	The teaching of evolution in science classes	The teacher was guilty. The decision was later overturned on a technicality.
Epperson v. Arkansas (1968)	Can the state ban the teaching of evolution?	The "anti-evolution" statute violated the Establishment Clause.
Edwards v. Aguillard (1987)	Can the state require that the teaching of creationism be given equal time with the teaching of evolution?	The Court ruled that the Arkansas legislature violated the Establishment Cause.
Kitzmiller v. Dover Area School District (2005)	Can a school board require its science teachers to discuss intelligent design?	The district judge ruled that "intelligent design cannot uncouple itself from its creationist, and thus religious, antecedents."

Segregation and Desegregation

A troublesome problem for U.S. society has been the history of legal and social separation of people based on their race—in other words, **segregation.** Up until the middle of the twentieth century, the public school systems in many states contributed to this problem through the operation of two separate sets of schools, one for whites and one for African Americans ("Negroes"). Segregated schools were supported by the court, state laws, and by the official actions of state and local government administrators. This kind of segregation, based in legal and official actions, is called **de jure segregation.**

Since 1954 the courts and communities have made intensive efforts to abolish the racial segregation of school students, a process that has been called **desegregation.**

FIGURE 6.4

Summary Statements on Church and State and the Practice of Religion in Public Schools

- To teach the Bible as a religion course in the public schools is illegal; to teach about the Bible as part of the history of literature is legal.
- To dismiss children from public schools for one hour once a week for religious instruction at religious centers is legal.
- Reading of scripture and reciting prayers as religious exercises are in violation of the Establishment Clause.
- Public schools can teach the scientific theory of evolution as a theory; a state cannot require that the biblical version of evolution be taught.
- If school facilities are made available to one group, then they must be made available to all other groups of the same general type.

segregation

Legal and/or social separation of people on the basis of their race.

de jure segregation

The segregation of students on the basis of law, school policy, or a practice designed to accomplish such separation.

desegregation

The process of correcting illegal segregation.

Should Science Teachers Be Required to Include Religion When Teaching about Evolution?

In the one-hundred-fifty years since Charles Darwin published the *Origin of the Species* some religious conservatives have challenged teaching evolution in public schools. The 1925 "monkey trial" in Tennessee found a high school science teacher guilty of teaching that humans and apes are related genetically. Since then state legislatures (Arkansas), state boards of education (Kansas), and school districts (Dover, PA) have directed that evolution not be taught or that an alternative perspective that advocates intelligent design be taught.

Most scientists believe in the factual evidence that documents the history of adaptive evolution. The courts have supported this view by rejecting most of these initiatives by, for example, arguing that intelligent design is not science but creationism in another form and that both are efforts to bring religion into the public school classroom, which would be in conflict with the Establishment Clause. In other words, public schools are not to be used to advance any particular form of religion.

Questions for Reflection

1. What are your thoughts about this dilemma? Regardless of your personal beliefs, do you see why the Establishment Clause is key to past court decisions?

2. A November 2004 Gallup poll found the following:

   13 percent of the respondents believed that God had no part in evolution or the creation of human beings.

   38 percent thought that humans evolved from less-advanced forms but that God guided the process.

   45 percent believe that God created humans in their present form within the last 10,000 years or so.

   What do these statistics suggest about citizens' personal views and understandings of science and religion?

To answer these questions on-line and e-mail your answers to your professor, go to Chapter 6 of the companion website (www.ablongman.com/johnson14e) and click on Professional Dilemma.

A major instrument the courts have used to accomplish this end has been **integration,** the busing of students to achieve a balanced number of students, in terms of race, in each school within a school district. A second instrument has been the use of magnet schools, which are schools that emphasize particular curriculum areas, disciplines, or themes. The hope is that these schools will attract a diverse set of students. These efforts to integrate the schools have had mixed success, and now there is increasing concern over the **resegregation** of schools based on where people live. Segregation—or resegregation—caused by housing patterns and other non-legal factors is called **de facto segregation.**

"SEPARATE BUT EQUAL": NO LONGER EQUAL

Before 1954 many states had laws either requiring or permitting racial segregation in public schools (de jure segregation). Until 1954 lower courts adhered to the doctrine of "separate but equal" as announced by the Supreme Court in *Plessy v. Ferguson* (1896). In *Plessy v. Ferguson,* the Court upheld a Louisiana law that required railway companies to provide separate but equal accommodations for the black and the white races. The Court's reasoning at that time was that the Fourteenth Amendment implied political, not social, equality.

THE FAILURE OF THE SEPARATE-BUT-EQUAL DOCTRINE This separate-but-equal doctrine appeared to be the rule until May 17, 1954, when the Supreme Court repudiated it in *Brown v. Board of Education of Topeka.* The Court said that in education the separate-but-equal doctrine has no place and that separate facilities are

integration

The process of mixing students of different races in school.

resegregation

A situation in which formerly integrated schools become segregated again because of changes in neighborhood population patterns.

de facto segregation

The segregation of students resulting from circumstances such as housing patterns rather than law or school policy.

One of the positive long-term effects of desegregation can be seen in today's highly diverse schools and classrooms.

inherently unequal. In 1955 the Court rendered the second *Brown v. Board of Education of Topeka* decision, requiring that the principles of the first decision be carried out with all deliberate speed.

From 1954, the time of the *Brown* decision, to 1964, little progress was made in eliminating segregated schools. On May 25, 1964, referring to a situation in Prince Edward County, Virginia, the Supreme Court said, "There has been entirely too much deliberation and not enough speed in enforcing the constitutional rights which we held in *Brown v. Board of Education*." The Civil Rights Act of 1964 added legislative power to the 1954 judicial pronouncement. The act not only authorized the federal government to initiate court suits against school districts that were laggard in desegregating schools but also denied federal funds for programs that discriminated by race, color, or national origin.

Subsequently, many efforts have been made to meet the expectations of the Court decisions and legislation. The objective of these initiatives has been to promote integration, that is, to achieve a representative mix of students of different races in schools. In the fifty years since *Brown,* there have been many efforts by school districts and communities and many additional lawsuits. Table 6.4 summarizes some key Supreme Court decisions on school desegregation and integration.

RELEASE FROM COURT ORDERS

After fifty-plus years of court actions related to desegregation and school district responses, questions were raised about the conditions that must be in place for a school district to be released from federal court supervision. Three cases in the 1990s offered instances of conditions under which the courts would back away. *Board of Education of Oklahoma City Public Schools v. Dowell* (1991) is important for at least three reasons: First, the U.S. Supreme Court made it clear that "federal supervision of local school systems was intended as a temporary measure to remedy past discrimination." Second, the Court stated that in relation to desegregation, "the District Court should look not only at student assignments, but to every facet of school operations—faculty, staff, transportation, extracurricular activities and facilities." Third, for the first time the Court defined what full compliance with a desegregation order would mean.

Two other cases added additional clarity to what the Court expects in order to release a school district from supervision. In *Freeman v. Pitts* (1992), the U.S. Supreme Court ruled that districts do not have to remedy racial imbalances caused

Multiethnic education requires reform of the total school.
James A. Banks

TABLE 6.4

TABLE 6.4 Selected U.S. Supreme Court Cases Related to School Desegregation and Integration

Case	Issue	Decision
Plessy v. Ferguson (1896)	Whether a railway company should be required to provide equal accommodations for African American and white races	The Court indicated in its decision that the Fourteenth Amendment implied political, not social, equality. Thus the doctrine of "separate but equal" was established.
Brown v. Board of Education of Topeka (1954)	Legality of separate school facilities	The separate-but-equal doctrine has no place in education, and dual school systems (de jure segregation) are inherently unequal.
Griffin v. County School Board of Prince Edward County (1964)	Whether a county may close its schools and provide assistance to private schools for whites only	The Court instructed the local district court to require the authorities to levy taxes to reopen and operate a nondiscriminatory public school system.
Board of Education of Oklahoma City Public Schools v. Dowell (1991)	The conditions under which a school district may be relieved of court supervision	Court supervision was to continue until segregation was removed from every facet of school operations.
Freeman v. Pitts (1992)	Whether court supervision may be withdrawn incrementally, and whether a school district is responsible for segregation based on demographic changes (de facto segregation)	A district court is permitted to withdraw supervision in discrete categories in which the district has achieved compliance; also "the school district is under no duty to remedy imbalance that is caused by demographic factors."

by demographic changes, but the districts still have the burden of proving that their actions do not contribute to the imbalances. The third case was a return to *Brown.* The Court had ordered the Court of Appeals for the Tenth Circuit to reexamine its 1989 finding that the Topeka district remained segregated. In 1992 the appellate court refused to declare Topeka successful. The court concluded that the district had done little to fulfill the duty to desegregate that was first imposed on it in 1954. The judges wrote that to expect the vestiges of segregation to "magically dissolve" with so little effort "is to expect too much."

These three cases in combination made it clear that it is possible for school districts to be released from court order. The decisions also made it clear that school districts have to make concerted efforts across time to address any and all remnants of de jure segregation. Further, it now appears that school districts are not expected to resolve those aspects of de facto segregation that are clearly beyond their control.

THE SUCCESSES OF THE DESEGREGATION AGENDA Desegregation has had some measurable benefits. For example, African Americans who graduated from integrated schools have higher incomes than those who graduated from segregated schools. They are more likely to graduate from college and to hold good jobs. In addition, the number of middle-class black families is growing. Still, there is a long way to go before the dream of full socioeconomic equality is achieved. It seems certain that schools will continue to be a primary vehicle for advancing this dream from the points of view of the courts.

ACHIEVING INTEGRATION IN TODAY'S DIVERSE SOCIETY

At present more than 500 school districts have experienced some form of federal court oversight to address segregation. At the same time instead of schools and communities becoming fully integrated there is a clear trend toward resegregation, especially in urban

FIGURE 6.5

Events in the History of Affirmative Action

1941   President Roosevelt issues an executive order prohibiting discrimination by government contractors.

1961   President Kennedy makes the first reference to affirmative action in an order mandating that federal contractors make employment practices free of racial bias.

1964   Congress passes the Civil Rights Act.

1965   President Johnson outlines specific steps federal contractors must take to ensure hiring equality.

1970   The Nixon administration orders federal contractors to set "goals and timetables" for hiring minorities.

1972   Congress passes Title IX of the Education Amendments Act that states that no person can be excluded from participation based on their sex.

1978   In *University of California v. Bakke,* the Supreme Court rules that colleges can consider race as one factor in admissions.

1995   The Supreme Court limits racial preferences in federal highway contracts.

2003   In *Grutter v. Bollinger* and *Gratz v. Bollinger* the Supreme Court rules that race can be considered by colleges in their efforts to have a diverse student body, but it cannot be done through a set formula or quota.

areas. As well intentioned as the efforts have been to erase de jure segregation, de facto segregation is increasing. There also is increasing diversity in the number of other racial and ethnic groups in most communities. Schools continue to be challenged to assure that all students have equal access to a quality education. The current strategy for achieving this end is some form of **race-conscious assignment** of students. Strategies such as magnet schools, including consideration of diversity in admissions, and giving priority to siblings in school assignment are being tried. As well intentioned as these efforts may be, some perceive inequities and each is being challenged in the courts.

Equal Opportunity

The Equal Protection Clause of the Fourteenth Amendment has been instrumental in shaping many court cases and federal statutes that are directed toward preventing discrimination in schools. Figure 6.5 is a summary of key events in the nation's efforts to eradicate discrimination. A judgment of **discrimination** can be defined as a determination that an individual or a group of individuals—for example, African Americans, women, or people with disabilities—has been denied constitutional rights. In common usage, the term applies to various minorities or to individual members of a minority who lack rights typically accorded the majority. The principle that discrimination violates the Equal Protection Clause was reinforced in Titles VI and VII of the Civil Rights Act of 1964 and in Title IX of the Education Amendments Act of 1972. Title VI of the Civil Rights Act states:

> No person in the United States shall, on the ground of race, color, or national origin, be excluded from participation in, be denied the benefits of, or be subjected to discrimination under any program or activity receiving federal financial assistance.

Title VII states:

> It shall be an unlawful employment practice for an employer (1) to fail or refuse to hire or to discharge any individual, or otherwise to discriminate against any individual with respect to his compensation, terms, conditions, or privileges of employment, because of such individual's race, color, religion, sex, or national origin; or (2) to limit, segregate,

All provisions of federal, state or local law requiring or permitting discrimination in public education must yield.

Earl Warren, Chief Justice, U.S. Supreme Court (1955)

race-conscious assignment

The strategy of taking race into account for placement of students without making it the primary or single consideration.

discrimination

Denial of constitutional rights to an individual or group.

or classify his employees or applicants for employment in any way which would deprive or tend to deprive any individual of employment opportunities or otherwise adversely affect his status as an employee, because of such individual's race, color, religion, sex, or national origin.

Title IX of the Education Amendments Act of 1972 states:

No person in the United States shall, on the basis of sex, be excluded from participation in, be denied the benefits of, or be subjected to discrimination under any education program or activity receiving federal financial assistance.

AFFIRMATIVE ACTION

In the years since the 1964 Civil Rights Act, numerous statutes and court cases have encouraged steps designed to ensure that underrepresented populations have equal opportunity. These **affirmative action** initiatives have included such actions as formalizing and publicizing nondiscriminatory hiring procedures and setting aside a certain number of slots in hiring or college admissions programs. Over time, concern has increased about the possibility of **reverse discrimination**—situations in which a majority or an individual member of a majority is not accorded equal rights because of different or preferential treatment provided to a minority or an individual member of a minority. This concern has resulted in a new set of court cases, each of which is attempting to redress what is perceived as a new imbalance.

The legal basis for affirmative action is found in Titles VI and VII of the Civil Rights Act of 1964 and in Title IX of the Education Amendments Act of 1972. However, affirmative action procedures and methods continue to be clarified and, in some instances, questioned. For example, in 1996 the citizens of California passed Proposition 209, which bans the state and its local governments from using racial and gender preferences in hiring, contracting, and college admissions. Proposition 209 and other legal initiatives will be examined in the courts.

OPPORTUNITIES FOR STUDENTS WITH DISABILITIES

The judicial basis for current approaches to the education of students with disabilities also is closely linked to the civil rights and equal opportunity initiatives. In addition, several specifically targeted statutes address the education of people with disabilities. Three particularly important statutes are Section 504 of the Rehabilitation Act; Public Law 94-142, the Education for All Handicapped Children Act (EAHCA); and the Individuals with Disabilities Education Act (IDEA).

SECTION 504 OF THE REHABILITATION ACT Under this civil rights act established in 1973, recipients of federal funds are prohibited from discriminating against "otherwise qualified individuals." Note that Section 504 is a federal statute and regulations, not a court decision. Three important themes addressed in Section 504 are equal treatment, appropriate education, and handicapped persons. Equal treatment, as in other civil rights contexts, must be addressed. However, this does not necessarily mean the *same* treatment. For example, giving the same assessment procedure to students with disabilities and other students may not be equal treatment. Educational judgments in relation to students with disabilities require a "heightened standard." The measures must fit the students' circumstances, and procedural safeguards must be employed. Appropriate education means that the school system and related parties must address individual needs of students with disabilities as adequately as do the education approaches for other students. In Section 504, a "handicapped person" is

Any person who (i) has a physical or mental impairment which substantially limits one or more major life activities, (ii) has a record of such an impairment, or (iii) is regarded as having such an impairment. (34 CFR 104.3)

PUBLIC LAW 94-142 (EAHCA) Passed by Congress in 1975, Public Law 94-142 has been amended several times since. This law assures "a free appropriate public

---

affirmative action

Policies and procedures designed to compensate for past discrimination against women and members of minority groups (for example, assertive recruiting and admissions practices).

reverse discrimination

A situation in which a majority or an individual of a majority is denied certain rights because of preferential treatment provided to a minority or an individual of a minority.

education" to all children with disabilities between the ages of three and twenty-one. Children with exceptional needs cannot be excluded from education because of their needs. The law is very specific in describing the kind and quality of education and in stating that each child with a disability is to have an individually planned education. Details of this plan must be spelled out in a written Individualized Education Plan (IEP), formulated by general and special education teachers, and subject to the parents' approval. Originally, the law provided for substantial increases in funding; in subsequent years, however, the funding authorizations have been lower than the original commitment. Two priorities for funding were identified: (1) the child who currently receives no education and (2) the child who is not receiving all the services he or she needs to succeed. These priorities place the emphasis on need rather than on the specific disability.

THE INDIVIDUALS WITH DISABILITIES EDUCATION ACT (IDEA)   This act (1992) developed tighter specifications for the delivery of educational services to children with disabilities. At the time, more than half of children with disabilities were not receiving appropriate educational services. The purpose of IDEA is to make available to all children with disabilities a free appropriate public education. IDEA establishes at the federal level an Office of Special Education Programs headed by a deputy assistant secretary. Further, the act makes clear that states are not immune under the Eleventh Amendment of the Constitution from suit in federal court for a violation of the act. The act encourages the education of individuals with disabilities by making grants to states and local education agencies for children ages three to five, requires the federal government to be responsive to the increasing ethnic diversity of society and those with limited English proficiency, and funds programs to provide education to all children with disabilities.

AIDS AS A DISABILITY

The 1990 Americans with Disabilities Act expanded the definition of *disability* in such a way as to include people with AIDS. Also, under IDEA the courts have found that AIDS is a disabling condition. But AIDS is an issue charged with emotion, as was desegregation. People do not always approach these difficult situations with calmness or equanimity. The courts, as well as school administrators and teachers, are constantly struggling to determine what is appropriate education for students with AIDS and what are suitable educational environments for children with AIDS-related disabilities. The Centers for Disease Control is a useful resource for information about AIDS (phone: 800-232-5636; website: www.cdc.gov/hiv/dhap.htm).

Journal for Reflection

The case study at the beginning of this chapter is a description of how one school district is requiring ninth graders to take a course on world religions and religious liberty. Take some time to write out what your thoughts are about this approach to increasing understanding of different perspectives. As a citizen what do you think about this initiative? As a parent would you want your ninth grade child to take this course? As a teacher what would be your expectations for student learning in this course? Also, what are some of the potential legal challenges that could be brought against this course?

Teachers' Rights and Responsibilities

Teachers have the same rights as other citizens. The Fourteenth Amendment gives every citizen the right to **due process** of law: both *substantive due process* (protection against the deprivation of constitutional rights such as freedom of expression) and *procedural due process* (procedural protection against unjustified deprivation of substantive rights). Most court cases related to teachers evolve from either liberty or property interests. Liberty interests are created by the Constitution itself; property interests are found in forms of legal entitlement such as tenure or certification.

Teachers also have the same responsibilities as other citizens. They must abide by federal, state, and local laws and by the provisions of contracts. As professionals they must also assume the heavy responsibility for educating young people. We will discuss specific court cases briefly here to illustrate some of the issues and decisions related to aspects of teacher rights and responsibilities. Note that the cases

due process

The legal procedures that must be followed to safeguard individuals from arbitrary, capricious, or unreasonable policies, practices, or actions.

TABLE 6.5	Selected U.S. Supreme Court Cases Related to Teachers' Rights and Responsibilities	
Case	**Issue**	**Decision**
Discrimination		
North Haven Board of Education v. Bell (1982)	Allegation by former women faculty members of sex discrimination in employment	Court ruled that school employees as well as students are protected under Title IX.
Cleveland Board of Education v. LeFleur (1974)	Rights of pregnant teachers	Court struck down the board policy forcing all pregnant teachers to take mandatory maternity leave.
Burkey v. Marshall County Board of Education (1981)	Paying female coaches half the salary of male coaches	Court ruled that the policy violated the Equal Pay Act, Title VII of the Civil Rights Act of 1964.
Contract Rights		
Board of Regents of State Colleges v. Roth (1972)	Rights of nontenured teachers	Teacher had been hired under a one-year contract. Court concluded that he did not have a property interest that would entitle him to procedural rights under the Fourteenth Amendment.
Perry v. Sindermann (1972)	Rights of nontenured teachers	Court ruled that a state employee may acquire the property interest if officially fostered customs, rules, understandings, and practices imply a contract promise to grant continuing contract status and thus establish a de facto tenure system.
Bargaining		
Hortonville Joint School District No. 1 v. Hortonville Education Association (1976)	Rights of boards of education to dismiss teachers who are striking illegally	Court said the law gave the board power to employ and dismiss teachers as a part of the municipal labor relations balance.
Academic Freedom		
Pickering v. Board of Education (1968)	Dismissal of an Illinois teacher for criticizing a school board and superintendent in a letter published by a local newspaper	Court upheld teacher's claim that his First and Fourteenth Amendment rights were denied.

selected do not necessarily constitute the last word regarding teacher rights but rather provide an overview of some of the issues that have been decided in the courts. Table 6.5 summarizes the issues and decisions in selected cases involving teacher rights and responsibilities. This summary table is not intended to provide a complete understanding of the court decisions cited; please read the text for better comprehension. Note also that most of the court cases were decided in the 1970s and 1980s; more recently, new federal statutes have been the defining force.

Conditions of Employment

Many conditions must be met for you to be hired as a teacher. These include your successful completion of a professional preparation program, being credentialed or licensed by the state, and receiving a contract from the hiring school district. In each of these instances, you have rights established in law and statute, as well as responsibilities.

TEACHER CERTIFICATION AND LICENSURE

The primary purpose of **teacher certification and licensure** is to make sure there are qualified and competent teachers in the public schools. Certification laws usually require, in addition, that the candidate show evidence of citizenship, good moral character, and good physical health. A minimum age is frequently specified. All states have established requirements for teacher certification and licensure. Carrying out the policies of certification is usually a function of a state professional standards board. The board first has to make certain that applicants meet legal requirements; it then issues the appropriate license/certificates. Certifying agencies may not arbitrarily refuse to issue a certificate to a qualified candidate. The courts have ruled that local boards of education may prescribe additional or higher qualifications beyond the state requirements, provided that such requirements are not irrelevant, unreasonable, or arbitrary. A teaching certificate or license is a privilege that enables a person to practice a profession—it is not a right. But teacher certification is a property interest that cannot be revoked without constitutional due process.

A big moment: signing a contract to teach is a professional commitment by the teacher and a legal one for the school district.

TEACHER EMPLOYMENT CONTRACTS

Usually, boards of education have the statutory authority to employ teachers. This authority includes the power to enter into contracts and to fix terms of employment and compensation. In some states, only specific members of the school board can sign teacher contracts. When statutes confer the employing authority to boards of education, the authority cannot be delegated. It is usually the responsibility of the superintendent to screen and nominate candidates to the board. The board, meeting in official session, then acts officially as a group to enter into contractual agreement. Employment procedures vary from state to state, but the process is fundamentally prescribed by the legislature and must be strictly followed by local boards. A contract usually contains the following elements: the identification of the teacher and the board of education, a statement of the legal capacity of each party to enter into the contract, a definition of the assignment specified, a statement of the salary and how it is to be paid, and a provision for signature by the teacher and by the legally authorized agents of the board. In some states, contract forms are provided by state departments of education, and these forms must be used; in others, each district establishes its own.

Teachers are responsible for making certain that they are legally qualified to enter into contractual agreements. For example, a teacher may not enter into a legal contract without having a valid teaching certificate issued by the state. Furthermore, teachers are responsible for carrying out the terms of the contract and abiding by them. In turn, under the contract they can legally expect proper treatment from an employer.

TEACHER TENURE

Teacher tenure legislation exists in most states. In many states, tenure or fair dismissal laws are mandatory and apply to all school districts without exception. In other states, they do not. The various laws differ not only in extent of coverage but also in provision for coverage.

Tenure laws are intended to provide security for teachers in their positions and to prevent removal of capable teachers by capricious action or political motive.

teacher certification and licensure

The process whereby each state determines the requirements for certification and for obtaining a license to teach.

tenure

A system of school employment in which educators retain their positions indefinitely unless they are dismissed for legally specified reasons through clearly established procedures.

Tenure statutes generally include detailed specifications necessary for granting tenure and for dismissing teachers who have tenure. These statutes have been upheld when attacked on constitutional grounds. The courts reason that because state legislatures create school districts, they have the right to limit their power.

BECOMING TENURED AND TENURE RIGHTS   A teacher becomes tenured by serving satisfactorily for a stated time. This period is referred to as the **probationary period** and typically is three years. The actual process of acquiring tenure after serving the probationary period depends on the applicable statute. In some states, the process is automatic at the satisfactory completion of the probationary period; in other states, official action by the school board is necessary. Teachers may be dismissed for any one of numerous reasons, including "nonperformance of duty, incompetency, insubordination, conviction of crimes involving moral turpitude, failure to comply with reasonable orders, violation of contract provisions or local rules or regulations, persistent failure or refusal to maintain orderly discipline of students, and revocation of the teaching certificate."[1]

A school board in Tennessee dismissed Jane Turk from her tenured teaching position after she was arrested for driving under the influence of alcohol (DUI).[2] Turk's appeal was upheld by the lower-court judge because there was no evidence of an adverse effect on her capacity and fitness as a teacher. The school board appealed to the Tennessee Supreme Court, which rejected the board's appeal, finding that the school board "acted in flagrant disregard of the statutory requirement and fundamental fairness in considering matters that should have been specifically charged in writing." Tennessee law requires that before a tenured teacher can be dismissed, "the charges shall be made in writing specifically stating the offenses which are charged." Nevertheless, teacher tenure may be affected by teacher conduct outside school as well as inside. This issue, in a sense, deals with the personal freedom of teachers: freedom to behave as other citizens do, freedom to engage in political activities, and academic freedom in the classroom.

Tenure laws are frequently attacked by those who claim that the laws protect incompetent teachers. There is undoubtedly some truth in the assertion, but it must be stated clearly and unequivocally that these laws also protect the competent and most able teachers. Teachers who accept the challenge of their profession and dare to use new methods, who inspire curiosity in their students, and who discuss controversial issues in their classrooms need protection from politically motivated or capricious dismissal. Incompetent teachers, whether tenured or not, can be dismissed under the law by capable administrators and careful school boards that allow due process while evaluating teacher performance.

RIGHTS OF NONTENURED TEACHERS   Although due process has been applicable for years to tenured teachers, nontenured teachers do not, for the most part, enjoy the same rights. As you can see in Table 6.6, there are significant differences from state to state. In general, tenured teachers enjoy two key rights: protection from dismissal except for cause as provided in state statutes and the right to prescribed procedures. Nontenured teachers may also have due process rights if these are spelled out in state statutes; however, in states that do not provide for due process, nontenured teachers may be nonrenewed without any reasons being given. If a nontenured teacher is dismissed (as distinguished from nonrenewed) before the expiration of the contract, the teacher is entitled to due process. Twenty-two states afford nontenured teachers the right both to know the reasons for their nonrenewal and to meet with the school board or superintendent to argue to keep their jobs. Cases in Massachusetts[3] and Wisconsin[4] point to the necessity of following due process in dismissing nontenured teachers. In the Massachusetts case, the court said: "the particular circumstances of a dismissal of a public school teacher provide compelling reasons for application of a doctrine of procedural due process."[5] In the Wisconsin case, the court said:

A teacher in a public elementary or secondary school is protected by the due process clause of the Fourteenth Amendment against a nonrenewal decision which is wholly

probationary period

The required time, typically one to three years, during which a beginning teacher must demonstrate satisfactory performance as a basis for seeking tenure.

TABLE 6.6   Employment Rights of Nontenured Teachers, K–12

	Right to Know Reasons for Nonrenewal	Right to Meet with Administration	Mandatory Evaluation of Job Performance	Mandatory Plan of Improvement	Violation of Evaluation Procedure Results in Contract Renewal	Union Can Bargain Just Cause Protection
Y Alabama						
X Alaska	✓	✓	✓	✓		✓
Arizona	✓		✓			
X Arkansas	✓	✓	✓	✓	✓	✓
Y California						
Y Colorado	✓		✓	✓		
Connecticut	✓	✓	✓			
X Delaware	✓	✓	✓	✓	✓	✓
Y Fed. Ed. Assn.			✓			
Y Florida			✓	✓		
Z Georgia	✓		✓	✓		
X Hawaii	✓	✓	✓		unclear	✓
X Idaho	✓	✓	✓		✓	✓
Y Illinois	✓		✓			
X Indiana	✓	✓	✓		✓	✓
X Iowa	✓	✓	✓		unclear	✓
Kansas			✓			✓
X Kentucky	✓		✓	✓	✓	✓
Louisiana	✓		✓	✓	✓	
Y Maine			✓			
Y Maryland			✓			
Y Massachusetts			✓			unclear
X Michigan			✓	✓	✓	✓
Minnesota	✓		✓			✓
Z Mississippi	✓	✓				
Y Missouri	✓		✓			
Montana						✓

(continued)

TABLE 6.6   (*continued*)

	Right to Know Reasons for Nonrenewal	Right to Meet with Administration	Mandatory Evaluation of job Performance	Mandatory Plan of Improvement	Violation of Evaluation Procedure Results in Contract Renewal	Union Can Bargain Just Cause Protection
X Nebraska	✓	✓	✓	✓	✓	unclear
X Nevada	✓		✓	✓	unclear	✓
Y New Hampshire						unclear
X New Jersey	✓	✓	✓	✓		
Y New Mexico	✓		✓			
New York	✓				✓	
Y North Carolina	✓		✓			
North Dakota	✓	✓	✓		unclear	✓
X Ohio	✓	✓	✓	✓	✓	✓
X Oklahoma	✓	✓	✓	✓	✓	
X Oregon	✓	✓	✓	✓		✓
X Pennsylvania	✓	✓	✓		✓	✓
Rhode Island	✓	✓				✓
South Carolina		✓	✓	✓		
Y South Dakota						unclear
Tennessee			✓	✓		unclear
Z Texas		✓	✓		✓	
Y Utah			✓	✓		
X Vermont	✓	✓				✓
Virginia	✓	✓	✓			
X Washington	✓	✓	✓	✓		unclear
X West Virginia	✓	✓	✓	✓	✓	
Wisconsin	✓	✓				✓
Y Wyoming	✓		✓			

Note:
X = States with substantial job protections for beginning teachers.
Y = States with few or no rights in connection with nonrenewal decisions.
Z = Three states have no state tenure laws, even for veteran teachers.

Source: "'Where Should I Teach?' How Each State Views New Teachers" (brochure). Washington, DC: National Education Association. Reprinted with permission.

without basis in fact and also against a decision which is wholly unreasoned, as well as a decision which is impermissibly based.

In 1972 the Supreme Court helped to clarify the difference between the rights of tenured and nontenured teachers. In one case (*Board of Regents v. Roth,* 1972), it held that nontenured teachers were assured of no rights that were not specified in state statutes. In this instance, the only right that probationary teachers had was the one to be notified of nonrenewal by a specified date. In a second case (*Perry v. Sindermann,* 1972), the Court ruled that a nontenured teacher in the Texas system of community colleges was entitled to due process because the language of the institution's policy manual was such that an unofficial tenure system was in effect. Guidelines in the policy manual provided that a faculty member with seven years of employment in the system acquired tenure and could be dismissed only for cause.

Whether or not a teacher is tenured, that person cannot be dismissed for exercise of a right guaranteed by the U.S. Constitution. A school board cannot dismiss a teacher, for example, for engaging in civil rights activities outside school, speaking on matters of public concern, belonging to a given church, or running for public office. These rights are guaranteed to all citizens, including teachers. However, if a teacher's behavior is disruptive or dishonest, a school board can dismiss the person without violating the right to freedom of speech.

DISCRIMINATION

School districts are prohibited from using discriminatory practices in hiring, dismissal, promotion, or demotion of school personnel. In addition to court decisions, federal statutes, such as the Civil Rights Acts of 1964 and 1991, have had a defining influence on the legal basis for judgments of discrimination. For example, the 1991 law expanded protection beyond race to include discrimination based on sex, disability, medical conditions, religion, and national origin. Further, employment decisions must be "job-related for the position in question." The 1991 law also places the burden on the defendant (schools) to show that a legitimate nondiscriminatory reason exists for any personnel decision that may be challenged.

RIGHT TO BARGAIN COLLECTIVELY

The right of teachers to bargain collectively has been an active issue since the 1960s. In the past, teacher groups met informally with boards of education to discuss salaries and other teacher welfare provisions. Sometimes the superintendent was even the spokesperson for such teacher groups. In more recent years, however, formal collective procedures have evolved. These procedures have been labeled collective bargaining, professional negotiation, cooperative determination, and collective negotiation. Teachers' groups have defined collective bargaining as a way of winning improved goals and not the goal itself. The right of employees to bargain collectively and the obligation of the district to bargain are not constitutionally granted but are typically guaranteed by statute.

A contract arrived at by a teachers' union means that salaries, working conditions, and other matters within the scope of the collective bargaining agreement can no longer be decided unilaterally by the school administration and board of education. Instead, the contract outlines how the teachers' union and its members will participate in formulating the school policies and programs under which they work.

The first teachers' group to bargain collectively with its local board of education was the Maywood, Illinois, Proviso Council of West Suburban Teachers, Union Local 571, in 1938. In 1957 a second local, the East St. Louis, Illinois, Federation of Teachers was successful in negotiating a written contract. The breakthrough, however, came in December 1961, when the United Federation of Teachers, Local 2 of the American Federation of Teachers (AFT), won the right to bargain for New York City's teachers. Since then, collective bargaining agreements between boards of education and teacher groups have grown phenomenally. Both the AFT and the National Education Association (NEA) have been active in promoting collective

Global Perspectives

Legal Aspects of Education in Other Countries

The legal aspects of school systems in other countries offer some interesting differences in comparison to the U.S. system. For example, other democratic countries do not have the apparently never-ending debates about the separation of church and state. As nearby as provinces of Canada and as far away as Belgium and the Netherlands, public dollars fund nondenominational and church-based schools. In the Dutch system, there are three separate school systems: public, Catholic, and Protestant. Each is supported with public funds, yet each is governed independently.

Germany incorporates instruction in religion in all schools. In fact, often one teacher is hired specifically to teach religion in regularly scheduled classes. Students have to take instruction on religion and are given a choice of Protestant or Catholic classes. In the higher grades, this instruction shifts toward more emphasis on human values.

Also, in Germany there are no school boards, and there are no publicly elected state boards of education. The school system is run by government bureaucracies. The curriculum and exams are set by the state. However, parents are actively involved in the education of their children at the school site. For example, when there is a parent evening, *both* parents will attend. At these evenings, much of the talk between parents will be about the homework assignments their children have been doing. This level of involvement is possible because parents are expected to help their children with homework. In Germany children have three to four hours of homework assignments *every day*. The school day ends at 1:00 P.M. Children return home and work on their homework during the afternoon.

Germany takes a different approach to consideration of special-needs children. These children either have tutors or are assigned to different schools. If a child cannot keep up with the others at a school, he or she is told, "You do not belong here." The parents and the child will then either have to work harder at keeping up or move to a different school.

Another legal aspect of the education system in Germany is that teachers, as government employees, cannot be sued. One consequence is that teachers do not supervise children during nonteaching times. Also, as government employees teachers are not evaluated after their first year of teaching. As this description of schooling in Germany illustrates, the legal aspects of education and schools can be very different from country to country. Be careful not to assume that schools are the same everywhere.

Questions for Reflection

1. Given the Establishment Clause, do you think it would be possible for schools in the United States to be both public and church-based as are found in Canada, Belgium, and the Netherlands?

2. How would you feel about the stance of German schools that if your child can't keep up, she or he needs to change schools?

---

bargaining. Today, approximately 75 percent of the nation's teachers are covered by collective bargaining agreements.

RIGHT TO STRIKE

Judges have generally held that public employees do not have the right to strike. For example, the Supreme Court of Connecticut[6] and the Supreme Court of New Hampshire[7] ruled that teachers may not strike. The court opinion in Connecticut stated:

Under our system, the government is established by and run for all of the people, not for the benefit of any person or group. The profit motive, inherent in the principle of free enterprise, is absent. It should be the aim of every employee of the government to do his or her part to make it function as efficiently and economically as possible. The drastic remedy or the organized strike to enforce the demands of unions of government employees is in direct contravention of this principle.

A few states permit strikes in their collective bargaining statutes. At least twenty states have statutes that prohibit strikes, however. Whether or not there are specific statutes prohibiting strikes, boards of education threatened by strikes can usually get a court injunction forestalling them. Both the NEA and the AFT view the strike as a last-resort technique, although justifiable in some circumstances.

In 1976, by a six-to-three vote, the U.S. Supreme Court ruled that boards of education can discharge teachers who are striking illegally. Ramifications of this decision, which involved a Wisconsin public school, are potentially far-reaching. The Court viewed discharge as a policy question rather than an issue for adjudication: "What choice among the alternative responses to the teachers' strike will best serve the interests of the school system, the interests of the parents and children who depend on the system, and the interests of the citizens whose taxes support it?" The Court said that the state law in question gave the board the power to employ and dismiss teachers as a part of the balance it had struck in municipal labor relations (*Hortonville Joint School District No. 1 v. Hortonville Education Association,* 1976).

One can argue that strikes are unlawful when a statute is violated, that the courts in their decisions have questioned the right of public employees to strike, and that some teachers and teacher organizations consider strikes unprofessional. In any given case, the question before teachers seems to be whether the strike is a justifiable and responsible means—after all other ways have been exhausted—of declaring abominable educational and working conditions and trying to remedy them.

Although the number of collective bargaining agreements between boards of education and teacher groups has grown phenomenally, many states have statutes that prohibit teachers from striking.

CROSS-REFERENCE

See Chapter 12 for information about how curriculum and instruction can be offered in ways that include teacher creativity.

Academic Freedom

A sensitive and vital concern to the educator is **academic freedom**—freedom to control what one will teach and to teach the truth as one discovers it without fear of penalty. Academic freedom is thus essentially a principle of pedagogical philosophy that has been applied to a variety of professional activities. A philosophical position, however, is *not necessarily* a legal right. Federal judges have generally recognized certain academic protections in the college classroom while exhibiting reluctance to recognize such rights for elementary and secondary school teachers. For example, the contract of a history teacher at the University of Arkansas–Little Rock was not renewed after he announced that he taught his classes from a Marxist point of view. The court ordered that the teacher be reinstated in light of the university's failure to advance convincing reasons related to the academic freedom issue to warrant his

academic freedom

The opportunity for a teacher to teach without coercion, censorship, or other restrictive interference.

nonrenewal.[8] In another case, a university instructor claimed that he was denied tenure because he refused to change a student's grade. He argued that awarding a course grade was the instructor's right of academic freedom. Because the university had given several valid reasons for the nonrenewal of the instructor's contract, however, the court did not order a reinstatement.[9]

ACADEMIC FREEDOM FOR ELEMENTARY AND SECONDARY TEACHERS

Although federal courts generally have not recognized academic freedom for elementary and secondary school teachers, the most supportive ruling was made in 1980[10] in a case that involved a high school history teacher whose contract was not renewed after she used a simulation game to introduce her students to the characteristics of rural life during the post–Civil War Reconstruction era. Although the role playing evoked controversy in the school and the community, there was no evidence that the teacher's usefulness had been impaired. Therefore, the school erred in not renewing the teacher's contract, and she was ordered reinstated.

In *Pickering v. Board of Education* (1968), the U.S. Supreme Court dealt with academic freedom at the public school level. Marvin L. Pickering was a teacher in Illinois who, in a letter published by a local newspaper, criticized the school board and the superintendent for the way they had handled past proposals to raise and use new revenues for the schools. After a full hearing, the board of education terminated Pickering's employment, whereupon he brought suit under the First and Fourteenth Amendments. The Illinois courts rejected his claim. The U.S. Supreme Court, however, upheld Pickering's claim and, in its opinion, stated:

> To the extent that the Illinois Supreme Court's opinion may be read to suggest that teachers may constitutionally be compelled to relinquish the First Amendment rights they would otherwise enjoy as citizens to comment on matters of public interest in connection with the operation of the public schools in which they work, it proceeds on a premise that has been unequivocally rejected in numerous prior decisions of this Court.

When standards are set in place, a successful school is one that provides both excellence and equity—a challenging education for every child. When a school adopts high standards for all, it is telling each of its students clearly, "We respect you and believe that you can learn."

Diane Ravitch

It is difficult to define precisely the limits of academic freedom. In general, the courts strongly support it yet recognize that teachers must be professionally responsible when interacting with pupils. In most instances, teachers are not free to disregard a school board's decision about which textbook to use, but they are able to participate more when it comes to their choice of supplementary methods. Teachers have usually been supported in their rights to criticize the policies of their local school boards, wear symbols representing stated causes, participate in unpopular movements, and live unconventional lifestyles. But when the exercise of these rights can be shown to have a direct bearing on a teacher's effectiveness, respect, or discipline, these rights may have to be curtailed. For example, a teacher may have the right to wear a gothic costume to class, but if wearing the outfit leads to disruption and an inability to manage students, the teacher can be ordered to wear more conventional clothes.

In summary, academic freedom for teachers is more limited than it is for higher education faculty. First Amendment protection of free speech is increasingly limited to a teacher's actions outside of the classroom and school. Before arguing for academic freedom and free speech in the classroom, a teacher must show that she or he did not defy legitimate state and local curriculum directives, followed accepted professional norms and acted in good faith when there was no precedent or policy.

BOOK BANNING AND CENSORSHIP

Ever since the United States has had public schools, some people have taken issue with what has been taught, how it has been taught, and the materials used. The number of people challenging these issues and the intensity of feelings have escalated since the mid-1970s. Well-organized and well-financed pressure groups have opposed the teaching of numerous topics, including political, economic, scientific, and religious theories; the teaching of values grounded in religion, morality, or ethnicity; and the portrayal of stereotypes based on gender, race, or ethnicity. Some complaints have involved differences of opinion over the central role of the school—whether the school's job is to transmit traditional values, indoctrinate students, or teach students to do their own thinking.

Several court cases since the 1970s have involved the legality of removing books from the school curriculum and school libraries. The courts have given some guidance but have not fully resolved the issue. In 1972 a court of appeals held that a book does not acquire tenure, so a school board was upheld in its removal of *Down These Mean Streets.* The Court of Appeals for the Seventh Circuit in 1980 upheld the removal of the book *Values Clarification,* ruling that local boards have considerable authority in selecting materials for schools. Removal of books on the basis of vulgar language has also been upheld.

The U.S. Supreme Court treated this issue in 1982.[11] The decision disappointed people who had hoped that the justices would issue a definitive ruling on the banning of books. Instead, Justice William Brennan ruled that students may sue school boards on the grounds of denial of their rights, including the right to receive information. The Court also indicated that removal of a book because one disagrees with its content cannot be upheld. The net effect of this decision was that the school board decided to return the questionable books to the library.

The latest censorship battleground has to do with limiting access to the World Wide Web. Many school districts and schools are applying filters that restrict access to particular types of websites. New questions related to defining what is meant by "responsible use" and who decides—teachers, principals, or school districts—are now occupying school boards, legislative bodies, and the courts.

FAMILY RIGHTS AND PRIVACY ACT

In 1974, Congress passed the Family Educational Rights and Privacy Act (FERPA), which also is called the **Buckley Amendment.** This statute addresses the maintenance of confidentiality of student records. The statute makes it clear that schools and teachers may not release any information or records of students without written permission of the parents. The statute also mandates that parents have the right to inspect the official records, files, and data related directly to their children, including academic and psychological test scores, attendance records, and health data. Parents must be able to challenge the content of their child's school records to ensure that they are accurate and that they are not misleading or in violation of the privacy or other rights of students. This statute does not prohibit teachers, principals, and other education professionals from making student information available for educational purposes as long as they take steps to maintain privacy of the information.

SCHOOL RECORDS   Before November 19, 1974, the effective date of the Buckley Amendment, the law regarding the privacy of student records was extremely unclear. Even today many school administrators—and most parents—do not realize that parents now have the right to view their children's educational records. Many teachers, too, are not yet aware that their written comments, which they submit as part of a student's record, must be shown at a parent's request, or at a student's request if the student is eighteen or older.

The law (P.L. 93-380 as amended by P.L. 93-568) requires that schools receiving federal funds must comply with the privacy requirements or face loss of those funds. What must a school district do to comply? According to a 1976 clarification by HEW, the Buckley Amendment requires that the school district

- Allow all parents, even those not having custody of their children, access to each educational record that a school district keeps on their child.
- Establish a district policy on how parents can go about seeing specific records.
- Inform all parents of what rights they have under the amendment, how they can act on these rights according to school policy, and where they can see a copy of the policy.

Buckley Amendment (Family Rights and Privacy Act, 1974)

Schools and teachers must maintain confidentiality of student records, and parents must be able to review and challenge the records for their children.

- Seek parental permission in writing before disclosing any personally identifiable record on a child to individuals other than professional personnel employed in the district (and others who meet certain specific requirements).[12]

STUDENTS GRADING ONE ANOTHER'S PAPERS   A common instructional practice for teachers is to have students grade one another's work. As common as the practice is, it resulted in a suit that went all the way to the U.S. Supreme Court. In *Owasso Independent School District v. Falvo,* the plaintiff alleged violations of FERPA in regard to "peer review." The suit was funded by the Rutherford Institute, a national conservative organization. The Court of Appeals for the Tenth Circuit agreed with an Oklahoma parent that students should not grade other students' work. In 2002 the Supreme Court was unanimous in overturning the circuit court and said that the privacy law was directed at records "kept in a filing cabinet in a records room or on a permanent secure database," not the grades on a classroom paper. The Court observed:

> Correcting a classmate's work can be as much a part of the assignment as taking the test itself. It is a way to teach material again in a new context, and it helps show students how to assist and respect fellow pupils. By explaining the answers to the class as the students correct the papers, the teacher not only reinforces the lesson but also discovers whether the students have understood the material and are ready to move on. We do not think FERPA prohibits these educational techniques.

Teacher Responsibilities and Liabilities

With about fifty-four million students enrolled in elementary and secondary schools, it is almost inevitable that some will be injured in educational activities. Each year, some injuries will occasion lawsuits in which plaintiffs seek damages. Such suits are often brought against both the school districts and their employees. Legal actions seeking monetary damages for injuries are referred to as *actions in tort*. Technically, a **tort** is a legal wrong—an act (or the omission of an act) that violates the private rights of an individual. Actions in tort are generally based on alleged negligence; the basis of tort liability or legal responsibility is negligence. Understanding the concept of negligence is essential to understanding liability.

Legally, *negligence* is a failure to exercise or practice due care. It includes a factor of foreseeability of harm. Court cases on record involving negligence are numerous and varied. The negligence of teacher supervision of pupils is an important topic that includes supervision of the regular classroom, departure of the teacher from the classroom, supervision of the playground, and supervision of extracurricular activities. **Liability** is the responsibility for negligence—responsibility for the failure to use reasonable care when such failure results in injury to another.

EDUCATIONAL MALPRACTICE

Culpable neglect by a teacher in the performance of his or her duties is called **educational malpractice.** The courts of California[13] and New York[14] dismissed suits by former students alleging injury caused by educational malpractice. The plaintiffs claimed that they did not achieve an adequate education and that this was the fault of the school district. In the California case, the student, after graduating from high school, could barely read or write. The judge in his opinion stated:

> The science of pedagogy itself is fraught with different and conflicting theories . . . and any layman might—and commonly does—have his own emphatic viewpoints on the subject. . . . The achievement of literacy in the schools, or its failure, is influenced by a host of factors from outside the formal teaching process, and beyond the course of its ministries.

tort

An act (or the omission of an act) that violates the private rights of an individual.

liability

Responsibility for the failure to use reasonable care when such failure results in injury to another.

educational malpractice

Culpable neglect by a teacher in the performance of his or her duties.

In essence, the judge stated that there was no way to assess the school's negligence. In the New York case, the judge said, "The failure to learn does not bespeak a failure to teach." In the twenty-first century, with the continuing push for accountability, there are likely to be more tests of the educational malpractice question.

NEGLIGENT CHEMISTRY TEACHER

In a California high school chemistry class, pupils were injured while experimenting with the manufacture of gunpowder.[15] The teacher was in the room and had supplemented the laboratory manual instructions with his own directions. Nevertheless, an explosion occurred, allegedly caused by the failure of pupils to follow directions. A court held the teacher and the board of education liable. Negligence in this case meant the lack of supervision of laboratory work, a potentially dangerous activity requiring a high level of "due care."

FIELD TRIP NEGLIGENCE

In Oregon a child was injured while on a field trip.[16] Children were playing on a large log in a relatively dry area on a beach. A large wave surged up onto the beach, dislodging the log, which began to roll. One of the children fell seaward off the log, and the receding wave pulled the log over the child, injuring him. In the subsequent court action, the teacher was declared negligent for not having foreseen the possibility of such an occurrence. The court said:

> The first proposition asks this court to hold, as a matter of fact, that unusual wave action on the shore of the Pacific Ocean is a hazard so unforeseeable that there is no duty to guard against it. On the contrary, we agree with the trial judge, who observed that it is common knowledge that accidents substantially like the one that occurred in this case have occurred at beaches along the Oregon coast. Foreseeability of such harm is not so remote as to be ruled out as a matter of law.

Although negligence is a vague concept, courts have ruled that teachers are responsible in specific cases of injury to students on school field trips.

Although liability for negligence is a vague concept involving due care and foreseeability, it is defined more specifically each time a court decides such a case.

GOVERNMENTAL IMMUNITY FROM LIABILITY

Historically, school districts have not been held liable for torts resulting from the negligence of their officers, agents, or employees while the school districts are acting in their governmental capacity. That immunity was based on the doctrine that the state is sovereign and cannot be sued without its consent. A school district, as an arm of state government, would therefore be immune from tort liability. Unlike school districts, however, employees of school districts have not been protected by immunity; teachers can be held liable for their actions. Teachers must act as reasonable and prudent people, foreseeing dangerous situations. The degree of care required increases with the immaturity of the pupil. Lack of supervision and foresight forms the basis of negligence charges.

Recent decades have seen a trend away from governmental immunity. As of 1986, more than half of the states had abrogated governmental immunity either judicially, statutorily, or through some form of legal modification. There has also been an increase in the number of lawsuits.

FIGURE 6.6

Summary Statements on Teachers' Rights and Responsibilities

- Prospective teachers must fulfill the requirements of laws and policies regarding certification before being employed as teachers.
- Boards of education have the authority to employ teachers, including authority to enter into contracts and to fix terms of employment and compensation.
- School districts are prohibited from use of discriminatory practices; discrimination in employment and salary of teachers on the basis of sex is in violation of Title IX of the Education Amendments Act.
- Most states have tenure laws that provide teachers with protection against arbitrary dismissal; rights of nontenured teachers are found in state laws.
- Teachers may speak out on matters of public concern, even in criticism of their school board, as long as their speech is not disruptive or a lie.
- Boards of education may remove books from library shelves under their authority to select materials for schools; however, the removal of a book merely because someone disagrees with its content was not upheld by the U.S. Supreme Court.
- Many states provide for school boards and teacher unions to bargain collectively on wages, hours, and terms and conditions of employment.
- Teacher strikes are unlawful when a statute is violated; in some states, it is legal for teachers to strike.
- Teachers are expected to exercise due care in foreseeing possible accidents and in working to prevent their occurrence; teachers may be sued for their negligence that led to pupil injury.

Journal for Reflection

Today's teachers have responsibilities never imagined in earlier times. School districts specify expectations and evaluate teachers—especially probationary teachers—clearly and closely. Teachers need to know about curriculum standards and be sure that their students have learned the material that will be on the tests. Always present is the possibility of legal action. Take a few minutes to summarize the key points you have learned from reading about teachers' rights and responsibilities. Which of these points had you not anticipated? Which will you need to be sure to learn more about?

LIABILITY INSURANCE

Many states authorize school districts to purchase insurance to protect teachers, school districts, administrators, and school board members against suits. It is important that school districts and their employees and board members be thus protected, either through school district insurance or through their own personal policies. The costs of school district liability insurance have increased so dramatically in recent years that many school districts are contemplating the elimination of extracurricular activities. Consequently, state legislatures are being pressured to fix liability insurance rates for school districts; they are also being asked to pass laws to limit maximum liability amounts for school-related cases. For teachers, membership in the state affiliates of the NEA and membership in the AFT include the option of liability insurance programs sponsored by those organizations.

In summary of the discussion of this section, Figure 6.6 lists brief statements related to the rights and responsibilities of teachers.

Students' Rights and Responsibilities

The rights of students have changed since the late 1960s. Before 1969, school authorities clearly had the final say as long as what they decided was seen as reasonable. A key U.S. Supreme Court decision in 1969 changed the balance by concluding that students do not "shed their constitutional rights to freedom of speech or expression at the schoolhouse gate." Going further on behalf of student rights, in 1975 the Court decided that the principle of due process applied to students.

These decisions led to several successful student challenges of school policies and procedures. In the late 1980s, Court decisions moved back toward increasing the authority of public school officials. Along the way, student life has become more complex, not only because of such threats as the increased use of drugs and the presence of weapons and gangs, but also because a diverse multicultural and shifting political context has made it more difficult to determine what is and what is not appropriate to do and say within a school environment.

To illustrate some of the issues and decisions related to student rights and responsibilities, we present specific court cases here. Note that the cases do not necessarily constitute the last word regarding student rights, but rather provide an overview of some of the issues that have been decided by the courts. Table 6.7 is

TABLE 6.7	Selected U.S. Supreme Court Cases Related to Students' Rights and Responsibilities	
Case	**Issue**	**Decision**
Plyler v. Doe (1982)	Rights to education of illegal aliens	Court struck down Texas law that denied a free public education to children of illegal aliens.
Goss v. Lopez (1975)	Suspension of high school students without a hearing	Court ruled that only in an emergency can a student be suspended without a hearing.
Wood v. Strickland (1975)	Question of whether school board members can be sued for depriving students of their constitutional rights (through suspension)	Students can seek damages from individual school board members but not from the school district.
Tinker v. Des Moines Independent Community School District (1969)	Free speech rights of students to wear black armbands to protest U.S. involvement in Vietnam	Court ruled against school district— recognized to an extent constitutional rights of pupils.
Board of Education, Island Trees Union Free District No. 26 v. Pico (1982)	School board's decision to remove books from the school library	Court issued decision that under certain circumstances, children may challenge board's decision to remove books.
Ingraham v. Wright (1977)	Power of states to authorize corporal punishment without consent of the student's parent	Court ruled that states may constitutionally authorize corporal punishment.
Bethel School District No. 403 v. Fraser (1986)	Power of school officials to restrain student speech	School officials may discipline a student for making lewd and indecent speech in a school assembly attended by other students.
Hazelwood School District v. Kuhlmeier (1988)	School district control of student expression in school newspapers, theatrical productions, and other forums	School administrators have broad authority to control student expression in the official student newspaper, which is not a public forum but is seen as part of the curriculum.
Honig v. Doe (1988)	Violation of the Education for All Handicapped Children Act (P.L. 94-142); school indefinitely suspended and attempted to expel two emotionally disturbed students	P.L. 94-142 authorizes officials to suspend dangerous children for a maximum of ten days. Justice Brennan said, "Congress very much meant to strip schools of unilateral authority to exclude disturbed students."
New Jersey v. T.L.O. (1985)	Search and seizure	School officials must have a reasonable cause when engaged in searches.

a summary of key cases; however, it is not intended to provide a complete under-standing of the court decisions. You should read the following subsections and pur-sue references provided in the notes and bibliography to learn more about these and other student rights issues.

Students' Rights as Citizens

Through a series of court decisions, all children in the United States have been granted the opportunity for a public school education. Further, although school of-ficials have a great deal of authority, children as students maintain many of the con-stitutional rights that adult citizens enjoy all the time. As obvious as each of these points might seem, each has been the subject of debate and court decision.

STUDENTS' RIGHT TO AN EDUCATION

Children in the United States have a right to an education; this right is ensured in many state constitutions. It has been further defined by court decisions and is now interpreted to mean that each child has an equal opportunity to pursue education.

The right to an education, however, is not without certain prerequisites. Citi-zenship alone does not guarantee a free education. Statutes that establish public school systems also generally establish how operating costs will be met. Real estate taxes are the usual source of funds, so proof of residence is necessary for school attendance without tuition. *Residence* does not mean that the student, parent, or guardian must pay real estate taxes; it means that the student must live in the school district in which he or she wants to attend school. Residence, then, is a prerequi-site to the right of a free public education within a specific school district.

ALIEN AND HOMELESS CHILDREN HAVE THE RIGHT TO GO TO SCHOOL   In 1982 the Supreme Court ruled that the children of illegal aliens had a right to a free pub-lic education. There are more than 500,000 homeless children in the United States. Because access to public school usually requires a residence address and a parent or guardian, as well as transportation, in the past homeless children were squeezed out of the system. Congress addressed this growing problem in 1987 with passage of the Stewart B. McKinney Homeless Assistance Act, which requires that "each State educational agency shall assure that each child of a homeless individual and each homeless youth have access to a free, appropriate public education." The law was amended in 1990 to require each school district to provide services to the homeless that are comparable to the services offered other students in the schools. These ser-vices include allowing homeless children to finish the school year in the school they were in before they lost their housing, providing transportation to school, tutoring to help catch students up, and giving homeless children the opportunity to take part in school programs offered to other children.

STUDENTS' RIGHT TO SUE

The U.S. Supreme Court has affirmed that students may sue school board members who are guilty of intentionally depriving students of their constitutional rights. In *Wood v. Strickland* (1975), the Supreme Court held that school officials who disci-pline students unfairly cannot defend themselves against civil rights suits by claim-ing ignorance of pupils' basic constitutional rights. As a result of this decision, Judge Paul Williams, a federal judge in Arkansas, ordered that certain students who had been suspended could seek damages from individual school board members—though not from the school district as a corporate body. The judge also ruled that the school records of these pupils must be cleared of the suspension incident. From these decisions, it is apparent that the U.S. Supreme Court is taking into account the rights of students.

Students have procedural due process rights, including the opportunity for some kind of hearing.

STUDENTS' RIGHT TO DUE PROCESS

Much of the recent involvement of the courts with student rights has concerned due process of law for pupils. Due process is guaranteed by the Fourteenth Amendment. The protection clause states, "nor shall any state . . . deny to any person within its jurisdiction the equal protection of the laws." Due process of law means following those rules and principles that have been established for enforcing and protecting the rights of the accused. As explained earlier, due process falls under two headings—procedural and substantive. *Procedural* due process has to do with whether the procedures used in disciplinary cases are fair; *substantive* due process is concerned with whether the school authorities have deprived a student of basic substantive constitutional rights such as personal liberty, property, or privacy.[17]

The application of due process to issues in schools is a recent phenomenon. Historically, schools functioned under the doctrine of **in loco parentis** ("in the place of a parent"). This doctrine meant that schools could exercise almost complete control over students because they were acting as parent substitutes. Under the doctrine of in loco parentis, the courts have usually upheld the rules and regulations of local boards of education, particularly about pupil conduct. However, the courts have not supported rules that are unconstitutionally "vague" and/or "overboard." The following cases illustrate the difficult balance between protecting students' right to due process and giving schools sufficient authority to pursue their mission.

PROCEDURAL DUE PROCESS IN CASES OF SUSPENSION AND EXPULSION   Zero tolerance policies have complicated the local schools' ability to balance students' right to due process and serving students' educational needs. Procedural due process is scrutinized especially in cases of suspension and expulsion. These cases most often result from disciplinary action taken by the school, which may or may not have violated a pupil's substantive constitutional rights. For example, in *Goss v. Lopez* (1975) the U.S. Supreme Court dealt with the suspension of high school students in Columbus, Ohio. In that case, the named plaintiffs claimed that they had been suspended from public high school for up to ten days without a hearing. The action alleged deprivation of constitutional rights. Two students who were suspended for a semester brought suit charging that their due process rights were denied—because they were not present at the board meeting when the suspensions were handed out.

in loco parentis
Meaning "in the place of a parent," this term describes the implied power and responsibilities of schools.

In ruling that students cannot be suspended without some kind of hearing, the Court said:

> The prospect of imposing elaborate hearing requirements in every suspension case is viewed with great concern, and many school authorities may well prefer the untrammeled power to act unilaterally, unhampered by rules about notice and hearing. But it would be a strange disciplinary system in an educational institution if no communication was sought by the disciplinarian with the student in an effort to inform him of his defalcation and to let him tell his side of the story in order to make sure that an injustice is not done. Fairness can rarely be obtained by secret, one-sided determination of the facts decisive of rights. . . . Secrecy is not congenial to truth-seeking and self-righteousness gives too slender an assurance of rightness. No better instrument has been devised for arriving at truth than to give a person in jeopardy of serious loss notice of the case against him and opportunity to meet it.

Procedural due process cases usually involve alleged violations of the Fourteenth Amendment, which provides for the protection of specified privileges of citizens, including notice to the student, impartiality of the hearing process, and the right of representation. These cases might also involve alleged violations of state constitutions or statutory law that call for specific procedures. For example, many states have procedures for expulsion or suspension. Expulsion usually involves notifying parents or guardians in a specific way, perhaps by registered mail, and giving students the opportunity for a hearing before the board of education or a designated hearing officer. Suspension procedures are usually detailed as well, designating who has the authority to suspend and the length of time for suspension. Teachers and administrators should know due process regulations, including the specific regulations of the state where they are employed.

SUBSTANTIVE DUE PROCESS AND STUDENTS' RIGHTS TO FREE SPEECH   Substantive due process frequently addresses questions of students' constitutional rights to free speech versus the schools' authority to maintain order in support of education. The *Tinker* case (*Tinker v. Des Moines Independent Community School District,* 1969) was significant. It involved a school board's attempt to keep students from wearing black armbands in a protest against U.S. military activities in Vietnam. In 1969 the U.S. Supreme Court ruled against the Des Moines school board. The majority opinion of the Court was that

> the wearing of armbands in the circumstances of this case was entirely divorced from actually or potentially disruptive conduct by those participating in it. It was closely akin to "pure speech" which, we have repeatedly held, is entitled to comprehensive protection, under the First Amendment. . . . First Amendment rights, applied in the light of the special characteristics of the school environment, are available to teachers and students. It can hardly be argued that either students or teachers shed their constitutional rights to freedom of speech or expression at the schoolhouse gate.

In the *Tinker* opinion, the Court clearly designated that the decision "does not concern aggressive, disruptive action or even group demonstrations." The decision did make it clear that whatever their age, students have constitutional rights, and the decision has had a widespread effect on the operation of schools in the United States. Schools have had to pay attention to U.S. law. Educators as well as lawyers have been guided by the principles set forth in the decision regarding the constitutional relationship between public school students and school officials.

A more recent U.S. Supreme Court decision appears to have at least narrowed the breadth of application of the *Tinker* ruling. The case involved Matthew Fraser, a high school senior in a school outside Tacoma, Washington. In the spring of 1983, Fraser was suspended from school for two days after he gave a short speech at a school assembly nominating a friend for a position in student government. School officials argued that Fraser's speech contained sexual innuendos that provoked other students to engage in disruptive behaviors unfavorable to the school setting. The U.S. District Court for the Western District of Washington held that Fraser's punishment violated his rights to free speech under the First Amendment and awarded him damages. The U.S. Court of Appeals for the Ninth Circuit affirmed the decision, holding that Fraser's speech was not disruptive under the standards of *Tinker*.[18] However, the Supreme Court reversed the decision. In the majority opinion in *Bethel School District No. 403 v. Fraser* (1986), Chief Justice Warren Burger wrote, "The determination of what manner of speech in the classroom or in school assembly is inappropriate properly rests with the school board."

Students' Rights and Responsibilities in School

The right, or privilege, of children to attend school also depends on their compliance with the rules and regulations of the school. To ensure the day-to-day orderly operation of schools, boards of education have the right to establish reasonable rules and regulations controlling pupils and their conduct. Boards' actions have been challenged in numerous instances, however. Challenges have concerned questions such as corporal punishment, the rights of married students, dress codes, student publications' freedom of expression, and involvement with drugs.

CROSS-REFERENCE
As is described in Chapter 10, a teacher's philosophy of education will influence what is seen as important student rights.

DRESS CODES AND GROOMING

Lower-court cases dealing with grooming have been decided in some instances in favor of the board of education—in support of their rules and regulations—and in other instances in favor of the student. A general principle seems to be that if the dress and grooming do not incite or cause disruptive behavior or pose a health or safety problem, the court ruling is likely to support the student. Dress codes, once very much in vogue, are less evident today. Although the U.S. Supreme Court has yet to consider a so-called long-hair case, federal courts in every circuit have issued rulings in such cases; half of them found regulations on hair length unconstitutional, and half upheld them. In all, over a two-decade period, federal and state courts decided more than 300 cases on this subject. If there is a trend, it is that students have won most of the cases that dealt with hairstyle. The courts have usually refused to uphold dress and hair length regulations for athletic teams or extracurricular groups unless the school proves that the hair or dress interfered with a student's ability to play the sport or perform the extracurricular activity.[19]

In the late 1970s and continuing through the 1980s, courts entertained fewer challenges to grooming regulations. The later decisions, however, continued to be consistent with earlier court rulings. Courts have supported school officials who attempted to regulate student appearance if the regulation could be based on concerns about disruption, health, or safety. Presumably, controversy over the length of students' hair or grooming in general is no longer critical because officials and students have a more common ground of agreement about what is acceptable. However, as the new century begins, new questions could be raised in relation to school efforts to control the clothing and other grooming symbols of gangs.

CORPORAL PUNISHMENT

In 1977 the U.S. Supreme Court ruled on and finally resolved many of the issues related to corporal punishment (*Ingraham v. Wright*, 1977). The opinion established that states may *constitutionally* authorize corporal punishment without prior hearing or notice and without

Court cases dealing with student grooming have found in favor of both school boards and students.

Would You Support the Use of Corporal Punishment in Your School?

In some states, spanking and paddling students is legal and, in some schools, is expected. From the teacher's perspective, corporal punishment may be seen as a last resort. However, some teachers, school administrators and parents hold other views.

YES

David Mason *teaches eighth-grade U.S. history at Spring Garden Middle School in St. Joseph, Missouri.*

Defiance, chaos, threats, cursing, assault. All these behaviors have risen from rare to frequent in many schools since the elimination of corporal punishment. I began teaching 29 years ago very opposed to corporal punishment. But I have come to see that caring parents and teachers set limits and should be able to back them with corporal punishment if necessary.

Once, parents held schools in such high esteem that children knew if they were in trouble at school they would be in even more trouble at home. Today, it is more common for a student to use his cell phone on his way to the office to call a parent to "bail him out."

A growing number of parents are so protective that they yell at teachers who dare to discipline their children, complain to administrators and school boards, and even threaten lawsuits. Few teachers and administrators can withstand such bullying. Paddling is legal in Missouri, but no administrator in my district will allow it.

NO

Noel Rosenbaum *is a technology teacher at the William D. Slider Middle School in El Paso, Texas.*

Corporal punishment is violence against children and has no place in a public school.

Middle school students often feel that a hit here, pull of hair there, stone thrown now and then are perfectly OK. As educators, we should be good role models and not add to the violence.

Corporal punishment is legal in Texas but in my district, we don't use it. So how do we keep unruly students from disrupting classes? Our school has an "In-School Suspension Room." If a student is out of control, an aide takes the student there for a "Time Out." Often, the student reflects and writes about why he or she acted inappropriately.

If that's not enough, we use a discipline plan with step-by-step, increasing consequences for misbehavior. For the most serious cases, we have an Alternative School where the student–teacher ratio is small and the primary focus is anger management and citizenship. There is a tradeoff: Academics take a back seat—although they are still present.

(continued)

consent by the student's parents, or may as a matter of policy elect to prohibit or limit the use of corporal punishment. It also held that corporal punishment is not in violation of the Eighth Amendment (which prohibits "cruel and unusual punishments").

In response to the greater sensitivity to student rights, many school districts have adopted administrative rules and regulations to restrict the occasions, nature, and manner of administering corporal punishment. Some school districts specify that corporal punishment can be administered only under the direction of the principal and in the presence of another adult. Still, as the Teacher Perspectives documents, there are two sides to this topic.

SEX DISCRIMINATION

Until relatively recently, educational institutions could discriminate against females— whether they were students, staff, or faculty. In 1972 the Ninety-Second Congress enacted Title IX of the Education Amendments Act to remove sex discrimination

TEACHER PERSPECTIVES

(continued)

YES

Misbehaving children have come to believe no one can stop them. Each year, when I tell students that state law allows spanking, they are incredulous. Their common taunt has become, "You can't touch me." Detention and suspension have no effect. Students carry these "punishments" as badges of honor in their negative peer group.

In a perfect world, parents would teach their children how to behave at home. Unfortunately, that often doesn't happen. If the nation wants orderly schools and higher test scores, it must allow educators a big toolbox of discipline methods in which corporal punishment continues to be an option. The occasional spanking of a boy or girl for bad behavior provides an immediate, painful consequence that can convince them and their friends to pay attention.

Even the threat of corporal punishment could be the one thing that keeps a boy or girl out of prison.

NO

On our campus, one boy started out the sixth grade with a noisy argument in the hall. He quickly progressed to disruptive classroom behavior and, ultimately, membership in a gang. We had to assign him to our Alternative School.

Several months later, he returned. He realized he had missed quite a bit of work. He said he had made very bad choices and was now determined to be a successful student. At his first award night he told me, "I never knew that if I gave of myself and really worked hard, I would receive far more back than I could ever expect!" What a beautiful smile he had, clutching his certificates for most improved student!

Not all students respond so well. But our Alternative School gave him a stronger and longer-lasting boost in the right direction than a paddle could have done.

Source: "Corporal Punishment Is Legal in 22 States. Would You Support Its Use in Your School?" *NEA Today* (September 2005), p. 38. Reprinted by permission of the National Education Association.

WHAT IS YOUR PERSPECTIVE ON THIS ISSUE?
Would you support the use of corporal punishment in your school?

To give your opinion, go to Chapter 6 of the companion website (www.ablongman.com/johnson14e) and click on Teacher Perspectives.

against students and employees in federally assisted programs. The key provision in Title IX states, "No person in the United States shall, on the basis of sex, be excluded from participation in, be denied the benefits of, or be subjected to discrimination under any education program or activity receiving federal financial assistance." Title IX is enforced by the Department of Education's Office of Civil Rights. An individual or organization can allege that any policy or practice is discriminatory by writing a letter of complaint to the secretary of education. An administrative hearing is the next step in the process. Further steps include suing for monetary damages under Title IX, which the U.S. Supreme Court affirmed in *Franklin v. Guinneth County Schools* (1992).

MARRIAGE AND PREGNANCY

In the past, it was not unusual for school officials to expel students who married. Some educators reasoned that marriage brought on additional responsibilities, such as the establishment of a household, and therefore that married students could not

> A recipient (e.g., a school district) shall not apply any rule concerning a student's actual or potential parental, family, or marital status which treats students differently on the basis of sex.
>
> ***Title IX of the Education Amendments Act of 1972***

perform well in school. They also believed that exclusion would help deter other teenagers from marrying. Courts tended to uphold school officials in these positions. Both courts and school officials acted consistently in not rigidly enforcing compulsory attendance statutes for underage students who married.

School officials today cannot prohibit a student from attending school merely because he or she is married. This position is based on the above-mentioned Title IX and on the notion that every child has a right to attend school. Public policy today encourages students to acquire as much education as they can. Not only are married students encouraged to remain in school, but they are also entitled to the same rights and privileges as unmarried students. Thus, they have the right to take any course the school offers and to participate in extracurricular activities open to other students. That is, participation in extracurricular activities cannot be denied a student solely on the basis of marital status. However, a student's attendance and participation rights can be removed if his or her behavior is deleterious to other students.

Today's schools also enroll more pregnant students than ever before. Title IX prohibits their exclusion from school or from participation in extracurricular activities. Many school systems have reorganized their school programs so that courses can be offered during after-school hours or in the evenings to accommodate married and pregnant students. This arrangement makes it easier for students to work during the day and complete their education at a time that is convenient for them. Such programs often include courses and topics aimed at the specific audience, as well as counseling programs to assist students with their adjustment to marriage and family life.

CHILD ABUSE AND NEGLECT

Government bodies in the United States have the right to exercise police power, which means that government is entrusted with the responsibility of looking after the health, safety, and welfare of all its citizens. In effect, each state acts as a guardian over all its people, exercising that role specifically over individuals not able to look after themselves. This guardianship extends to care for children who have been either abused or neglected by their parents. All fifty states have statutes dealing with this issue. These statutes generally protect children under the age of eighteen, but the scope of protection and definitions of abuse and neglect vary considerably among the states. In 1974, Congress passed the Child Abuse Prevention and Treatment Act, which provides financial assistance to states that have developed and implemented programs for identifying, preventing, and treating instances of child abuse and neglect.

The severity of this problem has been highlighted by the requirement of mandatory reporting of suspected abuse and neglect. Formerly, this reporting was limited mainly to physicians, but today educators are also required to report instances of suspected abuse and neglect. Some teachers are reluctant to do so because they fear a breakdown in student–teacher–parent relationships and the possibility of lawsuits alleging invasion of privacy, assault, or slander. Their fear should be diminished, however, by statutes that grant them immunity for acting in good faith.

STUDENT PUBLICATIONS

It is important that students bring a certain ragamuffin, barefoot irreverence to their studies; they are not here to worship what is known, but to question it.

Jacob Chanowski

A significant decision relative to "underground" student newspapers was made in Illinois in 1970.[20] Students were expelled for distributing a newspaper named *Grass High,* which the students produced at home and which criticized school officials and used vulgar language. The students were expelled under an Illinois statute that empowered boards of education to expel pupils guilty of gross disobedience or misconduct. A federal court in Illinois supported the board of education, but on appeal the Court of Appeals for the Seventh Circuit reversed the decision. The school board was not able to validate student disruption and interference as required by *Tinker.* The expelled students were entitled to collect damages. An implication is that the rights of students regarding newspapers they print at home are stronger than their rights of free expression in official school publications.

Early in 1988, in a landmark decision (*Hazelwood School District v. Kuhlmeier*), the U.S. Supreme Court ruled that administrators have broad authority to control student expression in official school newspapers, theatrical productions, and other forums that are part of the curriculum. In reaching that decision, the Court determined that the *Spectrum,* the school newspaper of the Hazelwood District, was not a public forum. A school policy of the Hazelwood District required that the principal review each proposed issue of the *Spectrum.* The principal objected to two articles scheduled to appear in one issue. One of the articles was about girls at the school who had become pregnant; the other discussed the effects of divorce on students. Neither article used real names. The principal deleted two pages of the *Spectrum* rather than delete only the offending articles or require that they be modified. He stated that there was no time to make any changes in the articles and that the newspaper had to be printed immediately or not at all.

Three student journalists sued, contending that their freedom of speech had been violated. The Supreme Court upheld the principal's action. Justice Byron White decided that the *Spectrum* was not a public forum, but rather a supervised learning experience for journalism students. In effect, the censorship of a student press was upheld by the Supreme Court. In Justice White's words,

> schools must be able to set high standards for the student speech that is disseminated under [their] auspices—standards that may be higher than those demanded by some newspaper publishers and theatrical producers in the "real" world—and may refuse to disseminate student speech that does not meet those standards.
>
> Accordingly, we hold that the standard articulated in *Tinker* for determining when a school may punish student expression need not also be the standard for determining when a school may refuse to lend its name and resources to the dissemination of student expression.

The issue of institutional control over publications has not yet been fully resolved. In response to questions about student publications and their distribution, school boards have endeavored to write rules and regulations that will withstand judicial scrutiny. A prompt review and reasonably fast appeal procedures are vital. Students should also be advised of distribution rules and abide by them.

RIGHTS OF STUDENTS WITH DISABILITIES

Before the early 1970s, the access to education of students with disabilities was left to the discretion of different levels of government. In the early 1970s, court decisions established the position that students with disabilities were entitled to an "appropriate" education and to procedural protections against arbitrary treatment. Congress subsequently specified a broad set of substantive and procedural rights via Section 504 of the Rehabilitation Act and Public Law 94-142, the Education for All Handicapped Children Act (EAHCA). Since that time there has been a continuing series of legislative and legal refinements and extensions of the intents to see that students with special needs have appropriate educational opportunities. The problem has been to define what is meant by "appropriate." This examination and clarification process continues to unfold.

One recent case regarding student rights dealt with a violation of P.L. 94-142. That law requires public school officials to keep disruptive or violent students with disabilities in their current classrooms pending hearings on their behavior. In the decision made in *Honig v. Doe* (1988), the U.S. Supreme Court upheld lower-court rulings that San Francisco school district officials violated the act in 1980 when they indefinitely suspended and then attempted to expel two students who were emotionally disturbed and dangerous as officials claimed.

The act authorizes officials to suspend dangerous children with disabilities for a maximum of ten days. Longer suspensions or expulsions are permissible only if the child's parents consent to the action taken or if the officials can convince a federal

Where reasonable suspicion exists, school authorities do not need a warrant to search a student's locker or a student's vehicle on campus.

district judge that the child poses a danger to himself or herself or to others. The rules under which school officials must operate also are more limiting if the misbehavior is a manifestation of the student's disability.

It is clear that Congress meant to restrain the authority that schools had traditionally used to exclude students with disabilities, particularly students who are emotionally disturbed, from school. But P.L. 94-142 did not leave school administrators powerless to deal with dangerous students.

STUDENT AND LOCKER SEARCHES

Most courts have refused to subject public school searches to strict Fourth Amendment standards. In general, the Fourth Amendment protects individuals from search without a warrant (court order). Many lower courts, however, have decided in favor of a more lenient interpretation of the Fourth Amendment in school searches. The rationale is that school authorities are obligated to maintain discipline and a sound educational environment and that that responsibility, along with their in loco parentis powers, gives them the right to conduct searches and seize contraband on reasonable suspicion without a warrant. First, however, school officials may only search for evidence that a student has violated a school rule or a law. Also, there must be a valid rule or law in place.

School authorities do not need a warrant to search a student's locker or a student vehicle on campus. For searches of a student's person, however, courts apply a higher standard. Where reasonable suspicion exists, a school official will likely be upheld. Reasonable suspicion exists when one has information that a student is in possession of something harmful or dangerous or when there is evidence of illegal activities such as drug dealing (money, a list of customers, or rolling papers). The second consideration is the way that the search of a student's person is conducted. School officials are advised to have students remove contents from their clothing rather than having a teacher or administrator do it. A further caution is not to force students to remove all their clothing or undress to their underwear. To date, courts have not upheld school officials in strip searches; these cases evoke the greatest judicial sympathy toward student claims for damages on grounds of illegal searches.[21]

PEER SEXUAL HARASSMENT

Title IX prohibits sex discrimination, and this includes students' harassing other students. Teasing, snapping bra straps, requesting sexual favors, making lewd comments about one's appearance or body parts, telling sexual jokes, engaging in physical abuse, and touching inappropriately are examples of peer sexual harassment. It is important for teachers to make it clear that sexual harassment will not be tolerated. School districts are supposed to have in place a grievance procedure for sex discrimination complaints. Students and/or their parents can file a complaint with the Office of Civil Rights also. All allegations must be investigated promptly, and schools must take immediate action in cases in which harassment behaviors have been confirmed. Keep in mind that sexual harassment is not limited to high school students; middle school and in some cases elementary school children are also sexually harassed. In summary of the topics covered in this section, Figure 6.7 lists brief statements related to the rights and responsibilities of students.

Journal for Reflection

Now it should be clear to you that students have rights and that teachers need to be aware of them. Teachers should always be sure that another teacher or administrator is present when disciplinary action is taken. When taking any such action, teachers must be sure that the principal or other administrators are informed. As a way of making the rights and responsibilities real for you, think back across your years as a student. Compare some of the things that you experienced or witnessed with what you have just read about the legal rights and responsibilities of students.

FIGURE 6.7

Summary Statements on Students' Rights and Responsibilities

- State constitutions provide that a child has the right to an education; to date, students have been unsuccessful in suing school board members on the ground that they have not learned anything.
- The due process clause provides that a child is entitled to notice of charges and the opportunity for a hearing prior to being suspended from school for misbehavior.
- Students enjoy freedom of speech at school unless that speech is indecent or leads to disruption; courts are in agreement that school officials can regulate the content of student newspapers. Underground newspapers are not subject to this oversight.
- Students may be awarded damages from school board members for a violation of their constitutional rights if they can establish that they were injured by the deprivation and that the school official deliberately violated those rights.
- The use of corporal punishment is not prohibited by the U.S. Constitution, but excessive punishment may be barred by the Fourteenth Amendment.
- Students may be restricted in their dress when there are problems of disruption, health, or safety.
- Assignments of students to activities or classes in general on the basis of sex is not consistent with Title IX. These assignments may be made in such areas as sex education classes or when sports are available for both sexes.
- Restricting a student's activities on the basis of marriage or pregnancy is inconsistent with the equal protection clause and Title IX.
- Teachers are required to report to proper authorities suspected instances of child abuse and neglect.
- Parents have the right to examine their children's educational records. Students age eighteen or older have the right to examine their records.
- School officials may search students, lockers, and student property without a search warrant, but they must have reasonable grounds for believing that a student is in possession of evidence of a violation of a law or school rule.

Summary

LEGAL ASPECTS OF EDUCATION. The U.S. Constitution is the starting point for viewing schools from the legal perspective. Interestingly, education is not mentioned directly in the Constitution, but the Tenth Amendment has been interpreted as assigning responsibility to each state for education of its citizens. Therefore, how education is addressed in each state's constitution is of paramount importance. Interpretations of law and the resolution of disputes, whether they be about separation of church and state, desegregation, or teachers' rights, ultimately are decided by the U.S. and state supreme courts.

TEACHERS' RIGHTS AND RESPONSIBILITIES. Teachers' rights as citizens and employees, including procedural and substantive due process, are protected. However, teachers do not have absolute academic freedom and must always be attentive to protecting the privacy of student records and guarding against negligence and malpractice.

STUDENTS' RIGHTS AND RESPONSIBILITIES. Students too have rights as citizens, including the right to an education. They have due process rights, protection from discrimination, and, within limits, freedom of expression. However schools have the authority to determine when student conduct is disruptive.

Discussion Questions

1. How do you view the continuing debate over the demand of some to include creationism/intelligent design with the teaching of evolution? Should science teachers and curriculum be required to include religion when teaching evolution?

2. The appropriate place for prayer in public schools continues to be a source of contention. What will you say and do if a parent wants you to have a moment of prayer in your classroom?

3. How should you as a teacher accommodate the religious interest of children in your class who are of a religion other than Christianity, such as Judaism, Islam, or Buddhism?

4. In *Ingraham v. Wright* (1977), the U.S. Supreme Court ruled that states may authorize the use of corporal punishment as school policy. The U.S. military has not allowed corporal punishment for 100 years; why should it be disallowed in the military but be permissible in schools? Is it ever appropriate in schools?

5. Each fall, teacher strikes somewhere in the country delay the opening of school. Have you ever been involved in a strike of any kind? What do you think are the most critical consequences of teacher strikes? If your association/union leaders called for a strike, would you join the picket line or teach your classes?

6. What are your thoughts about balancing student rights against school officials' need to maintain an environment conducive to learning? Should school officials have more authority? Should students have greater freedom?

7. AIDS is a legally recognized disability. If, as a teacher, you are to have an HIV-positive student in your classroom, what are that student's rights under the law? What are your responsibilities as a teacher?

School-Based Observations

1. Beginning teachers do not have the same rights as tenured teachers, but they do have rights. With a partner, compare and contrast the rights of beginning teachers in two school districts. Some of the items to check are length of the probationary period, the basis for tenure decision, how the tenure decision-making process works, and the rights of probationary teachers.

2. Interview an experienced teacher about students' rights. Ask him or her to provide examples of situations in which it was important for the teacher to be aware of student rights. What were the critical points to be considered? What were the related responsibilities of the teacher? What advice would this teacher have for today's beginning teachers?

Portfolio Development

1. Pick a school district where you think you would like to work as a teacher. Obtain a copy of the teacher employment contract from the district human resources/personnel office and study it. What does the contract say about your rights as a district employee and as a teacher? What does it say about your responsibilities? There may be references to other legal documents such as an employee handbook and board policies; if so, become familiar with those documents too. Together, these documents set the parameters for what you can, should, and should not do as a teacher. Place these documents and your notes in a folio file folder and save them for later use.

2. From time to time, newspapers and weekly newsmagazines carry reports about disagreements between students and school officials. Collect these reports, paying special attention to the legal interpretations drawn by each side, and consider the implications for you. In all instances, keep in mind that both teachers and students have legal responsibilities as well as rights. These clippings and notes may be a useful resource for you someday, when as a teacher you are confronted with a question about student and teacher rights.

Preparing for Certification

TEACHERS' AND STUDENTS' RIGHTS

1. The Praxis II Principles of Learning and Teaching (PLT) test includes cases and items that address "teachers' and students' legal rights inside and outside the classroom." Review the tables in this chapter that present key legal decisions affecting teachers' and students' rights, then list the five law-related parameters that you think will influence you the most in the subject area or geographical location in which you plan to teach.

2. Answer the following multiple-choice question, which is similar to items in Praxis and other state certification tests.

The Buckley Amendment

A. permits corporal punishment as long as district policies and procedures are in place.
B. allows all parents access to their children's academic records.
C. establishes that married or pregnant students have the same rights and privileges as other students.
D. states that all students with disabilities are entitled to an "appropriate" education.

3. Answer the following short-answer question, which is similar to items in Praxis and other state certification tests. After you've completed your written response, use the scoring guide in the ETS *Test at a Glance* materials to assess your response. Can you revise your response to improve your score?

What are the arguments for and against tenure for teachers? What is your position, and why?

Websites

http://catalog.loc.gov The Library of Congress Catalog provides a quick way to access the text of government bills, including those related to education.

http://janweb.icdi.wvu.edu *and* www.schoolnet.ca/sne There are many websites with information on special education topics. The ADA (Americans with Disabilities Act) Document Center and the Special Needs Education Network are two useful sites to check first.

www.abanet.org The American Bar Association's website provides access to its journal, analyses of court decisions, and a large database of court decisions.

www.dirksencongressionalcenter.org The Dirksen Congressional Center is a very useful resource for teachers. It offers a newsletter, curriculum resources, and links for educators to aid in improving understanding of Congress. One new feature describes how a bill becomes a law.

www.lawschool.cornell.edu The Cornell Law School website is easy to use and provides access to court decisions, news related to court cases, directories, and current awareness items.

www.cnn.com/LAW CNN operates a number of useful websites including Law Center, which reports on state, national, and international court proceedings.

www.nea.org The National Education Association website offers legal information and a number of teaching supports for beginning teachers.

Further Reading

Essex, Nathan L. (2005). *School Law and the Public Schools: A Practical Guide for Educational Leaders,* 3rd edition. Boston: Allyn & Bacon. This book presents issues and topics briefly, and for each it provides a table called "Administrative Guide" that summarizes legal points and suggests appropriate steps to take.

LaMorte, Michael W. (2005). *School Law: Cases and Concepts,* 8th edition. Boston: Allyn & Bacon. Each chapter presents an in-depth analysis of cases and points of law related to public education, teacher rights, and student rights.

Parker-Jenkins, Marie, Hartas, Dimitra, and Irving, Barrie A. (2005). *In Good Faith: Schools, Religion and Public Funding.* Burlington, VT: Ashgate. Sometimes it is useful to read how people in another country think about an issue. This book does that by examining issues in England, where different religious groups are advocating for their own schools with public support.

Zirkel, Perry A. "Courtside." *Phi Delta Kappan.* A regular column in the *Phi Delta Kappan* providing timely and pertinent information about legal issues.

(mylabschool
Where the classroom comes to life!

Go to Allyn and Bacon's MyLabSchool (www.mylabschool.com) and complete the following activity for Chapter 6. Click on **Courses;** click on **Foundations/Intro Teaching;** click on **MLS Video Lab;** then click on **Legal Foundations.**

Chapter 7
The Early History of
Education in a
Changing World

Chapter 8
Historical Perspectives
of Education

HISTORICAL PERSPECTIVES
OF EDUCATION

This part of the book briefly surveys the history of education. As you read these history chapters, remember that historians see past events from various perspectives. *Celebrationist* historians, for instance, tend to see the brighter side of historical events and may tend, for example, to praise schools for past accomplishments. By contrast, *liberal* historians tend to study educational history through perspectives that focus on conflict, stress, and inconsistencies. *Revisionist* historians use yet another perspective, seeing celebrationist history as fundamentally flawed and concluding that we often learn more by studying what has been wrong with education than by rehearsing what has been right. *Postmodernist* histo-

rians believe that a person sees the history of education through the unique perspectives of her or his social class, race, ethnicity, gender, age, and so on.

Some historians provocatively argue that it is really not possible to "know" history because it can only be viewed through somewhat clouded perspectives; we can only make assumptions about the past. Even though historians see history from different perspectives, they all work to document and interpret the history of education as it evolved in a changing world.

We challenge you to think critically as you read the next two chapters and to formulate your own perspective through which to view educational history.

CHAPTER 7

The Early History of Education in a Changing World

CASE STUDY

Teaching Patriotism—With Conviction
By Chester E. Finn, Jr., *Phi Delta Kappan*, April 2006

Americans will debate for many years to come the causes and implications of the September 11 attacks on New York City and Washington, D.C., as well as the foiled attack that led to the crash of United Airlines Flight 93 in a Pennsylvania field. Between the first and second "anniversaries" of 9/11, another development deepened our awareness of the dangerous world we inhabit and of America's role therein—the successful war to liberate Iraq from its dictator and his murderous regime. Of course, the consequences—and contentiousness—of that conflict continue to resonate daily in newspaper headlines and on the evening news. In these challenging times, educators rightly wonder about their proper role. What should they teach young Americans? How should they prepare tomorrow's citizenry? What is most important for students to learn?

These are weighty questions, and there is every reason to expect them to linger. But it is now clearer than ever that, if we wish to prepare our children for unforeseen future threats and conflicts, we must arm them with lessons from history and civics that help them learn from the victories and setbacks of their predecessors, lessons that, in Jefferson's words, "enable every man to judge for himself what will secure or endanger his freedom."

Jefferson was right when he laid upon education the grave assignment of equipping tomorrow's adults with the knowledge, values, judgment, and critical faculties to determine for themselves what

"will secure or endanger" their freedom and their country's well-being. The U.S. Supreme Court was right, half a century ago, when, in the epoch-shaping *Brown* decision, it declared education to be "the very foundation of good citizenship."

Teachers know this better than anyone, and many need no help or advice in fulfilling their responsibility. They're knowledgeable, savvy, creative, caring, and—may I say it?—patriotic, as many fine teachers have always been. They love our country and the ideals for which it stands. Teachers must communicate to their students the crucial lessons from history and civics that our children most need to learn. The events of 9/11 and the war on terrorism that has followed create a powerful opportunity to teach our daughters and sons about heroes and villains, freedom and repression, hatred and compassion, democracy and theocracy, civic virtue and vice.

On 10 April 2003, David McCullough told a Senate committee, "We are raising a generation of people who are historically illiterate. . . . We can't function in a society," he continued, "if we don't know who we are and where we came from." The solemn duty of all educators is to make certain that all our children know who they are. Part of that can be accomplished by teaching them about America's Founders, about their ideals, and about the character, courage, vision, and tenacity with which they acted. From that inspiring history, true patriotism cannot help but grow.

Questions for Reflection

1. What is your perspective on the need for schools to teach patriotism?

2. What are some of the ways teachers could do so if they wished?

3. What are some of the potential disadvantages to teaching patriotism in our schools?

Reprinted with permission.

INTASC

Learning Outcomes

After reading and studying this chapter, you should be able to:

1. List some of the most important early educators in the world and explain their contributions to education. (INTASC 4: Teaching Methods)

2. Detail the major educational accomplishments of the early Eastern societies, the ancient Greeks, the ancient Romans, and the Europeans of the Middle Ages, Renaissance, Reformation, and Age of Reason. (INTASC 3: Diversity)

3. Analyze what life was like for the colonial schoolteacher, student, and parent.

4. Articulate the roles government (local, state, and national) played in colonial America soon after winning the War of Independence, in the 1800s, and in the early twentieth century.

5. Analyze how an understanding of early U.S. educational history might be used to improve teaching today. (INTASC 9: Reflection)

historical interpretation

Different ways to study and understand history, such as celebrationist, liberal, revisionist, and post-modernist historical approaches.

The first part of this chapter will focus on some of the antecedents of our current U.S. educational systems. You can inform your own teaching experience by looking at past successes and failures in education. Remember that there are various perspectives of **historical interpretation,** and that historians often disagree when attempting to understand history. History is not an exact science by any means; rather, it is open to different interpretations.

Although this chapter presents detailed information about the development of education in what is now the United States, it does so around a number of major historical ideas. The first idea is that since the beginning of time, adults have always informally educated their children to prepare them for adult life. Another idea is that as people developed written language, they created a need for schools to teach these writing skills and pass on knowledge to succeeding generations. A third major historical idea presented in this chapter relates to the fact that early societies throughout the world developed unique educational programs to serve their perceived needs. For instance, the early American colonists brought their educational ideas and practices with them from Europe. In other words, nearly all of the educational practices and educational materials were essentially the same as those found in Europe at that time. The religious motive was extremely strong in colonial America, and it permeated colonial education.

The last big idea presented in this chapter is that education has played a critical role in the historical development of the United States. The framers of our Constitution clearly recognized that our new democracy was dependent on an educated citizenry. Progress and advancement in every society has been and still is, in large part, dependent on education.

The Beginnings of Education (to 476 CE)

Informal education has been provided for children down through the ages by aboriginal people throughout the world. All people, regardless of their time and place in history, have cared for their young and attempted to prepare them for lifes challenges. This was even true of the very earliest humans, who fed and protected their children and informally taught them—probably by example and admonition—the skills they needed to survive as adults. For instance, Native Americans, who lived and flourished in North America for thousands of years before the first Europeans arrived and established formal schools, educated generations of their children. Many other early societies, including those in China, Africa, and South America, for example, also successfully provided education that their children needed to help build their flourishing cultures. Unfortunately, records do not exist that would help us better understand these earliest informal educational systems. If such records did exist, we would probably be quite impressed with the educational efforts of our aboriginal ancestors.

Once there was written language, humans felt the need for a more formal education. As societies became more complex and the body of knowledge increased, people recognized a need for schools. What they had learned constituted the subject matter; the written language allowed them to record this knowledge and pass it from generation to generation.

Non-Western Education

It is impossible to determine when schools first came into existence. However, the discovery of cuneiform mathematics textbooks dated to 2000 BCE suggests that some form of school probably existed in Sumeria (now part of Iraq) at that time. There is also evidence to suggest that formal schools existed in China during the Hsia and Shang dynasties, perhaps as early as 2000 BCE. Let's briefly explore several examples of these early educational efforts.

HINDU EDUCATION

The ancient Hindu societies were deeply rooted in the caste system, in which family status determined a person's social and vocational position in life. The Hindu religion emphasized nonearthly values; this resulted in little interest in education for anyone but boys from the highest castes. Priests were in charge of what formal education existed. Clues from the writing of Buddha suggest that education involved a heavy emphasis on morals, writing with a stick in the sand, and frequent punishments with a rod. Further education was reserved for the priestly caste, which, over the ages, gradually cultivated such disciplines as logic, rhetoric, astronomy, and mathematics. Many of our contemporary educational values, including our European languages, are partially derived from those of the early Hindu societies.

HEBREW EDUCATION

Perhaps no culture has historically valued education more than the Hebrew societies. Hebrew

The aboriginal ancestors of today's Native Americans, like other aboriginal peoples, probably taught their children by admonition and example.

Global Perspectives

Educational Ideas Borrowed from around the World

The educational ideas now implemented in the United States had their inception a long time ago. Our contemporary schools are a mixture of educational perspectives, ideas, concepts, and practices borrowed from around the changing world. Much of whatever credit and accolades our current American educational system receives must be shared with those who long ago conceived the idea of formal education and who then slowly developed and refined their educational concepts.

Questions for Reflection

1. As you read this chapter, look for some examples of our current educational practices that were inherited from other countries.
2. Attempt to learn about the evolution of education in a foreign country of your choice.

---

education was derived from the Jewish scriptures, which taught religious faithfulness and strict adherence to Old Testament laws. Discipline was harsh both at home and in school and was justified by many Bible verses such as the proverb "He that spareth his rod, hateth his son." Early Hebrew schools taught boys to read and write and girls to prepare food, spin, weave, sing, and dance. Teachers were greatly respected; the Talmud dictates, "If your teacher and your father have need of your assistance, help your teacher before helping your father, for the latter has given you only the life of this world, while the former has secured for you the life of the world to come." From Hebrew society we have inherited, at least in part, the value we place on education.

CHINESE EDUCATION

It has been said that China has been civilized longer than any other society in the world. Chinese education has always been characterized by tradition, formality, and conformity—all designed to help students function in a regular, mechanical, and predictable routine.

In the sixth century BCE, two philosophers/reformers exerted enormous influence on Chinese thinking and education through their writings. One of these was Lao-tszu, who wrote,

> Certain bad rulers would have us believe that the heart and the spirit of man should be left empty, but that instead his stomach should be filled; that his bones should be strengthened rather than the power of his will; that we should always desire to have people remain in a state of ignorance, for then their demands would be few. It is difficult, they say, to govern a people that are too wise.
>
> These doctrines are directly opposed to what is due to humanity. Those in authority should come to the aid of the people by means of oral and written instruction; so far from oppressing them and treating them as slaves, they should do them good in every possible way.

Another Chinese reformer, K'ung-Fu-tzu (551–478 BCE), who later became known as Confucius, is perhaps the most famous Asian philosopher. Since his time, all Chinese students have been taught Confucius's five cardinal virtues (universal charity, impartial justice, conformity, rectitude of heart and mind, and pure sincerity) as well as many of his famous sayings, such as "There are three thousand crimes—of these no one is greater than disobedience to parents." Interestingly, early Chinese education did not include geography, history, science, language, or mathematics—all subjects that are highly valued by early Western societies. Also, unlike many of their Western counterparts, early Chinese educators placed little importance on the individual. From early Chinese educational traditions we have inherited our respect for others and for authority and patience, as well as advances in written language.

EGYPTIAN EDUCATION

In Egypt, civilization and intellectual advancement occurred very early. There, as in most early societies, education was provided only for privileged males. Several notable Greek philosophers, including Pythagoras, Plato, Lycurgus, and Solon, completed their education in Egypt.

Egyptian society was divided into castes, with priests holding the highest position and receiving instruction in philosophy, astronomy, geometry, medicine, history, and law. The priests also provided education for others who were considered worthy of that privilege.

Most of the great early Eastern civilizations developed educational systems long before Western civilizations did. Eastern civilizations contributed substantially to the development of knowledge, education, and schools in the world.

Western Education

It was not until about 500 BCE that a Western society advanced sufficiently to generate an organized concern for formal education. This happened in Greece during the **Age of Pericles,** 455–431 BCE. Greece consisted of many city-states, one of which was Sparta, a militaristic state whose educational system was geared to support military ambitions. The aims of Spartan education centered on developing such ideals as courage, patriotism, obedience, cunning, and physical strength. Plutarch (46–120 CE), a writer of later times, said that the education of the Spartans "was calculated to make them subject to command, to endure labor, to fight, and to conquer." There was relatively little intellectual content in Spartan education.

In sharp contrast to Sparta was Athens, another Greek city-state, which developed an educational program that heavily stressed intellectual and aesthetic objectives. Between the ages of eight and sixteen, some Athenian boys attended a series of public schools. These schools included a kind of grammar school, which taught reading, writing, and counting; a gymnastics school, which taught sports and games; and a music school, which taught history, drama, poetry, speaking, and science as well as music. Because all city-states had to defend themselves against aggressors, Athenian boys received citizenship and military training between the ages of sixteen and twenty. Athenian girls were educated in the home. Athenian education stressed individual development, aesthetics, and culture.

The Western world's first great philosophers came from Athens. Of the many philosophers that Greece produced, three stand out: Socrates (470–399 BCE), Plato (427–347 BCE), and Aristotle (384–322 BCE).

SOCRATES

Socrates left no writings, but we know much about him from the writings of Xenophon and Plato. He is famous for creating the **Socratic method** of teaching, in which a teacher asks a series of questions that leads the student to a certain conclusion. This method is still commonly used by teachers today.

Socrates traveled around Athens teaching the students who gathered about him. He was dedicated to the search for truth and at times was very critical of the existing government. In fact, Socrates was eventually brought to trial for inciting the people against the government by his ceaseless questioning. He was found guilty and given a choice between ending his teaching or being put to death. Socrates chose death, thereby becoming a martyr for the cause of education. Socrates' fundamental

The very spring and root of honesty and virtue lie in good education.
Plutarch

Age of Pericles

A period (455–431 BCE) of Greek history in which sufficiently great strides were made in human advancement to generate an organized concern for formal education.

Socratic method

A way of teaching that centers on the use of questions by the teacher to lead students to certain conclusions.

Of the many ancient Greek philosophers, Socrates stands out the most.

History illuminates reality, vitalizes memory, provides guidance in daily life. . . .

Marcus Cicero (first century BCE)

principle, "Knowledge is virtue," has been adopted by countless educators and philosophers throughout the ages. Incidentally, some historians speculate that Socrates might not really have existed, but rather might have been a mythical character created by other writers, which is something that many writers did at that time as evidenced by the rich Greek mythology we now treasure.

PLATO

Plato was a student and disciple of Socrates. In his *Republic,* Plato set forth his recommendations for the ideal society. He suggested that society should contain three classes of people: artisans, to do the manual work; soldiers, to defend the society; and philosophers, to advance knowledge and to rule the society. Plato's educational aim was to discover and develop each individual's abilities. He believed that each person's abilities should be used to serve society. Plato wrote, "I call education the virtue which is shown by children when the feelings of joy or of sorrow, of love or of hate, which arise in their souls, are made conformable to order."

ARISTOTLE

Like Plato, Aristotle believed that a person's most important purpose in life was to serve and improve humankind. Aristotle's educational method, however, was scientific, practical, and objective, in contrast to the philosophical methods of Socrates and Plato. Aristotle believed that the quality of a society was determined by the quality of education found in that society. His writings were destined to exert greater influence on humankind throughout the Middle Ages than the writings of any other person.

The early Greek philosophers, including Plato and Aristotle, articulated the idea that females and slaves did not possess the intelligence to be leaders and therefore should not be educated. Unfortunately, our world's current struggle with racism and sexism, deeply rooted in Western civilization, is traceable to the ancient world.

ROMAN SCHOOLS

In 146 BCE, the Romans conquered Greece, and Greek teachers and their educational system were quickly absorbed into the Roman Empire. Many of the educational and philosophical advances made by the Roman Empire after that time were actually inspired by enslaved Greeks.

Before 146 BCE, Roman children were educated primarily in the home, though some children attended schools known as *ludi,* where the rudiments of reading and writing were taught. The Greek influence on Roman education became pronounced between 50 BCE and 200 CE, when an entire system of schools developed. Some children, after learning to read and write, attended a *grammaticus* school to study Latin, literature, history, mathematics, music, and dialectics. These **Latin grammar schools** were somewhat like twentieth-century secondary schools in function. Students who were preparing for a career of political service received their training in schools of rhetoric, which offered courses in grammar, rhetoric, dialectics, music, arithmetic, geometry, and astronomy.

QUINTILIAN

One of the most influential Roman educators was a man named Quintilian (35–95 CE). In a set of twelve books, *The Institutes of Oratory,* he described current educational practices, recommended the type of educational system needed in Rome, and listed the great books that were in existence at that time.

Regarding the motivation of students, Quintilian stated,

> Let study be made a child's diversion; let him be soothed and caressed into it, and let him sometimes test himself upon his proficiency. Sometimes enter a contest of wits with him, and let him imagine that he comes off the conqueror. Let him even be encouraged by giving him such rewards that are most appropriate to his age.[1]

These comments apply as well today as they did when Quintilian wrote them nearly 2,000 years ago. Quintilian's writings were rediscovered in the 1400s and became influential in the humanistic movement in education.

Latin grammar school

An early type of school that emphasized the study of Latin, literature, history, mathematics, music, and dialectics.

The Romans had a genius for organization and for getting the job done. They made lasting contributions to architecture, and many of their roads, aqueducts, and buildings remain today. This genius for organization enabled Rome to unite much of the ancient world with a common language, a religion, and a political bond—a condition that favored the spread of education and knowledge throughout the ancient world.

Education in the Middle Ages (476–1300)

By 476 CE (the fall of the Roman Empire), the Roman Catholic Church was well on the way to becoming the greatest power in government and education in the Western world. In fact, the rise of the church to power is often cited as a main cause of the Western world's plunge into the Dark Ages. As the church stressed the importance of gaining entrance to heaven, life on earth became less important. Many people viewed earthly life as nothing more than a way to a better life hereafter. You can see that a society in which this attitude prevailed would be unlikely to make intellectual advances, except perhaps in areas tangential to religion.

This section will briefly review the history of education in the Dark Ages and the revival of learning that eventually followed. We begin by sketching the achievements of two educators who lived during the Dark Ages—Charlemagne and Alcuin.

The Dark Ages (400–1000)

As the name implies, the Dark Ages was a period in the Western world when human learning and knowledge didn't just stand still but actually regressed. This regression was due to a variety of conditions, including political and religious oppression of the common people. However, there were some examples of human progress during this time. In fact, some historians believe this historical period was not "dark" at all but rather an era of considerable human progress—another example of the differing perspectives with which historians view the past.

CHARLEMAGNE

During the Dark Ages, one of the bright periods for education was the reign of Charlemagne (742–814). Charlemagne realized the value of education, and as ruler of a large part of Europe, he was in a position to establish schools and encourage scholarly activity. In 768, when Charlemagne came into power, educational activity was at an extremely low ebb. The church conducted the little educating that was carried on, mainly to induct people into the faith and to train religious leaders. The schools where this religious teaching took place included *catechumenal schools,* which taught church doctrine to new converts; *catechetical schools,* which at first taught the catechism but later became schools for training church leaders; and *cathedral* (or *monastic*) *schools,* which trained clergy.

ALCUIN

Charlemagne sought far and wide a talented educator who could improve education in the kingdom, finally selecting Alcuin (735–804), formerly a teacher in England. While Alcuin served as Charlemagne's chief educational advisor, he became the most famous educator of his day. It is reported that Charlemagne himself often sat in the Palace School with the children, trying to further his own meager education.

Roughly during Alcuin's time, the phrase **seven liberal arts** came into common usage to describe the curriculum that was then taught in some schools. The seven liberal arts consisted of the *trivium* (grammar, rhetoric, and logic) and the *quadrivium*

seven liberal arts

A medieval curriculum that consisted of the trivium (grammar, rhetoric, logic) and the quadrivium (arithmetic, geometry, music, astronomy).

(arithmetic, geometry, music, and astronomy). Each of these seven subjects was defined broadly; collectively they constituted a more comprehensive study than today's usage of the term suggests. The phrase *liberal arts* has survived and is commonly used now as a reference to general education as opposed to vocational education.

The Revival of Learning

Despite the efforts of men such as Charlemagne and Alcuin, little educational progress was made during the Dark Ages. However, between 1000 and 1300—a period frequently referred to as the "age of the revival of learning"—humankind slowly regained a thirst for education. This revival of interest in learning was supported by the rediscovery of the writings of some of the ancient philosophers (mainly Aristotle) and renewed interest in them and in the reconciliation of religion and philosophy.

THOMAS AQUINAS

CROSS-REFERENCE
More information on important educational philosophy pioneers can be found in Part V.

Thomas Aquinas (1225–1274), more than any other person, helped to change the church's views on learning. This change led to the creation of new learning institutions, among them the medieval universities. The harmonization of the doctrines of the church with the doctrines of philosophy and education was rooted in the ideas of Aristotle. Himself a theologian, Aquinas formalized **scholasticism,** the logical and philosophical study of the beliefs of the church. His most important writing was *Summa Theologica,* which became the doctrinal authority of the Roman Catholic Church. The educational and philosophical views of Thomas Aquinas were formalized in Thomism—a philosophy that has remained important in Roman Catholic parochial education.

MEDIEVAL UNIVERSITIES

The revival of learning brought about a general increase in educational activity and the growth of educational institutions, including the establishment of universities. These medieval universities, the true forerunners of our modern universities, included the University of Bologna (1158), which specialized in law; the University of Paris (1180), which specialized in theology; Oxford University (1214); and the University of Salerno (1224). By the time Columbus sailed to North America in 1492, approximately eighty universities already existed in Europe.

Although the Middle Ages produced a few educational advances in the Western world, we must remember that much of the Eastern world did not experience the Dark Ages. Mohammed (569–632) led a group of Arabs who later captured northern Africa and southern Spain. The Eastern learning that the Arabs brought to Spain spread slowly throughout Europe over the next few centuries through the writings of such scholars as Avicenna (980–1037) and Averroës (1126–1198). These Eastern contributions to Western knowledge included significant advances in science and mathematics, including the Arabic numbering system.

Education in Transition (1300–1700)

Two very important movements took place during the educational transition period of 1300–1700: the Renaissance and the Reformation. The Renaissance represented the protest of individuals against the dogmatic authority the church exerted over their social and intellectual life. The Renaissance started in Italy (around 1300) when people reacquired the spirit of free inquiry that had prevailed in ancient Greece. The Renaissance slowly spread through Europe, resulting in a general revival of classical learning called *humanism.*

scholasticism

The logical and philosophical study of the beliefs of the church.

The second movement, the Reformation, represented a reaction against certain beliefs of the Roman Catholic Church, particularly those that discouraged learning and that, in consequence, kept lay people in ignorance.

The Renaissance

The common people were generally oppressed by wealthy landowners and royalty during the eleventh and twelfth centuries. In fact, the common people were thought to be unworthy of education and to exist primarily to serve landed gentry and royalty. The Renaissance represented a rebellion on the part of the common people against the suppression they experienced from both the church and the wealthy who controlled their lives.

VITTORINO DA FELTRE

An important and influential educator during the Renaissance was Vittorino da Feltre (c. 1378–1446),[2] a man from the eastern Alps region. Da Feltre studied at the University of Florence, where he developed an interest in teaching. He also developed a keen interest in classical literature and, along with other educators of that time, began to believe that people could be educated and also be Christians at the same time—a belief that the Roman Catholic Church generally did not share.

Da Feltre established several schools, taught in a variety of others, and generally helped to advance the development of education during his lifetime. He believed that education was an important end in itself and thereby helped to rekindle an interest in the value of human knowledge during the Renaissance.

ERASMUS

One of the most famous humanist educators was Erasmus (1466–1536), and two of his books, *The Right Method of Instruction* and *The Liberal Education of Boys,* formed a humanistic theory of education. Erasmus had considerable educational insight. Concerning the aims of education, he wrote:

> The duty of instructing the young includes several elements, the first and also the chief of which is that the tender mind of the child should be instructed in piety; the second, that he love and learn the liberal arts; the third, that he be taught tact in the conduct of social life; and the fourth, that from his earliest age he accustom himself to good behavior, based on moral principles.[3]

Erasmus (1466–1536) was one of the most famous educators of the Renaissance.

The Reformation

It is difficult for people today to imagine the extent to which the Roman Catholic Church dominated the lives of the common people through most of what is now Europe during the fifteenth and sixteenth centuries. The Roman Catholic Church and the pope had enormous influence over European royalty during this time. In fact, some historians suggest that the pope and other officials of the Roman Catholic Church were in some ways more powerful than many individual kings and queens. After all, the Roman Catholic Church could and frequently did claim that unless members of royalty abided by its rules, they were destined to spend eternity in hell—an extremely frightening prospect for any human being. Consequently, it is understandable that the church came to be a powerful influence throughout most of Europe.

LUTHER

The Protestant Reformation had its formal beginning in 1517. In that year, Martin Luther (1483–1546) published his ninety-five theses, which stated his disagreements with the Roman Catholic Church. One of these disagreements held great implications

Martin Luther (1483–1546) was an early supporter of state-sponsored, state-controlled education for all people.

> What can only be taught by the rod and with blows will not lead to much good; they will not remain pious longer than the rod is behind them.
>
> **Martin Luther**

for the importance of formal education. The church believed that it was not desirable for each person to read and interpret the Bible for himself or herself; rather, the church would pass on the "correct" interpretation to the laity. Luther felt not only that the church had itself misinterpreted the Bible but also that people were intended to read and interpret the Bible, for themselves. If one accepted the church's position on this matter, formal education remained relatively unimportant for the masses. If one accepted Luther's position, however, education became necessary for all people so that they might individually read and interpret the Bible for themselves. In a sense, education became important as a way of obtaining salvation.

IGNATIUS OF LOYOLA

To combat the Reformation movement, Ignatius of Loyola (1491–1556) organized the Society of Jesus (Jesuits) in 1540. The Jesuits worked to establish schools to further the cause of the Roman Catholic Church, and they tried to stem the flow of converts to the cause of Reformation. Although the Jesuits' main interest was religious, they soon grew into a great teaching order and were very successful in training their own teachers. The rules by which the Jesuits conducted their schools were stated in the *Ratio Studiorum;* a revised edition still guides Jesuit schools today. The improvement of teacher training was one of the Jesuits' main contributions to education.

COMENIUS

The textbooks written by Comenius (1592–1670) were among the first to contain illustrations.

Among many other outstanding educators during this transition period was Johann Amos Comenius (1592–1670). Comenius is perhaps best remembered for his many textbooks, including *Orbis Pictus,* his books were among the first to contain illustrations. The invention and improvement of printing during the 1400s made it possible to produce books, such as those of Comenius, more rapidly and economically, a development that was essential to the growth of education. Much of the writing of Comenius reflected the increasing interest that was then developing in science.

> My whole method aims at changing the school drudgery into play and enjoyment.
>
> **Comenius**

LOCKE

John Locke (1632–1704) was an influential English educator during the late seventeenth century. He wrote many important educational works, including *Some Thoughts on Education* and *Essay Concerning Human Understanding*. He viewed a young child's mind as a blank slate *(tabula rasa)* on which an education could be imprinted. He believed that teachers needed to create a nonthreatening learning environment—a revolutionary idea at that time.

Educational Awakening (1700)

As we have suggested, educational progress in the world was slow and developed in only a few places through the seventeenth century. This section will show why many of our current educational ideas can be traced to the early 1700s.

Age of Reason

The beginning of the modern period of educational thought, a period in which European thinkers emphasized the importance of reason. The writing of Voltaire strongly influenced the rationalist movement.

The Age of Reason

A revolt of the intellectuals against the superstition and ignorance that dominated people's lives at the time influenced education in this early modern period. This movement became the keynote of the period known as the **Age of Reason;** and François-Marie Arouet (1694–1778), a Frenchwriter who used the pen name Voltaire,

Is "Abstinence-Only" the Best Sex Education Policy for Schools to Implement?

Early school curricula were historically driven by a desire to help children read the Bible and develop strict moral standards. The debate about how to best help students develop socially acceptable sexual behavior carries on today, as shown in this debate.

YES

Elizabeth Bradley *teaches math at Lewiston High School in Lewiston, Maine, and won a Presidential Award in 2000 for her work. She has taught for 15 years, interrupted by eight years as a business applications programmer.*

Consider this:

"Good morning, class. Today we're going to talk about how to drive a car safely, even if you've been drinking. Now, it's really better not to drink and drive, because you might end up dead, but there are some ways to do it so that you cut your risk of becoming injured or dying."

The fact is that the true message sent by adults, the media, and the schools is the exact opposite: "Don't drink and drive." And we don't offer training in how to do it safely.

Now, let's change the scene just a little.

"Good morning, class. Today we're going to learn how to have safe sex (now referred to as "safer sex" because safe sex doesn't really exist).

"We'll show you how to put a condom on a banana, and some other things you can do to minimize your risk of contracting an incurable disease, which may make you sterile (chlamydia), be a precursor to cervical cancer (HPV), or cause death (HIV).

"Oh, and you might end up pregnant. Then your choices are abortion ("one dead, one wounded," to quote a recent bumper sticker), adoption (a lifelong hole in your heart), or parenthood (a 24/7 commitment that will make school, college, work, independence, and emotional stability very difficult)."

Why can't we take the drinking and driving approach of "Just don't do it"? Statistics show that kids do care about what the adults in their lives have to say.

NO

Eileen Toledo *has taught English in middle schools for 14 years, currently at the Pablo Avila Junior High School in Camuy, Puerto Rico. She runs the "Baby, Think It Over" program one period a week and wrote a master's thesis on it.*

The reality is that more students are becoming sexually active at earlier ages. As an educator, I had to get involved. I have been using "Baby, Think It Over" at my junior high school for five years. Pregnancy dropped from 15 the first year, to three last semester, and zero this year! This program has a "baby" simulator. Students, male and female, are given "baby" to take home for five days. They experience the endless cries, waking at night, feeding, changing diapers.

Meanwhile, at school, we talk about child abuse, how to place babies to sleep correctly, and more. Students budget the weekly costs of caring for a baby. They inquire about jobs available to them at their age (13–16). Students realize how hard raising a baby can be for them.

One girl who loved baby-sitting became so frustrated after two days that "baby" was thrown in a clothes hamper and covered to drown out the cries. Her parents explained the consequences had this been a real baby. The student learned that this is not the time for her to become a parent.

We also discuss STDs, and we talk about how making love is different from sex, which is what teens are having. Making love is a beautiful experience in a true relationship between adults ready and able to take on responsibilities, not teens who got pregnant by mistake. We do role-plays: You're with your boyfriend, lose control, go all the way and don't even think about birth

(continued)

Educational Awakening (1700)   **239**

(continued)

YES

To me, teen promiscuity is in the same category as Russian roulette, and promoting safe sex is just handing them the gun.

If you knew that within the next 12 months your child would have a child, an incurable disease, or be HIV positive, how far would you be willing to go today to prevent that? We are talking about 4 million teens a year who can expect to deal with these consequences.

Let's raise the standard and tell kids, unequivocally, what is in their best interest. Why is it that we want so much to protect their sexual activity, but not their very lives?

NO

control, and a while later the girl is pregnant and all dreams are now put on hold. Or, things get hot but you stop and say, "Wait a second, I'm not ready for this."

Yet I cannot be so naive as not to see that most teens become sexually active at an early age. So I must also talk about birth control. But schools that accept federal "abstinence-only" funds are not allowed to teach *any* factual information about the effectiveness of any form of birth control.

Students who have complete information about disease transmission and contraceptive use are the most likely to remain abstinent and will protect themselves if they choose to be sexually active. We have worked with over 400 students, and only three became pregnant in high school.

Source: "Is 'Abstinence-Only' the Best Sex Education Policy for Schools to Implement?" *NEA Today* (February 2003), p. 23. Reprinted by permission of the National Education Association.

WHAT IS YOUR PERSPECTIVE ON THIS ISSUE?
Is "abstinence-only" the best sex education policy for schools to implement?

To give your opinion, go to Chapter 7 of the companion website (www.ablongman.com/johnson14e) and click on Teacher Perspectives.

was one of its leaders. Those who joined this movement became known as *rationalists* because of the faith they placed in human rational power. The implication for education in the rationalist movement is obvious; if one places greater emphasis on human ability to reason, then education takes on new importance as the way that humans develop this power.

DESCARTES AND VOLTAIRE

The work of René Descartes (1596–1650) laid the foundations for rationalism. This philosophy evolved three axioms that gradually became well accepted by thinking people. These axioms were (1) that reason was supreme, (2) that the laws of nature were invariable, and (3) that truth could be verified empirically—verified by exact methods of testing. These ideas became the basis for disputing some of the traditional teaching of the church and for resisting the bonds that royalty had traditionally placed on the common people. These axioms also influenced the thinking of Voltaire. Voltaire was an articulate writer who was also brilliant, clever, witty, and vain—qualities that helped him become extremely influential. In fact, many authorities give him considerable credit for both the American and French Revolutions, which took place during his lifetime.

FREDERICK THE GREAT

One of the influential leaders during the Age of Reason was Frederick the Great (1712–1786). Frederick was a friend of Voltaire and supported the notion that education was of value. He was a liberal thinker for his time and one of the few leaders who did not attempt to force the common people into a particular form of religion. Frederick also permitted an unusual amount of free speech for his era and generally allowed the common people a degree of liberty that most rulers considered dangerous.

As a consequence, education had an opportunity to develop, if not flourish, during his reign as leader of Prussia. During Frederick's reign, Prussia passed laws regarding education and required teachers to obtain special training as well as licenses to teach.

Philosopher Jean-Jacques Rousseau (1712–1778) felt that education should seek to return humans to their natural state.

The Emergence of Common Man

The second pivotal trend of the early modern period that affected education was the concept sometimes called the **Emergence of Common Man.** Whereas the Age of Reason was sparked by a revolt of the learned for intellectual freedom, the thinkers who promoted the emergence of common man argued that common people deserved a better life—politically, economically, socially, and educationally.

ROUSSEAU

One of the leaders in this movement was Jean-Jacques Rousseau (1712–1778), whose *Social Contract* (1762) became an influential book in the French Revolution. Rousseau was a philosopher, not an educator, but he wrote a good deal on the subject of education. His most important educational work was *Émile* (1762), in which he states his views concerning the ideal education for youth. Rousseau felt that the aim of education should be to return human beings to their "natural state." His view on the subject is well summed up by the opening sentence of *Émile:* "Everything is good as it comes from the hand of the author of nature: but everything degenerates in the hands of man." Rousseau's educational views came to be known as *naturalism.*

> ### Emergence of Common Man
>
> A period during which developed the idea that common people should receive at least a basic education as a means to a better life.

Rousseau's most important contributions to education were his belief that education must be a natural process, not an artificial one, and his compassionate, positive view of the child. Rousseau believed that children were inherently good—a belief in opposition to the prevailing religiously inspired belief that children were born full of sin.

PESTALOZZI

Johann Heinrich Pestalozzi (1746–1827) was a Swiss educator who put Rousseau's theory into practice. Pestalozzi established two schools for boys, one at Burgdorf (1800–1804) and the other at Yverdun (1805–1825). Educators came from all over the world to view Pestalozzi's schools and to study his teaching methods. Pestalozzi enumerated his educational views in a book entitled *Leonard and Gertrude.* Unlike most educators of his time, Pestalozzi believed that a teacher should treat students with love and kindness.

Swiss educator Johann Heinrich Pestalozzi (1746–1827) put Rousseau's theory into practice.

Johann Friedrich Herbart (1776–1814) was a German philosopher, educator, and author who expanded the work of Pestalozzi.

Journal for Reflection

Select a person mentioned in this chapter (or another individual from the history of education who is of interest to you) and learn more about that person and her or his influence on today's schools. Make journal entry notes about what you learn.

Friedrich Froebel (1782–1852) was a German educator and author who founded the kindergarten.

Herbartian teaching method

An organized teaching method based on the principles of Pestalozzi that stresses learning by association and consists of five steps: preparation, presentation, association, generalization, and application.

Key concepts in the Pestalozzian method included the expression of love, understanding, and patience for children; compassion for the poor; and the use of objects and sense perception as the basis for acquiring knowledge.

HERBART

An educator who studied under Pestalozzi and was influenced by him was Johann Friedrich Herbart (1776–1841). Whereas Pestalozzi had successfully put into practice and further developed Rousseau's educational ideas, it remained for Herbart to organize these educational views into a formal psychology of education. Herbart stressed apperception (learning by association). The **Herbartian teaching method** developed into five formal steps:

1. *Preparation:* Preparing the student to receive a new idea
2. *Presentation:* Presenting the student with the new idea
3. *Association:* Assimilating the new idea with old ideas
4. *Generalization:* Generalizing the new idea derived from combination of old and new ideas
5. *Application:* Applying the new knowledge

Herbart's educational ideas are contained in his *Science of Education* (1806) and *Outlines of Educational Doctrine* (1835).

FROEBEL

Friedrich Froebel (1782–1852) was another European educator influenced by Rousseau and Pestalozzi who made a significant contribution to education. Froebel's contributions included the establishment of the first kindergarten (or *Kleinkinderbeschaftigungsanstalt*), an emphasis on social development, a concern for the cultivation of creativity, and the concept of learning by doing. He originated the idea that women are best suited to teach young children.

Evolving Perspectives of Education in Our Developing Nation

The earliest settlers to America from Europe brought with them a sincere interest in providing at least rudimentary education for their children. Naturally, they brought their European ideas about education with them and, soon after arrival, created educational programs throughout colonial America. This section will briefly examine these early colonial school programs.

Colonial Education

The early settlements on the East Coast were composed of groups of colonies: the Southern Colonies, centered in Virginia; the Middle Colonies, centered in New York; and the Northern Colonies, centered in New England. Each of these groups developed a somewhat unique educational system.

SOUTHERN COLONIES

The Southern Colonies soon were made up of large tobacco plantations. There was an immediate need for cheap labor to work on the plantations; in 1619, only twelve years after Jamestown was settled, the colony imported the first slaves from Africa.

Other sources of labor for the Southern Colonies included Europeans from a variety of backgrounds, people who purchased passage to the New World by agreeing to serve a lengthy period of indentured servitude on arrival in the colonies. There soon came to be two very distinct classes of people in the South—a few wealthy landowners and a large mass of laborers, most of whom were slaves.

The educational provisions that evolved from this set of conditions were precisely what one would expect. Few were interested in providing education for the slaves, with the exception of missionary groups such as the English Society for the Propagation of the Gospel in Foreign Parts. Such missionary groups tried to provide some education for slaves, primarily so that they could read the Bible. The wealthy landowners hired tutors to teach their children at home. Distances between homes and slow transportation precluded the establishment of centralized schools. When upper-class children grew old enough to attend college, they were usually sent to well-established universities in Europe.

MIDDLE COLONIES

The people who settled the Middle Colonies came from various national (Dutch, Swedish) and religious (Puritan, Mennonite, Catholic) backgrounds. This is why the Middle Colonies have often been called the melting pot of the nation. This diversity of backgrounds made it impossible for the inhabitants of the Middle Colonies to agree on a common public school system. Consequently, the respective groups established their own religious schools. Many children received their education through an apprenticeship while learning a trade from a master already in that line of work. Some people even learned the art of teaching school through apprenticeships with experienced teachers.

NORTHERN COLONIES

The Northern Colonies were settled mainly by the Puritans, a religious group from Europe. In 1630 approximately one thousand Puritans settled near Boston. Unlike people in the Southern Colonies, people in New England lived close to one another. Towns sprang up and soon became centers of political and social life. Shipping ports were established, and an industrial economy developed that demanded numerous skilled and semiskilled workers—a condition that eventually created a large middle class.

EARLY SCHOOL LAWS

These conditions of common religious views, town life, and a large middle class made it possible for the people to agree on common public schools and led to very early educational activity in the Northern Colonies. In 1642 the General Court of Massachusetts enacted a law that stated:

> This Co^t [Court], taking into consideration the great neglect of many parents & masters in training up their children in learning do hereupon order and decree, that in every towne y chosen men take account from time to time of all parents and masters, and of their children, concerning their ability to read & understand the principles of religion & the capitall lawes of this country.

This law did nothing more than encourage citizens to look after the education of children. Five years later (1647), however, another law was enacted in Massachusetts that required towns to provide education for their youth. This law, which was often referred to as the **Old Deluder Satan Act** because of its religious motive, stated:

> It being one chiefe proiect of y ould deluder, Satan, to keepe men from the knowledge of y Scriptures It is therefore orded [ordered], ye evy [every] towneship in this jurisdiction, aft y Lord hath increased y number to 50 household, shall then forthw appoint one w [with] in their towne to teach all such children as shall resort to him to write & reade & it is furth ordered y where any towne shall increase to y numb [number] of 100 families or househould, they shall set up a grammar schoole, y m [aim] thereof being able to instruct youth so farr as they shall be fited for y university [Harvard].

Old Deluder Satan Act

An early colonial educational law (1647) that required colonial towns of at least fifty households to provide education for youth.

Horace Mann (1796–1859) helped to establish common schools designed to provide a basic elementary education for all children in Massachusetts.

Beyond the power of diffusing old wealth, education has the prerogative of creating new. It is a thousand times more lucrative than fraud; and adds a thousand fold more to a nation's resources than the most successful conquest.

Horace Mann

dame school

A low-level primary school in the colonial and other early periods, usually conducted by an untrained woman in her own home.

common elementary school

Schools that originated in the mid-nineteenth century designed to provide a basic elementary education for all children.

These Massachusetts school laws of 1642 and 1647 served as models for similar laws that were soon created in other colonies.

TYPES OF COLONIAL SCHOOLS

Several different kinds of elementary schools sprang up in the colonies, such as the **dame school,** which was conducted by a housewife in her home; the writing school, which taught the child to write; a variety of church schools; and charity, or pauper, schools taught by missionary groups.

In 1635 the Latin Grammar School was established in Boston—the first permanent school of this type in what is now the United States. The grammar school was a secondary school. Its function was college preparatory, and the idea spread quickly to other towns. Charlestown opened its first grammar school one year later, in 1636, by contracting William Witherell "to keep a school for a twelve month." Within sixteen years after the Massachusetts Bay Colony had been founded, seven or eight towns had Latin grammar schools in operation. Transplanted from Europe, where similar schools had existed for a long time, these schools were aimed at preparing boys for college and "for the service of God, in church and commonwealth."

EARLY AMERICAN COLLEGES

Harvard, the first colonial college, was established in 1636 for preparing ministers. Other early American colleges included William and Mary (1693), Yale (1701), Princeton (1746), King's College (1754), College of Philadelphia (1755), Brown (1764), Dartmouth (1769), and Queen's College (1770). The curriculum in these early colleges was traditional, with heavy emphasis on theology and the classics. An example of the extent to which the religious motive dominated colonial colleges can be found in one of the 1642 rules governing Harvard College, which stated: "Let every Student be plainly instructed, and earnestly pressed to consider well, the maine end of his life and studies is, to know God and Jesus Christ."

The Struggle for Universal Elementary Education

When the colonists arrived in this country, they simply established schools like those they had known in Europe. The objectives of colonial elementary schools were primarily religious. These early colonial schools were meager by today's standards, but nevertheless, they were important forerunners of our contemporary schools.

MONITORIAL SCHOOLS

In 1805, New York City established the first *monitorial school* in the United States. The monitorial school, which originated in England, represented an attempt to provide economical mass elementary education for large numbers of children. Typically, the teacher would teach hundreds of pupils, using the better students as helpers. By 1840, however, nearly all monitorial schools had been closed; the children had not learned enough to justify continuance of this type of school.

HORACE MANN

Between 1820 and 1860, an educational awakening took place in the United States. This movement was strongly influenced by Horace Mann (1796–1859). As secretary of the state board of education, Mann helped to establish **common elementary schools** in Massachusetts. These common schools were designed to provide a basic elementary education for all children. Among Mann's many impressive educational achievements was the publication of one of the very early professional journals in this country, *The Common School Journal*. Through this journal, Mann kept educational issues before the public.

In 1852, Massachusetts passed a compulsory elementary school attendance law, the first of its kind in the country, requiring all children to attend school. By 1900, thirty-two other states had passed similar **compulsory education** laws.

Financing public education has always been a challenge in America. As early as 1795, Connecticut legislators decided to sell public land and create a permanent school fund to help finance public schools. As more and more children attended school, other states soon took action to establish school funding plans as well.

HENRY BARNARD

The first U.S. commissioner of education was a prominent educator named Henry Barnard (1811–1900). He was a longtime supporter of providing common elementary schools for all children and wrote enthusiastically about the value of education in the *Connecticut Common School Journal* and in the *American Journal of Education,* which he founded. He had also served as the Rhode Island commissioner of public schools and as the chancellor of the University of Wisconsin before holding the prestigious position of commissioner of education for the entire United States. Barnard also strongly supported kindergarten programs for very young children as well as high school programs for older students.

> The right beginning of this work of school improvement is in awakening, correcting, and elevating public sentiment in relation to it.
>
> *Henry Barnard*

REFLECTION ON EARLY U.S. ELEMENTARY EDUCATION

If we look back at the historical development of U.S. elementary education, we can make the following generalizations:

1. Until the late 1800s, the motive, curriculum, and administration of elementary education were primarily religious. The point at which elementary education began to be more secular than religious was the point at which states began to pass compulsory school attendance laws.
2. Discipline was traditionally harsh in elementary schools. The classical picture of a colonial schoolmaster equipped with a frown, dunce cap, stick, whip, and a variety of abusive phrases is more accurate than one might expect. It is no wonder that children historically viewed school as an unpleasant place. Pestalozzi had much to do with bringing about a gradual change in discipline when he advocated that love, not severe punishment, should be used to motivate students.
3. Elementary education was traditionally formal and impersonal. The ideas of Rousseau, Pestalozzi, Herbart, and Froebel helped change this condition gradually and make elementary education more student centered; this was becoming apparent by 1900.
4. Elementary schools were traditionally taught by poorly prepared teachers.
5. Although the aims and methodology varied considerably from time to time, the basic content of elementary education was historically reading, writing, and arithmetic.

> When any Scholar is able to understand Tully, or such Latine Author extempore, and make and speake true Latine in verse and Prose, suo ut aiunt marte, and decline perfectly the Paradigms of Nounes and Verbes in the Greek tonge, let him then, and not before, be capable of admission to the college.
>
> *Harvard admission requirement*

The Need for Secondary Schools

Contemporary U.S. high schools have a long and proud tradition. They have evolved from a series of earlier forms of secondary schools that were created to serve the needs of society at various points in the nation's history.

AMERICAN ACADEMY

By the middle of the eighteenth century, there was a need for more and better-trained skilled workers. Benjamin Franklin (1706–1790), recognizing this need, proposed a new kind of secondary school in Pennsylvania. This proposal brought about the establishment, in Philadelphia in 1751, of the first truly American educational institution—the *American Academy.* Franklin established this school because he

compulsory education

School attendance that is required by law on the theory that it is to the benefit of the state or commonwealth to educate all the people.

Global Perspectives

Educational Transplantation from Europe

The ideas of Pestalozzi and Herbart considerably affected elementary education when they were introduced into the United States in the late 1800s. Pestalozzianism emphasized teaching children with love, patience, and understanding. Furthermore, children should learn from objects and firsthand experiences, not from abstractions and words. Pestalozzian concepts soon spread throughout the country. Herbartianism was imported into the United States at the Bloomington Normal School in Illinois by students who had learned about the ideas of Herbart while studying in Germany. Herbartianism represented an attempt to make a science out of teaching. The more formal system that Herbartianism brought to the often disorganized elementary teacher was badly needed at the time. Unfortunately, Herbartianism eventually contributed to an extreme formalism and rigidity that characterized many U.S. elementary schools in the early 1900s. One school administrator of that time bragged that at a given moment in the school day he knew exactly what was going on in all the classrooms. One can infer from this boast that teachers and students often had a strict, rigid educational program imposed on them.

Questions for Reflection

1. What are some of your thoughts about the ideas of Pestalozzi and Herbart?
2. Of what value, if any, to contemporary educators are the ideas of Pestalozzi and/or Herbart?

> The excellent become the permanent.
>
> *Jane Addams*

thought the existing Latin grammar schools were not providing the practical secondary education that youth needed. The philosophy, curriculum, and methodology of Franklin's academy were all geared to prepare young people for employment. Eventually, similar academies were established throughout America, and these institutions eventually replaced the Latin grammar school as the predominant secondary educational institution. They were usually private schools, and many of them admitted girls as well as boys. Later on, some academies even tried to train elementary school teachers.

HIGH SCHOOL

> Comprehensive high school gave millions a shot at careers.
>
> *Mortimer B. Zuckerman*

In 1821 an *English Classical School* (which three years later changed its name to *English High School*) opened in Boston, and another distinctively American educational institution was launched. This first high school, under the direction of George B. Emerson, consisted of a three-year course in English, mathematics, science, and history. The school later added to its curriculum the philosophy of history, chemistry, intellectual philosophy, linear drawing, logic, trigonometry, French, and the U.S. Constitution. The school enrolled about one hundred boys during its first year.

The high school was established because of a belief that the existing grammar schools were inadequate for the day and because most people could not afford to send their children to the private academies. The high school soon replaced both the Latin grammar school and the private academy, and it has been with us ever since.

JUNIOR HIGH/MIDDLE SCHOOL

CROSS-REFERENCE
Information about current school organization is presented in Chapter 5.

About 1910 the first *junior high schools* were established in the United States. A survey in 1916 showed 54 junior high schools in thirty-six states. One year later a survey indicated that the number had increased to about 270. More recently, some school systems have abandoned the junior high school in favor of what is called the *middle school,* which usually consists of grades 6, 7, and 8.

Critiquing Historical Sources

STUDY PURPOSE/QUESTION: As you prepare for your teaching career, you should have an opportunity to read and think about original historical research sources. Such historical materials constitute the "relevant research" sources for those who strive to understand and learn from the past—something all educators should do.

STUDY DESIGN: The following letter, written in 1712 by Nathaniel Williams, briefly describes the curriculum of the first Latin grammar school established in the colonies—the Boston Latin Grammar School, which was created in 1635, soon after the first colonists settled in the area.

STUDY FINDINGS:

Curriculum of the Boston Latin Grammar School (1712)

The three first years are spent first in Learning by heart & then acc: to their capacities understanding the Accidence and Nomenclator, in construing & parsing acc: to the English rules of Syntax Sententiae Pueriles Cato & Cordcrius & Aesops Fables.

The fourth year, or sooner if their capacities allow it, they are entered upon Erasmus to which they are allou'd no English . . . & upon translating English into Latin out of m^r Garreston's Exercises.

The fifth year they are entred upon Tullies Epistles . . . the Elegancies of which are remarked and improv'd in the afternoon of the day they learn it, by translating an English which contains the phrase somthing altered, and besides recited by heart on the repetition day. . . .

The sixth year they are entred upon Tullies Offices & Luc: Flor: for the forenoon, continuing the use of Ovid's Metam: in the afternoon, & at the end of the Year they read Virgil. . . . Every week these make a Latin Epistle, the last quarter of the Year, when also they begin to learn Greek, & Rhetorick.

The seventh Year they read Tullie's Orations & Justin for the Latin & Greek Testam^t Isocrates Orat: Homer & Hesiod for the Greek in the forenoons & Virgil Horace Juyenal & Persius afternoons . . . Every fortnight they compose a theme. . . .

IMPLICATIONS: Each reader must deliberate and decide the implications of this small bit of original historical documentation of the Boston Latin Grammar School curriculum. What was the apparent function of the Boston Latin Grammar School? For whom was this curriculum apparently intended, and for what purpose? In what ways was this curriculum similar to that of secondary schools throughout the world today? In what ways was it different? What, if anything, can contemporary educators learn from the Boston Latin Grammar School?

Source: "Letter from Nathaniel Williams to Nehemia Hobart," in Robert F. Seybold, *The Public Schools of Colonial Boston.* Cambridge, MA: Harvard University Press, 1935, pp. 69–71.

The Evolution of Teaching Materials

The first schools in colonial America were poorly equipped. In fact, the first elementary schools were usually conducted by housewives right in their homes. The only teaching materials likely to be found then were a Bible and perhaps one or two other religious books, a small amount of scarce paper, a few quill pens, and perhaps hornbooks.

THE HORNBOOK

The **hornbook** was the most common teaching device in early colonial schools (see Figure 7.1). Hornbooks differed widely but typically consisted of a sheet of paper showing the alphabet, covered with a thin transparent sheet of cow's horn and tacked to a paddle-shaped piece of wood. A leather thong was often looped through a hole in the paddle so that students could hang the hornbooks around their necks. Hornbooks provided students with their first reading instructions. Records indicate that hornbooks were used in Europe in the Middle Ages and were common there until the mid-1700s.

As paper became more available, the hornbook evolved into a several-page "book" called a *battledore.* The battledore, printed on heavy paper, often resembled

hornbook

A single written page containing the alphabet, syllables, a prayer, and other simple words, tacked to a wooden paddle and covered with a thin transparent layer of cow's horn; used in colonial times as a beginner's first book or preprimer.

FIGURE 7.1

Hornbook
The hornbook was the most common teaching device in colonial American schools.

an envelope. Like the hornbook, it typically contained the alphabet and various religious prayers and/or admonitions.

THE NEW ENGLAND PRIMER

Very few textbooks were available for use in colonial Latin grammar schools, academies, and colleges, although various religious books, including the Bible, were often used. A few books dealing with history, geography, arithmetic, Latin, Greek, and certain classics were available for use in colonial secondary schools and colleges during the eighteenth century. The first real textbook to be used in colonial elementary schools was the *New England Primer.* Records show that the first copies of this book were printed in England in the 1600s. Copies of the *New England Primer* were also printed as early as 1690 in the American colonies. An advertisement for the book appeared in the *News from the Stars Almanac,* published in 1690 in Boston (see Figure 7.2). The oldest extant copy of the *New England Primer* is a 1727 edition, now in the Lenox Collection of the New York Public Library.

The *New England Primer* was a small book, usually about 2 by 4 inches, with thin wooden covers covered by paper or leather. It contained fifty to one hundred pages, depending on how many extra sections were added to each edition. The first pages displayed the alphabet, vowels, and capital letters. Next came lists of words arranged from two to six syllables, followed by verses and tiny woodcut pictures for each letter in the alphabet. Figure 7.3 shows a sampling of these pictures and verses. The contents of the *New England Primer* reflect the heavily religious motive in colonial education.

FIGURE 7.2

1690 Advertisement

This 1690 advertisement promotes the *New England Primer,* the first true textbook to be used in colonial American elementary schools.

> ADVERTISEMENT.
> There is now in the Press, and will suddenly be extant, a Second Impression of *The New-England Primer enlarged,* to which is added, more *Directions for Spelling :* the *Prayer of* K. *Edward* the 6th. and *Verses made by Mr.* Rogers *the Martyr, left as a Legacy to his Children.*
> Sold by *Benjamin Harris,* at the *London Coffee-House* in *Boston.*

FIGURE 7.3

Page from the *New England Primer*

How does this page from the *New England Primer* reveal the religious motive in colonial American education?

In Adam's Fall
We sinned all.

Thy Life to mend,
This Book attend.

The Cat doth play,
And after slay.

A Dog will bite
A Thief at Night.

An Eagle' flight
Is out of sight.

The idle Fool
Is whipt at School

BLUE-BACKED SPELLER

The primer was virtually the only reading book used in colonial schools until about 1800, when Noah Webster published *The American Spelling Book.* This book eventually became known as the *Blue-Backed Speller* because of its blue cover. It eventually replaced the *New England Primer* as the most common elementary textbook. Figure 7.4 shows a page from a *Blue-Backed Speller* printed about 1800. A later series of school books, commonly known as *The McGuffey Readers,* authored by William Holmes McGuffey, replaced the Blue-Backed Speller as the most commonly used school book—selling about sixty million copies. The speller was approximately 4 by 6 inches; its cover was made of thin sheets of wood covered with light blue paper. The first part of the book contained rules and instructions for using the book; next

FIGURE 7.4

Page from the *Blue-Backed Speller*

Noah Webster's *Blue-Backed Speller* came to replace primers around 1800. In addition to the alphabet, syllables, consonants, lists of words, and rules for reading and speaking, the *Speller* contained stories like the one shown here.

ᴏғ **PRONUNCIATION.** 85

FABLE I. *Of the Boy that ſtole Apples.*

AN old Man found a rude Boy upon one of his trees ſtealing Apples, and deſired him to come down; but the young Sauce-box told him plainly he wou'd not. Won't you? ſaid the old Man, then I will fetch you down; ſo he pulled up ſome tufts of Graſs, and threw at him; but this only made the Youngſter laugh, to think the old Man ſhould pretend to beat him out of the tree with graſs only.

Well, well, ſaid the old Man, if neither words nor graſs, will do, I muſt try what virtue there is in Stones; ſo the old Man pelted him heartily with ſtones; which ſoon made the young Chap, haſten down from the tree and beg the old Man's pardon.

M O R A L.

If good words and gentle means will not reclaim the wicked, they muſt be dealt with in a more ſevere manner.

came the alphabet, syllables, and consonants. The bulk of the book was taken up with lists of words arranged according to syllables and sounds. It also contained rules for reading and speaking, moral advice, and stories of various sorts.

TEACHING MATERIALS IN AN EARLY SCHOOL

By 1800, nearly two hundred years after the colonies had been established, school buildings and teaching materials were still very crude and meager. You can understand something of the physical features and equipment of an 1810 New England school by reading the following description written by a teacher of that school:

> The size of the building was 22 × 20 feet. From the floor to the ceiling it was 7 feet. The chimney and entry took up about four feet at one end, leaving the schoolroom itself 18 × 20 feet. Around three sides of the room were connected desks, arranged so that when the pupils were sitting at them their faces were toward the instructor and their backs toward the wall. Attached to the sides of the desks nearest to the instructor were benches for small pupils. The instructor's desk and chair occupied the center. On this desk were stationed a rod, or ferule; sometimes both. These, with books, writings, inkstands, rules, and plummets, with a fire shovel, and a pair of tongs (often broken), were the principal furniture.
>
> Instructors have usually boarded in the families of the pupils. Their compensation has varied from seven to eleven dollars a month for males; and from sixty-two and a half cents to one dollar a week for females. Within the past ten years, however, the price of instruction has rarely been less than nine dollars in the former case, and seventy-five cents in the latter. In the few instances in which instructors have furnished their own board the compensation has been about the same, it being assumed that they could work at some employment of their own enough to pay their board, especially the females.[4]

SLATES

About 1820 a new instructional device—the *slate*—was introduced in American schools. These school slates were thin, flat pieces of slate stone framed with wood. The pencils used were also made of slate and produced a light but legible line that was easily erased with a rag. The wooden frames of some of the slates were covered with cloth so that noise would be minimized as students placed the slates on the desk. Later on, large pieces of slate made up the blackboards that were added to classrooms.

By about 1900, pencils and paper had largely replaced the slate and slate pencil as the writing implements of students. The invention of relatively economical mass production of pencils in the late 1800s made them affordable for student use and led to their widespread use in schools.

McGUFFEY'S READERS

In the same way that Noah Webster's *Blue-Backed Speller* replaced the *New England Primer*, McGuffey's *Reader* eventually replaced the *Blue-Backed Speller*. These readers were carefully geared to each grade and were meant to instill in children a respect for hard work, thrift, self-help, and honesty. McGuffey's *Readers* dominated the elementary school book market until approximately 1900, when they were gradually replaced by various newer and improved readers written by David Tower, James Fassett, William Elson, and others.

One cannot help but be awed by the contrast and dramatic changes that have taken place in U.S. education today from its humble beginning centuries ago.

> ### Journal for Reflection
>
> 1. Try to learn more about the historical development of education in the particular grade or subjects you are thinking of teaching.
>
> 2. Record in your journal any especially pertinent things you learn.

Meager Early Education for Diverse Populations

It is sad but true that students of color, girls, and students with disabilities have been historically badly underserved by our educational system and typically not even allowed to attend school until relatively recently.

Early efforts to provide formal education for African American children were few. The African American Children's School, shown here, was one example.

Give me your tired, your poor, / Your huddled masses yearning to breathe free, / The wretched refuse of your teeming shore, / Send these, the homeless, tempest-tossed to me: / I lift my lamp beside the golden door.

Emma Lazarus

Education of African Americans

Unfortunately, general efforts have been made only recently in this country to provide an education for African Americans. In the following section, we will briefly explore why this was the case and discuss some of the early African American educators who struggled to correct this injustice.[5]

EARLY CHURCH EFFORTS TO EDUCATE AFRICAN AMERICANS

Probably the first organized attempts to educate African Americans in colonial America were by French and Spanish missionaries. These early missionary efforts set an example that influenced the education of both African Americans and their children. Educating slaves posed an interesting moral problem for the church. The English colonists had to find a way to overcome the idea that converting enslaved people to Christianity might logically lead to their freedom. The problem they faced was how to eliminate an unwritten law that a Christian should not be a slave. The church's governing bodies and the bishop of London settled the matter by decreeing that conversion to Christianity did not lead to formal emancipation.

The organized church nevertheless provided the setting where a few African Americans were allowed to develop skills in reading, leadership, and educating their brethren. Often African Americans and whites attended church together. Eventually, some preachers who were former slaves demonstrated exceptional skill in "spreading the gospel." The Baptists in particular, by encouraging a form of self-government, allowed African Americans to become active in the church. This move fostered the growth of African American congregations; thus, Baptist congregations gave enslaved as well as free African Americans an opportunity for education and development that was not provided by many other denominations.

EARLY SCHOOLS FOR AFRICAN AMERICAN CHILDREN

One of the first northern schools established for African Americans appears to have been that of Elias Neau in New York City in 1704. Neau was an agent of the Society for the Propagation of the Gospel in Foreign Parts.

In 1807 several free African Americans, including George Bell, Nicholas Franklin, and Moses Liverpool, built the first schoolhouse for African Americans in the District of Columbia. Not until 1824, however, was there an African American teacher in that district—John Adams. In 1851, Washington citizens attempted to discourage Myrtilla Miner from establishing an academy for African American girls. However, after much turmoil and harassment, the white schoolmistress from New York did found her academy; it is still functioning today as the School of Education at the University of the District of Columbia.

Boston, the seat of northern liberalism, established a separate school for African American children in 1798. Elisha Sylvester, a white man, was in charge. The school was founded in the home of Primus Hall, a "Negro in good standing." Two years later, sixty-six free African Americans petitioned the school committee for a separate school and were refused. Undaunted, the patrons of Hall's house employed two instructors from Harvard; thirty-five years later, the school was allowed to move to a separate building. The city of Boston opened its first primary school for the education of African American children in 1820—one more small milestone in the history of African American education.

CROSS-REFERENCE
The more recent role of the federal government in educational affairs is discussed in Chapters 5 and 6.

FREDERICK DOUGLASS

Born in slavery in Maryland in 1817, Frederick Douglass (1817(?)–1895) ran away and began talking to abolitionist groups about his experiences in slavery. He attributed his fluent speech to listening to his master talk. Douglass firmly believed that if he devoted all his efforts to improving vocational education, he could greatly improve the plight of African Americans. He thought that previous attempts by educators to combine liberal and vocational education had failed, so he emphasized vocational education solely.

JOHN CHAVIS

African Americans' individual successes in acquiring education, as well as their group efforts to establish schools, were greatly enhanced by sympathetic and humanitarian white friends. One African American who was helped by whites was John Chavis (1763–1838), a free man born in Oxford, North Carolina. Chavis became a successful teacher of aristocratic whites, and his white neighbors sent him to Princeton "to see if a Negro would take a college education." His rapid advancement under Dr. Witherspoon soon indicated that the venture was a success. He returned to Virginia and later went to North Carolina, where he preached among his own people. The success of John Chavis, even under experimental conditions, represented another step forward in the education of African Americans.

Frederick Douglass (1817(?)–1895) was an influential antislavery lecturer, writer, and consultant to President Lincoln.

PRUDENCE CRANDALL

A young Quaker, Prudence Crandall (1803–1890), established an early boarding school in Canterbury, Connecticut. The problems she ran into dramatize some of the Northern animosity to educating African Americans. Trouble arose when Sarah Harris, a "colored girl," asked to be admitted to the institution. After much deliberation, Miss Crandall finally consented, but white parents objected to the African American girl's attending the school and withdrew their children. To keep the school open, Miss Crandall recruited African American children. The pupils were threatened with violence; local stores would not trade with her; and the school building was vandalized. The citizens of Canterbury petitioned the state legislature to enact a law that would make it illegal to educate African Americans from out of state. Miss Crandall was jailed and tried before the state supreme court in July 1834. The court never gave a final decision because defects were found in the information prepared by the attorney for the state; the indictment was eventually dropped. Miss Crandall

Booker T. Washington (1856–1915), an early African American educator, founded the Tuskegee Institute in Alabama in 1880 to help African American children acquire the education they needed to compete in society.

continued to work for the abolition of slavery, for women's rights, and for African American education. Prudence Crandall became well known, and she deserves considerable credit for the advances made by minorities and women in the United States.

BOOKER T. WASHINGTON

Booker T. Washington (1856–1915) was one of the early African American educators who contributed immensely to the development of education in the United States. He realized that African American children desperately needed an education to compete in society, and he founded Tuskegee Institute in 1880. This Alabama institution provided basic and industrial education in its early years and gradually expanded to provide a wider-ranging college curriculum. It stands today as a proud monument to Booker T. Washington's vision and determination concerning the education of African American youth.

EARLY AFRICAN AMERICAN COLLEGES

Unfortunately, despite these efforts, African Americans received pathetically little formal education until the Emancipation Proclamation, issued by President Abraham Lincoln on January 1, 1863. At that time, the literacy rate among African Americans was estimated at 5 percent. Sunday school represented about the only opportunity most African Americans had to learn to read. In the late 1700s and early 1800s, some communities did set up separate schools for African Americans; however, only a very small percentage ever attended the schools. A few colleges such as Oberlin, Bowdoin, Franklin, Rutland, and Harvard admitted African American students, but, again, very few of them attended college then. There were even a few African American colleges such as Lincoln University in Pennsylvania (1854) and Wilberforce University in Ohio (1856); however, the efforts and opportunities for the education of African Americans were few relative to the size of the African American population.

Although there was no great rush to educate African Americans, the abolition of slavery in 1865 signaled the beginning of a slow but steady effort to improve their education. By 1890, African American literacy had risen to 40 percent; by 1910 it was estimated that 70 percent of African Americans had learned to read and write. These statistics showing the rapid increase in African American literacy are impressive; however, they are compromised by a report of the U.S. commissioner of education showing that by 1900, fewer than 70 of every 1,000 public high schools in the South were providing for African Americans. Even worse, while educational opportunities for African Americans were meager, for other minority groups such as Native Americans and Hispanic Americans they were practically nonexistent.

The number of Asian students is increasing rapidly throughout the United States.

Asian American Education

The Second World War brought about what many consider unwarranted discrimination against Japanese Americans when the U.S. government placed more than 100,000 Japanese American citizens in internment camps and in some cases confiscated their property. Not until 1990 did the government officially apologize and pay restitution for having done so. In hindsight, many believe that this treatment of U.S. citizens of Japanese background constituted a form of discrimination.

In the decades following the Korean and Vietnam wars, the number of Asian immigrants to the United States has increased dramatically. Large numbers of Vietnamese, Cambodians, Laotians, and Thais have been included in this recent migration. Although many of these Asian immigrants have experienced considerable success, the majority have struggled to receive an education and find suitable jobs. Many feel that they have been discriminated against and have not received equal educational and employment opportunities. Yet many of the highest-achieving high school students are Asian Americans, proof of the fact that their families typically place a high value on education.

Hispanic American Education

The number of Hispanic American students in U.S. schools has increased dramatically over the past seventy years. But the historical background of this increase can actually be traced to the very first formal schools in North America. The earliest formal schools on this continent were started and conducted by Spanish missionaries in Mexico and the southwestern part of what is now the United States in the sixteenth century. Some historians even assert that the Spanish had established several "colleges" in North America before Harvard was founded in 1636. This assertion is probably true if one defines a mission school as a college, because some of them prepared boys for the ministry. As with the other early schools in the Americas, the missionaries established these early Spanish schools primarily for religious purposes—to help people read the Bible and thus gain salvation. Early mission schools in what is now Mexico and in Florida, Cuba, California, Arizona, New Mexico, and elsewhere were taught by Catholic priests in the Spanish language. After the United States won its independence and grew to include what we now think of as the Southwest, these early Spanish schools gradually became part of the larger English-speaking U.S. school system.

Unfortunately, Hispanic American education did not develop as quickly or as well as that of the majority population. This discrepancy is due at least in part to the facts that many Hispanic Americans are in the lower income brackets, that many immigrated to the United States without well-developed English language skills, and that many suffered discrimination. Like other minority groups in the United States, Hispanic Americans have not historically been afforded equal educational opportunities. Schools in the southern and southwestern parts of the United States now have large numbers of Hispanic American students, and in many of these schools Hispanic American students are the majority or will become so in the relatively near future.

CROSS-REFERENCE
Multicultural education is presented in Chapters 2, 3, and 4.

Education of Women

Historically, women have not been afforded equal educational opportunities in the United States. Furthermore, many authorities claim that U.S. schools have traditionally been sexist institutions. Although there is much evidence to support both these assertions, it is also true that an impressive list of women have made significant contributions to educational progress.

Colonial schools did not provide education for girls in any significant way. In some instances girls were taught to read, but females could not attend Latin grammar schools, academies, or colleges. We will look briefly at a few of the many outstanding female educators who helped to develop our country's educational system, in spite of their own limited educational opportunity.

EMMA WILLARD

Whereas well-to-do parents hired private tutors or sent their daughters away to a girls' seminary, girls from poor families were taught only to read and write at home

Emma Willard (1787–1870) was a pioneer in female higher education who established Middlebury Female Seminary, Waterford Female Academy, and Troy Female Seminary.

Maria Montessori (1870–1952) developed a theory and methods for educating young children that are still practiced in the United States.

(provided someone in the family had these skills). Emma Willard (1787–1870) was a pioneer and champion of education for females during a time when there were relatively few educational opportunities for them. She opened one of the first female seminaries in 1821 in Troy, New York, and this school offered an educational program equal to that of a boys' school. In a speech designed to raise funds for her school, she proposed the following benefits of seminaries for girls:

1. Females, by having their understandings cultivated, their reasoning power developed and strengthened, may be expected to act more from the dictates of reason and less from those of fashion and caprice.
2. With minds thus strengthened, they would be taught systems of morality, enforced by the sanctions of religion; and they might be expected to acquire juster and more enlarged views of their duty, and stronger and higher motives to its performance.
3. This plan of education offers all that can be done to preserve female youth from contempt of useful labor. The pupils would become accustomed to it, in conjunction with the high objects of literature and the elegant pursuits of the fine arts; and it is to be hoped that both from habit and association they might in future life regard it as respectable.
4. The pupils might be expected to acquire a taste for moral and intellectual pleasures which would buoy them above a passion for show and parade, and which would make them seek to gratify the natural love of superiority by endeavoring to excel others in intrinsic merit rather than in the extrinsic frivolities of dress, furniture, and equipage.
5. By being enlightened in moral philosophy, and in that which teaches the operations of the mind, females would be enabled to perceive the nature and extent of that influence which they possess over their children, and the obligation which this lays them under to watch the formation of their characters with unceasing vigilance, to become their instructors, to devise plans for their improvement, to weed out the vices of their minds, and to implant and foster the virtues. And surely there is that in the maternal bosom which, when its pleadings shall be aided by education, will overcome the seductions of wealth and fashion, and will lead the mother to seek her happiness in communing with her children, and promoting their welfare.[6]

Many other female institutions were established and became prominent during the mid- and late 1800s, including Mary Lyon's Mount Holyoke Female Seminary;

 Global Perspectives

Maria Montessori

Maria Montessori (1870–1952), born in Italy, became first a successful physician and later a prominent educational philosopher. She developed her own theory and methods of educating young children. Her methods utilized child-size school furniture and specially designed learning materials. She emphasized independent work by children under the guidance of a trained directress. Private Montessori schools thrive in the United States today.

Questions for Reflection

1. Do a key word web search on "Montessori" and record in your journal some of your reactions to what you find.
2. What is your perspective on the strong points and weak points of the Montessori method?

Jane Ingersoll's seminary in Cortland, New York; and Julia and Elias Mark's Southern Carolina Collegiate Institute at Barhamville, to name just a few. Unfortunately, not until well into the twentieth century were women generally afforded access to higher education.

ELLA FLAGG YOUNG

Yet another example of an outstanding early female educator is Ella Flagg Young (c. 1845–1918). Overcoming immense obstacles, she earned a doctorate at the age of fifty under John Dewey, was appointed head of the Cook County Normal School in Illinois, and became superintendent of the gigantic Chicago public school system in 1909—all achievements that were unheard of for a female at that time. She was also elected the first female president of the male-dominated National Education Association.

MARY McLEOD BETHUNE

Mary McLeod Bethune (1875–1955) believed that education was the key to helping African American children move into the mainstream of American life.

Mary McLeod Bethune (1875–1955) was one of seventeen children born to African American parents in Mayesville, South Carolina, the first family member not born in slavery. She received her first formal schooling at age nine in a free school for African American children. It is reported that she would come home from school and teach her brothers and sisters what she had learned each day. She came to believe that education was the key to helping African American children move into the mainstream of American life, and she devoted her life to improving educational opportunities for young African American women. She eventually started the Daytona Normal and Industrial School for Negro Young Women and later Bethune-Cookman College, where she served as president until 1942. She also believed that education helps everyone to respect the dignity of all people, regardless of color or creed, and is needed equally by Caucasian Americans, African Americans, and all other Americans. Mary McLeod Bethune went on to serve as founder and head of the National Council of Negro Women, director of the Division of Negro Affairs of the National Youth Administration, President Franklin D. Roosevelt's special advisor on minority affairs, and special consultant for drafting the charter of the United Nations. Mary McLeod Bethune was an effective, energetic human rights activist throughout her life and also a dedicated and professional career educator.

THE NINETEENTH AMENDMENT

Various groups first took interest in advancing the cause of females in the United States in the mid-1800s. The women's rights convention held at that time passed twelve resolutions that attempted to spur interest in providing females more equal participation and rights in U.S. society. The Civil War also furthered interest in the rights of women throughout the country, very likely as a spin-off of the abolition of slavery. It is interesting to note that not all the people in favor of doing away with slavery supported improved rights for women. For instance, not until 1920, when the Nineteenth Amendment passed, did women have the right to vote.

Unfortunately, the right to vote did not necessarily do much to improve the status of women; females continued to be denied equal educational and employment opportunities. The civil rights movement after World War II served as another impetus to the women's movement and gave rise to an additional round of improvements for females in U.S. society. Some authorities would trace the emergence of the current feminist movement to the 1960s, when a variety of activist groups coalesced to work against discrimination of all kinds in U.S. society. Some groups and individuals feel that adequate educational provisions and opportunities for females, minorities, and those with disabilities are still lacking in our school systems today at all levels.

How Can the Busy Teacher Keep Up with Historical and Contemporary Research?

Ask any teacher what her or his major problems are and "not having enough time" will likely be near the top of the list. So it is perhaps not surprising that many teachers find it difficult to keep up with current research that may help educators do a better job. And yet one of the important hallmarks of a professional is finding, evaluating, and implementing the results of valid and reliable research. For instance, when a person goes to a medical doctor, he or she expects that physician to be using knowledge based on the most recent medical research. By the same token, parents have a right to expect, when they send their children to school, that teachers will be using the most recent educational research in their educational practice. Thus, the professional dilemma is: How do busy teachers locate, read, evaluate, and implement the best research results into their teaching? This task is made even more difficult by the fact that although a great volume of education research is constantly being conducted, a fair amount of it is not necessarily valid or reliable.

Teachers who are determined to put good research results into practice must first be able to read, understand, and evaluate educational research. To learn how to do this, you will probably need to take some basic research courses at a nearby college or university. You will also need to read research reports found in a variety of professional journals in your specialty fields. This may mean subscribing to such journals or getting your school to make them available. Probably you will also wish to attend a variety of professional meetings where research is presented and discussed. And after you locate good research findings, you will need to do careful planning when you implement these research results in your classroom.

Unfortunately, there is no simple solution to this professional dilemma. We know that because we, too, struggle with this problem. However, we are convinced that the first step to solving this dilemma is becoming determined to offer your clients (your students and their parents) the very best education possible. We also are convinced that to do so requires a knowledge of the best and most recent educational research.

Questions for Reflection

1. What are your feelings about this professional dilemma at this point in your career development?

2. What might you be able to do at this time to help you prepare to deal with this dilemma?

3. To what degree do you feel your current teachers are keeping up with, and using, research in their teaching?

To answer these questions on-line and e-mail your answers to your professor, go to Chapter 7 of the companion website (www.ablongman.com/johnson14e) and click on Professional Dilemma.

Private Education in America

Private education has been extremely important in the development of the United States. In fact, private schools carried on nearly all of the education in colonial times. The first colonial colleges such as Harvard, William and Mary, Yale, and Princeton were all private institutions. Many of the other early colonial schools, which can be thought of as **religion-affiliated schools,** were operated by churches, missionary societies, and private individuals.

religion-affiliated school

A private school over which, in most cases, a parent church group exercises some control or to which the church provides some subsidy.

The Right of Private Schools to Exist

In 1816 the state of New Hampshire attempted to take over Dartmouth College, which was a private institution. A lawsuit growing out of this effort ultimately resulted in the U.S. Supreme Court's first decision involving the legal rights of a private school. The Supreme Court decided that a private school's charter must be viewed as a contract and cannot be broken arbitrarily by a state. In other words, the Court decided that a private school could not be forced against its will to become a public school.

Subsequent court decisions have reconfirmed the rights of private education in a variety of ways. Generally speaking, for instance, courts have reconfirmed that private schools have a right to exist and in some cases even to share public funds, as long as these funds are not used for religious purposes. Examples of such actions include the use of state funds to purchase secular textbooks and to provide transportation for students to and from private schools.

Not until after the Revolution, when there was a strong sense of nationalism, did certain educators advocate a strong public school system for the new nation. However, such recommendations were not acted on for many years. In the meantime, some Protestant churches continued to expand their schools during the colonial period. For instance, the Congregational, Quaker, Episcopal, Baptist, Methodist, Presbyterian, and Reformed churches all, at various times and in varying degrees, established and operated schools for their youth. It was the Roman Catholics and Lutherans, however, who eventually developed elaborate **parochial school** systems operated by their respective denominations.

CROSS-REFERENCE
Additional information on legal aspects of education can be found in Chapter 6.

Parochial Schools

As early as 1820 there were 240 Lutheran parochial schools in Pennsylvania. Although the number of Lutheran schools in that particular state eventually dwindled, Henry Muhlenberg and other Lutheran leaders continued to establish parochial schools until the public school system became well established. The Missouri Synod Lutheran Church has continued to maintain a well-developed parochial school system. Currently, there are approximately 1,700 Lutheran elementary and secondary schools, which enroll about 200,000 pupils, in the United States, and most of these schools are operated by the Missouri Synod Lutheran Church.

The Roman Catholic parochial school system grew rapidly after its beginnings in the 1800s. Enrollment in Catholic schools mushroomed between 1900 and 1960 from about 855,000 to over five million students. The Roman Catholic parochial school system in the United States is now the largest private school system in the world.

A number of other religious groups have developed and operated their own parochial schools from time to time, and some of them still do today. Examples of such religious groups include the Mormons, Mennonites, and Quakers.

The Important Role of Private Education in America

The concept of public education—that is, education paid for by various governments (local, state, and federal)—is a relatively new idea in the history of U.S. education. For many years, if parents or religious groups wanted to provide education for their children, they had to do so with their own resources. In this part of the book, there have been many references to private schools and private education; at this juncture, we simply wish to reiterate the tremendous importance of private education. In fact, were it not for private education as the predecessor, it is difficult to imagine how we would have evolved a public education system. Private education still plays an enormously important role at all levels of education in the United States.

The major shift from private to public education occurred during the nineteenth century. For instance, in 1800 there was no state system of public education anywhere in the United States—no public elementary schools, secondary schools, or

parochial school

An educational institution operated and controlled by a religious denomination.

state colleges or universities. In fact, until the nineteenth century, all forms of education were private in nature—from elementary school through graduate school. By the year 1900, however, nearly all states had developed a public system of education running from elementary school through graduate school.

Many historians suggest that the overriding motive for private education has always been religious in nature. Initially, parents wanted their children to learn to read so that they could study and understand the Bible and thus gain salvation. Even the earliest colleges were designed primarily to prepare ministers.

Likewise, Benjamin Franklin created his unique academy as a private institution to provide technical training to young men because there was no public institution yet created to do so. It was not until 1874 that the Michigan State Supreme Court established that it was legal for school districts to tax citizens for general support of public high schools. By that time, private schools had been providing secondary education for our nation's youth for two centuries.

Summary

THE BEGINNINGS OF EDUCATION (to 476 CE). Any study of the beginnings of formal education should start with the fact that parents have always attempted to provide, in one way or another, the informal education their children need to survive in their society. Formal schools very likely did not come into existence until four or five thousand years ago, as humans developed written languages.

Current evidence suggests that one of the first well-organized educational systems was that evolved by the Greeks during what is today commonly called the Age of Pericles. Greek knowledge and schools eventually blended into Roman schools and libraries.

EDUCATION IN THE MIDDLE AGES (476–1300). During the later part of the Middle Ages, there was a revived interest in learning. This period of educational history is commonly marked by two historical movements: the Renaissance and the Reformation. The Renaissance represented a rebellion on the part of the common people against their economic, educational, and religious suppression under the royalty and landed gentry. These common people gradually demanded a better life and developed a spirit of inquiry, which created an interest in education and schooling.

EDUCATION IN TRANSITION AND EDUCATIONAL AWAKENING. The fourteenth through eighteenth centuries saw sometimes erratic, but nevertheless fairly continuous, progression of educational development and advancement throughout the world. In the Western world, this period is often divided into the Age of Reason, which emphasized people's rational and scientific abilities, and the Emergence of Common Man, which sought to create a better education and life for all people. The Protestant Reformation led by Martin Luther, and the work of Rousseau, Pestalozzi, Herbart, and Froebel, did much to improve education during this time.

EVOLVING PERSPECTIVES OF EDUCATION IN OUR DEVELOPING NATION, DIVERSE POPULATIONS, AND PRIVATE EDUCATION. Our earliest colonists brought their educational ideas and expectations with them from Europe and, soon after arriving in the New World, set about creating schools that fulfilled their needs. These efforts varied widely, from private tutorial education for plantation owners' children in the South, to religious schools in the Middle Colonies, to public schools in the North. Most education was driven by religious motives, and much of the formal education beyond that needed to read the Bible was provided only for boys from the more

Journal for Reflection

1. List some of the most important things you learned from this chapter.

2. Which, if any, of the items you listed will likely have practical value for you as a future educator?

3. In what ways?

well-to-do families. Early efforts to provide education for the poor, people of color, and women were nonexistent or, at the very least, meager. The earliest education was provided by private schools, which have remained a very important part of our educational system.

This chapter illustrates that there are many different perspectives on education throughout the ages. There are a number of big historical ideas that grow out of the more detailed history of education discussed in the chapter. These include the ideas that adults in early societies provided the informal education that they felt necessary for children to succeed in their society, that more formal schools likely came into existence only as people developed written languages, that all societies around the world have developed their own forms of education, down through the ages, designed to fulfill their unique needs, and that human progress has, in large part, depended on education.

Discussion Questions

1. What were the major contributions of several ancient societies to the development of education?
2. What factors contributed to the decline of education during the Dark Ages?
3. What were the strengths and weaknesses of Jean-Jacques Rousseau's ideas about children and education?
4. Discuss the evolution of elementary schools.
5. What historical conditions led to that uniquely U.S. institution, the comprehensive high school?
6. What are the highlights of the history of education of African Americans?
7. Discuss the roles that private schools have played in U.S. education.

School-Based Observations

1. Over two hundred years ago, Jean-Jacques Rousseau advocated that children be taught with love, patience, understanding, and kindness. As you work in the school, experiment with this basic approach to see whether it is effective. You might also wish to observe experienced teachers: To what extent do they teach children with love, patience, understanding, and kindness? We suggest that you experiment with other constructive ideas in this chapter as you observe and participate in the classroom.
2. As you work in schools, observe how they have changed relative to schools of the past. How are schools today similar to those of the past? How much and in what ways are students today similar to their historical counterparts? In what ways are they probably different?
3. While you are in the schools, visit with experienced teachers and administrators to discuss the ways that schools have changed over the years. Also ask how students, teaching methods, and parents have changed.

Portfolio Development

1. Make a list of historical educational ideas mentioned in this chapter that are still valid and useful for educators today.
2. Summarize the evolution of the goals of public schools in colonial America and the United States. Develop a chart that creatively portrays this evolution.
3. Write an essay on the importance of education in the historical development of the United States.

Preparing for Certification

THE EVOLUTION OF U.S. SCHOOLS

1. One of the topics in the Praxis II Principles of Learning and Teaching (PLT) test is "structuring a climate for learning (for example, attention to interpersonal relations, motivational strategies, questioning techniques, classroom and school expectations, rules, routines, and procedures)." In this chapter, you learned about the evolution of schools in the United States from colonial times to the present. Compare the climate for learning in early American schools with schools of today. How are schools' climates similar or different?
2. Answer the following multiple-choice question, which is similar to items in Praxis and other state certification tests.

The McGuffey readers were commonly used in U.S. schools in the 1800s. What was their major characteristic that contributed to modern curriculum development?

   A. The materials in each reader were sequenced by grade level and level of difficulty.
   B. They were the first materials to focus on phonics.
   C. They emphasized multicultural themes.
   D. They emphasized the concepts of learning by firsthand experience.

3. Answer the following short-answer question, which is similar to items in Praxis and other state certification tests. After you've completed your written

response, use the scoring guide in the ETS *Test at a Glance* materials to assess your response. Can you revise your response to improve your score?

Reread the Relevant Research feature of this chapter, which describes the curriculum of the Boston Latin Grammar School in 1712. List three ways in which the curriculum of the Boston Latin Grammar School is similar to that of U.S. secondary schools today and three ways in which it differs.

Websites

www.cedu.niu.edu/blackwell The Blackwell History of Education Museum and Research Collection is one of the largest collections of its kind in the world. Much of the collection is listed on this website. The Blackwell Museum has developed a variety of instructional materials (also listed on its site) designed to help you learn more about the antecedents of early American and U.S. education.

www.historyofeducation.org.uk The *History of Education* journal of the History of Education Society, located in England. A useful general source of educational history.

www.cpb.org/grants/historyandcivics A source of information about possible history and civics initiatives.

www.cr.nps.gov/nr/twhp/wwwlps/lessons58iron/58iron.htm A historical website about Iron Hill School, an African American one-room school in northern Delaware.

Further Reading

Cremin, Lawrence. (1961). *The Transformation of the School: Progressivism in American Education, 1876–1957*. New York: Knopf. This and the next two entries are authored by one of the most respected educational historians of the twentieth century.

Cremin, Lawrence A. (1970). *American Education: The Colonial Experience, 1607–1783*. New York: Harper & Row.

Cremin, Lawrence. (1990). *American Education: The National Experience, 1793–1976*. New York: Harper & Row.

Holmes, Madelyn, and Weiss, Beverly J. (1995). *Lives of Women Public Schoolteachers: Scenes from American Educational History*. New York: Garland. A well done book about the important role of women educators.

Johnson, Tony W., and Reed, Ronald F. (2002). *Historical Documents in American Education*. Boston: Allyn & Bacon. A compilation of many original resource documents pertaining to the history of education.

Morgan, Harry. (1995). *Historical Perspectives on the Education of Black Children*. Westport, CT: Praeger. A useful book containing a good deal of information about the history of African American children.

Szasz, Margaret Connell. (1988). *Indian Education in the American Colonies 1607–1783*. Albuquerque: University of New Mexico Press. An excellent source of information about the education of Native Americans during the colonial period.

mylabschool
Where the classroom comes to life!

Go to Allyn and Bacon's MyLabSchool (www.mylabschool.com) and complete the following activity for Chapter 7. Click on **Research Navigator** and then use the following search terms within the Education data base: **John Locke, Erasmus, Martin Luther.**

CHAPTER 8

Historical Perspectives of Education

Casualties of Segregation Receive Honorary Diplomas

By Justin Bergman, Associated Press, *St. Paul Pioneer Press*, June 16, 2003

FARMVILLE, VA.—Four decades after Prince Edward County, Va., closed its public schools rather than obey orders to integrate, the black students who were denied an education received honorary diplomas Sunday.

Ada Allen Whitehead said she was the kind of student who never missed a day of school. "I loved to learn," the 55-year-old said.

But she had to stop going to school in Prince Edward County after the seventh grade. She eventually earned her high school diploma outside the county in 1963 and is now working on her doctorate in special education.

"Today is extremely important to start to heal some of the wounds," said state Delegate Viola Baskerville, who is black. "Virginia didn't even want to discuss this for so many years. It was like it was swept under the rug."

To the students who received honorary degrees, the ceremony means "we haven't forgotten," Baskerville said.

Whitehead and other young blacks were forced from their classrooms from 1959 to 1964 when Prince Edward County simply closed its public schools rather than obey the U.S. Supreme Court's order to integrate them.

It was the only county in the nation to close its public schools for an extended period rather than integrate.

A private school was established for white students, while many black children never returned to school. Others, like Whitehead, finished school elsewhere.

Her brother, Ulysses S. Allen, 61, finished his senior year of high school in Washington, D.C.

He called Sunday's honorary graduation a nice gesture, but added: "I don't think you can ever really make amends. What's happened has happened. It's history."

In a gesture of reconciliation, the Virginia General Assembly this year passed a resolution expressing "profound regret" for the school closings.

Questions for Reflection

1. What is your reaction to the events reported in this news article?

2. What else might have been done to remedy this situation?

3. What role do you feel the government or courts should play in situations like this?

Reprinted by permission of the Associated Press.

Learning Outcomes

After reading and studying this chapter, you should be able to:

1. Decide, explain, and defend the degree to which you believe it is possible to know, understand, and profit from the history of education. (INTASC 10: Collaboration)

2. List and detail several of the most important improvements that have been made in the U.S. educational system over the past half century. (INTASC 2: Development and Learning)

3. Explain important educational contributions that have been made during the last sixty years by private schools, the federal government, researchers, teacher organizations, teacher educators, and other groups that have helped to improve U.S. schools.

4. List and explain several of the major ideas regarding the history of U.S. education.

5. Explain why knowledge of the history of education is important to educators and how it might be used to improve education today. (INTASC 7: Planning)

Many dramatic changes have occurred in education in the United States over the past half century. Examples of these rapid and often controversial changes that represent various perspectives will be briefly discussed in this chapter. However, the big historical ideas presented in this chapter are (1) the phenomenal change and growth in both the size and complexity of U.S. educational establishments; (2) the tremendous new demands and expectation on our schools and teachers placed by the current information age; (3) the major, yet unrealized challenge to our society and to our schools to provide excellent equal educational opportunities to all students; and, perhaps most important, (4) an understanding that the history of education is of very practical value in helping contemporary educators improve education.

More Students and Bigger Schools

Since World War II, U.S. education has been characterized by a great deal of growth and change: growth in terms of school enrollment, educational budgets, complexity, and federal influence, and change in terms of court decisions, proliferation of school laws, confusion about goals, school financial difficulties, struggles for control, and diversification of curricula.

Enrollment Growth

Perhaps the single most dramatic change that has occurred in education over the past sixty years is the sheer expansion in size of the educational enterprise, which took place in many ways. The total number of public school students in the United States has about doubled over the past seventy-five years. Although part of this rapid growth in school enrollment was attributable to overall population growth, a good part was due to the fact that greater percentages of people were going to school. Furthermore, people were staying in school much longer, as shown by the almost doubled enrollment in higher education.

Need for More Schools

As school enrollment dramatically increased, the need for new classrooms and buildings to house these students also increased. This need for new schools was generally concentrated in cities and suburbs. In fact, because of increased busing, school district consolidation, and shifting population, some smaller rural schools were no longer needed, whereas more densely populated areas saw a drastic shortage of classrooms. Many schools had to resort to temporary mobile classrooms. Other strategies for coping with classroom shortages included larger classes, split scheduling that started some classes very early and others very late in the day, and classes held in a variety of makeshift areas such as gymnasiums, hallways, and storage closets. Many schools also rented additional space in nearby buildings. Fortunately, over time taxpayers were generally willing to approve the necessary bond referenda to provide the needed additional schools during this period of rapid growth in student enrollment.

This is one of thousands of one-room country schools established to educate rural children during the westward movement in America.

Need for More Teachers

Naturally, this surge in student enrollment required many additional teachers, and at times colleges simply could not produce enough. In this situation, states lowered teacher certification requirements, sometimes to the point at which no professional education training was required at all. Over time, however, the nation managed to meet the demand for more teachers.

As one would expect, the increased numbers of students and teachers cost a great deal more money. More buses had to be purchased, more books and other instructional materials had to be obtained, more school personnel had to be hired—more of everything required to provide education was needed.

A person who wants to learn will always find a teacher.

Persian proverb

School District Consolidation

The consolidation of school districts was one notable administrative trend over the past seventy-five years. The number of separate school districts was reduced from 117,000 in 1940 to about 14,000 today. There was a corresponding decline in the number of one-teacher schools over this same period.

Growth of Busing

Both the number and the percentage of students who are bused has increased considerably over the past seventy-five years, as has the total cost and per-pupil cost of busing. In addition to the general busing of students necessitated by school district consolidation, integration efforts have often involved busing students away from their neighborhood schools. Busing students to school is still a big operation for the U.S. educational enterprise. It is estimated that about 60 percent of all students are bused to school by about 450,000 school buses.

Bigger School Budgets

CROSS-REFERENCE
See Chapter 5 for more information about the current costs of education.

Educational growth has driven the nation's public education costs to record heights. This rapid increase is illustrated by noting that the approximate cost of public education was $2 billion in 1940, $5 billion in 1950, $15 billion in 1960, $40 billion in 1970, $97 billion in 1980, and $208 billion in 1990. Even if the figures are corrected for inflation, public education has become considerably more expensive: The percentage of the gross domestic product spent on education rose from 3.5 percent in 1940 to 7 percent by 1980.[1]

Rapid Curricular Growth and Changes

As enrollments have increased and schools have grown larger, more diverse curricula and programs have been developed in U.S. schools. This rapid growth of programs places a great deal of work and pressure on teachers, school administrators, and school boards.

In the new brain-powered economy, education will be the world's largest, most important industry.

Morton Egol

Curricular growth, like most change, was the result of an accumulation of many smaller events. One such event was the publication in 1942 of the report of the Progressive Education Association's Eight-Year Study (1932–1940) of thirty high schools. The study showed that students attending "progressive" schools achieved as well as students at traditional schools. This report helped to create a climate that was more hospitable to experimentation with school curricula and teaching methodologies. The publication of a series of statements on the goals of U.S. education (the 1938 "Purposes of Education in American Democracy," the 1944 "Education for All American Youth," and the 1952 "Imperative Needs of Youth") helped broaden our schools' curricular offerings.

In 1958, shortly after the Soviet Union launched *Sputnik,* the world's first artificial satellite, Congress passed the National Defense Education Act (NDEA). This act provided a massive infusion of federal dollars to improve schools' science, mathematics, engineering, and foreign language programs. Eventually, innovative curricula such as SMSG mathematics, BSCS biology, and PSCS physics grew out of these programs. Other school programs, such as guidance, were later funded through the NDEA. Note that in the case of the NDEA the federal government called on the schools to help solve what was perceived to be a national defense problem. Regardless of the motive, the NDEA represented another milestone that contributed significantly to the growth of the U.S. educational enterprise.

If one were to compare today's school curriculum with that in any school seventy-five years ago, one would find impressive changes. The 1940 curriculum was narrow and designed primarily for college-bound students, whereas today's curriculum is broader and designed for students of all abilities. This growth in the school curriculum has come about through the dedicated work of many people and represents one of the truly significant accomplishments in U.S. education.

Growth of Special Education Programs

CROSS-REFERENCE
See Chapter 2 for more information about education and exceptionalities.

Perhaps curriculum growth is best illustrated in the area of special education. Public schools historically did not provide special education programs for children with disabilities; rather, they simply accommodated such children as best they could, usually by placing them in regular classrooms. Teachers had little or no training to help them understand and assist the special child. In fact, relatively little was known about common disabilities.

What Have We Learned about Homework and Students with Disabilities?

INTRODUCTION: Throughout history, teachers have worked to provide the right type and amount of homework for each student; and they are still striving to do so.

STUDY PURPOSE/QUESTION: Today, partly as a result of educational reform, many students are receiving increased amounts of homework. For students with disabilities, homework may pose significant challenges. Some of these problems are related to a student's ability to maintain attention, sustain acceptable levels of motivation, demonstrate effective study skills, and manifest positive attitudes toward homework. Others are related to factors such as how homework is assigned and the quality of communication between home and school about homework.

William Bursuck, researcher at Northern Illinois University, has been studying how practitioners and families can make homework a more successful experience for students with disabilities. One thing is clear—parent involvement is critical if homework is to be beneficial.

STUDY DESIGN: With his colleagues, Bursuck conducted a series of studies to identify problems parents and schools were experiencing in communicating about homework, as well as recommendations for ameliorating these problems.

STUDY FINDINGS: Teachers encountered the following problems:

- Insufficient time and opportunity to communicate.
- Too many students on a given teacher's caseload.
- Need for additional knowledge to facilitate communication (e.g., students' needs, whom to contact).
- Other factors that hindered communication, such as lack of phones in teachers' classrooms.

Recommendations for improvement grew out of the discussions.

Teachers identified useful adaptations for students with disabilities. They also suggested strategies for ensuring that homework was clear and appropriate.

In addition, the surveys indicated that teachers preferred the following strategies to maintain effective communication:

- Use technology to aid communication (e.g., use answering machines or e-mail, and establish homework hotlines).
- Encourage students to keep assignment books.
- Provide a list of suggestions on how parents might assist with homework. For example, ask parents to check with their children about homework daily.

Preferred Homework Adaptations

- Provide additional one-on-one assistance to students.
- Monitor students' homework more closely.
- Allow alternative response formats (e.g., audiotaping rather than writing an assignment).
- Adjust the length of the assignment.
- Provide a peer tutor or assign the student to a study group.
- Provide learning tools (e.g., calculators).
- Adjust evaluation standards.
- Give fewer assignments.

Tips for Assigning Homework

- Make sure the students can complete the homework assignment.
- Write the assignment on the chalkboard.
- Explain the assignment clearly.
- Remind students of due dates periodically.
- Assign homework in small units.
- Coordinate with other teachers to prevent homework overload.
- Make sure students and parents have information regarding your policy on missed and late assignments, extra credit, and available adaptations. Establish a set routine at the beginning of the year.
- Provide parents with frequent communication about homework.
- Use written modes of communication (e.g., progress reports, notes, letters, forms).
- Encourage the school administration to provide incentives for teachers to participate in face-to-face meetings (e.g., release time, compensation).
- Suggest that the school district offer after-school and/or peer tutoring sessions to give students extra help with homework.

(continued)

- Share information with other teachers regarding student strengths and needs and necessary accommodations.

IMPLICATIONS: If students, teachers, and parents do not find homework strategies palatable, they may not use them. "The ultimate impact of these homework practices on students may depend largely on how favorably teach-

ers, parents, and the students themselves perceive them," Bursuck adds. "Our research underscores the need to check out practices with all stakeholders. Simply put, practices that are not acceptable will not be used."

Source: ERIC Clearinghouse on Disabilities and Gifted Education, U.S. Office of Education, *Research Connections: In Special Education*, No. 8 (Spring 2001), pp. 2–3.

Journal for Reflection

1. Interview a retired teacher about the educational changes she or he has observed over a lifetime.

2. Ask what advice this retired educator has for beginning teachers today and record the answers.

Not until the federal government passed a series of laws during the later twentieth century—including Public Law 94-142, the Education for Handicapped Children Act—did schools begin to develop well-designed programs for students with disabilities. These new special education programs required teachers who had been trained to work with students with visual or hearing impairments, students with behavior disorders, and students with a range of other exceptionalities. States and colleges then developed a wide variety of teacher-training programs for special educators.

The Development of the Teaching Profession

The field of education has taken giant strides toward becoming a profession since World War II. In the following pages, we will briefly explore the increasing complexities of educational systems in the United States and look at some of the recent developments that have contributed to the professionalization of the field of education.

Increasing Federal Involvement

The federal government has played an important role in the development of national educational programs. This federal involvement in education has gradually increased over the years, and it reached a peak during the past seventy-five years.

The 1940s saw the nation at war, which provided the impetus for the federal government to pass a number of laws that affected education. The Vocational Education for National Defense Act was a crash program to prepare workers needed in industry to produce goods for national defense. The program operated through state educational agencies and trained more than seven million workers. In 1941 the Lanham Act provided funds for building, maintaining, and operating community facilities in areas where local communities had unusual burdens because of defense and war initiatives.

GI BILL

The GI Bill of 1944 provided for the education of veterans of World War II. Later, similar bills assisted veterans of the Korean conflict. The federal government recognized a need to help young people whose careers had been interrupted by military service. These federal acts afforded education to more than ten million veterans at a cost of almost $20 billion. Payments were made directly to veterans and to the colleges and schools the veterans attended. In 1966 another GI Bill was passed for veterans of the war in Vietnam. The initial cost of these acts amounted to a wonderful national investment because the government was repaid many times over by the increased taxes eventually paid by veterans who received this financial aid and later were employed.

NATIONAL SCIENCE FOUNDATION

The National Science Foundation, established in 1950, emphasized the need for continued support of basic scientific research. It was created to "promote the progress of science; to advance the national health, prosperity, and welfare; to secure the national defense; and for other purposes." The Cooperative Research Program of 1954 authorized the U.S. commissioner of education to enter into contracts with universities, colleges, and state education agencies to carry on educational research.

CATEGORICAL FEDERAL AID

Beginning in 1957, when the first Soviet space vehicle was launched, the federal government further increased its participation in education. The National Defense Education Act of 1958, the Vocational Education Act of 1963, the Manpower Development and Training Act of 1963, the Elementary and Secondary Education Act of 1965, and the International Education Act of 1966 are examples of increased federal participation in educational affairs. Federally supported educational programs such as Project Head Start, the National Teacher Corp, and Upward Bound are further indications of such participation.

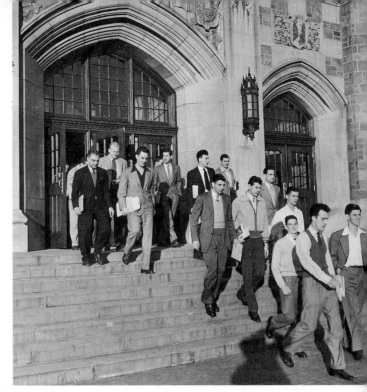

World War II veterans returned to college motivated by their war experiences and assisted by the federal GI Bill of Rights.

All these acts and programs have involved categorical federal aid to education—that is, aid for specific uses. Some people believe that federal influence on education has recently been greater than either state or local influence. There can be no denying that through federal legislation, U.S. Supreme Court decisions, and federal administrative influence, the total federal effect on education is indeed great. Indications are that this effect will be even more pronounced in the future. It will remain for historians to determine whether this trend in U.S. education is a beneficial one.

CROSS-REFERENCE

Chapters 5 and 6 present more information on the administrative and financial aspects of federal involvement in education.

THE STRUGGLE FOR EQUAL EDUCATIONAL OPPORTUNITY

The past half century has also been characterized by an increasing struggle for **equal educational opportunity** for all children, regardless of race, creed, religion, or gender. This struggle was initiated by the African American activism movement, given additional momentum by the women's rights movement, and eventually joined by many other groups such as Hispanic Americans, Native Americans, and Asian Americans. Other chapters of this book discuss the details of this relatively recent quest for equal educational opportunity. We mention it briefly at this point simply to emphasize that the struggle for equal educational opportunity represents an important but underrecognized recent historical movement in education. Today, many observers are pointing out that with the accelerated growth of minority subcultures within this nation, our economic and political survival depends to a great degree on educational opportunities and achievements for all segments of U.S. society.

NO CHILD LEFT BEHIND (NCLB)

One of the federal government's recent major efforts to improve education and help children learn, especially disadvantaged children, is the sweeping legislation commonly referred to as No Child Left Behind. While the goal of this law is admirable, it has been widely criticized, especially by the education profession. Examples of

equal educational opportunity

Access to a similar education for all students, regardless of their cultural background or family circumstances.

this criticism are that (1) sufficient funds have not been made available to effectively impliment the law, (2) the mandated testing required by the law is not sufficiently valid or reliable and is too time consuming, and (3) the law and testing does not take into account the extremely wide abilities of students. This law is discussed in more detail throughout this book, but it is mentioned here as yet another example of increasing federal involvement in education.

The Professionalization of Teaching

Formal teacher training is a relatively recent phenomenon. Teacher-training programs were developed during the late nineteenth century and the first half of the twentieth century. By the midpoint of the century, each state had established teacher certification requirements. Since then, teacher training and certification have been characterized by a "refinement" or "professionalization" movement.

In addition to teacher education, this professionalization movement touched just about all facets of education: curriculum, teaching methodology, training of school service personnel (administrators, counselors, librarians, media and other specialists), in-service teacher training, teacher organizations, and even school building construction. To understand clearly this professionalization movement, one need only compare pictures of an old one-room country school with a modern school building, read both a 1940 and a 2007 publication of the AFT or NEA, contrast a mid-twentieth-century high school curriculum with one from today, or compile a list of the teaching materials found in a 1940 school and a similar list for a typical contemporary school.

Continued Importance of Private Schools

As explained in Chapter 7, nearly all early schools in colonial America were private and religion was the main purpose of education. Children were taught to read primarily so that they could study the Bible, and most early colleges were private, established primarily to train ministers.

As the public school system developed, however, the religious nature of education gradually diminished to the point that relatively few U.S. children attended religious schools. There have always been certain religious groups, however, who have struggled to create and maintain their own private schools so that religious instruction could permeate all areas of the curriculum. The most notable of these religious groups has long been the Roman Catholic Church. Over the past twenty-five years, though, enrollment in non-Catholic religious schools has grown dramatically whereas Catholic school enrollment has declined.

Despite this recent trend, some Roman Catholic dioceses operate extremely large school systems, sometimes larger than the public school system in the same geographical area. The Chicago Diocese operates the largest Roman Catholic school system, enrolling approximately 150,000 students.

With rare exceptions, private and parochial schools struggle to raise the funds they need to exist. They typically must charge a tuition fee, rely on private contributions, and conduct various fund-raising activities. In recent years, some school districts have made tuition vouchers available to parents who choose not to send their children to public schools.

Home Schooling

Many years ago, with few exceptions the only parents who taught their children at home were those who lived so far from a school that it was impossible for their children to attend. In the past several decades, however, a growing number of parents have been choosing to educate their children at home—at least through the elementary grades and sometimes even through high school. The motivation for **home schooling** varies, but often it stems from a concern that children in the public schools may be exposed to problems such as drugs, alcohol, smoking, or gangs. Other parents have religious motives, wanting their children to be taught in a particular religious context. Still other parents, who may have had bad experiences with public schools, simply feel they can provide a better education for their children at home. Recent laws and court cases have generally upheld the right, within certain parameters, of parents to educate their children if they choose to do so. The number of parents providing home schooling has grown an estimated 15 percent each year in the last decade. A recent development among a minority of those who home school is a philosophy referred to as *unschooling* in which parents provide no instruction but allow their children to learn through whatever they naturally do. As one would expect, the value of home schooling is widely debated in our society.

Home schooling is a rapidly growing phenomenon.

home schooling
Teaching children at home rather than in formal schools.

Continuing/Adult Education

Many forms of education for adults have existed for at least two centuries in this country. Shortly after the United States became a nation, a need to help new immigrants learn English caused schools, churches, and various groups to offer English language instruction; factories found a need to offer job and safety training; churches taught adult religious instruction; and so forth. The New York public schools, as well as many other large schools, developed large English language programs as well as adult vocational programs for the unemployed. Adult education took a great variety of forms and quickly grew into a vast network of programs dealing with nearly all aspects of life in the United States.

An example of a large early adult education development can be found in the Chautauqua movement at Lake Chautauqua, New York. Started in 1874 by the Methodist Sunday school, this adult education effort expanded to include correspondence courses, lecture classes, music education, and literary study on a wide variety of subjects throughout the eastern part of the nation.

Public schools increasingly offered adult education classes during the nineteenth century. Some of the larger public school systems, such as in Gary, Indiana, developed adult educational programs with an emphasis on vocational and technical training. Gradually, nearly all schools serving rural areas developed adult agricultural programs to improve farming methods.

In 1964 the Economic Opportunity Act provided adult basic education funding to help adults learn to read and write. Since that time there has been a proliferation of continuing/adult education programs of all types throughout the United States. These programs serve an increasingly important purpose in our rapidly changing society. They help new immigrants learn the English language, provide job training for the unemployed, update job skills, teach parenting skills, enable

We should begin improving our schools by appreciating how well they have, in most places and most times, done so far.

Gerald W. Bracey

Adult education programs have been common in the United States since the seventeenth century, but they burgeoned during the late twentieth and early twenty-first centuries. Many such programs are offered through public schools.

CROSS-REFERENCE

Chapter 5 provides more information on private schooling in the United States.

people to move to higher-level employment, help people explore new hobbies, provide enrichment programs for retired folks, and generally make the world of education available to nearly all citizens regardless of age. The exploding popularity of the Elderhostel programs and other activities now offered for senior citizens and the crowded evening parking lots at high schools and colleges throughout the country attest to the popularity and success of continuing/adult education programs. In the future, as the world becomes increasingly complex and as more people remain active and healthy in old age, we predict that such adult/continuing education programs will continue to grow.

Evolution of Educational Testing

Educators have undoubtedly attempted to measure and assess student learning from the very beginning of formal education. However, it is only in the last sixty years that educational assessment has taken on vastly more importance, to the point in contemporary education that many feel assessment has become the tail that wags the educational dog. Let's briefly review this recent evolution of educational assessment.

Many historians suggest that the increased attention given to educational testing in the past sixty years was sparked by James Conant, who had become president of Harvard University in 1933. Conant and his colleagues were influenced by the developments in mental testing done by Alfred Binet in France and by Lewis Terman in the United States, which were used extensively by the U.S. Army to test recruits.

Through public education we can in this century hope in no small measure to regain that great gift to each succeeding generation, opportunity, a gift that once was the promise of our frontier.

James Conant

Conant seized on a relatively new test called the Scholastic Aptitude Test (SAT), developed by Carl Bright at Princeton University, as a way to assess a student's potential for success at Harvard. He also helped to create a new organization, called the Educational Testing Service (ETS), which became—and remains—the major power in the educational assessment area. By the 1960s, over a million high school students were taking the SAT test, which most colleges used as one criterion for admission.

Many so-called standardized tests have been developed over the past sixty years in an attempt to measure different kinds of aptitude, learning, motivation, and virtually every aspect of education. These standardized tests have come under much criticism by many educators, parents, and others, who question their fairness and accuracy. Even so they continue to be heavily used today.

Educators have faced increasing pressure in recent years to develop improved ways to assess student learning. Much of this pressure has come from taxpayers, government, and the industrial world, often in a demand for greater accountability. Most states have implemented a required system of achievement testing. The results of these achievement tests are commonly used to evaluate and compare schools— a controversial and unfair practice, according to many educators.

In fact, while agreeing that accurate educational assessment is absolutely essential to the educational enterprise, a growing number of educators are questioning many aspects of the increasing emphasis on educational assessment. This important topic is discussed more in various places throughout the text. Suffice it to point out here that educational assessment has grown rapidly and taken on increasing importance, for better or worse, in the past sixty years.

CROSS-REFERENCE

See Chapter 11 for more information on educational assessment.

Changing Aims of Education

The aims of education in the United States have reflected changing perspectives on education over the years. During colonial times, the overriding aim of education at all levels was to enable students to read and understand the Bible, to gain salvation, and to spread the gospel.

After the colonies won independence from England, educational objectives—such as providing U.S. citizens with a common language, attempting to instill a sense of patriotism, developing a national feeling of unity and common purpose, and providing the technical and agricultural training the developing nation needed—became important tasks for the schools.

Each generation must define afresh the nature, direction, and aims of education to assure such freedom and rationality as can be attained for a future generation.

Jerome S. Bruner

Committee of Ten

In 1892 a committee was established by the National Education Association (NEA) to study the function of the U.S. high school. This committee, known as the **Committee of Ten,** made an effort to set down the purposes of the high school at that time and made the following recommendations: (1) High school should consist of grades 7 through 12; (2) courses should be arranged sequentially; (3) students should be given very few electives in high school; and (4) one unit, called a Carnegie unit, should be awarded for each separate course that a student takes each year, provided that the course meets four or five times each week all year long.

The Committee of Ten also recommended trying to graduate high school students earlier to permit them to attend college sooner. At that time, the recommendation implied that high schools had a college preparatory function. These recommendations became powerful influences in shaping secondary education.

Seven Cardinal Principles

Before 1900, teachers had relatively little direction in their work because most educational goals were not precisely stated. This problem was partly overcome in 1918 when the Commission on Reorganization of Secondary Education published the report *Cardinal Principles of Secondary Education,* usually referred to as the Seven Cardinal Principles. In reality, the Seven Cardinal Principles constitute only one section of the basic principles discussed in the original text, but it is the part that has become famous. These principles stated that the student should receive an education in the following seven fields: health, command of fundamental processes, worthy home membership, vocation, civic education, worthy use of leisure, and ethical character.

Educational opportunity had become a measure of the aspirations and possibilities of American democracy.

Marvin Larerson

The Eight-Year Study

The following goals of education, or "needs of youth," were listed by the Progressive Education Association in 1938 and grew out of the Eight-Year Study of thirty high schools conducted by the association from 1932 to 1940:

1. Physical and mental health
2. Self-assurance
3. Assurance of growth toward adult status
4. Philosophy of life
5. Wide range of personal interests
6. Esthetic appreciations
7. Intelligent self-direction
8. Progress toward maturity in social relations with age-mates and adults
9. Wise use of goods and services
10. Vocational orientation
11. Vocational competence

Committee of Ten

A historic National Education Association (NEA) committee that studied secondary education in 1892.

"Purposes of Education in American Democracy"

Also in 1938, the Educational Policies Commission of the National Education Association set forth the "Purposes of Education in American Democracy." These objectives stated that students should receive an education in the four broad areas of self-realization, human relations, economic efficiency, and civic responsibility.

"Education for All American Youth"

In 1944 this same commission of the NEA published another statement of educational objectives, entitled "Education for All American Youth":

> Schools should be dedicated to the proposition that every youth in these United States—regardless of sex, economic status, geographic location, or race—should experience a broad and balanced education which will

1. equip him to enter an occupation suited to his abilities and offering reasonable opportunity for personal growth and social usefulness;
2. prepare him to assume full responsibilities of American citizenship;
3. give him a fair chance to exercise his right to the pursuit of happiness through the attainment and preservation of mental and physical health;
4. stimulate intellectual curiosity, engender satisfaction in intellectual achievement, and cultivate the ability to think rationally; and
5. help to develop an appreciation of the ethical values which should undergird all life in a democratic society.

"Imperative Needs of Youth"

In 1952 the Educational Policies Commission made yet another statement of educational objectives, entitled "Imperative Needs of Youth":

1. All youth need to develop salable skills and those understandings and attitudes that make the worker an intelligent productive participant in economic life. To this end most youth need supervised work experience as well as education in the skills and knowledge of their occupations.
2. All youth need to develop and maintain good health and physical fitness.
3. All youth need to understand the rights and duties of the citizen of a democratic society, and to be diligent and competent in the performance of their obligations as members of the community and citizens of the state and nation.
4. All youth need to understand the significance of the family for the individual and society and the conditions conducive to successful family life.
5. All youth need to know how to purchase and use goods and services intelligently, understanding both the values received by the consumer and the economic consequences of their acts.
6. All youth need to understand the methods of science, the influence of science on human life, and the main scientific facts concerning the nature of the world and of man.
7. All youth need opportunities to develop their capacities to appreciate beauty in literature, art, music, and nature.
8. All youth need to be able to use their leisure time well and budget it wisely, balancing activities that yield satisfactions to the individual with those that are socially useful.
9. All youth need to develop respect for other persons, to grow in their insight into ethical values and principles, and to be able to live and work cooperatively with others.
10. All youth need to grow in their ability to think rationally, to express their thoughts clearly, and to read and listen with understanding.

Education is not the filling of a pail, but the lighting of a fire.

William Butler Yeats

Should High Schools Prepare All Students for College?

You have learned in this and the last chapter that early secondary school programs were largely designed to prepare students for college. Since those early times, the goals of high schools have changed over time in an effort to offer something of value to all secondary students. The following debate between two contemporary teachers reflects two different perspectives concerning the most desirable goals for high schools today.

YES

BilliJo Saffold *teaches English at Riverside University High School in Milwaukee, Wisconsin.*

When you were in high school, were you told by a guidance counselor or teacher that you were not college material? Did you decide to defer college after high school graduation? Or perhaps you went to college right away, but then later decided to pursue another goal, with the possibility of returning to college afterward. In any case, I hope you were given the academic preparation and skills you would need to succeed in college. These skills are important for those who decide not to go to college as well.

As educators, we sometimes get caught up in the frustration of reminding students that they need to meet assignment deadlines and do a quality job. We have to prod lazy students who turn in mediocrity fully expecting to earn a top grade. This may cause us to have a negative outlook on such students' educational promise. However, the reality is that all students must come of their own volition to a place of willingness to do what's needed to reach the goal. When this happens, they begin to get more serious about school, meet those deadlines, and do their best work.

For many students, especially those of ethnic minority descent, college can be a lofty goal. Many have never known anyone to go to college. To enable those students to catch the dream, we must do all that we can to model education for them. I teach in a school with a large population of African-American and Hispanic students, along with a small Asian and Caucasian population. I personally take students on campus visits across the nation, and I try to bring in speakers of interest to my students every month, specifically seek-

NO

Bobbi Aschwanden Thomas *teaches computer skills at the Congress Middle School in Kansas City, Missouri.*

Traditional college is not for everyone. Our society needs people with a wide range of skills.

Although an advanced education is necessary for many jobs (doctors, lawyers, teachers), our society is dependent on more than white collar positions. Many students learn trades through experience. A number of jobs in these fields are not only satisfying but high paying.

Having grown up in the construction industry, I am the child of a "blue collar" employer. My father owned his residential painting business for 35 years. It did not require him to have a four-year degree. All of his education came on-the-job. His business was successful and rewarding and he provided first jobs for many of the kids in our neighborhood.

Traditional college is not the only place for students to learn skills. Trade schools help students in medical, technological, and other fields. My neighbor attended a trade school. He is a tool and die maker. He learned the skill in night classes. After spending time as an apprentice, he opened his own shop. It is now a multi-million dollar business.

This year, one of the teachers with whom I worked left education to pursue a career in massage therapy. This teacher spent evenings attending a trade school to learn a new occupation. This skill is now in high demand.

Let's also not forget about the young men and women who have chosen to serve our country in the military. Many of these young people are paying for college by serving our country, but

(continued)

TEACHER PERSPECTIVES

(continued)

YES

ing out people who have pulled themselves through the educational ranks to success and who look like my students.

Not all students will go on to college. However, as educators, we must do all that we can to ensure that students are prepared to handle the rigors of college, should they later decide that they want to attend.

NO

many will make a career out of the service. And of course, in our current state of affairs, many of these fine young people will not come home.

A solid K–12 education can and should prepare all of us for our next stage in life, be that college, trade school, military service, immediate employment, or to be a parent who chooses to stay home and raise the next generation. Our children need a variety of post-secondary opportunities in order to be productive members of society.

Source: "Should High Schools Prepare All Students for College?" *NEA Today* (November 2005), p. 45. Reprinted by permission of the National Education Association.

WHAT IS YOUR PERSPECTIVE ON THIS ISSUE?
Should high schools prepare all students for college?

To give your opinion, go to Chapter 8 of the companion website (www.ablongman.com/johnson14e) and click on Teacher Perspectives.

These various statements concerning educational objectives, made over the last century, sum up fairly well the history of the aims of U.S. public education. These changing aims also show how perspectives on the purposes of education have evolved over time.

Preparation of Teachers

Because present-day teachers have at least four—and often five to eight—years of college education, it is difficult to believe that teachers have historically had little or no training. One of the first forms of teacher training grew out of the medieval guild system, in which a young man who wished to enter a certain field of work served a lengthy period of apprenticeship with a master in the field. Some young men became teachers by serving as apprentices to master teachers, sometimes for as long as seven years.

Colonial Teachers

Elementary school teachers in colonial America were very poorly prepared; in fact, more often than not, they had received no special training at all. The single qualification of most teachers was that they themselves had been students. On the other

Global Perspectives

European Beginnings of Teacher Training

The first formal teacher-training school in the Western world of which we have any record was mentioned in a request to the king of England, written by William Byngham in 1438, requesting that "he may yeve withouten fyn or fee (the) mansion ycalled Goddeshous the which he hath made and edified in your towne of Cambridge for the free herbigage of poure scolers of Gramer."[2]

Byngham was granted his request and established Goddeshous College as a teacher-training institution on June 13, 1439. Students at this college gave demonstration lectures to fellow students to gain practice teaching. Classes were even conducted during vacations so that country schoolmasters could also attend. Byngham's college still exists today as Christ's College of Cambridge University. At that early date of 1439, Byngham made provision for two features that are still considered important in teacher education today: scheduling classes so that teachers in service can attend and providing some kind of student teaching experience. Many present-day educators would probably be surprised to learn that these ideas are nearly 600 years old.

Questions for Reflection

1. What are some of the probable reasons that any type of more formal teacher preparation was lacking in early history?

2. What is your perspective on Byngham's early efforts to provide teacher training?

---

hand, most colonial college teachers, private tutors, Latin grammar school teachers, and academy teachers had received some kind of college education, usually at one of the well-established colleges or universities in Europe. A few had received their education at an American colonial college.

Teachers in the various kinds of colonial elementary schools typically had only an elementary education themselves, but a few had attended a Latin grammar school or a private academy. It was commonly believed that to be a teacher required only that the instructor know something about the subject matter to be taught; therefore, no teacher, regardless of the level taught, received training in the methodology of teaching.

Because many colonial schools were conducted in connection with a church, the teacher was often considered an assistant to the minister. Besides teaching, other duties of some early colonial teachers were "to act as court messenger, to serve summonses, to conduct certain ceremonial services of the church, to lead the Sunday choir, to ring the bell for public worship, to dig the graves, and to perform other occasional duties."

Teachers as Indentured Servants

Sometimes the colonies used white indentured servants as teachers; many people who came to the United States bought passage by agreeing to work for some years as indentured servants. The ship's captain would then sell the indentured servant's services, more often than not by placing an ad in a newspaper. Such an ad, shown in Figure 8.1, appeared in a May 1786 edition of the *Maryland Gazette*.

Records reveal that there were many indentured servants and convicted felons among early immigrants who were advertised and sold as teachers. In fact, it has

FIGURE 8.1

1786 Advertisement for Indentured Servants

Men and Women Servants

JUST ARRIVED

In the ship *Paca,* Robert Caulfield, Master, in five Weeks from Belfast and Cork, a number of healthy Men and Women SERVANTS.

Among them are several valuable tradesman, viz.

Carpenters, Shoemakers, Coopers, Blacksmiths, Staymakers, Bookbinders, Clothiers, Diers, Butchers, Schoolmasters, Millrights, and Labourers.

Their indentures are to be disposed of by the Subscribers,

Brown, and Maris
William Wilson

been estimated that at least one-half of all the teachers in colonial America may have come from these sources. This is not necessarily a derogatory description of these early teachers when we remember that many poor people bought their passage to the colonies by agreeing to serve as indentured servants for a period of years and that in England at that time, hungry and desperate people could be convicted as felons and deported for stealing a loaf of bread.

Teaching Apprenticeships

Some colonial teachers learned their trade by serving as apprentices to schoolmasters. Court records reveal numerous such indentures of apprenticeship; the following was recorded in New York City in 1772:

> This Indenture witnesseth that John Campbel Son of Robert Campbel of the City of New York with the Consent of his father and mother hath put himself and by these presents doth Voluntarily put and bind himself Apprentice to George Brownell of the Same City Schoolmaster to learn the Art Trade or Mastery—for and during the term of ten years And the said George Brownell Doth hereby Covenant and Promise to teach and instruct or Cause the said Apprentice to be taught and instructed in the Art Trade or Calling of a Schoolmaster by the best way or means he or his wife may or can.

Teacher Training in Academies

One of Benjamin Franklin's justifications for proposing an academy in Philadelphia was that some of the graduates would make good teachers. Speculating on the need for such graduates, Franklin wrote,

> A number of the poorer sort [of academy graduates] will be hereby qualified to act as Schoolmasters in the Country, to teach children Reading, Writing, Arithmetic, and the Grammar of their Mother Tongue, and being of good morals and known character, may be recommended from the Academy to Country Schools for that purpose; the Country suffering at present very much for want of good Schoolmasters, and obliged frequently to employ in their schools, vicious imported servants, or concealed Papists, who by their bad Examples and Instructions often deprave the Morals and corrupt the Principles of the children under their Care.

The fact that Franklin said some of the "poorer" graduates would make suitable teachers reflects the low regard for teachers typical of the time. The academy that Franklin proposed was established in 1751 in Philadelphia, and many graduates of academies after that time did indeed become teachers.

First State Normal School was adopted from European teacher training schools and is still standing in Lexington, Massachusetts.

Normal Schools

Many early educators recognized this country's need for better-qualified teachers; however, it was not until 1823 that the first teacher-training institution was established in the United States. This private school, called a **normal school** after its European prototype, which had existed since the late seventeenth century, was established by the Reverend Mr. Samuel Hall in Concord, Vermont. Hall's school did not produce many teachers, but it did signal the beginning of formal teacher training in the United States.

The early normal school program usually consisted of a two-year course. Students typically entered the normal school right after finishing elementary school; most normal schools did not require high school graduation for entrance until about 1900. The nineteenth-century curriculum was much like the curriculum of the high schools of that time. Students reviewed subjects studied in elementary school, studied high school subjects, had a course in teaching (or "pedagogy" as it was then called), and did some student teaching in a model school, usually operated in conjunction with the normal school. The subjects offered by a normal school in Albany, New York, in 1845 included English grammar, English composition, history, geography, reading, writing, orthography, arithmetic, algebra, geometry, trigonometry, human physiology, surveying, natural philosophy, chemistry, intellectual philosophy, moral philosophy, government, rhetoric, theory and practice of teaching, drawing, music, astronomy, and practice teaching.

Horace Mann was instrumental in establishing the first state-supported normal school, which opened in 1839 in Lexington, Massachusetts. Other public normal schools, established shortly afterward, typically offered a two-year teacher-training program. Some of the students came directly from elementary school; others had completed secondary school. Some states did not establish state-supported normal schools until the early 1900s.

State Teachers' Colleges

During the early part of the twentieth century, several factors caused a significant change in normal schools. For one thing, as the population of the United States increased, so did the enrollment in elementary schools, thereby creating an ever-increasing demand for elementary school teachers. Likewise, as more people attended high school, more high school teachers were needed. To meet this demand, normal schools eventually expanded their curriculum to include secondary teacher education. The growth of high schools also created a need for teachers who were highly specialized in particular academic subjects, so normal schools established subject matter departments and developed more diversified programs. The length of the teacher education program was expanded to two, three, and finally four years; this longer duration fostered development and diversification of the normal school curriculum. The demand for teachers increased from about 20,000 in 1900 to more than 200,000 in 1930.

normal school

The first type of American institution devoted exclusively to teacher training.

The United States gradually advanced technologically to the point at which more college-educated citizens were needed. The normal schools assumed a responsibility to help meet this need by establishing many other academic programs in addition to teacher training. As normal schools extended their programs to four years and began granting baccalaureate degrees, they also began to call themselves *state teachers' colleges*. For most institutions, the change in name took place during the 1930s.

Changes in Mid-Twentieth Century Teacher Education

Universities entered the teacher preparation business on a large scale around 1900. Before then, some graduates of universities had become high school teachers or college teachers, but not until about 1900 did universities begin to establish departments of education and add a full range of teacher education programs to the curriculum.

Just as the normal schools expanded in size, scope, and function until they became state teachers' colleges, so the state teachers' colleges expanded to become *state colleges*. This change in name and scope took place for most institutions around 1950. The elimination of the word *teacher* really explains the story behind this transition. The new state colleges gradually expanded their programs beyond teacher education and became multipurpose institutions. One of the main reasons for this transition was that a growing number of students coming to the colleges demanded a more varied education. The state teachers' colleges developed diversified programs to try to meet their demands.

Many of these state colleges later became state universities, offering doctoral degrees in a wide range of fields. Some of our largest and most highly regarded universities evolved from normal schools. Figure 8.2 diagrams the evolution of U.S. teacher preparation institutions.

Obviously, establishing the teaching profession has been a long and difficult task. Preparation of teachers has greatly improved over the years from colonial times—when anyone could be a teacher—to the present, when people such as you must meet rigorous requirements for permanent teacher certification.

Journal for Reflection

1. Describe and evaluate a learning experience you remember from your own school days.

2. What made the experience memorable, and what role did the teacher play in the learning process?

FIGURE 8.2

Evolution of Teacher Preparation Institutions

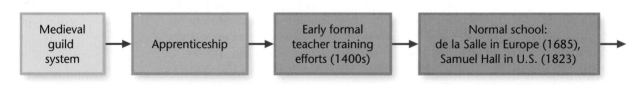

Private Colleges and Universities Enter Teacher Training on a Large Scale (1900s)

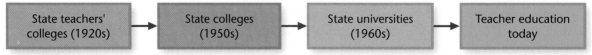

Recent Trends in Education

Education experienced major changes and a wide variety of perspectives following World War II when John Dewey, George Counts, William Bagley, W. W. Charters, Lewis Terman, and other intellectuals who had held sway during the first half of the twentieth century yielded to a somewhat less philosophically oriented breed of researchers represented by Abraham Maslow, Robert Havighurst, Benjamin Bloom, J. P. Guilford, Lee Cronbach, Jerome Bruner, Marshall McLuhan, Noam Chomsky, and Jean Piaget.[3] The Progressive Education Association closed its doors, and a series of White House conferences on children, youth, and education were inaugurated in an attempt to improve education.

No school system on earth has been scrutinized, analyzed, and dissected as profoundly and as mercilessly as that in the United States. From the late 1940s to the mid-1950s, educational institutions at all levels were not only flooded with unprecedented numbers of students but also censored and flailed unmercifully by self-ordained critics (Hyman Rickover, Arthur Bestor, and Rudolph Flesch). In retrospect this frantic rush to simultaneously patronize and criticize the institution seems a curious contradiction. The public schools were characterized as "godless, soft, undisciplined, uncultured, wasteful, and disorganized." Critics who remembered the high failure rates on tests given to World War II draftees were determined to raise the public's levels of physical fitness and literacy; others who detected a weakening of moral and spiritual values were eager to initiate citizenship and character education programs. The enrollments in nonpublic schools doubled, correspondence schools of all kinds sprang into existence, and the popular press carried articles and programs designed to help parents augment the basic skills taught within the school program. In 1955 there were an estimated 450 correspondence schools serving 700,000 students throughout the country.

> The schools have often attracted the zealous attention of those who wish to influence the future, as well as those who wish to change the way we view the past.
>
> *Diane Ravitch*

New Emphases in Education

Fortunately, although some people were highly critical of the schools, not everybody panicked. There were physical fitness programs, character education projects, a general tightening of educational standards, and much more. J. P. Guilford, E. Paul Torrence, Jacob Getzels, and others explored the boundaries of creativity; Alfred Barr and D. G. Ryans carried out exhaustive studies of teacher characteristics; and just about everybody experimented with new patterns of organization. There were primary block programs, inter-age groupings, plans devised by and named for George Stoddard and J. Lloyd Trump, core programs, and a host of other patterns or combinations of plans structured around subject areas, broad groupings of subjects, or pupil characteristics. There were programs for the gifted and the not-so-gifted, and there was a new concern for foreign language instruction as well as the functional use of English. There was also a limited resurgence of Montessori schools and several one-of-a-kind experimental schools such as Amidon and Summerhill. While all this was taking place within the schools, the school systems themselves were consolidating; by 1960 there were only about one-third as many school districts as had existed twenty years earlier.

> Education is a painful, continual, and difficult work to be done by kindness, by watching, by warning, by precept, and by praise, but above all— by love.
>
> *John Ruskin*

ANALYSIS OF TEACHING

Another emphasis found expression in the **analysis of teaching.** For half a century, researchers had been attempting to identify the characteristics and teaching styles that were most closely associated with effective instruction. Hundreds of studies had been initiated, and correlations had been done among them. During the 1950s, the focus began changing from identification of what ought to occur in

analysis of teaching
Procedures used to enable teachers to critique their own performance in the classroom.

Teaching is a complex process that requires continuous learning.

Ralph W. Tyler

teaching to scrutiny of what actually does occur. Ned Flanders and other researchers developed observational scales for assessing verbal communications between and among teachers and students. The scales permitted observers to categorize and summarize specific actions by teachers and students. These analyses were followed by studies of nonverbal classroom behaviors.

Another series of investigations involving the wider range of instructional protocols was patterned after the time-and-motion studies used earlier for industrial processes. Dwight Allen and several other educators attempted to analyze teacher behaviors, delineate the components of effective teaching, and introduce teacher candidates to the elements judged most important to good teaching. The change in focus from studies of teacher characteristics to analyses of what actually occurs in classrooms has offered educators highly fruitful insights into teaching and learning and has provided usable instruments for further investigations of classroom behavior. It is now possible to assess the logical, verbal, nonverbal, affective, and attitudinal dimensions of instruction, as well as the intricate aspects of cognition and concept development.

TEACHER EFFECTIVENESS

Research has focused even more closely on the instructional patterns of effective teachers. A review by Marjorie Powell and Joseph Beard, *Teacher Effectiveness: An Annotated Bibliography,* catalogs more than 3,000 investigations into instructional competencies. The **effective teaching** movement based on this research offers today's teachers important skills. In common with the schoolteachers of sixty years ago, today's teachers learn to be strong leaders who direct classroom activities, maximize the use of instructional time, and teach in a clear, businesslike manner.

Effective teachers now employ structured, carefully delineated lessons. They break larger topics into smaller, more easily grasped components, and they focus on one thought, point, or direction at a time. They check prerequisite skills before introducing new skills or concepts. They accompany step-by-step presentations with many probing questions. Teachers offer detailed explanations of difficult points and test students on one point before moving on to the next. They provide corrective feedback where needed and stay with the topic under study until students comprehend the major points or issues. Effective teachers use prompts and cues to assist students through the initial stages of acquisition.

This recent emphasis on demonstration, prompting, and practice is a far cry from the relatively unstructured classroom activities of the recent past. We now emphasize carefully created learning goals and lesson sequences. It will be interesting to see whether the educational pendulum swings back to a new focus on student concerns and initiatives at some time in the future.

STUDY OF THE LEARNING PROCESS

Several leading educational researchers in the United States and Europe have sought to analyze and describe how children learn. All of these investigators have stressed the importance of successful early learning patterns and the problems associated with serious learning deficits. They also believe that important elements within the environment may be changed or modified to promote learning. Lev Vygotsky, a Russian, developed a social development theory in the late 1800s that suggests social interaction among children plays a major role in cognitive development. His work contributed significantly to the founding of constructionist psychology.

Robert Havighurst, a University of Chicago professor, identified specific developmental tasks that he believes children must master if they are to develop normally. He even suggests there may be periods during which certain tasks must be mastered if they are to become an integral part of children's repertoire of responses. There may also be "teachable moments" (periods of peak efficiency for the acquisition of specific concepts/skills) during which receptivity is particularly high. Havighurst, like Piaget, has caused educators to look carefully at the motivations and needs of children.

effective teaching

A movement to improve teaching performance based on the outcomes of educational research.

Professional Dilemma

Can a Knowledge of History Help to Improve Multicultural Education?

When you become a teacher, you will be expected to provide multicultural education for your students, regardless of the age level or subjects you teach. Most teachers today face the dilemma of wanting to provide their students with a high-quality multicultural program, but being frustrated with the lack of time and support for doing so.

As you will learn, racial and ethnic prejudice and injustice have been present throughout U.S. educational history. Unfortunately, there is still considerable racial and ethnic strife in the United States today, and much of this strife has filtered into the halls of education. Debates rage about how schools should meet the educational demands of a complex multicultural society. As a teacher, you will be expected to join in this debate and help search for answers.

James Banks, a leading researcher in multicultural education at the University of Washington, feels past efforts have been too superficial. He asserts that "additive approaches" treat multicultural material as "an appendage to the main story of the development of the nation and to the core curriculum." Instead, multicultural education should integrate multicultural perspectives throughout the curriculum, on an equal footing with white European perspectives.

Despite the lack of time and adequate school district encouragement and support, there are many things that a determined and creative teacher can do to integrate multicultural education throughout the curriculum. Teachers can also encourage the school district to develop and support comprehensive programs for multicultural education and then participate in developing these plans.

Questions for Reflection

1. What are the historical antecedents that have contributed to the lack of racial and ethnic understanding in U.S. society?

2. Should education programs seek to eliminate cultural differences among individuals or to preserve and perhaps celebrate them?

3. What can you do in your classroom to improve multicultural education?

4. What additional information would you like about multicultural education, and where might you find such information?

To answer these questions on-line and e-mail your answers to your professor, go to Chapter 8 of the companion website (www.ablongman.com/johnson14e) and click on Professional Dilemma.

A contemporary of Havighurst, Jerome Bruner of Harvard, has also postulated a series of developmental steps or stages that he believes children encounter as they mature. These involve action, imagery, and symbolism. Bruner's cognitive views have stressed student inquiry and the breaking down of larger tasks into components.

Benjamin Bloom, author of Bloom's Taxonomy of Educational Objectives and distinguished service professor at the University of Chicago, has attempted to identify and weigh the factors that control learning. He believes that one can predict learning outcomes by assessing three factors: (1) the cognitive entry behaviors of a student (the extent to which the pupil has mastered prerequisite skills), (2) the affective entry characteristics (the student's interest in learning the material), and (3) the quality of instruction (the degree to which the instruction offered is appropriate for the learner). Bloom's research is reflected in models of direct instruction, particularly mastery learning, in which teachers carefully explain, illustrate, and demonstrate skills and provide practice, reinforcement, corrective feedback, and remediation.

Global Perspectives

Jean Piaget

Jean Piaget (1896–1980)
was a Swiss developmental
psychologist who researched
children's stages of learning.

Jean Piaget (1896–1980) was a Swiss psychologist educated at the University of Paris. Through his work with Alfred Binet, who developed one of the first intelligence tests, Piaget became interested in how children learn. He spent long hours observing children of different ages and eventually created a theory of mental or **cognitive development.** Piaget believed that children learn facts, concepts, and principles in four major stages. Up until about age two, he suggested, a child is at the *sensorimotor stage* and learns mainly through the hands, mouth, and eyes. From about two to seven years of age, a child is at the *preoperational stage* and learns primarily through language and concepts. Between ages seven and eleven, a child's learning is characterized by *concrete operations,* which involve the use of more complex concepts such as numbers. The final learning stage identified by Piaget is called the *formal operations* phase. This stage typically begins between ages eleven and fifteen and continues throughout adulthood. During this final stage, the learner employs the most sophisticated and abstract learning processes. Although children do not all fit neatly into these categories, Piaget's work has contributed much to educators' understanding of the learning process and has helped teachers develop more appropriate teaching strategies for students at different developmental stages.

Questions for Reflection

1. What is your perspective on Piaget's theory of cognitive development?
2. How might Piaget's ideas be useful today?

B. F. SKINNER

Psychologist B. F. Skinner
(1904–1990) developed a
behavioral theory that
suggested students could be
trained, or conditioned, to
learn just about anything a
teacher desired.

Burrhus Frederic (B. F.) Skinner (1904–1990) became one of the foremost early educational psychologists in U.S. education. He developed a **behavioral theory,** which was a theory focusing on outward behavior that suggested students could be successfully trained and conditioned to learn just about anything a teacher desired. This required the teacher to break down the learning into small sequential steps. Skinner even experimented with teaching machines that presented the learner with small sequential bits of information—an idea that has been revived today in computer-assisted instruction. Skinner published many works including *The Technology of Teaching, Beyond Freedom and Dignity,* and *Walden Two.* He contributed much to present-day understanding of human learning and helped to advance the technology of teaching.

Educational Critics

cognitive development

A learner's acquisition of facts, concepts, and principles through mental activity.

behavioral theory

A theory that considers the outward behavior of students to be the main target for change.

Another change in education was shown by a phalanx of critics, all holding differing perspectives, including Edgar Friedenberg (*Coming of Age in America*), Charles Silberman (*Crisis in the Classroom*), Jonathan Kozol (*Death at an Early Age*), Ivan Illich (*Deschooling Society*), John Holt (*How Children Fail*), and even the federal government (*A Nation at Risk,* 1983), all focusing on low educational standards. Some critics, such as Silberman, urge schools to refurbish what they already have; others, including Illich, want to abandon the schools altogether. These critics have not gone unnoticed. Friedenberg's call for alternatives to traditional education, Silberman's endorsement of open education, and Kozol's plea for equal opportunity are all reflected to some degree in innovative programs from coast to coast.

Changing Public Perspectives on Education

A public opinion survey, first conducted in 1950 and repeated in 1999, revealed the following interesting shifts over this sixty-year span: In 1950, 24 percent of those surveyed thought that teachers should be asked their political beliefs, whereas in 1999 only 9 percent thought so; in 1950, 39 percent said that religion should be taught in the public schools, whereas in 1999 the number had increased to 50 percent; in 1950, 44 percent said that teachers were underpaid, whereas in 1999, 61 percent said so; and in 1950, 67 percent of those polled thought that students were being taught more worthwhile and useful things in school than children twenty years before, but in 1999 only 26 percent thought so. These shifts in public opinion about public schools provide food for thought for contemporary educators.

Major Educational Events of the Past Century

As we moved into the twenty-first century, many people reflected on educational accomplishments in the United States over the past hundred years. As would be expected, opinions differ considerably on this subject. Ben Brodinsky, an education journalist, has suggested that the GI Bill of Rights should perhaps be considered the single most important educational event of the past century. He lists the desegregation of schools as the second most important and the federal Education for All Handicapped Children Act as the third most important educational event of the twentieth century.

Undoubtedly, many important educational events and accomplishments occurred during the twentieth century—the list could go on and on. One example of significant progress made by the U.S. educational system in the past seventy-five years is reflected in the increased percentage of students completing high school—from about 50 percent in 1940 to about 70 percent in 1990. What would you put on your list of the most important educational changes, events, and/or accomplishments of the last century?

It is difficult to draw meaningful inferences from recent events that have not yet stood the test of time. Implications of recent educational events will eventually be found in the answers to questions such as these: What should be the role of the federal government in education? How can equal educational opportunity be achieved in the United States? How professionalized should the school system be? To what degree should educational policy and practice be influenced by litigation? How will school reform movements change the practice of education? The answer to these questions, and other questions you may have in mind, will be colored by the perspectives through which people view the world, children, and schools. We believe that viewing all educational questions through well-informed historical perspectives yields more valid answers.

CROSS-REFERENCE
Appendix D at the back of this book presents a brief, selected chronology of the history of education.

Journal for Reflection
What are your perspectives on some of the trends in education that you have observed or experienced?

Summary

MORE STUDENTS AND BIGGER SCHOOLS.   Over the past seventy-five years the U.S. education system has experienced unprecedented changes and growth in both size and complexity. The great increase in numbers of students over these years has created a challenging need for more school buildings and many more teachers. Population increases and shifts from rural settings to cities require bigger schools and large, elaborate school busing systems. There has also been an amazing expansion of educational curricula and program diversification for different types of students at all levels over the past sixty years. All of this growth in size and programs has resulted in a tremendous increase in school budgets.

Programs for students with special needs have increased tremendously in recent history. There has also been notable growth in other educational programs designed to better serve the needs of the increasingly diverse student populations now found in our schools.

THE DEVELOPMENT OF THE TEACHING PROFESSION. There have been many changes and improvements in the teaching profession over the past seventy-five years, as U.S. educational systems have grown in complexity, especially in funding and control. The federal government has increased its involvement in public education through legislation such as the GI Bill, the National Science Foundation, the National Defense Education Act, the Elementary and Secondary Education Act, Project Head Start, Upward Bound, and the National Teacher Corps, to name just a few. And each of these federal acts, while providing funds for specific school programs, has also placed new demands and regulations on our schools.

CHANGING AIMS OF EDUCATION. This chapter also points out that here have been an impressive series of important statements made over the years in an attempt to determine and articulate the essential aims of education in the United States. These statements clearly show how perspectives on education have changed over time.

PREPARATION OF TEACHERS. The history of teacher preparation shows an evolution from a very meager and humble beginning centuries ago to a complex and professional state today. Educators should be proud of the history of advancement in the preparation of educators and be mindful and proud of the current rigorous professional training they receive.

RECENT TRENDS IN EDUCATION. Many other recent trends in education were also discussed in this chapter. These included professional advancements such as analysis of the teaching act, teacher effectiveness research, sociological studies, the development of new learning theories, and other research efforts designed to help us better understand and improve student learning. There have been an increasing number of widely read critics of our schools over the past sixty years; examples include Friedenberg, Silberman, Kozol, Illich, and Holt. Various governmental agencies at the state and national levels have also been critical of our schools in recent years, resulting in many reports and calls for school reforms.

Discussion Questions

1. Other than those mentioned in this chapter, what additional recent educational developments seem particularly important to you? Why are they important?
2. Has the increased federal involvement in education been good or bad for schools? How so?
3. In what respect, if any, has education become professionalized, in your opinion?
4. In your opinion, how much progress has the United States really made in providing equal educational opportunity? Defend your answer.
5. What is happening in education at this very moment that is likely to be written about in future history of education books?

School-Based Observations

1. As you work in the schools, look to see how the continuing struggle for equal educational opportunity is progressing. Also, analyze what you observe in order to determine the degree to which teaching has been professionalized—a movement that has gained impetus during the last sixty years. Finally, as you participate in classrooms, look for evidence that the work of educational pioneers discussed in this chapter (such as Bloom, Montessori, Skinner, and Piaget) has made an impact in U.S. classrooms.
2. Discuss with experienced educators the changes they have observed during their careers. Visit with veteran educational administrators to discuss changes they have seen in education over the years.

Portfolio Development

1. Prepare a creative educational history project (using a poster, videotape, audio recording, slide presentation, or some other creative medium) dealing with a topic, person, or idea that is of interest to you. Design your project so that it can be used as part of your job placement credentials.
2. Create a list of the most useful outcomes of U.S. education over the past sixty years. What can you as a beginning teacher learn, if anything, from your list?

Preparing for Certification

RESEARCH AND THEORIES OF LEARNING

1. One of the topics in the Praxis II Principles of Teaching and Learning (PLT) test is "encouraging students to extend their thinking" through an understanding of "stages and patterns of cognitive and cultural development." In this chapter, you learned about the several researchers who developed theories about child development and learning processes. Make a list of the theorists and write two or three sentences about how they contributed to our understanding of how students think and learn.
2. Answer the following multiple-choice question, which is similar to items in Praxis and other state certification tests.

   The effective teaching movement was based on research focusing on the instructional patterns of effective teachers. Which instructional pattern was *not* emphasized in the effective teaching movement?

   A. Teachers emphasize demonstration, prompting, and practice in their teaching.

   B. Teachers focus on student concerns and initiatives when constructing the lessons.
   C. Teachers check prerequisite skills before introducing new skills or concepts.
   D. Teachers emphasize carefully created learning goals and lesson sequences.

3. Answer the following short-answer question, which is similar to items in Praxis and other state certification tests. After you've completed your written response, use the scoring guide in the ETS *Test at a Glance* materials to assess your response. Can you revise your response to improve your score?

   Reread the 1952 list of "Imperative Needs of Youth." Think about the relevance of this list for students today. Select the two objectives that you believe are most important today and two of the objectives that you believe are least important today and explain your choices.

Websites

www.scholastic.com/Instructor The Scholastic Instructor site contains a variety of educational materials such as articles, contests, free materials for teachers, and chats with other educators on any subject, including the history of education.

www.si.edu This site provides links to each museum of the Smithsonian Institution in Washington, D.C. and includes much historical information.

www.cdickens.com/articles/dickjane.htm Information about the Dick and Jane readers that were used in many schools.

www.insight-media.com A wonderful source of information about history of education media.

Further Reading

Barton, Keith C. (2005). "Primary Sources in History: Breaking through the Myths." *Phi Delta Kappan* (June, 2005), pp. 745–757. A thought provoking but controversial article concerning historical research.

Campbell, John Martin. (1996). *The Prairie Schoolhouse.* Albuquerque: University of New Mexico Press. Contains information about rural schoolhouses common during the westward expansion of the United States.

Capella, Gladys, Geismar, Kathryn, and Nicoleau, Guitele (Eds.). (1995). *Shifting Histories: Transforming Schools for Social Change.* Cambridge, MA: Harvard Educational Publishing Group. A more detailed treatment of the history of education as it relates to social change in the United States.

Ravitch, Diane. (1983). *The Troubled Crusade: American Education 1945–1980.* New York: Basic Books. An excellent account of the history of relatively recent (1945–1980) education in the United States, written by a well-respected educational historian.

Spring, Joel. (1994). *The American School 1642–1990.* White Plains, NY: Longman. A useful survey of the history of education in the United States.

Web, L. Dean. (2006). *The History of American Education: A Great American Experiment.* Boston: Pearson Merrill Prentice Hall. A rather detailed treatment of the history of U.S. education.

mylabschool
Where the classroom comes to life!

Go to Allyn and Bacon's MyLabSchool (www.mylabschool.com) and complete the following activity for Chapter 8. Click on **Research Navigator** and then use the following search terms within the Education database: **BF Skinner, Jean Piaget, home schooling.**

PART V

Chapter 9
Philosophy: Reflections on the Essence of Education

Chapter 10
Building an Educational Philosophy for a Changing World

PHILOSOPHICAL FOUNDATIONS OF EDUCATION

The philosophical perspective provides a way to examine and interpret the world—to ask basic questions about human nature, beauty, principles of right and wrong, and how knowledge and reality are defined. Philosophical thinking helps to uncover the essentials—the basic principles that undergird teaching and learning.

The philosophical perspective is especially important because our personal philosophy of life is seldom explicit. Rather, philosophy lives in peoples' minds and hearts and is seldom expressed in words or specific ideas. Our personal philosophy becomes evident in the manner in which we respond to everyday problems and questions. The perspective of philosophy helps us to focus on the underlying issues and assumptions and beliefs that are not always evident to us in the hectic pace of contemporary life.

Because philosophy deals with underlying values and beliefs, it naturally pervades all aspects of education. The perspective of philosophy presents opposing views about human nature, knowledge, and the world in which we live. By examining these different, often opposing views, you will be able to identify your own philosophical position and state it in clearer language and concepts.

Finally, philosophy prepares you to fully participate in a changing world. Careful reflection about basic questions concerning human nature, principles of right and wrong, and the definition of knowledge prepares you to navigate calls for change in education. Your answers to these essential questions provide you tools to respond to concerns posed by parents, politicians, and reformers. Your answers will also help you determine which reforms make sense.

CHAPTER 9

Philosophy: Reflections on the Essence of Education

Teacher Resigns over Plagiarism Fight

CNN.com, February 7, 2002

PIPER, KANSAS (AP)—High school teacher Christine Pelton wasted no time after discovering that nearly a fifth of her biology students had plagiarized their semester projects from the Internet.

She had received her rural Kansas district's backing before when she accused students of cheating, and she expected it again this time after failing the 28 sophomores.

Her principal and superintendent agreed: It was plagiarism and the students should get a zero for the assignment.

But after parents complained, the Piper School Board ordered her to go easier on the guilty.

Pelton resigned in protest in an episode that some say reflects a national decline in integrity.

"This kind of thing is happening every day around the country, where people with integrity are not being backed by their organization," said Michael Josephson, founder and president of the Josephson Institute of Ethics in Marina del Rey, Calif.

Also in recent months, some of the nation's top historians, including Stephen Ambrose, have been accused of borrowing passages from other authors without proper credit.

Pulitzer Prize–winning historian Joseph Ellis was suspended without pay for a year from Mount Holyoke College after lying to his students about serving in Vietnam. Notre Dame University football coach George O'Leary resigned after falsifying his athletic and academic achievements on his resume.

"It's so hard to keep sending the message that character counts when you have officials saying it doesn't count that much," Josephson said.

In Piper, about 20 miles west of Kansas City, Mo., students got that message loud and clear, Pelton said.

"The students no longer listened to what I had to say," she said. "They knew if they didn't like anything in my classroom from here on out, they can just go to the school board and complain."

Piper High School junior Brandon Schmalz, 17, agreed. "That was bad. She was right, and they were wrong," Schmalz said of the board.

Pelton, 26, resigned days after the board ordered her to give the students partial credit and to decrease the project's value from 50 percent of the final course grade to 30 percent.

Board president Chris McCord did not give a reason for the Dec. 11 decision, which was made behind closed doors. He said it was not prompted by parents' complaints.

"If I had known all the publicity that would have come with this, I would still make the same decision," McCord said.

One of the complaining parents was Theresa Woolley, who told The Kansas City Star that her daughter did not plagiarize. Rather, her daughter was not sure how much she needed to rewrite research material, she said.

But Pelton said the course syllabus, which she required students to sign, warned of the consequences of cheating and plagiarism.

Rutgers University professor of management Donald McCabe, who has researched academic dishonesty in high schools and colleges, said many teachers ignore cheating, and the Kansas episode illustrates why.

Questions for Reflection

1. Do you think that the school board's order to give students partial credit for their plagiarized work was warranted? Why or why not?

2. What would you do in response to the school board's order if you were the teacher instead of Christine Pelton?

3. How would you operationally define plagiarism to high school students and what would you do to teach students about respect for the writings of others?

Copyright © 2002 the Associated Press. Reprinted with permission.

INTASC

Learning Outcomes

After reading and studying this chapter, you should be able to:

1. Define philosophy and describe methods of inquiry used by philosophers. (INTASC 1: Subject Matter)

2. List major philosophical questions associated with the three major branches of philosophy: metaphysics, epistemology, and axiology. (INTASC 1: Subject Matter)

3. Elaborate on the major tenets of idealism, realism, pragmatism, and existentialism. (INTASC 1: Subject Matter)

4. Relate philosophical concepts to teaching and learning. (INTASC 4: Teaching Methods; INTASC 5: Motivation and Management; INTASC 8: Assessment)

5. Compare writers from different schools of philosophy: Plato, Kant, Martin, Aristotle, Locke, Whitehead, Peirce, Dewey, Rorty, Sartre, Nietzsche, and Greene. (INTASC 1: Subject Matter)

6. Describe the characteristics of Eastern and Native North American ways of knowing. (INTASC 3: Diversity; INTASC 9: Reflection)

Although there are many different ways of defining philosophy, it is best thought of as a passion to uncover and reflect on the underlying meaning of things. Derived from the Greek *philos,* which means "love" and *sophos,* which means "wisdom," the word *philosophy* means "love of wisdom." Early philosophers did not claim to be wise; rather, they viewed themselves as reflective thinkers in search of wisdom. To many contemporary philosophers, conveying information or wisdom is not as important as helping others in their own search for wisdom.

In this chapter, you will explore different ways of looking at the world in which you live and work. Big ideas from metaphysics, epistemology, axiology, schools of philosophy, human nature, ways of knowing and analytic and prophetic thinking will offer very different perspectives about yourself and your place in the larger world. You will see how the art of asking larger questions about society and education can either clarify or challenge your personal beliefs about societal change, the role of schools, teaching and learning, values and societal norms, and discipline and motivation.

Structure and Methodology of Philosophy

Education presupposes ideas about human nature, the nature of reality, and the nature of knowledge. These questions are ultimately of a philosophical character. Teachers must constantly confront the underlying assumptions that guide conduct, determine values, and influence the direction of all existence. Philosophy reminds teachers to continue the search for truth and not be satisfied with pat answers, even answers that are provided by so-called experts. To a philosopher, an expert is not one who professes truth; an expert is one who searches, questions, and reflects. Hence, the study of philosophy is at the heart of education.

The Branches of Philosophy

Philosophy includes branches that investigate large and difficult questions—questions about reality or being, about knowledge, about goodness and beauty and living a good life. Throughout the centuries, entire branches of philosophy have evolved that specialize in and center on major questions. For example, questions about the nature of reality or existence are examined in metaphysics, questions about knowledge and truth are considered in epistemology, and questions about values and goodness are central to axiology.

METAPHYSICS

Metaphysics is a branch of philosophy that is concerned with questions about the nature of reality. Literally, *metaphysics* means "beyond the physical." It deals with such questions as "What is reality?" "What is existence?" "Is the universe rationally designed or ultimately meaningless?" Metaphysics is a search for order and wholeness—a search applied not to particular items or experiences but to all reality and to all existence.

The questions in metaphysics, especially those about humanity and the universe, are extremely relevant to teachers and students of education. Theories about how the universe came to be and about what causes events in the universe are crucial if scholars are to interpret the physical sciences properly.

A teacher's classroom approach will be linked to the teacher's metaphysical beliefs. If, for example, the teacher believes that very specific basic knowledge is crucial to the child's intellectual development, it is likely that this teacher will focus on the subject matter. If, on the other hand, the teacher holds that the child is more important than any specific subject matter, it is likely that this teacher will focus on the child and allow the child to provide clues as to how he or she should be instructed.

EPISTEMOLOGY

Epistemology is a branch of philosophy that examines questions about how and what we know. What knowledge is true, and how does knowledge take place? The epistemologist attempts to discover what is involved in the process of knowing. Is knowing a special sort of mental act? Is there a difference between knowledge and belief? Can people know anything beyond the objects with which their senses acquaint them? Does knowing make any difference to the object that is known?

Because epistemological questions deal with the essence of knowledge, they are central to education. Teachers must be able to assess what is knowledge to determine whether a particular piece of information should be included in the curriculum. How people know is of paramount importance to teachers because their beliefs about learning influence their classroom methods. Should teachers train students in scientific methods, deductive reasoning, or both? Should students study

Many important decisions we make have ethical dimensions: What should we teach? How should we treat students, parents, teachers, and administrators? In order to address such matters, we must conceive of moral bases on which to make these decisions and try to forecast the potential ramifications of them for individuals and society.

Gail McCutcheon

metaphysics

An area of philosophy that deals with questions about the nature of ultimate reality.

epistemology

An area of philosophy that examines questions about how and what we know.

Being a philosopher, I have a problem for every solution.

Robert Zend

logic and fallacies or follow intuition? Teachers' knowledge of how students learn influences how they will teach.

AXIOLOGY

Axiology is a branch of philosophy that deals with the nature of values. It includes such questions as "What is good?" and "What is beautiful?" Questions about what should be or what values we hold are highlighted in axiology. This study of values is divided into ethics (moral values and conduct) and aesthetics (values in the realm of beauty and art). Ethics deals with such questions as "What is the good life?" and "How should we behave?" One major question to be examined is "When does the end justify any means of achieving it?" Aesthetics deals with the theory of beauty and examines such questions as "Is art public and representative, or is it the product of private creative imagination?" Good citizenship, honesty, and correct human relations are all learned in schools. Sometimes these concepts are taught explicitly, but often students learn ethics from *who* the teacher is as well as from *what* the teacher says.

Both ethics and aesthetics are important issues in education. Should a system of ethics be taught in the public schools? If so, which system of ethics should be taught? Aesthetics questions in education involve deciding which artistic works should or should not be included in the curriculum and what kind of subject matter should be allowed or encouraged in a writing, drawing, or painting class. Should teachers compromise their own attitudes toward a piece of artwork if their opinion differs from that of a parent or a school board?

Thinking as a Philosopher

Philosophy provides the tools people need to think clearly. As with any discipline, philosophy has a style of thinking as well as a set of terms and methodologies that distinguish it from other disciplines. Philosophers spend much of their energy developing symbols or terms that are both abstract (apply to many individual cases) and precise (distinguish clearly). Developing ideas that embrace more and more instances (abstraction) while at the same time maintaining a clear and accurate meaning (precision) is difficult, but this tension is at the heart of the philosopher's task. The entire process is what is meant by understanding: uncovering the underlying, the foundational, and the essential principles of reality.

There is great variety in the ways philosophers think. Hence it is difficult to set forth a simple set of rules or thinking steps that can accurately be labeled philosophical thinking. To give you a sense of philosophical thinking, it is easier (and more accurate) to describe two different thinking styles that philosophers use interchangeably as they wrestle with large, unstructured questions. The first way of thinking can be labeled **analytic thinking.** Philosophers employ this style when they attempt to examine questions of the "what seems to be" type. A second philosophical style of thinking is called **prophetic thinking.** It focuses on questions of the "what ought to be" type.

ANALYTIC WAYS OF THINKING IN PHILOSOPHY

When philosophers encounter a contemporary problem, they often spend time analyzing it, attempting to clarify or find the "real" problem, not just the surface issues. To do so, philosophers use abstraction, imagination, generalization, and logic. These analytic thinking processes help focus the problem clearly and precisely.

ABSTRACTION   The notion of **abstraction** covers a multitude of meanings. The word *abstract* is derived from the Latin verb *abstrahere,* meaning to "draw away." Abstraction, then, involves drawing away from a concrete level of experience to a conceptual plane of principles or ideas. The process of abstraction can be thought of as a three-step process that moves thinking from singular concrete instances to

axiology

An area of philosophy that deals with the nature of values. It includes questions such as "What is good?" and "What is value?"

analytic thinking

A thinking strategy that focuses on questions of the "what seems to be" type; includes abstractions, imagination, generalization, and logic.

prophetic thinking

A thinking strategy that focuses on questions of the "what ought to be" type; includes discernment, connection, tracking hypocrisy, and hope.

abstraction

A thought process that involves drawing away from experiences to a conceptual plane.

more general, universal ideas. The three steps involve (1) focusing attention on some feature within one's experience, (2) examining the precise characteristics of the feature, and (3) remembering the feature and its characteristics later so as to apply them to other instances or combine them with other ideas.

When teachers are asked to examine a new textbook series, for example, they will often be presented with promotional material about the important subject matter and learning tools that the series contains. The process of abstraction helps teachers pull away from the "bells and whistles" or the concrete examples in the text. Abstraction enables teachers to consider the underlying themes that are implicit and that provide a cohesive structure to the entire text series. Abstraction helps teachers uncover hidden messages.

IMAGINATION AND GENERALIZATION   According to Herbert Alexander,[1] the second step of analytic thinking is the use of imagination. Imagination can be thought of as the altering of abstractions. In philosophy the use of imagination assists the process of abstraction by filling in the details of an idea, selecting details, and relating ideas to one another.

Imaginative explorations occur in many different ways. Usually, they occur when a person first focuses on some abstraction or idea. Ideas come when one makes observations, reflects about past experiences, reads, views a dramatic work or piece of art, or converses with others. Once ideas are selected, imaginative explorations can be made about them. Basic assumptions about things can be examined, arguments can be justified or clarified, and ideas can be distinguished from or related to other ideas. Experiential evidence, logical consistency, and a host of other criteria can be employed. The outcome of the whole imaginative process is the development of a system of ideas that has greater clarity and more interrelationships to other ideas or sets of propositions. This last step of the imaginative exploration process is sometimes referred to as *generalization,* because it ultimately results in the development of a comprehensive set of ideas.

Generalization sets ranges and limits to the abstractions that have been altered by imagination. As one's imagination relates more and more ideas to one another, the process of generalization determines which relationships should be emphasized or de-emphasized.

When teachers consider new ways to support student motivation, they can use these same processes. For example, teachers often imagine different types of mathematics contests or science Olympiads that might spur students' interests. As they imaginatively apply these contests to the classroom setting, teachers might abstract the competitiveness component as a necessary aspect of contests and Olympiads. Teachers might then wonder about the hidden messages of winning at the expense of others' losses. Teachers might generalize that the competitive approach could bring about knowledge wars; knowledge contests might make students less willing to share what they know with others. To complete this inquiry, teachers need to use logic.

LOGIC   Philosophy deals with the nature of reasoning and has designated a set of principles called *logic.* Logic examines the principles that allow us to move from one argument to the next. There are many types of logic, but the two most commonly studied are deductive and inductive logic. Deduction is a type of reasoning that moves from a general statement to a specific conclusion. Induction is a type of reasoning that moves in the opposite direction, from the particular instance to a general conclusion.

Philosophy provides tools that help people think clearly. It is important for educators to have a philosophy, both as a means of developing their ability to think clearly about what they do on a day-to-day basis and as a means of seeing how their workaday principles and values extend beyond the classroom to the whole of humanity and society. Figure 9.1 describes how analytic ways of thinking help teachers solve a classroom problem. Studying philosophy enables you to recognize the underlying assumptions and principles of things so you can determine what is significant.

Creativity consists largely of rearranging what we know in order to find out what we normally take for granted. Hence, to think creatively, we must be able to look afresh at what we normally take for granted.

George Kneller

FIGURE 9.1

Analytic Ways of Thinking: Focus and Solve Problems Clearly and Precisely

Specific Problem Confronts a Teacher
"Why do some students in my classroom fail to complete their homework?"

ABSTRACTION

Draw Away from the Specifics

- What motivates my students?
- What inhibits my students from completing any work at home?
- What motivates human beings?

IMAGINATION AND GENERALIZATION

Consider Possibilities

- People like freedom.
- People enjoy completing tasks that they do well.

LOGIC

Rationally Evaluate

- I need to allow more choices for students.
- I need to examine the home context of students who repeatedly fail to complete their homework.

PROPHETIC WAYS OF THINKING IN PHILOSOPHY

In contrast to the search for underlying universal principles that is the focus of an analytic way of thinking, *prophetic thinking* seeks to uncover multiple, even divergent realities or principles. Prophetic thinking has emerged as a counterpoint to the highly successful but rigid analytic thinking style. According to Cornel West, a prophetic thinker is one who goes beyond abstraction. A prophetic thinker lives in multiple realities, feeling and touching these realities to such a degree that understanding is ultimately achieved. And a prophetic thinker understands multiple realities so well that bridges can be built between and among the multiple worlds. In his book *Prophetic Thought in Postmodern Times,* West identifies four basic components of prophetic thinking: discernment, connection, tracking hypocrisy, and hope.[2]

CROSS-REFERENCE
For more about prophetic ways of thinking see Chapters 2 and 3.

DISCERNMENT Discernment is the capacity to develop a vision of what should be out of a sophisticated understanding of what has been and is. This first component of prophetic thought is quite different from the abstract approach of the analytic thinker. The prophetic thinker is more concerned with the concrete, specific aspects of reality. To discern a situation is to take the entire situation into account to get beyond abstract principles. A discerning teacher is one who sees beyond mere test scores, beyond simple classroom rules. A discerning teacher examines the total content of a child's life and makes decisions based on this context. An outsider could criticize a discerning teacher for bending rules or being inconsistent. Yet a prophetic thinker would applaud the teacher for being wise. The prophetic thinker is a bit of a historian, building the future on the best of the past and present.

CONNECTION A prophetic thinker must relate to or connect with others. Rather than considering humankind in the abstract, prophetic thinkers value and have empathy for other human beings. They show empathy, the capacity to get in contact with the anxieties and frustrations of others.

Hypocrisy—Prejudice with a halo.
Ambrose Bierce

Many teachers really do care and work hard to help students. However, they are often unable to make the connection that would complete caring relations with their students. Teachers' willingness to empathize with students is often thwarted by society's desire to establish teaching on a firm scientific footing. But to students, the failure to connect means that teachers sometimes look as though they simply do not care. According to Nel Noddings,[3] both teachers and students have become victims in the search for the one best method of instruction.

TRACKING HYPOCRISY Although the relationship between empathy and teaching is important, it is equally important for the prophetic teacher to identify and make known "the gap between principles and practice, between promise and performance, between rhetoric and reality."[4] Tracking hypocrisy ought to be done in a self-critical rather than in a self-righteous manner. It takes boldness as well as courage to point out inconsistencies between school policies and practices, but when doing so a prophetic teacher remains open to others' points of view. New

Teachers not only teach content but also find ways to help students seek connections to the world around them and apply ideas to their daily lives.

Should Morals and Values Be Taught in Public Schools?

Should a teacher instruct students about values and matters of right and wrong? You may feel that this question demands an obvious affirmative answer. A problem arises, however, when you are asked to clarify the specific values that should be taught. How do you, as a teacher in a multicultural school setting, determine what moral values should be the focus of instruction?

One school of thought, influenced largely by the work of Lawrence Kohlberg, endorses direct instruction in moral development. The educational theorists who endorse this position contend that there exists a body of morals that spans all cultures. This body of morals can be articulated at any point in time and should be taught directly to students in public schools. People—especially parents—may also feel that children are faced with an increasingly complex and dangerous society and cannot be expected simply to absorb the proper morals and values from the world around them. Because of this, the schools should step in.

In contrast to this point of view, those influenced by the educational theories proposed by Syd Simon in his text *Values Clarification* reject the direct instruction of morals on the grounds that democracy demands that its citizens be free to clarify their own sets of values. This school of thought calls for public schools to refrain from the direct instruction of morals and asks teachers to help students define their own sets of individually selected values. The approach requires teachers to remain neutral in their presentations of opposing value systems. The teacher's role is simply to assist students in the clarification of the consequences of selecting any one set of morals or values.

This difficult problem of teaching morals and values is especially problematic for a democracy.

Questions for Reflection

1. Who shall select the set of values to be taught?
2. If the majority is given this right, then what becomes of the individual rights of minorities?
3. Yet is it possible to teach a value-free curriculum?
4. Does the very act of instruction imply a certain value system expressed and upheld by the individual teacher?

To answer these questions on-line and e-mail your answers to your professor, go to Chapter 9 of the companion website (www.ablongman.com/johnson14e) and click on Professional Dilemma.

---

evidence might reveal that one's position is no longer valid, or it might enhance one's original thinking. Figure 9.2 describes how prophetic ways of thinking help teachers solve a classroom problem.

HOPE The fourth and perhaps most important component of prophetic thought is simply hope. West admits that given the numerous and horrific examples of people's inhumanity to one another, it is hard to take hope seriously. Still, without it, all thought is meaningless. West says:

> To talk about human hope is to engage in an audacious attempt to galvanize and energize, to inspire and to invigorate world-weary people. Because that is what we are. We are world-weary; we are tired. For some of us there are misanthropic skeletons hanging in our closet. And by misanthropic I mean the notion that we have given up on the capacity to do anything right; the capacity of human communities to solve any problem.[5]

West challenges educators to see "skeletons" as challenges, not as conclusions. Even when confronted with educators' failures at creating a better community of scholars, the prophetic teacher must remember that the world is unfinished, that the future is open-ended, and that what teachers think and do can make a difference.

Journal for Reflection

Classroom activities that deal with what is good and evil are in the realm of axiology. Prepare lists of the goods and the evils of the U.S. educational system. Then, propose recommendations for change that might counteract as many of the evils as possible.

FIGURE 9.2

Prophetic Ways of Thinking: Uncover Multiple Realities or Principles

Specific Problem Confronts a Teacher
"Why do some students in my classroom
fail to complete their homework?"

DISCERNMENT

Develop a Vision of What Should Be

Children and adults should be free to
develop in a variety of ways and
according to individual needs.

CONNECTION

Relate and Show Empathy to Others

I have felt constrained by school
assignments and rigid academic
requirements.

TRACKING HYPOCRISY

**What Is the Gap between Principles
and Practice?**

Why do I require homework? Do I allow
for student choice?

HOPE

The World Can Change for the Better

I will examine our school's philosophy
and mission and discuss the implications
for our children with my fellow teachers.

Schools of Philosophy and Their Influence on Education

As philosophers attempt to answer questions, they develop answers that are clustered into different schools of thought. These schools of philosophical thought are somewhat contrived; they are merely labels developed by others who have attempted to show the similarities and differences among the many answers philosophers develop. As you examine the schools of thought described in this section, keep in mind that the philosophers who represent these schools are individual thinkers, like yourself, who do not limit their thinking to the characteristics of any one label or school of thought. Four well-known schools of thought are idealism, realism, pragmatism, and existentialism. In addition to these, we will touch on Eastern thought and Native North American thought. Technically, these two final clusters of thought are not termed *schools* because they encompass greater diversity and often extend beyond the limits of philosophy into beliefs, customs, and group values.

Idealism

Idealism is a school of philosophy that holds that ideas or concepts are the essence of all that is worth knowing. The physical world we know through our senses is only a manifestation of the spiritual world (metaphysics). Idealists believe in the power of reasoning and de-emphasize the scientific method and sense perception, which they hold suspect (epistemology). They search for universal or absolute truths that will remain constant throughout the centuries (axiology).

EDUCATIONAL IMPLICATIONS OF IDEALISM

The educational philosophy of the idealist is idea-centered rather than subject-centered or child-centered because the ideal, or the idea, is the foundation of all things. Knowledge is directed toward self-consciousness and self-direction and is centered in the growth of rational processes about the big ideas. Some idealists note that the individual, who is created in God's image, has free will and that it is this free will that makes learning possible. The idealist believes that learning comes from within the individual rather than from without. Hence, real mental and spiritual growth do not occur until they are self-initiated.

Idealists' educational beliefs include an emphasis on the study of great leaders as examples for us to imitate. For idealists the teacher is the ideal model or example for the student. Teachers pass on the cultural heritage and the unchanging content of education, such as knowledge about great figures of the past, the humanities, and a rigorous curriculum. Idealists emphasize the methods of lecture, discussion, and imitation. Finally, they believe in the importance of the doctrine of ideas.

No one philosopher is an idealist. Rather, philosophers answer questions, and some of their answers are similar. These similarities are what make up the different schools of philosophy. To describe adequately any one school of philosophy, such as idealism, one needs to go beyond these general similarities to examine the subtle differences posed by individual thinkers. Plato and Socrates, Immanuel Kant, and Jane Roland Martin represent different aspects of the idealist tradition.

PLATO AND SOCRATES

According to Plato (c. 427–c. 347 BCE), truth is the central reality. Truth is perfect; it cannot, therefore, be found in the world of matter because the material world is

Idealists—Foolish enough to throw caution to the winds . . . have advanced mankind and have enriched the world.

Emma Goldman

Ideals are like stars: you will not succeed in touching them with your hands, but like the seafaring man on the desert of waters, you choose them as your guides, and following them you reach your destiny.

Carl Schurz

CROSS-REFERENCE
For more about the idealist curriculum see Chapters 11 and 12.

CROSS-REFERENCE
For more about Plato and Socrates see Chapter 7.

idealism
A school of philosophy that considers ideas to be the only true reality.

both imperfect and constantly changing. Plato did not think that people create knowledge; rather, they discover it. In one of his dialogues, he conjectures that humanity once had true knowledge but lost it by being placed in a material body that distorts and corrupts that knowledge. Thus, humans have the arduous task of trying to remember what they once knew.

The modern world knows the philosophy of Socrates only through Plato, who wrote about him in a series of texts called "dialogues." Socrates (c. 470–399 BCE) spoke of himself as a midwife who found humans pregnant with knowledge—knowledge that had not been born or realized. This Socratic "Doctrine of Reminiscence" speaks directly to the role of the educator. Teachers need to question students in such a way as to help them remember what they have forgotten. In the dialogue *Meno*, Plato describes Socrates' meeting a slave boy and through skillful questions leading the boy to realize that he knows the Pythagorean theorem, even though he does not know that he knows it. This emphasis on bringing forth knowledge from students through artful questioning is sometimes called the Socratic method.

Although the Socratic method dates back to 400 BCE, the art of asking probing questions and using dialogue to enhance learning is still widely used today.

IMMANUEL KANT

The German philosopher Immanuel Kant (1724–1804), in the *Metaphysics of Morals* and the *Critique of Practical Reason,* spelled out his idealistic philosophy. Kant believed in freedom, the immortality of the soul, and the existence of God. He wrote extensively on human reason and noted that the only way humankind can know things is through the process of reason. Hence, reality is not a thing unto itself but the interaction of reason and external sensations. Reason fits perceived objects into classes or categories according to similarities and differences. It is only through reason that we acquire knowledge of the world. Once again, it is the idea or the way that the mind works that precedes the understanding of reality.

JANE ROLAND MARTIN

Often labeled a feminist scholar, Jane Roland Martin (1929–) is a contemporary disciple of Plato's dialogues. In "Reclaiming a Conversation,"[6] Martin describes how women have historically been excluded from the "conversation" that constitutes Western educational thought. Martin advocates a return to Plato's approach. Dialogues such as the *Apology,* the *Crito,* and the *Phaedo* illustrate educated persons—well-meaning people of good faith, people who trust and like one another, people who might even be called friends—getting together and trying to talk ideas through to a reasonable conclusion. They engage in conversation, learning something from one another and from the conversation itself.

For Martin, to be educated is to engage in a conversation that stretches back in time. Education is not simply something that occurs in a specific building at a specific time. Nor is it simply training or preparation for the next stage in life. Education is the development of the intellectual and moral habits, through the give-and-take of the conversation, that ultimately give "place and character to every human activity and utterance." Education—the conversation—is the place where one comes to learn what it is to be a person.

German philosopher Immanuel Kant (1724–1804) believed in freedom, the immortality of the soul, and the existence of God.

The direction in which education starts a man will determine his future life.

Plato

Using Socratic Dialogue to Enhance Reflective Learning

STUDY PURPOSE/QUESTION: The ancient philosophers Socrates and Plato believed that learning is best achieved through dialogue. Both philosophers contended that a teacher's main task is to ask good questions. By so doing the learner would reason to new knowledge. Socratic dialogue has been the topic of research studies in contemporary education and is now described as a dual-way communication between a teacher or tutor and a learner. The teacher does not teach a subject by direct exposition. Instead, learners' beliefs are challenged by the teacher through a series of questions that lead learners to reflect on their beliefs, induce general principles, and discover gaps and contradictions in their beliefs.

Using this type of questioning strategy is difficult when attempting to teach precise mathematical, scientific relationships. Researchers have proposed a Pictorial Socratic Dialogue coined to refer to a Socratic dialogue involving only graphics (e.g., drawings of objects or Cartesian graphs).

STUDY DESIGN: All student participants were asked to investigate a Spring Balance System on their own. The Spring Balance System models an experimental apparatus employed for the verification of Archimedes' Principle in a physics laboratory. Students were randomly assigned to three different learning conditions. Prior to beginning the experiment, all students were pretested on the mathematical and physics principles surrounding Archimedes' Principle. One group of students investigated the Spring Balance System with the help of a teacher who assumed the role of a Socratic tutor and who prescribed immediate and intelligent feedback based on the Socratic questioning method. A second group of students investigated the Spring

Balance System with the help of a Socratic tutor as well as the assistance of an articulation tool. The articulation tool offers different problems that have similar solutions (DPSS) and similar problems with different solutions (SPDS). The Socratic tutor not only provided questions but also used the different DPSS and SPDS problems to guide the learning of the students.

STUDY FINDINGS: After both groups of students investigated the Spring Balance System, students were post-tested. Results showed that all students improved their understanding of Archimedes' Principle. However, students who only received the help of Socratic Dialogue improved their understanding on a surface level and did not achieve a more abstract understanding of critical attributes. Students who were assisted by both Socratic Dialogue and the DPSS and SPDS problems significantly improved both surface level and abstract understanding concerning Archimedes' Principle.

IMPLICATIONS: Socratic dialogue is an effective teaching tool. When teachers guide the development of students' understandings, learning occurs. However, when teachers wish to help students understand technical, abstract principles, Socratic dialogue needs to be enhanced by carefully structured, supporting problems that are designed to make explicit to the learner underlying critical entities that might be missed.

Source: Ah-Lian Kor, John Self, and Ken Tait, "Pictorial Socratic Dialogue and Conceptual Change," 2001 International Conference on Computers in Education, AACE-APC (Association for the Advancement of Computing in Education-Asia Pacific Chapter) Computer-Based Learning Unit, University of Leeds, Woodhouse Lane, Leeds LS29JT, UK, www.icce2001.org/cd/pdf/P02/UK002.pdf.

Realism

realism

A school of philosophy that holds that reality, knowledge, and value exist independent of the human mind. In contrast to the idealist, the realist contends that physical entities exist in their own right.

Realism's roots lie in the thinking of Aristotle. **Realism** is a school of philosophy that holds that reality, knowledge, and value exist independent of the human mind (metaphysics). In other words, realism rejects the idealist notion that ideas are the ultimate reality. Refer to Figure 9.3, which illustrates the dualistic position of idealism and realism.

EDUCATIONAL IMPLICATIONS OF REALISM

Realists place considerable importance on the role of the teacher in the educational process. The teacher should be a person who presents content in a systematic and organized way and should promote the idea that there are clearly defined criteria

FIGURE 9.3

Dualistic Position of Idealism and Realism

IDEALISM

a. Supernatural causes for creation of the universe

b. World of mental conceptions is the ultimate reality

c. Mind

REALISM

a. Natural causes for evolution of the universe

b. World of physical objects is the ultimate reality

c. Body

one can use in making judgments (axiology). Contemporary realists emphasize the importance of scientific research and development. Curriculum has reflected the impact of these realist thinkers through the appearance of standardized tests, serialized textbooks, and a specialized curriculum in which the disciplines are seen as separate areas of investigation.

Realists contend that the ultimate goal of education is advancement of human rationality. Schools can promote rationality by requiring students to study organized bodies of knowledge, by teaching methods of arriving at this knowledge, and by assisting students to reason critically through observation and experimentation (epistemology). Teachers must have specific knowledge about a subject so that they can order it in such a way as to teach it rationally. They must also have a broad background to show relationships that exist among all fields of knowledge.

Thus, the realist curriculum would be a subject-centered curriculum and would include natural science, social science, humanities, and instrumental subjects such as logic and inductive reasoning. Realists employ experimental and observational techniques. In the school setting, they would promote testing and logical, clear content. To understand the complexity of the realist philosophy, we must once again turn to the ideas of individual thinkers: Aristotle, Locke, and Whitehead.

CROSS-REFERENCE
For more about the realist curriculum see Chapters 11 and 12.

ARISTOTLE

Aristotle (384–322 BCE) thought that ideas (forms) are found through the study of the world of matter. He believed that one could acquire knowledge of ideas or forms by investigating matter. To understand an object, one must understand its absolute form, which is unchanging. To the realist, the trees of the forest exist whether or not there is a human mind to perceive them. This is an example of an independent reality. Although the idea of a flower can exist without matter, matter cannot exist without form. Hence, each tulip shares universal properties with every other tulip and every other flower. However, the particular properties of a tulip differentiate it from all other flowers.

Aristotle's writings are known for their analytic approach. In contrast to Plato, whose writings are in the form of a conversation, Aristotle took great care to write with precision.

Ancient Greek philosopher Aristotle (384–322 BCE) believed that one could acquire knowledge of ideas or forms through an investigation of matter.

John Locke (1632–1704) believed that a person's mind is like a blank tablet at birth and that a person's sensory experiences make impressions on this tablet.

Philosopher and mathematician Alfred North Whitehead (1861–1947) attempted to reconcile idealism and realism.

CROSS-REFERENCE
For more about the pragmatist curriculum see Chapters 11 and 12.

pragmatism
A late-nineteenth-century U.S. school of philosophy that stresses becoming rather than being.

JOHN LOCKE

John Locke (1632–1704) believed in the tabula rasa (blank tablet) view of the mind. Locke stated that the mind of a person is blank at birth and that the person's sensory experiences make impressions on this blank tablet. Locke distinguished between sense data and the objects they represent. The objects, or things people know, are independent of the mind or the knower insofar as thought refers to them and not merely to sense data. Ideas (round, square, tall) represent objects. Locke claimed that primary qualities (such as shapes) represent the world, whereas secondary qualities (such as colors) have a basis in the world but do not represent it.

> The little or almost insensible impressions on our tender infancies have very important and lasting consequences: and there it is, as in the fountains of some rivers, where a gentle application of the hand turns the flexible waters into channels, that make them at first, in the source, they receive different tendencies, and arrive at last at very remote and distant places.
>
> I imagine the minds of children as easily turned, this or that way, as water itself; and though this be the principal part and our main care should be about the inside yet the clay cottage is not to be neglected.[7]

ALFRED NORTH WHITEHEAD

Alfred North Whitehead (1861–1947), a philosopher and mathematician, attempted to reconcile some aspects of idealism and realism. He proposed "process" to be the central aspect of realism. Unlike Locke, Whitehead did not see objective reality and subjective mind as separate. He saw them as an organic unity that operates by its own principles. The universe is characterized by patterns, and these patterns can be verified and analyzed through mathematics.

> Culture is activity of thought and receptiveness to beauty and humane feelings. Scraps of information have nothing to do with it. . . . In training a child to activity of thought, above all things we must beware of what I will call "inert ideas"—that is to say, ideas that are merely received into the mind without being used, or tested, or thrown into fresh combinations.
>
> In the history of education, the most striking phenomenon is the schools of learning, which at one epoch are alive with a ferment of genius, in a succeeding generation exhibit merely pedantry and routine. The reason is that they are overladen with inert ideas. Education with inert ideas is not only useless: it is, above all things, harmful— *Corruptio optimi, pessima*.[8]

Pragmatism

Pragmatism is a late-nineteenth-century U.S. philosophy that affected educational and social thought. It differs from most forms of idealism and realism by a belief in an open universe that is dynamic, evolving, and in a state of becoming (metaphysics). It is a process philosophy, which stresses becoming rather than being. Wedded as they are to change and adaptation, pragmatists do not believe in absolute and unchanging truth. For pragmatists, truth is what works. Truth is relative because what works for one person might not work for another, just as what works at one time or in one place or in one society might not work in another (axiology).

EDUCATIONAL IMPLICATIONS OF PRAGMATISM

Like the realist, the pragmatist believes that we learn best through experience, but pragmatists are more willing to put that belief into practice. Whereas realists are concerned with passing organized bodies of knowledge from one generation to the next, pragmatists stress applying knowledge—using ideas as instruments for problem solving (epistemology). Realists and idealists call for a curriculum centered on academic disciplines, but pragmatists prefer a curriculum that draws the disciplines together to solve problems—an interdisciplinary approach. Refer to Figure 9.4, which illustrates the relationships among realism, idealism, and pragmatism.

FIGURE 9.4

Relationship of Realism, Idealism, and Pragmatism

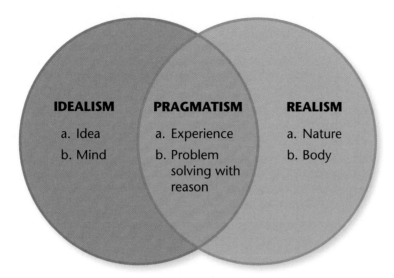

IDEALISM

a. Idea

b. Mind

PRAGMATISM

a. Experience

b. Problem solving with reason

REALISM

a. Nature

b. Body

CHARLES SANDERS PEIRCE

Charles Sanders Peirce (1839–1914) is considered the founder of pragmatism. He introduced the principle that belief is a habit of action undertaken to overcome indecisiveness. He believed that the purpose of thought is to produce action and that the meaning of a thought is the collection of results of actions. For example, to say that steel is "hard" is to mean that when the operation of scratch testing is performed on steel, it will not be scratched by most substances. The aim of Peirce's pragmatic method is to supply a procedure for constructing and clarifying meanings and to facilitate communication.

JOHN DEWEY

Early in his philosophical development, John Dewey (1859–1952) related pragmatism to evolution by explaining that human beings are creatures who have to adapt to one another and to their environments. Dewey viewed life as a series of overlapping and interpenetrating experiences and situations, each of which has its own complete identity. The primary unit of life is the individual experience.

Dewey wrote the following passage early in his career. In it he shows his zeal for education as a social force in human affairs.

> I believe that all education proceeds by the participation of the individual in the social consciousness of the race. This process begins unconsciously almost at birth, and is continually shaping the individual's powers, saturating his consciousness, forming his habits, training his ideas, and arousing his feelings and emotions.
>
> In sum, I believe that the individual is a social individual and that society is an organic union of individuals. If we eliminate the social factor from the child we are left only with an abstraction; if we eliminate the individual factor from society, we are left only with an inert and lifeless mass.[9]

RICHARD RORTY

Richard Rorty (1931–) is a contemporary pragmatist philosopher who has spent much of his life reinventing the work of John Dewey in light of the chaotic, ever-changing view of the world. Rorty contends that reality is not fixed, and it is the task of thinkers to come up with a procedure for correctly describing the nature of the

Charles Sanders Peirce (1839–1914) believed that the purpose of thought is to produce action.

real. He argues that reality is the outcome of inquiry, and as human inquiry shifts so too will shift the nature of what we call real. Rorty contends that different disciplines have different avenues for studying the world and therefore these avenues of inquiry create different realities. The way an artist looks at the world and creates a work of art and the way a chemist looks at the world and develops a new way of looking at molecules both affect the very nature of what is. Essential to this point of view is the understanding that disciplines such as science, mathematics, art, and history are not rooted in a fixed reality but are constructed by groups of people who are trying to make sense of the world. Hence, disciplines are arbitrary contrivances and one discipline is as good as another. Also, because disciplines are created by persons, they are subject to all the foibles, limitations, and prejudices of any human convention.

Although Rorty has not spoken directly to the field of education, his work provides a significant challenge to teachers. No longer can teachers represent expert knowledge as accurate or as true. Rather, expert knowledge is the current agreement of scholars at this point in time. Expert knowledge is simply a set of ideas and procedures that have been found to be useful. Rorty contends that a thinker should no longer be represented as a discoverer; rather, a thinker is more of a maker or cobbler who crafts meaning. People come together, agree on certain things, and then try to talk or reason their way to a sensible conclusion. Expertise is more a matter of "usefulness" than truth.

Existentialism

In **existentialism,** reality is lived existence, and the final reality resides within the individual (metaphysics). Existentialists believe that we live an alien, meaningless existence on a small planet in an unimportant galaxy in an indifferent universe. There is no ultimate meaning. Whereas some people might be paralyzed by this view, existentialists find the definition of their lives in the quest for meaning (epistemology). The very meaninglessness of life compels them to instill life with meaning.

The only certainty for the existentialist is that we are free. However, this freedom is wrapped up in a search for meaning. We define ourselves; that is, we make meaning in our world by the choices we make. In effect we are what we choose (axiology).

EDUCATIONAL IMPLICATIONS OF EXISTENTIALISM

The existentialist believes that most schools, like other corporate symbols, deemphasize the individual and the relationship between the teacher and the student. Existentialists claim that when educators attempt to predict the behavior of students, they turn individuals into objects to be measured, quantified, and processed. Existentialists tend to feel that tracking, measurement, and standardization militate against the creation of opportunities for self-direction and personal choice. According to the existentialist, education ought to be a process of developing a free, self-actualizing person—a process centered on the feelings of the student. Therefore, proper education does not start with the nature of the world and with humankind, but with the human individual or self.

The existentialist educator would be a free personality engaged in projects that treat students as free personalities. The highest educational goal is to search for oneself. Teachers and students experience existential crises; each such crisis involves an examination of oneself and one's life purposes. Education helps to fill in the gaps with understanding that the student needs in order to fulfill those purposes; it is not a mold to which the student must be fitted. Students define themselves by their choices.

The existentialist student would have a questioning attitude and would be involved in a continuing search for self and for the reasons for existence. The existentialist teacher would help students become what they themselves want to become, not what outside forces such as society, other teachers, or parents want them to become.

CROSS-REFERENCE
For more about the existentialist curriculum see Chapters 11 and 12.

existentialism
A school of philosophy that focuses on the importance of the individual rather than on external standards.

Existentialist thinkers are as varied as the notions of individual thought and self-defined meaning would suggest. There are atheistic existentialists as represented by Jean-Paul Sartre, critical existentialists as exemplified by Friedrich Nietzsche, and humanistic existentialists such as Maxine Greene.

JEAN-PAUL SARTRE

Modern existentialism was born amidst the pain and disillusionment of World War II. Jean-Paul Sartre (1905–1980) broke with previous philosophers and asserted that existence (being) comes before essence (meaning).

Sartre saw no difference between being free and being human. This view opens great possibilities; yet it also creates feelings of dread and nausea as one recognizes the reality of nonbeing and death as well as the great responsibilities that accompany such radical freedom to shape oneself out of one's choices. The process of answering the question "Who are we?" begins at a crucial event in the lives of young people called the existential moment—that point somewhere toward the end of youth when individuals realize for the first time that they exist as independent agents.

FRIEDRICH NIETZSCHE

Friedrich Nietzsche (1844–1900) is an existential philosopher who stresses the importance of the individuality of persons. Throughout his writings, Nietzsche indicts the supremacy of herd values in modern democratic social systems. He criticizes the way social systems such as modern educational institutions foster a spirit of capitalistic greed. When Nietzsche turns his attention primarily to social systems, human beings are portrayed much more as victims of social dynamics than as inferior or superior beings.

In Nietzsche's texts there is a strategy to liberate people from the oppression of feeling inferior within themselves, a teaching of how not to judge what one is in relation to what one should be. Although Nietzsche did not author a comprehensive teaching methodology, he teaches how to cultivate a healthy love of self-care, a taste for solitude, a perspective on perspective, literacy as a vital capacity, and an overall gratitude for one's existence.

Nietzsche observed that most teachers and parents

> hammer even into children that what matters is something quite different: the salvation of the soul, the service of the state, the advancement of science, or the accumulation of reputation and possessions, all as the means of doing service to mankind as a whole; while the requirements of the individual, his great and small needs within the twenty-four hours of the day, are to be regarded as something contemptible or a matter of indifference.[10]

MAXINE GREENE

A theme that permeates most of Maxine Greene's work is her unyielding faith in human beings' willingness to build and transcend their lived worlds. To Greene (1917–) philosophy is a deeply personal and aesthetic experience. Her writing blurs the distinction between philosophy and literature. This is appropriate because Greene contends that living is philosophy. Greene asserts that schools must be places that offer "an authentic public space where diverse human beings can appear before one another as best they know to be."[11]

Philosopher Maxine Greene (1917–) contends that living is philosophy and that freedom means overcoming obstacles that obstruct our attempts to find ourselves and fulfill our potential.

Eastern Ways of Knowing

Most studies of Western philosophy typically begin with the Greek philosophers. Yet there is evidence that Platonic philosophy owed much of its development to Eastern thinkers who emphasized the illusory quality of the physical world. Although there are many different philosophical writings among the Far Eastern and Near Eastern philosophers, **Eastern ways of knowing** as a group stress inner peace, tranquility,

Eastern ways of knowing

A varied set of ideas, beliefs, and values from the Far and Near East that stress inner peace, tranquility, attitudinal development, and mysticism.

Does Prepping for High-Stakes Tests Interfere with Teaching?

More and more states require students to pass tests in order to graduate or to receive a diploma. Some states offer different types of diplomas based on how well a student performs on a test. This type of testing is called high-stakes testing and it poses several philosophical questions. What do high-stakes tests say about the nature of knowledge? What does it mean to be educated in a high-stakes testing environment? What behaviors do high-stakes testing encourage? How do high-stakes tests influence teaching? The following debate raises these types of questions.

YES

Nancy Buell teaches fourth grade at the Lincoln School in Brookline, Massachusetts. She has taught for thirty-two years and serves on the state Board of Education's Advisory Council for Mathematics and Science.

As I watch my students debate how much taller fourth graders are than first graders, I am struck by their intuitive use of significant features of the data. As in:

Lee: Fourth graders are 10" taller because the tallest fourth grader is 64" and the tallest first grader is 54".

Tamara: A first grader is about 5" shorter. I found the middle height for each and just subtracted. The middle for the fourth graders is 57" and the middle for the first graders is between 51" and 52".

Dana: 5" or 4", because the most common height for first graders is 53" and the most common height for fourth graders is 58" or 57".

These students are exploring ideas involving maximum, median, and mode. They are considering what features to use to tell what is typical of the two groups so they can be compared. Students support their ideas with information in the data itself. They are developing ways to think about data that will lead to deep understanding of more formal statistics.

The rich mathematical discussions in my class are an outgrowth of my participation in professional development that focused on inquiry-based teaching and the big ideas we should be teaching.

But since high-stakes testing arrived, professional development meetings often focus on how to improve test scores, not on how to improve learning.

NO

Charlotte Crawford teaches fourth grade at Coteau-Bayou Blue School in Houma, Louisiana. A twenty-seven-year teaching veteran, she helped set the cut scores for her state's high-stakes fourth-grade test and now serves on a state panel for staff development.

Preparing students to take high-stakes tests does not interfere with teaching. It enhances teaching. When used properly, high-stakes tests can focus attention on weaknesses in the curriculum and in the teaching of it, as well as furnish an assessment of student progress. Once identified, student weak areas can be strengthened.

When the new high-stakes tests and revised curriculum were introduced in Louisiana, along with new accountability standards, many teachers were bewildered at the prospect of being held accountable for teaching a new curriculum without being told how to teach it.

Yet many of these teachers were also open to the new ideas and began working to find ways to implement them. They were aided by funding from the state for additional reading materials and in-service training.

Teachers often feel overwhelmed by the changes involved in our state's rigorous new standards, but many Louisiana educators are beginning to take ownership of their new curriculum. They're growing confident when making scope and sequence decisions. They're consistently reevaluating what they have taught, and how they have taught it, so they can do better next time.

These educators are revamping their classroom activities and their teacher-made tests to match them more closely to the format and tone of the state-mandated tests.

(continued)

(continued)

YES

Teaching that concentrates on improving test scores is very limited—by the nature of both testing and teaching. Testing involves sampling student knowledge. It is fragmented and only examines learning outcomes. It seldom looks at how well a student understands complex ideas.

A typical test item might give students a set of data and ask for the median. Students would not be asked to select the appropriate statistic to address a question and justify their choice. Yet knowing how to find the median, without knowing when to use it, is useless, except on tests.

If we teach facts and procedures likely to be on the test, without the deeper understanding behind them, we shortchange our students. We must not limit what we teach to what will be tested.

Many teachers feel pressured to choose teaching techniques that help with testing more than learning. They're urged to spend more time on information that mimics test items.

Students should, of course, know how to answer multiple choice, short answer, and open response questions, but teaching these test-taking skills should not be confused with teaching a subject. Some teachers spend a day a week using test-like items, not to sample what children know, but to try to teach the content.

Teaching should build on what students already know and help them develop a rich web of interconnected ideas. Real learning involves inquiry, hypothesis testing, exploration, and reflection.

Teaching to the test will not help my students think about how to use features of data sets to answer real questions. Teaching to the test is not teaching.

NO

Helping students become familiar with the state-mandated test formats, by using them in the classroom, prevents having to spend valuable class time to "practice" for the high-stakes tests.

Learners, meanwhile, are reaping the benefits of having teachers who are determined that their students will be as prepared as possible to relate the skills they learn in school to real-life situations. They're becoming lifelong learners, besides performing well on standardized tests.

Some educators complain that they must "teach to the test."

But others consider this to be a weak objection since the state tests focus on information and skills students are expected to know at certain points in their schooling.

These educators say the curriculum objectives covered by the state tests should be taught before the tests are given, with the remaining objectives covered afterwards. This is a very workable arrangement when high-stakes tests are given early in the spring.

To be sure, some Louisiana educators are still resisting the changes that come with the state tests.

But most realize this is an idea whose time has come.

In 1998, my school helped pilot the fourth-grade language arts test. I was nervous about how my students would fare. When they finished, I asked for reactions.

Much to my surprise, students calmly informed me that the state test was "kind of hard, kind of easy, kind of fun."

That day, my students unwittingly reassured me that learners who are prepared for high-stakes tests need not fear them.

Source: "Does Prepping for High-Stakes Tests Interfere with Teaching?" *NEA Today* (January 2001), p. 11. Reprinted by permission of the National Education Association.

WHAT IS YOUR PERSPECTIVE ON THIS ISSUE?
Does prepping for high-stakes tests interfere with teaching?

To give your opinion, go to Chapter 9 of the companion
website (www.ablongman.com/johnson14e) and click on Teacher Perspectives.

attitudinal development, and mysticism. Western philosophy has tended to emphasize logic and materialism; on the other hand, Eastern ways of knowing, in general, stress the inner rather than the outer world, intuition rather than sense, and mysticism rather than scientific discoveries. This has differed from school to school, but overall Eastern ways of knowing begin with the inner world and then reach to the outer world of phenomena. Eastern ways of knowing emphasize order, regularity, and patience that is proportional to and in harmony with the laws of nature.

Eastern thinkers have always concerned themselves with education, which they view as a way of achieving wisdom, maintaining family structure, establishing law, and providing for social and economic concerns. Instruction includes the things that one must do to achieve the good life, and education is viewed as necessary not only for this life but also for achievement of the good life hereafter.

One good reason to study Eastern ways of knowing is that they offer vantage points from which to examine Western thought. Eastern ideas encourage one to question seriously the Western world's most basic commitments to science, materialism, and reason.

INDIAN THOUGHT

Far Eastern Indian thought has a long, complex history and is permeated by opposites. To Western philosophers, opposites need to be reconciled, but to the Eastern mind, this need for consistency is unimportant. For example, great emphasis is placed on a search for wisdom, but this does not mean a rejection of worldly pleasures. Though speculation is emphasized, it has a practical character. Far Eastern Indian thinkers insist that knowledge be used to improve both social and communal life and that people should live according to their ideals. In Far Eastern Indian thought, there is a prevailing sense of universal moral justice, according to which individuals are responsible for what they are and what they become.[12]

CHINESE THOUGHT

The emphasis of Far Eastern Chinese philosophy is on harmony; correct thinking should help one achieve harmony with life. This harmony of government, business, and family should then lead toward a higher synthesis. Confucianism and Taoism provide two major contexts for Chinese thought.

For more than two thousand years, Confucian thought has influenced education, government, and culture in China. Confucius (551–479 BCE) believed that people need standards for all of life, so rules were developed for a wide range of activities. Confucian thought gives education a high place but stresses building moral character more than merely teaching skills or imparting information. This moral approach has a practical component. Children should obey and defer to parents and respect the wisdom adults have gained in their journey through life. Following these principles enables children to become *chun-tzu,* persons distinguished by faithfulness, diligence, and modesty.

The central concept of Taoism is that of the "Tao," the Way or Path. The Tao is the way the universe moves, the way of perfection and harmony. It is conformity with nature. Perhaps the most significant aspect of the Tao is letting things alone, not forcing personal desires onto the natural course of events. It is a noncompetitive approach to life. Taoists believe that conflict and war represent basic failures in society, for they bring ruin to states and a disrespect for life.

JAPANESE THOUGHT

Japanese thought is rooted in Shinto, a way of thinking that recognizes the significance of the natural world. This respect for all nature permeates Japanese thought and life. Shinto accepts the phenomenal world (the world people apprehend through their senses) as absolute; this acceptance leads to a disposition to lay greater emphasis on intuitive, sensible, concrete events rather than on universal ideas. On the social level, Japanese express this focus on the natural world through many artifacts, including the patterns of traditional kimonos. Within the house, flowers are

When a man has pity on all living creatures, then only is he noble.
Buddha

Everything has beauty, but not everyone sees it. Wheresoever you go, go with all your heart.
Confucius

Ancient Chinese philosopher Confucius (551–479 BCE) believed that people need standards for all of life so he developed rules for a wide range of activities.

Global Perspectives

The Fabric of Eastern Ways of Knowing

As you can see, Eastern thought is like a rich fabric of diverse ideas. It emphasizes sets of views that are quite different from the neat categorizations of Western thought. Eastern thought suggests that cohesive views can be achieved without the necessity of neat, hierarchically distinct categories. Although they are quite difficult to summarize, the philosophy and thought of the East suggest new ways of looking at long-accepted meanings and assumptions. As such, the study of Eastern thought is an important part of all future educators' preparation in an increasingly multicultural society.

Questions for Reflection

1. In what ways do Eastern ways of knowing affect character education programs?
2. What values would receive greater or lesser emphasis?

arranged in vases and dwarf trees placed in alcoves, flowers and birds are engraved on lintels, and nature scenes are painted on sliding screens.

EDUCATIONAL IMPLICATIONS OF EASTERN WAYS OF KNOWING

Eastern educational thought places great emphasis on the teacher–student relationship. Change springs from this relationship; that is, the student is changed as a result of contact with the guru, master, or prophet. Eastern educational thought emphasizes transformation: The individual must be transformed to face life. Attitude shaping is important because the attitude a person holds toward life will determine the individual's levels of goodness and wisdom.

A recurring educational aim in Eastern ways of knowing is to put humanity in tune with nature. There is great emphasis on observing nature and learning through wanderings and pilgrimages. The importance of achieving wisdom, satori, enlightenment, or nirvana is supreme. All paths must lead to this, and from this wisdom spring virtue, right living, and correct behavior.

Native North American Ways of Knowing

Just as the rich past and diverse cultures make it difficult to summarize Eastern thought, Native North American ways of knowing are equally difficult to synthesize. **Native North American ways of knowing** include a varied set of beliefs, positions, and customs that span different tribes in North America. These beliefs, positions, and customs center on the relationship of humans to all of nature, including the earth, the sun, the sky, and beyond. Because Native North American ways of knowing center on the relationship of humans to all of nature, it is sometimes difficult to separate knowing from a way of life. In fact, to understand is to live and to develop an ever closer, more profound human-to-nature relationship. The types of relationships and the symbols that inform these human-to-nature relationships differ widely among tribes.

Although Native North American ways of knowing are as different as the four hundred–plus tribes in North America, these ways of knowing do have similar elements. They all include traditional stories and beliefs that dictate a way of knowing and living. All include a reverence for nature and a sense of humans' responsibility to nature. And all groups make reference to a supreme being—although the names are different, the relationships vary, and the expectations of some supreme beings

CROSS-REFERENCE
For more about Native North American ways of knowing see Chapters 3 and 4.

Traditionally, Native Americans view time as a flow of events with no beginning or end.

Lee Little Soldier, Native American educator

Native North American ways of knowing

A varied set of beliefs, philosophical positions, and customs that span different tribes in North America.

are interpreted through natural elements. Thus, the Black Hills are sacred to the Lakota, the turtle is revered as Mother Earth by the Ojibwa, and so on. Native North American ways of knowing are orally developed rather than written. Hence, they change slightly from age to age. Additionally, the ways of knowing are subject to interpretation by the shaman, or holy one.

NAVAJO THOUGHT

The Navajo nation is the largest tribe in the United States. The Navajos' early history was nomadic, and their thoughts and customs are known for their unique ability to assimilate with and adapt to the thought and customs of other tribes. As with most Native North American cultures, the Navajo universe is an all-inclusive unity viewed as an orderly system of interrelated elements. At the basis of Navajo teachings and traditions is the value of a life lived in harmony with the natural world. Such a view enables one to "walk in beauty." To understand the Navajo worldview, one must note the teachings of the "inner forms" of things. These inner forms were set in place by First Man and First Woman. The concept of inner form is similar to the concept of a spirit or soul; without it, the Navajos say, the outer forms would be dead.[13]

Native North American ways of knowing provide a perspective that connects knowledge to the earth that surrounds us and of which we are a part.

LAKOTA THOUGHT

The Native American culture of the Great Plains, of which the Lakota form part, is based on mystical participation with the environment. All aspects of this ecosystem, including earth, sky, night, day, sun, and moon, are elements of the oneness within which life was undertaken. The Lakota celebrate the "sacred hoop of life" and observe seven sacred rites toward the goal of ultimate communion with Wakan-Tanka, the great Spirit.[14]

HOPI THOUGHT

The Hopi follow the path of peace, which they believe is a pure and perfect pattern of humankind's evolutionary journey. The Road of Life of the Hopi is represented as a journey through seven universes created at the beginning. At death the conduct of a person in accordance with the Creator's plan determines when and where the next step on the road will be taken. Each of the Hopi clans has a unique role to play, and each role is an essential part of the whole. Hopis must live in harmony with one another, with nature, and with the plan. Out of this complex interplay, then, the plan is both created and allowed to unfold.

> We feel that the world is good. We are grateful to be alive. We are conscious that all men are brothers. We sense that we are related to other creatures. Life is to be valued and preserved. If you see a grain of corn on the ground, pick it up and take care of it, because it has life inside. When you go out of your house in the morning and see the sun rising, pause a moment to think about it. When you take water from a spring, be aware that it is a gift of nature. (Albert Yava, Big Falling Snow, Hopi)[15]

EDUCATIONAL IMPLICATIONS OF NATIVE NORTH AMERICAN WAYS OF KNOWING

Journal for Reflection

Consider the four components of prophetic thinking: discernment, empathy, tracking hypocrisy, and hope. Select one of these components and apply it to the educational controversy over school prayer. Record your thoughts, feelings, and observations.

Native North American educational thought emphasizes the importance of nature. The pursuit of knowledge and happiness must be subordinate to a respect for the whole universe. To know is to understand one's place in the natural order of things. To be is to celebrate through ritual and stories the spirit that informs all reality. These principles encourage educators to study the physical and social world by examining the natural relationships that exist among things, animals, and humans. Studying ideas in the abstract or as independent entities is not as important as understanding the relationships among ideas and the physical reality. Hands-on learning, making connections, holding discussions, and celebrating the moment are essential components of an educational experience.

Summary

STRUCTURE AND METHODOLOGY OF PHILOSOPHY. The study of philosophy permeates every aspect of the teacher's role and provides the underpinning for every decision. This chapter describes how philosophy is related to daily teaching decisions and actions, and it clarifies some of the major ideas that different philosophers have developed in their private quest for wisdom.

Philosophy revolves around three major types of questions: those that deal with the nature of reality (metaphysics), those that deal with knowledge and truth (epistemology), and those that deal with values (axiology). Successful teachers are those who are dedicated to and thoroughly understand their preferred beliefs. Decisions about the nature of the subject matter emphasized in the curriculum are metaphysical commitments to reality—what is real? Questions related to what is true and how we know are epistemological. Classroom methods are practices that aim to assist learners in acquiring knowledge and truth in the subject area. Classroom activities that deal with ethics (what is right or wrong), beauty, and character are in the realm of axiology (values). The task of the teacher is to identify a preferred style, understand that style as thoroughly as possible, and use that style with each unique group of learners.

Analytic and prophetic thinking provide two approaches to the process of philosophy. Analytic thinking provides clarity and precision, whereas prophetic thinking fosters breadth and sensitivity. Both thinking approaches are valuable and help educators understand the essential and critical features of situations or problems.

SCHOOLS OF PHILOSOPHY AND THEIR INFLUENCE ON EDUCATION. Four classical Western schools of philosophical thought (realism, idealism, pragmatism, and existentialism) were introduced. For each school of philosophy, representative philosophers and their ideas were provided to give prospective teachers a sense of how they might develop their own educational philosophy.

The chapter concluded with overviews of Eastern and Native North American ways of knowing. The Eastern and Native North American ways of knowing are varied and diverse. Despite such diversity, many of these ways of knowing share an underlying sensitivity to nature and an emphasis on wisdom, virtue, spirituality, and harmony within the larger universe. The educational implications of these ways of knowing include the importance of teaching respect for the earth and awareness of the interrelationships among all things.

Discussion Questions

1. How would you describe philosophy to a young child?
2. In your opinion, which is the most important aspect of a given philosophy (for the teacher): the metaphysical component, the epistemological component, or the axiological component? State the rationale for your choice.
3. Early Greek philosophers suggest that all knowledge is based on experience. Discuss the implications of this statement for teaching methodology.
4. Describe the ways that Eastern and Native North American ways of knowing might influence what and how you teach.

School-Based Observations

1. As you visit schools and classrooms, be alert for indications of philosophical concepts and different philosophical views. Examine the lesson plans that teachers have developed and consider whether their focus is on subject matter acquisition, the development of character, or the development of skills. These emphases can be a clue to the type of philosophy that teacher endorses. You might wish to talk with teachers about their educational ideas.
2. Many schools have written statements describing their philosophy of education. Ask several schools to send you a copy of their philosophy of education. When you receive them, look for similarities and differences among the philosophical statements.
3. As you visit schools and classrooms, focus on the discipline approaches that teachers employ. What do these approaches imply about teachers' views of human nature?

Portfolio Development

1. According to idealistic philosophy, character education can be enhanced through study and imitation of exemplars/heroes in the historical record. Identify an exemplary educator from history and describe how you could teach character through that persons example. Place your essay in your folio as an example of your teaching methodology.
2. Assist a student as a mentor or tutor. Before beginning, gather samples of the student's thinking and schoolwork. Try to think like the student and by so doing uncover areas in which the student needs help. Develop a diagnosis that details what changes will be beneficial. Place these ideas in your folio as an example of your diagnostic and metacognitive skills.

Preparing for Certification

PHILOSOPHICAL THINKING

1. One of the topics in the Praxis II Principles of Learning and Teaching (PLT) test is using "teacher self-evaluation to enhance instructional effectiveness." In this chapter, you learned about two approaches to philosophical thinking—analytic and prophetic—that are useful tools to enhance instructional effectiveness. Think about a specific problem you might face in the subject or grade level you plan to teach. Analyze that problem using the two approaches. How does each approach contribute to your understanding of the problem?
2. Answer the following multiple-choice question, which is similar to items in Praxis and other state certification tests.

Two middle school teachers are discussing their philosophical beliefs about teaching and learning. Jan says, "I think it is very important that all students master an essential body of knowledge; I would like to teach a unit in my subject area that focuses on specific content and make sure that all students master it." Lee says, "I disagree. I think it is more important that students are able to apply knowledge to solve problems. I would teach an interdisciplinary unit that focuses on real issues so students can see how what they are learning applies to the real world." Lee's position more closely resembles

A. realism
B. idealism
C. pragmatism
D. existentialism

3. Answer the following short-answer question, which is similar to items in Praxis and other state certification tests. After you've completed your written response, use the scoring guide in the *Test at a Glance* materials to assess your response. Can you revise your response to improve your score?

Some school districts have established mandatory service-learning programs to encourage students to develop an ethic of caring, involvement in the community, and citizenship. Do you believe service-learning projects should be a requirement for graduation? What are the benefits of such a requirement? What are the arguments against such a requirement?

Websites

webs.csu.edu/~big0ama/mpes/mpes.html The Midwest Philosophy of Education Society (MPES) comprises educators who are committed to the critical normative and interpretive aspects of education. The mission of MPES is to encourage scholarship in the field of philosophy of education; to discuss curricular, methodological, and institutional issues in the field; and to offer educators at large a forum for the philosophical analysis of educational issues. The site provides Internet resources, papers, and discussions that help teachers understand questions and concerns that flow from a philosophic perspective on education.

www.apped.org The Association for Process Philosophy of Education (APPE) provides an opportunity to meet, discuss, share papers, and publish your thinking about and the connections between philosophy and educational theory and practice. The news, articles, essays, and announcements on these pages are influenced by the process philosophies of Henri Bergson, John Dewey, and Alfred North Whitehead, and by the work of contemporary philosophers and educators who have explored the relevance of these ideas for educational theory and prac-

tice. APPE members include those who teach at every level of school from kindergarten through the baccalaureate, those involved in adult learning, academic administrators, education theorists, and philosophers. The site offers educators an opportunity to meet, discuss, share papers, and publish their thinking about effective pedagogy and the connections between process philosophy and educational theory and practice.

www.pdcnet.org The Philosophy Documentation Center (PDC) is a nonprofit organization dedicated to providing affordable access to the widest possible range of philosophical materials. Established in 1966, the PDC provides access to scholarly journals, reference materials, conference proceedings, and instructional software. This site provides easy access to the ideas and writings of a wide variety of philosophers of education.

http://busboy.sped.ukans.edu/~rreed/NAedPhilosophy. html This is the Native American educational philosophy website maintained by the University of Kansas. This site emphasizes that Native American educational philosophy encompasses the education of the whole child with many types of learning styles and teaching styles.

Further Reading

Abel, Donald C. (1992). *Theories of Human Nature.* New York: McGraw-Hill. Describes different views of human nature and discusses the implications for teaching, working, and living in society.

Bahm, Archie J. (1995). *Comparative Philosophy: Western, Indian, and Chinese Philosophies Compared,* rev. edition. Albuquerque, NM: World Book. Compares different thinkers, ideologies, and philosophies from both the West and the East.

Cromer, Alan H. (1997). *Connected Knowledge: Science, Philosophy, and Education.* New York: Oxford University Press. Written by a physicist, this text argues that students' understanding needs to be connected; it provides practical suggestions that advance students' understanding in an orderly manner.

Littleton, Scott C. (1996). *Eastern Wisdom.* New York: Henry Holt. Describes Eastern thought drawn from India, China, and Japan and shows how such ideas enhance life.

Nerburn, Kent, and Mengelkoch, Louise. (1991). *Native American Wisdom.* Novato, CA: The Classic Wisdom Collection. Describes the contributions of different Native American thinkers and suggests that their ideas need to be integrated into schools of learning.

Palmer, Parker. (1997). *To Know as We Are Known: Education as Spiritual Journey.* San Francisco: Harper. Shows the close relationship between learning and becoming a person. Provides both spiritual and practical suggestions that challenge views of knowledge.

Sassone, Leslie. (2002). *The Process of Becoming: A Democratic Nietzschean Philosophical Pedagogy for Individualization.* Chicago: Discovery Association. This book explores in detail the many Nietzschean perspectives on education. It also offers a democratic Nietzschean pedagogy supplemented by contemporary radical democratic education reformers Paulo Freire, Ivan Illich, Jonathan Kozol, and Neil Postman.

❰mylabschool
Where the classroom comes to life!

Go to Allyn and Bacon's MyLabSchool (www.mylabschool.com) and complete the following activity for Chapter 9. Click on **Research Navigator,** and then use the following search terms within the Education database: **axiology, epistemology, metaphysics.**

CHAPTER 10

Building an Educational Philosophy for a Changing World

Scientists Explore the Molding of Children's Morals

By Susan Gilbert, *New York Times,* March 18, 2003

Along with their academic education, students in kindergarten through 12th grade in the Metropolitan School District of Lawrence Township in Indianapolis have another field of study: character education.

Each school displays a poster listing what the district has identified as the "life skills for building character," including honesty, fairness and trustworthiness. Teachers look for ways to reinforce these traits each day.

Classroom discussions focus on the moral strengths and weaknesses of characters in the books that students have read. Students make quilts and write songs celebrating the life skills. They get buttons and other rewards for putting the skills into practice.

While the Lawrence Township schools are exceptional in the scope of their initiative, they are not alone in their effort to calibrate the moral compasses of their students. Over the last few years, schools in 48 states have introduced character education programs in the hope of bolstering students' resolve to resist the temptation to lie, cheat, bully, use drugs and behave immorally in other ways. The Department of Education has promoted these efforts by giving $27 million in character education grants since 1995.

Many of the programs draw on some recent research showing that although all children are born with the capacity to be moral, it needs to be nurtured by parents, schools and the community at large. Otherwise, its development is stunted.

Without a firm sense of right and wrong, some experts say, children tend to become cynical, alienated and extremely selfish. They cheat to get ahead, rationalizing that "everybody does it." They lack the social obligation to control their anger when they feel that they have been wronged. In the extreme, tragedies happen, like the massacre at Columbine.

Much of the impetus for character education in schools is a perception that the moral fiber of children as well as adults is unraveling. Two-thirds of Americans think that society is less honest and moral than it used to be, according to *Bowling Alone,* published in 2000, by Dr. Robert Putnam, a professor of public policy at Harvard.

Last year, a poll of 12,000 high school students by the Josephson Institute of Ethics, a nonprofit organization in Marina del Rey, Calif., found that 74 percent admitted cheating on a test in the previous year.

But some researchers—while not denying that there is considerable room for improvement—say children today are no less moral than their parents, grandparents and great-grandparents were as children.

Dr. Elliot Turiel, the author of *The Culture of Morality,* published last year, says cheating is just as common today as it was in the 1920's. He compared surveys of students done then with the findings of recent surveys like those of the Josephson Institute and found that the percentage of students who admitted to cheating was roughly the same.

"It may be that kids today are fresh and disobedient in fairly large numbers," said Dr. Turiel, a psychologist at the University of California at Berkeley, "but was it really different in the past? It wasn't with cheating."

Dr. Turiel and other researchers criticize many of the character education programs in schools for being superficial and ineffective. "Morality isn't traits of character but a complicated set of judgments," he said.

Dr. John M. Doris, a philosophy professor at the University of California at Santa Cruz, goes as far as to question whether there is such a thing as a moral character. He says that the existence of moral character, described by philosophers as far back as Aristotle, is not supported in the scientific literature today.

Questions for Reflection

1. In this article, Dr. Elliot Turiel describes moral character as a complicated set of judgments while the Lawrence Township School District identifies specific life skills for building character, including honesty, fairness and trustworthiness. How would you describe moral character and what evidence do you have to support your description?

2. Dr. John M. Doris questions that there is such a thing as moral character. What is your position on the existence of moral character?

3. Describe how your position about moral character affects your approach to teaching.

Copyright © 2003 by the New York Times Co. Reprinted with permission.

INTASC

Learning Outcomes

After reading and studying this chapter, you should be able to:

1. Identify the major tenets of authoritarian educational philosophies of essentialism, behaviorism, and positivism. (INTASC 1: Subject Matter)

2. Identify the major tenets of nonauthoritarian educational philosophies of progressivism, humanism, and constructivism. (INTASC 1: Subject Matter)

3. Relate educational philosophies to learning and curriculum development. (INTASC 2: Development and Learning)

4. Relate the tenets of critical pedagogy to societal change. (INTASC 3: Diversity; INTASC 9: Reflection)

5. Relate educational philosophy to classroom organization, discipline practices, motivation, and classroom climate. (INTASC 5: Motivation and Management; INTASC 9: Reflection)

6. List the characteristics of teachers as change agents. (INTASC 9: Reflection; INTASC 10: Collaboration)

7. State the components of a personal philosophy of education (INTASC 2: Development and Learning; INTASC 9: Reflection)

There is a plethora of divergent views about teaching and learning expressed in philosophy, psychology, and education journals. Today's classroom teachers must identify their own beliefs about educating young people. Although labeling the classroom practice of any one teacher is not easy, we recommend that you, as a prospective teacher, carefully identify a personal set of operational principles with regard to classroom techniques. This identification task is an excellent first step toward developing a dynamic, ever-developing philosophy of education.

A philosophy of education is not a set of written words. It is a platform on which decisions are made and life is led. A teacher's practices in the classroom reflect her or his personal philosophy. The best goal for beginning educators is to become comfortable with a variety of classroom practices that address the needs of learners. It is not a matter of selecting one methodology over another but rather of understanding these different approaches and using them responsibly. We believe that a sound preparation for teaching addresses the need to develop a workable classroom philosophy—one that incorporates the larger role of teaching in a complex society as well as the microrole of the teacher working with students in the classroom setting.

One strategy that can help you develop your own personal philosophy of education is to build on the educational philosophies of others. These educational philosophies emerged over time as educators applied their philosophic views to education. Six major educational philosophies will be described in the first part of the chapter to show you how different philosophies give rise to divergent philosophies of education. We believe that this examination of different educational philosophies will prepare you, in the second part of the chapter, to develop your own philosophy of education.

The Dynamic Relationship between Philosophy and Education

Educational philosophy can be analyzed as the application of philosophy to the classroom. The way curriculum is organized, the manner in which instruction is delivered, the character of school environments, and the processes used in testing and grading are informed by the philosophical views held by educators, parents, and legislators. Such views vary greatly among school districts and states. Table 10.1 describes the relationships between four schools of philosophy—idealism, realism, pragmatism, and existentialism—and education.

The four schools of philosophy described in Table 10.1 give rise to different, sometimes competing, learning foci, curricular goals, teaching methods, and approaches to character and aesthetic development. Educational philosophers attempt to develop cohesive ideas about teaching and learning by drawing on one or more compatible philosophies. They also attempt to clarify how these different approaches to curriculum, instruction, and assessment work or do not work together. For example, a behaviorist educational philosopher could focus on the mind, the physical world, or the social world. On the other hand, it would be inappropriate for the behaviorist to focus on personal choice because behaviorism essentially aims to control human behavior through teacher-directed reinforcement.

Six educational philosophies are presented according to the degree to which they rely on external (teacher-based) versus internal (student-based) authority. This distinction between a teacher-centered versus a student-centered locus of control can also be used to group schools of philosophy. As indicated in Table 10.1, the ideas and principles that surround idealism and realism imply that external authority is important to the attainment of truth and goodness, whereas pragmatism and existentialism focus more on the innate worth of the individual.

Educational philosophies explain how teacher-centered locus-of-control teaching and learning principles differ from those of student-centered locus-of-control principles. They also help clarify how each set of teaching and learning principles forms a cohesive whole. The six educational philosophies considered here are essentialism, behaviorism, positivism, progressivism, humanism, and constructivism. To varying degrees, each of these educational views is used by classroom teachers

Journal for Reflection

Schools are being challenged to develop students who can succeed in a complex business world. Interview business executives from two different companies to determine the importance of ethics in their business operations. Determine the extent to which the executives' ethical values were influenced by teachers. In your journal, list recommendations for teachers made by the executives. Describe a teaching approach that responds to these recommendations.

TABLE 10.1 Educational Implications of Philosophy

Educational Aspect	Teacher-Centered Locus-of-Control Philosophies		Student-Centered Locus-of-Control Philosophies	
	Idealism	Realism	Pragmatism	Existentialism
Learning focus	Subject matter of the mind: literature, intellectual history, philosophy, religion	Subject matter of the physical world: mathematics, science	Subject matter of social experience	Subject matter of personal choice
Curriculum goal	The same education for all	Mastery of laws of the universe	Creation of a new social order	Personal freedom and development
Preferred teaching method	Teaching for the handling of ideas: lecture, discussion	Teaching for mastery of information and skills: demonstration, recitation	Problem solving: project method, product development	Individual exploration: discovery method, authentic pedagogy
Character development	Imitation of exemplars, heroes	Training in rules of conduct	Group decision making in light of consequences	Development of individual responsibility for decisions and preferences
Aesthetic development	Study of the masterworks; values of the past heritage	Study of design in nature	Participation in art projects based on cross-cultural and universal values	Development of a personal view of the world; self-initiated activities

Source: Adapted from Van Cleve Morris and Young Pai, *Philosophy and the American School,* 2nd edition. Boston: Houghton Mifflin, 1976. Copyright 1976 by Houghton Mifflin Company. Reprinted with permission.

and applied to the way teachers organize their classroom, their instruction, and their assessments. As you study these different educational philosophies, you will find that one or more of them clearly meshes with your own views.

Teacher-Centered Locus-of-Control Educational Theories

Essentialism, behaviorism, and positivism are educational philosophies that espouse a teacher-centered locus of control. Each theory's approach to subject matter, classroom organization, teaching methods, and assessment places most of the responsibility on the teacher, whose job it is to enable students to learn what is important. Although each educational theory forms a distinct cohesive whole, all three are rooted in an authoritarian principle—that is, that truth and goodness are entities best understood by the person with expertise who is in authority. The students' role is, then, to attempt to master and follow the directions of those in power who have experience and authority.

This chapter presents each educational philosophy's perspectives on curriculum, teaching, and learning. In addition, for each theory we will describe a representative program along with an illustrative class activity. The class activity is further analyzed according to the nature of the learner (active or passive), the nature of the subject matter, the use of the subject matter, and the type of thinking that is emphasized (convergent—focused on right answers—or divergent—focused on developing multiple perspectives).

Essentialism

Essentialism holds that there is a common core of information and skills that an educated person in a given culture must have. Schools should be organized to transmit this core of essential material as effectively as possible. There are three basic principles of essentialism: a core of information, hard work and mental discipline, and teacher-centered instruction. Essentialism seeks to educate by providing training in the fundamentals, developing sound habits of mind, and teaching respect for authority. The back-to-the-basics movement is a truncated form of essentialism because it focuses primarily on the three Rs and discipline. Essentialism draws equally from both idealism and realism.

Essentialists are not so intent on transmitting underlying, basic truths; rather, they advocate the teaching of a basic core of information that will help a person live a productive life today. Hence, this core of information can and will change. This is an important difference in emphasis from the notions of everlasting truths that characterize the idealist. Essentialism stresses the disciplined development of basic skills rather than the idealist goals of uncovering essences or underlying principles. (See the Essentialist Class Activity.)

ESSENTIALIST FOCUS OF LEARNING

Essentialism's goals are to transmit the cultural heritage and develop good citizens. It seeks to do this by emphasizing a core of fundamental knowledge and skills, developing sound habits of mental discipline, and demanding a respect for authority in a structured learning situation. The role of the student is that of a learner. School is a place where children come to learn what they need to know, and the teacher is the person who can best instruct students in essential matters.

ESSENTIALIST CURRICULUM

The essentialist curriculum focuses on subject matter that includes literature, history, foreign languages, and religion. Teaching methods require formal discipline and feature required reading, lectures, memorization, repetition, and examinations. Essentialists differ in their views on curriculum, but they generally agree about teaching the laws of nature and the accompanying universal truths of the physical world. Mathematics and the natural sciences are examples of subjects that contribute to the learners' knowledge of natural law. Activities that require mastering facts and information about the physical world are significant aspects of essentialist methodology. With truth defined as observable fact, instruction often includes field trips,

> The business of education is not to make the young perfect in any one of the sciences, but so to open and dispose their minds as may best make them capable of any, when they shall apply themselves to it.
>
> *John Locke*

ESSENTIALIST CLASS ACTIVITY

Mr. Jackson's second graders had just learned to count money. He decided to let them play several games of "musical envelopes." There was one envelope per student, each containing a different amount of paper "nickels," "dimes," "quarters," and "pennies." When the music stopped, students had to count the money in their envelopes. The one with the most money for each game got a special prize.[1]

In this essentialist class activity, the nature of the learner is *passive*, the nature of the subject matter is *structured*, the use of the subject matter is *cognitive*, and the thinking approach is *convergent*.

essentialism
An educational theory that holds that there is a common core of information and skills that an educated person must have; schools should be organized to transmit this core of essential material.

Essentialist teaching methods require formal discipline through emphasis on required reading, lectures, memorization, repetition, and examination.

laboratories, audiovisual materials, and nature study. Habits of intellectual discipline are considered ends in themselves.

Essentialism envisions subject matter as the core of education. Severe criticism has been leveled at U.S. education by essentialists who advocate an emphasis on basic education. Essentialism assigns to the schools the task of conserving the heritage and transmitting knowledge of the physical world. In a sense, the school is a curator of knowledge.

With the burgeoning of new knowledge in contemporary society, essentialism may be contributing to the slowness of educational change. In this context, essentialism has been criticized as obsolete in its authoritarian tendencies. Such criticism implies that essentialism does not satisfy the twenty-first-century needs of U.S. youth. Essentialist educators deny this criticism and claim to have incorporated modern influences in the system while maintaining academic standards.

CROSS-REFERENCE

For more about the essentialist curriculum see Chapters 11 and 12.

Education makes a people easy to lead, but difficult to drive, easy to govern, but impossible to enslave.

Franklin Delano Roosevelt

ESSENTIAL SCHOOLS MOVEMENT

The Essential Schools movement is a contemporary school reform effort developed by Dr. Theodore Sizer. Sizer contends that students need to master a common core of information and skills, and he encourages schools to strip away the nonessentials and focus on having students "use their minds well." The Essential Schools movement does not specify what content is essential in a given culture at a given time. Rather, "essential schools" are required to analyze clearly what this core of information should be and to change the curriculum to emphasize this core.

The Coalition of Essential Schools (www.essentialschools.org) promotes a vision of schooling in which students engage in in-depth and rigorous learning. Essential schools select a small number of core skills and areas of knowledge that they expect all students to demonstrate and exercise broadly across content areas. Ten common principles have been developed by Dr. Sizer in collaboration with essential school participants to guide the efforts of the coalition. These principles include using the mind well; a focus on clear, essential learning goals; an attempt to apply these goals to all students; personalized teaching and learning; emphasis on student-as-worker; student performance on real tasks with multiple forms of evidence; values of un-anxious expectation; principal and teachers as generalists first and specialists second; budgets that do not exceed traditional schools by more than 10 percent; and nondiscriminatory policies and practices.

behaviorism

A psychological theory that asserts that behaviors represent the essence of a person and that all behaviors can be explained as responses to stimuli.

Behaviorism

B. F. Skinner (1904–1990), the Harvard experimental psychologist and philosopher, is the recognized leader of the movement known as **behaviorism.** Skinner verified Pavlov's stimulus-response theory with animals and, from his research, suggested that human behavior could also be explained as responses to external stimuli. (See the Behaviorist Class Activity.) Because of its focus on the careful examination of environment, behaviors, and responses, behaviorism is closely linked to realism.

BEHAVIORIST CLASS ACTIVITY

Students in Mr. Drucker's civics class were given merit tokens for coming into the room quietly, sitting at their desks, preparing notebooks and pencils for the day's lesson, and being ready to begin answering comprehension questions in their workbooks. On Fridays students were allowed to use their tokens at an auction to buy items that Mr. Drucker knew they wanted. Sometimes, however, students had to save tokens for more than two weeks to buy what they liked best.

In this behaviorist class activity, the nature of the learner is *passive*, the nature of the subject matter is *amorphous* (unstructured), the use of the subject matter is *affective* (having to do with feelings) or *cognitive*, and the thinking approach is *convergent*.

Other behaviorists' research expanded on Skinner's work in illustrating the effect of the environment, particularly the interpersonal environment, on shaping individual behavior.

BEHAVIORIST FOCUS OF LEARNING

Behaviorism is a psychological and educational theory that holds that one's behavior is determined by environment, not heredity. This suggests that education can contribute significantly to the shaping of the individual because the teacher can control the stimuli in a classroom and thereby influence student behavior. Behaviorists believe that the school environment must be highly organized and the curriculum based on behavioral objectives, and they hold that knowledge is best described as behaviors that are observable. They contend that empirical evidence is essential if students are to learn and that students must employ the scientific method to arrive at knowledge. The task of education is to develop learning environments that lead to desired behaviors in students.

A teacher affects eternity; he can never tell where his influence stops.

Henry Adams

REINFORCEMENT: A BEHAVIORIST PRACTICE

The concept of reinforcement is critical to teacher practices in behaviorism. The behaviorist teacher endeavors to foster desired behaviors by using both positive reinforcers (things students like, such as praise, privileges, and good grades) and negative reinforcers (things students wish to avoid, such as reprimands, extra homework, and lower grades). The theory is that behavior that is not reinforced (whether positively or negatively) will eventually be "extinguished"—will cease to occur. In general, behaviorists contend that learning takes place when approved behavior is observed and then positively reinforced.

A teacher may provide nonverbal positive reinforcement (smiling, nodding approval) or negative reinforcement (frowning, shaking the head in disapproval). Similarly, nondirective statements, questions, and directive statements may be positive or negative. Both children and adults respond to the models other people (peers, adults, heroes) represent to them by imitating the model behavior. Behaviorists contend that students tend to emulate behaviors that are rewarded.

The behaviorists have supplied a wealth of empirical research that bears on the problems of attaining self-control, resisting temptation, and showing concern for others. Behaviorists do not attempt to learn about the causes of students' earlier problems. Rather, the teacher must ascertain what is happening in the classroom environment to perpetuate or extinguish students' behavior.

Positivism

The educational theory of positivism stems from what the social scientist Auguste Comte (1798–1857) described as "positive knowledge." Comte divided the thinking

Positivism focuses learning on acquisition of facts based on careful, empirical observation and measurement of the world.

of humankind into three historical periods, each of which was characterized by a distinct way of thinking. The first was the theological era, in which people explained things by reference to spirits and gods. The second was the metaphysical era, in which people explained phenomena in terms of causes, essences, and inner principles. The third was the positive period, in which thinkers did not attempt to go beyond observable, measurable fact.

The positivist position rejects essences, intuition, and inner causes that cannot be measured. Empirical verification is central to all proper thinking. This theory rejects beliefs about mind, spirit, and consciousness and holds that all reality can be explained by laws of matter and motion. In sum, **positivism** limits knowledge to statements of observable fact based on sense perceptions and the investigation of objective reality. Positivism became a rallying point for a group of scholars in Vienna. Because the group consisted largely of scientists, mathematicians, and symbolic logicians, positivism became known as logical positivism.

POSITIVIST FOCUS OF LEARNING

Practiced as an educational theory, positivism focuses learning on the acquisition of facts based on careful empirical observation and measurement of the world. Positivism requires schools to develop content standards that represent the best understandings of experts who have already uncovered important ideas based on their own observation and measurement. Students are encouraged both to master these expert understandings and to develop their own skills of observation, classification, and logical analysis.

OBJECTIVE FORCED-CHOICE TESTING: A POSITIVIST REQUIREMENT

Testing students' acquisition of content standards is a valued activity for the positivist educator. Creating objective tests that are free from bias is critical to education. Because empirical knowledge is proven by years of careful analysis, there is a set of truths that students should master and understand according to a clear set of criteria. The only way to ensure that such knowledge has been attained and understood is to test all students according to the same objective set of criteria. (See the Positivist Class Activity.)

DIRECT INSTRUCTION: A POSITIVIST APPROACH TO TEACHING AND LEARNING

Direct instruction is a teaching and learning approach that requires teachers to clearly and precisely identify and state what a student needs to learn and master, as well

What we have to learn to do, we learn by doing.

Aristotle

positivism

A social theory that limits truth and knowledge to what is observable and measurable.

POSITIVIST CLASS ACTIVITY

Humberto Diaz introduced the meaning of surface tension to his junior high science students. During class he then distributed eyedroppers, water, and pennies to the students. He directed the students to determine how many drops of water could fit on the surface of the penny before spilling over. Students were to collect data and develop a data table and corresponding charts. At the end of the class, Mr. Diaz asked the students to discuss their findings and draw a conclusion.

In this positivist class activity, the nature of the learner is *active,* the nature of the subject matter is *structured,* the use of the subject matter is *cognitive,* and the thinking approach is *convergent.*

as to restate this expectation through different media and assignments. It is a teaching and learning approach that places the responsibility for clear, precise expectations on the teacher. Once a teacher has identified precisely what students should know and be able to do, the teacher is expected to clearly describe to students exactly what they should know and be able to do. Teachers are encouraged to use repetition and have students practice and practice again, recite and recite again, what is to be learned. Teachers are further encouraged to have students repeat the main ideas of the instruction by using different media: oral recitation, writing, restating, drawing, and so forth. The key ingredient for this approach is the use of clear, uncluttered statements and restatements about the focus of learning.

This approach to teaching and learning fits the positivist educational theory because in such an educational approach knowledge is considered something that is clear and precise. If all knowledge is clear, precise, and the same for all, then teachers can be expected to require all students to learn the same knowledge. Direct instruction is possible because all knowledge that is worthy is also clear and precise.

Journal for Reflection

Consider the different teacher-centered educational philosophies and recall a teacher you know who seems to follow one of these educational philosophies. Describe the ways that the teacher's actions represent the teacher-centered locus of control educational philosophy.

Student-Centered Locus-of-Control Educational Theories

Progressivism, humanism, and constructivism espouse a student-centered authority approach to subject matter, classroom organization, teaching methods, and assessment. Although each educational philosophy forms a distinct cohesive whole, all three are rooted in an internal locus-of-control principle, that is, the belief that truth and goodness belong to all persons no matter what their station. Teachers are learners and learners are teachers, and education is the process through which individuals help one another to clarify personal meaning.

As with the teacher-centered positions, we will present each student-centered locus-of-control theory's ideas on curriculum, teaching, and learning. In addition, for each theory we will describe a representative program along with an illustrative class activity. The class activity is further analyzed according to the nature of the learner (active or passive), the nature of the subject matter, the use of the subject matter, and the type of thinking that is emphasized (convergent—focused on right answers, or divergent—focused on developing multiple perspectives).

Progressivism, the educational theory developed by philosopher John Dewey (1859–1952), emphasizes that ideas should be tested by experimentation and that learning is rooted in questions developed by the learners.

Progressivism

In the late 1800s, with the rise of democracy, the expansion of modern science and technology, and the need for people to be able to adjust to change, people in Western societies had to have a new and different approach to acquiring knowledge in order to solve problems. A U.S. philosopher, Charles S. Peirce (1839–1914), founded the philosophical system called *pragmatism*. This philosophy held that the meaning and value of ideas could be found only in the practical results of these ideas. Later, William James (1842–1910) extended Peirce's theory of meaning into a theory of truth. James asserted that the satisfactory working of an idea constitutes its whole truth. Pragmatism was carried much further by John Dewey (1859–1952), who was a widely known and influential philosopher and educator. Dewey insisted that ideas must always be tested by experiment. His emphasis on experiment carried over into his educational philosophy, which became the basis for what was usually described as progressive education. **Progressivism** is an educational theory that emphasizes that ideas should be tested by experimentation and that learning is rooted in questions developed by learners.[2]

progressivism

An educational theory that emphasizes that ideas should be tested by experimentation and that learning is rooted in questions developed by the learner.

The one real object of
education is to have a
man in the condition of
continually asking
questions.

**Bishop Mandell
Creighton**

From its establishment in the mid-1920s through the mid-1950s, progressivism
was the most influential educational view in the United States. Progressivists basi-
cally oppose authoritarianism and favor human experience as a basis for knowledge. Progressivism favors the scientific method of teaching and learning, allows for
the beliefs of individuals, and stresses programs of student involvement that help
students learn how to think. Progressivists believe that the school should actively
prepare its students for change. Progressive schools emphasize learning *how* to
think rather than *what* to think. Flexibility is important in the curriculum design,
and the emphasis is on *experimentation,* with no single body of content stressed
more than any other. This approach encourages *divergent thinking*—moving beyond conventional ideas to come up with novel interpretations or solutions. And
because life experience determines curriculum content, all types of content must be
permitted. Certain subjects regarded as traditional are recognized as desirable for
study as well. Progressivist educators would organize scientific method-oriented
learning activities around the traditional subjects. Such a curriculum is called
experience-centered or student-centered; the essentialist and positivist curricula are
considered subject-centered. Experience-centered curricula stress the *process* of
learning rather than the result.

Progressivism as a contemporary teaching style emphasizes the process of education in the classroom. It is more compatible with a core of problem areas across
all academic disciplines than with a subject-centered approach to problem solving.
It would be naive to suggest that memorization and rote practice should be ruled
out. In progressive teaching, however, they are not stressed as primary learning techniques. The assertion is that interest in an intellectual activity will generate all the
practice needed for learning. (See the Progressivist Class Activity.)

PROGRESSIVISM AND DEMOCRACY

A tenet of progressivism is that the school, to become an important social institution, must take on the task of improving society. To this end, progressivism is
deemed a working model of democracy. Freedom is explicit in a democracy, so it
must be explicit in schools. But freedom, rather than being a haphazard expression
of free will, must be organized to have meaning. Organized freedom permits each
member of the school society to take part in decisions, and all must share their
experiences to ensure that the decisions are meaningful. Pupil–teacher planning is

---

PROGRESSIVIST CLASS ACTIVITY

Mr. Brandese Powell asked his second graders to look at a cartoon that pictured a
well-dressed man and woman in an automobile pulled by a team of two horses.
The highway they were traveling along passed through rolling farmland with un-
crowded meadows, trees, and clear skies in the background. He led a discussion
based on the following questions:

1. What is happening in this picture?
2. Do you like what is happening in the picture? Why or why not?
3. What does it say about the way you may be living when you grow up?
4. Are you happy or unhappy about what you have described for your life as an
   adult?
5. How can we get people to use less gasoline now?
6. What if we could keep companies from making and selling cars that could not
   travel at least forty miles on one gallon of gasoline?

In this progressivist class activity, the nature of the learner is *active,* the nature
of the subject matter is *structured,* the use of the subject matter is *cognitive,* and
the thinking approach is *divergent.*

---

the key to democracy in classrooms and is the process that gives some freedom to students, as well as teachers, in decisions about what is studied. For example, the teacher might ask students to watch a film about an issue of interest and have them list questions about the issue that were not answered by the film but that they would like to investigate. Students and the teacher can then analyze the questions and refine them for research. Such questions can become the basis for an inquiry and problem-solving unit of study.

Progressivism views the learner as an experiencing, thinking, exploring individual. Its goal is to expose the learner to the subject matter of social experiences, social studies, projects, problems, and experiments that, when studied by the scientific method, will result in functional knowledge from all subjects. Progressivists regard books as tools to be used in learning rather than as sources of indisputable knowledge.

CRITICAL PEDAGOGY: A PROGRESSIVIST CURRICULUM

Many people believe that the socialization aspect of progressivism—the fact that it represents the leading edge of society and helps students learn how to manage change—is its most valuable aspect. However, progressivism is criticized for placing so much stress on the processes of education that the ends are neglected. Its severest critics contend that progressive educators have little personal commitment to anything, producing many graduates who are uncommitted and who are content to drift through life. Progressivists counter by stating that their educational view requires that students be taught to analyze world events, explore controversial issues, and develop a vision for a new and better world. Teachers would critically examine cultural heritages, explore controversial issues, provide a vision for a new and better world, and enlist students' efforts to promote programs of cultural renewal. Although teachers would attempt to convince students of the validity of such democratic goals, they would employ democratic procedures in doing so.

A contemporary version of progressivism is rooted in the work of Henry Giroux, who views schools as vehicles for social change. He calls teachers to be transformative intellectuals and wants them to participate in creating a new society. Schools should practice "critical pedagogy," which unites theory and practice as it provides students with the critical thinking tools to be change agents.[3]

CROSS-REFERENCE
For more about critical pedagogy see Chapter 14.

humanism

An educational theory that contends that humans are innately good—that they are born free but become enslaved by institutions.

Humanism

Humanism is an educational approach that is rooted both in the writings of Jean-Jacques Rousseau and in the ideas of existentialism. Rousseau (1712–1778), the father of romanticism, believed that the child entered the world not as a blank slate but with certain innate qualities and tendencies. In the opening sentence of *Émile*, Rousseau's famous treatise on education, he states that "God makes all things good; man meddles with them and they become evil."[4] Thus, Rousseau believed in basic goodness at birth. He also believed that humans are born free but become enslaved by institutions. Humanistic education mingles some of these ideas from Rousseau with the basic ideas of existentialism.

Humanistic educational theory is concerned with enhancing the innate goodness of the individual. It rejects a group-oriented educational system and seeks ways to enhance the individual development of the student. (See the Humanist Class Activity.)

Humanists believe that most schools de-emphasize the individual and the relationship between the teacher and the student. Humanists claim that as educators attempt to predict behavior of students, they turn individuals into objects to be measured. According to the humanist, education should be a process of developing

Jean-Jacques Rousseau (1712–1778) is the father of romanticism and believed that humans are born free but become enslaved by the structures of society.

Ms. Fenway wanted her ninth graders to think about the effectiveness of television and radio advertising. She asked students to write down any five slogans or jingles they could remember and the products advertised. Ms. Fenway selected from their items at random and tested the class. For each slogan, class members had to identify the product advertised. The test was corrected in class by the students, who were very surprised to find the grading scale reversed. Those who had all correct answers received Fs, and those who had only one correct answer received As. When asked why she'd reversed the grades, Ms. Fenway responded, "Why do you think advertising is so effective?" She asked whether students resented some companies' selling tactics. Then she and the class made a list of questions to ask themselves in order to avoid spending money in ways they might later regret. She also asked for specific examples of spending money for items they later wished they hadn't bought.[5]

In this humanist class activity, the nature of the learner is *active,* the nature of the subject matter is *structured,* the use of the subject matter is *affective,* and the thinking approach is *divergent.*

---

a free, self-actualizing person—a process that is centered on the student's feelings. Therefore, education should not start with great ideas, the world, or humankind, but with the individual self.

HUMANISTIC CURRICULUM

Because the goal of humanism is a completely autonomous person, education should be without coercion or prescription. Students should be active and should be encouraged to make their own choices. The teacher who follows humanistic theory emphasizes instruction and assessment based on student interests, abilities, and needs. Students determine the rules that will govern classroom life, and they make choices about the books to read or exercises to complete.

Humanists honor divergent thinking so completely that they delay giving their own personal opinions and do not attempt to persuade students to particular points of view. Even though they emphasize the affective and thereby may make students feel a certain urgency about issues, it is always left to the individual student to decide when to take a stand, what kind of stand to take, whether a cause merits action, and, if so, what kind of action to engage in.

HUMANISTIC SCHOOL ENVIRONMENTS

Martin Buber's writings describe the heart of humanistic school environments. In *I and Thou,* Buber portrays two different ways in which individuals relate to the outside world. In the I–It relationship, one views something outside oneself in a purely objective manner, as a thing to be used and manipulated for selfish ends. In contrast, I–Thou relationships are characterized by viewing other people as sacred entities who deserve profound respect. Such relationships focus on the importance of understanding and respecting diverse, subjective, personal meanings. Buber was deeply concerned that people were treated as objects (Its) rather than as Thous, especially in business, science, government, and education.[6]

Many students today believe that educators treat them as Social Security numbers stored in a computer. In college classes of 100 or more, it is difficult for teachers to remember students' names, let alone get to know them as individuals. Often teachers assign material, mark papers, and give grades without ever really conversing

Humanists believe that education should be without coercion or prescription and that students should be active learners and make their own choices.

with students. When the semester ends, students leave class and are replaced by other, equally anonymous students. Buber did not believe that schools had to be this way. He contended that in a proper relationship between teacher and student, there is a mutual sensibility of feeling. There is empathy, not a subject–object relationship.

A humanistic school environment is one in which people (both teacher and student) share their thoughts, feelings, beliefs, fears, and aspirations with one another. Nel Noddings labels this *an environment of caring*. According to humanists, this kind of caring relationship should pervade the educational process at all levels as well as society at large.

Inspired by humanism, many educators attempt to personalize education in less radical ways. Examples include individualizing instruction, open-access curriculum, nongraded instruction, and multi-age grouping. Each of these approaches attends to the uniqueness of the learner. Block scheduling permits flexibility for students to arrange classes of their choice. Free schools, storefront schools, schools without walls, and area vocational centers provide humanistic alternatives to traditional school environments.

Educational programs that address the needs of the individual are usually more costly per pupil than traditional group-centered programs. Consequently, as taxpayer demands for accountability mount, humanistic individualized programs are often brought under unit-cost scrutiny. Nonetheless, growing numbers of educators are willing to defend increased expenditures to meet the needs of the individual learner within the instructional programs of the schools.

Constructivism

Constructivism is an educational theory that emphasizes hands-on, activity-based teaching and learning. Constructivism is closely associated with existentialism. The American Psychological Association (APA) has encouraged teachers to reconsider the manner in which they view teaching. The APA contends that students are active learners who should be given opportunities to construct their own frames of thought. Teaching techniques should include a variety of different learning activities during which students are free to infer and discover their own answers to important questions. Teachers need to spend time creating these learning situations rather than lecturing. Constructivist educators consider true learning to be the active framing of personal meaning (by the learner) rather than the framing of someone else's meaning (the teacher's).

Such a view of teaching and learning has profound ramifications for the school curriculum. If students are to be encouraged to answer their own questions and develop their own thinking frame, the curriculum needs to be reconceptualized. Constructivist theorists encourage the development of critical thinking and the understanding of big ideas rather than the mastery of factual information. They contend that students who have a sound understanding of important principles that were developed through their own critical thinking will be better prepared for the complex, technological world.

CONSTRUCTIVIST CURRICULUM

Constructivist ideas about curriculum stand in sharp contrast to the authoritarian approaches we described earlier. Traditionally, learning has been thought of as a mimic activity, a process that involves students repeating newly presented information. Constructivism, on the other hand, focuses on the personalized way a learner internalizes, shapes, or transforms information. Learning occurs through the construction of new, personalized understanding that results from the emergence of new cognitive structures. Teachers and parents can invite such transformed understandings, but neither can mandate them.

Accepting this simple proposition—that students learn by shaping their own understandings about their world—makes the present structure of the school

Few high school students look upon the language which they speak and write as an art, not merely a tool, yet it ought to be, the noblest of all arts, looked upon with respect, even with reverence, and used always with care, courtesy, and deepest respect.

Mary Ellen Chase

CROSS-REFERENCE
For more about the constructivist curriculum see Chapters 11 and 12.

constructivism

An educational theory that emphasizes hands-on, activity-based teaching and learning during which students develop their own frames of thought.

Should I Use Homogeneous or Heterogeneous Ability Grouping?

The issue of how to group students for instruction can be very controversial. Some propose homogeneous grouping and others argue for heterogeneous grouping. Homogeneous ability grouping is a practice that seems to have merit. Permitting students who require the same level of instruction to be clustered in a single setting makes planning and resource allocation much easier. Such grouping patterns permit students to receive instruction that is tied to their specific needs, because they are with others who need the same information or skill development.

Those who oppose homogeneous ability grouping contend that labeling students and placing them in similar ability groups based on their academic skill sets up structures that often inhibit future growth and development. Both teachers and parents begin to view students according to these labels; once tracked by ability, students seldom break out of the initial labels assigned at an early age. These critics call for multiability or heterogeneous grouping. They believe that having students from a variety of backgrounds and ability levels work together is more in keeping with a democratic society. Furthermore, such multiability grouping permits students to help one another, fostering cooperativeness and caring among those from different backgrounds. Indeed, opponents of tracking programs have pointed to the disproportionate number of minority and low-income students who seem to make up the lower-level groups.

Questions for Reflection

1. List other pros and cons of homogeneous ability grouping that you can think of. List other pros and cons of heterogeneous ability grouping.

2. Should one type of grouping be used in all instructional settings or circumstances, or should the types of grouping be varied according to task and context?

To answer these questions on-line and e-mail your answers to your professor, go to Chapter 10 of the companion website (**www.ablongman.com/johnson14e**) and click on Professional Dilemma.

---

problematic. According to constructivist principles, educators should invite students to experience the world's richness and empower them to ask their own questions and seek their own answers. The constructivist teacher proposes situations that encourage students to think. Rather than leading students toward a particular answer, the constructivist teacher allows students to develop their own ideas and chart their own pathways. But schools infrequently operate in such a constructivist way. Typically, schools determine what students will learn and when they will learn it.

PROBLEM-BASED LEARNING: A CONSTRUCTIVIST PEDAGOGY

Problem-based learning has recently emerged as a student-centered teaching and learning approach that is in keeping with constructivist tenets. Based on Dewey's concept of teaching through student-centered problems, this educational methodology centers student activities on tackling authentic contemporary problems. Problem-based learning is a radical approach in that it challenges educators to focus curriculum on student interests and concerns rather than on content coverage. (See the Constructivist Class Activity.)

In a problem-based experience, students are presented with a "hook." The hook might be a letter from a civic group, a request from an environmental agency, or any other motivating beginning. The hook describes a contemporary dilemma and requests students to take on some real-life role to solve the problem. Problem-based learning usually

Journal for Reflection

Choose and write down a metaphor for each of the educational philosophies you have studied so far. For example, "constructivism is a shared voyage into new and uncharted territory." Then design a metaphor for your personal educational philosophy and clarify how it compares to the other metaphors.

CONSTRUCTIVIST CLASS ACTIVITY

Reiko Nishioka's sophomore biology class had just completed reading Michael Crichton's novel *Jurassic Park* when a letter from movie producer Steven Spielberg arrived addressed to each student in the class. The letter requested each student's assistance in Spielberg's effort to determine what aspects of the novel were or were not scientifically accurate with regard to dinosaurs. The letter asked students to prepare a written summary and to send the summary, along with proper documentation, to Spielberg's production company. Because time was limited, Spielberg requested that the summaries be completed within three weeks. Reiko provided time for her students to think about the letter and then asked them to determine what they would do next.

In this constructivist class activity, the nature of the learner is *active,* the nature of the subject matter is *unstructured,* the use of the subject matter is *authentic* to real life, and the thinking approach is *divergent.*

Constructivist educators invite students to experience the world's richness and empower them to ask their own questions and seek their own answers. Problem-based learning is an example of constructivist pedagogy.

requires students to spend time finding the core problem, clarifying the problem, assessing what is and is not known about the problem, gathering needed data to complement what has been uncovered, and finally presenting a position statement and/or suggesting a solution. Throughout the process, teachers act as guides or coaches and give great latitude to student interest. Students learn content and skills within the problem context. Teachers spend time selecting problems that are compatible with student maturity levels and curricular needs.

Developing Your Own Philosophy of Education

This section helps you to clarify your role as a teacher in society and identify effective classroom practices. It offers a number of big ideas or key concepts that will challenge your image of what constitutes a good teacher. Ideas such as classroom environment or climate, voice and space, community of learners, and teacher as leader are presented to help you clarify your own approach to education. Which type of environment is best for today's students? How much teacher control is needed? Whose voices are predominant and whose voices are muted in today's classrooms? These questions are examined and shown to be important to the development of a classroom climate that is either open and authentic or directed and didactic.

As you examine and refine your own philosophy of education, it is helpful to review how the six different educational philosophies relate to the contemporary classroom. Figure 10.1 summarizes how teacher-centered locus-of-control philosophies versus student-centered locus-of-control philosophies affect classroom organization, motivation, discipline, classroom climate, learning focus, teaching styles and leadership styles. You may find that this chart quickly provides you a starting point for the clarification of your personal philosophy of education.

FIGURE 10.1

Teacher-Centered Locus-of-Control versus Student-Centered Locus-of-Control Classroom Approaches

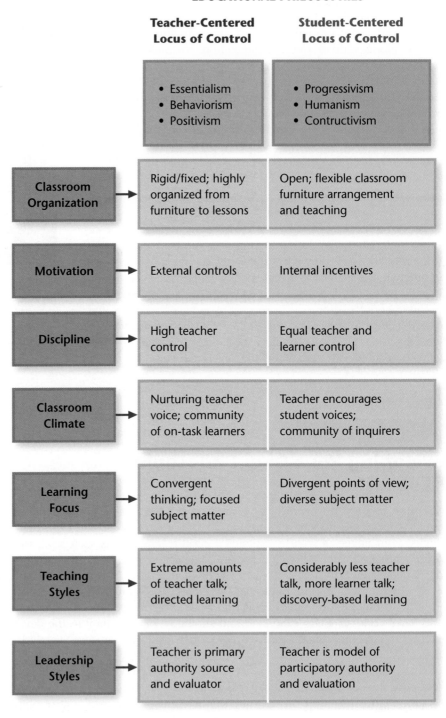

EDUCATIONAL PHILOSOPHIES

	Teacher-Centered Locus of Control	Student-Centered Locus of Control
	• Essentialism • Behaviorism • Positivism	• Progressivism • Humanism • Contructivism
Classroom Organization	Rigid/fixed; highly organized from furniture to lessons	Open; flexible classroom furniture arrangement and teaching
Motivation	External controls	Internal incentives
Discipline	High teacher control	Equal teacher and learner control
Classroom Climate	Nurturing teacher voice; community of on-task learners	Teacher encourages student voices; community of inquirers
Learning Focus	Convergent thinking; focused subject matter	Divergent points of view; diverse subject matter
Teaching Styles	Extreme amounts of teacher talk; directed learning	Considerably less teacher talk, more learner talk; discovery-based learning
Leadership Styles	Teacher is primary authority source and evaluator	Teacher is model of participatory authority and evaluation

Classroom Organization

All teachers must be able to organize the classroom in such a way that it is conducive to teaching and learning. In fact, many school principals are quick to assert that the easiest way to predict the success of a beginning teacher is to evaluate his or her ability to organize the classroom. A common misconception is that good classroom organization means maintaining a controlled atmosphere and refusing to allow any behavior that even looks ungoverned or unplanned. Actually, **classroom organization** is a multifaceted dimension of teaching that includes the content, methods, and values that infuse the classroom environment. It is a dimension of teaching that requires analysis and selection similar to that used in the identification of a preferred teaching philosophy. Figure 10.1 shows how closely one's teaching philosophy affects the different components of classroom organization.

A teacher's practices in the classroom reflect his or her personal philosophy.

LESSON PLANNING

Careful lesson planning is mandatory if effective teaching and learning are to follow. If the learners are considered to be passive, the lesson plan might emphasize students' absorption of the factual content of the subject matter. Adherents of teaching styles that consider the learners to be active participants (student-centered locus-of-control) would tend to emphasize processes and skills to be mastered and view the factual content of the subject matter as important but variable.

Regardless of the expectation for the learner, active or passive, the teacher needs to plan sound lessons. Every lesson should be built from a basic set of general objectives that correspond to the overall goals of the school district. This is not to suggest that every third-grade classroom in a school district should have the same daily learning objectives for the students. Daily lesson objectives can vary from classroom to classroom depending on the particular needs of the students being served. However, if those daily teaching objectives are closely related to the overall objectives of the school district, then cross-district learning will reflect the school district's overall goals.

Lessons should be tied to some form of teaching units. These units should be planned in detail to include suggestions for teaching the lessons, types of materials to be used, and specific plans for evaluation. Initially, these are all philosophical questions for the classroom teacher. The way the teacher approaches these questions says a lot about his or her classroom philosophy.

THE PHYSICAL SETTING

The mere arrangement of classroom furniture and the use of classroom materials may be predicated on the teacher's perception of the learners as passive or active. Traditionally, the classroom has tended to be arranged in rows and columns at the elementary and secondary levels of schooling. This type of classroom arrangement has often been thought to be the best for classroom control and supervision. Often, however, the elementary teacher will rearrange the classroom into a series of small circles for special groupings in reading, mathematics, and other specific subjects.

Student-centered locus-of-control theories tend to support more open classrooms. The teacher intends learning for the students to be divergent in nature, and

classroom organization

A multifaceted dimension of teaching that includes the content, method, and values that infuse the classroom environment, planning, and discipline practices.

We not only want students to achieve, we want them to value the process of learning and the improvement of their skills, we want them to willingly put forth the necessary effort to develop and apply their skills and knowledge, and we want them to develop a long-term commitment to their learning.

Carole A. Ames

CROSS-REFERENCE

For more about student assessment and evaluation see Chapter 12.

the student is expected to be more active in the learning process. This is not to suggest that one type of classroom arrangement is better than another or that one theory is superior to another, but we do suggest that the teacher in training examine classroom theory as it relates to the physical environment for learning.

STUDENT ASSESSMENT AND EVALUATION

In assessing student progress and assigning grades, most teachers use a variety of techniques including examinations, term papers, project reports, group discussions, performance assessments, and various other tools. If the subject matter is treated as a bundle of information, teacher-made tests will tend to seek certain facts and concepts as "right" answers, suggesting emphasis on convergent thinking. However, if the subject matter is treated as big ideas that are applicable to problem solving, and if students are expected to engage in processes and develop skills to arrive at several "right" answers, teacher-made tests will tend to allow for divergent thinking.

How you develop your classroom philosophy will also dictate the emphasis you place on a student's academic performance. You must decide whether a student is to be compared with his or her peers or with a set of expectations based on individual needs and differences. Generally, teachers who support student-centered authority and look for divergence in learning will tend to place less emphasis on group norms. Teachers who favor teacher-centered authority for the classroom with a stress on convergence in learning will be more apt to favor student evaluation strategies that are based on group norms.

Motivation

motivation

Internal emotion, desire, or impulse acting as an incitement to action.

The concept of **motivation** is derived from the word *motive,* which means an emotion, desire, or impulse acting as an incitement to action. This definition of motive has two parts: First, the definition implies that motivation is internal because it relates to emotions, desires, or other internal drives; second, it implies that there is an accompanying external focus on action or behavior. Organizing a learning environment so that it relates to student needs and desires (internal) and also permits active participation in the learning process (external) is important to student motivation.

Teachers want students to be motivated to do many things: complete homework, be responsible, be lifelong learners, be on time, have fun, care about others, become independent. However, it is not always clear how one sets up a classroom environment that ultimately promotes these desired outcomes. For example, in a teacher-dominant orientation, control is primarily in the hands of the teacher. In such an authoritarian setting, motivation tends to come in the form of rules and regulations. Students are given clear directions concerning their responsibilities; and they are expected to follow these directions because the teacher is in charge. For some students, this clarity of expectations and rules is comfortable. Students achieve because they must; in such a setting, the second half of motivation (external action) is achieved, but not the first (internal desire).

The physical setting of the classroom tends to reflect whether the teacher follows a directive or nondirective theory of education.

Relevant Research

Can Children Philosophize?

STUDY PURPOSE/QUESTION: Philosophy for Children is an instructional program developed by Mathew Lipman and Ann Sharp more than 30 years ago. The instructional program is designed to help students think critically about the world. Students are provided novelettes about fundamental philosophical controversies. They discuss these stories, use logical reasoning and judgment, and enter into meaningful dialogue about moral issues. This study was designed to investigate whether the use of newly created stories that incorporate specific notions of non-violence into the discussions have an impact on moral autonomy, judgment, empathy, and emotion-recognition of five-year-old children.

STUDY DESIGN: This was an experimental study involving 39 kindergarten children in three schools in Montreal, Canada. All 39 children participated in a philosophy-for-children session once a week. Experienced teachers directed the hour-long sessions that included the reading of an episode of a novel (read by the teacher), followed by questions suggested by the children for discussion. The control group consisted of 42 children in kindergarten classes in the same 3 schools. These children were similar to children in the experimental group and were subjected to the same curriculum (other than the philosophy for children sessions). Four tests focusing on moral autonomy, judgment, empathy, and the recognition of emotion were administered in October as pretests and then again in April of the next year as posttests to all children in both the experimental and control groups in the three schools. In the moral autonomy test, children were presented with a number of moral dilemmas and choose what to do. In the judgment tests, children were asked to consider like and unlike situations and relationships. In the empathy measure, a problem is posed regarding whether to buy a dog for a friend whose dog had recently died. In the emotion-recognition measure, two

short story vignettes are presented for each of four emotions. After each vignette children are asked to tell how the child in the story feels. The experimental and control group scores were analyzed via an analysis of variance to determine if either of the two groups displayed significantly different results.

STUDY FINDINGS: The analysis of variance for moral autonomy and emotion recognition revealed that both the experimental and control group showed significant progress from the pretest to the posttest. However, there was no significant difference between the progress of the experimental and control groups on these measures. The analysis of variance for empathy also revealed significant progress over time for both groups of students, but in this test the experimental group displayed significantly greater improvement than the control group. As for children's judgment, both experimental and control groups showed a highly significant change over time. With regard to judgment as it relates to violence, children in the experimental group improved significantly more than children in the control group.

IMPLICATIONS: This study indicates that the use of philosophy-for-children readings and discussion enhance the natural development of children's empathy and judgment. Additionally, the study shows that children's natural development in all four areas of moral autonomy, emotion recognition, empathy, and judgment are not harmed by philosophical discussions and readings. However, given the small size of the sample and the short duration of the study, more studies are needed.

Source: Michael Schleifer, Marie-France Daniel, Emmanuelle Peyronnet, and Sarah LeComte, "The Impact of Philosophical Discussion on Moral Autonomy, Judgment, Empathy and the Recognition of Emotion in Five-Year Olds," *The Journal of Philosophy for Children, 16*(4), pp. 4–12.

The reason students' internal motivation may suffer is that they recognize that both the task of teaching and the responsibility for their learning belong primarily to the teacher.

In a learner-dominant setting, the responsibility for learning is primarily borne by the students. The teacher attempts to produce a climate of warmth and mutual respect. Students are encouraged to achieve specific outcomes, but ultimately, they are free to select those that most interest them. In this type of setting, the first aspect of motivation (internal desire) is achieved, in that students select the learning

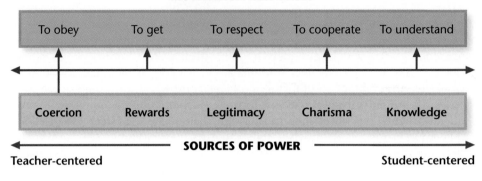

FIGURE 10.2

Sources of Power and Types of Motivation Responses

MOTIVATION RESPONSES

| To obey | To get | To respect | To cooperate | To understand |

| Coercion | Rewards | Legitimacy | Charisma | Knowledge |

SOURCES OF POWER

Teacher-centered   Student-centered

Journal for Reflection

Think about the different student seating arrangements in various classrooms. Sketch each seating arrangement and describe the types of student interaction and the types of learning that each seating arrangement supports. Draw the seating arrangement that you prefer, and describe the types of student interaction and learning that it encourages.

In every real man a child is hidden that wants to play.

Friedrich Nietzsche

outcomes and processes that interest them; however, the second aspect of motivation (external action) is not as clearly achieved, in that students act according to their personal desires and these desires do not always match those of the teacher.

As a teacher, you should arrange the classroom environment so that it matches your personal philosophy. Your task here is to consider carefully the "sources of power" that best reflect your philosophy of education. Figure 10.2 illustrates as many as five different power sources that relate to five different levels of motivation.[7] Power can be coercive when the motivation is "to obey." Power can take the form of rewards when the motivation is "to get." Power can be seen as legitimate when motivation is "to respect." Power can be in the form of charisma when the motivation is "to cooperate." Finally, power can be knowledge when the motivation is "to understand." Your philosophy of teaching could include all of these sources of power. All of them might be necessary at one time or another. On the other hand, it is important to assess how you set up your classroom rules and environment and make certain that they match your personal understanding of where power should lie in the teaching and learning process.

Discipline

The attention given by the national media to disruptive behavior in the classroom has rekindled conflicting views regarding discipline. Polls of parents and teachers alike list discipline among the top issues confronting the schools. The main source of dissatisfaction for nearly two-thirds of today's teachers is their inability to manage students effectively. Teachers also are concerned about the effect disruptive behavior has on learning. The discipline dilemma—how to achieve *more* teacher control in the classroom while adhering to a more open philosophy that advocates *less* teacher control—precludes the development of a school discipline policy that would satisfy both views. Depending on the school district's expectations, the teacher might be caught between conflicting demands. Whatever the personal philosophy of the teacher, he or she must address the wishes of the district when establishing classroom management schemes. The division of views on classroom discipline has inspired numerous books to assist teachers with discipline problems,

FIGURE 10.3

Teacher–Student Control Continuum

TEACHER CONTROL →

STUDENT CONTROL

Low Teacher Control	Equal Teacher Control	High Teacher Control
High Student Control	Equal Student Control	Low Student Control
↓	↓	↓
Noninterventionists	Interactionists	Interventionists

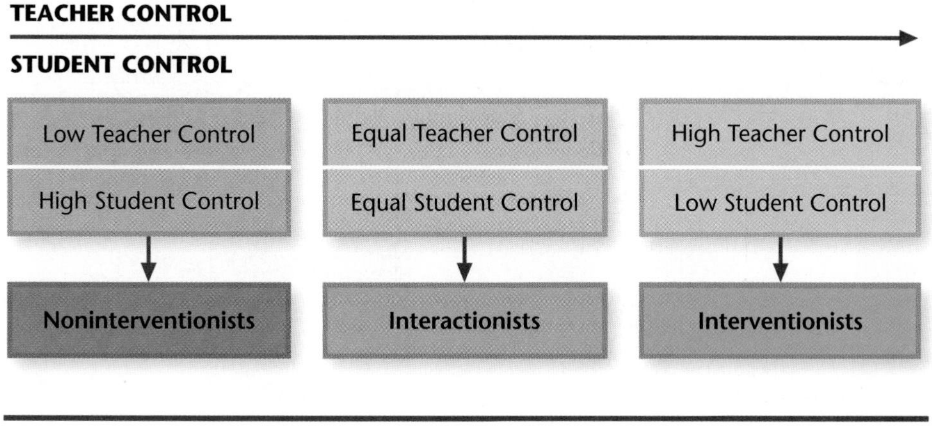

and many special courses and workshops have been developed to deal with classroom discipline strategies. But because very few beginning teachers are given extensive exposure to discipline strategies in teacher preparation programs, the vast range of alternatives makes the choice of strategies difficult for teachers who have yet to develop their own styles.

Carl Glickman and Charles Wolfgang have identified three schools of thought along a teacher–student control continuum (Figure 10.3).[8] Noninterventionists hold the view that teachers should not impose their own rules; students are inherently capable of solving their own problems. Interactionists suggest that students must learn that the solution to misbehavior is a reciprocal relation between student and teacher. Interventionists believe that teachers must set classroom standards for conduct and give little attention to input from the students.

As you prepare to be a teacher, you need to identify your own beliefs regarding discipline in the classroom. The goal is to keep disruptive behavior at a minimum, thus enhancing the students' potential for learning as well as your own job satisfaction. Where maintenance of discipline is the primary concern, one might choose from among the entire range of possibilities along the Glickman–Wolfgang continuum regardless of one's own teaching style preference. Figure 10.4 illustrates how the major theories and behaviors of classroom management relate in terms of control issues along the teacher–student control continuum. It is the professional responsibility of each classroom teacher to understand how each behavior can be used to support his or her preferred teaching philosophy.

CONTROL OR CHOICE THEORY

The psychiatrist William Glasser has advanced **control theory** as a requisite for classroom discipline practices. He suggests that a person's total behavior is composed of feelings, physiology, actions, and thoughts. How a person manages these aspects of behavior makes up an operational definition of control theory. Glasser asserts, "Control theory contends that we choose most of our total behaviors to try to gain control of people or ourselves."[9]

Over time, Glasser realized that the term *control theory* was subject to misinterpretation, so he retitled his theory *choice theory*. He felt that the term *choice* reflected a better understanding of his ideas. Glasser states that people are driven by six basic needs. All of our choices and behaviors are based on the urgency for survival, power, love, belonging, freedom, and fun. If there is an unbalance in any of these six basic needs, people act out.

control theory

A theory of discipline that contends that people choose most of their behaviors to gain control of other people or of themselves.

FIGURE 10.4

Teacher Behavior Continuum

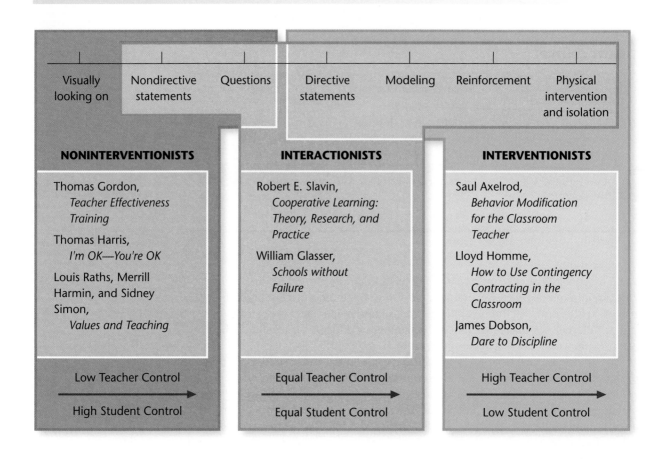

| Visually looking on | Nondirective statements | Questions | Directive statements | Modeling | Reinforcement | Physical intervention and isolation |

NONINTERVENTIONISTS

Thomas Gordon,
Teacher Effectiveness Training

Thomas Harris,
I'm OK—You're OK

Louis Raths, Merrill Harmin, and Sidney Simon,
Values and Teaching

Low Teacher Control

High Student Control

INTERACTIONISTS

Robert E. Slavin,
Cooperative Learning: Theory, Research, and Practice

William Glasser,
Schools without Failure

Equal Teacher Control

Equal Student Control

INTERVENTIONISTS

Saul Axelrod,
Behavior Modification for the Classroom Teacher

Lloyd Homme,
How to Use Contingency Contracting in the Classroom

James Dobson,
Dare to Discipline

High Teacher Control

Low Student Control

As a beginning teacher thinking about classroom discipline, you will find that choice theory encourages you to realize that it is somewhat natural and human for students not to take responsibility for disrupting class or deviating from classroom norms. As a matter of fact, even teachers often find it difficult to take responsibility for some of their own behaviors that deviate from the norm. Choice theory requires teachers to consider the many factors that can account for problem behaviors: physiology, feelings, urges, and so forth. Finally, teachers are encouraged to seek the assistance of counselors, social workers, and parents to fully understand what is causing the problem behavior and only then design an appropriate response.

Choice theory is one of the most difficult management approaches for a new teacher to implement. The majority of discipline problems in the classroom derive from the misguided efforts of students to achieve control. Unfortunately, many teachers think they must have complete control over the classroom. This type of classroom management allows no room for other individuals to have their need for control met. Consequently, student acting out behaviors increase. The first challenge to a new teacher is to evaluate the inappropriate behavior exhibited by the student, determine which need the student thinks is being met by that behavior, and think of appropriate replacement behaviors. The next step, according to choice theory, is to help the student identify the inappropriate behavior and the natural consequences of that behavior. This is done through a series of questions:

- What are you doing?
- What are you supposed to be doing?
- What is the rule?
- Are you making the best choices?

It is important for teachers not to impose artificial consequences. The final challenge is to get students to design a plan on their own. This can be accomplished by follow-up questions such as:

- What is your plan?
- What choices do you need to make?
- What are you going to do to bring your plan into action?

As a prospective teacher, you will need to evaluate whether control or choice theory is compatible with your view of human nature. If you believe that problem behavior is a natural consequence of our need to balance and fulfill natural urges for survival, power, love, belonging, freedom, and fun, then control theory will fit your philosophy of education. If, however, you believe that humans are blank tablets who simply need to be directly taught the proper ways of acting, this approach probably won't be for you. You may find the next discipline approach more conducive to your beliefs.

ASSERTIVE DISCIPLINE

Assertive discipline is a teacher-in-charge, structured classroom management approach designed to encourage students to choose responsible behavior. Developed by Lee Canter over twenty years ago, this discipline approach is based on consistency, follow-through, and positive relationship building. The underlying tenet of this approach is that teachers have a right to teach and pupils have a right to learn.

Assertive discipline contends that the teacher has the right to determine what is best for students and to expect compliance. No pupil should prevent the teacher from teaching or keep another student from learning. Student compliance is imperative in creating and maintaining an effective and efficient learning environment. To accomplish this goal, teachers must react assertively, as opposed to aggressively or nonassertively.

Assertive discipline requires teachers to develop a clear classroom discipline plan. The classroom plan must clarify behaviors that are expected of students and clarify what students can expect from the teacher in return. The aim of the plan is to have a fair and consistent way to establish a safe, orderly, positive classroom in which teachers teach and pupils learn. The plan consists of three parts:

- *Rules* that students must follow at all times
- *Positive recognition* that students will receive for following the rules
- *Consequences* that result when students choose not to follow the rules

According to assertive discipline, students cannot be expected to guess how a teacher wants them to behave in all situations. If students are to succeed in the classroom, they need to know, without doubt, what is expected of them. When students are not given the limits they need, they will act up in order to make the adults around them take notice. A student's disruptive behavior is often a plea for someone to care enough to make him or her stop.

Assertive discipline is not without critics. Some contend that assertive discipline is undemocratic. It conveys a message that only those with power have the right to make rules. Some teachers have responded to this criticism by allowing students to enter into the rule-making process. However, in the end, the assertive discipline teacher makes the final decision.

Other critics of assertive discipline claim that it is simplistic. Assertive discipline does not get at the root of some discipline problems. It assumes that by simply setting up clear rules and consequences along with providing positive feedback, all problem behaviors can be expunged.

In addition, some critics contend that children should obey rules because that is the right thing to do, not because there is some reward associated with obeying or some punishment for not obeying. The long-term implications of rewarding behavior as suggested by the assertive discipline model is that children obey because of positive feedback or because they are told to obey by an authority figure. Real discipline, according to the critics of assertive discipline, should be internal. Responsible behavior should be based on doing what is right.

As a prospective teacher, you will need to assess to what degree assertive discipline fits your philosophy of education. If your philosophy tends to be focused on the teacher's responsibility to control students, assertive discipline is compatible. If your philosophy is focused on students' authority, you would need to modify some of the assertive discipline tenets or not use this discipline.

> The mediocre teacher tells. The good teacher explains. The superior teacher demonstrates. The great teacher inspires.
>
> **William Arthur Ward**

DISCIPLINE WITH DIGNITY

Richard Curwin and Allen Mendler suggest that it is not enough to simply "control" students. Educators on all levels must help students learn to become decision makers and critical thinkers about their own actions. Their approach, a program called Discipline with Dignity, provides a method for teaching students to take responsibility for their own behavior. The approach offers essential skills and strategies for dealing with angry, disruptive behavior while positively affecting the lives of students. The students learn to manage themselves as stress and pressures mount. The program emphasizes prevention by fostering a positive classroom environment and sensitive communication. Students are viewed as partners in the process of ensuring positive, productive classroom environments.

CONFLICT RESOLUTION

Another approach to discipline, conflict resolution focuses on the process of teaching students how to recognize problems and then solve them constructively. Students are taught to be conflict managers and are trained to deal with difficulties on the playground, in the hallways, and in the classroom. The student "managers" learn specific skills that enable them, for example, to guide a discussion about a problem between two people who are fighting. There are a variety of ways to train the students, but the underlying benefit is that the students solve their own problems with minimal assistance of adults. Advocates of conflict resolution contend that permitting students to share in the structure and even the enforcement of discipline policies helps them learn to contribute to the school and to society as a whole.

PEER MEDIATION

Peer mediation programs are closely associated with conflict resolution approaches. The focus of peer mediation is not so much the resolution of conflict but rather the proactive cultivation of a climate of peace. In these programs, students receive training in empathy development, social skills, and bias awareness. The overall goal of peer mediation training is to help students develop a social perspective wherein joint benefit is considered over personal gain.

RULES FOR DISCIPLINE

There is no cookbook formula for classroom discipline rules and procedures. There are, however, some general guidelines that will help the beginning teacher to establish some operating rules that will be accepted and practiced by students. These guidelines are as follows:

1. Students and teachers need to learn the importance of considerate behavior and communication.
2. Students need to be treated with respect. Students who are treated with respect develop strong self-esteem.
3. Teachers need to apply critical thinking skills when creating disciplinary rules or analyzing needed disciplinary action.

4. Teachers need to examine how their actions of a social or instructional nature may have helped trigger misbehavior.

The way the teacher introduces and uses these general principles for establishing rules for discipline will set the tone for classroom interactions, creating an environment that is conducive to learning and that minimizes classroom interruptions.

Classroom discipline strongly reflects the teacher's operating classroom philosophy. As you examine the educational philosophy that wins your interest and support, search for its applications to discipline in your classroom.

By creating an environment in which students listen to each other with respect and build on one another's ideas, a teacher helps students build a community of inquiry.

Classroom Climate

John Goodlad, in his observation of more than one thousand classrooms, found that differences in the quality of schools have little to do with teaching practices. Differences come from what Goodlad called an overall **classroom climate**.[10] Classroom climate is not a simple set of rules or ways of acting; it is a holistic concept, one that involves a set of underlying relationships and an underlying tone or sense of being and feeling.

Different types of classroom climate have been found to be successful. Goodlad's research showed that successful schools are ones with favorable conditions for learning, parent interest in and knowledge of the schools, and positive relationships between principals and teachers and teachers and students. S. M. Johnson identified school climate as one of the most important components contributing to effective learning and high levels of student motivation.[11] In *The Schools We Deserve*, Diane Ravitch defined a positive school climate as relaxed and tension-free. Teachers and students alike know that they are in a good school, and this sense of being special contributes to high morale.[12]

Vito Perrone set out to uncover the underlying characteristics of a classroom climate that could be linked to increased student achievement. After examining hundreds of studies, Perrone determined that a successful learning climate was one in which (1) students have time to wonder and find a direction that interests them; (2) topics have an "intriguing" quality, something common seen in a new way; (3) teachers permit—even encourage—different forms of expression and respect students' views; (4) teachers are passionate about their work; (5) students create original or personal products; (6) students do something—they participate in activities that matter; and (7) students sense that the results of their work are not predetermined.[13]

The problem with establishing a certain type of school climate is that climate is not something that can be developed artificially. Climate arises from the interactions of all the things that teachers do in the classroom. There are two concepts, however, that can help you examine climate a little more closely: voice and space.

VOICE

Voice is a term brought to education by Henry Giroux.[14] Giroux's concept of **voice** refers to the multifaceted and interlocking set of meanings through which students and teachers actively engage in dialogue with one another. Each individual voice is shaped by its owner's particular cultural history and prior experience. Voice, then, is the means that students have at their disposal to make themselves "heard" and to define themselves as active participants in the world. Voice is an important pedagogical concept because it alerts teachers to the fact that all learning is situated historically and mediated culturally and derives part of its meaning from interaction with others.

classroom climate

A holistic concept that involves a set of underlying relationships and a tone or sense of being and feeling in the classroom.

voice

The multifaceted interlocking set of meanings through which students and teachers actively engage with one another.

You can teach a student a lesson for a day; but if you can teach him to learn by creating curiosity, he will continue the learning process as long as he lives.

Clay P. Bedford

CROSS-REFERENCE

For more about voice see Chapter 4.

Teacher voice reflects the values, ideologies, and structuring principles teachers use to understand and mediate the histories, cultures, and subjectivities of their students. For instance, teachers often use the voice of common sense to frame their classroom instruction. It is often through the mediation of teacher voice that the very nature of the schooling process is either sustained or challenged. The power of teacher voice to shape schooling is inextricably related not only to a high degree of teacher self-understanding but also to the possibility for teachers to join together in a collective voice for social betterment. Thus, teacher voice is significant in terms of its own values as well as in relation to the ways it functions to shape and mediate school and student voices.

Teachers need to be aware of the voices of their students as well as their own voice. Too often the teacher's voice is the only voice that counts in a classroom. Teachers must analyze the interests that different voices represent less as oppositional components and more as a medley that shapes the individual meanings of all participants in the learning process.

SPACE

"Authentic public space" is a concept developed by Maxine Greene.[15] She contends that a climate consists of spaces between and among people. The manner in which this space is maintained and the type of space that is created determine the climate. Space that permits students to explore, take risks, make mistakes, and take corrective action is an authentic space—one in which people do not have to engage in pretense. Space that requires perfection, does not tolerate divergent responses, and is limited is a space that restricts freedom.

Another way of creating space is by developing a "community of inquiry." This phrase, coined by Charles Sanders Peirce, has come to mean an environment in which students listen to one another with respect, build on one another's ideas, challenge one another to supply reasons for their opinions, assist one another in drawing inferences, and seek to identify one another's assumptions.[16] Teachers ask questions and students answer them without either party feeling the least twinge of embarrassment, because the process of such thinking and rethinking is natural. An ongoing dialogue ensues and a community of inquiry forms.

Ultimately, classroom climate arises from the beliefs and values held by teachers and students. Your understanding of your own views and beliefs is critical to the climate that will ultimately emerge in your classroom. Your clarity about your most deeply held views on the nature of knowledge, the nature of reality, and the importance of teacher-led versus student-led actions will ensure that your classroom climate authentically represents you.

Learning Focus

Journal for Reflection

Describe the teaching method and classroom environment that you believe has been most effective for you as a learner. Identify the educational philosophy or philosophies that would encourage the teaching method and environment you have selected. Create a graphic that visually represents your own theory of teaching and learning.

As you consider the components of your personal philosophy of education, you will face the question of student learning. What constitutes your vision for a learned person? Is it learning about the acquisition of knowledge? Is it concerned with good thinking? Or is it concerned with good character? An easy answer, of course, is that learning includes all these things: knowledge, thinking, and dispositions. However, as a teacher you will need to determine what is the proper mix: how much learning time should be spent on knowledge acquisition, how much time should be devoted to practicing skills, and how much time should be spent on the development of character traits or values. To make this question even more difficult, you will need to consider what types of knowledge, skills, and dispositions are appropriate. Unfortunately, you will not find easy answers to these questions in your district's curriculum guide or textbooks. These tools provide only a set of opportunities for learning; your philosophy of education will be the force that guides you in determining which of all these things you wish to emphasize in your teaching.

Using Philosophy of Education beyond the Classroom

The way you manage your classroom and the content, teaching methods, and values you stress will be based on your personal view of the proper role of the teacher in society. A classroom philosophy must incorporate this larger societal view into other views that relate to student learning and behavior in the classroom.

Schools play a role within the larger society. This role is determined by a number of factors: the expectations of society's leaders, economic conditions, the ideologies of powerful lobbying groups, and the philosophies of teachers. It is especially important for educators to examine the role of the school in terms of the larger society—because if such reflection does not occur, schools will merely reflect the status quo or the needs and desires of a single powerful group.

Teachers as Change Agents

An age-old question about the role of schools in a changing society concerns the proper role of the school and the teacher in relation to change. Should teachers be **change agents,** actively working for changes in the existing scheme of things? Or should they reemphasize eternal truths and cultural positions? This question of change versus transmission of ongoing values has been articulated in a variety of ways.

CHANGE AS ADAPTATION

Isaac L. Kandel (1881–1965) was a leader in the essentialist movement who advocated change as a process of **adaptation.** The adaptation approach emphasized the importance of promoting stability in schools and enabling the individual to adapt to the larger environment. The school should provide students with an unbiased picture of the changes that occur in society. But schools cannot educate for a new social order, nor should teachers use the classroom to promote doctrine. Change occurs first in society. Schools follow the lead.[17]

CHANGE AS RATIONAL PROCESS

John Dewey believed that schools have a part in social change. He contended that change continually occurs, often without a clearly defined direction. Schools need to assume a leadership role in this change because educators have the time to study newer scientific and cultural forces, estimate the direction and outcome, and determine which changes may or may not be beneficial. Schools need to provide an environment in which students can learn these analytic skills and participate in helping society determine the direction that is of most worth.[18]

CHANGE AS RECONSTRUCTION

The reconstructionist Theodore Brameld contended that every educational system should help diagnose the causes of world problems. Schools need to do more than assess scientific and technological change; they should be places where teachers and students alike can reconsider the very purpose of schooling and study new ways of formulating goals and organizing subject matter. Schools and society alike need

CROSS-REFERENCE
For more about teachers as change agents see Chapter 14.

change agent
A person who actively endeavors to mobilize change in a group, institution, or society.

adaptation
In the context of social change, an educational approach that favors the promotion of a stable climate in schools to enable students to obtain an unbiased picture of changes that are occurring in society and thus to adapt to those changes.

to be reconstructed according to a set of human goals based on cross-cultural, universal values.[19]

CHANGE AS DIALECTIC

Samuel Bowles and Herbert Gintis[20] call for a dialectical humanism through which teachers can help students explore the tension between the individual and society. They identify a conflict, or **dialectic,** between the reproductive needs of society and the self-actualizing needs of the individual. Bowles and Gintis claim that entities such as schools, churches, peer groups, and town meetings attempt to mediate this tension between individual freedom and responsibility for the community. The problem schools face is that they are often unaware that they are mediating this underlying tension, and teachers are often caught in the middle of the dilemma. Teachers are asked to respond to the unique needs of the individual while simultaneously answering to the conflicting needs of society. Bowles and Gintis call on teachers to develop a participatory democracy in which all interested parties learn both to pursue their interests and to resolve conflicts rationally. Educators must develop a dialectical educational philosophy that seeks a new synthesis between the individual and the community.

As a teacher, you will become part of the educational system. As part of this system, you will be asked to make decisions about student outcomes, discipline procedures, instructional methodologies, and assessment methods. Your decisions regarding these educational issues will be greatly influenced by how you perceive teachers as change agents. You will make different decisions depending on whether you determine that teachers need to help schools adapt, rationally change the social order, reconstruct, or participate in a dialectic. Your task is to consider carefully each of these change paradigms and select the one that matches your personal system of beliefs.

A good teacher is first of all a good human being—someone who in personality, character, and attitude exercises a wholesome and inspiring influence on young people.

Norman Cousins

dialectic

A conflict between opposing forces or ideas; in change theory, this conflict is the one between individual needs and the needs of society.

Teachers as Leaders

Teachers serve as leaders for their students. Evidence of this can be found in the testimonials that are offered by former students when they have become adults.

Teaching can be looked at in a variety of ways, ranging from helping students create their own meaning to taking a deliberate stand and arguing for social change.

Should Teachers Express Their Views on Controversial Topics in Class?

YES

Rachael Rice is an artist and activist who teaches fifth- to eighth-grade art at Barre City Elementary and Middle School in Barre, Vermont.

If those views support civil and human rights, of course they should!

I believe one cannot advocate for children anywhere without advocating for children everywhere. This means advocating for children in Iraq, Afghanistan, and Palestine as well as in Western and European countries.

Advocating for peace is now considered controversial in my district, as are rainbows and pink triangles ("pro-gay"). Here at Barre City School, I have had a "Safe Space Ally" sign illegally stolen off my door by a former school board member. Our administration forbade me to replace it, citing "controversy."

At one time, the abolition of slavery, desegregation, and women voting were considered controversial topics. But today, we as teachers are freely encouraged to support equal rights around Dr. Martin Luther King's birthday, and to examine the effects of prejudice as we study the Holocaust or slavery. We are encouraged to educate students for participation in the democratic process, which depends so much upon the freedom to express dissent.

So the truth is that teachers are supported when they express controversial views, as long as their opinions are aligned with those of the majority.

Of course, it is extremely important for teachers who express strong opinions to respect the fact that some students may feel intimidated. That's why I tell all my students on the first day of school not to believe anything I say just because I say it.

I urge them to turn a critical eye toward their teachers as well as toward their studies.

They trust me to help create a safe environment in which unpopular sentiments may be expressed and responded to in appropriate, kind ways.

NO

Lacey Pitts is an NEA Student member in Americus, Georgia.

I do not believe teachers should share their opinions on controversial topics in the classroom. Too often teachers attempt to share their views to stimulate conversation, but only end up alienating students.

I am in college and still in a student's position, and I am not far removed from being a high school student. I was in a classroom where a teacher attacked my personal view and I remember how terrible it felt.

I was in tenth grade. The teacher opened a discussion of homosexuality in the classroom by stating that she felt homosexuality was wrong and a sin, implying that supporting such an alternative lifestyle was also wrong.

I was crushed, having family members and very close friends who were homosexual. I felt attacked for my love of these people and for accepting their lifestyle choices.

My teacher was supported by other students, but no one, not even I, advocated homosexuality. I was afraid of being told I was wrong and feared a personal attack by the teacher or other students. My voice was silenced in the classroom.

As educators, we must never allow this stifling to occur. Instead, we must strive to construct and foster environments that support differences in views and opinions by informing students of all arguments involved. We are in the classroom to guide, inform, and inspire our students.

When I become a teacher, I plan to play devil's advocate on controversial topics. I want my students to hear and consider all sides of an issue.

Impartiality is the key to allowing our students to think and decide their own stances on these topics individually.

(continued)

TEACHER PERSPECTIVES

(continued)

YES

The best teachers teach students to think for themselves.

NO

Teachers must correct misstatements of facts, but a student's individual opinion should be allowed expression without fear of judgment.

Source: "Should Teachers Express Their Views on Controversial Topics in Class?" *NEA Today* (October 2005), p. 40. Reprinted by permission of the National Education Association.

WHAT IS YOUR PERSPECTIVE ON THIS ISSUE?
Should teachers express their views on controversial topics in class?

To give your opinion, go to Chapter 10 of the companion website (www.ablongman.com/johnson14e) and click on Teacher Perspectives.

Most students, whether they have achieved graduate degrees or have followed vocational pursuits immediately after high school, report remembering teachers who had a personal impact on their lives. These students will usually discuss the leadership and modeling behaviors of the teachers they remember.

The idea of teachers as leaders suggests that the new teacher should be aware of the need to develop a beginning repertoire of leadership qualities to which students can look for guidance during their developmental years. These leadership qualities—and the practice of them—are highly dependent on the classroom philosophy that the new teacher puts into practice. Some beginning concepts for teacher leadership are vision, modeling behaviors, and use of power.

VISION

Classroom leadership behaviors begin when a teacher possesses both a vision and the intent to actualize that vision for the students. How a teacher actually puts his or her vision into practice depends wholly on the teacher's philosophical convictions. A **vision** is a mental construct that synthesizes and clarifies what you value or consider to be of highest worth. The clearer the vision or mental picture, the easier it is for a leader to make decisions or persuade or influence others. Formulating a vision requires reflection concerning what you believe about truth, beauty, justice, and equality. It is important to consider these issues and formulate a vision about how schools and classrooms should be organized and what ideas should be implemented.

Linda Sheive and Marian Schoenbeit offer five steps to help leaders put their visions into action:[21]

1. Value your vision.
2. Be reflective and plan a course of action.
3. Articulate the vision to colleagues.
4. Develop a planning stage and an action stage.
5. Have students become partners in the vision.

If teachers reflect on their vision, they can plan the course of action they need to use with their learners. Articulation provides teachers with an opportunity to share

vision

A mental construction that synthesizes and clarifies what a person values or considers to be of highest worth.

their vision with colleagues. Inservice or staff development sessions are excellent times to articulate a classroom vision. Visions require a planning stage and an action stage if they are to become reality. Planning and action stages should involve the students who are intended to be the receivers of this vision. For example, if a teacher wishes students to be reflective in their learning environment, then the teacher needs to help the students understand the benefits of reflectiveness and become partners in the planning. The teacher might engage the students in free and open discussions of the vision and its importance to the learning environment in the classroom.

MODELING

If teachers hold certain expectations of learner behaviors in the classroom, it is imperative that they model those behaviors with the students. If the classroom teacher is rigid and fixed in his or her classroom practices and creates an authoritarian atmosphere, then the students will probably respond accordingly. On the other hand, if the teacher provides a more democratic classroom, the students will respond similarly in their classroom encounters. We would caution that a laissez-faire environment will probably produce a classroom where learners have little or no direction. Teachers should consider the modeling effect on the classroom environment and exhibit behaviors consistent with their philosophy of education.

EMPOWERMENT

The concept of power in the classroom should not be considered good or bad; power in itself has no value structure. The use of power, however, gives it a good, poor, or bad image. All leaders have power that is associated with their position, but the successful leader is judicious in its use. The nature of the teaching position entrusts a teacher with power both within and outside the classroom. How a teacher uses power in the classroom or in the school building is wholly determined by the classroom philosophy the teacher wants to project.

Teachers' use of power can be classified into two different styles: teacher-dominant and learner-supportive. Past and present practices in schools tend to lean heavily on the teacher-dominant style. Therefore, although many teachers in training study both categories of teaching styles, they tend to see only one major type in practice when they visit schools. We suggest that you continually study both major styles so that you can apply either one as needed on the basis of your classroom objectives for students and your classroom philosophy.

A teacher-dominant power style is based on an authoritarian construct for the classroom. Learners are not expected to be active verbally in the learning process but are generally expected to be receivers and practicing users of teacher-given information. Learning is very convergent. It is selected and given to the learner in the particular way in which the teacher wishes the student to acquire it.

A learner-supportive power style views the learner as someone who is verbally active and who seeks divergence in learning. Learner-supportive power styles encourage the active participation of the learner in exploring learning and helping to determine the extent to which he or she will engage in alternative approaches. Learning is very divergent. These power styles tend to recognize differences in learning, individual interests, and higher-order learning.

Teachers' use of power extends beyond the classroom. Teachers, by their very occupation, are empowered with both rights and responsibilities. They have a unique obligation to advocate for the needs of children, to remind society of its obligations to coming generations, to look beyond material wealth, and to consider the spiritual wealth of knowledge. Teachers, by virtue of their occupation, are given certain rights to speak and be heard. The greater society looks to teachers for guidance concerning the future health of the world.

Journal for Reflection

Develop a statement that depicts how you intend to function as a teacher/leader within the larger society. Describe one position you support related to a political action.

Global Perspectives

The World as a Classroom

This chapter encourages you to examine your beliefs and assumptions in an effort to develop a personal philosophy of education. It is also important, however, to consider the limitations that such a philosophy can impose. For example, to what degree does your philosophy of education incorporate the larger world of thinkers? Does your philosophy affirm or disaffirm varied thinking schemes, varied beliefs, and varied ways of arriving at answers? Relating to global neighbors is no longer a matter of respecting differences. If educators are truly to relate and work collaboratively, their thinking schemes need to intermingle with those of other educators, educators who may have vastly different ways of thinking. Yet a personal philosophy implies the development of a cohesive set of views about knowledge and the nature of the world. Teachers must balance this need to intermix against the importance of clarifying an individual point of view; this is the challenge the world classroom presents to every teacher.

Questions for Reflection

1. How might you present to another teacher your own views about what knowledge is of most worth?

2. What can you do if you are asked to team teach with another educator who views knowledge differently than you do?

Summary

THE DYNAMIC RELATIONSHIP BETWEEN PHILOSOPHY AND EDUCATION. A philosophy of education is not a set of written words. It is a platform on which decisions are made and life is led. A teacher's practices in the classroom reflect her or his personal philosophy. One strategy that can help teachers develop their personal philosophy of education is to build on the educational philosophies of others.

TEACHER-CENTERED LOCUS-OF-CONTROL EDUCATIONAL THEORIES. This chapter provided an overview of six leading educational views that are held in part or entirely by teachers in U.S. schools. The teacher-centered locus-of-control educational theories include essentialism, behaviorism, and positivism. Each of these theories emphasizes the importance of controlling the subject-matter content, thinking processes, and discipline procedures within the classroom setting. Teachers are held responsible for controlling these areas of the school environment.

STUDENT-CENTERED LOCUS-OF-CONTROL EDUCATIONAL THEORIES. The student-centered locus-of-control educational theories include progressivism, humanism, and constructivism. Each of these theories places less emphasis on the external control of the teacher and more emphasis on student control. Progressivism promotes individual student inquiry, humanism stresses student freedom, and constructivism emphasizes the importance of supporting personal meaning. This chapter further illustrates the relationship of current educational views to the classical philosophies and describes educational views in terms of the learner, subject-matter orientation, and external versus internal locus-of-control tendencies. Although your ultimate teaching style might not be completely committed to a single educational theory, the basic description of these views will help you to identify your personal preferences.

DEVELOPING YOUR OWN PHILOSOPHY OF EDUCATION.   One way of clarifying your philosophy of education is to examine the different aspects of teaching and determine your own preferences for classroom organization, student motivation, discipline, and classroom climate. Each of these aspects of teaching will take on a different character based on your personal preference for a specific educational philosophy. Remember, that most teachers pull aspects of different educational philosophies as they determine the specific type of classroom organization, discipline, motivation, and classroom climates that they prefer. For this reason, we encourage an eclectic approach—an approach that draws on many different sets of ideas.

USING PHILOSOPHY OF EDUCATION BEYOND THE CLASSROOM.   Finally, to perceive a philosophy of education is one thing; to live according to the philosophy is another. In teaching, one must exhibit behavior that is compatible with a personal educational philosophy. In life, one must consider the implications of a philosophy of education for acting responsibly in society. What types of societal change match your philosophy of education, and what type of responsible leadership does your philosophy compel you to assume?

Discussion Questions

1. What were the characteristics and behaviors of a favorite teacher who was authoritarian toward students? Of a favorite teacher who was focused on student-centered locus of control?
2. When might a teacher focus on personalized situations involving such things as death or injustice to stimulate student learning? How would such a strategy relate to the back-to-basics expectations of many U.S. schools?
3. Experienced teachers often advise a beginning teacher: "Be firm with the students and let them know at the beginning how you intend to teach your classes." Is this advice good or bad? Discuss the pros and cons of such a procedure.
4. Constructivism rules out some of the conventional notions about educating youth. It emphasizes students' construction of personalized understandings of the world rather than an established curriculum. What implications does constructivism have for grouping students?
5. Teachers must be able to manage the classroom in such a way that the environment created is conducive to teaching and learning. How do you plan to organize your classroom to set up such an environment?
6. What is your vision of democracy in the classroom? To what degree should students be permitted to decide what they will study, when they will study, and how they will study? Why?

School-Based Observations

1. This chapter contains examples of classroom activities associated with various educational theories. As you work in the schools, take the class activity features with you and see whether you can determine which educational philosophies you observe in use. Then decide which educational philosophy you subscribe to and determine whether your own classroom activities are consistent with your personal educational philosophy.
2. Interview several teachers who organize their classrooms and teaching materials differently. Using probing questions, try to uncover the educational philosophy or philosophies that account for the differing teaching approaches.
3. Prepare a synopsis of your overall philosophy of education. Then interview a teacher who seems to teach and organize the classroom the way you would. Ask the teacher to review your synopsis.

Portfolio Development

1. Develop a hands-on, activity-based lesson in a subject that you enjoy. Type up the entire lesson, with teacher and student directions and activity pages. Then write an introductory rationale that describes which educational theories are supported by the way you designed the lesson. Include this lesson in your portfolio as an example of your ability to analyze lessons in terms of theories.
2. Select one major concept from one of the national standards documents (available at your college library). Describe the teaching methods you would use to help students attain an understanding of that particular concept. Then annotate the teaching methods, explaining their theoretical foundations. Include this in your portfolio to illustrate your ability to apply theory to practice.
3. Prepare a synopsis of your overall philosophy of education perspective. Include your views about classroom organization, motivation, discipline, and climate. Try to develop a graphic that clearly shows how all these components connect and are consistent with your overall perspective.
4. Develop a statement that depicts how you intend to function as a teacher/leader within the larger society. Describe one position you support related to political action.

Preparing for Certification

EDUCATIONAL THEORIES AND LEARNING CLIMATES

1. One of the topics in the Praxis II Principles of Learning and Teaching (PLT) test is "encouraging students to extend their thinking" through the use of a "repertoire of flexible teaching and learning strategies" (for example, teacher-directed instruction, cooperative learning, independent study, laboratory/hands-on approaches). In this chapter, you learned about six major educational theories and the various teaching and learning approaches, classroom practices, and educational programs of study related to each theory. Review each of the theories, paying particular attention to the relationship between how students learn and the teaching and learning strategies consistent with each theory. Which theory seems most compatible with your own beliefs and philosophy? Which theory seems least compatible?

2. Answer the following multiple-choice question, which is similar to items in Praxis and other state certification tests.

Ms. Jones, a second-grade teacher, began a language arts lesson by reading the beginning and middle of a story to the children. Instead of reading the end of the story, however, she asked the students to create an ending of their own. The children wrote their own endings and then read them aloud. Ms. Jones then read the story's ending, and she and the class talked about the many ways a story can end. Which educational theory appears to guide Ms. Jones's lesson?

    A. Behaviorism
    B. Constructivism
    C. Positivism

3. Answer the following short-answer question, which is similar to items in Praxis and other state certification tests. After you've completed your written response, use the scoring guide in the *Test at a Glance* materials to assess your response. Can you revise your response to improve your score?

What is meant by the terms *teacher-centered locus of control* and *student-centered locus of control?* Give three examples of teaching practices or learning activities that you might observe in two classrooms—one dominated by teacher-centered locus of control and the other dominated by student-centered locus of control.

4. Several topics in the Praxis II Principles of Teaching and Learning (PLT) test relate to the contents of this chapter, including "structuring a climate for learning," developing "strategies to maintain discipline to promote student learning," and becoming skilled in "allocation of time for instructional activities, including transition time." Review the Classroom Climate section of this chapter. How will you build on John Goodlad's findings about positive classroom climate, Henry Giroux's conception of voice, and Maxine Greene's conception of space in your own classroom?

5. Answer the following multiple-choice question, which is similar to items in Praxis and other state certification tests. If you are unsure of the answer, review the opening section of this chapter.

Which of the following activities would most clearly be an inappropriate activity to encourage divergent thinking in a mathematics lesson on patterns and shapes?

    A. Children will identify and match pictures of three-dimensional shapes while playing a board game with peers.
    B. Children will create patterns using different shapes of pasta noodles and write how many pieces are in their designs.
    C. Children will use an online program in which they correctly identify shapes.
    D. Children will search for shapes in the classroom and make a chart listing the types and numbers of shapes found.

6. Answer the following short-answer question, which is similar to items in Praxis and other state certification tests. After you've completed your written response, use the scoring guide in the *Test at a Glance* materials to assess your response. Can you revise your response to improve your score?

The Jefferson Elementary School staff is debating the merits of the assertive discipline program developed by Lee Canter. One of the teachers, Leslie Brown, is strongly in favor of the program. Another teacher, Robin James, strongly opposes the program. What arguments might Leslie make in favor of the assertive discipline program? What arguments might Robin make against the program?

Websites

www.ed.uiuc.edu/EPS/Educational-Theory/purpose.asp
Educational Theory is a quarterly publication that fosters the continuing development of educational theory and encourages wide and effective discussion of theoretical problems within the education profession. You will find this journal filled with contemporary concerns that relate to teaching and learning.

www.funderstanding.com/constructivism.cfm
Funderstanding contains a variety of theories on learning, instruction, assessment, influences, history of education, learning patterns, educational reforms, as well as additional links.

www.imsa.edu/team/cpbl/cpbl.html The Illinois Mathematics and Science Academy Center for Problem-Based

Learning offers programs, ideas, examples of problem-based learning in classrooms, access to a problem-based learning teachers' network, and other resources that relate to the use of problem-based learning in contemporary schools.

www.criticalthinking.org The Foundation for Critical Thinking is dedicated to providing educators, students, and the general public with access to information about critical thinking, theory and practice, concepts, techniques for learning and teaching, and classroom exercises.

www.theteachersguide.com The Teachers Guide is a web-based company that provides information, professional articles, resources, books, virtual field trips, and educational software related to classroom management, educational psychology, special education, and so on. Click on Class Management for more information.

www.nwrel.org/scpd/sirs/5/cu9.html The School Improvement Research Series website provides introductions, definitions, and research on discipline practices. Discussions include research findings, teacher training in classroom management, discipline of multicultural students, specific discipline programs, and ineffective discipline practices. The site also includes a summary of research perspectives on improving school and classroom discipline.

Further Reading

Campbell, D. M., Cignetti, P. B., Melenyzer, B. J., Nettles, D. H., and Wyman, R. M., Jr. (1997). *How to Develop a Professional Portfolio: A Manual for Teachers.* Boston: Allyn & Bacon. This booklet provides a comprehensive look at what is needed to develop a professional portfolio for education professionals.

Carlson, Richard. (2003). *The Don't Sweat Guide for Teachers: Cutting through the Clutter so That Every Day Counts.* New York: Hyperion. How to deal with the demands of teaching and still enjoy the job. Gives strategies for creating surprise, modeling respect, and being a talent scout.

Joyce, B. R., Weil, M., and Calhoun, E. (2000). *Models of Teaching,* 6th edition. Boston: Allyn & Bacon. This book describes the relationship between different approaches to teaching and various educational theories. It shows that most teaching methods tend to draw from several related educational theories rather than a single educational theory.

Kohn, Afie. (1993). *Punished by Rewards: The Trouble with Gold Stars, Incentive Plans, A's, Praise, and Other Bribes.* Boston: Houghton Mifflin. Dr. Kohn describes the unexpected consequences of using reinforcement practices and cautions against the dangers of providing rewards to enhance good behavior.

Ladson-Billings, G. (1994). *The Dreamkeepers: Successful Teachers of African American Children.* San Francisco: Jossey-Bass. A reflective look at different teaching strategies in terms of their effectiveness with African American students.

MacKenzie, Robert J. (2003). *Setting Limits in the Classroom.* Roseville, CA: Prima. Offers up-to-date alternatives to punishment and permissiveness beyond the usual methods. Also offers special tools for handling the "strong-willed" student.

Martin, Jane Roland. (1995, January). "A Philosophy of Education for the Year 2000." *Phi Delta Kappan,* 77(1), pp. 21–27. This article describes the work of an existentialist and how to develop a philosophy of education that is consistent with existential principles.

Strike, Kenneth A., and Soltis, Jonas F. (1985). *The Ethics of Teaching.* New York: Teachers College Press. A careful analysis of the ethics surrounding the life of a teacher. Drs. Strike and Soltis provide thoughtful questions and ideas that help teachers reassess their own ethical positions.

Torp, Linda, and Sage, Sara. (2002). *Problems and Possibilities: Problem-Based Learning for K–16 Education,* 2nd edition. Alexandria, VA: Association for Supervision and Curriculum Development. Provides a specific approach to the implementation of problem-based learning. The approach is supported by educational theories, and a clear set of steps for developing a problem-based learning unit is presented.

⦿mylabschool
Where the classroom comes to life!

Go to Allyn and Bacon's MyLabSchool (**www.mylabschool.com**) and complete the following activity for Chapter 10. Click on **Courses;** click on **Foundations/Intro Teaching;** click on **MLS Video Lab;** then click on **Module 4: Philosophical Foundations.**

PART VI

Chapter 11
Standards-Based Education and Assessment of Student Learning

Chapter 12
Designing Programs for Learners: Curriculum and Instruction

Chapter 13
Technology in a Changing World

Chapter 14
Education in the Twenty-First Century

CURRICULAR FOUNDATIONS OF EDUCATION

In the preface of this edition of our book, your authors identified the key challenge for educators in the twenty-first century—responding to multiple perspectives in a changing world. In the first five parts (Chapters 1 to 10), different perspectives for viewing and understanding today's schools and the education system were presented. Each of these parts and chapters represents a different foundation and way of thinking about and describing the opportunities and issues facing today's teachers. In Part VI, Chapters 11 through 13 address the contemporary subjects and priority themes in today's schools. Chapter 14 presents ideas about where schools and education are headed in the near future.

The world of teaching has changed from the teacher-centered view of the past. Today teaching begins with developing understanding of what students need to learn. The desired learning is described in terms of standards. Also, teachers and students today are fully aware that learning will be assessed by teachers and tested by school districts and states. These two components—standards and assessments—are the starting blocks for developing curriculum materials and preparing lessons.

Another dramatic way that the world is changing is in terms of technology. Teachers have technology resources that were unimaginable even ten years ago. Making best use of these technologies will be a continuing challenge and opportunity for teachers.

An interesting dimension of the "multiple perspectives in a changing world" theme is envisioning how education, schools, and teaching will evolve from here. Teachers of tomorrow's schools will most certainly have new opportunities and different challenges. The ideas presented in Chapter 14 are intended to stimulate you to think about implications for teachers as well as to inspire you to think more imaginatively about what education, schools, and teaching will be like in ten to twenty years.

CHAPTER 11

Standards-Based Education and Assessment of Student Learning

State's Kids Rate Low on Reading Test, National Exam Results Disappoint After Schools' Efforts to Improve

Nanette Asimov, Chronicle Staff Writer, *San Francisco Chronicle,* October 20, 2005

California has been unable to raise students' reading scores from near the bottom nationally despite a decade of trying, including overhauling the way children are taught to read.

The 2005 results of the National Assessment of Educational Progress, released Wednesday, show that California's fourth-graders scored an average of 207 out of 500 points on a reading test last spring—tying for next-to-last place with students in Arizona, Nevada and New Mexico and falling well below the national average of 217. Only fourth-graders in Mississippi and Washington, D.C., scored lower.

Eighth-graders, the only other students tested on the exams sponsored by the U.S. Department of Education, scored higher than the younger children in reading. California again was near the bottom, however, its eighth-graders scoring an average of 250 points, 10 points below the national figure.

Students in Hawaii and Washington, D.C., were the only ones to average a lower score than California eighth-graders, at 238 points.

California students fared slightly better in math. The fourth-graders scored 230, tying with Arizona, Hawaii, Louisiana and Nevada to beat out Mississippi, Alabama, New Mexico and Washington, D.C. The national average was 237.

California eighth-graders scored 269 in math, topping children in Hawaii, Alabama, Mississippi and Washington, D.C. The national average was 278.

"It is clear that California must do more to improve student achievement," state schools chief Jack O'Connell said. "The scores released today are not surprising and are another indication of the challenges we face."

But O'Connell also questioned the fairness of state-by-state comparisons that make California schools look like slackers despite years of trying to raise test scores and improve instruction.

He said California had the nation's highest proportion of English learners, which can bring reading scores down. About one in every four California students is an English learner. The highest scorers in the country—Vermont and New Hampshire among the fourth-graders, and Massachusetts among eighth-graders—have relatively few students learning the language.

In addition, only a sampling of students in each state takes the test, and while California excused about 12 percent of its English learners, O'Connell said Texas excused 37.5 percent and New York 29 percent.

The superintendent also pointed out that California's instruction is aligned to its own state exam, on which students have improved. He said the national test contains material with which students may not be familiar.

But Russlynn Ali, executive director of the Education Trust West, an Oakland think tank devoted to closing the academic achievement gap among ethnic groups, dismissed O'Connell's remarks as excuses.

"No matter how you cut it, it is not OK that California, the fifth-largest economy in the world, is only doing better than poor (places) like Alabama and Mississippi and Washington, D.C.," Ali said. "It's simply not tolerable."

Ali said her group had crunched data showing that even California's white children, traditionally among the highest-scoring groups, were among the worst reading and math students in the country.

Hopes in California had been high that 10 years of intense efforts to improve kids' academic skills would pay off on the national test.

Questions for Reflection

1. What do you think; are students in California really doing that bad?

2. Do you think that schools and states should be judged based on how students perform on a single test?

3. If you were a teacher in California when this newspaper article was published, how would you respond to questions from the parents of your students?

Copyright © 2005 by the *San Francisco Chronicle*. Reprinted by permission of the *San Francisco Chronicle* via the Copyright Clearance Center. To read the rest of this story, go to the archives for the *San Francisco Chronicle*: www.SFGate.com.

INTASC

Learning Outcomes

After reading and studying this chapter, you should be able to:

1. Identify different conceptions of standards and analyze the consequences that these conceptions have for teaching and learning.

2. Compare different sources of standards and describe the conflicts that result from the varied interests of these sources.

3. Identify problems that surround standards-based assessment practices and predict their influence on teachers and classroom practices. (INTASC 8: Assessment)

4. Define accountability for student learning and describe how the No Child Left Behind Act is holding schools, school districts, and states accountable for student achievement.

5. Understand the meaning of "helping all students learn" and explain how standards and assessments may increase or limit the chances of schools to meet this goal. (INTASC 8: Assessment)

The leading theme for this text is "perspectives on education in a changing world." The reality of this theme for teachers and schools comes alive in the Case Study from the *The San Francisco Chronicle*. The world is indeed changing and the expectations for schools are changing too. One major theme in the article is student performance on a national test. But note also that references are made to a specific state test. The state superintendent was interviewed for this article, as was a citizen advocate advocating for efforts to reduce the achievement gap. Reference also is made to the ten-plus-year effort to improve schools by changing instruction.

All of the themes in the *Chronicle* article relate to a major way the world has changed for education. Today, there are greater expectations for **accountability** of states, school districts, schools, and teachers. The tool for measuring performance and judging success is student scores on state and national tests. These are major changes from the past when *local control* was the norm, as was described in Chapter 5.

accountability

Setting expectations for education, specifying the means for judging.

Not only has the locus of control moved beyond the classroom and school, there has been a profound change in thinking and setting of expectations for teachers and teaching. In the past, the teacher was placed at the center of thinking about the classroom and teaching. Now student learning is at the center. In the past the focus was on the "inputs," such as curriculum materials, the age of the textbook, and how teachers taught. Now the focus is on the "outputs," which is narrowly targeted on the available evidence that the students learned the specified knowledge and skills.

These changes in expectations for teachers and students truly constitute a **paradigm** change. A new way of thinking about teaching is now expected in all classrooms and across all schools, districts, and states. Two complementary strategies are at the center of today's education paradigm: **standards** and **assessments.** In combination these comprise today's preferred instructional model, **standards-based education.** These two strategies are the subject of this chapter.

Four big ideas surround and inform the standards movement. First is the articulation of rigorous standards for student achievement. A second is the increased demand from policymakers and the public for accountability—that students meet these standards. A third big idea is an emphasis on the importance of authentically assessing what students have learned. Fourth, standards require a major change in the curriculum and the way teachers and students think and work in classrooms. In total, the emphasis on standards-based education represents a major shift in thinking about accountability, teaching, and learning.

A number of important challenges and critical issues have emerged around the standards and assessment movement. Some of the questions that will be explored in this chapter include:

- What type of standards and assessments are appropriate for today's schools?
- Who determines the content of standards and assessments?
- How fair is a common set of standards and assessments for a diverse population?
- How can assessments be made authentic to the contexts of the community and the world of work?
- When should assessments be tailored to individual development and when should they be standardized?
- What is the role of the teacher in today's standards and assessment environment?
- What is the role of students and parents in today's standards and assessment environment?

We will also tackle issues and questions that surround standards-based education and assessment. At every turn, we place the emphasis on what teachers need to know and understand about this important education movement.

Traditional versus Standards-Based Education

The paradigm change that we are experiencing can easily be seen in the classroom. Put simply, today's teachers must think about teaching in terms of outputs instead of inputs. Some of the indicators of the differences in thinking between these two paradigms are listed in Table 11.1. Check your own thinking at this time by asking these questions related to the bulleted lists in Table 11.1.

1. What do you think about first in preparing to teach: the topic you will teach or what is expected for student learning?
2. Do you first talk with your students about what they already know or do you immediately move into planning the lesson?

paradigm

A particular perspective or conceptual model with unique assumptions and expectations.

standards

A statement of the desired outcome, which in education is normally a description of student learning.

assessments

The use of multiple methods, including tests, to evaluate the current level of student learning; used in planning future steps in instruction.

standards-based education

Using descriptions of student learning in terms of standards as the basis for instruction and assessment.

TABLE 11.1	Comparing Traditional Instruction with Standards-Based Education

Teacher-Centered	Standards-Based
• Teacher selects topic	• Teacher reviews state/district standards and benchmarks
	• Dialogue with students about current understanding and expectations for new learning
• Teacher prepares lesson based on textbook or topics of greater personal interest	• Teacher prepares lesson based on district/state identified student learning expectations
• Teacher-centered presentation	• Instruction is interactive with ongoing checks on student understanding
• Test developed by teacher after lesson is taught	• Assessment is based on learning expectations, known by teacher and student ahead of time
• Tests are returned and grade distribution may be displayed	• Teacher and students compare performance to public expectations for learning

3. Do your students know what the learning expectations are *before* the lesson is taught?
4. Do you think about "teaching" as being centered in the teacher, or is it more based on two-way interaction with the students?
5. Is testing of student learning based on what you taught or what the district and state expect students to learn?
6. Do you give back the tests with a score/grade and move to the next topic, or do you and your students first reflect on their learning against the district and state expectations?

Chances are you had to think hard to answer each question, trying to understand the differences between teacher-centered and standards-based teaching. This is one of the very real challenges in making a paradigm change. It is hard to think and act in a new way. Most of the teachers you have had probably have taught in the teacher-centered way. To be successful in today's schools teachers need to think in terms of outputs (What did my students learn?) rather than in terms of inputs (What am I teaching?) One of the important tools for teaching in this way is understanding standards and their role in standards-based education.

In order to ensure that our children receive a better education, higher standards need to be set for all students—not just the academic elite—and schools need to be held accountable for helping their students meet those standards.

Achieve, Inc. (an organization committed to raising standards)

Standards-Based Education

Standards-based education is a systemic approach to the entire teaching and learning process. Systemic implies that the entire school system (including the curriculum, instruction, assessments, and professional development) is driven and linked by a set of standards that the community of teachers, administrators, parents, and learners endorse. As an instructional approach, standards-based education places student learning at the center. Achievement of the standards is paramount and is increasingly linked to a student being promoted or receiving a diploma. Student achievement of the standards, which is often measured by performance on standardized tests, sometimes determines the jobs and salaries of teachers and principals.

Differing Conceptions of Standards

Standards are a popular topic in both the business and education worlds. Policymakers at the state and federal levels are concerned about standards, their rigor, and student achievement as measured against them. School administrators, teachers, curriculum developers, and education reformers are expected to implement the standards and show evidence that students meet them. Interestingly, among people using the term *standards,* definitions of the term can be quite different. Some people view standards as

Students must meet high standards before they can graduate from high school. A growing number of states are requiring students to pass a test before they receive a diploma.

synonymous with rigor and the setting of high expectations for schools, teachers, and students. Others focus on the specification of learner outcomes or use the term in relation to a particular approach to instruction. Still others equate standards with high-stakes tests.

At their simplest, standards are statements that describe an expected level of attainment or performance. Standards are developed for school construction, program accreditation, teacher credentials, and for student learning. They also can range in scope from being extremely global and ambitious to very narrow and specific.

WORLD-CLASS STANDARDS

National Educational Technology Goals

Goal 1: All students and teachers will have access to information technology in their classrooms, schools, communities, and homes.

Goal 2: All teachers will use technology effectively to help students achieve high academic standards.

Goal 3: All students will have technology and information and literacy skills.[1]

A common goal of many is that students, teachers, and schools in the United States will be the best in the world. Others are most concerned that U.S. students are competitive with students from countries that score highest on international comparisons, such as Germany, Korea, Japan, and Sweden. Either way, the aspiration is to be among the best in the world. These standards cannot be met in a single elementary or secondary school setting. Rather, they are visionary statements of aspiration and accomplishment; they are not intended to be met within a single school year. Instead educators need to set the accomplishments of their students in comparison to world-class standards and aspire over time to see greater student successes. Some question whether our nation really should aspire to be world-class, especially when the social costs are considered. Myron Lieberman, for example, argues that unlike South Korea, people in the United States are not ready to have the 300 test-makers sequestered in a hotel for twenty-nine days (so that test items will be secure), or to have offices open at 10:00 a.m. the day of testing (to facilitate student transportation), or to avoid driving near schools or to have nearby

World-class standards describe the high levels of performance necessary to be competitive at national and international levels.

plane departures rescheduled on the test day (so as not to cause noise).[2] Still world-class standards set high level goals and remind us that international comparisons are being made and that being able to compete in a global economy is important.

REAL-WORLD STANDARDS

Creating Tomorrow's Citizens

A core belief in AISD [Austin Independent School District] is that effort creates ability. Sustained effort in an instructional environment that is rich in rigor, relevance, and positive relationships results in achievement at high levels. However, students who are absent from the core instruction due to truancy and misbehaviors resulting in serious discipline or inappropriate referrals to special education cannot sustain the effort required for achievement at high levels. Minimizing these distracters to student effort requires campuswide involvement in actively teaching, reinforcing and modeling character skills in a positive learning environment.[3]

Another segment of the public believes that standards should be real-world goals. This conception of standards places primary emphasis on the necessary knowledge and skills that will make students employable and enable them to live independent lives. Assessments of reading, writing, and computing skills show that too many high school graduates lack these skills. Major U.S. firms report that 34 percent of tested job applicants lack the basic skills necessary for the job.[4] In contrast to world-class standards, real-world standards are seen as being achievable in schools. Real-world standards set the expectation that students learn the basic skills of reading, writing, and computing that allow them to balance checkbooks, prepare for job interviews, manage their daily lives, and maintain employment.

DISCIPLINE-BASED OR CONTENT STANDARDS

English Language Standard

Students read a wide range of print and non-print texts to build an understanding of texts, of themselves, and of the cultures of the United States and the world; to acquire new information; to respond to the needs and demands of society and the workplace; and for personal fulfillment. Among these texts are fiction and nonfiction, classic and contemporary works.[5]

Should We Reward Good Grades with Money and Prizes?

There is a wide range of perspectives about rewarding students for good grades. There also are differences in views about what is appropriate for teachers to do versus what parents should do.

YES

Margo Ungricht, *seventh-grade English teacher, Lehi, Utah*

I believe we can offer prizes, food, money, or field trips to students for good grades. I don't see the difference between offering students prizes and money for good grades and having a "3.0 dance" or special assembly. A reward is a reward.

Most students who work hard for good grades would do it without the prizes and dances, so the prizes and money are simply an added bonus that they can choose to accept or decline.

Students who cheat, beg, badger, and whine for a good grade in order to earn money or prizes generally do not maintain a good grade for long. Intrinsic values usually have the upper hand in the end.

Tennille Jones-Lewis, *high school guidance counselor, Alliance, Ohio*

Students should be rewarded for good grades. I view school for students similar to the way I view a job for an adult, and I believe it's appropriate for parents to provide monetary rewards for good work and penalties for poor performance. If you are late for school, money is deducted. If you miss a day for illness, money is deducted. If your performance suffers, so will your pay. It gives students a chance to relate real-world experiences to school-related tasks.

This may not work for every family or for every child, but it's one of many things a parent can do.

My husband and I reward our eight nieces and nephews for earning good grades on their report cards. We give them $5 for each A and $3 for each B. Money is deducted for each C, D, and F. When their report cards come out, they call us immediately. They all do well in school and we want to show them we value their achievements, the same way a future employer will when they perform well in their jobs.

NO

Karen Barksdale, *ninth-grade English teacher, Memphis, Tennessee*

The only money and prizes a student should be given for good grades are the better money they will earn as adults and the prizes of self-esteem, pride, and commitment to attaining the highest level of their educational and intellectual development.

Instead of the student asking, "What will you give me for trying?" we should be asking students, "What will you be giving yourself for your future if you apply yourself?" The ultimate reward for a good education is a secure and rewarding future.

Brenda Nelson, *social worker, Barrington, Illinois*

External rewards undermine students' natural eagerness to learn. When we offer kids money and prizes, we cheapen the value of learning. We have all seen kids who become so accustomed to external rewards that the presents, candy, or money are what they want, rather than the academic achievement itself. I recently overheard a teenage girl and her father arguing about how high her grades needed to be in order to get a car, and what kind of car it would be. The conversation had everything to do with the prize and nothing to do with learning.

Our ultimate goal is to create citizens who make decisions for the right reasons—not because someone is dangling a prize in front of them.

Mary Bungert, *special education teacher, Topeka, Kansas*

When students receive good grades, it is because of a team effort. The parents in most cases have worked diligently in the evenings with homework,

(continued)

(continued)

YES

However, I don't think it is appropriate for teachers to use money as a reward. There's a fine line—a teacher giving the whole class a pizza party for a job well done could be appropriate, but a teacher giving money as a reward would cross the line.

NO

the paraprofessionals have put in time and effort, the teachers do the same. How do we determine who made that achievement possible?

We had a second-grade student who knew seven sight words when he came to our school. He was on target by the end of third grade. That happened because of his parents, classroom teacher, paraprofessionals, and the special education teacher who kept him focused, as well as the student's own motivation to learn. Who deserved a prize?

Source: "Should We Reward Good Grades with Money and Prizes?" *NEA Today* (May 2004), p. 39. Reprinted by permission of the National Education Association.

WHAT IS YOUR PERSPECTIVE ON THIS ISSUE?
Should we reward good grades with money and prizes?

To give your opinion, go to Chapter 11 of the companion website (www.ablongman.com/johnson14e) and click on Teacher Perspectives.

Numbers and Operations Standard

Instructional programs from prekindergarten through grade 12 should enable all students to understand numbers, ways of representing numbers, relationships among numbers, and number systems.

The setting of standards requires understanding different expectations, learning new things, and extensive discussions about the content.

- **Pre–K–2 Expectations:** In prekindergarten through grade 2 all students should count with understanding and recognize "how many" in sets of objects . . .
- **Grades 3–5 Expectations:** In grades 3–5 all students should understand the place-value structure of the base-ten number system and be able to represent and compare whole numbers and decimals . . .
- **Grades 6–8 Expectations:** In grades 6–8 all students should work flexibly with fractions, decimals, and percents to solve problems . . .
- **Grade 9–12 Expectations:** In grades 9–12 all students should develop a deeper understanding of very large and very small numbers and of various representations of them.[6]

Standards are listed with the permission of the National Council of Teachers of Mathematics (NCTM). NCTM does not endorse the content or validity of these alignments.

Other people think of standards as discipline based. These standards describe what teachers and students should know and be able to do in various subject areas such as science, mathematics, history, geography, social studies, physical education, and the arts. Usually, these **content standards** emphasize the core components and big ideas of the discipline that should be known at a specific age or grade level. They are often accompanied by standards for what teachers should know about the content or subject to teach at the preschool, elementary, middle, or secondary level.

At a meeting of the U.S. state governors in 1989, the first President George Bush supported the development of content standards to ensure that the nation's students would be first in international academic competitions. The first set of student standards was released in 1989 by the National Council of Teachers of Mathematics (NCTM). With federal support, standards for P–12 students were developed by professional associations and other groups such as the National Research Council in subsequent years. Today, all states have developed their own content standards or adapted the national standards to their own state contexts.

Content standards establish the knowledge that should be learned in various subject areas. These standards are often linked to big ideas, themes, or conceptual strands that should be nurtured throughout a student's education. For example, in the national science standards, the big ideas of evolution and equilibrium, form and function, systems, and the nature of science are explicitly described, along with specific grade-level **benchmarks** that are linked to these bigger ideas. The same is true in the standards for social studies; the big ideas of community, scarcity of resources, and democracy are specified in statements concerning what students should know in primary, elementary, middle, and secondary schools. The NCTM standards, furthermore, state that students should be able to understand and use numbers and operations; specifically, they should

- *Understand numbers,* ways of representing numbers, relationships among numbers, and number systems;
- *Understand meanings* of operations and how they relate to one to another;
- *Compute fluently* and make reasonable estimates.[7]

In addition to knowledge acquisition statements, content standards often specify what thinking and process skills and strategies students and/or teachers should acquire. These skills and strategies might include developing a plan and hypothesis; interpreting, extrapolating, and drawing conclusions; and communicating results. Standards may also include statements about the habits or dispositions that should be nurtured in students. These habits or **dispositions** include curiosity, perseverance, tenacity, caring, and open-mindedness. For instance, the INTASC standards for state licensure expect new teachers to demonstrate the following dispositions related to individual and group motivation and behavior:

- The teacher takes responsibility for establishing a positive climate in the classroom and participates in maintaining such a climate in the school as a whole.
- The teacher understands how participation supports commitment and is committed to the expression and use of democratic values in the classroom.
- The teacher values the role of students in promoting each other's learning and recognizes the importance of peer relationships in establishing a climate of learning.
- The teacher recognizes the value of intrinsic motivation to students' lifelong growth and learning.
- The teacher is committed to the continuous development of individual students' abilities and considers how different motivational strategies are likely to encourage this development for each student.[8]

Other Uses of Standards in Education

The standards movement has resulted in standards being developed not only for K–12 students, but for teachers, administrators, and program accreditations. Examples of

content standards

Standards that specify learning outcomes in a subject or discipline (for example, mathematics or social studies).

benchmarks

A level of performance at which a standard is met. Examples of levels include "proficient" and "correct response on 80 percent of questions or performances."

dispositions

The values, commitments, and professional ethics that influence beliefs, attitudes, and behaviors.

Opportunity-to-learn standards identify the resources and support needed to ensure all students can meet content and performance standards.

each are described next. As you read about each of these sets of standards look for the common themes.

STANDARDS FOR BEGINNING TEACHERS (INTASC)

Principle 1
The teacher understands the central concepts, tools of inquiry, and structures of the discipline(s) he or she teaches and can create learning experiences that make these aspects of subject matter meaningful for students.[9]

Early in the standards movement (1987) a network of state education department teacher licensing professionals formed the *Interstate New Teacher Assessment and Support Consortium (INTASC)*. One premise guides their work: "An effective teacher must be able to integrate content knowledge with the specific strengths and needs of students to assure that *all* students learn and perform at high levels." This group developed standards for beginning teachers and gradually these have become the foundation not only for state initial teacher licensure tests, but also for the substance of teacher education programs. Therefore the INTASC standards also have been a guide for writing this text.

CROSS-REFERENCE
INTASC is described in Chapter 1.

STANDARDS FOR EXPERT/MASTER TEACHER CERTIFICATION (NBPTS)

VIII. Assessment
Accomplished teachers understand the strengths and weaknesses of different assessment methods, base their instruction on ongoing assessment, and encourage students to monitor their own learning.[10]

Also established in 1987 was the *National Board for Professional Teaching Standards (NBPTS)*. Its purpose has been to set standards for and to recognize accomplished teachers. It now has standards in twenty-seven fields. Teachers prepare and submit a portfolio which includes samples of student work, assessments, and videos of their teaching. Upon careful review the selected teachers receive national board certification. Now, just as the medical profession has board certification for various specialties, so does the teaching profession.

TEACHER EDUCATION PROGRAM ACCREDITATION STANDARDS (NCATE)

Standard 1: Candidate Knowledge, Skills, and Professional Dispositions
Candidates preparing to work in schools as teachers or other professionals know and demonstrate the content knowledge, pedagogical content knowledge and skills, pedagogical and professional knowledge and skills, and professional dispositions necessary to help all students learn. Assessments indicate that candidates meet professional, state, and institutional standards.[11]

National and state accreditation of teacher education programs is based on statements of standards. Teacher education faculty in colleges and universities have to prepare a report and document that their candidates meet the standards. This requires evidence of each candidate's knowledge, skill, dispositions, and ability to make a difference in student learning.

OPPORTUNITY-TO-LEARN STANDARDS

CROSS-REFERENCE
As is described in Chapter 5, the financing of schools affects the opportunity for all students to learn.

Teachers' and students' awareness of content and performance standards will do little to ensure achievement unless supports and resources are provided by the district and the community. Hence, some experts have advocated for opportunity-to-learn standards, which are sometimes called input or delivery standards. These standards address the need for the provision of adequate and appropriate instructional resources, assessments, and system structures to create the proper conditions for students to achieve the standards. Examples include guaranteeing that students have sufficient opportunities to relearn when a standard is not achieved, ensuring that sufficient time is offered to students so that they can achieve various standards at their own pace, offering alternative ways to achieve a standard based on individual needs, specifying the types of technology to be available in schools and classrooms, and regularly providing staff inservice that helps teachers fine-tune instructional techniques that lead to student achievement of specific standards. Students with disabilities and English language learners should be provided appropriate accommodations to support their learning of the proficiencies outlined in standards.

The Common Theme across Standards

What has been the common theme in the examples of standards presented here? The theme reflects the paradigm shift that was introduced in the introduction to this chapter—the focus on student learning. In each case the standards address student learning. Even the teacher education program accreditation standards address learning. Candidate learning is not sufficient; there needs to be evidence that each candidate can "help all students learn." Inputs, such as the number of books in the library, are less important than there being evidence that teacher education candidates, beginning teachers, and master teachers can make a difference in student learning. The student learning that is being addressed is what has been described in the district, state, and national professional association standards.

NO CHILD LEFT BEHIND AND STANDARDS

To help ensure that all students will learn at acceptable levels, Congress enacted legislation entitled No Child Left Behind (NCLB) in 2001. This act required all states to set standards for what a child should know and learn for all grades in mathematics, reading, and science. In addition, the states were required to set a level of proficiency for determining whether the standards are met by students. As was described in Chapter 5, schools are expected to make adequate yearly progress (AYP) as shown by their students achieving at the state's proficiency level or above on the state test. Federal expectations are that low-income students, students with disabilities, English language learners, and students from different racial and ethnic backgrounds will meet state proficiencies. If AYP is not achieved by one or more of these groups for more than two years, the school will be identified as needing improvement. Student performance will be publicly reported for schools in district report cards. By 2013 all students are expected to be at the proficiency level for their grade level.

The purpose of this title is to ensure that all children have a fair, equal, and significant opportunity to obtain a high-quality education and reach, at a minimum, proficiency on challenging state academic achievement standards and state academic assessments.

No Child Left Behind Act

CROSS-REFERENCE
NCLB is described in Chapters 1 and 5.

Why Standards Differ

These diverse conceptions of standards stem from differing expectations. Business leaders tend to want high school graduates who are ready for work by being able to read, write, and compute. They expect schools to prepare a supply of future workers. Businesses are willing to provide specific job training, but they do not want to teach what they consider basic skills that all students should have before entering the world of work.

Policymakers think about the larger, long-term needs of society. They promote more rigorous academic standards that will ensure that students perform at high levels on international comparisons, maintaining world-class status for the United States. They want students to know more science, history, mathematics, literature, and geography than students in other countries.

FIGURE 11.1

Differing Expectations for Standards

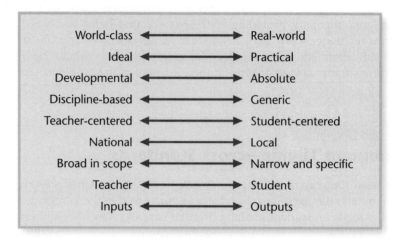

World-class	Real-world
Ideal	Practical
Developmental	Absolute
Discipline-based	Generic
Teacher-centered	Student-centered
National	Local
Broad in scope	Narrow and specific
Teacher	Student
Inputs	Outputs

Parents choose standards based on their own personal goals and family histories. Some parents want their children to go to prestigious colleges; others want their children to obtain a job immediately after high school; still others want their offspring to prepare for a professional career such as a medical doctor, lawyer, or engineer. These expectations influence the type of standards that parents support.

Figure 11.1 is a summary of the different dimensions and tensions that those who develop standards must consider. School districts wrestle with these differing expectations for schools when they adopt a set of learning standards. It is not easy to have a clearly articulated, coordinated set of standards that meets the expectations of all members of a community. The process of setting standards is not a simple one, and those who write standards often receive criticism from various dissatisfied community members. Despite these difficulties, the development of clear standards enables different constituencies within the school community to clarify their needs and their aspirations. The process of selecting and adapting standards also provides a forum for conducting dialogues and negotiating what schools should do and for what schools, teachers, and students should be held accountable.

The Future of Standards-Based Education

There is no escaping standards in schools today. They are not abstract statements of ideals that teachers can simply ignore. They are now driving what teachers teach and, in many districts, how schools—and in some cases teachers—are evaluated. Moving from a traditional to standards-based education requires a great deal of time, the involvement of all constituencies (teachers, administrators, parents, and community members), and good communications among the stakeholders.

Standards-based education is a complex and sophisticated approach to teaching and learning. It is a professional challenge for beginning teachers, as well as experienced teachers, to learn to teach this way. The teacher's role shifts from conveyor of knowledge and dispenser of grades to coach and facilitator of students as they engage in learning. The expectations and checkpoints are stated and known by the teacher and students before instruction begins. Students not only know beforehand what is to be learned, but they also know what the assessment tasks will be like—that is, the types of performances described in the expectations.

Many questions color the future of standards. How will school organization, use of time, graduation requirements, and power relationships change because of the standards movement? Can the same standards really be put in place everywhere without also bringing opportunity-to-learn standards to the front and center? How can the plethora of standards be managed by teachers and still be integrated with the move toward thematic and interdisciplinary instruction? If the standards movement is to be worth the upheaval it has generated, such questions must be answered by thoughtful, knowledgeable participants who are engaged in the process of changing what students learn and how they learn. One important step is the compilation of data about student learning related to standards. Therefore, one of the early efforts in the standards movement has been significantly increased attention to methods for assessing student learning.

Journal for Reflection

Consider the types of assessments that have been used throughout your college studies. Select one assessment experience that you have found to be especially helpful in displaying what you believe you really know and can do. Describe the assessment, and then list what characteristics of the assessment enabled you to express your understanding.

Assessment: The Other Side of Standards

Standards are not an end unto themselves. Simply listing standards in a school brochure will make little difference in the way students learn and achieve. If standards are to have any real effect on schools and on student achievement, they need to be supported by other elements in a school's structure: an articulated curriculum, professional development sessions focused on improving student achievement, and a well-thought-out array of assessments that match the standards.

rubric

Scoring guides that describe what learners should know and be able to do at different levels of competence.

When assessments are linked to standards, changes will occur in the types of measures used, the kinds of data collected, and the ways in which assessment results are used to enhance student achievement. These changes in the assessment process can be quite dramatic, since assessment in the past has often meant little more than teachers producing grades or students doing well on paper-and-pencil achievement tests. When assessments are interwoven into standards-based frameworks, they become much more varied and meaningful to teachers and students alike. The following section examines the changing face of assessment and the ways in which it should enhance the teaching and learning process.

What Is Assessment?

Assessment in education implies many things: evaluation, grades, tests, performances, criteria, **rubrics,** and more. To adequately encompass its many dimensions, it is helpful to examine assessment in a broader sense by analyzing its root meanings. The term *assessment* is derived from the Latin word *assessio,* which means "to sit beside." This image provides an excellent metaphor. Ultimately, assessment can be thought of as the act of sitting beside oneself and analyzing what one observes. In a sense, all assessment is based on this image: the examination of oneself through

Paper-and-pencil tests remain the major type of standardized assessments used to measure student achievement.

the perception of an examiner who sits beside you and provides feedback. Some theorists contend that all true assessment is ultimately self-assessment. Assessors can provide information, but in the end it is the person being assessed who accepts the information or rejects it, using the information to further his or her development or setting aside the information as unimportant.

The image of an assessor sitting beside a learner also implies the use of tools or measuring devices that enable the assessor to gather different types of information. Paper-and-pencil tests, performance assessments, portfolios, journals, and observation checklists are examples of different assessment measures. Often these tools are labeled assessments, but in fact they are merely measures that assessors use to provide feedback. Keep in mind that assessment is really the larger process of gathering information, interpreting the information, providing feedback, and ultimately using or rejecting the feedback.

Purposes for Assessment

The ultimate reason for assessment in the classroom is to help students learn. However, assessments of students and teachers today are being used for a number of other purposes as well. It is important to clarify these different purposes before attempting to interpret assessment results.

EVALUATING STUDENT LEARNING

formative assessment

Collection of data to show what a student has learned in order to determine the instruction required next.

summative assessment

Data about student performance that are used to make a judgment about a grade, promotion to the next grade, graduation, college entrance, etc.

Put simply, for teachers and students, assessing in classrooms is done for two purposes. The first is a **formative assessment** to determine what the student has learned and provide feedback to the learner so that both the teacher and the student can understand where to next focus their energies. The second is a **summative assessment** to make a final judgment about whether a certain level of accomplishment has been attained, such as passing a course. Most assessments for these purposes have been developed by teachers for use in their own classrooms. In standards-based education, teachers are checking throughout the year for evidence that students are meeting the standards through tests and a variety of other sources.

Student essays, projects, and portfolios are also valuable resources for knowing how deeply students understand the content of a subject. Observing students as they conduct experiments, demonstrate how to solve a mathematics problem, or interact with other students on a group project provides additional information about student learning. More and more teachers are recording their observations of student learning throughout the school year in journals that can show growth over time. These formative assessments help teachers know which students know the content at the expected level and which students need additional assistance.

DIAGNOSING

Assessment is an ongoing process in which teachers collect data on student progress toward meeting standards as they interact with, listen to, and observe students on a regular basis.

Diagnostic assessments are used to determine at what level a student is functioning compared to the level at which he or she should be able to function developmentally. Tests and other assessments can be used to help determine whether students are performing at grade level. The feedback from these sources should help teachers design new or different instructional strategies that will assist students who are having difficulty. These types of assessments provide an array of questions and tasks for a student to perform in a specific area such as reading, writing, mathematics, or motor skills. In such assessments, the questions and tasks might be organized by difficulty. As the student performs each task successfully, she or he is given another, more difficult question. Eventually, the student will be unable to answer or perform any tasks successfully.

Diagnostic assessments are also used to determine the need for special services or accommodations and are usually conducted by a special education teacher, school psychologist, speech/language pathologist, occupational therapist, or regular teacher trained to administer a specific test. Most school districts require these tests of students who have been referred by teachers or parents for special education or gifted and talented services. If a student is identified as needing special education services, an individualized education plan (IEP) is developed collaboratively by the regular teacher, a special education teacher, parents, and appropriate specialists such as a reading specialist or speech/language pathologist. The goal of the IEP is to identify appropriate instruction to support student learning at a level and pace that is appropriate to a student's specific needs.

GATEKEEPING

Assessments are often used as gatekeepers to determine who moves to the next grade or is admitted to a profession. For example, college admissions offices have a long history of using students' performance on standardized tests such as the ACT and SAT to determine who can be admitted. Professions such as law, medicine, nursing, physical therapy, certified public accountancy, and architecture require persons to pass a standardized test before they are admitted to the profession and allowed to work in a specific state. Most state departments of education require new teachers to pass a standardized test to be eligible for a license to teach. The use of standards for gatekeeping purposes is also becoming a way of life at the P–12 level. One of the first steps for children entering some of the prestigious preschools in a number of metropolitan areas is passing a test. A growing number of states require students to pass a test before a diploma of graduation is granted. Some school districts expect students to pass a test to move to the next grade.

Traditional Assessments

Educators use different types of assessments depending on the purpose of the assessments. The types described next are among the most common. Many are manifested in paper-and-pencil formats; others take the form of a demonstration of skills. Educators and parents should know the type of assessments being administered to their students and children. Are the assessments designed to compare students across the state or to determine if students have developed the core knowledge and skills expected in standards? The second design could be very helpful to a teacher and parents in knowing whether students are learning.

NORM-REFERENCED ASSESSMENTS

Sometimes assessments are used to demonstrate who is best in some area. In a norm-referenced assessment, the individual's performance is compared with that of a norm group of similar individuals. After these types of assessments are developed, they are carefully revised on a regular basis to ensure that the tests yield varied test scores from low to high. These types of assessment do not reveal all that an individual child knows or is able to do. They are not the appropriate assessment to use to determine whether students meet proficiencies outlined in standards. In some ways, norm-referenced assessments are like a contest, and it is expected that some students will excel and others fail.

Norm-referenced assessments are misused more often than most other assessments. Teachers must be cautious in concluding that individual students who score low are not doing well. Norm-referenced tests typically sample only a portion of what students in a particular class are expected to know and do. Therefore, the student might not be performing well in those areas assessed by the tests but be doing better in other areas that were not tested.

Sometimes state authorities penalize a school district or school whose students as a group perform below a specific level on a norm-referenced test. This is a flawed practice because norm-referenced tests are designed such that 50 percent will score below the fiftieth percentile. In fact, when schools begin to score regularly above this percentile, the test is made more difficult. A related problem is that the nature of the test prevents the inclusion of questions on some of the core, most important concepts in content standards. Too many students select the correct answer because their teachers focused on this key concept in their teaching to ensure that students learned it. If a large number of students select the correct answer, the test question is revised. As a result, many of the items on the test address peripheral areas of the standards, avoiding the important knowledge and skills at the heart of the standards. The goal is not to determine if most students meet standards but to make sure there is an appopriate distribution of scores.

CRITERION-REFERENCED ASSESSMENTS

Instead of comparing a student's performance with that of a group of students, criterion-referenced assessments compare a student's performance with a specific type of accomplishment or criterion. For instance, one can assess whether students can add two-digit numbers without regrouping. To measure this skill, a student could be asked to answer ten different questions. If a child successfully answers all ten, or nine or even eight of the ten questions, a teacher can state with some degree of confidence that the child knows how to add two-digit numbers without regrouping. This type of assessment is similar to a competency-based assessment; the major difference is that the criterion may be a very narrow competency, such as adding two-digit numbers, in contrast to a competency such as driving a car.

Most classroom tests should measure students' knowledge in a criterion-referenced manner; that is, a student should be asked to answer questions a number of times that measure the same learning. Then, instead of scoring the test by using some sort of A through F range, the teacher sets an acceptable score that determines that the student really understands a concept at an acceptable level.

CAPSTONE/SUMMATIVE ASSESSMENTS

Summative or capstone assessments can be developed to celebrate a milestone accomplishment or to demonstrate how well a person has mastered something. These types of assessments are used near the end of some major accomplishment such as recitals or graduation. For instance, after completing courses in education, a teacher candidate student teaches to show that he or she can help students learn the subject matter. Hence, student teaching is a capstone-type assessment. This capstone assessment is evaluated by a master teacher who notes all the accomplishments that are shown by the student teacher throughout the performance. In such an assessment, deficiencies can also be identified, but the major focus is to uncover what a teacher candidate has mastered throughout a program of study.

At the school level, a capstone assessment can be used at the end of a school year. Students can be asked to apply all they have learned in science by completing a science project or in language by writing a short story or a research paper. Some schools require a comprehensive test, presentation of student work in a portfolio, or essay as the capstone experience for graduation.

Performance Assessment

The notion of assessment is changing. For decades, educators have called for better testing, but the response was the proliferation of a number of different kinds of

Observing students at work is a very useful form of assessment.

tests with different emphases. Tests of achievement, basic skills tests, criterion-referenced tests related to specific objectives, tests of cognitive ability, tests of flexibility, and tests of critical thinking were developed. Despite these worthy attempts, these tests provide a limited view of what students know. Many educators viewed these paper-and-pencil instruments as an intrusion and not directly related to what was really happening in the classroom.

Instead, educators want assessments that allow students to demonstrate in a number of ways that they met standards in real-world or authentic settings—in other words, **performance.** The best performance assessments are designed to promote student understanding, learning, and engagement rather than simply the recall of facts.

Performance assessments can be used to demonstrate a specific competence. For example, if students have been taught a specific method for using a piece of science equipment, such as a gram balance, a competency-based assessment would include having the learner weigh several objects on a balance. The teacher would typically observe the learner to see whether all the specific techniques in accurately weighing a sample were used. Assessments of specific competencies in schools include many teacher-made assessments that focus on the specific things a learner has studied. An example of a competency-based assessment outside the classroom is the road test employed in most states as a prerequisite to receive a driver's license. The critical characteristic of such an assessment is that the assessment is closely related to something the learner must be able to do. Hence, in the road test, a person drives a car in situations that the driver will typically experience: turning left or right, backing up, parking, and so forth. The person is usually scored through an observation checklist that the assessor uses.

These performance assessments are examples of another important characteristic of good assessing. The tasks that students are asked to perform are **authentic.** They are realistic in terms of being as close as possible to how the learning would be applied in a real-world setting. Too often test items and activities are seen as being remote from what a learner would need to do in life. When assessments are authentic the tasks are based in problems and contexts that are clearly seen as relevant and real. Some possibilities for authentic performance tasks are presented in Table 11.2.

> I hear and I forget. I see and I remember. I do and I understand.
>
> *Chinese proverb*

performance
Demonstration of learning through doing.

authentic
Assessment tasks that are grounded in real-world settings and applications of what has been learned.

			Tips for the Teacher
Type	**What It Is**	**Uses**	**for Effective Use**
Learning Logs and Journals	Notes, drawings, data, charts, artwork, and other notes written by the student	• To reflect as one is learning • Also provides a record of questions and thoughts	• Generate questions for students to ponder and respond to. • The more varied the questions, the better.
Folios and Portfolios	Folio is the storage bin, box, or file. Portfolio is the organization and presentation of selected folio artifacts for a particular purpose.	• Document learning and growth over time • Encourages self-assessment • Show student's best work	• Have students explain why they have Included the various items. • Works should be tied to standards. • Teacher should provide feedback. • Both should discuss the portfolio.
Interviews	Peers and/or the teacher asking a set of questions	• Can determine what has been learned	• A variety of question types should be used to obtain a range of responses.
Observation with Anecdotal Record	Observing and note taking during day-to-day activities	• Provides documentation of performance and learning over time	• Needs to be done regularly. • Notes need to be written clearly and include specific descriptions. • Notes need to be reviewed. • Be careful to distinguish between facts and interpretations.
Student Products and Projects	Specific products such as lab reports, presentations, and digital productions	• Provides cumulative evidence about the extent of learning	• Can be displayed. • Review and discuss.

Table caption (top): **TABLE 11.2** Types of Performance Assessment Tasks

DESIGNING AUTHENTIC PERFORMANCE ASSESSMENTS

There are three major areas to consider in developing authentic assessments for standards. First, a rich context needs to be designed, one that permits inquiry to occur. Second, it is important to fill the context with a wide variety of questions so that different types of thinking can occur. Finally, the critical indicators for learning need to be identified.

BASING ASSESSMENT IN STANDARDS

Developing a performance assessment task begins by considering the learning standards, benchmarks, and objectives that are the intended outcomes of instruction. It is critical that students be assessed on the intended outcomes as described in the district/state standards and benchmarks.

SELECTING AN AUTHENTIC CONTEXT

An important step in developing authentic assessments is to structure the tasks so that they are complex enough to permit students to show important learning, motivating enough to encourage students to think, rich enough to offer multiple opportunities to show how and what students have shaped into an understanding, and relevant enough that students can use their own experience. Some writers call the structure of the task the **context,** by which they mean the various activities, hands-on experiences, and questions that encourage learners to think and show how they can apply what they know.

context

The various elements of the experience, questions asked, and setting.

FIGURE 11.2

A Simple Version of a Rubric as Described by Dr. Elliott Asp, Assistant Superintendent, Cherry Creek (CO) School District

Absolutely ——— Kind of ——— Not Sure ——— No Way
     4   **3**   **2**   **1**

MAKING THE ASSESSMENT REFLECTIVE OF THE INSTRUCTION

Too often teachers assess one way but teach in another. For example, assessing by using paper-and-pencil tests or using single-answer questions when instruction has been emphasizing inquiry is inappropriate. The reverse is also true. Assessing students in a hands-on inquiry mode when all instruction was lecture and reading/writing is equally incorrect.

RUBRICS

In its simplest and most basic sense, a rubric is a scoring guide. It is a way of describing different levels of accomplishment or degrees of being proficient. A rubric is not the measure; it is a way of interpreting, scoring and summarizing how well a student has performed. Figure 11.2 represents one way of thinking about a rubric. Rubrics are a tool for focusing on the important elements in an assessment and to combine these elements into a single score. They also provide guidance to ensure that different assessors rate in the same manner.

Rubrics can be analytic or holistic measures. *Analytic* means looking at each dimension of the performance and scoring each. *Holistic* refers to considering all criteria simultaneously and making one overall evaluation. You might sum all the analytic scores for a total score, or you might have one holistic dimension within an analytic rubric to provide an overall impression score. By doing this, assessors can access the benefits of both analytic and holistic scoring procedures. Analytic scoring, of course, provides the most specific data for use as a diagnostic assessment; it also limits flexibility because the dimensions are prescribed ahead of time. Holistic scoring does not require specific dimensions to be assessed; as such, it provides more flexibility and allows an assessor to give credit for unexpected dimensions that may contribute to the overall success of a performance. However, holistic scoring provides less direction for students than analytic scoring does. Table 11.3 and Table 11.4 are examples of analytic and holistic scoring rubrics.

BASING ASSESSMENT IN THE DISCIPLINE

The teacher needs to consider how the learning goals and standards relate to the lives and actions of scientists, writers, historians, and mathematicians. Consider what professionals do and how they use their different ways of knowing. Together, these considerations will often trigger ideas for the performance context.

To illustrate this way of determining a context, consider a curriculum that is filled with learning experiences focused on food chains, prey and predator relationships, and the balance of nature. How does this translate into a real-world context? Having students dissect owl pellets and analyze findings in light of the previous concepts provides one such context that is closely tied to the real world and to environmental issues. Like practicing scientists, students could be asked to

The rubric below uses a scale of one to four. Level 1 is a beginning or low level of performance; level 4 is a high level of performance.

Experiment Design	Scientific Results
4 Design shows student has analyzed the problem and has independently designed and conducted a thoughtful experiment.	4 Pamphlet explained with convincing clarity the solution to the problem. Information from other sources or other experiments was used in explaining.
3 Design shows student grasps the basic idea of the scientific process by conducting experiment that controlled obvious variables.	3 Pamphlet showed that student understands the results and knows how to explain them.
2 Design shows student grasps basic idea of scientific process but needs some help in controlling obvious variables.	2 Pamphlet showed results of experiment. Conclusions reached were incomplete or were explained only after questioning.
1 Design shows student can conduct an experiment when given considerable help by the teacher.	1 Pamphlet showed results of the experiment. Conclusions drawn were lacking, incomplete, or confused.

Data Collection	Verbal Expression
4 Data were collected and recorded in an orderly manner that accurately reflects the results of the experiment.	4 Speech presented a clearly defined point of view that can be supported by research. Audience interest was considered, as were gestures, voice, and eye contact.
3 Data were recorded in a manner that probably represents the results of the experiment.	3 Speech was prepared with some adult help but uses experiment's result. Speech was logical and used gestures, voice, and eye contact to clarify meaning.
2 Data were recorded in a disorganized manner or only with teacher assistance.	2 Speech was given after active instruction from an adult. Some consideration was given to gestures, voice, and eye contact.
1 Data were recorded in an incomplete, haphazard manner or only after considerable teacher assistance.	1 Speech was given only after active instruction from an adult.

Source: G. Wiggins, *Educative Assessment.* San Francisco: Jossey-Bass, 1998, p. 167. Copyright © 1998 Jossey-Bass. Reprinted by permission of John Wiley & Sons, Inc.

investigate a set of owl pellets that have been collected from a specific area of the country. Students can apply what they know and use skills and thinking processes throughout the investigation. The assessment should provide students with opportunities to take measurements, make observations, and record observations about the owl pellets. Students can be asked to create data tables that summarize the types of prey that were consumed, make inferences and draw conclusions about food availability, and finally even answer direct questions about food chains.

STUFFING THE CONTEXT WITH MULTIPLE OPPORTUNITIES   Once a context has been selected, it needs to be structured and filled with opportunities to show how and what students have learned. Asking students to display their cognitive abilities in as many ways as possible enhances the teacher's understanding of students' unique ways of knowing. This is where assessment tools are helpful. Observing students in action and recording these observations in a variety of ways are critical.

ASKING DIFFERENT TYPES OF QUESTIONS   Teachers have long been aware that questioning is an important way to cue students to display their understanding. Research indicates that the types of questions students are asked determine the

TABLE 11.4	Holistic Oral Presentation Rubric
5—Excellent	The student clearly describes the question studied and provides strong reasons for its importance. Specific information is given to support the conclusions that are drawn and described. The delivery is engaging and sentence structure is consistently correct. Eye contact is made and sustained throughout the presentation. There is strong evidence of preparation, organization, and enthusiasm for the topic. The visual aid is used to make the presentation more effective. Questions from the audience are clearly answered with specific and appropriate information.
4—Very Good	The student describes the question studied and provides reasons for its importance. An adequate amount of information is given to support the conclusions that are drawn and described. The delivery and sentence structure are generally correct. There is evidence of preparation, organization, and enthusiasm for the topic. The visual aid is mentioned and used. Questions from the audience are answered clearly.
3—Good	The student describes the question studied and conclusions are stated, but supporting information is not as strong as a 4 or 5. The delivery and sentence structure are generally correct. There is some indication of preparation and organization. The visual aid is mentioned. Questions from the audience are answered.
2—Limited	The student states the question studied but fails to describe it fully. No conclusions are given to answer the question. The delivery and sentence structure are understandable, but with some errors. Evidence of preparation and organization is lacking. The visual aid may or may not be mentioned. Questions from the audience are answered with only the most basic response.
1—Poor	The student makes a presentation without stating the question or its importance. The topic is unclear, and no adequate conclusions are stated. The delivery is difficult to follow. There is no indication of preparation or organization. Questions from the audience receive only the most basic or no response.
0	No oral presentation is attempted.

Source: G. Wiggins, *Educative Assessment.* San Francisco: Jossey-Bass, 1998, p. 166. Copyright © 1998 Jossey-Bass. This material is used by permission of John Wiley & Sons, Inc.

academic culture of a classroom. Questions that focus on a single aspect of knowing (knowledge or skills) limit the opportunities for showing understanding (the interactions of knowledge, skills, and habits of mind). Having a clearer picture of the multidimensionality of understanding (ways of knowing) directs teachers to ask a wide variety of questions. This is especially true during an assessment experience. Students should be asked many different types of questions within a rich, hands-on context. Figure 11.3 presents examples of the variety of question types that allow students multiple opportunities to show their various ways of knowing.

ASSESSING THE IMPORTANT ELEMENTS Once students are engaged in a motivating inquiry, they will be better able to exhibit learning development. It is important that teachers focus on all aspects of learning when they examine student performance and not simply focus on those aspects that are easy to assess. If a context is truly authentic, there should be ample opportunities for students to display what they know and can do across a variety of different standards:

- Knowledge and comprehension of concepts, application of concepts, and connection of concepts to real-world contexts
- Ability to solve problems and exercise thinking skills
- Ability to perform and apply process skills
- Ability to structure thinking
- Collaboration and other dispositions
- Communication and ability to modify ideas on the basis of new evidence

FIGURE 11.3

Examples of the Types of Questions That Encourage Students to Show Different Ways of Knowing

- Analysis Questions: What are the key parts? Which parts are essential and why?
- Comparison Questions: How are these alike? What specific characteristics are similar? How are these different? In what way(s) are they different?
- Classification Questions: Into what groups could you organize these things? What are the rules for membership in each group? What are the defining characteristics of each group?
- Connections Clarification Questions: What does this remind you of in another context? To what is this connected?
- Constructing Support Questions: What data can you cite that support this conclusion? What is an argument that would support this claim?
- Deduction Questions: On the basis of this rule, what would you deduce? What are the conditions that make this inevitable?
- Inferring and Concluding Questions: On the basis of these data, what would you conclude? How likely is it that this will occur?
- Abstracting Questions: What pattern underlies all these situations? What are the essential characteristics of this thing?
- Error Analysis: How is this conclusion misleading? What does not match?

A rich assessment context allows students to display many of these components of understanding and skill. The art of assessing well includes identifying indicators—things that can be observed that relate to different aspects of some important standard. Identifying indicators in a performance task is much like acting as an X-ray; teachers need to notice what behaviors count and how successful ways of doing and knowing look. To do this, teachers need to step back from the performance, much like a physician, and identify those actions that are meaningful and, more important, the learning that those actions indicate. Once teachers develop lists of indicators, they can easily assess what a child knows and does not know. These lists can form the basis for assigning grades, discussing student progress, and making decisions about student needs.

Authentic assessment is both an art and a science. As an art, assessment is like the world of a play. Placing students in the proper context is like situating characters to play a particular role; once in this context, students cannot help but display the knowledge, thinking, and habits of mind they have developed. On the other hand, authentic assessment is also like a science in that the educator needs to meticulously identify and examine the important questions and other types of learning indicators that are important to the task.

As can be seen, authentic assessment is an attempt to make testing both in and out of the classroom more closely grounded in the context of student learning and less narrowly focused on a few aspects of what has been learned. Its very name implies trying to better determine what children have really learned.

Professional Aspects of Good Assessments

Thus far, we have examined the purposes and described a variety of the methods being applied to performance assessment. However, assessing student learning has more to it than the mechanics of constructing authentic tasks. Assessing student learning is an activity that influences and affects many people. Therefore, there are professional and ethical considerations. A number of very technical issues are also related to whether each assessment task is fair and truly assesses what was intended.

PRINCIPLES FOR HIGH-QUALITY ASSESSMENTS

Like other professionals who have knowledge that their clients do not have and whose actions and judgments affect their clients, classroom teachers are responsible for conducting themselves in an ethical manner. This responsibility is particularly important in education because, unlike other professions, students have no choice about whether they will or will not attend school. The following principles are keys to developing and using powerful and responsible assessments:

- Base assessments on standards for learning.
- Represent performances of understanding in authentic ways.
- Embed assessments in curriculum and instruction.
- Provide multiple forms of evidence about student learning.
- Evaluate standards without unnecessary standardization.
- Involve local educators in designing and scoring assessments.
- Let the innovators of the system lead.
- Provide professional development that builds the capacity of teachers and schools to enact new teaching and assessment practices.
- Judge school performance based on practices as well as longitudinal performance data for individuals.[12]

FAIRNESS

Some of the attractions of state tests are that they are standardized, perceived as objective, and inexpensive in comparison to performance assessments. One of the problems is that they ignore the lived experiences of many test takers, resulting in biases that give students from one group an advantage over another. Analyses of test items show that many of them are biased against students from low-income families. Basing assessments on a set of standards provides appropriate standardization. Performance assessments, unlike standardized tests, can take into account the variations in students' learning contexts while still holding to the levels of achievement expected to meet standards.[13]

RELIABILITY AND VALIDITY OF ASSESSMENTS

Two critical aspects of any effort to assess student learning, whether the assessment items have been developed by an individual teacher or a national testing company, are reliability and validity. Each of these terms is regularly used in professional discussions; however, their meaning and implications might not be appreciated. The only way in which any assessment of student learning can be counted on to be fair is if each and every item is both valid and reliable.

Validity refers to whether the assessment item measures what it is intended to measure. All too frequently, test items do not measure what the test maker had in mind. For example, a history teacher could have a learning objective related to students being able to describe key social, economic, and political causes of the Civil War. If the teacher then uses a test item that asks students to describe the results of key

Communicating with all constituencies, including taxpayers, parents, and students, is an essential part of developing standards and having a shared understanding about assessment methods and the meaning of results.

battles during the Civil War, the test item would not be valid. It did not ask students to demonstrate what they had learned in relation to the stated learning objective. This is a simple and obvious example of an assessment item that is not valid. Problems related to validity are many and can be extremely complex. Still, it is essential that teachers make every effort in the construction of assessment items to make sure that what students are being asked to do is closely aligned with the statement of standards and learning objectives.

Reliability is an equally important technical aspect of having high-quality assessments. Reliability has to do with the consistency of information about student learning that results from repeated use of each assessment item or task. If two students who have learned the same amount complete the same assessment, do they receive identical scores? If they do, then the item has high reliability. If two students with the same level of learning receive discrepant scores, then the item is not consistent or reliable. Test makers often check for reliability of their items in another way, called test–retest. In this approach to checking reliability, the same student responds to the same test item after a carefully selected time interval, typically a week or two. Here too the reliability question is "How consistent are the results from both administrations of the assessment?" If both assessments have similar results, then the assessment is considered to be reliable.

Journal for Reflection

Obtain a copy of your state's learning standards for one discipline. Examine the framework in which the standards are described. Do they have related goals, benchmarks, or other dimensions? Focus on one standard and identify all of the components that relate to that learning standard. In your journal, draw a diagram or create a mind map or concept map that shows the interrelationships of all the supporting pieces that surround the standard.

Accountability

Schools will be responsible for improving the academic performance of all students, and there will be real consequences for districts and schools that fail to make progress.

No Child Left Behind Act

As is illustrated in the case study at the beginning of the chapter, parents and policymakers in many areas of the country are holding their teachers, schools, and school districts accountable for student learning as measured on standardized tests. The federal legislation No Child Left Behind requires schools to annually test all students in grades 3 through 8 on their achievement of standards in math, reading, and science. Secondary students must be tested at least once. One of the purposes is to provide feedback on student learning to students, parents, and teachers. Data are publicly reported in district and state report cards that show how students in local schools perform in comparison to students in other schools. The legislation allows parents to remove their children from a local school that has been found in need of improvement for two consecutive years and send them to a school at which students are achieving at a higher level.

I believe that we should get away altogether from tests and corelations among tests, and look instead at more naturalistic sources of information about how people around the world develop skills important to their way of life.

Howard Gardner

Student assessments can provide important information on whether school programs are effective. One way of assessing the success of a school program is through norm-referenced assessments, but these assessments are quite limited. They measure only how well a group of students does on a standardized paper-and-pencil task in comparison to other groups of students across the country. To determine how well a program is doing, it is important to use **multiple assessments.** For example, one additional way to assess a school program would be to regularly gather information about how graduates are performing in the real world. Information about how many students successfully graduate without being retained could be another useful indicator. Having a broad array of assessment data can enable school districts to take stock and redirect efforts such as changing the types of instruction being used and the types of learning being emphasized.

multiple assessments

Using more than one measure and type of measure in making a judgment.

Testing Ups and Downs

The nationwide movement toward standards, performance, and a variety of assessment strategies is a good one, especially for teachers and their students. The goals

Similar Students, Different Results: Why Do Some Schools Do Better?

STUDY PURPOSE/QUESTION: Whenever student test data are examined for several schools there will appear to be schools where students do well and other schools where the same type of students do not do as well. Lower scores on tests are expected for schools with large proportions of low-income students. However, some schools with large proportions of low-income students score well. Why is this?

STUDY DESIGN: A team of researchers examined the data for 257 of California's elementary schools. The schools were selected based on their having higher proportions of low-income students. Teachers and principals were then surveyed "to explore school qualities, policies, and practices related to school success." Topics sampled included: having a standards-based instructional program, involving and supporting parents, using assessment data to improve student achievement and instruction, and encouraging teacher collaboration and professional development. The other important source of data was California's Academic Performance Index (API), which ranks all schools in the state based on the performance of students on the state content tests.

STUDY FINDINGS: The findings indicated that in schools where low-income students scored higher the following elements were in place:

- *Prioritizing Student Achievement.* Both teachers and principals had higher expectations for student performance and there were well defined plans for instructional improvement.

- *Implementing a Coherent, Standards-Based Curriculum and Instructional Program.* In higher performing schools teachers reported school-wide instructional consistency within grades, curricular alignment from grade-to-grade, classroom instruction guided by state academic standards, and districtwide commitment to address the instructional needs of English learners in their schools.

- *Using Assessment Data to Improve Student Achievement and Instruction.* The district and school used assessments that were highly correlated with the API tests. Principals, as well as teachers, used these data to develop strategies to follow up on the progress of selected students to help them reach goals.

- *Ensuring Availability of Instructional Resources.* In schools where more teachers held regular certification and had more years of teaching experience student success was higher. The districts for these schools provided sufficient and up-to-date instructional materials.

IMPLICATIONS: Among the many important implications that can be drawn from this study for teacher education candidates are the following:

1. *Low-income students can succeed.* Teachers, schools and school districts have to set and make clear the expectations that low-income students can learn.

2. *Alignment is important.* Having content standards, state testing, and district, school, and teacher tests that are aligned is important. In other words, teacher tests and school/district interim assessments should predict how well each student and school will do on the once-a-year state test.

3. *Standards-based education is a key.* Having and using standards, aligning instruction within and across grade levels, and using assessments makes a positive difference in learning for low-income students.

4. *Teachers and Principals are Proactive.* Rather than accepting the status quo, teachers and their principals use assessment information to make changes in instruction with the intent of improving student learning.

5. *Teachers did not work alone.* Rather, teachers and the principal worked together to continually improve.

Source: T. Williams, M. Kirst, E. Haertel, et al. *Similar Students, Different Results: Why Do Some Schools Do Better? A Large-Scale Survey of California Elementary Schools Serving Low-Income Students.* Mountain View, CA: Ed Source, 2005.

---

of teaching and learning are made clear, which then makes it easier for teachers to know what to teach and how. Having standards certainly aids students in understanding what is most important to learn. And having standards helps teachers, schools, school districts, and states in determining the learning outcomes that should be assessed. Still, as with any education initiative, the standards movement has had a number of unintended consequences that need to be considered. Several of the

What Is the Proper Way to Prepare for High-Stakes, State-Mandated Tests?

Schools across the country are now required to administer state assessments linked to learning standards. The assessments tend to be paper-and-pencil, multiple-choice examinations of reading, mathematics, science, social studies, and writing. The assessments are given annually to students in grades 3–8. Teachers within these targeted grade levels are required to interrupt their regular school instruction to administer these state examinations.

The state-mandated assessments are comprehensive in nature; that is, they cover a wide variety of topics that relate to the state standards. This often poses a dilemma for teachers who instruct at one of the targeted grade levels. Students in their classrooms might show that they have not had proper instruction in one or more aspects of the state content. This can and does occur because the district curriculum might not fully represent state standards, because individual students do not develop at the same pace, or because students transfer from school districts that have diverse curricula.

What can or should a teacher at a targeted grade level do to assist students on these state examinations? Some teachers attempt to teach to the test. That is, they try to get sample test items, and they clarify what was on the prior year's examination. These teachers may even develop teacher-made test questions that mimic the state examination and require students to practice taking these preparation tests. In some states, practice tests can be purchased from private publish-

ing companies. Teachers who teach to the test in this way are sometimes criticized because they take time out of the regular school curriculum. They are also criticized because some educators consider teaching to the test to be improper.

Other teachers do not try to teach to the test, but they do have students practice test-taking techniques. They teach students strategies that could assist them in taking any standardized multiple-choice examination. They too take time out of the normal curriculum, but these teachers contend that the acquisition of such test-taking skills assists in all areas of learning.

A third group of educators refuse to do any test preparation other than to teach the required curriculum for their grade level. These educators believe that state tests should not affect the normal instructional process. If students do not perform well, then the curriculum should be officially changed.

Questions for Reflection

1. What will you do if you are teaching in one of these target grade levels?
2. Should you teach to the test?
3. Should you teach test-taking techniques?
4. Should you ignore the test and simply follow the normal curriculum?
5. What approach can you defend as the proper one?

To answer these questions on-line and e-mail your answers to your professor, go to Chapter 11 of the companion website (www.ablongman.com/johnson14e) and click on Professional Dilemma.

more important of these consequences with direct impact on teachers and students in classrooms are discussed next.

HIGH-STAKES TESTING

As the focus on student performance has intensified, policymakers have mandated that students be tested annually. Testing of this type is called **high stakes** because of the consequences for the test taker or school once the test results are known. At a minimum, the student test results are compiled by schools and reported to the public. Schools are named and ranked in the newspaper, and sharp questions are asked about those schools that are not meeting adequate yearly progress.

high stakes

Decisions that have major consequences/implications.

Another way in which testing can be high stakes is through the assignment of rewards and sanctions. In a few states, "high-performing" schools receive additional funds. In some districts, teachers and/or principals receive salary bonuses if test

FIGURE 11.4

Criteria for High-Stakes Testing Practices

Source: Denise McKeon, Marcella Dianda, and Ann McLaren, *Advancing Standards: A National Call for Midcourse Corrections and Next Steps.* Washington, DC: National Education Association, 2001, p. 8.

The American Educational Research Association's (AERA) *Public Policy Statement on High-Stakes Testing in PreK–12 Education,* adopted in July 2000, provides twelve criteria, based on solid research, that state education leaders, local school leaders, parents, and others can use to assess the assessments. AERA states that every high-stakes testing program should ensure:

- Protection against high-stakes decisions based on a single test
- Adequate resources and opportunity to learn
- Validation for each separate intended use
- Full disclosure of likely negative consequences of high-stakes testing programs
- Alignment between the test and the curriculum
- Validity of passing scores and achievement levels
- Opportunities for meaningful remediation for examinees who fail high-stakes tests
- Appropriate attention to language differences among examinees
- Appropriate attention to students with disabilities
- Careful adherence to explicit rules for determining which students are to be tested
- Sufficient reliability for each intended use
- Ongoing evaluation of intended and unintended effects of high-stakes testing

For more information, visit AERA's website at www.aera.net.

---

scores improve. Some states provide rewards to high-performing schools, but much more likely is some sort of sanctioning of the low-performing schools. On the positive side, Kentucky and North Carolina provide assistance to schools that are "in need of improvement" by assigning an experienced master teacher or principal to work with the schools. In other cases, principals are reassigned and entire school staffs replaced. In states such as New Jersey, Massachusetts, and Ohio, an entire school district that is designated low performing can be taken over by the state. Criteria for high-stakes testing are listed in Figure 11.4. Tests can be high stakes for students and their future as well. Many states now use standardized exams to determine graduation from high school.

PRESSURES TO CHEAT

In high-stakes conditions, we can expect teachers and principals to invest concerted effort in helping their students do well on the tests. In nearly every school and classroom, teachers stop their regular instruction for a week or more to help students prepare for the test. These preparations can be as practical as practicing answering multiple-choice questions and reviewing what has been taught during the year. The problem arises when teachers—and in some cases principals—help their students cheat. Cheating ranges from telling students how to answer specific test items to teachers, principals, and school district administrators actually changing students' responses on individual tests. In other instances, schools have encouraged some students, such as those with learning disabilities, to stay at home on the day of testing.

TEACHING TO THE TEST

A related issue has to do with balancing the time teachers spend on topics that are likely to be on the test versus instructional time spent on the rest of the curriculum.

High-stakes conditions have led to an increase in student pressure to cheat.

About two-thirds of teachers indicate that their instruction is too focused on content that will be tested, to the detriment of covering other material. Almost 80 percent of teachers report that they teach test-taking skills to students,[14] reducing the amount of time to teach the content itself.

Any single test is bound to sample a very limited part of what students learn. Also, state tests might have little overlap with the various sets of content standards and the emphasis in district curriculum materials. Time spent on preparing for high-stakes tests reduces the time available to teach related material and other subjects, such as the performing arts, that are not being tested or for which the stakes are not as high. Teaching to the test also often means that the development of critical-thinking and higher-order thinking skills is neglected. If the whole of the district curriculum is aligned with state standards, then those students whose instruction covers more of the standards should perform better on the tests.

ONE-SIZE-FITS-ALL

Another critical issue related to the heavy focus on testing is the assumption that the same test is appropriate for all students, schools, and states. Historically, in the U.S. system of education heavy emphasis has been placed on the importance of attending to individual differences and emphasizing that all students do not develop at the same rate. Now policymakers are mandating that one test be given to all students at a certain grade level at a specified time—in other words, "one-size-fits-all." No matter what the uniqueness of individuals might be, all are to take the same relatively narrow test, and major decisions about individual students and/or schools are based on the test results. Academically able students take the same test that poor urban students take. This practice undermines the credibility of the test and its results clearly disadvantage some students and schools.

THE THREAT OF A NATIONAL EXAM

A growing concern of some people is that the practice of many states using the same tests is just one step away from a national exam, which will lead shortly thereafter to a national curriculum. This is the one-size-fits-all concern taken to the extreme. Others believe that there already is a national curriculum and that national requirements are appropriate. A key target of this perspective is the National

Assessment of Student Learning across Nations

National assessment is not limited to the United States; it is a worldwide phenomenon that has blossomed over the past decade. Participants in the World Education Forum adopted a World Declaration on Education for All in Jomtien, Thailand, in 1990 and ratified the declaration in Dakar, Senegal, in 2000. The declaration recognized that periodic student assessments make a valuable contribution toward the improvement of educational quality. Many countries consider academic achievement as pivotal in establishing a highly qualified labor force that attracts foreign capital and allows them to be competitive in the global martketplace.[15] To promote these efforts, the World Bank, Inter-American Development Bank, United Nations Educational, Scientific, and Cultural Organization (UNESCO), and the U.S. Agency for International Development (AID) have invested in the design and implementation of national assessments.

What assessments are required in other countries? England has a national examination for students at ages seven, eleven, fourteen, and sixteen that measures the effectiveness of schools in delivering the national curriculum. Schools in England set targets for student growth. France conducts national assessments at grades 3, 6, and 9 for diagnostic and planning purposes. The tests at the end of grade 9 and the end of high school measure student achievement.[16]

National examinations in Hong Kong dictate instruction in schools. China views its National College Entrance Examination as critical to the nation's development. Much of the population sees the national test as providing opportunities for the oppressed to achieve an elite education. The only national test in Japan is for college entrance. However, Japanese students take other high-stakes tests to gain admission to high schools.[17]

Students in Argentina are tested annually in grades 3, 6, 7, 9, and 12 in mathematics, language, science, and social studies. All twelfth graders are tested, but testing at the other grades is conducted through a sampling process. Chile assesses all students in grades 4 and 8 in language and mathematics, and samples 10 percent of the students in natural sciences, history, and geography. Uruguay tests students in mathematics and language in grades 3, 6, and 9. Each of these three South American countries compiles data on the school and family socioeconomic conditions of test takers and develops individualized school reports. Argentina and Chile have disseminated test results publicly for nearly a decade.[18]

Questions for Reflection

1. What benefits do you see in the high-stakes testing that students are experiencing? Is your reasoning different for the United States than for other countries? Why?

2. In the United States, the states are spending over two billion dollars each year on testing. Do you see this as a good use of tax dollars? Why or why not?

3. Should high-stakes tests accommodate for English language learners? How?

Assessment of Educational Progress (NAEP), which is administered each year to students in a sample of schools in each state. One of its purposes is to make it possible for policymakers and educators to view nationally how well students are doing. Comparisons then are made with student achievement in other countries, and most assuredly comparisons are made from state to state in this country. NAEP is designed to make inferences about student achievement within states. It is not designed to make judgments about individual students or schools. Unfortunately, although NAEP has existed for several decades and its findings are very useful, school districts and schools are increasingly unwilling to participate owing to the mounting pressure and time demands of the many other required tests.

INCREASED TEACHER BURDEN

As exciting and important as the new approaches to assessment are, one of the downsides is the increased work for teachers. Developing more authentic tasks takes more time than does constructing multiple-choice and true/false test items. Deriving scoring devices for authentic tasks is added work too. Holistic scoring entails first developing a scoring rubric and then examining each student's response in sufficient detail to be able to determine a total score. The load on teachers becomes even heavier in secondary schools because each teacher has contact with more students. One of the important solutions to the risk of an increased burden is for teachers within a school or school district to collaborate in the development of assessment tasks. There also is national sharing of assessment items through discipline-based professional associations and various chat rooms on the web. A related key for individual teachers is to keep in mind that many of the traditional activities that teachers have been doing to assess student learning, such as noting their performance in laboratories and in the field, have become more legitimate with the move to authentic assessment.

Equity within Accountability

There's something wrong with imposing universal standards on a state or nation until, prior to that time, we have given the children genuinely equal resources. The way it is being done today is invidious, punitive, and humiliating.

Jonathan Kozol

No Child Left Behind expects schools to help all students meet standards at defined proficiency levels regardless of their socioeconomic status, ethnicity, race, first language, disability, migrant status, or gender. In fact, performance by students from each of these groups must be reported on the school's and district's annual report card. Thus, teachers are held responsible for helping all students learn as reflected on a single assessment—the state content test. Meeting this goal will be more difficult in some settings than others, especially when resources are limited or nonexistent for providing students with the facilities and support necessary to promote learning at a high level and providing teachers the necessary professional development. Nevertheless, it is a goal worth achieving.

A continuing point of criticism about these traditional tests is that they do not address or accommodate the diversity of students in today's classrooms. Each student brings a unique set of background experiences, prior knowledge, and cultural perspectives to learning. Asking all students to show what they know on a narrow standardized test is a very real problem.

The gap between the test scores of white students and most students of color remains wide. The data collected from the fifty states and the District of Columbia for *Education Week*'s annual *Quality Counts 2003* showed that the achievement gap between white and African American or Latino students in twenty-five states on the NAEP eighth-grade math test was 20 percentage points or more.[19] Ironically, many researchers have found that state tests are much better determiners of the family's socioeconomic level than of academic ability. Students who perform poorly on these tests are disproportionately from low-income families.

Supporters of NCLB argue that black and Latino students will perform at a more equal level over time because schools will be able to raise their test scores by hiring only **highly qualified teachers,** teaching reading more effectively, basing instruction on what is known to work from "scientifically based research," and allowing parents to remove their children from low-performing schools and place them in higher-performing schools. Critics also believe that all students can learn and that highly qualified teachers are essential, but they worry about the use of a single standardized test rather than multiple assessments to determine whether a student can be promoted or graduate. They also question the ability of schools, especially in high-poverty areas, to raise test scores without intensive professional development

highly qualified teachers

Teachers who are licensed without a provision and have passed a standardized content test in the subject they teach or for the grades they teach.

of teachers, reduction of student-to-teacher ratios, greater involvement of parents, and more stimulating curriculum and instruction—all areas that require financial resources that are not usually available in communities with the greatest need.

These issues become even more glaring for students who are English language learners and those with special needs and learning disabilities. State assessments usually allow for exemptions from taking the test for some students and require appropriate accommodations for others. Often, simply changing the way in which learning is assessed can provide significant new opportunities for these students to demonstrate their knowledge and skills against a set of standards.

Journal for Reflection

Standards-based education and new approaches to assessing learning are being applied in higher education, especially in teacher education programs. The same ideas apply in both P–12 and higher education settings. In what courses have you seen standards-based education reflected? In what ways? How would you compare the effectiveness of a standards-based approach to a traditional approach to teaching and learning?

Summary

STANDARDS-BASED EDUCATION. A new paradigm has arrived in U.S. schools. No longer is the focus on the inputs, what teachers teach. Now the focus is on the outputs, evidence that students have learned. Expectations for learning are being described in the form of standards, which have been developed for all subject areas and grade levels. In addition, there are specific INTASC Standards for what is now expected of beginning teachers. Even the national accreditation of teacher education programs is based on standards of what has been learned by candidates.

ASSESSMENT: THE OTHER SIDE OF STANDARDS. Once the standards of learning have been set, teachers, as well as curriculum developers and policymakers, want to know how well students are doing. Assessing is more than testing. It entails developing and using good measures along with making interpretations and judgments about what has been accomplished and what needs to be done next. Assessment of student learning has become very important and increasingly technical. Using multiple measures to make judgments about the amount of student learning is very important for teachers and when making high stakes decisions.

ACCOUNTABILITY. The pressures on states, school districts, schools, and teachers has never been higher. Everyone wants to see higher levels of student learning. Two tools are being used to hold educators accountable: standards and testing. The stakes of testing can be high for states, school districts, schools, teachers, and students. Every effort must be taken to insure that the tests are of high quality and that high stakes decisions are based upon multiple sources of evidence.

Discussion Questions

1. Standards-based education is now the paradigm that teachers are expected to use. Using the elements identified in Table 11.1 as a guide, where would you place teachers you have had? Which approach have you found most helpful in your learning?
2. Assessing has been described as being more than testing. What does this mean for you as a teacher? How will you know if you are assessing, rather than simply testing?
3. Standards-based education calls for the use of performance assessments in determining whether students meet standards. How could student portfolios be used to show what students have learned? What problems might such assessments cause?
4. How fair is it to demand that all students, no matter what their ability or socioeconomic status, master a common set of learning standards before obtaining a diploma? In what cases do you think students should be exempt from testing requirements for graduation?
5. What do you see as your role as a teacher in a standards-based education classroom? What professional development will you need as a new teacher in order to implement standards-based curriculum and performance assessments in your classroom?

School-Based Observations

1. Talk with teachers in the schools that you are observing and review the school district's website; then identify the standards that teachers are supposed to use. During your observations, record the evidence that convinces you that standards are (or are not) integrated into classroom instruction. Also indicate how the school is (or is not) supporting teachers in preparing students to meet the standards.
2. Interview several teachers who are required to administer state assessments that reflect standards. Ask the teachers to identify what they do to help students prepare for the assessments. Record the results of your interviews and then write your own stance (from an educator's perspective) with regard to the value of statewide and high-stakes assessment.
3. One of the distinguishing characteristics of standards-based education is that students, regardless of grade level, are supposed to be able to describe the expectations for learning (standards and benchmarks). Interview some students and see how they describe what they are doing in a particular lesson. Do they tend to describe the instructional activity ("We are studying the Civil War"), or do they describe what they are supposed to be learning ("We are learning about the economic factors that led to the Civil War"). Can they describe how much they have learned?

Portfolio Development

1. Authentic assessments attempt to provide students with opportunities to show what they know and can do within a real-world setting. Within your major subject area, develop an authentic assessment that would enable students to demonstrate what they have learned in relation to one of the national standards.
2. Use the library, the web, or a faculty member to search out information about the activities in one school district regarding their use of standards and their assessment of learning related to those standards. Look closely at the standards and assessments for your planned teaching area. Develop a page of notes about what you would say in a job interview related to their use of standards-based education. Also note three or four questions for which you would need to find additional information or develop better understanding before you went to the interview.

Preparing for Certification

STANDARDS AND ASSESSMENT

1. Two topics in the Praxis II Principles of Learning and Teaching (PLT) test relate to this chapter: "monitoring students' understanding of content through a variety of means" and "reflecting on the extent to which learning goals were met." In this chapter, you learned about the importance of the standards movement in establishing curriculum goals and assessing student learning. Learn more about the national standards for the subjects and grade levels you plan to teach. What goals for learning are contained? What are some ways you might assess those goals?

2. Answer the following question, which is similar to items in Praxis and other state certification tests.

   Mr. Harding has just completed a unit on sonnets. To assess students' understanding of the structure of sonnets, he constructed a quiz of ten poems and asked students which poems were sonnets. He expected students to be able to classify the poems with at least 80 percent accuracy. This assessment is an example of

   A. norm-referenced assessment
   B. criterion-referenced assessment

C. authentic assessment

D. summative assessment

3. Answer the following short-answer question, which is similar to items in Praxis and other state certification tests. After you've completed your written response, use the scoring guide in the *Test at a Glance* materials to assess your response. How can you revise your response to improve your score?

Reread the case study at the beginning of the chapter, which reports on how California fourth- and eighth-graders scored on the National Assessment of Educational Progress. As a teacher, your students' performance will be compared to how the students of other teachers and students in other school districts and other states are doing. Take a position for or against these comparisons and provide your reasons.

Websites

www2.edtrust.org/edtrust Education Trust's site provides data, policies, and recommendations related to academic achievement with an emphasis on students who have not been served well in the educational system.

www.nces.ed.gov/nationsreportcard The National Assessment of Educational Progress website provides information about the national testing programs and national report card.

www.relearning.org This site for Relearning by Design provides information on standards and authentic assessment and is hosted by the Coalition for Curriculum and Assessment (CCA).

www.nctm.org Information about the National Council of Teachers of Mathematics and its standards can be found at this website.

www.ccsso.org The Council of Chief State School Officers is the professional association for all state superintendents of education. The web site provides links to each state where it is possible to explore that state's standards and information about test results.

www.edform.com The Center for Educational Reform provides summaries of test results as well as statistics from the National Center for Education Statistics. There also is news and information about each state.

Further Reading

Kohn, Alfie. (1999). *Schools Children Deserve: Moving beyond Traditional Classrooms and "Tougher Standards."* Boston: Houghton Mifflin. A discussion of the overemphasis on achievement and standardized testing. The author calls for intellectually stimulating classrooms and provides examples from classrooms.

Lazear, Edward (ed.). (2002). *Education in the Twenty-First Century.* Stanford, CA: Hoover Institution Press. In this book of edited papers various scholars examine issues related to national exams, accountability, performance and school funding. Throughout is the theme of the importance of education to the individual and society.

Popham, W. James. (2001). *The Truth about Testing: An Educator's Call to Action.* Alexandria, VA: Association for Supervision and Curriculum Development. A critique of the tests being used by states for high-stakes testing programs. Guidelines are included to help teachers use tests for instructional benefits.

Sacks, Peter. (1999). *Standardized Minds: The High Price of America's Testing Culture and What We Can Do to*

Change It. Cambridge, MA: Perseus Books. A critique of standardized testing and its negative impact on teaching and learning, especially for students from low-income families.

Symcox, Linda. (2002). *Whose History? The Struggle for National Standards in American Classrooms.* New York: Teachers College Press. A discussion and analysis of the drafting of the history standards, the controversy, and their subsequent rejection by Congress. The analysis provides valuable insights into how decisions are made about the history to be taught in schools and about developing national content standards.

Wiggins, Grant, and McTighe, Jay. (1998). *Understanding by Design.* Alexandria, VA: Association for Supervision and Curriculum Development. This book is a key reference on how to think about assessment and to make connections between assessments, the design of instruction, and student learning.

mylabschool
Where the classroom comes to life!

Go to Allyn and Bacon's MyLabSchool (**www.mylabschool.com**) and complete the following activity for Chapter 11. Click on **MyLabSchool Simulations;** then click on **Classroom Assessment and Content Standards.**

CHAPTER 12

Designing Programs for Learners: Curriculum and Instruction

CASE STUDY

Guidelines for Teaching English Are Adopted

By Carla Rivera, *Los Angeles Times,* April 18, 2006

A divided state Board of Education on Monday adopted far-reaching new guidelines for reading and English language arts textbooks aimed at California's elementary and middle school students despite objections that the materials do not do enough to help students struggling to learn English.

The new curriculum, passed on a 6–4 vote, is critical because it will be used to provide detailed guidance for textbook publishers who will supply the books, teacher guides and other instructional materials for classrooms over much of the next decade.

The guidelines specify criteria for oral and written vocabulary development, writing and reading comprehension.

For the first time, the criteria seek to incorporate the needs of English learners, with additional instruction and assessments before and after regular classroom time.

Supporters contend that the curriculum will provide California with some of the most rigorous standards in the nation and ensure equity for all students.

But in a packed hearing room, opponents told board members that the guidelines do not go far enough in addressing the needs of the 1.6 million students who speak little or no English. They proposed an additional option that would allow school districts to incorporate extra instruction for English learners during regular class periods.

"We're outraged and can't believe that the state of California is prepared to say that one program fits all of the kids," said Shelly Spiegel-Coleman, a member of the group Californians Together, an English-learners advocacy group.

Earlier in the hearing, Darline P. Robles, superintendent of the Los Angeles County Office of Education, told the board that school districts must have flexibility.

And state Assemblywoman Judy Chu (D-Monterey Park) told board members that the new guidelines represent the "status quo" that has not addressed the needs of the residents in her district, many of whom are English learners.

She noted that California spends more than $500 million on new textbooks every six years.

"As chair of the Assembly Appropriations Committee, I do not believe in wasting money that does not support a large percentage of the students in this state," Chu said.

Board members who voted against the guidelines said they were undecided on other options and sought further review.

But many other speakers supported the new curriculum and voiced concerns that other options might lead to segregating English learners from other students.

"These criteria ensure that all students are held to the same standard," said Michael Romero, director of reading for the Los Angeles Unified School District. "The additional vocabulary instruction will be greatly appreciated and effectively utilized by thousands of students in our district."

Textbook selection in California is a complex, yearlong process layered by multiple committees and reviews. The final product is a framework, which includes textbook criteria, that is submitted to the state Board of Education for approval or modification.

Textbook publishers then shape their materials to meet the criteria. Panels check content accuracy, scholarship and adherence to state standards. Committees also review social content, such as gender roles and depictions of racial, religious and ethnic groups. The board then makes final selections. New materials are adopted on a six-year cycle. The new selection will be used starting in 2008 and will be standard through 2014.

Elementary and middle schools must spend most of their textbook funds on state-approved materials.

In recent decades, publishers—seeking a foothold in the state's lucrative market—have been willing to adapt materials in an effort to meet California standards.

Questions for Reflection

1. Did you know that in many states local school districts are not free to choose textbooks? Instead, the state board of education selects them. What do you consider the pros and cons of this approach?

2. If textbook publishers "adapt" their materials to fit the adoption specifications for large markets, such as Texas and California, what do you see as possible implications for other states with smaller markets?

3. Education is often criticized for being slow to change. In the case of textbook selections in California, how much time does it take to go through the whole cycle? What are some of the consequences of this lengthy process?

Reprinted with permission.

INTASC

Learning Outcomes

After reading and studying this chapter, you should be able to:

1. Analyze the effects of different influences on the selection and design of curricula in your state. (INTASC 10: Collaboration)

2. Describe and compare different curriculum designs. (INTASC 1: Subject Matter; INTASC 4: Teaching Methods; INTASC 7: Planning; INTASC 8: Assessment)

3. Identify and apply different types and forms of learning objectives to instruction. (INTASC 4: Teaching Methods; INTASC 7: Planning)

4. Describe and analyze characteristics of direct and indirect teaching strategies. (INTASC 4: Teaching Methods)

5. Compare the learning needs of different types of learners and the relative effectiveness of different teaching strategies. (INTASC 2: Development & Learning; INTASC 4: Teaching Methods)

The content taught, the materials selected, the teaching strategies used, and the activities in which children engage are elements of the curriculum. Deciding on these elements is a complex process. Most major decisions about the curriculum are made a long way from the classroom. As a result, contrary to what you might expect, today's teachers have a limited say in selection of the curriculum. Many others—including policymakers, parents, advocacy groups, and publishers—are involved in determining the curriculum.

However, teachers continue to have major responsibility for and autonomy in the *delivery* of the curriculum. Which content is taught, how much time it receives, and student perceptions of the importance of particular subject areas are determined by the classroom teacher. The real-time delivery of a lesson, how the classroom is managed, the responses made to student statements, and the day-to-day assessment of student work are also in the hands of the teacher. Determining which students respond to questions, whose work is displayed, and which students are selected to be group leaders are key elements of instruction and primarily, if not solely, the responsibility of the teacher. All of these decisions and actions are elements of the curriculum. Likewise, the teacher decides how much of the textbook to use and the extent to which the teacher, or the students, touch the manipulative materials. Because teachers control the delivery of the curriculum in the classroom, also known as *instruction*, the role of the teacher is probably more significant than ever.

The major theme of this textbook, "perspectives on education in a changing world," applies doubly when it comes to the discussion of curriculum and instruction. As the case study illustrates, everyone has a perspective about what should be in, and not in, the curriculum. Also, curriculum and instruction (C&I) are very expensive components of education. So taxpayers, as well as textbook publishers, are interested in how well the money is spent. Adding to these themes is the way the world is changing, which has significant implications for today's learners who will be tomorrow's adult citizens. The importance of careful consideration of all perspectives is a critical part of the curriculum selection process. However, before curriculum can be selected, it must be developed, which entails many steps. Once developed and selected the curriculum has to be taught in each classroom and across all schools, which requires highly skilled teachers who understand their subjects and know how to teach their students in interesting ways.

This chapter presents two important topics—curriculum and instruction. Both topics build on the content of earlier chapters, especially Chapters 2, 3 and 4 that dealt with the sociological foundations, and Chapters 9, 10, and 11 that described the philosophical foundations. These different perspectives come to life when a curriculum is being developed, as well as when it is time to select what will be taught. These perspectives also influence how the selected curriculum will be taught—that is, instruction.

One big idea has to do with diagramming the many constituents and interest groups that have a hand in determining the curriculum. A second has to do with the fact that much of the curriculum is not readily visible or even understood by teachers, parents, and community members. Of course, the important responsibilities and role of the teacher in planning, delivery, and assessing instruction are covered. What teachers decide to do and not do makes significant differences in what students learn.

> Curriculum is the substance of schooling—the primary reason why people attend school.
> **M. Francis Klein**

Curriculum: Relating Expectations for Learning to What Is Taught

The **curriculum** is anything and everything that supports student learning. Certainly, curriculum includes the materials and teaching processes that are described in various documents such as curriculum guides and textbooks. The curriculum also includes statements for student learning and the methods used to assess student learning. It includes the informal and less visible parts of the school day. Deciding on the curriculum is an important beginning. However, choosing certain learning outcomes—in other words, standards—and describing the particular subject content and perhaps some of the teaching activities are only the beginning. An important next step is curriculum development. In developing curriculum, there are a number of basic designs to choose from. Once selected and developed, the whole of the curriculum for each state and each school district must be managed and evaluated. Each of these steps and processes is of critical importance, and each must be done well in order for teachers to do the most they can to help all of the students in their classrooms learn. Over the next several pages, we describe each of the steps in the curriculum development process along with direct implications for classrooms, teachers, and their students.

curriculum

Standards, teacher resources, classroom materials, and teaching processes that in combination support student learning.

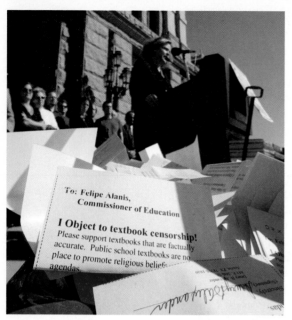

Special interest groups are a powerful influence on the selection of curriculum.

Developing Curriculum Is a Process Involving Different Perspectives

The various curriculum resources such as standards, textbooks, lab materials, and technology that are available to teachers had to be developed. In most cases a number of people will have been involved in creating and trying out curriculum resources before they are made available to teachers and schools in general. Some materials will have been developed by a single teacher and then made available on the web or through a curriculum library located in a school district office or in a college of education curriculum resources center. Regardless of who did the development a number of important tasks had to be accomplished and a number of critical questions about what is truly important had to be addressed.

STEPS IN THE CURRICULUM DEVELOPMENT PROCESS

Curriculum theorists of the past identified a logical sequence of steps to accomplish when developing new curriculum; see Table 12.1.[1,2] The steps may seem overly simple, logical, and sequential; however, they continue to be as essential as they were in the past. The development of any curriculum should incorporate each of these steps. When one or more of these steps is neglected, teachers and their students will have to struggle to fill in the missing pieces.

PERSPECTIVE MATTERS

As was described in the sociology and philosophy chapters, those who are engaged in developing curriculum will bring their own views and beliefs to the effort. For example, people who believe that students can be trusted will press for activities that allow for student initiative and open-ended explorations, whereas the developers who believe that students will make a mess and break manipulative materials will develop activities that rely more on the teacher and are more structured for the students.

Beliefs about student learning and effective teaching come into play as well. Some theorists believe that what is to be learned should be broken down into subparts and each of these taught separately and sequentially, whereas others will advocate for presenting the whole and letting the students "figure it out." For example, perspective makes a difference in teaching addition. Should students be taught a single way to do addition and be expected to always do it that way, or should they be encouraged to do addition in different ways, as long as they can explain how they obtained the correct answer? There is not a single correct answer to any of these questions; the best answer is a matter of perspective. Depending on the perspectives of the developers, curricula they produce can be quite different.

SOME DIFFICULT CURRICULUM DEVELOPMENT QUESTIONS

The seven steps to curriculum development outlined in Table 12.1 make the work look easy. However, the reality is that developing curriculum is hard work and there are a number of very important value-laden questions that will either be addressed explicitly or implicitly. These questions are not only important for curriculum developers to ask; they also are important for each teacher to consider in bringing the curriculum to life in the classroom.

Three key questions must be addressed for each curriculum development initiative:

TABLE 12.1	Basic Steps of the Curriculum Development Process	
Step	**Name/Purpose**	**Example Activity**
1	Determining what needs to be learned and why	Surveying parents or business leaders about what future citizens/workers will need to know; or, identifying the big ideas in a discipline
2	Describing the desired learning outcome(s)	Writing standards, benchmarks, and objectives for each grade level
3	Selecting the specific content	Relating what is expected in the standards with what are the important topics in the discipline
4	Organizing the content	Designing a topic and objectives sequence so that what is learned first builds toward what will be learned later
5	Selecting the learning activities	Identifying the specific lesson activities, tasks, and materials that will engage the learner and be congruent with the core ideas of the discipline
6	Organizing the learning activities into a whole	Sequencing the learning from the early grades through high school and organizing the topics within each year so that they are coherent and rigorous, with objectives that can be learned
7	Evaluating the effectiveness of the materials, instruction, and student learning	Collecting evidence from teachers about instruction and from students about learning outcomes

1. What should be taught?
2. Who should decide?
3. How will it be taught?

Think about each of these questions. Determining what will be taught has serious implications for the learner, the teacher, and society. Should the content prepare students for work? Should it contribute to their being "good" citizens? To what extent should the selected content prepare the student to learn advanced content? Who should make these decisions—teachers, experts, politicians, or citizens? Getting agreement on the third question is difficult too. Each teacher will have his or her own views about which way is best. What is to be done when the curriculum developers and teachers have different views? Answering each of these questions begins with philosophical assumptions and beliefs about what is important for society and individuals, as well as understanding the discipline. What should happen during instruction also requires careful deliberation.

The following questions also must be addressed by curriculum developers. Answering them is not easy for one person; it is even more difficult for a curriculum development team to come to consensus about them. Still, each has to be addressed in each curriculum development effort.

TABLE 12.2   The Variety of Curriculum Designs

Curriculum Design Name	Design	Role of the Teacher	Role of the Student
Subject-Centered	Selected subjects are identified. Organization is tight and narrow, and the sequence is specified.	Primary strategy is lecture. Teachers are expected to teach to the prescribed sequence and use the prescribed materials.	Students learn the content. The narrow focus allows students to learn more content in less time.
Broad Fields	A number of subjects are integrated and theme generalizations from each subject become the big ideas.	Teachers may lecture. Focus is on the broad generalizations instead of depth in a particular content.	Students are expected to develop a broad understanding across a number of contents. Students may not understand the broad themes and simply memorize them.
Core	Includes some contents all students should know. Depending on the philosophical perspective, a set of subjects is selected to be the center of the curriculum.	Rather than discrete content courses, integrated blocks may be offered. The content is taught in relation to problems or topics. Each problem uses each of the content areas. Typically, teachers teach as interdisciplinary teams.	Students learn through the study of interdisciplinary problems. Accompanying this learning is learning in related subjects.
Spiral	The curriculum is viewed across the P–12 continuum, the assumption being that key content will be taught more than once. In an early grade, a particular topic will be introduced in a general way. Several years later, the subject will be taught a second time with more depth. Then in the high school years, the topic will be taught again with even greater depth.	Teachers will use a variety of teaching strategies. The key is that teachers must have sufficient depth of knowledge to offer more content depth with each cycle in the spiral. Teachers also must make a concerted effort to add depth to student understanding with each subsequent pass.	Students are expected to learn the content at the depth taught each time. The risk is that they will not retain the knowledge and understanding developed in the previous cycle.
Problem-Based	Students work in groups and are presented with a problem. Solving the problem requires that they learn new content.	The teacher is guide and coach rather than dispenser of content. Only when the need arises does the teacher present content.	Students are expected to be able to work cooperatively as members of problem-solving teams. They must be self-starters and motivated to study the problem.
Mastery	Levels of learning that all students are to reach are identified. Students are given as much time as they need and a variety of activities to aid their reaching mastery.	Teachers must be able to provide a variety of activities and ways for students to reach mastery. Teachers also must be skilled at assessing what students do and do not know.	Once students have met the criterion for a particular learning, they move on to addressing the next learning target.

(continued)

TABLE 12.2	(continued)		
Standards-Based	The standards of learning become the content.	Student learning is placed at the center rather than the topic being taught. Teachers use a wide variety of lessons and assessment strategies, all of which are aimed at assisting students in constructing their own understanding.	Students know the standards and specific benchmarks they are studying. They self-assess in relation to these.

1. To what extent should the learning outcomes support preserving a democratic society?
2. Which outcomes are important for the individual learner's self-worth?
3. Is the curriculum biased in some way against certain individuals or groups?
4. Will the curriculum be available to all? Or is it too expensive, hard to teach, or does it have components that are inaccessible to some?
5. Is it built around the essential center of the discipline or is it composed of peripheral and isolated elements?

As challenging as these questions are, coming to consensus about their answers is central to the curriculum development process.

CURRICULUM DESIGNS

Several basic designs for curricula exist. Each design has particular strengths and weaknesses; each has different implications for teachers. Some designs are typically found in U.S. schools, whereas others are more apt to be seen in schools in other countries. Each design is based on assumptions about what is important for students to learn as well as particular philosophies about teaching and how students learn best. Summaries of common designs are presented in Table 12.2.

The earliest schools in America were **subject-centered.** There were three subjects: religion, Latin, and Greek. The only teaching style was lecture. The students were expected to learn—in other words, memorize—the content. Since that time, a series of evolutions in curriculum design have occurred. One theme of change is an increase in the number of content areas taught. A second theme is developing curriculum designs that are of more interest to students. The move toward various types of integrated and problem-centered curricula is a reflection of the first theme, whereas the decreasing popularity of teacher lecture is seen as an effective way to increase student motivation.

COCURRICULUM AND EXTRA-CURRICULUM

When most teachers, parents, and the public think about curriculum, they think about the core academic subjects of language arts, science, mathematics, and social studies. However, school includes other subjects, such as world languages, physical education, and, especially in secondary schools, athletics, band, drama, choir, and many clubs. These other subjects, after-school activities, and clubs make up the **cocurriculum,** which sometimes is called the **extra-curriculum.** In many ways, it can be argued that the cocurriculum is of equal importance as the basic subject areas. The cocurriculum is especially important in high schools. Unfortunately, during times of budget cuts, various pieces of the cocurriculum are targeted. For example, driver education used to be a free component of the cocurriculum in most public high schools. Now, if it is offered through the school at all, it requires a fee. This is unfortunate because for many students participation in the cocurriculum is a prime reason for staying in school. Cocurriculum teachers are excited about their programs and spend long hours after school, at night, and on weekends working

subject-centered

Curriculum that is organized around a finite and limited set of core subjects.

cocurriculum/extra-curriculum

School activities and programs, before, during, and after regular school class hours, that enrich the curriculum and provide extended opportunities for student participation.

Student participation in the cocurriculum and extra-curriculum can provide important opportunities for learning, as well as encouragement for staying in school.

with students to publish the student newspaper or yearbook or to prepare the team or band for the next competition. These highly dedicated teachers and their programs provide students with experiences and skills they will carry with them throughout their adult lives.

Selecting Curriculum Is a Complex Business

At the beginning of this chapter, we observed that in today's schools teachers play a limited role in select-ing the curriculum. In the past, teachers could teach their favorite lessons without worrying that there would be dire consequences for them or their students as a result of not following the guide or syllabus. As was illustrated in the case study, teachers today do not have this flexibility; they are responsible for helping all students achieve in terms of the published standards and benchmarks. So then, who does select the curriculum?

DIFFERENT LEVELS OF INFLUENCE

As befits our democracy, many people and groups have a say in selecting the cur-riculum for public schools. Figure 12.1 illustrates the many different actors and forces involved in determining the curriculum. Around the outer circle is the array of forces and interest groups that represent the macro view. The middle ring summarizes many of the local factors and conditions that influence curriculum decisions. The inner ring shows the school context and influences. The product of this array of forces and interests is the curriculum that is selected and implemented in each classroom.

LARGE SCALE INFLUENCES ON CURRICULUM SELECTION   The primary effect of the various elements that form the outer ring in Figure 12.1 is to influence what will be common for curriculum in all states and school districts. Court cases, state and fed-eral legislation, national reports, and educational research, as well as textbook pub-lishers, determine much of what will be taught and learned in all schools and classrooms. In fact, this set of influences works against local control of schools. In-stead of local control, there is a steadily growing movement toward the establish-ment of a statewide and even national curriculum.

Another macro-level influence on the curriculum are the various **interest groups,** such as teacher and administrator organizations, political parties, and reli-gious advocacy groups. These groups pay close attention to the work of commit-tees charged with developing standards, curriculum guides, and test items. Each group is likely to have its own unique perspective and agenda. For example, teacher associations tend to resist any accountability moves that would link student performance on tests with the identity of the teachers who taught them. Many religious groups advocate that their positions, such as intelligent design, be included and that contrary positions, such as evolution, receive less emphasis. A different per-spective might be represented by administrator associations, which are concerned more about costs and being asked to implement **unfunded mandates.**

The various accrediting bodies, such as the Southern Association of Colleges and Schools (SACS) and the New England Association of Schools and Colleges (NEASC), influence the curriculum through their standards for all schools they accredit. These standards in some ways set a common curriculum for all schools. For example, school accrediting bodies require each school to have a **school improvement process (SIP).** A SIP usually is written by a school committee and

interest groups

Informal and formal orga-nizations of individuals who hold a common in-terest and shared agenda in regard to a particular topic or policy.

unfunded mandates

Policies that are required to be implemented for which no financial support is forthcoming.

school improvement process (SIP)

A plan for future action that results from a school leadership team review of current successes and needs.

FIGURE 12.1

Influences on Curriculum Selection and Development

Source: F. W. Parkay and B. H. Stanford, *Becoming a Teacher,* 5th edition, p. 378. Published by Allyn and Bacon, Boston, MA, 2001. Copyright © 2001 by Pearson Education. Reprinted by permission of the publisher.

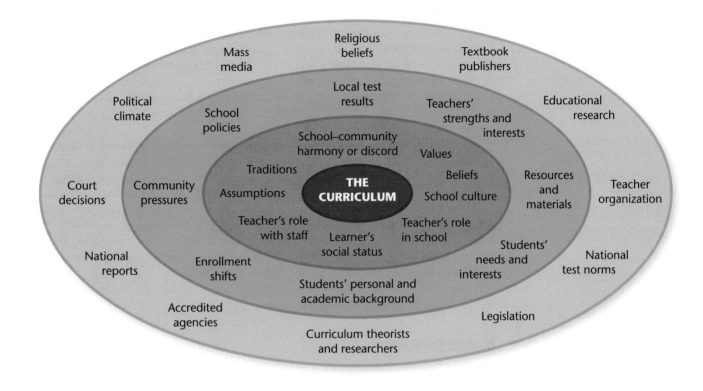

the principal during the spring of the year. The plans include analyses of data about student learning, reports about the year's efforts to improve the school, and specific plans for the next year. Key expectations for these plans include analyses of student success on state tests such as those in mathematics, literacy, and, in some states, writing. The accrediting body expects improved student performance on state tests; a direct consequence of this expectation is that each school and teacher is expected to provide curriculum and instruction designed to enhance student achievement on the prescribed test. In ways such as this, a common curriculum is defined and implemented for all accredited schools.

INTERMEDIATE INFLUENCES ON CURRICULUM SELECTION   At the local school district level, many additional factors influence the curriculum. Clearly, community interests and priorities are an influence. If the community values high school football and marching band, these two program areas will be an integral part of the cocurriculum. The personal background of students also influences the curriculum. For example, in most school districts a significant proportion of the students might be **English language learners (ELLs).** ELL students are in middle and high school classrooms as well as elementary school classrooms. Curriculum influences of this population are many. There is more demand for teachers who speak their native languages. ELL students also need more assistance in learning academic subjects because they are learning English at the same time. One likely consequence is that ELL students do less well on high-stakes tests, especially if they are expected to read

English language learners (ELLs)

Students whose first language is other than English and who therefore are learning English at the same time they are learning the content specified in the curriculum standards.

Curriculum: Relating Expectations for Learning to What Is Taught   **399**

and respond in English. The overall result is that the curriculum in the classroom needs to be adjusted in response to these influences.

SCHOOL SITE INFLUENCES   The inner circle of Figure 12.1 summarizes some of the school's influences on the curriculum. Assumptions about learning, for example, make a significant difference in which subjects are emphasized, what is taught, and how. For example, if teachers in a particular school truly believe that all students can learn, then the curriculum is organized and delivered in ways that support all students learning: Students are grouped according to their needs; regular classrooms include students with special needs; and most group activities are organized to take advantage of the diverse talents and interests of students rather than having like students grouped together. In comparison, if teachers in a particular school believe that some of the children can't learn, then "those" children are given less opportunity and more limited access to the curriculum. The result confirms the teacher's beliefs: Those students do less well.

In spite of the many influences on curriculum selection, its development, and its implementation, it is clear that in the end the curriculum is delivered in classrooms. This has two important implications. The first is that the role of the teacher in implementing today's curriculum is enormous. Although teachers have relatively little say in curriculum selection, they have the primary responsibility for helping students learn and achieve the desired outcomes. The second implication is that teachers have a plethora of curriculum resources to work with: curriculum guides, teacher-training sessions, and textbooks, as well as standards and benchmarks. All of these curriculum resources assist teachers in understanding what they should be teaching, and help them see what came before and what will happen next year with the students they teach this year.

Curriculum Resources and Selection

The curriculum delivered in each classroom has a rich and complex foundation. The tangible items for the teacher and the students include curriculum guides, textbooks, student workbooks, available technologies, and manipulative materials and lab supplies. However, the curriculum is more than printed documents. It also encompasses schoolwide resources and special-purpose facilities such as the media/resource center, playground and athletic facilities, cafeteria, auditorium, band practice hall, and arts and crafts classroom. As stated previously, the curriculum also includes the expectations for student learning. Each of these curriculum resources is important for teachers to understand, carefully examine, and use wisely.

CURRICULUM LIBRARIES AND THE WEB

Today's teachers have many easy-to-access supplementary resources to help them understand the curriculum and to obtain ideas for teaching to the standards. One invaluable resource now is the web. For any subject matter or topic there will be a large number of websites. Professional associations, regional education laboratories, intermediate agencies, and individual teachers and professors have made available tips and full lesson plans. The school resource center and the curriculum resources in the district office and at the nearby college will have much useful information. In addition are the textbooks and activities that are used during the teacher preparation program. Having these to refer back to can save the day, or night, sometimes.

TEXTBOOKS

For teachers, one of the primary sources of information about the curriculum is the commercially published textbook. Textbook publishers employ expert author teams and invest large sums of money to provide students and teachers with

German Education

Education programs in the United States always suffer in comparisons with other schools of the world, particularly those in Europe. A recent comparison of German and American schools, however, gives a more accurate analysis of the two systems and what they produce. Before comparing the two systems, the analysis places the systems on the same playing field. For example, U.S. schools, in addition to the major charges of teaching the three Rs, must provide social education, including understanding and appreciating differences in ethnicities, races, creeds, and cultures; recreation; avocational education; vocational education; art; music; and theater—and the list goes on. German schools have a much narrower mission. Their focus is on the three Rs, special education, and socialization. Extracurricular activities, from music to sports, are the responsibility of the communities, churches, and amateur athletic associations. Vocational education is the primary responsibility of business and industry. Health and safety are the responsibility of health maintenance organizations (HMOs), government, churches, private institutions, and the home.

After the sixth grade, German students elect, by choice and examination, the main school, *Hauptschule* (about a third of the students), the *Realschule* (about one-fourth of the students), or the *Gymnasium* (about one-third of the students). Whereas the *Hauptschule* and *Realschule* prepare students for vocational education and apprenticeship programs, the *Gymnasium* is the academic school for the development of the mind and preparation for college attendance for professional careers. Special education students, about 10 percent of the student body, attend well-supported special schools called *Sonderschule*. Although a comprehensive-type high school, *Gesamtschule,* which is patterned after the American comprehensive high school, has been started, fewer than 10 percent of the students attend it.

There is little or no heterogeneous grouping in German schools, and teachers are firmly supportive of ability grouping. In the college preparatory schools, students can shift programs on the basis of interest and societal need, but the longer they wait to do that, the longer it takes them to complete their education because they must make up deficient prerequisites. Classes are spread over twelve months of the year and meet six days a week. However, with time allowed for vacations and holidays, German schools are open about 180 days a year, much like those in the United States. College-bound high school students experience a program that is closer to that of the U.S. college than of the U.S. high school.

Teachers in Germany are better paid and more respected than their U.S. counterparts. Recently, a German poll ranked teachers second behind judges in the list of most respected professionals. As a profession, teaching maintains a type of guild that is somewhat similar to the teaching ranks in U.S. colleges. Most master teachers in the *Gymnasium* have earned a doctorate along the way up their career ladder. The state, Germany, pays teacher salaries, but the communities are responsible for the construction, care, and maintenance of the various schools in their community. Businesses and industries provide the financial support for vocational education.

To compare the students of these two countries requires that similar students be compared. The best of the U.S. academically talented students compare most favorably with the students of the *Gymnasium*. German students who are not in that school are not used for comparison purposes with American students, but all American students of the U.S. comprehensive high schools become data for comparison with foreign students. Therefore, most comparisons are not apples to apples, but rather apples to sauerkraut.

Questions for Reflection

1. Do you think that American schools should be organized into the three types of schools: *Hauptschule, Realschule,* and *Gymnasium*? Why or why not?

2. In German schools students are ability grouped. Why is this a good idea? What is wrong with it?

up-to-date and well-designed materials. In U.S. schools, for most subjects textbook packages provide the bulk of the content, lesson objectives, and audiovisual resources, as well as student assignments. Most textbooks have an accompanying instructor's guide that provides the teacher with additional background subject information, lesson plans, suggestions for extensions and special assignments, and test items. A number of additional resources exist for teachers who use textbooks in the major subject areas such as science, mathematics, and English. These additional resources include training workshops, access to supporting websites, and perhaps videos of classroom lessons in which the textbook is used.

CURRICULUM GUIDES AND COURSE SYLLABI

Another important curriculum resource consists of the support materials for the teacher prepared by the school district and state. These include syllabi and curriculum guides for each subject area and grade level. Curriculum guides and syllabi draw the connections between what is to be taught at each grade level and the expectations for student learning in state and district standards. These guides also provide a vertical view of how the subject is to be covered from grade level to grade level. This is important because students experience school one year at a time, but their learning needs to be cumulative across the years. Teachers need to see how what they are teaching this year relates to what students learned last year and what they will be expected to learn next year. District and state curriculum guides are very useful for teachers as they plan daily lessons, especially when information is provided about the specific benchmarks for student learning that must be addressed and assessed at each grade level and for each subject. In some cases, such as in California, instead of having guides the state curriculum is organized around the **big ideas** for each subject area and published as Curriculum Frameworks. For example, in describing the nature of science, three broad assumptions are stated:

> The scientific method is a process for predicting, on the basis of a handful of scientific principles, what will happen next in a natural sequence of events. Because of its success, this invention of the human mind is used in many fields of study. The scientific method is a flexible, highly creative process built on the broad assumptions:
>
> - Change occurs in observable patterns that can be extended by logic to predict what will happen next.
> - Anyone can observe something and apply logic.
> - Scientific discoveries are replicable.[3]

STANDARDS ARE THE FIRST PLACE TO LOOK

Of all the resources available to teachers the most important are the standards. As has been described earlier, for most subject areas there will be at least three sources of standards: (1) those published by the professional associations such as the National Council of Teachers of English (www.ncte.org); (2) the statement of standards developed within each state, and available through each state's department of education website; (3) a school district's own list of standards, often called **power standards,** which are a reduced or more focused set of the state and national standards. These standards will clearly identify the subject matter and content that should be taught. The standards will not describe how to teach to the standard; teachers will need to turn to the many other curriculum materials and resources to plan instruction.

TESTS

How often in your career as a student have you thought about asking or heard someone else ask the teacher, "Will this be on the test?" An important indicator of which elements of the curriculum are seen as most important is what is actually tested.

big ideas

The organization of content around major themes and principles.

power standards

A reduced set of standards that focuses on the most critical learning outcomes that must be taught and learned within each school year.

With the continuing emphasis on high-stakes testing, teachers and their students must be knowledgeable about what is tested. A core assumption in some school districts and states, such as Texas, that have "no-pass-no-play" rules is that students will work harder to learn the material if they are tested and experience the direct consequences of the results.

For you as a teacher, understanding what is on the test is important for at least two reasons: (1) Your students will be highly motivated to learn what will be on the test; and (2) you will quickly discover that for your grade level or subject, some critical topics are not covered on the high-stakes test. Both of these reasons illustrate an important aspect of the curriculum: The curriculum is not just what is in the textbook, nor just what is in the classroom lessons; it also is embedded in the expectations for learning and related assessments.

Managing Curriculum

Clearly, many levels of interest and many perspectives directly influence the selection of a curriculum. This large and diverse set of influences also affects the processes for designing curricula. Without some sort of control mechanisms or an organized authority, it would be impossible for each teacher to choose what to teach and how to teach in ways that satisfy a majority of the influences. Without some sort of overall authority, there would be no continuity in the curriculum from teacher to teacher, grade level to grade level, or school to school.

In the United States, the legal responsibility for schools, and therefore for the curriculum, lies with each state. In large part, state legislatures and state boards of education determine the curriculum. Additional structures exist to set and support the curriculum at the school district level. In addition, even with the centralizing roles of the state and district, schools and teachers retain a number of important roles and responsibilities.

THE STATE ROLE IN MANAGING CURRICULUM

Because each state has the primary responsibility for setting the curriculum for schools within that state, teachers need to know how this is done and what they can do to contribute to the process. The states have assumed two major areas of responsibility for curricula. The first is establishing what students are expected to learn, and the second is determining the instructional materials that can be used.

STATES SET STANDARDS The statements of expectation for student learning are determined at the state level. However, the statements of content standards that have been developed by the various national associations, such as the National Council of Teachers of Mathematics (NCTM), are a major resource for the states. The typical process is to establish a statewide committee comprising teachers, school administrators, higher education faculty, and state policymakers, such as a representative state board of education member or a legislator, such as chair of the House Education Committee. Standards committees with similar composition are established for each content area. Each committee reviews the national curriculum standards for its content area. These committees hold public hearings around their state so that the various interest groups (remember the different circles in Figure 12.1) can present their positions. When each of these committees completes its work, members recommend a set of state standards to the state board of education. Once the state board approves them, all districts, schools, and classrooms in the state are required to teach to those standards.

STATES MAY CHOOSE CURRICULUM MATERIALS There is some variation from state to state in the extent of state-level involvement in selecting curriculum materials.

The main area of involvement is in selecting textbooks. States have either **open adoption** or **state adoption** policies. Most southeastern states as well as Texas and California have formal state-level processes for adopting textbooks; these are state adoptions. In these states, a committee is charged with reviewing the various available textbooks and establishing an adoption list. School districts and schools then select the textbooks they will use from this list of approved materials. If schools wish to select curriculum materials from the adoption list, they receive state funding to support the purchase. If a district or school decides to select materials not on the state's adoption list, it will have to pay the full cost. In open states, the adoption of textbooks is a matter of local choice; the state leaves responsibility for the selection of curriculum materials to each school district, even when there is state funding for their purchase.

THE DISTRICT'S ROLE IN MANAGING CURRICULUM

Regardless of whether a school district is located in an adoption state or an open state, major curriculum-related tasks and responsibilities are assumed by each school district.

DISTRICT TEXTBOOK SELECTION   One obvious district task is to select the textbooks and related curriculum materials to be purchased and used within the district. Typically, a district will use a process similar to that used at the state level. A curriculum committee is established that includes teachers, principals, parents, and perhaps higher education faculty. The committee reviews the current status of the subject area, including how well students are doing on tests. The committee examines available text and materials options, and then recommends to the district superintendent and school board which materials should be purchased. Teacher participation on these committees is important. Teachers are concerned about the textbooks and other curriculum materials they will have to use. Therefore, they have a strong interest in and pay close attention to what the district curriculum selection committee does.

DISTRICT OFFICE CURRICULUM SPECIALISTS   School districts also employ a number of professional specialists whose responsibility it is to see that each curriculum area is supported and that teachers are prepared. One important role is that of curriculum coordinator/liaison/specialist. Typically, earlier in their careers these individuals were master teachers. Now their role is to guide, support, and champion their subject areas. In smaller districts, an individual might have responsibility for a number of content areas, such as language arts and social studies. Larger school districts have curriculum specialists assigned for at least each of the "big four" areas: reading, mathematics, science, and social studies. There are also specialists for special education, bilingual/ELL education, compensatory education, and other need areas.

DISTRICT OFFICE TEACHER DEVELOPMENT SPECIALISTS   In addition to the subject-specific specialists, most school district office staffs include **generalists.** Instead of being experts in a particular content area, these individuals are experts in helping teachers learn and apply different teaching strategies, assessment procedures, and use of technology. District office generalists include:

- Experts in general teaching strategies, such as cooperative grouping and assessment methods, that can be used in most content areas.
- Induction specialists, who are responsible for offering workshops, mentoring, and other supports for beginning teachers.
- Staff developers, who coordinate and present teacher inservice workshops, including those offered districtwide at the beginning of each school year.
- **Teachers on special assignment (TOSAs)** are expert teachers who leave the classroom for one to three years to participate in a curriculum review,

open adoption

A state text adoption policy that allows each school district the autonomy to review and select whichever textbooks it chooses.

state adoption

A state textbook adoption policy that limits financial support and selections to those that are included on a state-approved list.

generalists

Professional educators housed in the district office who provide classroom support across a number of content areas.

teachers on special assignment (TOSAs)

Teachers who are assigned to the district office for a limited time in order to accomplish a specified curriculum support task.

including selection of new materials, and to support teachers during the implementation phase. These teachers then return to the classroom, although some move on to other leadership positions, such as department head and assistant principal.

MANAGING THE CURRICULUM WITHIN THE SCHOOL   Even with all of the activities done at the national, state, and district levels, each school has major tasks and responsibilities for managing the curriculum. It still is up to each school and teacher to bring the curriculum alive in each and every classroom. Each teacher must do his or her part by being informed about the state standards and the benchmarks for their students' grade level, and they must teach with the materials and strategies that will help all students learn. In secondary schools, an important curriculum management structure is the department. When teachers for one subject are organized as a department, they can easily seek ideas from colleagues who know the content, and they can coordinate across grade levels what is taught in each course. The same ends are obtained in elementary schools by having grade-level teams and in larger schools by establishing content-specific curriculum committees.

Evaluating Curricula

How do we know if the selected and implemented curriculum is making any difference? The obvious answer is that without systematic and well-organized evaluation studies, we cannot know. Evaluation of the curriculum has to be done carefully and at all levels, from teachers in classrooms, to school- and district-level evaluation, to statewide evaluation. In addition, national and international curriculum evaluation studies are conducted.

CLASSROOM-BASED CURRICULUM EVALUATION

Curriculum evaluation is based on what occurs in the classroom. Until the curriculum is implemented and student learning is assessed, direct evidence of effectiveness cannot be obtained.

TEACHER EVALUATION OF THE CURRICULUM   The first evaluation step is done by each teacher who implements the curriculum. Teachers' informal assessments of how easy it is to teach, the effectiveness of textbooks and materials, and the amount of student interest and motivation are early indicators of how effective any curriculum will be. Another early indicator is teacher assessments of the extent of student learning. Through informal teacher assessments and the formal testing done in the classroom, teachers and curriculum specialists can obtain early evidence of how well a curriculum is working.

CLASSROOM IMPLEMENTATION STUDIES   Researchers and curriculum evaluators also focus on classrooms to determine curriculum effectiveness. Whereas the teacher examines only his or her classroom, researchers systematically document use of the curriculum and related student learning in a large number of classrooms. For example, in a study of teaching and learning mathematics with a curriculum designed around the NCTM standards, the researchers documented classroom processes and student learning in over one hundred classrooms. The results of their study included the following findings: (1) Classrooms where the teaching most closely approximated the best practices as outlined in the NCTM standards had the highest levels of student performance, the corollary being that in classrooms with less use of the new curriculum, students achieved less; (2) students in classrooms with teachers who were collaborating with other teachers in teaching the new curriculum had higher levels of achievement.[4]

Relevant Research

Some Achievement Gaps Are Narrowing

STUDY PURPOSE/QUESTION: One of the major concerns and priorities for schools has been implementing strategies that will reduce, and ultimately eliminate, the gap in achievement that is regularly observed between white and minority students, and between rich and poor students. Policy initiatives such as No Child Left Behind and the many curriculum reform efforts are in large part intended to reduce the gap. Given all of the efforts over the last two decades, are there any indications that the gap is being reduced?

STUDY DESIGN: Answering a question that asks about change over time requires having data from at least two points in time. Answering a question that encompasses all schools requires data that represents all schools. The National Assessment of Educational Progress (NAEP) is such a data source. In NAEP samples of students in all states are given the same tests and the tests are designed to be comparable across years. Therefore it is possible to explore whether or not the achievement gap has remained the same across the more than twenty years that NAEP tests have been administered. The Center on Education Policy used these data to see if there any trends in the size of the gap across the last twenty years.

STUDY FINDINGS: The following are some of the encouraging trends:

- The black–white gap in average math scale scores for nine-year-olds shrank from twenty-nine points in 1982 to twenty-three points in 2004.
- The gap for nine-year-old Hispanic students widened between 1982 and 1994 and has narrowed significantly since. However for thirteen-year-olds the gap has changed very little.

- The gap in reading achievement for nine-year-olds has shrunk. The white–Hispanic gap reduced from thirty-two points in 1982 to twenty-one points in 2004.
- The gaps in reading scores for both black and Hispanic students have narrowed since 1994.
- There has been a reduction in the gap in the writing assessments as well. The gap between black and white grade four students declined from twenty-six points in 1998 to twenty-one points in 2000.
- The gap has narrowed for low-income fourth-grade students in math and in reading.
- The researchers also noted that the gap reduction has occurred while the scores have gone up for all three groups.

IMPLICATIONS: This is a different type of research. Rather than conducting a study with a small sample of students, classrooms, or schools, this study uses nationally representative samples. The data also cover a time span of over twenty years. Clearly the findings indicate a positive trend in that the achievement gap appears to be getting smaller. Notice that these findings were for fourth grade. The findings are not as encouraging for the upper grades. Hopefully, the narrowing of the gap for grade four will mean that today's elementary school students will be better prepared to enter the upper grades. Regardless of the grade level, however, the gap still exists. This means that policymakers, curriculum developers and teachers cannot relax in their efforts to reduce and, ultimately, eliminate the achievement gap.

Source: Based on *Do You Know . . . The Latest Good News About American Education?* Washington, DC: Center on Education Policy, August 2005.

DISTRICT AND STATE CURRICULUM EVALUATION PRACTICES In today's high-stakes testing environment, school districts and states are focusing on student performance on standardized tests. Unfortunately, there is little examination of what goes on in classrooms. Instead, schools and school districts are being judged and labeled based on overall test score results. NCLB mandates that the test scores for each school be published in the local newspaper. In extreme situations, when test scores are at the bottom year in and year out, (such as in Hartford, Connecticut; Compton, California; and Trenton, New Jersey), the state may "take over" operation of the school district. The results of these state takeovers are mixed, at best. In some districts, such as Hartford Public Schools, student test scores have gone up. In other districts, they have remained low.

NATIONAL CURRICULUM STUDIES Two important national approaches to curriculum evaluation are the National Assessment of Educational Progress (NAEP) and the testing at most grade levels mandated in the No Child Left Behind Act (NCLB). These approaches reflect two very different philosophies about curriculum evaluation. In NAEP a random sample of students is selected from across each state. The sample is drawn from all students in the state but does not include all of the students in one school or from one classroom. Therefore, the findings from NAEP indicate how well students are doing in reading, science, or mathematics by state. NAEP cannot make judgments about the effectiveness of particular schools or school districts.

In No Child Left Behind, Congress has mandated that all public school students be tested each year in grades three through eight and in one year of high school. Each state can select the test, but the major content areas must be tested. These data will allow the labeling of schools and districts, even ranking each in terms of student performance on the selected tests.

CROSS-REFERENCE
Key requirements of NCLB are described in Chapter 5.

INTERNATIONAL CURRICULUM EVALUATION STUDIES

Over the last twenty years, there has been escalating concern about how well U.S. students do in comparison with students from other countries. Here again, student performance on standardized tests is the benchmark. The most widely reported study is the Trends in International Mathematics and Science Study (TIMSS) (see http://nces.ed.gov/timss). In this major study, the performance of students in grade four and/or eight in the different countries is compared. The study was first done in 1995 and has been repeated in 1999, 2003 and 2007. In the 2003 study forty-six countries participated.

Each country is required to draw a random sample of students and schools. All students take the same test and scores are compared across countries. For example, in 2003, U.S. fourth-grade students scored 518, on average, in mathematics while the international average was 495. U.S. students outperformed students in Australia, Italy, and Norway, but did less well than students in Belgium-Flemish, England, Hungary, Japan, and the Netherlands. Eighth grade U.S. students performed above the international average but were outperformed by students in nine countries including Japan, Korea, Singapore, Belgium-Flemish, Hungary, and the Netherlands.

Journal for Reflection
Use Table 12.2 to think about a subject area that you plan to teach. Which curriculum design(s) did you experience when you were in school learning this subject? What do you see as the strengths and weaknesses of that design(s)?

Instruction: Turning Curriculum into Classroom Activities

Once the influences and committees have converged and a curriculum has been selected, teachers have the responsibility to bring it to life in classrooms. This is extremely important work. If teachers fail in the delivery of the curriculum, students cannot learn material required in the stated benchmarks and standards. One dire consequence of students not learning is failure—failure for the students and the teacher as well as for the school and community that have supported development of the curriculum.

Thus, as is true for curriculum development, instruction begins with consideration of what students need to learn. Teachers need to think about student learning in relation to each lesson and how lessons will unfold across days and weeks. Based on the expectations for learning and the characteristics and interests of the students, particular teaching strategies can be selected. Another important influence on instruction is the schoolwide effort to improve learning that includes components

Analysis of the various skills that students are to learn is an important early step in planning instruction.

that are expected to be implemented in all classrooms. For example, all elementary teachers in a school or school district may be expected to use the same instructional approach in teaching reading. Fortunately, many instructional resources are available for teachers.

Instructional Objectives for Student Learning

Standards and benchmarks are descriptions of expected student learning that represent relatively long-term steps. Teachers and their students need more focused and short-term statements in order to focus individual lessons and the accumulation of several weeks of lessons. The instructional tools for creating this focus are called **objectives;** these are the statements of expected student learning for each lesson. The difference between objectives and standards is the size and scope of learning described. Standards represent the broad learning outcomes that students are expected to achieve across several years. Benchmarks address parts of standards, but they still are quite broad and can describe learning accomplishments that can take months. Instructional objectives, on the other hand, help the teacher and students identify each lesson's focus.

AIMS, GOALS, AND OBJECTIVES

Before the term *standards* was applied to student learning, three kinds of outcomes for education were used: aims, goals, and objectives. **Aims** are general, long-term aspirations for education. In fact, they are so general and long term that they are not seen as direct outcomes of attending school. Instead, these are statements that apply to lifelong aspirations. Aims also tend to be thought of as something that a group, rather than an individual, can accomplish. For example, an aim for many people is to complete high school and be the first in their family to graduate from college.

Goals are statements of educational aspirations, again related to group accomplishment but somewhat narrower in scope and with a shorter timeline. Goals typically cover two to four years and address a major area of educational accomplishment. For example, many school districts and states set a goal to reduce the dropout rate by 10 percent. Or they may establish a goal to increase the high school graduation rate from 87 percent to 97 percent. Accomplishing these goals takes several years, and not everyone accomplishes them.

Objectives address the daily learning expectations for students. Tests, daily lessons, and classroom activities need to be clearly tied to the important expectations for learning. Contrary to what some teachers practice, objectives for instruction should be known and understood by *both* the teacher and the students.

THE HIDDEN CURRICULUM

As the name implies, the **hidden curriculum** is not readily seen. In fact, it is invisible! At the same time it is a very critical and significant component of teaching and schools. The hidden curriculum is experienced through the messages that are sent to students about expectations for what they should do and what is important to succeeding with each teacher and across the school. The hidden curriculum can be detected through examining the meaning behind the rules of the classroom and school, noting what is celebrated, what is deemed to be important, and what is rewarded, punished, and ignored. For example, are academic accomplishments celebrated as well as athletic? Are special education students included or isolated? Do all students have equal access to algebra and AP classes or just certain groups of

objectives

Statements of learning outcomes for a lesson or several weeks of lessons.

aims

General, long-term aspirations for education.

goals

Expectations for education that typically cover two to four years of accomplishments.

hidden curriculum

The implicit values and expectations that teachers and schools convey about what is important for students to learn.

Should Teachers Allow Students to Use Profanity in Their Writing?

Students are regularly exposed to profanity in music, on television, in books, and in peer conversations. That this is the case does not necessarily mean that teachers should permit, or encourage, students to use profanity in their writing.

YES

Rob Koplan *teaches English and Social Studies at Stone High School, an alternative public school in Ann Arbor, Michigan.*

I never announce to my students, "Please include profanity in your writing!" But I don't ban it.

We want to encourage students to write. My students in particular—at-risk, older teens—have felt disenfranchised from our public education system, and that includes writing. They have spent most of their years in schools being told what not to do. So many come to my school afraid to write, or with other negative attitudes about writing.

There is the old saying, "Pick your battles!" I would rather win the writing battle than the profanity one.

We often ask students to write from their personal knowledge and experiences. Many of my students come from homes where they hear profanity used freely and frequently. And it has also been proven that writing can be a tool for releasing emotional pain.

When I see profanity in students' writing and don't feel it's appropriate, I use it as a teaching moment. It gives me an opportunity to cover such topics as the power of words and the power of using certain ones sparingly rather than frequently. It also comes up in government classes when we talk about the First Amendment.

We have discussions about where profanity might be appropriate and where it isn't. In my students' home lives, profanity is so pervasive that I actually have to teach them why it is not acceptable in certain places and situations (a job interview, for example).

But because I don't ban it, I really don't see it that often. When I do, if I feel that other words would be better choices, then I gently offer

NO

Nellie Ugarte *teaches English at Montwood High School, El Paso, Texas.*

Have I come to a point in my career where I am comfortable allowing my students to express themselves in any way they deem appropriate, including profanity? My answer is irrefutably and decisively no! Students should not be allowed under any circumstances to use profanity in their writing while they are in a public school.

One of the most important lessons I teach my students is that writing is a moral exercise. This influential tool can inspire and shape an individual's perspective. Words then become the source of nourishment for this inspiration. Words can soothe and caress the core of an individual. Words can sting and inflame the spirit. Words are power.

My problem as an educator is not about censorship, but about exposing this generation to something they might otherwise not see—the power to create imaginative essays with words of substance. It is almost too simplistic to allow students to use profanity. It does not take any real effort on the students' part to use vulgarity in writing. They are exposed to it daily by the media. The real test is to challenge them to find other ways to express themselves that have the same effect as these profane words.

Profanity in writing is at times merely used as a shock element. Some students actually believe it is an expression of their generation. They think their generation invented profanity. My students find it humorous when I tell them I can easily conjugate those words in more creative ways than they ever knew existed.

Students will argue that it is their right to express themselves as they see fit. They may be right

(continued)

(continued)

YES

NO

alternatives. I treat the profanity as I would any other word where a different word could be better. It works.

We have to prepare students to deal with the real world. In the real world, sometimes they will hear or see profanity, and at other times it is definitely unacceptable. They need to know the difference.

in a way, but reality is colored quite differently. Young kids still need to be guided by the adults in their lives.

When they spill into the community as adults, they will have choices to make for themselves. Wouldn't it be fabulous if they had a wealth of words with which to express those choices?

Source: "Should Teachers Allow Students to Use Profanity in Their Writing?" *NEA Today* (November 2004), p. 47. Reprinted by permission of the National Education Association.

WHAT IS YOUR PERSPECTIVE ON THIS ISSUE?
Should teachers allow students to use profanity in their writing?

To give your opinion, go to Chapter 12 of the companion website (www.ablongman.com/johnson14e) and click on Teacher Perspectives.

students? When a teacher emphasizes neatness, speaking one at a time, or is open to divergent student talk, messages are made clear about what is important for students to do and not do. Social behavior, dress codes, and rules about how to behave in the corridors become important ways that students learn about expectations. Whatever teacher's value about learning, the subject matter, and the uniqueness of their students become elements of the hidden curriculum. Students learn what is important or not important through this invisible curriculum, even though it is not written down.

The level and complexity of student learning that are stated in learning objectives should be reflected in the assessment method.

OBJECTIVES ARE ABOUT STUDENT LEARNING

One of the important elements of writing objectives is understanding their purpose. Frequently, when teacher education candidates first write objectives they write them as *input statements,* which describe what the teacher will do and what will happen in the lesson. The following objective is one example: "The students will be assigned to groups and they will read the chapter in the text." Such an objective is incorrect in instruction today.

Objectives should be written as *output statements,* which describe what students are to learn as a result of experiencing the lesson or lessons. For example, "As a result of this lesson, students will be able to compare and contrast the reasoning behind the economic and political arguments for and against sending troops into Iraq."

The difference between thinking in terms of inputs and outputs is crucial to becoming a successful teacher (see Figure 12.2). The natural tendency of teachers and professors is to think in terms of "what I am teaching." They may even say things such as "I teach English." In

FIGURE 12.2

Two Emphases to Teacher Thinking: Which Should Be First?

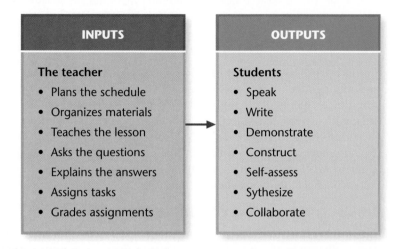

INPUTS	OUTPUTS
The teacher • Plans the schedule • Organizes materials • Teaches the lesson • Asks the questions • Explains the answers • Assigns tasks • Grades assignments	**Students** • Speak • Write • Demonstrate • Construct • Self-assess • Sythesize • Collaborate

the past, this way of thinking about instruction was acceptable; however, in today's schools teachers need to be thinking and talking in terms of what their students are learning. "My students have been learning about the Civil War and the terrible cost of life that occurred." Fortunately, the use of instructional objectives can help teachers make this important shift in thinking.

Different Kinds of Instructional Objectives

As an additional support for teachers, scholars have identified different ways of describing learning outcomes. The development and refinement of these typologies has occurred over the last thirty to forty years. Each type addresses a different kind of learning, and assessing student learning requires different methods, depending on the type of objective. For most lessons, teachers will likely have at least two kinds of learning objectives, which also means that careful thought has to be given to how the learning outcomes will be assessed.

BEHAVIORAL OBJECTIVES

Behavioral objectives, as the name implies, focus on observable performance. In fact, the proponents of behavioral objectives advocate that if the learning cannot be described in terms of observable behaviors, then there is no way to tell if learning took place. From this point of view, student learning is to be described in terms of behaviors. This means that in behavioral objectives, the verb, or *action word,* is key. The objective needs to focus on a behavior, such as to observe, classify, name, or interpret, and not on words, such as *appreciate* and *understand.*

Behavioral objectives are a useful instructional tool for teachers in planning, teaching, and assessing student learning. A useful approach to identifying student behaviors is to perform a **task analysis,** which is the systematic identification of the key skills that someone needs to be able to do to complete a task or satisfy a benchmark. The typical steps for a teacher in doing a task analysis include:

- Examine the related standards and benchmarks in order to identify the observable skills that students must demonstrate.
- Identify the small learning steps that in combination would result in students being able to do the whole task.

behavioral objectives

Expectations for student learning that are stated in terms of observable behaviors.

task analysis

The process of systematically identifying and sequencing the small learnings that must be accomplished in order for students to demonstrate mastery of a particular task or benchmark.

- Describe each step in terms of behaviors that can be observed.
- Determine the sequence in which students will need to learn the behaviors.
- Write behavioral objectives for the most central and important of these behaviors.
- Be attentive as the lesson unfolds to facilitating students acquiring those behaviors.
- Create an end-of-lesson, or unit, test that focuses on whether the students can exhibit the behaviors described in the behavioral objectives.

This approach to thinking about learning and teaching has been criticized as too linear and rational. Still, it is a useful way for teachers and students to maintain a focus on the key elements of a lesson. The real risk with behavioral objectives is having too many objectives and objectives that are so specific and narrow that they are trivial. It is one thing to write a behavioral objective that describes what both hands are doing when a person is touch typing, but it's another thing—and on a much more micro level of task analysis—to have an individual objective for the placement of each finger on the keyboard.

LEARNING OBJECTIVES FOR THE COGNITIVE DOMAIN

In 1956 a significant small book was published titled *Taxonomy of Educational Objectives: The Classification of Educational Goals Handbook 1: Cognitive Domain*.[5] The lead author of this book was a scholar named Benjamin Bloom. He and his coauthors had developed a typology of different types of learning objectives in the area of knowledge. The basic premise was that educational objectives should be classified according to the type of knowledge the learner was acquiring. This book and the classification system it introduced has become a cornerstone of curriculum and instruction; the classification system is known as **Bloom's Taxonomy.** Rather than treating all knowledge that is learned as being the same, Bloom and his colleagues identified six different levels of learning and therefore educational objectives. These six levels are summarized in Table 12.3.

In Bloom's Taxonomy, each of the six levels of the cognitive domain represent different amounts of complexity of knowledge and different extents of knowledge use. Teachers require different types of learning of students, depending on which level of the taxonomy is being addressed. In addition, teachers must keep in mind that this taxonomy is also a learning hierarchy. Students cannot perform at the higher levels unless they have already learned the necessary knowledge at the lower levels. The level of learning must be reflected in the way the learning objective is written. Simple memory and recall is a very different level of learning than is Application or Analysis.

LEARNING OBJECTIVES FOR THE AFFECTIVE DOMAIN

The **affective domain** of student learning also is important for teachers to consider as they plan instruction, teach lessons, and assess student learning. The affective domain addresses human reactions and responses to the content and subject matter. Student attitudes, feelings, and dispositions are a key component of instruction. Shortly after the development of the cognitive domain taxonomy, a parallel effort was underway to develop a taxonomy of educational objectives in the affective domain. The leader of this team was David Krathwohl.[6]

An unavoidable part of instruction is consideration of students' attitudes and beliefs because these affective elements are related to classroom behaviors. Krathwohl's Affective Domain Taxonomy provides an analytical tool for planning instruction and an aid for teachers to think about different levels of student learning in terms of values and beliefs (see Table 12.4 on p. 414). In planning instruction and during teaching, the affective domain can be used to assess the openness to and interest of students in learning about a particular topic. If certain students are at level 1.0, Receiving (Attending), the lesson will need to be aimed at having students become more engaged with the topic and opening a willingness to move toward level 2.0, Responding, and

Bloom's Taxonomy

A system for classifying knowledge learning outcomes in terms of the complexity of mental activity required.

affective domain

A system for classifying learning outcomes in the area of human reactions and responses.

TABLE 12.3	The Six Levels of Bloom's Taxonomy of the Cognitive Domain
1.00 Knowledge	Knowledge and behaviors that emphasize remembering and recall. This could be relatively simple memorization such as facts, word spelling, and the multiplication tables. This domain also includes knowledge of criteria, rules, principles, methods, and theories.
2.00 Comprehension	Students being able to understand communication and making some use of the idea. The communication may be oral, written, or an equation or some other symbolic form. Three types of comprehension are translation, interpretation, and extrapolation. Translation entails the ability to understand an idea presented in one form, such as a graph, and be able to describe its meaning in another form, such as a written paragraph. Interpretation moves beyond translation to being able to weigh the different parts of a communication and to identify and understand the major ideas as well as the interrelationships. Extrapolation is extending beyond the presented communication by predicting consequences or likely next steps.
3.00 Application	The student is able to apply learning to a new situation. Furthermore, the student is able to select the correct application without coaching by the teacher or other students. Using a principle to predict what will happen when a certain factor is changed is application.
4.00 Analysis	Analysis addresses the ability to break something down into its parts or pieces. Analysis also deals with detection of the relationships between the parts and how the whole is organized. Analysis begins with identifying the elements and then the relationships and interactions between the elements. Analysis goes beyond the stated and also includes recognition of the implicit.
5.00 Synthesis	This is the process of putting together the parts to make a whole. Bloom points out that this is the level of the taxonomy that addresses creative behavior. This does not mean completely free creative effort, as there are likely lesson and problem contexts that set outside limits. At this level, the learner is working with a given situation. The product of synthesis might be an original idea.
6.00 Evaluation	Evaluation is about making judgments about the value or worth of ideas, products, or problem solutions. Although evaluation is presented as the last level, Bloom emphasizes that some effort at evaluation is a component of most of the other levels as well. At this level, evaluation is seen as a considered process based on criteria. It is not a simplistic rush to opinion. Instead, there is a reasoned analysis of all facts and weighing of alternatives and the consequences of each.

TABLE 12.4	The Five Levels of Krathwohl's Taxonomy of Affective Domain
1.0 Receiving (Attending)	The learner is sensitized to the condition, phenomenon, or stimulus that is the aim of the lesson or topic of study. At the most basic level, the learner is *aware* of the object or phenomenon. For example, in music students are aware of differences in mood or rhythm. Another component of this level is the *willingness to receive* or to attend to the topic of study. If there is not openness to learning more, then higher levels of the affective domain cannot be reached.
2.0 Responding	At this level, the learner is motivated beyond simply attending and is actively attending. At the lowest level of responding, there is *acquiescence in responding;* in other words, the learner is willing to go along. Slightly higher is the *willingness to respond,* in which the student looks for additional information or experience. A higher level of responding is indicated when the student shows *satisfaction in response.*
3.0 Valuing	At this level, the student is behaving in ways that reflect a sense of belief or attitude. Within this level, there is the range of behavior from *testing for acceptance of a value* to *commitment.* Actions of reaching out to learn more about a new topic, such as asking questions or searching out the topic on the web, are indicative of acceptance. With commitment there is a conviction and loyalty to the topic, position, or group.
4.0 Organization	As more than one value becomes relevant, there is a need to develop an internal system of organization of values. Organization begins with *conceptualization* of particular values and beliefs. This does not necessarily require verbal expression, but the learner is able to compare one value or belief to another. This process leads to *organization of a value system,* which brings together a number of values and their relationships.
5.0 Characterization by a Value or Value Complex	At this level, the learner has a set of values in place, the values are organized into some kind of internal system, and behaviors are consistent over time in relation to these values. The values represent a *generalized set,* and there is a *characterization* of the person in terms of the internal consistency of thought and an external consistency of action that is characteristic of the person.

level 3.0, Valuing. If students are already at level 4.0, Organization, then the learning objectives can ask students to weigh, compare, and form judgments. Values and beliefs, as well as motivation and interests, are a core component of learning. Students of teachers who continually attend to the affective domain will have greater learning success in the cognitive domain. When students are interested in learning and see the value of learning certain content, they will more intensely engage with the curriculum, which makes instruction more interesting and successful.

LEARNING OBJECTIVES FOR THE PSYCHOMOTOR DOMAIN

Another domain, which has received much less attention, is related to learning physical skills, which require the mind and body to work together. Music, art, drama, industrial arts, and other vocational courses require students to perform tasks physically. The corresponding taxonomy, the **psychomotor domain,** has received attention from curriculum theorists and was developed by E. J. Simpson.[7] The first two levels are Perception and Set, which address the learner becoming aware of a particular stimulus and becoming ready to act. For example, the band director raises the baton and all members prepare to play the first note. Levels 3 and 4 of Simpson's psychomotor domain taxonomy address Guided Response and Mechanisms. When trying something for the first time, it helps to have suggestions and directions as a guide. With time the steps become automatic. At Level 5, Complex Overt Response, the learner can accomplish more complex tasks and movements. At the still higher level, Adaptation, the learner is able to adjust his or her behavior and accommodate its application in different settings or under different conditions. At the highest level, Origination, creativity is demonstrated. For example, the trumpet student moves beyond playing the written music to improvisation.

> Children engaged in daily physical education show superior motor fitness, academic performance, and attitude toward school as compared to their counterparts who do not participate in daily physical education.
>
> *James Pollalschele and Frank Hagen*

Teaching Strategies

Once the curriculum has been established and instructional objectives have been written, it is time to plan for and teach lessons that will help students learn the knowledge, dispositions, and skills identified in the objectives, benchmarks, and standards. Two hundred years ago, there was only one teaching strategy—lecture; the teacher talked and the students memorized. Today this "stand and deliver" strategy has fallen into disrespect. Students are not willing to sit through continuous lectures, and a variety of teaching strategies have been demonstrated to be significantly more effective in engaging students and having students achieve at higher levels.

DIRECT INSTRUCTION

Although the lecture method continues to receive criticism, there is an appropriate time for teachers to impart information directly. Over the last thirty years, extensive research has been done on the behaviors of the teacher and the effectiveness of direct instruction.[8] When direct instruction is done well and with appropriate learning objectives, students learn. A basic, underlying assumption of this teaching strategy is that the teacher knows the content and the easiest way for students to learn it is for the teacher to directly communicate it to them.

Although with direct instruction information is passed from teacher to students, additional ways to communicate information exist besides teacher lecture. Reading the textbook, questions and answers, as well as different applications of technology such as videos, television programs, and information searches on the web are ways to impart information and to make direct instruction more interesting and motivating for students.

To be most effective in using direct instruction, the teacher must manage a number of important steps (see Figure 12.3). With direct instruction, the teacher is at the center and maintains full control of the lesson. The teacher must control the flow and keep all talk focused. Sidebars and off-topic discussion are discouraged. A primary purpose of direct instruction is to maintain a high amount of on-task learning time, or **active learning time (ALT).** Higher proportions of class time in which students are engaged will yield higher levels of student learning.

INDIRECT INSTRUCTION

The opposite approach to direct instruction is indirect instruction, which covers a large number of teaching strategies in which students have greater responsibility for structuring tasks and managing their own learning. The teacher still has overall responsibility, but students have to initiate more, to organize more of the tasks and their thinking, and in the end be able to construct their own product or way of

psychomotor domain

A system for classifying learning outcomes that require physical activity and performance.

active learning time (ALT)

The proportion of time within a lesson that students are actively engaged with the task of learning the objectives.

FIGURE 12.3

Key Characteristics of Effective Direct Instruction

1. Direct instruction works best when the learning objectives are clear and narrow in scope.
2. Information and/or tasks should be presented in sequence and one step at a time.
3. The teacher should check carefully for student understanding as the presentation unfolds.
4. Build in student practice with corrective feedback.
5. Avoid negative criticism.
6. Include review at key points.
7. Tasks and assignments should be clearly structured.

demonstrating what they have learned. Key characteristics of indirect instruction are presented in Figure 12.4.

INQUIRY   Inquiry lessons begin with a problem or puzzle being posed by either the teacher or students. Then the students initiate investigations or problem-solving strategies in an effort to construct an answer. *Problem solving* is another name for this general approach. Students assume major responsibility for their learning with this approach. In an inquiry lesson, the first phase is to define the problem. The teacher might pose a dilemma, or in a science lesson do a demonstration, for which the answer is not obvious. The students then have to define the specific question or problem. The second major phase in inquiry lessons is discovery of the solution. The discovery phase might include conducting an experiment, seeking out information from reading or on the web, or, in a mathematics lesson, using manipulative materials. In the end, the students will have constructed new understanding and have learned new concepts and principles.

PROBLEM-BASED LEARNING   One innovative adaptation of the inquiry approach, which was first used in medical education, is problem-based learning (PBL). In this approach, a real or simulated problem is posed, and students work in groups to develop a solution. The problem does not have a quick or obvious answer, nor is it one about which the students will already have sufficient knowledge. The purpose of PBL is to engage a team of four to six students in systematic inquiry, decision making, and problem solving. The result is deeper understanding of the subject as well as the development of skills in inquiry and collaborative work. In medical education, the students will need to seek out information in journals, attend lectures

FIGURE 12.4

Key Characteristics of Effective Indirect Instruction

1. The teacher or students pose a problem or puzzle.
2. The problem or puzzle is one that stimulates student interest and inquisitiveness.
3. The teacher does not provide the answer or problem solution.
4. Students initiate activities and investigations to analyze the problem or puzzle.
5. The teacher serves as a guide or coach only when students are stymied.
6. All possible solutions/answers are given open consideration.
7. Students articulate orally, in writing, and/or through presenting the reasoning behind their answer/solution.

by professors, meet in their group to analyze the problem, and pool their developing understanding. Many medical schools have small seminar rooms reserved for PBL teams to study the problem and concentrate their efforts for weeks. The evaluations of the use of PBL in medical education have demonstrated that the future MDs do just as well on the standardized licensure exams and they are better at information retrieval and problem solving.

MODEL-CENTERED INSTRUCTION Models are an important device for organizing and explaining knowledge, and they are used widely in science. In the model-centered approach to teaching, a twelve- to fourteen-week curriculum allows the students to explore and evaluate models and to create their own models for explaining and predicting phenomena (such as force and motion in astronomy). Research on this approach shows improvements in student content knowledge.[9]

STUDENT GROUPING

One important component of all teaching strategies has to do with how students are grouped. Should students be taught as a whole class? When should students be divided into groups? What should be the size of the groups? Should the groups be kept the same? What should be done about the different ability levels and skills of students? All of these questions must be answered in relation to student grouping.

HOMOGENEOUS OR HETEROGENEOUS GROUPING Grouping together students who have similar levels of achievement and abilities is called **homogeneous grouping.** Grouping together students with different levels of achievement and different abilities is called **heterogeneous grouping.** The best way to group depends to some extent on the task. Deciding on which way to group students is philosophical too. Proponents of heterogeneous grouping point out that high-achieving students help the lower-achieving ones and that everyone learns. On the other hand, the proponents of homogeneous grouping believe that mixed-ability grouping slows down the fast learners. Note that the unstated assumption in this debate is that the only learning that counts is that of each student individually. The accomplishment of the group also should be considered.

COOPERATIVE LEARNING A widely used approach to grouping is **cooperative learning,** in which students are expected to work together to accomplish tasks and are held accountable for both individual and group achievement. In this approach, the general plan is to have a mix of students, so that each group will include students with high, middle, and lower abilities. An alternative is to have students grouped according to interest and assign them activities according to those interests. Typically, cooperative learning groups work together for several weeks or longer. Each group member has an assigned role, including group leader, monitor, resource manager, recorder, and reporter. In this way, leadership and task responsibilities are shared. Extensive research has been done on this approach to grouping. Some of the outcomes are improvement in understanding of content, development, and support of using acceptable social skills; opportunities for student decision making; and encouragement of student responsibility.[10] Criticisms of cooperative learning include the arguments against homogeneous grouping cited previously. Other critics, including many parents, object to grading students based on group accomplishments.

Teaching Strategies for Addressing Students with Exceptionalities

A central consideration in selecting teaching strategies is how well they match up with the learning needs of diverse students. In many ways, each student in a classroom is

homogeneous grouping

Grouping together students who are alike in terms of their ability to learn or interests.

heterogeneous grouping

Grouping together students who are diverse in their interests and ability to learn.

cooperative learning

A strategy for grouping that provides specific roles and responsibilities for each member.

unique. Effective teachers use strategies that take advantage of each student's strengths and that accommodate areas of need. Students will vary in their ability to read and calculate. They will vary in their ability to use English and in how well they can communicate orally and through writing. Some will be exceptionally fast at learning, and others will be slow.

One important component of instruction that teachers must examine and understand is how best to address the array of students with special needs and those who are English language learners. For example, students with learning disabilities are apt to have difficulty with direct instruction strategies, especially lecture. However, they benefit from having clear and concrete teacher directions and activities that are well structured and sequenced. ELL students can be very successful with strategies that facilitate their interaction with other students and that provide ample time for processing what is happening. ELLs also benefit from indirect instruction strategies, because their learning is less dependent on understanding everything the teacher says. ELL students in secondary school classes in particular do not benefit from direct instruction. Fortunately, a number of well-developed approaches exist for accommodating the needs of diverse learners.

WHICH APPROACH IS BEST—TRANSITIONAL OR IMMERSION? A seemingly never-ending debate has to do with selecting the best instructional approach for ELL students. Some advocate **immersion** programs, or English as a second language (ESL), in which students are taught primarily in English, and their native language is limited and used only on a case-by-case basis to clarify instructions. Other experts advocate that ELL students be placed in **transitional** programs, also called **bilingual** education, in which their native language is used along with English to ensure content understanding, but only until the student can make the full transition to all-English instruction. The Institute for Education Sciences (IES) of the U.S. Department of Education is currently funding a major research study related to this debate. Table 12.5 was developed by IES as a summary of distinctions between these two program models.

RESOURCES FOR TEACHING ELL STUDENTS Among the many resources for teachers who have ELL students are several federally funded centers. One of these is the National Clearinghouse for English Language Acquisition (www.ncela.gwu.edu). The NCELA is a repository for best practices, research, and related information for teachers who work with ELL, dual language, and migrant education. Subjects on the NCELA website include assessment and accountability, curriculum and instruction, and parent and community involvement. The website also includes links to legislation and regulations related to the No Child Left Behind Act, searchable databases, and strategies and activities for ELL teachers.

In practice, teachers of ELL students should include two kinds of objectives: language and content. Content objectives are established for all students. For the ELL students, adding a language objective helps with their language development. For example, a language objective could be that the ELL students will be able to identify and say vocabulary words when shown a picture.

During an elementary school lesson, the teacher could speak the key words while pointing to them in a Big Book or writing them on the whiteboard. In a secondary classroom, the teacher could use a worksheet that has sentences with blanks where the key vocabulary words should go. This task will help the ELL student focus on the key words and concepts. Another useful technique in both elementary and secondary classrooms is to have one or two of the students model the task before the whole class begins individual or group work. ELLs, as well as all the other students, are able to see what is expected of them. Figure 12.5 (p. 420) presents another useful set of tips for assisting ELL students.

ACCOMMODATING STUDENTS WITH SPECIAL NEEDS

There is a wide range of variability in student needs and the resources that teachers have to address them. In the past, most students with special needs were isolated and placed in "special education" classrooms. This self-contained model came under

immersion

A program approach in which ELL students are taught primarily in English, with use of their native language only on a case-by-case basis.

transitional/bilingual

A program approach in which ELL students are taught in their native language along with English.

TABLE 12.5   Comparison of English Immersion and Transition Programs

	Structured English Immersion	Transition
Content Instruction	Instruction is in English with adjustments to proficiency level so that subject matter is comprehensible. Instruction is supplemented by visual aids and gestures.	Literacy and academic content areas begin in student's primary language and continue to grade-level mastery of academic content. As proficiency in oral English develops, the language gradually shifts to English. The transition usually begins withmath computation, followed by reading and writing, then science, and finally social studies. Students transition to mainstream classes in which all academic instruction is in English once they acquire sufficient English proficiency.
Language Arts Instruction	English is taught through content areas. Subject matter knowledge and English are taught together by teaching content through learner-appropriate English. A strong language development component is included in each content lesson.	Begins in student's primary language with instruction in English oral language development. The goal is to achieve both basic oral English proficiency and content knowledge, mainstreaming to an all-English program by the end of grade 3.
Language Goals	English acquisition and content knowledge by grade 3.	English acquisition and content knowledge by grade 3.
How Primary Language Is Used	Primary language is limited to use on a case-by-case basis, primarily to clarify English instruction.	Primary language is used to ensure grade-level mastery of academic content but only until the student can make a full transition to all-English instruction.
How English Is Used	To teach content instruction, adjusted to proficiency level.	Shifts from student's primary language to English as proficiency in oral English develops. English is frequently used in nonacademic subjects such as art, music, and physical education.

Source: U.S. Department of Education, Institute of Education Sciences.

heavy criticism for a number of reasons, including the absence of contact with general education student role models and special education students losing out on many school activities and events. One consequence of P.L. 94-142 was establishment of the resource room and a major change in philosophy. Now there is an expectation that special-needs students are members of the general education classroom and go to the resource room only for special instruction—in other words, inclusion.

DISPOSITIONS ARE IMPORTANT   The first step in addressing teaching and learning for special-needs students is appropriate attitude. There is a strong tendency on the part of all students to look for differences and to prefer to interact with peers who are like themselves. Rather than accepting and valuing diversity (here is a hint of the need for affective learning objectives), students may have a predisposition to reject and isolate peers who are different in gender, race, socioeconomic class, or ability to learn. The expectations that students in any classroom hold and act on in regard to students with special needs begins with the attitudes and behaviors of the teacher. There is no escaping the fact that how well students in a classroom value

FIGURE 12.5

Entrees to English: Tips for Assisting Language Learners

Source: Judith Lessow-Hurley, "Entrees to English: Tips for Assisting Language Learners," *Curriculum Update* (Fall 2002). Copyright © 2002 Association for Supervision and Curriculum Development. Reprinted by permission. The Association for Supervision and Curriculum Development is a worldwide community of educators advocating sound policies and sharing best practices to achieve the success of each learner. To learn more, visit ASCD at www.ascd.org.

- **Engage cooperative groups of English language learners (ELLs) and English speakers in common tasks.** This gives students a meaningful context for using English.
- **Develop content around a theme.** The repetition of vocabulary and concepts reinforces language and ideas and gives ELLs better access to content.
- **Allow student nonverbal ways to demonstrate knowledge and comprehension.** For example, one teacher has early primary students hold up cardboard "lollipops" (green or red side forward) to indicate "Yes" or "No" to questions.
- **Don't constantly correct students' departure from standard English.** It's better to get students talking; they acquire accepted forms through regular use and practice. A teacher can always paraphrase a student's answer to model standard English.
- **Consider using visual aids and hands activities to deliver content.** Information is better retained when a variety of senses are called upon.
- **Use routines as way to reinforce language.** This practice increases the comfort level of second language learners; they then know what to expect and associate the routine with language.

and respect diversity is in large part related to the values and behaviors of the teacher. This is true for each school as a whole. In schools where the principal and teachers all share the belief that all students can learn and there is a shared responsibility for helping all students learn, all students do learn more. This is a matter of disposition and begins with the adults in the school. A useful set of questions for assessing how well students are doing to promote a sense of community and social acceptance is presented in Figure 12.6.

FIGURE 12.6

Questions for Determining the Extent to Which a School/ Classroom Is Promoting a Sense of Community and Social Acceptance

Source: D. Voltz, N. Brazil, and A. Ford, "What Matters Most in Inclusive Education: A Practical Guide for Moving Forward," *Intervention in School and Clinic, 37* (2001), pp. 23–30.

- Are students with disabilities disproportionately teased by other students?
- Do students with disabilities seem to enjoy being in the general education classroom?
- Do students without disabilities voluntarily include students with disabilities in various activities?
- Do students without disabilities seem to value the ideas and opinions of students with disabilities? Do students with disabilities seem to value the ideas and opinions of students without disabilities?
- Do students with disabilities consider the general education classroom to be their "real class"? Do they consider the general education teacher to be one of their "real teachers"? (p. 25).

Often, determining students' dispositions is as easy as looking at each student individually. Deciding what to do is more complex.

CLASSROOM MANAGEMENT

A critical component of instruction for all students is managing materials, organizing of tasks, scheduling, monitoring the flow of activities, and setting rules of behavior. Classroom management is even more important when addressing the needs of special students, whether they are gifted or have a disability. The following are some useful tips:

- Involve the students in setting classroom rules and expectations.
- Be careful not to have too many or too few general rules. A total of six to eight seems to be about right.
- Post the general rules and always refer to them when correcting behavior.
- Create a safe, supportive, and welcoming environment.
- Strive to have the students assume responsibility for their own behavior and do their part to establish and maintain the general norms of the classroom.
- Seat students who tend to be disruptive close to you.
- Keep in mind that students with hearing and vision impairments need to be seated where they can see and hear.
- Regularly evaluate classroom arrangements to be sure there are no hazards and that any students with disabilities have ready access to instruction, materials, and activities.
- Use a variety of techniques to reinforce positive behaviors. Be sure that your reinforcers are meaningful to individual students.
- When there are behavior problems, think about what is going on in the classroom that is encouraging the student to do the behavior.
- Strive to have all students become self-managers of appropriate behaviors.
- Keep the teacher's desk organized, as well as all of the classroom materials and supplies. High and tilting stacks of paper are a temptation.

This list of classroom management tips is just a beginning. In order for all students to learn, there first has to be organization, order, and predictability in the rules of behavior, schedule of activities, location and access to manipulative materials, and sanctions for misbehaviors.

Adjusting the Attitude of Learners

Teachers in today's schools meet face-to-face with increasing attitude problems of some learners. These problems are manifested in a lack of respect for teachers, visual boredom in learning, and a lack of work ethic for career. The lack of respect may come from a societal image of teachers as "Those who can't, teach!" Additionally, whatever is wrong in society tends to be blamed on the teacher and the school program. Teacher authority is usurped by parents and the society, which challenge the teacher's right to discipline students, even the unruly ones. Some students call into question the worthiness of professional teachers, who are considered to have lower status when compared with other professions. The fact that teachers tend to be grossly underpaid for the type of workload they face may be questioned.

Some students exhibit boredom and are not motivated to learn because they do not see the relevance of what they are studying. To them, much of what they study seems to be important only for the tests they take and has no relevance to their lives. They yearn for assurance that teachers not only are competent but also care. The lack of a work ethic may be attributable to an environment that provides everything material they need and want. This student problem may be related to the "good life" quality of a society that tends to have everything it needs. Many students have economically secure homes, are provided with an overabundance of goods and services, and are not held accountable for responsible activities in the family.

This dilemma does not paint a glowing picture of what is waiting for the teacher when she or he enters the classroom. If this picture is accurate and is to be altered, then the teacher needs to actively develop with the students a common ground for the establishment of respect for each other.

Questions for Reflection

1. How can the teacher show respect for the students and have the students show respect for the teacher?

2. How does the teacher prepare a learning environment that has meaning to the everyday life of the learner?

3. How does the teacher work with the home and community in providing a learning atmosphere in which students develop a work ethic and recognize its value?

To answer these questions on-line and e-mail your answers to your professor, go to Chapter 12 of the companion website (www.ablongman.com/johnson14e) and click on Professional Dilemma.

Models for School Reform

Over the last three decades, there has been continuing and ever-increasing frustration with U.S. schools. National, state, and local policymakers frequently use criticism of schools in their campaigns for political office. Education researchers and leading educators also regularly express concern about the quality of schools and the readiness of high school graduates to enter the workforce. In response, educators have developed a number of **school reform** models. These are comprehensive schoolwide efforts to change curriculum and instruction with the expressed intent of increasing student test scores. School reforms are systematic, multiyear, involve all school staff and all subject areas, and are organized to focus all efforts on curriculum and instruction in order to increase student learning. The most widespread approach is generally called school improvement. Ten or more different reform models are based on particular philosophies of education, research findings, and specialized processes that the school staff must move through. Each of these reform models is led by a university scholar, and the participating schools

school reform

The use of comprehensive programs that are intended to bring about schoolwide changes in curriculum and instruction and thereby increase learning outcomes for all students.

will belong to a regional or national network of schools that are engaged with the same approach. Teachers will receive special training and they will be expected to use certain instructional approaches. Each approach involves a number of schoolwide elements including acceptance of certain beliefs about students and learning, use of specified curriculum and teaching strategies, and a special vocabulary that draws attention to the core philosophy and principles of the reform model. For most models, there is a leading scholar of national prominence who originated the basic principles for the reform approach and is the national spokesperson for the model. Many of these school reform models have been designed especially to serve urban schools and schools with a high proportion of at-risk students. Most of the models have been designed to be used in elementary schools, although several can be applied in secondary schools and at least one was designed explicitly for high schools. A sampling of these models is described briefly in the next few paragraphs.

Power does not always welcome a challenge. There have always been and will always be entrenched systems, institutions, and structures that resist change, that punish dissent and innovation. Whenever there is a challenge to the patriarchal status quo, the old dogs in positions of power start howling, trying vainly to hold onto their comfortable lives.

Sister Monica Weiss

SCHOOL IMPROVEMENT

The most widespread approach for gradual improvement of schools is generally the School Improvement Process (SIP). An example of an organizing framework for school improvement is presented in Figure 12.7. Note what is placed at the center of this framework, as well as how arrows are used to indicate the importance of drawing connections between goals, data about past performance, and action plans for next steps. The typical SIP requires a number of steps, including principal leadership, and the establishment of a school SIP team composed of teachers, department chairs or grade-level team leaders, and parents. School improvement processes have an annual rhythm to them. During spring the SIP team will hold meetings and

FIGURE 12.7

Hartford (Connecticut) Public Schools' Organizing Framework for School Improvement

Source: Italia Negroni, Hartford Public Schools, and Jonathan Costa, Performance Innovations. Reprinted with permission.

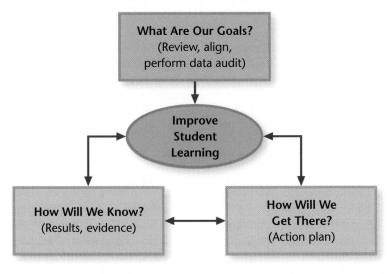

THREE BASIC QUESTIONS OF SCHOOL IMPROVEMENT

examine test scores and other data about how well students are performing. The SIP team produces a school improvement plan that identifies specific targets that everyone in the school will work on during the next year. The intention behind the selection of the targets is to identify specific areas, such as writing, algebraic reasoning, or SAT vocabulary, in which a schoolwide effort should be able to lead to increases in student learning. The SIP plan will be reviewed and approved by district office staff. As schools open in August, the school staff may receive related professional development, and during the entire school year the specific objectives stated in the SIP plan will be monitored. The following spring the SIP team will meet and start the school improvement process cycle all over again. Ideally, there will be data documenting gains in the target areas, and for the next year a different set of specific targets will become the focus of improvement efforts.

ACCELERATED SCHOOLS

SIP is a widespread generalized approach to improving schools. The various reform models are more customized. Each reform model is based on a particular philosophy of teaching and learning. Each reform model is also based on a particular line of research, which was directed by the lead proponent of the reform model. For example, Henry Levin, formerly of Stanford University and more recently Teachers College of Columbia University, is the founder and conceptual leader for the Accelerated Schools approach to school reform. Professor Levin proposed that rather than slowing down instruction for low-achieving students, teachers should *accelerate* their expectations for students as well as the way they teach. For more information and print materials related to Accelerated Schools, see the website www.creativelearningpress.com.

SUCCESS FOR ALL (SFA)

The leading scholar for the Success For All (SFA) school reform model is Robert Slavin of Johns Hopkins University.[11] The foundations for SFA demonstrate another important feature of school reform models—they are based on the findings from classroom research. In the case of SFA, much of the research was done in inner-city schools with children who were truly at risk of failure and in schools with track records of failure. As a result, SFA was developed around the core assumption that every child can read. Implementation of SFA begins with implementation of a structured approach to the curriculum and support for children as they learn to read. For example, the first step is *prevention*—strategies to have children ready for school, including strong preschool and kindergarten reading readiness programs. Curriculum instruction and classroom management are addressed through training for all teachers. The approach includes specific reading books, the use of reading tutors, and eight-week reading assessments. All reading teachers employ a prescribed strategy. For example, reading time begins by having the teacher read children's literature to the students and engage them in a discussion of the story. Another component is Story Telling and Retelling (STaR), which engages the students in listening, retelling, and dramatizing literature. Each of these components has been derived from earlier research studies, and SFA is regularly evaluated to assess how well it is working in terms of increasing student achievement.

INSTITUTE FOR LEARNING

The Institute for Learning (IFL), which is housed at the University of Pittsburgh, is directed by Lauren Resnik. As with SFA, the IFL approach is based on decades of research in classrooms. The IFL model is grounded in a set of Principles of Learning, which have been derived from the many research studies. In the IFL model, there are clear and high expectations for student work. Curriculum and instruction are tied to standards, as are evaluations. There is an expectation of academic rigor and a thinking curriculum. The curriculum is to focus on a Knowledge Core that is to "progressively deepen" understanding of core concepts. This approach also expects students to self-manage their learning.

SCHOOL REFORM MODELS FOR HIGH SCHOOLS

School reform models for high schools are fewer in number but equally challenging for teachers and students. One of the most extensively applied models was developed by Theodore Sizer.[12] The participating high schools belong to a national network called the Coalition of Essential Schools. Members of this coalition subscribe to a set of common principles:

1. Learning to use one's mind well
2. Less is more, depth over coverage
3. Goals apply to all students
4. Personalization
5. Student-as-worker, teacher-as-coach
6. Demonstration of mastery
7. A tone of decency and trust
8. Commitment to the entire school
9. Resources dedicated to teaching and learning
10. Democracy and equity

Another approach to reform in high schools is the International Baccalaureate Diploma Program. This program is a comprehensive two-year curriculum, which has high academic rigor. The curriculum emphasizes critical thinking, intercultural understanding, and exposure to a variety of points of view. Typically, this program will be offered as an option within a high school rather than instituted as the only route for all students. High school students who have an IB diploma are readily accepted at universities around the world.

MULTIPLE INTELLIGENCES

Another approach to school reform and thinking differently about instruction is based on Howard Gardner's theory of multiple intelligences (MI).[13] Gardner argues that there is not a single form of intelligence such as that measured in traditional IQ tests. In other words, there are many ways to be "smart." In his most recent works, Gardner identifies eight different intelligences (see Figure 12.8). Each of these represents

FIGURE 12.8

Howard Gardner's Multiple Intelligences

Source: Project SUMIT (Schools Using Multiple Intelligence Theory), "Theory of Multiple Intelligences."

Linguistic Intelligence uses language to communicate and make sense of the world.

Musical Intelligence involves creation, communication, and understanding of sound.

Logical-Mathematical Intelligence uses abstract relations.

Spatial Intelligence addresses perceiving visual and spatial information, transforming this information, and recreating visual images from memory.

Bodily-Kinesthetic Intelligence uses all or part of the body to create products and solve problems.

Interpersonal Intelligence entails recognizing and making distinctions about others' feelings and intentions.

Intrapersonal Intelligence entails recognizing and making distinctions about ones own feelings.

Naturalist Intelligence includes distinguishing, classifying, and using features of the environment.

a unique way that students, and adults, can excel. Gardner's theory at a minimum should be a cautionary reminder to teachers not to oversimplify examination of the intelligence of students. If there are many ways to be smart, or at least multiple dimensions to intelligence, then one clear implication is that classrooms and schools can be organized to help students learn in relation to each form of intelligence.

An important implication of Gardner's model is the importance of appreciating how assessment of learning changes in an MI classroom or school. Tests of reading, writing, and calculations are no longer sufficient. Student performance in athletics, music, communication with others, and self-assessment of feelings will be equally important forms of assessment. Each classroom and the school will be striving to help students learn in relation to each of the eight intelligences.

Summary

CURRICULUM: RELATING EXPECTATIONS FOR LEARNING TO WHAT IS TO BE TAUGHT. Establishing the curriculum is a complex and dynamic process that takes place well before teachers plan for instruction. The process includes extensive involvement of the many interest groups within the education profession and citizens at large. The important beginning step is developing consensus about desired learning outcomes. The actual development of the curriculum entails identifying the many possible resources that can be made available to teachers and their students and describing teaching approaches. Strategies for evaluating the effectiveness of the curriculum and student learning must also be designed. Two other significant components of the curriculum are the cocurriculum and the hidden curriculum. For many students these are their reasons for staying in school or dropping out.

INSTRUCTION: TURNING CURRICULUM INTO CLASSROOM ACTIVITIES. Teachers have primary responsibility for translating the standards for learning and the curriculum into minute-to-minute and day-to-day learning experiences for students—in other words, instruction. Following analysis of the standards and benchmarks, teachers must develop instructional objectives for each lesson and employ teaching strategies that will engage the students. Teachers must make sure that all students, including ELLs and special needs students, are able to participate and develop understanding. Many schools are implementing one of the reform models which provide teachers with additional curriculum resources and instructional strategies. A useful reminder of the uniqueness of each student is offered in the multiple intelligences theory of Howard Gardner. At its simplest, Gardner's theory points out that students can be smart in many different ways, which means that in order for students to learn the most, instruction needs to be designed and delivered in a variety of ways.

Journal for Reflection

An important part of teacher success is related to how well they manage the classroom. In the section that described classroom management (page 421) there is a list of tips. Review this list and note those you believe you can do well now, and also note those where you need to learn more.

Discussion Questions

1. Revisit the case study presented at the beginning of this chapter. Identify the different interest groups that spoke to the state board of education. What about their views were different, and in what ways were they the same? Where do each of the views fit in Figure 12.1?
2. The curriculum comprises not only the formal statement of standards, materials, and teacher guides, but also the cocurriculum and the hidden curriculum. For a particular subject such as literacy, mathematics, or science, how have you seen these three types of curriculum affect you and other students? What roles did your teachers play with each type of curriculum?
3. Today's teachers have the major responsibility for instruction. For the most part the curriculum is set. What do you see as being keys to teachers being effective in instruction? What can you do to be sure that the instructional objectives you set for a given lesson engage all your students?

School-Based Observations

1. During practicum and other classroom observation experiences, be sure to examine the curriculum materials provided for the teacher. Which elements of the curriculum designs can you trace back to the various sources and influences on curriculum development?
2. Examine a teacher's lesson plans in order to see the connections to state and district standards, to yearly benchmarks, and to the learning objectives for the lesson(s) you are observing. What are the clear themes in terms of expectations for student learning? In what ways does the lesson facilitate students learning the stated objectives?
3. When observing classrooms, look for the students who have limited English language skills. What special steps does the teacher take to facilitate these students' learning? What are these students doing to learn the content of the lesson as well as the English language?
4. Technology can be used in a wide variety of ways in classrooms and within lessons. In classrooms where you are observing, how is technology used? Which forms are supports for the teacher? Which have direct uses by the students? In what ways are there integrated uses of technology?

Portfolio Development

1. Find a copy of a curriculum guide for a subject that you plan to teach. As you study the guide make notes about the topics you already know well enough. Also identify those topics where you will need to learn more before you can be an effective teacher. Make a table with these two lists. Have a "comments column" so that in the future you can make notes about what you have learned as you continue with your teacher education program.
2. At the library or when visiting a school curriculum resource room, examine the curriculum materials for a subject that you plan to teach. For one lesson, use Bloom's Taxonomy as a guide and write a set of learning objectives. This task will provide you with experience and a sample product that you can use as you are planning lessons in the future.

Preparing for Certification

CURRICULUM AND INSTRUCTION

1. A topic in the Praxis II Principles of Learning and Teaching (PLT) test related to curriculum and instruction is "creating or selecting teaching methods, learning activities, and instructional materials or other resources that are appropriate for the students and are aligned with the goals of the lesson." Praxis II also has tests in academic disciplines; most states require prospective teachers to take the appropriate subject

matter tests as well as the PLT. Go to the Praxis website (www.ets.org/praxis) and review the *Tests at a Glance* materials for the test in your subject area or teaching field. What is the structure of the test (e.g., multiple-choice, essay, or both)? What topics does the test cover? Can you answer the sample questions?

2. Answer the following multiple-choice question, which is similar to items in Praxis and other state certification tests.

Ms. Sanchez, a second-grade teacher, after assessing the reading levels of students in her classroom, brought a group of five low-achieving students to work with her on the \ea\ sounds. She asked students to brainstorm words that contained \ea\ and recorded students' responses on the board. She then asked, "Does the \ea\ in all of these words have the same sound? How many sounds do you think \ea\ makes in English? Today you will find out how many different sounds \ea\ can make." After working with students on the concept, she showed a series of flashcards with words containing \ea\ and asked students to read the words. She recorded the number of correct responses each child made on an informal assessment sheet. This assessment is an example of

A. homogeneous grouping and direct instruction
B. heterogeneous grouping and indirect instruction
C. homogeneous grouping and direct instruction
D. heterogeneous grouping and indirect instruction

3. Answer the following short-answer question, which is similar to items in Praxis and other state certification tests. After you've completed your written response, use the scoring guide in the *Test at a Glance* materials to assess your response. Can you revise your response to improve your score?

Some states have passed legislation requiring that all schools use immersion programs rather than bilingual programs for English as a second language (ESL) students. Define the immersion and bilingual approaches to teaching students who are not proficient speakers of English. What are the arguments for and against each approach? Which position do you support, given your current level of knowledge?

Websites

www.csrclearinghouse.org A one-stop site to learn about many of the school reform models, including an "ask-the-expert" link.

www.emsc.nysed.gov/guides Many of the states have websites for accessing their curriculum guides. This is New York's state website and includes "working drafts" of resource guides for most subjects, as well as "other Internet links."

www.ncela.gwu.edu The website of the National Clearinghouse for English Language Acquisition, sponsored by the U.S. Department of Education, is a great resource for information about teaching ELL learners.

www.acceleratedschools.org An informative site for learning about Accelerated Schools that includes descriptions of schools and a Q&A link.

Further Reading

Educational Leadership, the journal of the Association for Supervision and Curriculum Development. This periodical is designed for teachers who are interested in learning about the latest curriculum and instruction ideas, approaches, and issues.

Joyce, Bruce, Weil, Marsha, and Calhoun, Emily. (2003). *Models of Teaching,* 7th edition. Boston: Allyn & Bacon. An entire book devoted to description and analysis of different teaching strategies and how to use them in instruction.

Kelly, A. V. (2004). *The Curriculum: Theory and Practice,* 5th edition. Thousand Oaks, CA: Sage Publications. An informative text that addresses what is entailed in developing curriculum and the central role that teachers play. There also is an examination of the meaning of knowledge.

Smith, Tom E., Polloway, Edward, Patton, James R., and Dowdy, Carol A. (2004). *Teaching Students with Special Needs in Inclusive Settings,* 4th edition. Boston: Allyn & Bacon. This text is a useful resource for teaching students with special needs. There are chapters devoted to suggestions for each type of disability as well as chapters on teaching in elementary and secondary school classrooms.

Tanner, Daniel, and Tanner, Laurel. (2006). *Curriculum Development: Theory into Practice,* 4th edition. Upper Saddle River, NJ: Prentice Hall. Information about the historical roots of current curriculum, connections to today's reforms, along with descriptions of applications in the classroom.

mylabschool
Where the classroom comes to life!

Go to Allyn and Bacon's MyLabSchool (**www.mylabschool.com**) and complete the following activity for Chapter 12. Click on **Courses;** click on **Foundations/Intro Teaching;** click on **MLS Video Lab;** then click on **Module 6: Curriculum Development and Classroom Management.**

CHAPTER 13

Technology in a Changing World

Technology: A Class Act

By Garance Burke, Associated Press, December 19, 2005

OLATHE, KAN.—Aesop's fables came beaming across the classroom and landed in Eva Hernandez's Palm handheld.

On the bottom floor of Ridgeview Elementary School, she sat scrolling, using her stylus to navigate through "The Flies and the Honeypot."

"Hmmm," said the 12-year-old. "I think I can animate the flies."

Eva, a sixth-grader, is part of a new generation of kids using handhelds to read, write, do math, take pictures of the human eye or research Egyptian hieroglyphics—all as a regular part of their curriculum.

As school districts scout ways to engage students already accustomed to instant messaging and interactive video games, they're buying up the kind of tech tools once reserved for jet-setting corporate executives.

Educational sales of personal digital assistants, laptop computers and handheld remote controls called "clickers" are ballooning nationwide. Last year, a survey by Quality Education Data Inc. found that 28 percent of U.S. school districts offered handhelds for student and teacher use. One of every four computers purchased by schools was a laptop.

One of the frontrunners was Yankton High School in South Dakota, which adopted Palm handhelds in 2001 and found they improved students' grades.

Electronic learning has become so popular that one school in Arizona went textbook-free this year, instead equipping its students with laptops. Seventeen schools outside Eugene, Ore., now use handhelds on most science field trips.

Eva Hernandez's district has spent $1.84 million to build "smart classrooms" with electronic interactive whiteboards, handheld computers, DVD-VHS players, high-definition sound and video systems and wireless keyboards and mice, all of which connect to the teacher's desktop computer. High schoolers use their Palms to write college applications and work through calculus problems. Nine-year-olds routinely "beam" in their homework, making the district a poster child for the digital classroom.

For Eric Johnson, who directs educational sales for Palm Inc., the manufacturer of Eva's Zire 71 model, public schools represent a $300 million market. And as schools purchase handhelds, dozens of spin-off industries are racing to integrate themselves into teachers' lesson plans.

Ridgeview Elementary, which sits in a squat building on the edge of this booming Kansas City suburb, bought Zire 71 and Zire 72 models for the fourth and sixth grades. Aside from their basic functions, the handhelds boast color screens, digital cameras, Internet capabilities and MP3 players. They can be easily hooked up to wireless keyboards.

Eva's teacher, Regan Veach, was one of the first in Kansas to embrace handhelds and now trains educators across the state.

Veach touts a new generation of educational software that makes the devices worthwhile. Using a drawing and graphics application called TealPaint, students can animate their versions of Aesop's tales to transform a fable into a digital flipbook. Another program, Inspiration, lets students create clickable "mindmaps" to diagram ideas before they start writing, while Quizzler gives children instant feedback on multiple choice tests.

Veach's instructional process illustrates just how crucial the handhelds have become to everyday learning in Olathe schools.

First, she downloaded Aesop's Fables from a free online site and reformatted it using a program called ebookstudio that crunches it into a format the handhelds can read. That left Eva and her classmates fidgeting with anticipation. Then, once Veach "synched" her Palm to her desktop and "beamed" the fables from student to student, excitement spilled through the room.

"My stepdad, he was like freaked out because he didn't get to use (the devices)," said Alejandro Najera, 11, as he selected colors from a rainbow template on his 3-inch screen. "Now whenever I go home, he's like, 'What did you do with the Palms today'?"

Next was an exercise with the "clickers," handheld remotes that Veach uses to gauge students' progress. As pupils took a quiz to instantly test their understanding of Greek mythology, Veach got out a wireless whiteboard to write up the day's homework.

The day's assignments—90 minutes of reading and a few multiplication exercises—were then wirelessly projected onto a roll-down screen at the front of the classroom and onto her desktop. The kids copied those notes down on paper—in the sixth grade, they're not allowed to take the handhelds home.

Studies show that when used regularly, such media-rich instructional tools can work well to assess student performance.

But some worry that while children may learn to beam in their papers, this generation of "digital natives" could come up short in learning basic math, science and English.

"Despite the fact that we have spent gazillions of dollars in schools on technology, it's still just a leap of faith that kids are better educated because of that," said Robin Raskin, the founder and former editor of FamilyPC magazine. "Students need to have some opportunity to digest material serially, like reading a book from end to end. A tiny screen might stop you from being an analytic thinker, because you just can't see enough of a thing at once."

Ridgeview's principal, Kelly Ralston, is aware that technology won't erase the difficulties faced by her students, over half of whom come from low-income families.

Last year, she spent just one-third of her annual $63,000 budget for handhelds; the district has spent at least $952,000 to equip 4,000 students with the devices in the last four school years. "The overall achievement is rising and the Palms have been a piece in keeping our kids engaged," said Ralston.

Questions for Reflection

1. Why are students excited about doing school work on handheld devices?

2. Why are manufacturers of handheld devices and other technology becoming so interested in the school market?

3. Why are some adults questioning the extensive use of technology in the curriculum?

Reprinted with permission.

INTASC

Learning Outcomes

After reading and studying this chapter, you should be able to:

1. Describe the fundamental concepts of computer technology. (INTASC 9: Reflection and Professional Growth)

2. Determine how to use technology to support student learning. (INTASC 4: Instructional Strategies; INTASC 5: Motivation and Behavior)

3. Direct students to technology resources that will help them learn the subject matter you are teaching. (INTASC 1: Subject Matter)

4. Identify some of the major issues that arise as technology is integrated into the education process. (INTASC 9: Reflection and Professional Growth)

5. Think about the technology that may be available in schools of the future. (INTASC 9: Reflection and Professional Growth)

The rapidity with which **technology** changes our world can produce extremes in terms of both excitement and anxiety. A new technological innovation that can instill thrilling optimism in one person can be viewed by another as a serious threat. One person's perspective about technology could be optimistic and another's skeptical. Nevertheless, there is little doubt that it plays a significant and sometimes defining role in our society.

In today's world, it is difficult to imagine U.S. schools and classrooms without technology. An expectation exists that nearly all schools and classrooms will have access to computers in some form. Other technologies such as videotapes, DVDs, television, calculators, digital cameras, and overhead projectors are found in most schools and available to most classrooms. We are teaching and learning in a technology-rich environment.

It is much more difficult to imagine what teachers and students are actually doing with the available technology resources. Teachers and students may be limited by what technology is available, but an even bigger limitation is in imagining what can be done with technology. In far too many classrooms, technology resources are mainly on display rather than in use. In other classrooms, a particular type of technology can become the content instead of a tool for teaching established goals, standards, and curriculum. All too frequently, teachers and their students become specialists in one or another technology or a narrow set of applications.

The term *technology* is, contrary to popular usage, a very generic term that can refer to any tool used by people to accomplish a task. Thus, such common educational materials as chalkboards and three-ring notebooks could be considered educational technologies. More contemporary uses of the term are likely referring to **information technology.** This chapter will utilize the latter, more contemporary meaning. Interestingly, it is worth keeping the chalkboard in mind as one example of technology because it has some clear advantages when used in support of teaching and learning.

> When I took office, only high energy physicists had ever heard of what is called the Worldwide Web. . . . Now even my cat has its own page.
>
> **Bill Clinton**

Technology Basics

A foundational knowledge of educational technologies can enhance a teacher's capacity to meet any number of goals related to teaching. In addition, a comfort with technology can help teachers quickly adapt to the changing needs of students and expectations of society. A set of knowledge and skills as they relate to educational needs are described in general terms in this section.

Standards

The International Society for Technology in Education (ISTE) has developed a set of standards that delineate what knowledge and skills teachers should possess to effectively integrate technology into the classrooms. The resulting National Educational Technology Standards for Teachers (NETS-T) consist of six general areas:

1. Technology Operations and Concepts
2. Planning and Designing Learning Environments and Experiences
3. Teaching, Learning, and the Curriculum
4. Assessment and Evaluation
5. Productivity and Professional Practice
6. Social, Ethical, Legal, and Human Issues[1]

The first area, Technology Operations and Concepts, consists of the general skills and knowledge that any professional would need to utilize technology. This area

CROSS-REFERENCE
Standards are also discussed in Chapter 11.

technology
A tool such as a computer or a chalkboard used to complete a task.

information technology
Computer, software, telecommunications, and multimedia tools used to input, store, process, and communicate information.

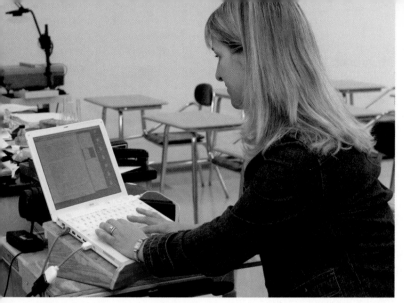

Most people do not innately know how to use a computer or make a software program work. Experimenting with the equipment and software is the best way to become comfortable with using them.

will be addressed in more depth in the Fundamental Concepts section of this chapter. The next four areas deal directly with the common activities of the professional teacher and how technology is used to support those activities. These areas will be briefly described in the second section of the chapter. The final area deals with a number of general issues that arise in the final section of the chapter.

Fundamental Concepts

One way to increase your comfort with computers and other technologies is to play with them. Some of the more apprehensive computer users are concerned that they might somehow harm the computer if they make a mistake. In reality, computers have now advanced to the point where it is quite difficult to do any significant harm. Another way to increase your comfort with computers is to learn more about how they work. Although computers have become very complicated, they are really based on some simple concepts that deserve a bit of attention to help overcome the black box mentality that they are magical.

Every task that a computer completes is a result of a series of on and off switches that are not much more complicated than that used to control a room light. These switches are found on computer microchips which can now contain the equivalent of billions of switches. If the switch is *on* the computer views that as a 1. Off equals 0. Each 0 or 1 is termed a **bit.** Since it is difficult to describe too many things as simply yes and no (or on and off), bits are generally combined into segments of eight, or a **byte.** Computers use codes to convert bytes to more useful items such as letters. For example, the code 0100 0001 is equivalent to the letter *A*. Similar conversions can be made for visual elements such as color and size as well as auditory elements such as pitch and volume.

Programmers use these codes and related procedures to develop useful **software** tools such as word processors and spreadsheets. Computers simply react to the instructions the programmer provides. At its most fundamental level, a computer simply accepts some input (e.g., keystrokes from a keyboard), processes that input, and finally produces some form of output. A simple handheld calculator is a computer that reflects each of these steps. To complete a calculation, you input data by pressing several keys (e.g., 2 + 2 =), the calculator processes the input (e.g., determines that 2 + 2 = 4), and produces some output (e.g., displays 4 on the screen).

COMPUTER HARDWARE

All input and output tasks are largely the function of **hardware,** or the tangible objects that make up the computer. Each of the **peripherals** described in this section are examples of computer hardware.

An obvious place to begin exploring hardware is with the personal computer. The evolution of the PC clearly illustrates the ever-expanding application possibilities and exponential increases in speed and size. The first PC used widely in schools was the Apple I, which was introduced in the early 1980s. Curiously, the term *personal computer* was coined after the introduction of the Apple and originally referred to the IBM versions. Apple I's were useful for basic word processing as long as the document wasn't too big, and they had a calculator. As innovative teachers adopted Apples, they quickly started creating new programs and even establishing

bit

One unit of information represented as a 1 or 0 on a microchip by being either on or off.

byte

A computer code that combines eight bits into segments that convert into letters, colors, font sizes, pitches, volumes, etc.

software

Programs and procedures that direct the computer to perform a specific task such as word processing or browsing the web.

hardware

Physical components of a computer such as the CPU, monitor, mouse, and keyboard.

peripherals

Components of a computer such as a mouse or keyboard that are separate from the CPU.

classes to teach students programming in BASIC (a computer language) so that special applications could be done by computer. Almost as quickly as the PC was introduced, educators were confronted with the age-old question about applying a new technology in the classroom: Was the primary purpose of this new educational technology to learn *about* computers or to use computers *to learn?* Fortunately, classes in writing programming code did not last long. Today, PCs are smaller than the early ones, but now they can store enormous amounts of information in digital form and are faster each year.

The input of a personal computer is most often accomplished with the keyboard and mouse. Other common input devices include scanners, microphones, and digital cameras. The most common output device is the monitor, followed closely by printers and speakers. Storage devices such as the computer hard drive and disk drives often serve as input and output devices. Retrieving (or opening) a file from a disk is an example of using a storage device for input. After making changes to the file, you save (or output) the file back to the original disk.

PROCESSING HARDWARE   The processing of information on your computer is done through a combination of hardware and software. The central device that accomplishes much of the processing work on a computer is the central processing unit (CPU) or processor. Common processor manufacturers include Intel and AMD. One other processing component that is vital to consider with today's computer is the graphics processor. With more and more classrooms making and using video technologies, the graphic capability of a computer becomes critical.

STORAGE HARDWARE   A wide variety of storage devices now exists for computers. Each of these devices is rated in terms of their capacity. As noted above, information is viewed by the computer as a series of bits or zeros and ones. This results from the computer using a binary number system. This system also benefits from viewing information as a series of eight bits or a byte. Thus, you will often see references to bits and bytes as they pertain to computers and their peripherals. Since bits and bytes are relatively small units you will most commonly see them preceded by a metric prefix. A metric prefix review might be helpful. The most common metric prefixes are kilo = thousand (1,000), mega = million (1,000,000) and giga = billion (1,000,000,000). This information is organized into files and directories or folders. Files might be best thought of as individual documents and directories as organizational folders. Files are generally of a certain type, such as a word processing file or a video file.

The most common (and essential) devices include the computer hard drive and **RAM.** The hard drive is a persistent storage device in that it will store information even while the computer is off. The hard drive is not a permanent storage device because files can be modified and erased. Since this is the primary storage device on most computers, it is most often measured in giga-bytes (GB). A 100-GB hard drive can store the equivalent of about 50,000,000 pages of text. Other more intense storage needs such as audio and video can fill up a hard drive very quickly.

RAM, or random access memory, functions as the real-time storage device for the computer. RAM is not persistent and thus will depend upon power to maintain its current data. This is why it is important to save prior to turning off a computer. Saving your work commonly refers to saving what you have in RAM to a persistent storage device such as a hard drive. The amount of RAM in your computer will dictate how much your computer can do at one time—and, to some degree, how fast. The amount of RAM is generally much less than the size of the hard drive.

COMPUTER SOFTWARE

The term software refers to the components of the computer that are instructional rather than mechanical. These are essentially the plans provided to the computer that guide the functions of the hardware. Two of the most familiar types of software include application software and operating system (OS) software.

Hardware: the parts of a computer that can be kicked.
Jeff Pesis

The great thing about a computer notebook is that no matter how much you stuff into it, it doesn't get bigger or heavier.
Bill Gates

RAM (random access memory)

Real-time storage in which files are saved while working on the computer. Its size determines how many programs and files the user can be working on at the same time.

APPLICATION SOFTWARE   The most common software application in the world is likely the web browser. Internet Explorer, Netscape Navigator, and Mozilla Firefox are all examples of web browser software. Other types of application software include word processing (e.g., Microsoft Word), spreadsheet (e.g., Microsoft Excel), and database (e.g., Filemaker Pro). You can operate many applications simultaneously (with some limitations). Running multiple applications is referred to as multitasking and can be very useful. For example, tasks such as word processing can be completed while waiting for the download of a large file from the web to finish.

OPERATING SYSTEM (OS) SOFTWARE   Your computer's operating system is tasked with managing all the resources associated with your computer. It is used to facilitate communication between all of your application software and your hardware. Common operating systems include Windows XP, Mac OS 10, and Linux. An example of the type of communication directed by your OS includes printing from different applications. We need printing functions from most of our application software. A print request from your browser is sent to the OS rather than directly to the printer. This might seem like a wasted step unless you consider the large number of applications and printers in existence. Having only one software program communicate with the printer (and all other peripherals) is actually much more efficient.

Knowledge of the role of the OS when compared to application software can be very useful when you are troubleshooting a variety of errors. Consider a music program as an example. For some unknown reason, the music is not coming out of your speakers when you play a song. After checking the hardware (i.e., speakers are on and plugged into the appropriate jack on your computer), you turn to the software. In this instance, both the OS and the application software likely have settings for volume. Thus, you'll need to check that each have the volume up. Where to check this varies for different operating systems and applications but they are often labeled with clearly marked language such as control panel or settings.

Networks

The need to have computers be able to exchange information quickly and easily has been critical to the successful utilization of computers in supporting our personal, workplace, and educational needs. A **network** refers to two or more interconnected computers. Most networks found in schools are based upon the use of Ethernet technology which uses cables to connect each computer to a central location. This interconnected group of computers is often referred to as a Local Area Network or LAN. Wide Area Networks, or WANs, refer to networks where multiple buildings or LANs are interconnected. School districts often have LANs in each school building and have each building in the district connected to a WAN.

The Internet

The **Internet** refers to the global network that currently connects many of the computers in the world. The Internet was originally designed in the United States to ensure communication could be maintained in a time of war. This original Internet was called the ARPA-NET. The tremendous growth of the Internet is due in large part to the introduction of a common protocol or language that made it possible for any network computer to share information (or bits) with any other networked computer. In addition to a common language, the Internet shares a common addressing scheme as well. The use of Internet Protocol (IP) addressing enables special computers called **routers** to direct information to the appropriate computer.

network

Two or more computers that are interconnected, allowing files to be shared among users.

Internet

Global network that currently connects many of the computers in the world.

routers

Special computers or hardware devices that direct information from the Internet to the appropriate computer so that it can be read by a user.

The early use of the Internet was largely restricted to large universities and research labs. In those environments the exchange of email and data files constituted the majority of the use of the Internet. However, in the early 1990s, Tim Berners-Lee developed a new protocol for formatting text files that accommodated visual elements, such as headings, and functional elements such as hyperlinks.[2] Soon after, Marc Andreessen while working at the National Center for Supercomputing Applications (NCSA) developed an application called a browser, named Mosaic, that used the codes developed by Berners-Lee to visually display text, hyperlinks and images. Current browsers like Internet Explorer, Netscape, and Firefox are all based upon the original designs of Berners-Lee and Andreessen. The Internet has become a critical component of all facets or our society as it enables any Internet-connected computer to communicate quickly and easily with any other Internet-connected computer in the world.

Journal for Reflection

1. What is your level of proficiency in relation to ISTE Standard One and the fundamental concepts introduced in this section?

2. What technologies did you use in high school? What additional ones are you using for your college work?

3. How do you use the Internet for learning purposes?

Teachers' Use of Technology

Technology is having a tremendous impact on teaching today. Spiral-bound grade books have given way to computer-based grading software. Hand-written report cards have been replaced by computer-generated printouts. When one considers the large amount of information that teachers must manage, it is easy to see how computers can be an invaluable support tool. Additionally, computers can now facilitate much more streamlined communication with parents, administrators, and in some instances students. However, the power of computers can go far beyond supporting the many administrative tasks a teacher faces. Much of the enthusiasm for technology in education is directed towards student uses of computers.

Of course the teacher plays a pivotal role in establishing the environment that is conducive to learning and thus must be comfortable with the technology. We know that not all teachers enter classrooms ready to integrate technology. Most teachers progress through several phases of use before they are able to integrate technology effectively. Much of our understanding of teacher development comes from research conducted very early in the history of the personal computer through the Apple Classrooms of Tomorrow project. Apple computers outfitted a large number of schools, classrooms, and homes with personal computers to investigate how they would impact the learning environment. The researchers found that teachers moved through five phases of varying sophistication in terms of how to use the integrated technology. Early phases such as *entry* and *adoption* are characterized by familiarization with the technology and implementation with rote tasks such as drill and practice software. Teachers in advanced stages such as *appropriation* were more likely to use technology supported strategies that included collaboration and projects.[3]

> The proper artistic response to digital technology is to embrace it as a new window on everything that's eternally human, and to use it with passion, wisdom, fearlessness and joy.
>
> *Philip Greenspun*

Outside the Classroom

Technology for many teachers has become an instrumental part of their teaching within and beyond the classroom. Many teachers are introduced to the potential of technology in endeavors that are unrelated to their professional life. Using email to communicate with family and friends has quickly become a common way for much of our society to keep in touch. Similarly, using the Internet has become the tool to plan travel, conduct research for a car purchase, and solicit restaurant recommendations. Once teachers see the value of technology in their personal lives they quickly look for opportunities to utilize it in support of their classroom goals.

iPods and similar devices can be used for more than listening to one's favorite music. They are now being used by teachers for instructional purposes and their own professional development.

TEACHER–FAMILY COMMUNICATION

Email is often referred to as the *killer app* in technology circles. This is due to its tremendous usefulness that quickly rendered it an application we could not live without. Teachers have also found tremendous value in this tool. Teachers may use email to communicate with other educators within and beyond their school. This has helped many educators overcome the isolation of being physically separated from colleagues for much of the day.

Teachers also find online discussion forums, weblogs (or **blogs**), and **podcasts** to be useful tools for communicating with colleagues throughout the world. Online discussion forums can be very valuable for new teachers as a place to post questions and find new ideas. Blogs are now easily established and thus more and more teachers are using them to chronicle their ideas, experiences, and challenges regarding life as a teacher. In addition, there are a number of potential applications of these tools with students.

Regular and consistent communication with parents has long been considered vital to the success of students. In the past, teachers were dependent upon mail, phone, and students to facilitate this communication. Internet technologies augment these standard tools in some exciting ways. The most common example of parent communication in use today is the school or classroom website. Even the most basic of websites can provide valuable information for parents and students. Contact information and a staff directory can be very helpful. In addition, schools find that providing significant information on their website reduces the number of phone calls to school staff for frequently asked questions (also known as FAQs).

Providing basic information regarding the school is only the beginning of what the Internet may provide in terms of parent communication. Some school districts are now making homework assignments available via the web. This can give the parent up-to-date information regarding the activities of their child. Some schools are also utilizing the Internet to share students' grades with parents.

TRACKING STUDENT LEARNING

Student assessment is also being supported by technology. A critical and often missing component of an effective lesson is addressing the individual needs of students. Inevitably, teachers are faced with a very diverse class of students in terms of their understanding of any particular concept. Many schools now have database systems that collect and report student assessment results in a format that is easy to access. For example, teachers can view reports of their students that list how each student performed on assessment items specific to a standard or topic on recent district or state assessments. This information can then be used to guide decisions such as where the lesson should begin and what sort of student groupings might be most appropriate.

Many schools and school districts are purchasing database services to help them manage and retrieve all of the data that had been stored in file cabinets and unique databases set-up by teachers or school administrators. They are purchasing assessment systems from companies such as Northwest Evaluation Association (NWEA), Plato Learning, and Tungston Learning, which allow teachers to regularly assess students against state and district standards. Some schools test their students monthly, using systems that make performance data available immediately to teachers. Sophisticated systems are able to track student growth from year to year.[4] These assessments and their instantaneous feedback are allowing teachers to intervene in the learning

CROSS-REFERENCE

Chapter 11 examines the assessment of student learning.

blog

A chronological publication on the Internet of personal thoughts about a subject to which participants contribute the content online. It is sometimes called a weblog.

podcasts

Multimedia files such as audio programs or music videos that are available on the Internet for playback on personal computers and mobile devices such as the iPod.

These elementary teachers are reviewing reports of how their students performed on the most recent district assessment. They have decided to do some team teaching with different groups of students to ensure students learn the concepts and skills on which they did not perform well.

process to assist students in improving their academic performance. These assessments can also be designed to test other knowledge and skills such as critical thinking and problem solving that may not be assessed on the state tests.

LESSON PLANNING

Computer-based technologies have become essential components of efficient and effective lesson planning. When you consider the tasks that need to be accomplished in planning a lesson, it is clear that computer software and the Internet can be invaluable contributors. The teacher must first clearly describe the goal(s) of the lesson in terms of student outcomes, which often are derived from national, state, and local standards. Although teachers are likely given a copy of these standards when they begin teaching, it is much more convenient to utilize electronic versions of these documents when building lessons. The standards may be available on the web via the school or district home page. These same sites may also provide links to sample lessons that address a particular standard or group of standards.

Lesson plan ideas are plentiful on the web. The problem is finding plans that are effective and appropriate to one particular situation. Teachers will find that the sites that are the most valuable to them for this purpose provide more than just a listing and categorization of lessons; they also include some mechanism for evaluation and/or rating.

Teachers also utilize the web to a great degree to gather information about lesson topics, including the discovery of different media to support instruction. A number of sites now provide access and rights to images, sound, and video files that can be used to develop documents and presentations. As with lesson ideas, you will find sites that provide quick access to media resources that are of high quality and have undergone some level of evaluation or rating. Additionally, it is vital that the media author has granted the appropriate rights for teachers to use the media.

Inside the Classroom

The potential for technology to support learning is substantial and a large reason why so many educators are excited about its use. This look at some of the uses of technology in the classroom will use potential tasks as the frame of reference rather

CROSS-REFERENCE
No Child Left Behind and its expectations for students to meet standards at their grade level is discussed in greater detail in Chapter 11.

CROSS-REFERENCE
Lesson planning is also discussed in Chapter 12.

FIGURE 13.1

Classroom Tools on the Web

INTERNET SEARCH ENGINES

- **Google, Google.com**
  Hands down the best search engine on the web. The advanced search functions will allow you to search only certain sites and/or Creative Commons licensed resources.

- **Yahoo, Yahoo.com & Yahooligans.com**
  A close second in terms of search engines. Yahooligans restricts results to those most appropriate for younger audiences.

COLLABORATION TOOLS

- **Skype, Skype.com**
  This free voice conferencing tool allows students and teachers to talk with anyone else on an Internet connected computer.

- **Odeo, Odeo.com**
  Online podcasting tool allows teachers and students to record and share audio files over the Internet.

- **iTunes, Apple.com**
  This popular media manager originally served music but has expanded into podcasts and videos.

- **Blogger, Blogger.com**
  A popular free blogging service that is very powerful and easy to use.

ENCYCLOPEDIAS

- **Britannica, Brittanica.com**
  Online version of the popular print encyclopedia.

- **Encarta, Encarta.com**
  Electronic only encyclopedia that is also available as a DVD.

- **Wikipedia, En.wikipedia.org (English version)**
  The popular and controversial online community-built encyclopedia.

TEACHER GUIDED RESEARCH

- **Webquest, Webquest.com**
  Teachers use this to organize lessons and point out helpful sites for students to use.

- **Delicious, Del.icio.us**
  Teachers can use this social bookmarking tool to tag sites that are appropriate for a particular topic or assignment.

PROJECT DEVELOPMENT TOOLS

- **KidPix, http://riverdeep.net**
  Powerful multimedia development tool for elementary age students.

- **PowerPoint, http://microsoft.com**
  Presentation program that can be used as an interactive multimedia development tool.

- **iMovie, Apple.com**
  This easy to use video editing program is included with all new Macintosh computers.

than the tools themselves. Beginning with the instructional goal in mind rather than the technology may seem obvious but can get lost when educators learn of new and exciting technologies. Examples of online tools for classroom use are found in Figure 13.1.

Research has also supported the value of technology in classrooms but with a very important caveat, which is that the strategies used to integrate technology are

Social Context in the Use of Computers

STUDY PURPOSE/QUESTION: Do small groups or individual work have a more favorable effect on learning through computer technology?

STUDY DESIGN: This study used a special research method called meta-analysis. Instead of analyzing the data from a single study, with meta-analysis it is possible to summarize the findings of many different studies. In this case, 122 studies involving 11,317 learners were analyzed.

STUDY FINDINGS: The first finding was that social context played an important role when students learn with computer technology (CT). In other words, students who worked in small groups learned more than those students who worked alone. "In general, small group learning with CT had more favorable effects than individual learning with CT on student cognitive, process and affective outcomes" (p. 476).

The results from working in small groups were positive across several types of learning outcomes. "These positive results indicate that when working with CT in small groups, students in general produced substantially better group products than individual products and they also gained more individual knowledge than those learning with CT individually" (p. 476).

There were a number of instructional features that made a positive difference: (a) students had experience in working in groups, (b) students were instructed in specific cooperative learning strategies, (c) the group size was small, and (d) the content was tutorials, practice software, learning computer skills, or social sciences. However, there was a small negative effect when the subject matter involved mathematics, science, or language arts. Also the best group size is two, which probably is as many as can easily see the CT screen at one time.

IMPLICATIONS: The findings from this meta-analysis indicate that teachers should plan carefully and organize instruction differently depending on the number of students, the number of CT stations, and the subject area. Ideally there should be no more than two students per station, and the students should have had prior instruction and experience with doing group work. The subject area being taught could make a difference; however, the meta-analyses seemed to indicate that the negative effects from small group versus individual work was quite small and probably could be offset by better organization and structuring of the tasks. Preparing students to use cooperative learning strategies would appear to be important for a number of different teaching strategies and subject areas, as well as with small group work at CT stations. It probably is worthwhile to teach children skills for cooperative grouping early in the school year.

Source: Based on Yiping Lou, Philip C. Abrami, and Sylvia d'Apollonia, "Small Group and Individual Learning with Technology: A Meta-Analysis," *Review of Educational Research, 71*(3) (Fall 2001), pp. 449–521.

---

consistent with what we know about student learning. More specifically, when technology is used to actively engage students in learning, applying, and analyzing important concepts, achievement gains result. For example, researchers have found that in classrooms in which computer simulations are used to support higher-level cognitive tasks, subsequent achievement gains can result.[5] The same cannot be said for more rote learning activities where engagement of the learner is less. Keep this important distinction in mind as you review the tools described below and consider how they could be implemented effectively.

INFORMATION RESOURCES

It should not be surprising that gathering information is such an important task in classrooms. Many now refer to our society as a knowledge or information-based economy. Good information was once only accessible by a few. Even the best public libraries, while plentiful, could house only a fraction of the world's books and periodicals. Now, with the Internet, information is plentiful. So plentiful that evaluating information has become a critical skill for students.

Some school districts are providing both teachers and students with computers as part of ubiquitous computing plans to encourage the use of technology in their work.

In classrooms, students have always had a variety of needs regarding information. This might be as simple as looking up the spelling of a word in the dictionary or as involved as the development of a report on a large topic such as global warming. Now, with virtually every classroom in the country connected to the Internet, many teachers and students are looking online for information. The ease with which anyone can post information to the Internet has led to an explosion of web pages that presents as many challenges as it does opportunities. One of the greatest challenges for teachers is sifting through the over 11.5 billion web pages[6] to find the most accurate and relevant information. Teachers will often use one of three strategies to help students deal with the tremendous amount of information available online. These strategies include the use of search engines, encyclopedias, and teacher-guided research.

INTERNET SEARCH ENGINES Internet search engines attempt to index web pages in ways that are meaningful to users. The hope is that the search engine can retrieve the most useful pages on the Internet based on a few words supplied by the user. Search engines have improved tremendously over the past few years—mostly due to advances introduced by Google. The most important thing Google introduced was a human element to the ranking of the results. They did this by counting links from one site to another as a *vote* for the site. Not surprisingly, this greatly improved the ranking of results.

Most search engines now have the capability to filter results so that they do not include adult content. Many also feature specialized searches that will only return Creative Commons licensed content. The authors of this content grant certain permissions for further use of the content. This can be valuable for students and teachers who would like to use the content for other purposes.

ENCYCLOPEDIAS Encyclopedias have long been considered an essential component of any school library. Most school encyclopedias are now available via computer through the school network or through an online subscription with a publisher. Traditional encyclopedia companies such as Encyclopedia Britannica offer online versions of their well respected print series. Microsoft has also developed a very popular encyclopedia series entitled Encarta. The online versions

Global Perspectives

China's Filtering of the Internet

Most of us see Internet search engines as assisting us in the organization of the billions of resources available worldwide on the topics in which we are interested. We probably also think that the Internet lets anyone in the world access information that they might not otherwise be able to find, especially if they live in rural or isolated areas of the world. Thus, we were surprised to learn that Chinese officials had negotiated with Cisco Systems, Google, Microsoft, and Yahoo to filter information for the potential 111 million Chinese users by limiting access to material on the Internet. In his annual news conference, Premier Wen Jiabao indicated that available websites should "convey the right message and information." Many advocates of free speech are saying that China has placed a firewall on the Internet to curtail the questioning of government policies and practices by its citizens.[7]

Questions for Reflection

1. Why would companies that provide Internet access agree to filter the information available to users in China?

2. How might such filtering of information accessible on the Internet contribute to oppression and inequality in a country?

have the advantage of access throughout the school (versus only the library) and much easier searching.

A newcomer to the encyclopedia market is Wikipedia. This online encyclopedia is unique in that anyone can contribute content to its pages. By allowing everyone to contribute, Wikipedia has quickly become the world's largest encyclopedia with the English version cataloging over one billion articles. Most of the articles are written by individuals with significant experience in the respective topic and have been discussed, reviewed, and revised hundreds of times. Wikipedia's open nature has also resulted in it being a target for vandalism and sharp criticism, requiring users to cross-check facts for accuracy.

TEACHER-GUIDED RESEARCH   Teacher-guided research strategies involve the use of a selected number of sites for students to use in their search on a topic. This strategy can alleviate many of the concerns that arise from the use of other web-based research strategies. One of the strengths of this approach is that it allows the teacher to identify credible and useful resources for students. This can often be more efficient in that the amount of time students spend searching for information is reduced. It also reduces the possibility that students will find inappropriate and/or inaccurate information.

One common model teachers use to develop these types of lessons is the WebQuest. These inquiry-based lessons were conceived by Bernie Dodge as a way to incorporate web-based content into learning activities. The model includes the development of clear learning objectives, specific tasks to be accomplished by the group, and a listing of web-based resources that the students should use in accomplishing the task. One of the many strengths of this model is that it is familiar to many teachers and thus they are able to easily incorporate other teachers' WebQuests into their own classrooms.

Assigning Homework That Uses Technology

Ninety-nine percent of the schools in the United States are wired for the Internet, and most classrooms have one or more computers with software for the subject and grade level being taught. The computers may have graphics capability that allow students to design interesting presentations with audio and video clips. Math teachers have graphic calculators. Students can edit their own videotapes to produce a movie instead of a traditional written paper for a class project. The school district is offering professional development courses on the use of handheld devices and podcasting for instruction. Teachers are being encouraged to communicate with parents and guardians via email and postings on the school's website. Students are excited about having the opportunity to work on the computers. They like the interactivity of many of the software packages. The challenge for teachers is to figure out how best to use the technology for learning, not just for entertainment and fun.

One of the values of the Internet is to search for information about almost any subject. Search engines identify resources from many different sources and multiple perspectives. One of the skills that students should develop is how to sort through multiple sources for the information they need and how to test its accuracy. Students could use the Internet to explore topics and concepts being presented in a unit. Class time can be spent for such research activities, but it may be difficult for all students to spend the time needed, especially if a classroom has a limited number of computers. Thus, a teacher may be tempted to assign homework that requires using the Internet. A problem with assigning homework on the Internet, however, is that not all students have computers at home. Even if an assignment does not require the use of the Internet, those students who have access to it at home have an advantage in completing school projects.

Questions for Reflection

1. What are the problems that could result from assigning homework that requires the use of the Internet?

2. How could a teacher overcome the inequities that exist when some students have computers at home and others do not?

3. What would be the advantage of a program that allows all students access to a laptop? What are the disadvantages?

To answer these questions on-line and e-mail your answers to your professor, go to Chapter 13 of the companion website (www.ablongman.com/johnson14e) and click on Professional Dilemma.

PROJECT DEVELOPMENT TOOLS

Classroom teachers will frequently design project-based activities for students with the outcome being a report or other project. Many are now using educational technology tools to enable students to produce creative multimedia products. Students often find the use of the computer in this manner more motivating than the traditional report. It also gives students the chance to be more creative in the presentation of their work.

Common multimedia development applications include KidPix for elementary age students and PowerPoint for older students. Each of these programs gives students the capacity to incorporate text, sound, images, and movies into presentations (or shows) that can be shared. More recently, teachers are asking students to develop their own topical movies for projects. This has only recently become feasible for the classroom as the required equipment (digital video camera and a powerful computer with movie editing software) has become much more accessible.

An important consideration classroom teachers must make in using these types of projects is how much time will be dedicated to learning the software versus engaging in the desired learning activities. This is an area where collaboration with other teachers in the school is critical. If teachers can agree on some common tools for project development activities, it reduces the time any one class must spend on learning the tools.

COLLABORATION TOOLS

Classroom teachers are always looking for ways to extend student learning beyond the walls of the classroom. This makes the learning more valuable and motivating for students as they see the connections to their own life. In the past, this goal was met most directly through the use of field trips and possibly guest speakers. Each of these options required significant funding and planning. In addition they were often limited in scope and time. Many have now looked to the Internet as a way to extend the classroom in powerful and authentic ways.

Email is the most commonly used method for collaborating with others. It is easy to use and does not require any specialized software. Teachers can partner with classrooms to learn more about other countries, collaborate on projects, or simply exchange messages. In addition to text, email can be used to exchange pictures and other files. In some instances, email is giving way to real-time (or synchronous) tools such as instant messaging and voice or video conferencing. As computers become more powerful, the Internet connections become faster and the necessary software becomes more easily accessible.

Podcasting and Blogs are two more recent technologies that have been utilized by classroom teachers to facilitate collaboration among students. New technologies on the web (specifically Really Simple Syndication or RSS) have made it possible for students to publish their podcasts and subscribe to the podcasts of others. Apple's iTunes software and iPod music players have helped to make this technology very popular. However, one only needs an Internet-connected computer to develop, distribute, and listen to podcasts.

Blogs are being used to streamline collaboration via the Internet. Blogs are content-rich sites that are easy to setup and contribute to. Most of them make it easy for novice computer users to submit postings to a website that can then be read by anyone. Readers can also comment on postings. The posting and subsequent comments can frequently generate meaningful discussions around the original topic. Blogger.com is one example of many free services that allow anyone to start a blog.

> Home computers are being called upon to perform many new functions, including the consumption of homework formerly eaten by the dog.
> *Doug Larson*

Distance Education

Distance education typically describes learning experiences in which the teacher and student are geographically separate. While distance education has experienced a recent resurgence in popularity, it is not a recent phenomenon. Correspondence courses have long been popular options for individuals seeking postsecondary learning opportunities when they did not have easy access to higher education. Military personnel and people living in rural areas often benefit from educational opportunities that do not require *face-to-face* classroom meetings. While distance education is most commonly associated with learning beyond high school, there are examples of students using distance education to meet goals such as earning a high school diploma. Nebraska's Independent Study High School has been offering courses since 1929.

Advances in computer and communications technologies are largely responsible for the renewed interest in distance education. The Internet in particular has dramatically increased the communications opportunities between teachers and students. Email alone was a tremendous advance over the use of postal mail. More recent advances in Internet communication tools such as instant messaging and audio conferencing have also contributed to the increased interest in distance education.

Thirty-eight percent of all U.S. public high schools offered distance education courses during the 2002–2003 academic year.[8] Over 325,000 students were

distance education
Learning experiences in which the teacher and student are geographically separate.

enrolled in these courses.[9] The vast majority of these schools are delivering courses electronically. While definitive data are difficult to come by, there is little doubt that these offerings are expanding rapidly. Some states and districts have expanded their online distance education offerings to include the entire curricula. According to one estimate, as many as 2,400 **virtual schools** were operating in 2005.[10]

There are a number of reasons high schools are offering distance education courses. One of the most common is to provide more opportunities to students. Schools can offer a wider variety of courses to students if they can combine enrollments from multiple locations. For example, while a Russian language class may not draw enough interest from students in one high school, offering it as a distance education course that can be taken by students in any high school in that school district (or beyond) may make the offering more feasible.

Educators have different perspectives on the appropriateness of distance education, especially for younger students. Certainly, today's students are becoming more and more accustomed to socializing through electronic tools such as cell phones and instant messaging programs. However, there is little doubt that some degree of face-to-face interactions among teachers and students can be valuable.

Distance education has also become an important means for many teachers to continue their learning while teaching. These experiences range from short professional development workshops to entire graduate degree programs. Most school districts now take advantage of web-based learning to provide some proportion of their professional development programs to teachers. Most colleges and universities provide graduate courses in education; they offer either courses or entire graduate programs through the Internet. Classroom teachers find the flexibility inherent in distance education very helpful in their efforts to continue their education.

Journal for Reflection

1. How could immediate access to how students have performed on standards-based assessments be helpful to a teacher?

2. How could a teacher use email for instructional purposes?

3. What would teaching in a virtual school be like? How would you get to know your students? Why (or why not) would you be interested in such a teaching assignment?

Issues Related to the Use of Technology

Up to this point, this chapter has painted a rather optimistic picture of the potential of technology to support teaching and learning. In many ways the optimism is justified. Of course, that optimism must be balanced with some professional skepticism. Each of the opportunities described earlier in the chapter present significant challenges to classroom teachers, administrators, parents, and students. Many of these issues cut across all of the technology-related topics. This section will briefly address five of the social, ethical, legal, and human issues that educators are being faced with as a result of technology in our quickly changing world.

Equality in Access

Although the number of Internet users is growing exponentially each year, most of the world's population do not have access to computers or the Internet. People in developing nations have limited access to what most of us would consider a basic communications necessity—the telephone. In fact, the disparity across nations in telephone, cell phone, and computer access is quite great as shown in Figure 13.2 (p. 449). Countries in Africa and Southeast Asia are least likely to have phones and computers.[11] In many parts of the world cell phones are becoming the cheaper and faster way to expand communication systems. "Between 1997 and 2002 the number of telephone lines [in the world] grew by 40% and the number of cell phone

virtual schools

Schools in which all of the curriculum is delivered via distance learning.

Should School Computer Labs Be Phased Out?

As technologies develop and their applications expand, educators try to determine the best way to integrate them into daily teaching and learning. This debate focuses on one question that arises from such attempts to use technology effectively in education.

YES

Barbara Barr is a K–1 teacher at Brookside Elementary School in Nicholasville, Kentucky. This twenty-four-year teaching veteran teaches nearly all lessons using classroom computers. In the fall, Barr will work in her district's technology office training teachers to integrate computers into the curriculum.

Computers belong in all classrooms, not held captive in the computer lab and taught as a specialized subject area at a scheduled time.

All staff and students need to learn how to effectively use this instrument. This can most realistically happen when computers are conveniently accessible in a classroom.

Computer labs have a number of drawbacks. In a lab setting, the computer is learned apart from other subjects and activities. It is much more difficult to integrate technology into other areas of the curriculum within the lab setting. The computer becomes a separate course or activity, rather than a tool used to enhance learning in other areas.

Time limits are another disadvantage to computer labs. Most educators have an assigned time to use the lab. This restricted access limits activities a teacher can conduct with students.

The time limits affect students, too. For example, a student doing a research project on World War II using computers in the classroom has instant access to major databases and can use the Internet to get resources. Research can be performed instantly and on an ongoing basis.

Scheduled time to conduct research in a lab a few times a week doesn't allow ample time to work on projects like this.

Even the physical location of computer labs causes problems in many schools. It is just too inconvenient to have educators take away from their classroom time to shuttle students down the hall or to another part of the school building. Once they get to the lab, there is no access to regular classroom materials.

NO

Ferdi Serim taught computer lab at John Witherspoon Middle School in Princeton, New Jersey, until his recent move to New Mexico. Serim is coauthor of the book NetLearning: Why Teachers Use the Internet *and editor of* MultiMedia Schools Magazine.

I call this the "right shoe vs. left shoe" debate. You need both kinds of shoes to get anywhere. In an ideal world, computers belong on every student's lap. But rather than focusing on where we put them, we need to focus on how the computers will be used. Once we know that, we can make better decisions about how they'll be deployed.

For the past ten years, I've worked as an educator in computer labs, in two different districts. I've seen labs used well, and I've seen them used in ways that make me cringe. There is indeed a push by some to get rid of labs. Computer labs should not be phased out. Rather, they should be used in ways that make educational sense.

There is great value in having spaces where entire classes can use technology at the same time, whether it's a computer lab or a library/media center.

Computer labs are effective places to give all students adequate access to technology to perform meaningful work.

A good example of this is when Shannon Dahl, an eighth-grade language arts teacher at my school, had her kids create books using the computer. Students gathered autobiographical information, pictures, and relics. They used a range of desktop publishing technologies to print, bind, and produce these one-of-a-kind heirlooms. The project ended in an "author's breakfast" for 125 kids, their families, and the community.

It took Shannon Dahl three weeks to complete the project using the computer lab. If she had only two computers in her room, the project would take all year. Having six machines would

(continued)

TEACHER PERSPECTIVES

(continued)

YES

Having computers located within an educator's classroom setting has a number of advantages. With just one computer in the classroom, we can:

- Create a spreadsheet of students' names and have each student enter data for daily attendance, lunch count, and records of monies received.

- Use a scrolling marquee screen saver for spelling words, new vocabulary, announcements, or information.

- Replace messy chalk boards or overheads with PowerPoint presentations or a simple text program using enlarged fonts.

- Instantly access encyclopedia programs, museums, libraries, and universities.

Not only are computers convenient, they are the only teaching instrument that can handle all subjects on every developmental level and still keep up with the latest information. When the student is ready to learn, the classroom computer is there!

Teachers must become comfortable with computers in order to use them effectively. This will happen when computers are available in the classroom on a consistent daily basis.

In my 24 years teaching, I've seen programs come and go with varying degrees of success. Never have I found one simple item that added so much to instruction, while instilling a passion for knowledge in students. Why limit this tremendous tool to scheduled sessions in a room at the other end of the building?

NO

have allowed her to complete it in 15 weeks. That doesn't make educational sense.

Before getting rid of labs and putting more computers in classrooms, educators should consider these additional benefits of computer labs:

- Most classroom computers are not networked to other school computers. Computer labs allow teachers and students to make projects and information available for collaboration via the school network.

- Classroom computers don't often allow for projection devices to support group activity.

When teachers used my lab, I'd make "housecalls" to other computers with my laptop and an LCD panel for wider viewing by groups of students. The teachers I worked with would rather have a machine that let "everybody" observe a demonstration than five or six machines that only served a fraction of their class.

I will say that simply having a computer lab within a school is not enough. The spectre of the empty, locked lab is responsible for much of the impulse to do away with labs and put the machines back into the classroom.

The lab must be viewed as a shared resource for both the classroom teacher and the computer lab teacher. Computer labs will only work when there are people who know how to use them, and who are empowered to make them serve educators' needs.

Source: "Should School Computer Labs Be Phased Out?" *NEA Today* (September 1999), p. 11. Reprinted by permission of the National Education Association.

WHAT IS YOUR PERSPECTIVE ON THIS ISSUE?
Should school computer labs be phased out?

To give your opinion, go to Chapter 13 of the companion website (www.ablongman.com/johnson14e) and click on Teacher Perspectives.

users grew by 547%."[12] The move to wireless connections may eliminate the need for telephone lines, but it does not remove the barrier of equipment costs.

Sixty-two percent of U.S. students have access to personal computers at home and 55 percent have Internet access.[13] Who has these technologies depends on a

FIGURE 13.2

Telephones and Computers by Country in 2003

Source: U.S. Census Bureau, *Statistical Abstract of the United States: 2006,* 125th edition. Washington, DC: U.S. Government Printing Office, 2006, Table 1364.

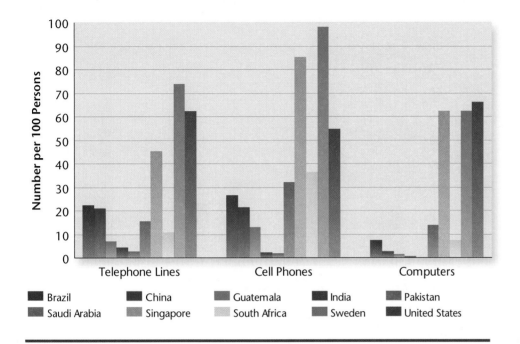

number of factors. Fifty-one percent of households with incomes less than thirty thousand dollars a year have a computer. Ninety-six percent of households with incomes greater than seventy-five thousand dollars have a computer. Similar disparities exist in terms of race: 87 percent of white, non-Hispanic, households have a computer compared to 54 percent of African Americans and 55 percent of Latinos. Rural households are less likely to have access to high-speed Internet connections such as cable and DSL. Twenty-four percent of Internet connected rural households have highspeed connections as compared to 40 percent of urban households.[14]

The **digital divide** between the populations who have access to the Internet and information technology tools and those who don't is based on the same factors. Children in 68 percent of the families with an income over $75,000 connect to the Internet at home as compared to 31 percent of the children in families with incomes under $20,000. Over 60 percent of children with parents who are college graduates use the Internet at home as compared with 40 percent of those whose parents have finished high school but not attended college. Only 24 percent of students with parents who dropped out of high school connect to the Internet at home.[15] Differences are also found among households and families from different racial and ethnic groups. Fifty-seven percent of white children, 28 percent of African American children, and 27 percent of Latino children have access to the Internet.[16]

Another problem that exacerbates these disparities is that African Americans, Latinos, and American Indians hold few of the jobs in information technology. Twenty-seven percent of the people working in professional computer and mathematical occupations are women.[17] African Americans and Latinos are also underrepresented in this field as shown in Figure 13.3. Women receive only 28 percent of the bachelor's degrees in computer and information science—a figure that has doubled since 1971.[18] The result is that women and members of the most oppressed ethnic groups are not eligible for these jobs, which offer among the highest salaries at graduation.

CROSS-REFERENCE
Issues of equality are discussed in greater detail in Chapter 3.

digital divide
The difference in access to technology tools and the Internet between those with economic advantages and those without them.

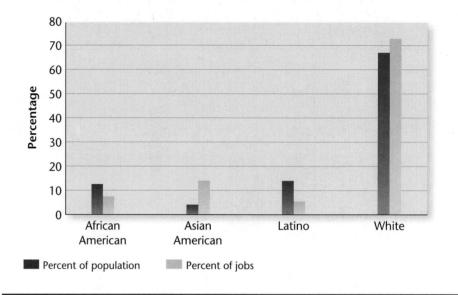

FIGURE 13.3

Participation in Professional Computer and Mathematical Occupations

Source: U.S. Census Bureau, *Statistical Abstract of the United States: 2006,* 125th edition. Washington, DC: U.S. Government Printing Office, 2006, Tables 14 and 604.

Do similar disparities exist in schools? Almost all schools in the country have Internet access. However, the number of classrooms with Internet connections differs by the income level of students. Using the percentage of students who are eligible for free or reduced-price lunches at a school to determine income level, we find that 95 percent of the schools with more affluent students have wired classrooms as compared to 90 percent of the schools with the highest concentrations of low-income students.[19] Figure 13.4 shows a similar disparity in the number of students per computer in schools with student populations who are students of color or from high poverty areas. Thus, the students who are most likely to have access at home also are more likely to have access in their schools.

Stipulating Student Use

With the tremendous growth in the access to and use of computers in the classroom, a number of concerns arise regarding the use of the Internet by students. One of the obvious and common concerns of parents is the ease of access to inappropriate content. Parents expect schools to closely monitor what students have access to online. Most schools use a number of strategies to address these concerns. The foundation of these strategies is often an Acceptable Use Policy or AUP that delineates what constitutes an acceptable and unacceptable use of school or district computing resources. These policies include guidance about software use, acceptable websites, and the types of activities that the computer resources are intended to support. Also included are acceptable activities for different groups in the school. Expectations for teachers are generally different from the students.

Policies generally include some stipulations regarding when a student can access the Internet. Some schools require direct adult supervision of any student computer

FIGURE 13.4

Student Access to Computers

Note: For this chart, high-poverty schools are those in which more than half the students are eligible for the federal free or reduced-price lunch program. High-minority schools are those in which more than half the students belong to minority racial or ethnic groups.

Source: Christopher B. Swanson, "Tracking U.S. Trends," *Technology Counts 2006: The Information Edge: Using Data to Accelerate Achievement.* Bethesda, MD: *Education Week,* Editorial Projects in Education, 2006, p. 51. Data from Market Data Retrieval public school technology surveys, 1999–2005. Used by permission of MDR, a company of D&B, 1 Forest Parkway, Shelton, CT 06484. www.schooldata.com.

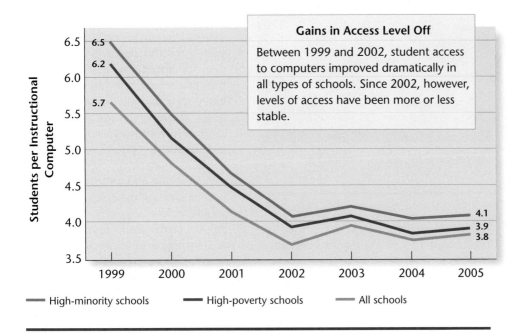

Gains in Access Level Off

Between 1999 and 2002, student access to computers improved dramatically in all types of schools. Since 2002, however, levels of access have been more or less stable.

use. Others only allow student Internet use with explicit parental permission. In addition to acceptable use policies, schools employ other technological safeguards to their computer systems. Safeguards that are often used on the computers include tools that restrict the modifications that can be made to a computer system. Think of the havoc that would ensue if students could install their own software onto school machines. Another important safeguard includes the use of filtering software for the Internet. These tools will allow only Internet traffic into the school that comes from approved websites. These restrictions are not without costs. The more stringent the requirements regarding student computer use, the more likely teachers will consider it not worth the effort to introduce students to some of the powerful resources available on the Internet.

Plagiarism

Advances in computer technologies in general and the Internet in particular have resulted in an apparent rise in plagiarism. This is due in large part to the ease with which a person can copy one person's work and claim it as their own. Additionally, it is easy to find just the type of content that a person needs to complete an assignment. Like many ethical issues, teachers find that a proactive approach can greatly reduce the frequency with which students engage in inappropriate activities.

The computer has become a primary resource to support learning in today's classrooms.

Presenting students with a variety of scenarios related to using, citing, and quoting sources can help clarify what is and is not ethical when it comes to using works created by others.

While a proactive approach is often effective, there are times when a teacher would like to investigate some suspicious assignments. One strategy that teachers can use is to simply copy small bits of text from an assignment into a search engine (using quotes around the text to search for the entire phrase rather than the specific words). If the text was taken from the Internet, it will likely appear at the top of the search results. More sophisticated tools such as Turn It In (www.turnitin.com) are also available. These services will conduct extensive searches for matching text and return detailed reports regarding the originality of the assignment.

These challenges are not unique to children. You have likely seen media reports related to plagiarism in books and on the Internet. It is important that you model ethical behavior in how you conduct yourself. Classroom teachers often excel at collaborating and sharing powerful ideas. When you are using lesson plans provided by others, acknowledging the contributions of others sends a powerful message to students.

Copyright

As with plagiarism, technological advancements have presented educators with a number of additional challenges as they attempt to conform to current copyright laws. These challenges are nowhere more apparent than the Internet. The very structure of the Internet is based upon copying. When you request a page on the Internet, your browser will copy the requested page (or file) to your computer for viewing. Of course, few people would quarrel with your right to view a page copied to your computer given that this was clearly the intent of the author. However, your rights are not always clear. Can you print out the page that you have just viewed? Can you print it and copy it for your class? These and other questions can be difficult.

In the United States, as in most countries, the intent of copyright law is to encourage authors and artists to produce creative works of value to society. This is done by providing the copyright owner with certain rights regarding how a work can be used. Giving copyright owners control over the use of the work enables them to profit from the work and thus encourages and supports further work. Earlier versions of United States copyright law codified these rights for a limited amount of time, after which the work would become a part of the public domain. Subsequent revisions to copyright law have greatly extended the amount of time copyright owners control the work. Additionally, copyright is now assumed rather than claimed. In other words, it is not necessary for someone to include a copyright statement or symbol on the work for it to be protected.[20]

This poses a number of challenges for educators who are always searching for supporting resources. For example, a lesson on a website that you feel would be appropriate for your class is by default protected from uses other than that explicitly provided by the copyright holder. Thus, if the promising lesson you found does not include a statement that indicates you can copy the lesson for classroom use, you may be violating the rights of the copyright holder. However, the likelihood that someone who posts lesson plans would view that as a violation of their rights is slim.

The determination of whether a use is appropriate can be supported through the application of *fair use guidelines*. Fair use guidelines emerged from court cases involving copyright law in determining whether certain uses violated the rights of copyright holders. Fair use is determined by addressing four questions regarding the nature of the work and its use:

1. The purpose and character of the use, including whether such use is of a commercial nature or is for nonprofit educational purposes.
2. The nature of the copyrighted work.
3. The amount and substantiality of the portion used in relation to the copyrighted work as a whole.
4. The effect of the use upon the potential market for or value of the copyrighted work.[21]

Responding to each of these considerations involves a certain degree of judgment. Each of these questions must be addressed. A use deemed educational or nonprofit does not alone justify its use. If after reviewing the fair use guidelines the use is not clearly appropriate you should either seek permission of the copyright holder or not use the material.

Globalization

The world is quickly shrinking. While many people predicted this inevitable globalization of our society, few recognized the rapidity with which the media in general and the Internet in particular would have made it a reality. The ramifications for schools are significant. It is as easy to communicate with someone in Bangladesh as is it is with our next-door neighbor. The classroom teacher who integrates the Internet into instruction will be faced with an increasing number of important issues resulting from this shrinking of our world. Imagine your students corresponding (possibly in real time) with students from Bangladesh. The disparities between the two countries in terms of economics, values, and government are tremendous.

Journal for Reflection

1. Why should educators be concerned about equality of access to technology for their students and parents?

2. Why are parents concerned about schools controlling their children's access to some websites?

3. Why does a teacher need to be aware of copyright laws?

A Look Ahead

The past decade has seen tremendous change in terms of the technologies available to classroom teachers and students. However, many feel that the changes we have seen thus far are minimal compared to what lies ahead. Much of this optimism is based upon the promise of **ubiquitous computing** initiatives. Eight percent of U.S. schools indicated that they had such a program in place in 2003. An additional six percent had future plans for a laptop initiative.[22] Once every child has his or her own computer, the context changes dramatically.

Many are also encouraged by the prospect of computers helping teachers better manage the administrative tasks that can detract from instruction time. Attendance records, seating charts, and parent contact information all become much

> It would appear that we have reached the limits of what it is possible to achieve with computer technology, although one should be careful with such statements, as they tend to sound pretty silly in 5 years.
>
> **John Von Neumann**

ubiquitous computing
Initiatives in which students are provided laptops to use during and after school.

Schools must decide how to prevent students from visiting inappropriate websites and from loading their own software onto school computers while still encouraging them to be engaged with computer technology for learning purposes.

Journal for Reflection

1. What are the potential advantages of ubiquitous computing? What are the disadvantages or potential problems?

2. How do you feel about having the learning of your students tracked to your teaching? Why?

3. What emerging technologies do you know about? How might they be used in the classroom?

easier to access as web-based information systems mature into robust tools. More importantly, teachers will be able to monitor student learning related to standards, compare performance to other students in the school district or state, and access lesson plans for addressing areas in which students are having problems. When teachers are able to commit more time to planning they are better able to develop learning activities that are more engaging and effective.

Technology is allowing school districts and states to track students as they move from school to school. Sophisticated data management systems are including identifiers for both students and teachers so that school officials can match student achievement gains to specific teachers. A growing number of districts may be using the data on student gains to determine salary increments for teachers. For example, the Florida State Board of Education agreed in 2005 to give bonuses to up to 10 percent of the teachers based on the greatest gains in achievement as measured on the state test.[23]

Maybe the most exciting changes ahead are related to communications tools. The prospect of being able to easily communicate with anyone, anywhere has intrigued educators for a long time. The opportunities for learning experiences to be more distributed and less dependent upon everyone meeting in a classroom is quickly becoming commonplace. There is little doubt that the Internet will serve as a catalyst for much of this change.

Summary

TECHNOLOGY BASICS. Teachers often learn the fundamental concepts about computer technology as they use it for email, PowerPoint presentations, and other personal needs. The Internet has made it convenient to communicate with people all over the world. For classroom use, it allows students and teachers to easily search for information to which they would have had limited access in the past. Mobile digital devices, wireless connections, and a computer's growing capacity for audio, photo, and video storage are also lending themselves to instructional uses.

TEACHERS' USE OF TECHNOLOGY. Technology is one of the important resources that today's teachers have. The particular types and the quantity may vary, but most classrooms are supplied with a variety of technologies. The teacher has the major responsibility for seeing that each technology is used effectively with the goal of helping students learn. Technology is allowing teachers more opportunities to interact with families. It also makes it easier to assess student learning and track students' progress at meeting standards.

ISSUES RELATED TO THE USE OF TECHNOLOGY. Bridging the digital divide between students who have access to computers and the Internet and those who do not is one of the challenges faced by educators in providing equity and social justice. Schools also need policies for controlling student use of school computers so that they are used appropriately. Other issues that teachers need to be aware of as they integrate technology into their instruction are plagiarism, copyright, globalization, and the accuracy of the information on the Internet.

A LOOK AHEAD. Knowing how the Internet has changed many of our personal lives and the way we do research for school projects over the past ten years, it is difficult to imagine the technology that will impact the future. Teachers will need to be open to learning the technologies of the future and adapting them appropriately to classroom instruction. The possibilities in our changing world are both limitless and exciting.

Discussion Questions

1. Technology appears to have potential for both improving student learning and making learning more exciting. What do educators mean when they say that "technology is sometimes the content rather than the tool" for instruction?
2. Almost all schools are wired for the Internet and most classrooms have computers. Why then do we hear reports that the computer technology is not being used by teachers? What could change this situation?
3. Many of your future students are likely to be engaged with blogs and Podcasts. How could you integrate their interest in the interactivity of the web into a lesson?
4. The data reported in this chapter indicate that a digital divide exists between white middle-class students and students from low-income families. How can schools help narrow the access gap that could lead to the most underserved students being economically disadvantaged in the future?
5. Based on what you learned in this chapter and know from your own experience, how do you see technology affecting education over the next ten years?

School-Based Observations

1. In one or more of the schools you are visiting, ask the principal and teachers if they have easy access to data on the academic performance of their students. How do they know how students in their school or class are performing on state tests? Are they using any assessment databases that allow them to regularly assess students against benchmarks? If so, which ones and what are they learning from them?
2. Technology can be used in a wide variety of ways in classrooms and within lessons. In classrooms that you are observing, how is technology being used? Which technology supports the teacher? Which have direct uses by the students? In what ways is technology being integrated into the curriculum?

Portfolio Development

1. Teachers need to have skills for using a variety of technologies. Learn to use a technology that you have not used before, or learn a new application of a technology you have used before. Use the technology to develop a teaching product that you might be able to use in student teaching or in your first year of teaching.
2. Technology in classrooms should be used to help students learn. For your portfolio, develop a lesson plan in your subject area that requires students to use the Internet. Be clear about the objectives for the lesson and guidance that you will provide students to assist them in using the Internet effectively.

Preparing for Certification

TEACHERS AND TECHNOLOGY

1. The Praxis II Principles of Learning and Teaching (PLT) test, which assesses a prospective teacher's knowledge about a variety of teaching-related skills, is required in many states. The test covers four broad categories: organizing content knowledge for student learning, creating an environment for student learning, teaching for student learning, and teacher professionalism. Learn more about the PLT test by reviewing the ETS *Test at a Glance* materials at www.ets.org/praxis.
2. Answer the following question, which is similar to items in Praxis and other state certification tests.

   Students in a sixth-grade class are trying to find a way to deal with the problem of wasted paper in the school computer labs. They have invited the director of the local recycling facility to speak with the class. The students are at which of the following steps in the problem-solving process?

   A. Develop criteria to evaluate possible solutions to the problem.
   B. Brainstorm possible solutions to the problem.
   C. Gather facts and information about the problem.
   D. Develop a plan to implement the best solution to the problem.

3. Answer the following short-answer question, which is similar to items in Praxis and other state certification tests. After you've completed your written response, use the scoring guide in the *Test at a Glance* materials to assess your response. Can you revise your response to improve your score?

Reread the chapter-opening case study. The students in Eva Hernandez's school district have access to a wide variety of classroom technologies. How do these technologies affect the teachers in the district? How do these technologies affect student performance in the district? What technology resources will you have access to in your classroom?

Websites

www.edweek.org/techcounts06 Online components that accompany *Education Week's Technology Counts 2006* are available at this website. It also includes reports on the use of technology to collect and manage data in each state.

www.iste.org The website of the International Society for Technology in Education gives information about the society's mission and projects, including technology standards for students and teachers.

www.pbs.org/teachersource The PBS website includes a wide variety of lesson plans and activity suggestions. Many of these are associated with PBS videos although they are not required for most activities.

http://rubistar.4teachers.org This site features a powerful rubric building tool that can be used for assessing a wide variety of student products.

www.readwritethink.org This website includes high quality reading and language arts lessons.

http://school.discovery.com/lessonplans This website provides hundreds of lesson plans categorized by grade and subject. It also includes resources for *Discovery Channel* videos.

http://school.discovery.com/schrockguide This lesson planning website includes a variety of resources including assessment and rubric tools and critical evaluation forms for web resources.

http://webquest.org This website includes a directory of good WebQuests as well as tools to build your own.

Further Reading

Grabe, Mark, and Grabe, Cindy. (2004). *Integrating Technology for Meaningful Learning,* 4th edition. Boston: Houghton Mifflin. An informative text with practical examples of integrated applications of technology.

International Society for Technology in Education. (2000). *National Educational Technology Standards for Students: Connecting Curriculum and Technology.* Eugene, OR: Author. Teacher-created lesson plans that integrate technology with English language arts, foreign language, mathematics, science, and social studies. Each lesson is accompanied by appropriate standards, a narrative by the teacher, and performance indicators.

International Society for Technology in Education. (2006). *National Educational Technology Standards for Students: Resources for Student Assessment.* Eugene, OR: Author. Strategies and tools for measuring students' ability to use technology for learning. It includes guidelines for creating and choosing reliable tests of technology literacy for various grades along with case studies and best practices.

Leu, Donald J., and Leu, Deborah Diadiun. (2000). *Teaching with the Internet Lessons from the Classroom,* 3rd edition. Norwood, MA: Christopher-Gordon. A book filled with interesting ways to use the Internet in instruction. Chapters provide examples of activities to use in different subject areas and applications that work well with students who have special needs.

Technology Counts 2006: The Information Edge: Using Data to Accelerate Achievement. (2006). Bethesda, MD: *Education Week,* Editorial Projects in Education. This report analyzes state and district efforts to manage data of student learning. Articles also address the ways teachers are using these databases to plan instruction.

ᵐmylabschool
Where the classroom comes to life!

Go to Allyn and Bacon's MyLabSchool (www.mylabschool.com) and complete the following activity for Chapter 13. Click on **Courses**; click on **Foundations/Intro Teaching**; click on **MLS Video Lab**; then click on **Module 8: Technology.**

CHAPTER 14

Education in the Twenty-First Century

Take a Hike

By Susan Brenna, *Edutopia*, March 2006

Though his parents once lived in the country-side in Mexico, Juan Martinez grew up in crowded Los Angeles, barely noticing the earth and sky that was masked by the concrete and smog. Six years ago, when Martinez was fifteen, his science teacher proposed he earn extra credit and raise his failing grade by joining the school's ecology club. He found he liked working in the school yard, which led to a trip to the Teton Science Schools, in Wyoming's Grand Teton National Park. It changed his life. Today he leads overnight camping trips for nature-deprived LA teens and helps them restore their neighborhood parks even as he studies to become an environmental lawyer. "I can't live without nature," he says, "I've got to have it in my life."

But nature is exactly what's missing from the lives of many urban and suburban and even rural American children and teens, according to the San Diego journalist Richard Louv. In his book, *Last Child in the Woods: Saving Our Children from Nature Deficit Disorder,* Louv presents evidence that American children are losing a vital aspect of healthy development as they spend increasingly less time riding bikes, climbing trees, fishing, or doing much of anything outdoors.

Louv notes a number of trends that have converged over decades to create the modern indoor-centric family: residential development patterns have consumed the bits of forest and empty lots where young baby boomers used to meet and play. Ubiquitous air-conditioning has made homes into comfort cocoons. As more parents have gone to work, they have enrolled their children in supervised after school programs, many of them conducted indoors. "The average child thirty years ago was spending four to five hours a day outdoors, while the child today is spending all that time inside—including nearly six and half hours a day with electronics," says Kevin Coyle, vice president for education at the National Wildlife Federation.

"It's not just that the outdoors is uncool to kids who prize gaming devices over games of catch," says Martin LeBlanc, national youth director of the Sierra Club. "It's that it doesn't exist for them." And the unknown is scary. When teens from many of Chicago's Boys and Girls club took an overnight trip to the Indiana Dunes National Lake Shore, last fall, many feared going on a night hike and encountering critters in the dark.

As families have increasingly stayed inside in recent decades, behavioral scientists have shown that children and teens are less stressed, and physically and emotionally healthier, when they are regularly exposed to nature. Scientists at Cornell University have found that children who have more contact with nature—even a view of something green from their bedrooms—expressed less stress than those with less contact. At the University of Illinois, scientists found that children as young as five engaged with plants and nature showed reduced signs of attention deficit hyperactivity disorder. Pediatricians warn parents that low academic achievement and obesity are linked to hours spent indoors watching TV.

Kathy Lineberger, a 3rd grade teacher at Marvin Ward Elementary School, in suburban Winston-Salem, North Carolina, doesn't need to see studies to conclude that children learn better when they get exercise and fresh air. Lineberger and her fellow teachers raised money from local businesses and the National Science Foundation to create a wildlife preserve and nature trail behind their five-year old school. Every Wednesday, Lineberger lets her students spend twenty minutes scampering on the trail. Then she puts them to work counting animal tracks, or trying to see that boggy woods through the eyes of nature-lover Lady Bird Johnson whose biography they recently read.

"Kids who are sick on Tuesday and are sick on Thursday are not sick on Wednesday, because that is nature-trail day," Lineberger says. When they return to the classroom to write in their journals, she adds, "they are much more settled. I know it calms them, because I see it."

Louv's invention of the term "nature deficit disorder" got a national conversation started. Schools are developing on-site gardens and wildlife habitats where students learn hands-on science, and parents are bucking the indoor trend household by household.

But there still are attitudes left to change. Remember that nature trail in Winston-Salem? Custodians covered it with cedar chips so it would be easier to clean. "It broke my heart," teacher Kathy Lineberger says, "because the students could no longer see where deer and raccoons had walked before them."

Questions for Reflection

1. How comfortable or uncomfortable would you be teaching in a school that required students to participate in outdoor activities every day? Why do you feel the way you do?

2. What types of learning would be possible that are currently difficult in today's schools? What types of learning might suffer as a result of this focus on the outdoors?

3. Should schools focus exclusively on academic achievement or should schools be responsible for helping students appreciate the outdoors? Explain the reasons for your answer.

Reprinted by permission of Susan Brenna.

INTASC

Learning Outcomes

After reading and studying this chapter, you should be able to:

1. Identify the characteristics of twenty-first-century change and articulate how these change characteristics affect schools, teachers, and students. (INTASC 2: Development and Learning; INTASC 3: Diversity; INTASC 4: Teaching Methods)

2. Describe the ways that futurism anticipates contemporary trends in education. (INTASC 4: Teaching Methods)

3. Analyze contemporary educational reform initiatives and distinguish those reforms that are transforming from those that merely extend existing school structures. (INTASC 7: Planning)

4. Conceptualize a professional development profile for yourself as educator. (INTASC 2: Development and Learning)

5. Develop a personal, preferable vision for twenty-first-century schools that is based on contemporary trends. (INTASC 9: Reflection)

The new millennium has ushered in major shifts, changes, and a reexamination of values in the United States and the world. All professions are now caught up in this confusing, fast-paced time of change. Robotics and handheld computer devices may abound in schools of the future. Information and technology are growing at exponential rates, and access to information is as immediate as the Internet. Relativity governs the actions of society.

This text explores and reflects on schools, students, teaching, and assessment because teachers must be able to anticipate, understand, and manage change throughout their careers. As one of these teachers, you will become the agent of change. Not only will the complexity and makeup of U.S. society change ethnographically, but so also will society across the globe, where, despite differences, we interact more and more. Schools, which once had the primary purpose of educating the masses in the fundamentals of learning—namely, the three Rs—now additionally must focus on how to live in and protect our world. What values will enhance all peoples' lives? What ecological issues and practices must we adopt if the planet is to survive?

Teachers are prepared better than ever before for their careers. Students are more capable and demanding than ever before. And the school, despite constant attacks on it by critics, is better prepared to respond to the demands of a fast-paced society. The system is not perfect, but it has proven to be resilient and has carefully survived and adjusted to become what society wants. However, schools still face tremendous difficulties associated with their readiness and continuing ability to identify and conceptualize just what it is we want for society and the schools.

This final chapter examines the possibilities for schools as they push forward into the next century. As such, it is a chapter of intelligent predictions, predictions that are by no means certainties but that provide a reasonable set of possibilities for the students and teachers of the immediate tomorrow. Change, transformation, reform, futurism, and twenty-first-century professionalism provide the framework for this chapter. Diverse perspectives about these ideas provide exciting challenges that we believe you and other professionals will respond to and ultimately create exciting new visions for schools, students, learning, and society.

The Nature of Change in the Twenty-First Century

There is no escaping change in today's world. In the first few years of this century, we have witnessed horrors and amazing acts of courage. As a nation of free and independent thinkers, we have had to consider the proper, human response to the events of September 11, 2001. We have had to determine our own thinking with regard to ongoing conflict in Afghanistan and Iraq, and we have had to cope with a struggling economy that has put enormous limitations on school programs.

One of the biggest challenges for twenty-first-century teachers is to respond to societal change intelligently. Information continues to increase in both amount and speed. Instant messaging, Internet news, and satellite communications have made global consciousness a reality. Reporters provide instant reports about happenings around the world as they occur. Distinctions have begun to fade. The home is the workplace; what happens in one nation instantly affects another; national banks are giving way to world banks. Yet, despite the blurring of borders and time, there exists greater diversity than ever. What we once considered to be a single nation with an

CROSS-REFERENCE
The various roles that teachers play as change agents in contemporary society are discussed in Chapter 11.

Involving students in solving real-world problems such as dealing with waste enables them to apply school content to their lives and the world around them.

Be the change you want to see in the world.

Mahatma Gandhi

Never let the future disturb you. You will meet it, if you have to, with the same weapons of reason which today arm you against the present.

Marcus Aurelius

transformational changes

Changes that influence the shape, structure, and operations of schools and classrooms.

ethnic identity has given way to multiple identities working with and against other identities. We no longer think of a country as a nation-state of similar peoples; rather, we see nations as a complex of interconnecting groups with divergent identities, values, histories, and perspectives.

Innovative ideas, reforms, and practices abound, and teachers are constantly being asked to make them work for the betterment of students. This section provides a perspective on twenty-first-century change, a perspective that helps you determine what type of change is being proposed and how to cope with change requests.

Characteristics of Change

Changes come in various sizes. As with business and industry, change in schools can be vast and sweeping or small and insignificant. Another aspect of change is that, in many instances, planned changes are not actually implemented; there is a great deal of talk, but the change itself is never put into practice. In other cases, small changes occur that do not make a major difference in what students learn. Therefore, a distinction can be made between talking about change and tinkering with relatively small changes.

Changes that provide a different way of thinking or acting—changes that really make a difference—are called transformational. **Transformational changes** are changes that dramatically influence the shape, structure, and operations of schools and classrooms.

Size of Educational Change

One way to view the different magnitudes of change is illustrated in Figure 14.1. This ten-point scale goes from "talking" to "thinking" to "transforming." At the talking end of the scale are speeches, press announcements, and published commission reports; these result in little if any change in classrooms. As one moves toward the thinking section, changes take place in schools and in classrooms; however, the changes are of modest impact. These changes do not affect the structures of the school or its essential orientation. The categories of change at the transforming end represent major, wide-ranging restructurings, redesigns, and alternative configurations of what schools and school practices can be like.

Think about the changes in schools that you are aware of and the ones you have read about in this text. How many of the ideas have been put into practice? Often good ideas are never implemented in schools. This is because change is difficult, and large-scale change is personally uncomfortable. Also, the truly transforming changes tend to be seen as reckless. Ideas such as having schools replaced by large, open centers for learning or schools embedded into the life of the community with students, businesses, and community centers working collaboratively represent major shifts from schools as we know them. Transforming ideas, such as having public schools begin with children at birth or having a high school student take two months to do an independent project away from the school, are hard to accept as realistic. Yet an increasing number of transforming innovations are being tried.

The remainder of this chapter describes futurism, the teaching profession, and various transforming types of educational innovations. The purpose is to stretch

FIGURE 14.1

Hall's Innovation Category Scale (HICs)

Source: G. E. Hall, "Examining the Relative Size of Innovations: A Scale and Implications."
Greeley, CO: College of Education, University of Northern Colorado, 1993.

	LEVEL	NAME	EXAMPLES
Talking	0	Cruise control	• 1950s • Teacher in same classroom for many years
	1	Whisper	• Pronouncements by officials • Commission reports
	2	Tell	New rules and more regulations of old practices
	3	Yell	Prescriptive policy mandates
Thinking	4	Shake	• New texts • Revised curriculum
	5	Rattle	• Changing principal • Team teaching
	6	Roll	• Change teacher's classroom • Change grade configurations
	7	Redesign	• Evening kindergarten • Integrated curriculum
Transforming	8	Restructure	• Site-based decision making • Differentiated staffing
	9	Mutation	• Teacher and principal belong to the same union • Changing the role of school boards • Coordinated services
	10	Reconstitution	• Local constitutional convention • Glasnost

your thinking and to increase your awareness of the vast variety of major changes that already exist in some U.S. schools. As the twenty-first century continues to unfold, more of these transforming innovations will take place, and in your career as a teacher you will have the opportunity to participate in the implementation of many of them. At the very least, you will likely experience working in a school district where one or more schools will be incorporating some of these practices. Perhaps, as your career unfolds, you will have the opportunity to create additional innovations in teaching, curriculum, and classroom school operations.

Journal for Reflection

Consider the changes you have personally witnessed in schools. What was the magnitude of the educational change and what evidence do you have to support your choice? Identify a transformational change that has occurred in schools. In what ways did this change influence the shape and structure of schools?

How Do I Create an Authentic Learning Environment in the Twenty-First Century Classroom?

Real-world learning, engaging students in authentic performance situations, and encouraging students to construct their own meanings are often proclaimed as hallmark characteristics of contemporary, future-based classrooms. Real-world problems are problems that are current, unsolved, and important to the contemporary world. Examples of real-world problems include issues such as where to locate waste sites, what to do about car pollution, and how to deal with a growing over-weight population. Real-world problems are messy, involving uncertainty and complexity. They don't mesh well with mandated curricula, textbooks, standardized tests, and the seven-period day. Teachers who actually try using real-world problems with their students tend to be those few who thrive on change and risk-taking. As educators search for ways to make curricula and learning more relevant, the question of whether curricular rigor is maintained as new delivery systems are explored always surfaces. There's always too much to teach with too little time.

Still, teachers of the future will be challenged by the fast-paced, technologically sophisticated society to create more dynamic learning environments. Students will increasingly demand to see how their work in school is related to the real world. You will need to meet this authentic learning challenge while remaining vigilant about the importance of students' mastery of important, sometimes mandated, academic content and skills. How you accomplish this will require sophisticated evaluation and practice. Designing challenges to develop the understandings, skills, and dispositions necessary to be successful with real-life problems requires practice, trial and error, and, most important, good judgment about the nature of a worthy problem versus a problem that does not lead to the development of relevant, new understandings and skills.

Questions for Reflection

1. What are the characteristics of a worthy authentic problem of study?

2. What types of assessments can be embedded in an authentic problem-solving activity?

3. How do you motivate students to get involved in an authentic problem-solving activity?

To answer these questions on-line and e-mail your answers to your professor, go to Chapter 14 of the companion website (www.ablongman.com/johnson14e) and click on Professional Dilemma.

Futurism and Transformational Trends in Twenty-First-Century Education

Futurism is the science of strategically analyzing trends, ideas, and movements to bring about futures that are preferable for the welfare of society. Futurists identify and study trends, interpret the trends, attempt to forecast their future effects on society, and generate alternative courses of action that might achieve the desired effects. Alvin Toffler notes the importance of futuristic thinking when he states:

futurism

The science of strategically analyzing trends, ideas, and movements to bring about futures that are preferable for the welfare of society.

> Every society faces not merely a succession of probable futures, but an array of possible futures, and a conflict over preferable futures. The management of change is the effort to convert certain possibles into probables, in pursuit of agreed-on preferables. Determining the probable call for a science of futurism. Delineating the possible calls for an art of futurism. Defining the preferable calls for a politics of futurism.[1]

Futuristic thinking, therefore, includes not only studying and considering the knowledge of the past and present but also conjuring up alternative futures. It further involves using values in choosing a desired alternative and then planning and acting to create the preferred alternative.

Our ability to forecast the future of schools is limited, like our ability to generate possible alternative futures. Furthermore, choosing preferred alternatives from possible alternatives is likely to be challenging; and finally, creating the desired state of the future may be impossible. Yet a basic assumption is that the future will be different from the past and the present, and we have a responsibility to try to shape it. As a member of the teaching profession, you cannot escape the responsibility to enter into discussions about changes that will bring about a better future. Whether you do so by active discussion and engagement or by passive acceptance of the trends of the day, you do influence the future of schools. The following sections discuss possible future trends in education that may or may not materialize. No matter what your response to the pressures that surround these trends, you will help determine if the trends come to be and do or do not provide a preferable future.

Increased Accountability and Testing Focused on Student Achievement

A contemporary trend is the expectation of data-driven results. This expectation permeates much of today's school legislation. Teachers are increasingly held accountable for their students' development. Teachers are challenged to show evidence that students have achieved specific learning outcomes. There is less interest in what teaching skills were employed and more interest in whether the teaching techniques actually improved student learning.

Some states reward teachers whose students show improvement on state tests and other learning performance measures. Schools are required to publish annual reports that describe students' performance on various tests. Schools can be punished for low performance by allowing parents to remove their children from a low-performing school. Sometimes schools are taken over by the state department of education if they continue to show low student achievement.

Along with the increased focus on student achievement results, teachers are required to collect supporting evidence of student growth. To collect this evidence, they may develop pre- and postassessments that show students have achieved specific learning outcomes based on their participation in classroom activities. Student logs, portfolios, observation checklists, and test results are increasingly important aspects of a teacher's evidence repertoire.

CROSS-REFERENCE
The roots and importance of accountability as well as school district report cards are discussed in Chapter 5.

Providing Safe Schools

Providing safe schools is an increasingly important characteristic of twenty-first-century schools. A **safe school** is one that provides a secure environment that makes learning possible in any given situation. If students and staff do not feel safe, learning cannot occur. All schools are vulnerable to a variety of threats to the security of students and staff—threats that stem from within the school, such as student misbehavior, to threats that extend to the building perimeter, such as the intrusion of outsiders into school buildings. There is an increased interest and concern to reduce these internal and external threats and adapt safety procedures by implementing facilities standards, policies and procedures standards, equipment standards, staff certification standards, and safety planning and crisis response training standards.[2]

Statistics at the K–12 level indicate that attention to school safety can make a difference. According to the federal government's "Indicators of School Crime and Safety" (2003) violent crime victimization rates for students age twelve through eighteen declined from forty-eight incidents per thousand students in 1992 to twenty-eight

safe school

A school that provides a secure environment that makes learning possible in any given situation.

incidents per thousand students in 2001. On the other hand, 71 percent of public schools reported at least one violent incident in 1999 through 2000 and 20 percent of public schools experienced one or more serious violent crimes.[3]

A variety of approaches are employed to enhance the safety of school environments and at times, these approaches may seem inconvenient or frustrating. Therefore, it is important that the entire school community understand the reasons for safety procedures so that a commitment to their importance develops.

Safe environmental design is one approach that greatly affects the overall safety of a school building. Building layouts and establishing features that promote desirable behavior is the basis of this type of design. Some of these features include limiting the number of entrances to buildings and ensuring that administrative offices have clear sightlines of the main entry, parking lots, and play areas, as well as establishing boundaries between a school and adjacent properties.

Designing smaller schools is another factor that contributes to school safety. Larger schools allow students to be anonymous or ignored. Feelings of unimportance contribute to alienation which can lead to violence.

Lighting and cameras enhance school safety as well. Lighting helps administrators monitor outside areas of school property and wards off trespassers. Cameras help schools monitor property and student behavior in hallways, parking lots, cafeterias, and other areas. In Biloxi, Mississippi, some schools have installed cameras in every classroom to improve safety and, in some cases, to keep students focused on academic work.

In some environments with high crime, metal detectors, resource officers, and access control is warranted. Police presence can make a school community feel safer, and across the nation thousands of school resource officers provide onsite service to students and staff to discuss safety concerns and report potential trouble. Access control systems can alert security personnel of potential breaches such as when a door is propped open. Some schools use cards in combination with an access code entered into a touch pad. Others have adopted biometric systems that identify students and staff through fingerprints and facial scanning.

Ultimately, school safety is a twenty-first-century trend that continues to grow in importance. Teachers are often asked to include safety as part of the curriculum, because without the support of the entire school community these approaches will fail.

Schools as the Center for Delivery of Coordinated Service

Twenty-first-century schools are gradually changing from single-purpose to full-service centers. Increasingly, schools will be the center for access to many types of services including emotional, health, welfare, educational, criminal justice, and dental. Instead of attempting to address the educational needs of children and families in isolation from other needs, some schools have already become such holistic family resource centers.

This approach is a dramatic move away from the array of individual agencies that have dealt with distinct parts of the child. Each of these agencies may have been performing well, but none dealt with the child as a whole person. In fact, it is not uncommon to have an average of five different social service agencies addressing the needs of one child who is at risk. Typically, none of these agencies communicates with the others concerning their knowledge of the child or the child's family, nor do they communicate about the interventions implemented. In addition, the various levels of federal, state, and local human service agencies complicate the delivery of services. For example, in the California state government, 160 different programs and thirty-five state agencies deal with services to children. The whole child is not seen by one agency, as each agency specializes in the delivery of its specific service.

Emphasis on Character Development

Since the origin of the common school, character development has been an important aspect of a child's education. Throughout the last century, this emphasis declined in favor of academic achievement. However, the tragic events of 9/11 coupled with increased school violence have brought character development to the forefront of American consciousness. A recent poll found that violence, fighting, gangs, and drugs ranked in the top five problems faced by schools.[4] Whereas society's typical responses to student violence are increased restrictions and law enforcement measures, character development advocates call for smaller classes and mutual respect among all school constituents, reciprocity among students, and the development of reverence for the dignity of others.[5]

In response to these issues, character education programs have emerged with great support. A Forest of Virtues, Character Counts, and many other programs claim that by incorporating character education lessons in the curriculum, students' character will be enhanced. Unfortunately, little research has yet been completed to support these claims. Additionally, critics have raised serious concerns about character education, citing the problem of superficial obedience to rules of conduct versus the development of authentic character traits.[6]

Despite the debate that surrounds the proper conduct of character education, the importance of including moral development or some sort of character development in the school curriculum remains strong in the United States. Most experts advocate a comprehensive approach to the development of character in educational settings. Such an approach goes beyond direct instruction to incorporate the development of democratic classroom practices, cooperative learning, conflict resolution, moral reflection, caring, altruistic behavior, and the inclusion of ethical concerns within science, social studies, and other academic disciplines.

CROSS-REFERENCE
Developing character in students is discussed as part of a humanistic educational theory in Chapter 10 and as part of discipline in Chapter 11.

Journal for Reflection

Analyze a character development program that you believe has the potential for developing students into good citizens. Describe the characteristics of a good citizen in the twenty-first century and then describe why the character development program you selected might enhance these characteristics.

Increased Competition among Schools

Schools are increasingly feeling the pressures of a competitive environment. Public displays of school and district report cards, annual comparisons of state test results in newspapers, and legislation that permits students to transfer from low-performing schools are changing the vision of stable neighborhood school settings. Schools are slowly feeling the effects of a results-oriented workplace with competitive vendors vying for customers.

Examples of school choice include open-enrollment options, privately and government-funded vouchers, tax credits, and charter schools. Philanthropists in many locations provide vouchers to enable students to attend nonpublic schools. The most notable examples of these privately funded choice ventures can be found in New York City and Chicago. In New York, a group of business executives provided funding for scholarships that enabled 2,200 students to attend nonpublic schools, while another group of citizens raised millions of dollars for a national program to provide inner-city students with similar scholarships.

Another trend that ultimately increases competition in public schools is privatization. Privatization occurs when the operation of public schools is contracted out to business corporations. A well-known, controversial privatization initiative is the Edison School Corporation. In 1995, Edison won contracts to operate four schools. The company has since contracted with school districts to operate more than a hundred public schools. Although the success of Edison has not yet been established, private contractors are increasingly taking over all or some school operations. Sylvan Learning Corporation and other private companies provide tutoring assistance to at-risk students in public schools across the country. Private firms have also taken over the financial operations of some school districts.

In a time of drastic change it is the learners who inherit the future. The learned usually find themselves equipped to live in a world that no longer exists.

Eric Hoffer

The Changing Profession of Education

CROSS-REFERENCE
The many responsibilities that accompany the profession of teaching are discussed in Chapter 1.

The profession of education is changing. There is no longer a single path or description of the twenty-first-century educator. Rather, a career in education involves a wide variety of possibilities and develops with increased responsibilities that range far beyond the presentation of content or developing discipline approaches.

Career Development Continuum

The notion that becoming a teacher involves obtaining a degree in education followed by state licensure is obsolete. As in the medical profession, teachers grow into their profession and gradually develop their skills along a novice-to-master career continuum. For example, beginning teachers focus on fine-tuning their skills in the classroom. This developmental opportunity involves personal assessment of daily interventions with students, journaling, and discussing classroom events with other teachers. Mentoring is also a major component of the novice teacher's professional life. As you move from the novice teacher stage to the experienced teacher stage, you will find yourself involved in more and more activities that go beyond the classroom. You will likely be a member of various school program committees and take on leadership roles that provide direction for the larger school program.

As teaching careers evolve, some teachers find it interesting to complete an administrative internship. This provides teachers an opportunity to see school through the eyes of administration. Other teachers explore a curricular internship that allows them to provide leadership in the development of different curricular projects such as designing a scope and sequence for the science program or developing a school mission statement. These experiences provide veteran teachers an opportunity to see school life outside the classroom.

As teachers develop into master teachers, they often take on the role of mentors. Some master teachers spend time in other teachers' classrooms providing expert advice and modeling sophisticated teaching approaches. Other master teachers do not even have their own classrooms but spend their entire day working in the classrooms of other teachers and providing leadership in various school program initiatives. Master teachers also develop ideas for grants and spend time working with local businesses and other community groups helping to develop meaningful partnerships.

During this advanced developmental phase, teachers often seek National Board certification and complete advanced degree programs. These external awards and certifications provide further evidence of professional career standing.

Developing professional learning communities provides personal growth and enhances the quality of projects.

Professional Collaboration

Teaching today requires working with colleagues in a number of activities. In the classroom, teachers may team teach or plan with other teachers who are teaching the same grade or subject. Teams work together to plan curriculum and assessment activities. Teachers support one another through professional development activities and peer evaluations in a number of schools.

Special educators, bilingual educators, school psychologists, and other professionals serve as resources for teachers who are planning for individualized student learning as well as physical and emotional development. Support personnel in schools include custodians, secretaries, principals, other administrators, and parent or community liaison people. These support personnel can be helpful to teachers in maintaining a positive learning environment, understanding the community, and contacting families. They can serve as resources in planning events and making appropriate contacts in the community.

Teachers are also expected to work with families in support of student learning. Parental involvement is no longer limited to parent–teacher conferences scheduled periodically during the school year. Teachers and other school officials contact parents to confer about students and to prevent potential problems that could interfere with learning.

> Progress is impossible without change, and those who can change their minds can change anything.
> *George Bernard Shaw*

Participating in the Profession

One of the rewarding aspects of becoming a teacher is the opportunity to work with other well-educated and highly dedicated professionals. There are many types of professional organizations and associations that teachers can join. In most school districts, teachers are represented by a teachers' organization or union that is responsible for negotiating contracts and setting working conditions. These organizations and associations have had a major influence on the development of national education policy; in the determination of state policies, laws, rules, and regulations related to schooling; and (at the local level) in curriculum decisions and labor contract negotiations. At all of these levels, teachers are actively involved and are responsible participants as well as part of the membership that works with the resultant policy decisions and curriculum products.

Teachers have opportunities to become involved in professional or specialty associations as well. These associations deal directly with issues such as the development of student and teacher standards, the design of curriculum, innovation in teaching, improving instructional processes, and so forth. They provide teachers with the opportunity to collaborate with other teachers who have like concerns and interests; they also enable teachers to participate in various professional leadership activities. Some specialty associations focus on teaching specific subjects, such as science, math, literature, and reading, or specific grade levels, such as middle school and early childhood education. These associations usually have national, state, and local chapters. Clearly, teachers can profit from membership and participation in both professional organizations and professional or specialty associations.

TEACHER UNIONS

Teacher unions were organized to improve working conditions. The National Education Association (NEA) and the American Federation of Teachers (AFT) are the two major unions for teachers in the United States. Some teachers have chosen to join other state or local organizations that are not affiliated with the NEA or the AFT but operate similarly to a union. The unions provide a number of services for their members, leadership on a number of professional issues, and a political presence at the local, state, and national levels.

NATIONAL EDUCATION ASSOCIATION (NEA) The National Education Association is by far the largest teachers' organization, with 2.5 million members, including teachers, administrators, clerical and custodial employees, higher education faculty, and other school personnel. Teacher education candidates can join the NEA's Student Program. More than a million teacher education candidates have joined the student group since it was formed in 1937. You might wish to explore the advantages of joining this organization on your campus.

The NEA is committed to advancing public education. The organization was founded in 1857 as the National Teachers' Association (NTA). In 1870 the NTA united with the National Association of School Superintendents, organized in 1865, and the American Normal School Association, organized in 1858, to form the National Education Association. The organization was incorporated in 1886 in the District of Columbia as the National Education Association and was chartered in 1906 by an act of Congress. The charter was officially adopted at the association's annual meeting of 1907, with the name National Education Association of the United States.

The Representative Assembly (RA) is the primary legislative and policymaking body of the NEA. NEA members of state and local affiliates elect the 9,000 RA delegates who meet annually in early July to debate issues and set policies. The president, vice president, and secretary-treasurer are elected at the annual RA. The top decision-making bodies are the Board of Directors and the Executive Committee. An executive director has the primary responsibility for implementing the policies of the association, and standing committees and ad hoc committees carry out much of the work.

Given its long history of advocacy of teaching as a profession, it should not be surprising to learn that the NEA sponsors many professional initiatives designed to disseminate best practices, facilitate teacher leadership, and empower teachers to reform schools. The NEA has organized to provide professional help in student assessment and accountability; professional preparation, state licensure, and national certification; and governance and member activities. The NEA also initiated in 1954, along with four other associations, the accrediting body for teacher education, NCATE, and continues today to provide leadership through appointments to NCATE's governance board and board of examiners, the practitioners who visit college campuses to apply the standards. These and other program areas offer an array of activities and initiatives to further advance teacher professionalism.

Members of the NEA receive its newsletter, *NEA Today,* and have access to numerous other publications and products, including publications that are available online through its professional library. Recent reports from the association address diversity, portfolios, student assessment, school safety, cooperative learning, discipline, gender, inclusion, reading and writing, and parent involvement. Handbooks published by the NEA and written by experienced teachers are helpful resources for new teachers.

AMERICAN FEDERATION OF TEACHERS (AFT)   The second largest teachers' union is the American Federation of Teachers, with national headquarters in Washington, D.C. It was organized in 1916 by teachers in Winnetka, Illinois, to establish an organization to meet their needs and to create a strong union affiliation. The Chicago Teachers' Federation preceded the AFT, having been established in 1897 and affiliating with the American Federation of Labor (AFL) in 1902. Since 1916, AFT membership has grown steadily. The late Albert Shanker, who was AFT president from 1964 until his death in 1997, is given much of the credit for the growth and success of the AFT, including its national involvement in political discussions related to education. In 1965, membership was at 110,500; by 2000, membership exceeded one million. The organization of the AFT includes a president, numerous vice presidents, a secretary-treasurer, and administrative staff. The membership serves on standing committees and council committees.

Since its inception, the AFT has boasted of its affiliation with the AFL, and later the AFL-CIO. AFT has stressed that organized labor was an important force in establishing our system of free public schools and that it has actively supported school improvement programs. Affiliation with organized labor gives the AFT the support of the more than fifteen million members of the AFL-CIO. Support from local labor unions has often worked to the advantage of local AFT unions in their efforts to gain better salaries and improved benefits from local boards of education.

The AFT has diverse resources available to its members. Its lobbying and political action activities support a number of professional issues, in addition to bargaining issues at the local, state, and national levels. Its publications include the journal *American Educator.* Jointly with the NEA, the AFT conducts the annual QUEST conference to convene the leadership of both organizations to discuss professional issues. The Educational Research and Dissemination Program helps make selected findings from recent research on classroom management and effective teaching available to teachers.

POLITICAL ACTION   Both the NEA and AFT have political action committees and government relations departments. **Political action committees** are engaged in action to elect political candidates who are sympathetic to education and teachers' issues. They monitor elected officials' voting records on education bills and analyze the platforms of new candidates. They actively participate in the election campaigns of the president, governors, and key legislators. The state and national political action committees of the NEA and AFT have a common aim: to promote education by encouraging teachers to participate in the political life of their local, state, and national communities. These committees throughout the states are responsible for recommending political endorsements to their respective boards of directors.

PROFESSIONAL ASSOCIATIONS

Teachers can join, participate in, and provide leadership for many professional associations that focus on their chosen professional interests. These associations are organized around academic disciplines and specific job assignments, such as science teaching, mathematics teaching, special education, school psychology, reading, cooperative learning, and multicultural education. Over five hundred organizations focusing on some aspect of education exist in the United States. A selected list of professional associations with website addresses is found in Appendix E at the end of this book.

PHI DELTA KAPPA INTERNATIONAL   The professional association Phi Delta Kappa International (PDK) is one of the largest and most highly regarded organizations for educators in the world. Today it is open to all educators, although in its earlier years women were not allowed to join. It publishes excellent professional material, including the journal *Phi Delta Kappan,* a newsletter, *Fastback* booklets on timely educational topics, research reports, books, and various instructional materials. The organization also sponsors many surveys, research projects, grants, awards, conferences, training programs, and trips. Local PDK chapters bring together teacher candidates, higher education faculty, and local teachers and administrators. You might want to consider a student membership and become involved in your local chapter.

SPECIALTY PROFESSIONAL ASSOCIATIONS

There are over five hundred specialty associations in education based on different academic disciplines, different types of students, and different instructional approaches. Over time, you will find those specialties that apply to your unique role in education. Participation in these associations will enable you to network with others who have similar interests and focus.

Of the specialty associations that could be described, the Association for Supervision and Curriculum Development (ASCD) is profiled here because it provides an international forum focused on all aspects of effective teaching and learning. Founded in 1943, ASCD is a nonprofit, nonpartisan organization representing 175,000 educators from more than 135 countries and more than sixty affiliates. Members span the entire profession of education—superintendents, supervisors, principals, teachers, professors of education, and school board members. ASCD offers broad, multiple perspectives in reporting key policies and practices. The association focuses on professional practice within the context of public and private schools and cites as its primary goal to build an engaged diverse community to improve learning and teaching for each student.

political action committees
Committees focused on electing political candidates who are sympathetic to education and teachers' issues.

Education International

In January 1993, Education International (EI) officially replaced the World Confederation of Organizations of the Teaching Profession (WCOTP), which had worked vigorously to improve the teaching profession and educational programs around the world. EI has united more than 240 national educator unions and professional associations from around the world. This new organization brings together more than twenty million elementary, secondary, and higher education professionals. In the United States, this merger brings the NEA and the AFT together under a world umbrella. The EI is focusing its efforts on improving the quality of education throughout the world, upgrading education employee working conditions and compensation, fighting for adequate educational funding, sharing curricula, safeguarding human rights, fighting for gender equality, and building stronger educational organizations.

Question for Reflection

1. To what degree do you think the working conditions of public school teaching in the United States should provide a model for working conditions in schools in other countries?

Journal for Reflection

Develop a profile of your interest areas as a twenty-first-century teacher. What subject areas, instructional approaches, or reform issues do you wish to develop? Examine the many professional organizations and associations that are available. Which ones might you join and why?

RELIGIOUS EDUCATION ASSOCIATIONS National and regional religious education associations are under denominational or interdenominational control. These organizations might represent sectarian schools attended by students whose families prefer them to public schools or secular private schools. Some religious groups or clubs supplement the public or private school program by offering educational activities for youth and adults. Examples of religious organizations include the Association of Seventh-Day Adventists Educators, Catholic Biblical Association of America, Council for Jewish Education, National Association of Episcopal Schools, Association of Christian Schools International, and Religious Education Association.

A Vision for Twenty-First-Century Schools

This last section posits a possible and preferable future for schools. It is by no means presented as a certainty, but using the tools of futurism, it presents a possible vision for twenty-first-century schools.

Professional Learning Communities

Coming together is a beginning, staying together is progress, and working together is success.

Henry Ford

Professional learning communities is a concept that positions teachers as inquirers. The distinction between teacher and learner is blurred in this vision of a teacher. A professional learning community is characterized by collaboration, a commitment to a shared vision and mission, a focus on learning, shared leadership, continuous school improvement, celebration, and persistence.[7] In this culture, teachers and administrators work together to enhance learning across the entire school community.

Relevant Research

Can Groups Learn?

STUDY PURPOSE/QUESTION: Learning in groups can encourage student creativity and imaginative problem solving; it also provides a productive exchange of ideas. However, groups with assigned tasks often have only a vague idea about the criteria that will be used to assess their group projects. The researchers contended that lack of clarity about the group project criteria diminished the quality of group learning and the quality of the final project. This study sought to answer the proposition that providing students with specific guidelines as to what makes an exemplary group product improves the character of group discussion as well as the quality of the group project.

STUDY DESIGN: This was an experimental study of five sixth-grade classrooms located in California's Central Valley. All five participating teachers were skilled in using complex instruction, a special set of instructional strategies enabling heterogeneous classrooms to work at a high intellectual level. Groups in the different classrooms carried out the same tasks using the same curricular material. The researchers assessed the work of creative problem-solving groups who were studying the same social studies unit on ancient Egypt. The measures for creative problem solving focused on the nature of the group discussion, the quality of the group product, and essays written by the students upon completing the unit.

After careful preparation and practice on three prior instruction units, the focal unit on ancient Egypt required five days of implementation. Each group worked on five different tasks, gave a presentation on their group product, and received feedback from the teacher and their classmates. In three of the five classrooms, groups worked with explicit evaluation criteria provided with their instructions and resource materials. With this one exception, the instructions to groups in the other two classrooms were the same. Following the completion of the learning tasks, all students wrote essays on the relationship of specific group activities and products to the central idea of the unit.

STUDY FINDINGS: The researchers found that groups that used evaluation criteria were more self-critical, more task focused, had better quality group products, and had higher essay scores. The amount of evaluative and task-focused talk and the quality of the group products were independent predictors of the group's aggregate score on the essays. When groups were more focused on the content of the product, they created a better group product. This assisted their understanding and grasp of academic content as measured by the essays. In addition, the more the group evaluated their product and performance, the higher their essay scores.

IMPLICATIONS: Providing evaluative criteria helps groups to become more self-critical and to increase their effort. Such increased effort leads to superior group products, thereby strengthening students' written performance. By holding groups accountable for their products, the teacher can do much to ensure the kind of group performance that will lead to individual learning. Teachers can and should assess group products and provide feedback based on the evaluation criteria clearly presented to the groups prior to their activity.

Source: Elizabeth G. Cohen, Rachel Lotan, Beth Scarloss, Susan E. Shultz, and Percy Abram, "Can Groups Learn?" *Teachers College Record* 104(6) (2002), pp. 1045–1068.

Inquiry is at the center of everyone's life. Teachers collaborate in advancing new ideas, actualizing these ideas, and collecting evidence to determine if the ideas are helping students learn. Principals collaborate with teachers and other principals in the same endeavor. Celebrations occur as the results of ongoing inquiries are shared. Such celebrations enable others to know what has or has not been fruitful, and thus new ideas are generated. School improvement occurs naturally through this process of shared inquiry.

In such a culture, teachers are in other teachers' classrooms on a regular basis. No longer is the classroom an isolated community. Rather, teachers work together as part of the larger learning community. Change occurs because of this collaboration.

Classrooms as Dynamic Centers of Learning

If you want to know your past, look into your present conditions. If you want to know your future, look into your present actions.

Buddhist saying

In this vision of a preferable future, the walls of individual classrooms disappear. Classrooms are merely centers for learning—places where information is shared and assessed. Learning occurs beyond the classroom in laboratories, in the community, in businesses, and in technology centers. Learning is authentic, and students construct their own meaning as they attain new knowledge, solve real-world problems, gather data, make inferences, and draw conclusions. These conclusions are shared in the classroom. Through this sharing, conclusions are challenged and students learn to shift their thinking in response to legitimate criticism and questions.

Mentoring is the primary teaching technique in such a vision. Teachers mentor other teachers, teachers mentor students, students mentor other students, and parents and community members mentor as well. Dialogue across the community occurs on a regular basis because so many constituents of the community are involved with students.

Yearlong schools are the norm. The school schedule closely relates to the calendar of the community. Breaks in the school year correspond to the holidays and work schedule of community members. Schooling also occurs outside the school. Computers provide access to learning opportunities at home, at places of worship, and at community centers. There is no need to stop learning just because the school has closed its doors for vacation.

The curriculum is integrated. Ideas interrelate as they are studied in different problems and contexts. Thinking strategies, content acquisition, the practice of valued dispositions (cooperation, listening to others' ideas, curiosity, perseverance), play, exercise, sports, and community service are part of the school day. More important, learning is viewed as natural and lifelong.

New Forms of Teacher Leadership

Across the country a growing number of school districts offer new avenues for expert teachers to provide leadership to other teachers. In Hartford, Connecticut, *turnaround specialists* provide assistance to classrooms with struggling students. These expert teachers model different teaching strategies in classrooms where students are at-risk. The classroom teacher meets with the turnaround specialist to plan instruction and to discuss the individual needs of students. Schools in Utah employ *site-based staff developers*. These master teachers meet with classroom teachers and discuss their unique needs and concerns. They offer advice and also design staff development opportunities based on teachers' needs. In Douglas County, Colorado, *building resource teachers* support student learning, mentor new teachers, assist with data analysis, plan and implement staff development, provide resources, and build collegial relationships. Although the titles differ, these emerging teacher leadership roles share a common strategy: Master teachers are assigned to provide professional development, instructional leadership, and collaboration with other teachers in a building or district to improve teaching practice and student learning.

Journal for Reflection

Consider the characteristics of an ideal school—one that helps students prepare for life in the twenty-first century. Describe this ideal school and clarify what role teachers would perform on a typical school day.

These changing times are exciting times for teachers. There are new challenges and new possibilities. Teachers are called to transform, to improve, and ultimately to prepare students to be change agents in a fast-paced world of diversity.

Will Public Education Survive the Next Century?

As the pace of change escalates and the future becomes more and more uncertain, the relevance of public schools is called into question. Has society so changed that requiring students to come to a specific place called school and earn elementary, middle school, and high school degrees is unnecessary? Ivan Illich thought that society would be better if it were de-schooled.

YES

Dr. Barbara Smith Palmer is an elected member of the United Teachers of Los Angeles House of Representatives and Political Action Committee, the California Teachers Association State Council, and a UTLA delegate to the NEA Representative Assembly.

I'm excited about the prospects for teaching and learning in the 21st Century. But for public education to truly survive in the 21st Century, we will need to make some adjustments in our efforts at reform, in our philosophy, and in our teaching.

• **Reform.** How schools are structured has complicated our attempts at innovation. The relationship between knowledge and power, within the social and political contexts for our schools, has placed burdensome external controls on teachers and students, controls ranging from excessive regulation to massive testing.

Current policies that focus on national testing and national standards are too narrow. There is no one approach that can work for all kids. Our testing and standards policies must take into account the many diverse learning styles in our student population.

• **Learning Approaches.** Our presuppositions commonly prevent us from thinking effectively about education issues—and from committing ourselves to equity and excellence for all. We must put an end to deficit terminology and labeling. Terms like "at-risk" marginalize kids into categories and make assumptions about their learning capabilities that aren't true. Children are capable of much more than teachers and parents generally realize.

• **Teaching.** In the school of the 21st Century, teachers will have to challenge traditional approaches to teaching and learning by

NO

Cynthia Russ is a curriculum coach for Residence Park Latin Grammar Classical Studies Magnet School in Dayton, Ohio. A teacher for more than 26 years, Russ is an alternate member of the Resolutions Committee for both the Ohio Education Association and the NEA.

As I look ahead to the next century and think about the fate of our public education system, I feel discouraged. I do not think public education will, in fact, survive the next century.

Public schools, to be sure, have always faced challenges. As public educators, we've always had to battle to make sure all children have the rights and opportunities they deserve. We had to fight to end segregation, fight for equity for Native American children schooled on reservations, and fight to get adequate funding for inner-city schools.

But the opponents we face now seem tougher than ever, and we find ourselves battling on so many different fronts.

• **Vouchers.** The increasing clamor for private-school tuition vouchers is a direct threat to public education's survival in the next century.

Vouchers siphon off much needed funding from public schools. In a voucher-friendly America, those who remain in an underfunded public system will face a vicious downward spiral of deteriorating buildings, out-of-date materials, overcrowded classrooms, and uncertified teachers. This downward spiral will only create pressure for more vouchers.

• **Charter Schools.** Charters today are too often run by businesses out to make a buck, not educators with visions they want to try to realize. The results are predictable. Children become

(continued)

(continued)

YES

modeling a collaborative form of practitioner inquiry.

Teachers need to encourage students to question answers and to express their own viewpoints. They have to provide ways for students to participate in the discourse that shapes their lives. Curiosity, industry, and imagination should be encouraged and rewarded.

Teachers need more autonomy and the ability to create exciting educational experiences for students. By encouraging democratic dialogue among educators, we can empower teachers.

We can excel in the new century if teachers function as a community of scholars, engaging in collaborative diagnostic and problem-solving work to create alternative approaches for designing tasks and assessing activities.

In the classroom of the 21st Century, teachers need to involve students in interesting project-based assignments so that they can learn by doing.

Students should become more engaged readers. Activities like peer-assisted reading, classroom discussions about texts, and book club projects can allow students to become leaders on their own terms.

Students will reach their personal goals through the gentle guidance of teachers, who hold themselves and their students accountable to high standards for all.

Educators joining with each other and with their students to explore a critical pedagogy of group work, collaboration, and serious individualized attention will create a revolutionary classroom where all children learn at the highest levels.

If that happens, public education will not only survive through the 21st Century, it will thrive!

NO

mere moneymakers for the companies involved. But what happens when the money runs out?

If charters continue, with little public oversight, we won't have much in our education budgets left in the next century for children to receive the education they deserve.

• **Lack of Parental Involvement.** The absence of parents in our schools is another factor that leads me to believe that public education may not survive.

Parental support has always been the backbone for public education. With dwindling parental support, lines of communication tend to close. Schools are then left subject to gossip, innuendo, misconceptions, and bad feelings.

Schools that do not have a strong communication link with parents will not survive. We cannot survive in the next century if parents and the community do not understand what is really happening in our schools today.

If public education is to survive into the next century, we need to rebuild general public support. We must not let vouchers and other schemes take away the resources we need to help our public schools thrive.

There are problems, of course, in our public school system. But American public education—available to everyone, without regard to race, color, creed, economic status, or physical and mental ability—remains our nation's greatest contribution to democracy.

Society needs to understand that our children are our future. If we continue diluting public education, we will no longer have a viable method to educate all children. And without a focus on all children, public education will cease to exist.

Source: "Will Public Education Survive the Next Century?" *NEA Today* (January 2000), p. 11. Reprinted by permission of the National Education Association.

WHAT IS YOUR PERSPECTIVE ON THIS ISSUE?
Will public education survive the next century?

To give your opinion, go to Chapter 14 of the companion website (www.ablongman.com/johnson14e) and click on Teacher Perspectives.

Summary

THE NATURE OF CHANGE IN THE TWENTY-FIRST CENTURY. Change is constant and there are no guarantees concerning the precise direction of the future. One of the biggest challenges for twenty-first-century teachers is to respond to societal change intelligently. Change can be measured by the degree of impact on an organization. Talking, thinking, and transforming types of change are described. Often good ideas are never implemented in school because large-scale change is often uncomfortable and messy.

FUTURISM AND TRANSFORMATIONAL TRENDS IN TWENTY-FIRST-CENTURY EDUCATION. Futuristic thinking is the science of strategically analyzing trends, ideas and movements to bring about futures that are preferable for the welfare of society. Futuristic thinking includes not only studying and considering knowledge of the past and present but also conjuring up alternative futures and choosing a desired or preferable alternative. Several trends for the twenty-first century include increased accountability and testing, providing safe schools, transforming schools as centers for delivery of coordinated service, increased emphasis on character development, and increased competition among schools. Some of these trends may be preferable alternatives and others may not. It is important for you to determine which trends are worthy and which ones are not.

THE CHANGING PROFESSION OF EDUCATION. The teacher as a professional is described as a developing process moving from novice to expert. Professional collaboration and participation in the profession involves a wide variety of activities. Working with other teachers on teams or on a project, supporting one another throughout curriculum and assessment planning, and accessing other professionals as resources encompass one aspect of collaboration. Joining different professional organizations and associations is another level of professional collaboration. Participating in political action initiatives provides another avenue for involvement in the profession.

A VISION FOR TWENTY-FIRST-CENTURY SCHOOLS. Exciting new visions for schools include professional learning communities, classrooms as centers for dynamic learning, and new forms of teacher leadership. However, this vision for education is by no means certain. Rather, it provides a possible and preferable future for you in collaboration with other educators to discuss, debate, and ultimately recreate new visions for schools, students, learning, and society. We wish you the best in such a future and look for your leadership in making the twenty-first century an exciting world of peace, justice, and learning.

Discussion Questions

1. What types of change do you observe in your college or university? Are they talking, thinking, or transforming?
2. Recall a character education learning experience from your high school. Describe the experience and explain why it was worthwhile or not.
3. List the reasons you intend to join or not join a specific professional organization.
4. Consider a transforming change that you believe would be good for your college. Why do you think this transforming change would be difficult to implement?
5. What vision for schools do you have for the future? What obstacles might inhibit your vision from materializing?

School-Based Observations

1. Ask teachers to describe educational initiatives that are being implemented in the school. Ask if they think any of these initiatives affects their role, how they teach, or how they relate to students. Based on the teachers' responses, determine if any of the educational initiatives are thinking, talking, or transforming.
2. Check the teachers' lounge for publications or announcements from professional organizations. If so, read through those that relate to your area of study and summarize current key issues.

Portfolio Development

1. Visit a school setting that you believe exhibits a teacher-friendly culture. Describe what constitutes this culture and what variables make this culture possible.
2. Develop a sample lesson that incorporates some sort of character development activity embedded in an academic subject.
3. Develop a research project about your future students. Provide a rationale for your research question and outline the types of data you would collect in order to answer the question.

Preparing for Certification

PROFESSIONAL RELATIONSHIPS AND STANDARDS

1. One of the topics in the Praxis II Principles of Learning and Teaching (PLT) test is "building professional relationships with colleagues to share teaching insights and coordinate learning activities for students." Think about people you have worked with so far in your teacher preparation program—fellow students, teachers, professors, and others in the field of education. How has each contributed to your insights about teaching and learning? Can you build on those relationships and interactions to make them even more professionally beneficial for you and for them?
2. One of the themes of this book has been the importance of understanding the role of standards, assessment, and accountability in education today. When used well, standards provide a common language for teachers, students, parents, and the community in the shared goal of students' learning and growth. Standards for teachers, such as the INTASC standards and the principles underlying Praxis and other state-mandated teacher licensure tests, serve a similar purpose. When used well, INTASC standards, Praxis, and other tests provide a common language for prospective teachers' learning and growth.

As stated in Chapter 1, the best way to prepare for Praxis or any other standardized certification test is to understand the concepts covered in the test and how they relate to the content in each of your courses and field experiences. At the end of each chapter, you were encouraged to relate what you learned to concepts in the Praxis test and to try a few sample questions. As a final reflective activity, return to the ETS *Test at a Glance* materials for the PLT test. Read through the topics covered and think about how they relate to the ideas in this book. Are you now better prepared to address some of those topics? Think ahead to future courses and experiences in your teacher preparation program. Which topics do you need to learn more about? Make a plan for how you will continue to relate the content of future courses and field experiences to the test you will eventually take.

Websites

www.ilt.columbia.edu/publications/index.html The Institute for Learning Technologies website hosted at Columbia University provide papers, ideas, and visions of an idealized system of U.S. twenty-first-century schools.

www.ratical.org/many_worlds/PoL.html The Paths of Learning Resource Center provides a free online tool that can assist in your educational explorations. You can now search over five hundred indexed books, magazines, and journals.

www.rethinkingschools.org Rethinking Schools began as a local effort led by classroom teachers dedicated to equity in public education. It is now a prominent organization and publisher focused on providing new visions for public education and the creation of a humane, caring, and multiracial democracy. The site provides provocative articles, innovative projects, and its own search engine.

www.pdkintl.org The Phi Delta Kappa International website provides educational resources, papers, and discussions about best practices in education.

www.ei-ie.org Education International is an international federation of educators. Its website provides ideas, projects, and visions for education across the globe and is an excellent resource for viewing education in a broader context.

Further Reading

Fullan, Michael. (1991). *The New Meaning of Educational Change*. New York: Teachers College Press. Excellent analysis of both the theoretical basis and the practical implications of research on the school change process.

Palmer, P. J. (1998). *The Courage to Teach: Exploring the Inner Landscape of a Teacher's Life*. San Francisco: Jossey-Bass. A reflective look at the life of a teacher from the inside out.

Scapp, Ron. (2003). *Teaching Values: Critical Perspectives on Education, Politics, and Culture*. New York: Routledge and Farmer Press. A provocative text that raises questions about values and morality embedded in our curriculum but often hidden from discussion.

Witte, John F. (2000). *The Market Approach to Education*. Princeton, NJ: Princeton University Press. Concentrating on but not limiting his attention to the Milwaukee voucher program, Witte assesses both the promises and dangers of vouchers, open enrollment, and other choice mechanisms.

---

mylabschool
Where the classroom comes to life!

Go to Allyn and Bacon's MyLabSchool (www.mylabschool.com) and complete the following activity for Chapter 14. Click on **MyLabSchool Case Archive;** then click on **Teaching as a Profession.**

State Certification and Licensure Offices throughout the United States

A teaching certificate or license is valid only in the state for which it is issued. Certification and testing requirements are never static. States are changing requirements constantly. If you are planning to move to another state, you should contact that state's certification/licensure office as the first step. Below are websites to guide you.

When you contact a state office, indicate the type of certificate you are receiving, your state, and the tests you have taken. You may also find information at www.nasdtec.org, and click on the Interstate Agreement to look at states that cooperate with licensure transfer. School districts that want to employ you may also have methods of hiring you on a temporary license for 1–2 years.

Alabama
www.alsde.edu/html/sections/section_detail.asp?
section=66&footer=sections

Alaska
www.educ.state.ak.us/teachercertification

Arizona
www.ade.state.az.us/certification

Arkansas
http://arkedu.state.ar.us/teachers/teachers_licensure.html

California
www.ctc.ca.gov or www.calteach.com

Colorado
www.cde.state.co.us/index_license.htm

Connecticut
www.state.ct.us/sde/dtl/cert/index.htm

Delaware
www.doe.k12.de.us/info/certification

District of Columbia
www.k12.dc.us/dcsea/certification/licensing/licensing.html

Florida
www.fldoe.org/edcert

Georgia
www.gapsc.com/TeacherCertification.asp

Hawaii
http://doe.k12.hi.us/teacher/index.htm

Idaho
www.sde.state.id.us/certification

Illinois
www.isbe.net/teachers.htm

Indiana
www.doe.state.in.us/dps/licensing/welcome.html

Iowa
www.state.ia.us/educate/programs/boee/index.html

Kansas
www.ksbe.state.ks.us/cert/cert.html

Kentucky
www.kyepsb.net/certification/certstandardroutes.asp

Louisiana
www.louisianaschools.net/lde/tsac/home.html

Maine
www.maine.gov/education/cert/index.html

Maryland
http://certification.msde.state.md.us

Massachusetts
www.doe.mass.edu/educators/e_license.html

Michigan
www.michigan.gov/mde/0,1607,7-140-5234_
5683_14795---,00.html

Minnesota
www.education.state.mn.us/mde/Teacher_Support/
Educator_Licensing/index.html

Mississippi
www.academploy.com/cert/certms.htm

Missouri
www.dese.mo.gov/divteachqual/teachcert/index.html

Montana
www.opi.state.mt.us/index.html

Nebraska
www.nde.state.ne.us/tcert/tcmain.html

Nevada
www.academploy.com/cert/certnv.htm

New Hampshire
www.academploy.com/cert/certnh.htm

New Jersey
www.state.nj.us/njded/educators/license/index.html

New Mexico
www.sde.state.nm.us/div/ais/lic/index.html

New York
http://usny.nysed.gov/teachers/teachercertlic.html

North Carolina
www.ncpublicschools.org/employment.html

North Dakota
www.nd.gov/espb/licensure

Ohio
www.ode.state.oh.us/GD/Templates/Pages/ODE/
ODEPrimary.aspx?Page=2&TopicRelationID=513

Oklahoma
www.sde.state.ok.us/home/defaultie.html

Oregon
www.tspc.state.or.us/default.asp?op=1&id=0

Pennsylvania
www.teaching.state.pa.us/teaching/site/default.asp?g=0

Rhode Island
www.ridoe.net/teachers

South Carolina
www.scteachers.org/cert/index.cfm

South Dakota
http://doe.sd.gov/oatq

Tennessee
http://state.tn.us/education/lic

Texas
www.sbec.state.tx.us/SBECOnline/default.asp

Utah
www.usoe.k12.ut.us/cert/require/reqs.htm

Vermont
www.state.vt.us/educ/new/html/maincert.html

Virginia
www.pen.k12.va.us/VDOE/newvdoe/teached.html

Washington
www.k12.wa.us/certification

West Virginia
http://wvde.state.wv.us/certification

Wisconsin
www.dpi.state.wi.us/dpi/dlsis/tel/index.html

Wyoming
www.ptsb.state.wy.us

U.S. Department of Defense Dependents' Schools
www.dodea.edu/offices/hr/onlineapplication/default.htm

Source: Adapted from "Locating U.S. State Certification Offices."
2006 AAEE Job Search Handbook, American Association for
Employment in Education, Inc.

Code of Ethics of the Education Profession

Preamble

The educator, believing in the worth and dignity of each human being, recognizes the supreme importance of the pursuit of the truth, devotion to excellence, and the nurture of the democratic principles. Essential to these goals is the protection of freedom to learn and to teach and the guarantee of equal educational opportunity for all. The educator accepts the responsibility to adhere to the highest ethical standards.

The educator recognizes the magnitude of the responsibility inherent in the teaching process. The desire for the respect and confidence of one's colleagues, of students, of parents, and of the members of the community provides the incentive to attain and maintain the highest possible degree of ethical conduct. The code of Ethics of the Education Profession indicates the aspiration of all educators and provides standards by which to judge conduct.

The remedies specified by the NEA and/or its affiliates for the violation of any provision of this Code shall be exclusive and no such provision shall be enforceable in any form other than the one specifically designated by the NEA and/or its affiliates.

Principle I

Commitment to the Student

The educator strives to help each student realize his or her potential as a worthy and effective member of society. The educator therefore works to stimulate the spirit of inquiry, the acquisition of knowledge and understanding, and the thoughtful formulation of worthy goals.

In fulfillment of the obligation to the student, the educator—

1. Shall not unreasonably restrain the student from independent action in the pursuit of learning.
2. Shall not unreasonably deny the student's access to varying points of view.

3. Shall not deliberately suppress or distort subject matter relevant to the student's progress.
4. Shall make reasonable effort to protect the student from conditions harmful to learning or to health and safety.
5. Shall not intentionally expose the student to embarrassment or disparagement.
6. Shall not on the basis of race, color, creed, sex, national origin, marital status, political or religious beliefs, family, social or cultural background, or sexual orientation, unfairly—
   a. Exclude any student from participation in any program
   b. Deny benefits to any student
   c. Grant any advantage to any student
7. Shall not use professional relationships with students for private advantage.
8. Shall not disclose information about students obtained in the course of professional service unless disclosure serves a compelling professional purpose or is required by law.

Principle II

Commitment to the Profession

The education profession is vested by the public with a trust and responsibility requiring the highest ideals of professional service.

In the belief that the quality of the services of the education profession directly influences the nation and its citizens, the educator shall exert every effort to raise professional standards, to promote a climate that encourages the exercise of professional judgment, to achieve conditions that attract persons worthy of the trust to careers in education, and to assist in preventing the practice of the profession by unqualified persons.

In fulfillment of the obligation to the profession, the educator—

9. Shall not in an application for a professional position deliberately make a false statement or fail to disclose a material fact related to competency and qualifications.
10. Shall not misrepresent his/her professional qualifications.
11. Shall not assist any entry into the profession of a person known to be unqualified in respect to character, education, or other relevant attribute.
12. Shall not knowingly make a false statement concerning the qualifications of a candidate for a professional position.
13. Shall not assist a noneducator in the unauthorized practice of teaching.
14. Shall not disclose information about colleagues obtained in the course of professional service unless disclosure serves a compelling professional purpose or is required by law.
15. Shall not knowingly make false or malicious statements about a colleague.
16. Shall not accept any gratuity, gift, or favor that might impair or appear to influence professional decisions or action.

Adopted by the NEA 1975 Representative Assembly. Reprinted by permission of the National Education Association.

Teaching Job Websites

The Web has quickly become the major resource for finding education vacancies: through your college's career center website, school district websites, and state departments of education or related organizations. Many commercial sites also exist; be aware that some may have fees attached.

AAEE sponsors two web-based services. First is Project Connect, a year-round vacancy listing service. Just go to www.aaee.org, click on Project Connect and follow the links. You will need a username (teacher) and password (aswan) to search for positions.

Alabama
www.alsde.edu/html/sections/section_detail.asp?
section=66&footer=sections

Alaska
www.akeducationjobs.com

Arizona
www.arizonaeducationjobs.com

Arkansas
www.as-is.org/classifieds

California
www.calteach.com

Colorado
https://gateway.cde.state.co.us/portal/page?_pageid=
33,34440&_dad=portal&_schema=PORTAL

Connecticut
www.state.ct.us/sde

Delaware
www.teachdelaware.com

Florida
www.teachinflorida.com

Georgia
www.teachgeorgia.org

Hawaii
http://doe.k12.hi.us/personnel/jobopportunities.htm

Idaho
www.jobservice.us/iw/jobsearch/js.asp

Illinois
www.isbe.state.il.us

Indiana
http://ideanet.doe.state.in.us/peer/welcome.html

Iowa
www.iowaeducationjobs.com

Kansas
www.kansasteachingjobs.com

Kentucky
www.kde.state.ky.us

Louisiana
www.louisianaschools.net/lde/index.html

Maine
www.state.me.us/education/jobs1.htm

Maryland
www.msde.state.md.us

Massachusetts
www.doe.mass.edu/jobs

Michigan
http://mtn.merit.edu/joblistings.html

Minnesota
www.mnasa.org/masa_mnjobs.html

Mississippi
www.mde.k12.ms.us/mtc/vacancy.html

Missouri
www.moteachingjobs.com

Montana
http://jobsforteachers.opi.state.mt.us

Nebraska
www.nebraskaeducationjobs.com

Nevada
www.doe.nv.gov/teachers/
employmentopportunities.html

New Hampshire
www.ed.state.nh.us/education/doe/employ.htm

New Jersey
www.njhire.com

New Mexico
www.nmsba.org

New York
www.highered.nysed.gov/tcert/index.html

North Carolina
www.dpi.state.nc.us/employment.html

North Dakota
https://onestop.jobsnd.com

Ohio
www.ode.state.oh.us/jobs

Oklahoma
www.sde.state.ok.us/pro/job.html

Oregon
www.teachoregon.com

Pennsylvania
www.teaching.state.pa.us/teaching/
site/default.asp

Rhode Island
www.ridoe.net/teachers/ed_employment.htm

South Carolina
www.cerra.org/cerraapp/SearchJobPostings.do

South Dakota
www.asbsd.org/default.asp?wppk=4

Tennessee
www.state.tn.us/education/mtjobs.htm

Texas
www.sbec.state.tx.us

Utah
www.utaheducationjobs.com

Vermont
www.state.vt.us/educ

Virginia
www.pen.k12.va.us/VDOE/JOVE/home.shtml

Washington
www.wateach.com

West Virginia
http://wvde.state.wv.us/jobs

Wisconsin
www.wisconsin.gov/state/app/employment

Wyoming
http://onestop.state.wy.us/appview/tt_home.asp

U.S. Department of Defense Dependents' Schools
www.dodea.edu/offices/hr/onlineapplication/default.htm

Important Dates in the History of Western Education

ca. 4000 BCE	Written language developed
ca. 2000	First known schools
1200	Trojan War
479–338	Period of Greek brilliance
469–399	Socrates
445–431	Greek Age of Pericles
427–346	Plato
404	Fall of Athens
384–322	Aristotle
336–323	Ascendancy of Alexander the Great
303	A few private Greek teachers set up schools in Rome
167	First Greek library in Rome
146	Fall of Corinth: Greece fell to Rome
31–476 CE	Empire of Rome
35–95	Quintilian
40–120	Plutarch
70	Destruction of Jerusalem
476	Fall of Rome in the West
734–804	Alcuin
800	Charlemagne crowned Emperor
980–1037	Avicenna
1100–1300	Crusades
1126–1198	Averroes
ca. 1150	Universities of Paris and Bologna
1209	Cambridge founded
1225–1274	St. Thomas Aquinas
1295	Voyage of Marco Polo
1384	Order of Brethren of the Common Life founded
ca. 1400	Thirty-eight universities; 108 by 1600
ca. 1423	Printing invented
ca. 1456	First book printed
1460–1536	Erasmus
1483–1546	Martin Luther
1487	Vasco da Gama discovered African route to India
1491–1556	Ignatius of Loyola
1492	Columbus landed in America
ca. 1492	Colonists began exploiting Native Americans
ca. 1500	250 Latin grammar schools in England
1517	Luther nailed theses to cathedral door; beginning of Reformation
1519–1521	Magellan first circumnavigated the globe
1534	Founding of Jesuits

1536	Sturm established his Gymnasium in Germany, the first classical secondary school
1568	Indian school established in Cuba by the Society of Jesus
1592–1670	Johann Comenius
1601	English Poor Law established principle of tax-supported schools
1618	Holland had compulsory school law
1620	Plymouth Colony, Massachusetts, settled
1635	Boston Latin Grammar School founded
1636	Harvard founded
1642	Massachusetts law of 1642 encouraged education
1632–1704	John Locke
1647	Massachusetts law of 1647 compelled establishment of schools
ca. 1600s	Hornbooks evolved
1661	First newspaper in England
1672	First teacher-training class in France, Father Demia, France
1684	Brothers of the Christian Schools founded
1685	First normal school, de la Salle, Rheims, France
1697	First teacher training in Germany, Francke's Seminary, Halle
1700–1790	Benjamin Franklin
1712–1778	Jean-Jacques Rousseau
1723	Indian student house opened by College of William and Mary
1746–1827	Johann Pestalozzi
1751	Benjamin Franklin established first academy in the United States
1758–1843	Noah Webster
1762	Rousseau's *Émile* published
1775–1783	Revolution, United States
1776–1841	Johann Herbart
1782–1852	Friedrich Froebel
1778–1870	Emma Willard
1789	Adoption of Constitution, United States
1796–1859	Horace Mann
1798	Joseph Lancaster developed monitorial plan of education
1799–1815	Ascendancy of Napoleon, Waterloo
1804	Pestalozzi's Institute at Yverdon established
1806	First Lancastrian School in New York
1811–1900	Henry Barnard
1819	Dartmouth College Decision
1821	First American high school
1821	Troy Seminary for Women, Emma Willard; first higher education for women in United States
1823	First private normal school in United States, founded by Rev. Hall in Concord, Vermont
1825	Labor unions came on the scene
1826	Froebel's *The Education of Man* published
1827	Massachusetts law compelled high schools
1837	Massachusetts had first state board, Horace Mann first secretary
1839	First public normal school in United States, Lexington, Massachusetts
1855	First kindergarten in United States, based on German model, founded by Margarethe Meyer Schurz at Oshkosh, Wisconsin
1856–1915	Booker T. Washington
1857–1952	John Dewey
1861–1865	Civil War
1861	Oswego (New York) Normal School, Edward Sheldon
1862	Morrill Land Grant Act: college of engineering, military science, agriculture in each state

1868	Herbartian Society founded
1870–1952	Maria Montessori
1872	Kalamazoo Decision made high schools legal
1875–1955	Mary Bethune
1888	Teachers College, Columbia University, founded
1892	Committee of Ten established
1896–1980	Jean Piaget
1904–1990	B. F. Skinner
1909–1910	First junior high schools established at Berkeley, California, and Columbus, Ohio
ca. 1910	First junior colleges established at Fresno, California, and Joliet, Illinois
1917	The Smith-Hughes Act encouraged agriculture, industry, and home economics education in the United States
1932–1940	The Eight-Year Study of thirty high schools completed by the Progressive Education Association
1941	Japanese bombed Pearl Harbor
1941	Lanham Act
1942	Progressive Education Association published the findings of the Eight-Year Study; reported favorably on the modern school
1944–1946	Legislation by 78th U.S. Congress provided subsistence allowance, tuition fees, and supplies for the education of veterans of World War II, the GI Bill
1945	The United Nations Educational, Scientific, and Cultural Organization (UNESCO) initiated efforts to improve educational standards throughout the world
ca. 1946–1947	Beginning of U.S. "baby boom"; eventually caused huge increase in school enrollments
1948	*McCollum v. Board of Education;* U.S. Supreme Court ruled it illegal to release children for religious classes in public school buildings
1948	Fulbright programs began; by 1966 involved 82,500 scholars in 136 nations
1950	National Science Foundation founded
1952	GI Bill's educational benefits extended to Korean War veterans
1954	*Brown v. Board of Education;* U.S. Supreme Court decision required eventual racial integration of public schools
1954	Cooperative Research Program
1957	Soviet Union launched *Sputnik*
1958	Federal Congress passed the National Defense Education Act
1959	James B. Conant wrote *The American High School Today*
1961	Federal court ruled *de facto* racial segregation illegal
1961	Peace Corps established
1961	Approximately four million college students in the United States
1962	In *Engle v. Vitale,* U.S. Supreme Court ruled compulsory prayer in public school illegal
1963	Vocational Education Act
1963	Manpower Development and Training Act
1964	Economic Opportunity Act provided federal funds for such programs as Head Start
1964	Civil Rights Act
1965	Elementary and Secondary Education Act allowed more federal funds for public schools
1965	Higher Education Act
1966	GI Bill's educational benefits extended to Vietnam war veterans
1966	One million Americans travel abroad

1966	U.S. International Education Act
1966	Coleman Report suggested that racially balanced schools did not necessarily provide a better education
1967	Education Professions Development Act
1972	Indian Education Act, designed to help Native Americans help themselves
1972	Title IX Education Amendment outlawing discrimination on the basis of sex
1973	In *Rodriguez v. San Antonio Independent School,* U.S. Supreme Court ruled that a state's system for financing schools did not violate the Constitution although there were large disparities in per-pupil expenditure.
1975	Indochina Migration and Refugee Assistance Act (Public Law 94-23)
1975	Public Law 94-142, requiring local districts to provide education for children with special needs
1979	Department of Education Act
1980	U.S. Secretary of Education position became a cabinet post
1983	*High School: A Report on Secondary Education in America* by the Carnegie Foundation
1983	*A Nation at Risk: The Imperative for Educational Reform,* report by the National Commission on Excellence in Education
1983	Task Force on Education for Economic Growth, Action for Excellence, Education Commission of the States Report
1983	Task Force on Federal Elementary and Secondary Education Policy, Making the Grade, the Twentieth Century Fund Report
ca. 1980–1984	Fundamentalist religious movement advocating prayer in the schools and teaching of Biblical creation story
1984	Public Law 98-377 added new science and mathematics programs, magnet schools, and equal access to public schools
1984	Perkins Vocational Education Act to upgrade vocational programs in schools
1984	Public Law 98-558 created new teacher education scholarships and continued Head Start and Follow Through programs
1985	NCATE Redesign Standards published
1986	Holmes Group report published
1986	Carnegie Report of the Task Force on Teaching as a Profession
1989	Presidential Education Summit with governors
1990	U.S. Supreme Court decision to allow Bible clubs in schools
1992	U.S. Supreme Court decision finds officially sanctioned prayers or invocations unconstitutional
1994	National Educational Goals: 2000 adopted by federal government
ca. 1990s	Development of school voucher plans and charter schools
2001	President George W. Bush promises to push school reform
2001	Federal No Child Left Behind Act
2003	U.S. Supreme Court reaffirms and clarifies affirmative action
2006	Intelligent design versus evolution debate intensifies in education

APPENDIX E

Professional Education Associations: A Selected List

American Association for Health Education (AAHE)
www.aahperd.org/aahe

American Association of Physics Teachers (AAPT)
www.aapt.org

American Comparative Literature Association (ACLA)
www.acla.org

American Council on the Teaching of Foreign Languages (ACTFL)
www.actfl.org

American Federation of Teachers (AFT)
www.aft.org

American Library Association (ALA)
www.ala.org

American Speech-Language-Hearing Association (ASHA)
www.asha.org

American Association for Health Education (AAHE)
www.aahperd.org/aahe

Association for Childhood Education International (ACEI)
www.acei.org

Association for Education in Journalism and Mass Communications (AEJMC)
www.aejmc.org

Association for Educational Communications and Technology (AECT)
www.aect.org

Association for Supervision and Curriculum Development (ASCD)
www.ascd.org

Association of Christian Schools International (ACSI)
www.acsi.org

Council for Exceptional Children (CEC)
www.cec.sped.org

Education International (EI)
www.ei-ie.org/en/index.php

International Reading Association (IRA)
www.reading.org

International Society for Technology in Education (ISTE)
www.iste.org

International Technology Education Association (ITEA)
www.iteaconnect.org

Interstate New Teacher Assessment and Support Consortium (INTASC)
www.ccsso.org/Projects/interstate_new_teacher_assessment_and_support_consortium/780.cfm

Modern Language Association of America (MLA)
www.mla.org

Music Teachers National Association (MTNA)
www.mtna.org

National Art Education Association (NAEA)
www.naea-reston.org

National Association for Bilingual Education (NABE)
www.nabe.org

National Association for the Education of Young Children (NAEYC)
www.naeyc.org

National Association for Gifted Children (NAGC)
www.nagc.org

National Association for Multicultural Education (NAME)
www.nameorg.org

National Association for Sport & Physical Education (NASPE)
www.aahperd.org/naspe

National Association of Biology Teachers (NABT)
www.nabt.org

National Association of Episcopal Schools (NAES)
www.naes.org

National Board for Professional Teaching Standards (NBPTS)
www.nbpts.org

National Business Education Association (NBEA)
www.nbea.org

National Catholic Educational Association (NCEA)
www.ncea.org

National Council for Accreditation of Teacher Education (NCATE)
www.ncate.org

National Council for the Social Studies (NCSS)
www.ncss.org

National Council of Teachers of English (NCTE)
www.ncte.org

National Council of Teachers of Mathematics (NCTM)
www.nctm.org

National Education Association (NEA)
www.nea.org

National Middle School Association (NMSA)
www.nmsa.org

National Science Teachers Association (NSTA)
www.nsta.org

Phi Delta Kappa
www.pdkintl.org

Teachers of English to Speakers of Other Languages (TESOL)
www.tesol.org

Notes

CHAPTER 1

1. Recruiting New Teachers, Inc., *The Essential Profession: A National Survey of Public Attitudes toward Teaching, Educational Opportunity and School Reform*. Belmont, MA: Author, 1998.
2. Ibid.
3. Carol A. Langdon and Nick Vesper, "The Sixth Phi Delta Kappa Poll of Teachers' Attitudes toward the Public Schools," *Phi Delta Kappan, 81*(8) (April 2000), pp. 607–611.
4. Recruiting New Teachers, Inc., ibid.
5. Debra E. Gerald and William J. Hussar, *Projections of Education Statistics to 2009*. Washington, DC: National Center for Education Statistics, U.S. Department of Education, 1999.
6. Recruiting New Teachers, Inc., ibid.
7. Linda Darling-Hammond, "Teaching for America's Future: National Commissions and Vested Interests in an Almost Profession," *Educational Policy, 14*(1) (January/March 2000), pp. 162–183.
8. National Commission on Teaching and America's Future, ibid.
9. "Who Should Teach? The States Decide," *Education Week, XIX*(18) (January 13, 2000), pp. 8–9.
10. Richard Wolf, quoted in Paul Leavitt, "Capitol Roundup," *USA Today* (March 13, 2000).
11. "Who Should Teach? The States Decide," ibid.

CHAPTER 2

1. Milton M. Gordon, *Assimilation in American Life: The Role of Race, Religion, and National Origins*. New York: Oxford University Press, 1964.
2. U.S. Census Bureau, *Statistical Abstract of the United States: 2006,* 125th edition (Table 604). Washington, DC: U.S. Government Printing Office, 2006.
3. Stephen J. Rose, *Social Stratification in the United States: The New American Profile Poster*. New York: New Press, 2000.
4. U.S. Census Bureau, 2006, Table 678.
5. Ibid.
6. Sarah Anderson, John Cavanagh, Scott Klinger, and Liz Stanton, *Executive Excess 2005: Defense Contractors Get More Bucks for the Bang: Twelfth Annual CEO Compensation Survey*. Washington, DC: Institute for Policy Studies and United for a Fair Economy, August 2006.
7. U.S. Census Bureau, 2006, Table 693.
8. National Center for Children in Poverty, "Basic Facts about Low-Income Children: Birth to Age 18." Retrieved on May 7, 2006, from www.nccp.org/pub_lic06.html.
9. U.S. Census Bureau, 2006, Table 696.
10. U.S. Census Bureau, 2006, Table 679.
11. U.S. Census Bureau, 2006, Table 686.
12. National Center for Children in Poverty, 2006.
13. "Children's Progress Elsewhere," *U.S. News & World Report* (August 28, 1995), p. 24.
14. National Center for Children in Poverty, 2006.
15. U.S. Bureau of the Census, American FactFinder, "Ancestry: 2000" [Census 2000 Summary File 3 (SF3)—Sample Data]. Retrieved May 9, 2006, from http://factfinder.census.gov/servlet/QTTable?_bm=y&-geo_id=01000US&-qr_name=DEC_2000_SF3_U_QTP13&-ds_name=DEC_2000_SF3_U.
16. M. Kelley, "Indian Affairs Head Makes Apology" *The Free Press* (September 8, 2000).
17. U.S. Census Bureau, American FactFinder, "Language Spoken at Home" (2004 American Community Survey). Retrieved May 7, 2006, from http://factfinder.census.gov/servlet/STTable?_bm=y&-geo_id=01000US&-qr_name=ACS_2004_EST_G00_S1601&-ds_name=ACS_2004_EST_G00_.
18. W. P. Thomas and Virginia P. Collier, *School Effectiveness for Language Minority Students*. Washington, DC: National Clearinghouse for Bilingual Education, 1997.
19. Michael Gurian and Patricia Henley, *Boys and Girls Learn Differently! A Guide for Teachers and Parents*. San Francisco: Jossey-Bass, 2001, pp. 54–55.
20. Ibid.
21. Barrie Thorne, "Do Girls and Boys Have Different Cultures?" *The Jossey-Bass Reader on Gender in Education* (pp. 125–150). San Francisco: Jossey-Bass, 2002.
22. United Nations Educational, Scientific and Cultural Organization, *Education for All: Is the World on Track?* Paris, France: Author, 2002, p. 68.
23. United Nations Development Fund for Women, *Progress of the World's Women 2002: Volume 2: Gender Equality and the Millennium Development Goals*. New York: Author, 2002.

24. U.S. Census Bureau, 2006, Tables 286 and 289.

25. United States Department of Education, Office of Civil Rights, "Additional Clarification of Intercollegiate Athletics Policy: Three-Part Test—Part Three" (March 17, 2005). Retrieved on May 9, 2006, from www.ed.gov/print/about/offices/list/ocr/docs/title9guidanceadditional.html.

26. Women's Sports Foundation, "State of Women's Sports." Retrieved on May 9, 2006, from www.womenssports foundation.org/binary-data/WSF_ARTICLE/pdf_file/1109.PDF.

27. Francis Mark Mondimore, *A Natural History of Homosexuality.* Baltimore: Johns Hopkins University Press, 1996.

28. Jason Ost and Gary J. Gates, *The Gay & Lesbian Atlas.* Washington, DC: Urban Institute, 2004.

29. Ibid.

30. Joseph G. Kosciw and Elizabeth M. Diaz, *The 2005 National School Climate Survey: The Experiences of Lesbian, Gay, Bisexual and Transgender Youth in Our Nation's Schools.* New York: Gay, Lesbian and Straight Education Network, 2006.

31. Ibid.

32. U.S. Census Bureau, American FactFinder, "Disability Characteristics" (2004 American Community Survey). Retrieved on May 7, 2006, from http://factfinder.census.gov/servlet/STTable?_bm=y&geo_id=01000US&-qr_name=ACS_2004_EST_G00_S1801&-ds_name=ACS_2004_EST_G00_&-redoLog=false.

33. U.S. Census Bureau, "Facts & Features: 12th Anniversary of Americans with Disabilities Act (July 26)," Press Release. Washington, DC: Author, July 12, 2002.

34. Dorothy Kerzner Lipsky and Alan Gartner, "Inclusion, School Restructuring, and the Remaking of American Society," *Harvard Educational Review* 66(4) (Winter 1996), pp. 762–796.

35. U.S. Department of Education, National Center for Education Statistics, *The Condition of Education 2005.* Washington, DC: Author.

36. Gallup Organization, "Gallup Poll: How Important Would You Say Religion Is in Your Own Life?" Princeton, NJ: Author, 2006.

37. U.S. Census Bureau, 2006, Table 69.

CHAPTER 3

1. U.S. Census Bureau, *Statistical Abstract of the United States: 2006,* 125th edition (Table 60). Washington, DC: U.S. Government Printing Office, 2006.

2. M. D. Bramlett and W. D. Mosher, *Cohabitation, Marriage, Divorce, and Remarriage in the United States.* Washington, DC: National Center for Health Statistics, 2002.

3. U.S. Census Bureau, 2006, Table 51.

4. U.S. Census Bureau, 2006, Table 60.

5. Sharon Vandivere, Kathryn Tout, Martha Zaslow, Julia Calkins, and Jeffrey Capizzano, "Unsupervised Time: Family and Child Factors Associated with Self-Care" (Occasional Paper Number 71). Washington, DC: The Urban Institute, November 2003.

6. U.S. Department of Education, National Center for Education Statistics, *The Condition of Education 2004* (NCES 2004-077), Indicators 33 and 34. Washington, DC: Author, 2004.

7. U.S. Census Bureau, 2006, Table 19.

8. U.S. Census Bureau, 2006, Table 22.

9. U.S. Census Bureau, 2006.

10. U.S. Census Bureau, "Table 8. Poverty of People, by Residence: 1959 to 2004." Retrieved on May 7, 2006, from www.census.gov/hhes/www/poverty/histpov/hstpov8.html.

11. U.S. Department of Education, National Center for Education Statistics, "Navigating Resources for Rural Schools." Washington, DC: Author, 2006. Retrieved on May 22, 2006, from http://nces.ed.gov/surveys/RuralEd/Tables HTML.

12. National Center for Children in Poverty. "Basic Facts about Low-Income Children: Birth to Age 18." New York: Author, 2006. Retrieved on May 7, 2006, from www.nccp.org/pub_lic06.html.

13. U.S. Census Bureau, 2006, Tables 42 and 213.

14. Children's Defense Fund, *The State of America's Children: 2005.* Washington, DC: Author, 2005.

15. National Center for Children in Poverty, 2006.

16. National Law Center on Homelessness and Poverty, "Homelessness and Poverty in America: Overview." Retrieved on May 11, 2006, from www.nlchp.org/FA%5FHAPIA.

17. National Law Center on Homelessness and Poverty, "Key Data Concerning Homeless Persons in America," New York: Author, July 2004. Retrieved from www.nlchp.org/FA_HAPIA/HomelessPersonsinAmerica.pdf.

18. Ibid.

19. Ibid.

20. Homes for the Homeless, "Facts." Retrieved on May 7, 2006, from www.homesforthehomeless.com/index.asp?CID=3&PID=20.

21. James Alan Fox and Marianne W. Zawitz, *Homicide Trends in the United States.* Washington, DC: U.S. Department of Justice, Bureau of Justice Statistics, 2005. Retrieved from www.ojp.gov/bjs/pub/pdf/htius.pdf.

22. UNICEF, *Domestic Violence: An Epidemic.* New York: Author, 2000.

23. Homes for the Homeless.

24. U.S. Census Bureau, 2006, Table 333.

25. Fox and Zawitz, 2005.

26. U.S. Census Bureau, 2006, Table 332.

27. Centers for Disease Control, National Center for Injury Prevention and Control, "Sexual Violence: Fact Sheet." Retrieved on May 15, 2006, from www.cdc.gov/ncipc/factsheets/svfacts.htm.

28. N. H. Cambron-McCabe, M. M. McCarthy, and S. B. Thomas, *Public School Law: Teachers' and Students' Rights,* 5th edition. Boston: Pearson, 2004.

29. American Association of University Women Educational Foundation, "Harassment-Free Hallways: How to Stop Sexual Harassment in Schools: A Guide for Students, Parents, and Teachers, Section III for Schools." Washington, DC: Author, 2002, p. III-2.

30. Joseph G. Kosciw and Elizabeth M. Diaz, *The 2005 National School Climate Survey: The Experiences of Lesbian, Gay, Bisexual and Transgender Youth in Our Nation's Schools.* New York: Gay, Lesbian and Straight Education Network, 2006.

31. Tonja R. Nansel, Mary D. Overpeck, Denise L. Haynie, June Ruan, and Peter C. Scheidt, "Relationships between Bullying and Violence among US Youth," *Archives of Pediatrics and Adolescent Medicine, 157*(4) (April 2003), pp. 348–357.

32. Ibid.

33. American Association of University Women Educational Foundation, 2002.

34. Centers for Disease Control and Prevention, Morbidity and Mortality Weekly Report, *Youth Risk Behavior Surveillance—United States 2003*. Atlanta: Author, 2004. Retrieved from www.cdc.gov/mmwr/PDF/ss/ss5302.pdf.

35. The National Campaign to Prevent Teen Pregnancy, "Fact Sheet: How is the 34% Statistic Calculated?" Washington, DC: Author, February 2004. Retrieved from www.teen pregnancy.org/resources/reading/pdf/35percent.pdf.

36. Centers for Disease Control and Prevention, 2004.

37. The National Campaign to Prevent Teen Pregnancy, 2004.

38. Bill Albert, Sarah Brown, and Christine M. Glanigan, *14 and Younger: The Sexual Behavior of Young Adolescents*. Washington, DC: National Campaign to Prevent Teen Pregnancy, 2003.

39. The Annie E. Casey Foundation, "Kids Count Indicator Brief: Reducing the Teen Birth Rate." Baltimore, MD: Author, July 2005. Retrieved from www.aecf.org/kidscount/sld/auxiliary/briefs/teenbirthrateupdated.pdf.

40. Ibid.

41. Gregory Acs and Heather Koball, "TANF and the Status of Teen Mothers under Age 18," *New Federalism: Issues and Options for States,* Series A, No. A-62. Washington, DC: Urban Institute, 2003.

42. The Annie E. Casey Foundation, *Kids Count Data Book 2003*. Baltimore, MD: Author, 2003, p. 44.

43. The Annie E. Casey Foundation, 2006.

44. U.S. Census Bureau, 2006, Table 260.

45. Gary Orfield, Daniel Losen, Johanna Wald, and Christopher B. Swanson, *Losing Our Future: How Minority Youth are Being Left Behind by the Graduation Rate Crisis*. Cambridge, MA: The Civil Rights Project at Harvard University with Contributions from Urban Institute, Advocates for Children of New York, and The Civil Society Institute, 2004.

46. U.S. Department of Education, National Center for Education Statistics, *Condition of Education 2005*. Washington, DC: Author, 2005.

47. U.S. Department of Education, 2004.

48. The Annie E. Casey Foundation, "Kids Count Indicator Brief: Reducing the High School Dropout Rate." Baltimore, MD: Author, July 2005. Retrieved from www.aecf.org/kidscount/sld/auxiliary/briefs/hsdropoutsupdated.pdf.

49. U.S. Census Bureau, 2006, Table 580.

50. Lowell C. Rose and Alec M. Gallup, "The 37th Annual Phi Delta Kappa/Gallup Poll of the Public's Attitudes Toward the Public Schools," *Phi Delta Kappan, 87*(1) (September 2005), pp. 41–57.

51. L. D. Johnston, P. M. O'Malley, J. G. Bachman, and J. E. Schulenberg, *Monitoring the Future—National Results on Adolescent Drug Use: Overview of Key Findings, 2005*. Bethesda, MD: National Institute on Drug Abuse, 2006.

52. National Center for Health Statistics, *Health, United States, 2002 with Chartbook on Trends in the Health of Americans* (Table 65). Hyattsville, MD: Author, 2002.

53. Howard N. Snyder and Melissa Sickmund, *Juvenile Offenders and Victims: 2006 National Report*. Washington, DC: U.S. Department of Justice, Office of Justice Programs, Office of Juvenile Justice and Delinquency Prevention, 2006.

54. U.S. Census Bureau, 2006, Table 316.

55. Howard N. Snyder and Melissa Sickmund, 2006.

56. Laudan Y. Aron and Daniel P. Mears, "Addressing the Needs of Youth with Disabilities in the Juvenile System: The Current Status of Evidence-Based Research" (A Research Report). Washington, DC: National Council on Disability, 2003.

57. Howard N. Snyder and Melissa Sickmund, 2006.

58. Ibid.

59. Arlen Egley, Jr. and Christine E. Ritz, "Highlights of the 2004 National Youth Gang Survey" (OJJDP Fact Sheet). Washington, DC: U.S. Department of Justice, Office of Juvenile Justice and Delinquency Prevention, April 2006.

60. Centers for Disease Control and Prevention, 2004.

61. U.S. Department of Education, 2005.

62. U.S. Census Bureau, 2006, Tables 263 and 264.

63. Robert I. Lerman, "Are Teens in Low-Income and Welfare Families Working Too Much?" Washington, DC: Urban Institute, November 2000. Retrieved on May 22, 2006, from www.urban.org/publications/309708.html.

64. Barry van Driel, "Coming to Justice: A Program for Youth around Issues of International Justice," *Intercultural Education, 16*(2), (May 2005), pp. 161–169.

65. Elizabeth Cove, Michael Eiseman, and Susan J. Popkin, "Resilient Children: Literature Review and Evidence from the HOPE VI Panel Study." Washington, DC: Urban Institute, December 2005.

66. Ibid.

CHAPTER 4

1. David F. Labaree, "Public Goods, Private Goods: The American Struggle over Educational Goals," *American Educational Research Journal, 34*(1) (Spring 1997), p. 81.

2. Carolyn Cottom, "A Bold Experiment in Teaching Values," *Educational Leadership, 53*(8) (May 1996), p. 54.

3. Ibid, p. 56.

4. Donna M. Gollnick and Philip C. Chinn, *Multicultural Education in a Pluralistic Society,* 7th edition. New York: Merrill, 2006.

5. Recruiting New Teachers, Inc., *The Essential Profession: American Education at the Crossroads*. Belmont, MA: Author, 2004.

6. Andrew Sum, Irwin Kirsch, and Robert Taggart, *The Twin Challenges of Mediocrity and Inequality: Literacy in the U.S. from an International Perspective*. Princeton, NJ: Educational Testing Service, 2002, pp. 31–32.

7. Sharon Nelson-Barber and Elise Trumbull Estrin, "Bringing Native American Perspectives to Mathematics and Science Teaching," *Theory into Practice, 34*(3) (1995), pp. 174–185.

8. U.S. Census Bureau, *Statistical Abstract of the United States: 2006,* 125th edition (Table 291). Washington, DC: U.S. Government Printing Office, 2006.

9. Ibid.

10. American Association of University Women (AAUW), *Tech-Savvy: Educating Girls in the New Computer Age*. Washington, DC: Author, 2000.

11. University of California Linguistic Minority Research Institute, "The Intersection of Language, Race/Ethnicity, Immigration Status and Poverty" (EL Facts, Number 5). Berkeley, CA: Author, September 2005.

12. The Civil Rights Project, Harvard University, *What Works for the Children? What We Know and Don't Know about Bilingual Education.* Cambridge, MA: Author, September 2002, p. 5.
13. Ibid.
14. Fred Genesee, ed., *Program Alternatives for Linguistically Diverse Students.* Washington, DC: Center for Research on Education, Diversity and Excellence, 1999.
15. Ibid.
16. Darren E. Lund, "Educating for Social Justice: Making Sense of Multicultural and Antiracist Theory and Practice with Canadian Teacher Activists," *Intercultural Education, 14*(1) (March 2003), pp. 3–16.
17. Ibid.

CHAPTER 5

1. B. Fuller, E. Burr, L. Huerta, S. Puryear, and E. Wexler, *School Choice: Abundant Hopes, Scarce Evidence on Results.* Berkeley, CA: Policy Analysis for California Education, 1999.
2. D. Goldhaber, "School Choice: An Examination of the Empirical Evidence on Achievement, Parental Decision Making, and Equity," *Educational Researcher* (December 1999), pp. 16–25.
3. B. Nelson, P. Berman, J. Ericson, N. Kamprath, R. Perry, D. Silverman, and D. Solomon, *The State of Charter Schools 2000.* Washington, DC: Office of Educational Research and Improvement, U.S. Department of Education, 2000.
4. *Private Independent Schools 2002, 55th Annual Edition.* Wallingford, CT: Bunting and Lyon, 2002.
5. Bobette Reed and William L. Dandridge, *Minority Leaders for Independent Schools.* Boston: National Association of Independent Schools.
6. Richard C. Hunter, "The Mayor versus the School Superintendent," *Education and Urban Society, 29*(2) (February 1997), pp. 217–232.
7. U.S. Department of Education, National Center for Education Statistics. *National Public Education Financial Survey. School Year 2002–2003.* Washington, DC.
8. *Helena Elementary School District v. State* (1989).
9. Consumers Union Education Services, *Captive Kids: Commercial Pressures on Kids at School.* Yonkers, NY: Consumers Union, 1996.

CHAPTER 6

1. Michael LaMorte, *School Law: Cases and Concepts,* 8th edition. Boston: Allyn & Bacon, 2005, p. 195.
2. *Turk v. Franklin Special School District* (1982).
3. *Lucia v. Duggan* (1969).
4. *Gouge v. Joint School District No. 1* (1970).
5. Haskell C. Freedman, "The Legal Rights of Untenured Teachers," *Nolpe School Law Journal, 1* (Fall 1970), p. 100.
6. *Norwalk Teachers Association v. Board of Education* (1951).
7. *City of Manchester v. Manchester Teachers' Guild* (1957).
8. *Cooper v. Ross* (1979).
9. *Hillis v. Stephen F. Austin University* (1982).
10. *Kingsville Independent School District v. Cooper* (1980).
11. *Board of Education, Island Trees Union Free District No. 26 v. Pico* (1982).
12. Lucy Knight, "Facts about Mr. Buckley's Amendment," *American Education, 13* (June 1977), p. 7.
13. *Peter W. v. San Francisco Unified School District* (1976).
14. *Donahue v. Copiague Union Free School District* (1978).

15. *Mastrangelo v. West Side Union High School District* (1935).
16. *Morris v. Douglas County School District* (1966).
17. Lee O. Garber and Reynolds C. Seitz, *The Yearbook of School Law, 1971.* Danville, IL: Interstate, 1971, p. 253.
18. Thomas J. Flygare, "De Jure," *Phi Delta Kappan, 68* (October 1986), pp. 165–166.
19. *Long v. Zopp* (1973).
20. *Scoville v. Board of Education* (1970).
21. William D. Valente, *Law in the Schools.* Columbus, OH: Merrill, 1980, p. 282.

CHAPTER 7

1. Quintilian, *The Institutes of Oratory,* trans. W. Guthrie. London: Dewick and Clark, 1905, p. 12.
2. Glenn Smith et al., *Lives in Education.* Ames, IA: Educational Studies Press, 1984, pp. 84–88.
3. Gabriel Compayre, *History of Pedagogy,* trans. W. H. Payne. Boston: Heath, 1888, pp. 12–13, 88–89.
4. Paul Monroe, *History of Education.* New York: Macmillan, 1905, p. 282 .
5. Portions of the material dealing with the history of African Americans up to the signing of the Emancipation Proclamation (1863) was adapted from the doctoral dissertation of Samuel David, *Education, Law, and the Negro.* Urbana: University of Illinois, 1970.
6. Emma Willard, "A Plan for Improving Female Education" in *Women and the Higher Education.* New York: Harper & Brothers, 1893, pp. 12–14.

CHAPTER 8

1. U.S. Dept. of Commerce, Bureau of the Census, *Digest of Education Statistics 1982.* Washington, DC: U.S. Government Printing Office, 1982, p. 23.
2. W. H. G. Armytage, "William Byngham: A Medieval Protagonist of the Training of Teachers," *History of Education Journal, 2* (Summer 1951), p. 108.
3. We thank Dr. Donald Barnes for many of the ideas presented in this section.

CHAPTER 9

1. Herbert G. Alexander, *The Language and Logic of Philosophy.* Lanham, MD: University Press of America, 1987, pp. 107–108.
2. Cornel West, *Prophetic Thought in Postmodern Times.* Monroe, ME: Common Courage Press, 1993.
3. Nel Noddings, *The Challenge to Care in Schools.* New York: Teachers College Press, 1993, p. 2.
4. West, *Prophetic Thought,* p. 5.
5. West, *Prophetic Thought,* p. 6.
6. Jane Roland Martin, "Reclaiming a Conversation," in *The Ideal of the Educated Woman.* New Haven, CT: Yale University Press, 1985, pp. 1–7.
7. John Locke, "Some Thoughts Concerning Education," in *The Works of John Locke,* Volume X. London: Printed for W. Otridge and Son et al., 1812, pp. 6–7.
8. Alfred North Whitehead, *The Aims of Education.* New York: Free Press, 1929/1957, pp. 1–2.
9. John Dewey, "My Pedagogic Creed," *The School Journal, 54*(3) (January 16, 1989), pp. 77–80.
10. Friedrich Nietzsche, "The Wanderer and His Shadow," in *Human All Too Human,* trans. R. J. Hollingdale. Cambridge: Cambridge University Press, 1986, p. 6. This section on the writing of Nietzsche was developed by Dr. Leslie A. Sassone

from the Foundations of Education faculty at Northern Illinois University.

11. Maxine Greene, *The Dialectic of Freedom.* New York: Teachers College Press, 1988.

12. Howard A. Osman and Samuel M. Craven, *Philosophical Foundations of Education.* Columbus, OH: Merrill, 1986, pp. 66–85.

13. Terry P. Wilson, *Navajo: Walking in Beauty.* San Francisco: Chronicle Books, 1994.

14. Terry P. Wilson, *Lakota: Seeking the Great Spirit.* San Francisco: Chronicle Books, 1994.

15. Terry P. Wilson, *Hopi: Following the Path of Peace.* San Francisco: Chronicle Books, 1994.

CHAPTER 10

1. Lloyd Duck, *Instructor's Manual for Teaching with Charisma.* Boston: Allyn & Bacon, 1981, Item 4, p. 40.

2. John Dewey, *Democracy and Education.* New York: Macmillan, 1916, pp. 1–9.

3. Henry A. Giroux, "Teachers as Transformative Intellectuals," *Social Education, 49* (1985), pp. 376–379.

4. Jean-Jacques Rousseau, *Émile,* trans. Alan Bloom. New York: Basic Books, 1979.

5. Duck, *Instructor's Manual,* Item C, pp. 50–51.

6. Martin Buber, *I and Thou,* trans. Ronald G. Smith. New York: Charles Scribner, 1958.

7. R. Schmuck and P. A. Schmuck, *Group Processes in the Classrooms.* Dubuque, IA: Wm. C. Brown, 1983.

8. Carl D. Glickman and Charles H. Wolfgang, "Conflict in the Classroom: An Eclectic Model of Teacher–Child Interaction," *Elementary School Guidance and Counseling, 13* (December 1978), pp. 82–87.

9. William Glasser, *Control Theory in the Classroom.* New York: Harper & Row, 1986, p. 47.

10. John Goodlad, *A Place Called School: Prospects for the Future.* New York: McGraw-Hill, 1984.

11. S. M. Johnson, *Teachers at Work: Achieving Success in Our Schools.* New York: Basic Books, 1990, pp. xvii–xix.

12. Diane Ravitch, *The Schools We Deserve: Reflections on the Educational Crisis of Our Times.* New York: Basic Books, 1985, p. 303.

13. Vito Perrone, ed., *Expanded Student Assessment for Supervision and Curriculum Development.* Alexandria, VA: Association for Supervision and Curriculum Development, 1991.

14. Henry Giroux, *Ideology, Culture and the Process of Schooling.* Philadelphia: Temple University Press, 1981.

15. Maxine Greene, "Curriculum and Consciousness," in William Pinar, ed., *Curriculum Theorizing: The Reconceptualists.* Berkeley, CA: McCutchan, 1975, p. 12.

16. C. S. Peirce, "The Fixation of Belief," in Justus Buchler, ed., *Philosophical Writings of Peirce.* New York: Dover, 1955, pp. 5–22.

17. Isaac L. Kandel, *Conflicting Theories of Education.* New York: Macmillan, 1938, pp. 77–88.

18. John Dewey, "Education and Social Change," *The School Frontier III* (1937), pp. 235–238.

19. Theodore Brameld, "Imperatives for a Reconstructed Philosophy of Education," *School and Society, 87* (1959), pp. 18–20.

20. Samuel Bowles and Herbert Gintis, *Schooling in Capitalistic America.* New York: Basic Books, 1975, pp. 18–20.

21. Linda Tinelli Sheive and Marian Beauchamp Schoenbeit, "Vision and the Worklife of Educational Leaders," in *Leadership: Examining the Elusive.* Alexandria, VA: Association for Supervision and Curriculum Development, 1987, p. 99.

CHAPTER 11

1. U.S. Department of Education, *e-Learning: Putting a World-Class Education at the Fingertips of All Children.* Washington, DC: Author, January 1, 2004. www.ed.gov.

2. Myron Lieberman, "World-Class Standards: Rhetoric and Reality," *School Reform News* (May 1, 2005).

3. Austin Independent School District, *Character Education Creating Tomorrow's Citizens.* Austin, TX: Author. www.austin.isd.tenet.edu.

4. American Management Association, *AMA Survey on Workplace Testing: Basic Skills, Job Skills, Pyschological Measurement.* New York: Author, 2001.

5. *Standards for the English Language Arts,* by the International Reading Association and the National Council of Teachers of English. Copyright © 1996 by the International Reading Association and the National Council of Teachers of English. Reprinted with permission. For the full list of standards, please go to www.ncte.org/about/over/standards/110846.htm.

6. Reprinted with permission from *Principles & Standards for School Mathematics.* Copyright 2000 National Council of Teachers of Mathematics. All rights reserved.

7. Ibid, p. 29.

8. Interstate New Teacher Assessment and Support Consortium, *Model Standards for Beginning Teacher Licensing, Assessment, and Development: Resource for State Dialogue.* Washington, DC: Author, 1992.

9. Council of Chief State School Officers, *Model Standards for Beginning Teacher Licensing, Assessment and Development: A Resource for State Dialogue.* Washington, DC: Author, 1992. www.ccsso.org/content/pdfs/corestrd.pdf. Reprinted with permission.

10. Reprinted with permission from the National Board for Professional Teaching Standards, Middle Childhood/Generalist Standards. www.nbpts.org. All rights reserved.

11. National Council for the Accreditation of Teacher Education, The NCATE Unit Standards (Proposed Revisions UAB March 2006). Washington, DC: Author. www.ncate.org.

12. S. Linda Darling-Hammond and Beverly Falk, "Supporting Teaching and Learning for All Students: Policies for Authentic Assessment Systems," in A. Lin Goodwin, ed., *Assessment for Equity and Inclusion: Embracing All Our Children.* New York: Routledge, 1997.

13. Ibid.

14. Lynn Olson, "Overboard on Testing?" *Quality Counts 2001: A Better Balance [Education Week, 20(7)]* (January 22, 2001), available at www.edweek.org/sreports/qcol/articles/qcolstory.cfm?slug=17test.h20.

15. Luis Benveniste, "The Political Structuration of Assessment: Negotiating State Power and Legitimacy," *Comparative Education Review, 46(2)* (February 2002), pp. 89–118.

16. John A. Holloway, "A Global Perspective on Student Accountability," *Educational Leadership, 60(5)* (February 2003), pp. 74, 76.

17. Ibid.

18. Benveniste, "Political Structuration."

19. Kathryn M. Doherty and Ronal A. Skinner, "State of the States," *Quality Counts 2003: "If I Can't Learn from You . . ." [Education Week, 22(17)]* (January 9, 2003).

CHAPTER 12

1. R. W. Tyler, *Basic Principles of Curriculum Development.* Chicago: University of Chicago Press, 1950.
2. H. Taba, *Curriculum Development Theory and Practice.* New York: Harcourt, Brace & World, 1962.
3. California Department of Education, *The Nature of Science and Technology.* Sacramento, CA: Author, 2003, p. 9.
4. Archie A. George, Gene E. Hall, and Kay Uchiyama, "Extent of Implementation of a Standards-Based Approach to Teaching Mathematics and Student Outcomes," *Journal of Classroom Interaction, 35*(1) (Spring 2000), pp. 8–25.
5. Benjamin S. Bloom, ed., *Taxonomy of Educational Objectives: The Classification of Educational Goals Handbook 1: Cognitive Domain.* New York: David McKay, 1956.
6. David R. Krathwohl, Benjamin S. Bloom, and Bertram B. Masia, *Taxonomy of Educational Objectives: The Classification of Educational Goals Handbook II: Affective Domain.* New York: David McKay, 1964.
7. E. J. Simpson, *The Classification of Educational Objectives in the Psychomotor Domain: The Psychomotor Domain,* Vol. 3. Washington, DC: Gryphon House, 1972.
8. Barak Rosenshine and R. Stevens, "Teaching Functions," in M. C. Wittrock, ed., *Handbook of Research on Teaching,* 3rd edition. New York: Macmillan, 1986, pp. 376–391.
9. Christina V. Schwarz, Using Model-Centered Science Instruction to Foster Students' Epistemologies in Learning with Models. Paper presented at the annual meeting of the American Educational Research Association, New Orleans, April 2002.
10. David W. Johnson and Roger T. Johnson, *Learning Together and Alone: Cooperative, Competitive and Individualistic Learning,* 5th edition. Boston: Allyn & Bacon, 1999.
11. Robert Slavin, *Education for All.* Exton, PA: Swets & Zeitlinger, 1996.
12. Theodore R. Sizer, *Horace's Hope: What Works for the American High School.* Boston: Houghton Mifflin, 1997.
13. Howard Gardner, *The Disciplined Mind: What All Students Should Understand.* New York: Simon & Schuster, 1999.

CHAPTER 13

1. International Society for Technology in Education, *National Educational Technology Standards for Teachers,* Eugene, OR: Author, 2000.
2. T. Berners-Lee and M. Fischetti, *Weaving the Web: The Original Design and Ultimate Destiny of the World Wide Web by Its Inventor.* San Francisco: HarperSanFrancisco, 1999.
3. D. C. Dwyer, C. Ringstaff, and J. H. Sandholdtz. "Changes in Teachers' Beliefs and Practices in Technology-Rich Classrooms," *Educational Leadership, 48*(8) (1991), pp. 45–52.
4. Rhea R. Borja, "Risk and Reward," *Technology Counts 2006: The Information Edge: Using Data to Accelerate Achievement.* Bethesda, MD: *Education Week,* Editorial Projects in Education, 2006.
5. H. Wenglinsky, *Using Technology Wisely: The Keys to Success in Schools.* New York: Teachers College Press, 2005.
6. A. Gulli and A. Signorini, "The Indexable Web Is More Than 11.5 Billion Pages." Paper presented at the 14th International World Wide Web Conference, May 2005. Retrieved from www.cs.uiowa.edu/~asignori/pubs/web-size.
7. Tim Johnson, "Chinese Premier Defends Nation's Internet Policy," *Knight Ridder Newspapers.* Posted in the *San Jose*

Mercury News, March 14, 2006. Retrieved June 28, 2006, from www.mercurynews.com/mld/mercurynews/news/world/14092424.htm.

8. J. C. Setzer, and L. Lewis, *Distance Education Courses for Public Elementary and Secondary School Students: 2002–2003* (NCES 2005-010). Washington, DC: U.S. Department of Education, National Center for Education Statistics, 2005.
9. U.S. Census Bureau, *Statistical Abstract of the United States: 2006,* 125th edition (Table 248). Washington, DC: U.S. Government Printing Office, 2006.
10. L. Pape, "High School on the WEB." *American School Board Journal, 192*(7) (2005), pp. 12–16.
11. Dan Smith, *The Penguin State of the World Atlas,* 7th edition. New York: Penguin, 2003, p. 96.
12. Ibid.
13. U.S. Census Bureau, 2006, Table 1150.
14. J. Cheeseman, A. Janus, and J. Davis, *Computer and Internet Use in the United States: 2003.* Washington DC: U.S. Census Bureau, 2005.
15. U.S. Census Bureau, 2006, Table 247.
16. Ibid.
17. U.S. Census Bureau, 2006, Table 244.
18. U.S. Census Bureau, *Statistical Abstract of the United States: 2004–2005,* 124th edition (Table 285). Washington, DC: U.S. Government Printing Office, 2005.
19. U.S. Census Bureau, 2006, Table 244.
20. L. Lessig, *The Future of Ideas: The Fate of the Commons in a Connected World.* New York: Random House, 2001.
21. U.S. Code, Title 17, Ch. 1, Sec. 107.
22. B. Parsad and J. Jones, *Internet Access in U.S. Public Schools and Classrooms: 1994–2003* (NCES 2005-015). Washington, DC: Department of Education, National Center for Education Statistics, 2005.
23. David J. Hoff, "Keeping Track," *Technology Counts 2006: The Information Edge: Using Data to Accelerate Achievement.* Bethesda, MD: *Education Week,* Editorial Projects in Education. 2006.

CHAPTER 14

1. Alvin Toffler, *Future Shock.* New York: Bantam, 1971, p. 460.
2. Association of Supervision and Curriculum Development, "The Definition of School Safety," *Safe Schools America, Inc.,* 2006, www.ascd.org.
3. Mike Kennedy, "Providing Safe Schools," *American School and University,* January 2004, Retrieved from http://asump.com/mag/university.
4. Lowell D. Rose and Alec M. Gallup, "The 34th Annual Phi Delta Kappa/Gallup Poll of the Public's Attitudes toward the Public School," *Phi Delta Kappan, 83* (September 2002), p. 52.
5. Mary Anne Raywid and Libby Oshiyamam, "Musing in the Wake of Columbine," *Phi Delta Kappan, 81* (February 2000), p. 449.
6. Alfie Kohn, "How Not to Teach Values: A Critical Look at Character Education," *Phi Delta Kappan, 78* (February 1997), pp. 428–439.
7. Robert Eaker, Echard Dufour, and Rebecca DuFour, *Getting Started: Restructuring Schools to Become Professional Learning Communities.* Bloomington, IN: National Educational Service, 2003, pp. 9–29.

Name Index

Abel, Donald C., 317
Abram, Percy, 473
Abrami, Philip C., 441
Adams, Henry, 325
Adams, John, 166, 253
Addams, Jane, 246
Alcuin, 235–236
Alexander, Herbert, 297
Alger, Horatio, 51
Ali, Russlynn, 357–358
Allen, Dwight, 284
Allen, Ulysses S., 265
Ambrose, Stephen, 293
Ames, Carole A., 336
Andreessen, Marc, 437
Aquinas, Thomas, 236
Aristotle, 233, 234, 305–306, 326
Arouet, François-Marie, 238–240
Asimov, Nanette, 357–358
Aurelius, Marcus, 462
Averroës, 236
Avicenna, 236
Axelrod, Saul, 340

Bachman, J. G., 92
Bagley, William, 283
Bahm, Archie J., 317
Baldaro, Aaron, 31
Banks, James A., 196, 285
Barksdale, Karen, 363
Barnard, Henry, 154, 245
Barr, Alfred, 283
Barr, Barbara, 447–448
Barton, Keith C., 290
Baskerville, Viola, 265
Beard, Joseph, 284
Beauvoir, Simone de, 118
Bedford, Clay P., 344
Bell, George, 253
Bergman, Justin, 265
Bergson, Henri, 317
Berliner, David C., 145
Berners-Lee, Tim, 437
Bestor, Arthur, 283
Bethune, Mary McLeod, 257
Biddle, Bruce J., 145
Bierce, Ambrose, 299
Binet, Alfred, 286
Bloom, Benjamin, 283, 285, 412, 413
Bolman, Lee G., 179
Bonhoeffer, Dietrich, 83
Borton, Terry, 10
Bowles, Samuel, 346
Bracey, Gerald W., 273
Bradley, Elizabeth, 239–240

Brameld, Theodore, 345–346
Brazil, N., 420
Brenna, Susan, 459–460
Brennan, William, 209
Bright, Carl, 274
Brodinsky, Ben, 287
Bruner, Jerome S., 275, 283, 285
Buber, Martin, 330–331
Buddha, 312
Buell, Nancy, 310–311
Buendia, Edward, 56
Bungert, Mary, 363–364
Burke, Garance, 431–432
Bursuck, William, 269
Bush, George W., 19, 155
Byngham, William, 279

Calhoun, Emily, 354, 428
Campbell, D. M., 354
Campbell, John Martin, 290
Canter, Lee, 341
Capella, Gladys, 290
Carlson, Richard, 354
Carter, Jimmy, 154
Carter, Robert T., 98
Chanowski, Jacob, 220
Charlemagne, 235, 236
Charters, W. W., 283
Chase, Mary Ellen, 331
Chavis, John, 253
Chinn, Philip C., 73
Chisolm, Shirley, 97
Chomsky, Noam, 283
Chu, Judy, 391
Cicero, Marcus, 234
Cignetti, P. B., 354
Clinton, Bill, 433
Cohen, Elizabeth G., 473
Comenius, Johann Amos, 238
Comte, Auguste, 325–326
Conant, James, 274
Confucius, 123, 232, 312
Coolidge, Calvin, 184
Counts, George, 283
Cousins, Norman, 346
Coyle, Kevin, 459
Crandall, Prudence, 253–254
Crawford, Charlotte, 310–311
Creighton, Mandell, 328
Cremin, Lawrence A., 263
Crichton, Michael, 333
Cromer, Alan H., 317
Cronbach, Lee, 283
Crosland, Kristin, 56
Cross, W. E., Jr., 98

Cuomo, Andrew, 32
Curwin, Richard, 342

Dahl, Shannon, 447–448
Daniel, Marie-France, 337
d'Apollonia, Sylvia, 441
Darwin, Charles, 190–191, 194
Davis, Wendy N., 189
Deal, Terrence E., 179
Descartes, René, 240–241
Dewey, John, 257, 283, 307, 308, 317, 327, 345
Dianda, Marcella, 383
Diaz, Humberto, 326
Dobson, James, 340
Dodge, Bernie, 443
Doris, John M., 320
Douglass, Frederick, 253
Doumbia, Fode, 56
Dowdy, Carol A., 428

Edelman, Marion Wright, 53
Edmonds, Ron, 143
Egol, Morton, 268
Ellis, Joseph, 293
Elson, William, 251
Emerson, George B., 246
Emery, Suzanne, 60–61
Erasmus, 237
Essex, Nathan L., 225
Estrin, Elise, 122

Fassett, James, 251
Feltre, Vittorino da, 237
Ferdman, B. M., 98
Ferraro, Geraldine A., 37
Fine, Michelle, 98
Finn, Chester E., Jr., 229
Flanders, Ned, 284
Flesch, Rudolph, 283
Flores-Gonzalez, Nilda, 103
Ford, A., 420
Ford, Henry, 472
Forster, Nancy, 140
Fountaine, Joshua, 75
Frank, Anne, 99
Franklin, Benjamin, 245–246, 260, 280–281
Franklin, Nicholas, 253
Fraser, Matthew, 216–217
Frederick the Great, 241
Friedenberg, Edgar, 286
Froebel, Friedrich, 242
Fullan, Michael, 479

Gallegos, P. I., 98
Gallup, Alec M., 8, 39
Gandhi, Mahatma, 462
Gardner, Howard, 380, 425–426
Gates, Bill, 435
Geismar, Kathryn, 290
Getzels, Jacob, 283
Gilbert, Susan, 319–320
Gintis, Herbert, 346
Giroux, Henry, 343
Gitlin, Andrew, 56
Glasser, William, 339–341
Glickman, Carl, 339
Goethe, Johann Wolfgang von, 58
Goldman, Emma, 302
Gollnick, Donna M., 73
Goodlad, John L., 17, 343
Gordon, Thomas, 340
Grabe, Cindy, 457
Grabe, Mark, 457
Grant, Carl A., 135
Greene, Maxine, 309, 344
Greenspun, Philip, 437
Gregory, Dick, 83
Grubman, Barbara Joan, 116–117
Guilford, J. P., 283

Haertel, E., 381
Hagen, Frank, 415
Hall, G. E., 463
Hall, Primus, 253
Hall, Samuel, 281
Hamilton, Edith, 175
Harmin, Merrill, 340
Harris, D., 145
Harris, Sarah, 253
Harris, Thomas, 340
Hartas, Dimitra, 225
Havighurst, Robert, 283, 284
Hehir, Thomas, 73
Helms, J. F., 98
Herbart, Johann Friedrich, 242, 246
Hernandez, Eva, 431
Hilliard, Asa, 122
Hobart, Nehemia, 247
Hoffer, Eric, 467
Holmes, Madelyn, 263
Holt, John, 286
Homme, Lloyd, 340
Hoover, Virginia, 33–34

Ibrahim, Ibrahim, 43
Ignatius of Loyola, 238
Ingersoll, Jane, 257
Irving, Barrie A., 225

Jackson, B. W., III, 98
Jacobson, Linda, 39
James, William, 327
Jefferson, Thomas, 184, 229
Johnson, Eric, 431
Johnson, Lyndon, 155, 197
Johnson, Tony W., 263
Johnston, L. D., 92
Jones-Lewis, Tennille, 363
Josephson, Michael, 293
Jovanovic, Jasna, 125
Joyce, B. R., 354
Joyce, Bruce, 428

Kandel, Isaac L., 345
Kant, Immanuel, 303
Kaplan, Bob, 33–34
Kelly, A. V., 428
Kennedy, John F., 96, 197
King, Martin Luther, Jr., 55, 347

King, R. A., 179
King, Sally Steinbach, 125
Kirst, M., 381
Klein, M. Francis, 393
Kneller, George, 297
Kohlberg, Lawrence, 300
Kohn, Alfie, 354, 389
Koplan, Rob, 409–410
Kor, Ah-Lian, 304
Kozol, Jonathan, 103, 286, 386
Krathwohl, David, 412–414
K'ung-Fu-tzu, 232–233

Ladson-Billings, G., 354
LaMorte, Michael W., 225
Langdon, Carol A., 9, 39
Lao-tszu, 232
Lardner, James, 73
Larerson, Marvin, 275
Larson, Doug, 445
Lazarus, Emma, 252
Lazear, Edward, 389
Leavitt, Grace, 162–163
LeBlanc, Martin, 459
LeComte, Sarah, 337
Lessow-Hurley, Judith, 420
Lester, Emile, 181
Leu, Deborah Diadiun, 457
Leu, Donald J., 457
Levin, Henry, 424
Lieberman, Myron, 361–362
Lincoln, Abraham, 254
Lindsay, Samuel M., 8
Lineberger, Kathy, 460
Lipman, Mathew, 337
Little Soldier, Lee, 313
Littleton, Scott C., 317
Liu, Jing-Qui, 112
Liverpool, Moses, 253
Locke, John, 238, 306, 323
Losen, Daniel, 91
Lotan, Rachel, 473
Lou, Yiping, 441
Louv, Richard, 459–460
Luke, Bettie Sing, 116–117
Luther, Martin, 237–238
Lycurgus, 233
Lyon, Mary, 256

MacKenzie, Robert J., 354
Maddox, Sheila, 139–140
Males, Mike A., 103
Malloy, Wendy, 105–106
Mann, Horace, 244, 281
Mark, Julia and Elias, 257
Marshall, Thurgood, 168–169
Martin, Jane Roland, 303, 354
Martinez, Juan, 459
Maslow, Abraham, 283
Mason, David, 218–219
McCabe, Donald, 294
McCord, Chris, 293
McCullough, David, 229
McCutcheon, Gail, 295
McGuffey, William Holmes, 250, 251
McKeon, Denise, 383
McLaren, Ann, 383
McLuhan, Marshall, 283
McTighe, Jay, 389
Mead, Margaret, 129
Melenyzer, B. J., 354
Mendler, Allen, 342
Mengelkoch, Louise, 317
Miller, D. C., 177
Millett, Kate, 62
Miner, Myrtilla, 253

Mohammed, 236
Mohl, John, 89–90
Montessori, Maria, 113, 256
Moody, Dorothy, 162–163
Morgan, Harry, 263
Morris, Jerome E., 82
Morris, Van Cleve, 322
Moyers, Bill, 52
Muhlenberg, Henry, 259
Muir, E., 31
Mukhtar, Habiba, 43

Najera, Alejandro, 432
Neau, Elias, 253
Negroni, Italia, 423
Nelson, Brenda, 363
Nelson, F. Howard, 31
Nelson-Barber, Sharon, 122
Nerburn, Kent, 317
Netterville, Claude, 28
Nettles, D. H., 354
Nicoleau, Guitele, 290
Nietzsche, Friedrich, 309, 338
Nishioka, Reiko, 333
Nixon, Richard, 197
Noddings, Nel, 10, 299, 331

O'Connell, Jack, 357
O'Connell, Suzanne, 140
O'Leary, George, 293
O'Malley, P. M., 92
Orfield, Gary, 91
Ovid, 247

Pai, Young, 322
Palmer, Barbara Smith, 475–476
Palmer, P. J., 479
Palmer, Parker, 317
Parkay, F. W., 399
Parker-Jenkins, Marie, 225
Partelow, L., 177
Patton, James E., 428
Peirce, Charles Sanders, 307, 327, 344
Pelton, Christine, 293
Perrone, Vito, 343
Pesis, Jeff, 435
Pestalozzi, Johann Heinrich, 241–242, 246
Peyronnet, Emmanuelle, 337
Piaget, Jean, 283, 286
Pickering, Marvin L., 208
Pitts, Lacey, 347–348
Plank, D., 145
Plato, 233, 234, 302–304
Plutarch, 233
Pollalschele, James, 415
Polloway, Edward, 428
Popham, W. James, 389
Powell, Brandese, 328
Powell, Lewis F., Jr., 168–169
Powell, Linda C., 98
Powell, Marjorie, 284
Putnam, Robert, 319
Pythagoras, 233

Quintilian, 234–235

Ralston, Kelly, 432
Randolph, A. Philip, 114
Raskin, Robin, 432
Rathbone, Charles H., 39
Raths, Louis, 340
Ravitch, Diane, 208, 283, 290, 343
Reed, Ronald F., 263
Reeve, Christopher, 65
Resnik, Lauren, 424
Rice, Rachael, 347–348

Richards, Jennifer Smith, 43–44
Rickover, Hyman, 283
Ritchie, Joy, 43
Rivera, Carla, 391–392
Roberts, Patrick S., 181
Robles, Darline P., 391
Roosevelt, Franklin Delano, 197, 257, 324
Rorty, Richard, 308
Rose, Lowell C., 8, 39
Rosenbaum, Noel, 218–219
Rousseau, Jean-Jacques, 241, 242, 329
Ruskin, John, 283
Russ, Cynthia, 475–476
Ryans, D. G., 283

Saavedra, Sherry, 139–140
Sacks, Peter, 389
Saffold, BilliJo, 277–278
Sage, Sara, 354
Sartre, Jean-Paul, 309
Sassone, Leslie, 317
Scapp, Ron, 479
Scarloss, Beth, 473
Schleifer, Michael, 337
Schmalz, Brandon, 293
Schoenbeit, Marian, 348
Schulenberg, J. E., 92
Schurz, Carl, 302
Scopes, John, 192, 193
Self, John, 304
Sen, A., 177
Serim, Ferdi, 447–448
Seybold, Robert F., 247
Sharp, Ann, 337
Shaw, George Bernard, 469
Sheive, Linda, 348
Shepard, Matthew, 75
Shultz, Susan F., 473
Silberman, Charles, 286
Simon, Sidney, 340
Simon, Syd, 300
Singnysane, Myra, 44
Sizer, Theodore, 324, 425
Skinner, B. F., 286, 324–325
Slavin, Robert E., 340, 424

Sleeter, Christine E., 135
Slifer, Jennifer, 89–90
Smith, David, 73
Smith, Tom E., 428
Socrates, 233–234, 303, 304
Solon, 233
Soltis, Jonas F., 354
Spiegel-Coleman, Shelly, 391
Spielberg, Steven, 333
Spring, Joel, 290
Stanford, B. H., 399
Stoddard, George, 283
Strike, Kenneth A., 354
Swanson, Christopher B., 91, 451
Sylvester, Elisha, 253
Symcox, Linda, 389
Szasz, Margaret Connell, 263

Tait, Ken, 304
Tanner, Daniel, 429
Tanner, Laurel, 429
Tatum, Beverly Daniel, 98
Terman, Lewis, 283
Thomas, Bobbi Aschwanden, 277–278
Toffler, Alvin, 464
Toledo, Eileen, 239–240
Torp, Linda, 354
Torrance, E. Paul, 283
Tower, David, 251
Trump, J. Lloyd, 283
Turiel, Elliot, 319–320
Turk, Jane, 202
Twain, Mark, 155
Tyler, Ralph W., 284

Ugarte, Nellie, 409–410
Ungricht, Margo, 363
Unz, Ron, 127

Van Vooren, Carol, 139–140
Veach, Regan, 431–432
Vesper, Nick, 9
Vodicka, Devin, 139
Voltaire, 240–241
Voltz, D., 420

Von Neumann, John, 453
Vygotsky, Lev, 284

Wald, Johanna, 91
Ward, Douglas, 60–61
Ward, William Arthur, 342
Warren, Earl, 197
Washington, Booker T., 254
Weaver, Reg, 3–4, 10
Web, L. Dean, 290
Webster, Noah, 250–251
Weil, M., 354
.Weil, Marsha, 428
Weis, Lois, 98
Weiss, Beverly J., 263
Weiss, Monica, 423
White, Edward, 221
Whitehead, Ada Allen, 265
Whitehead, Alfred North, 306, 317
Wiggins, Grant, 376, 377, 389
Wijeyesinghe, C. L., 98
Willard, Emma, 255–256
Williams, Barbara, 75
Williams, Nathaniel, 247
Williams, Paul, 214
Williams, T., 381
Witherell, William, 244
Witte, John F., 479
Wolfgang, Charles, 339
Wong, L. Mun, 98
Woodard, Ken, 44
Woolley, Theresa, 293
Wyman, R. M., Jr., 354

Xenophon, 233

Yava, Albert, 314
Yeats, William Butler, 276
Young, Ella Flagg, 257

Zehr, Mary Ann, 75
Zend, Robert, 296
Zirkel, Perry A., 225
Zuckerman, Mortimer B., 246

Subject Index

Ability grouping, 332, 417
Ableism, 99
Abstinence-only sex education policy, 239–240
Abstraction, 296–297, 298
Abuse, 85–86, 220
Academic achievement
  achievement gaps and, 155, 386, 406
  schools and, 110–111
Academic freedom
  book banning and censorship, 208–209
  defined, 207
  privacy rights and, 209–210
  of teachers, 200, 207–210
Accelerated Schools, 424, 428
Acceptance, encouraging attitude of, 105–106
Accountability, 380–387
  defined, 175, 358
  equity within, 386–387
  in financing education, 175–176, 177
  nature of, 175–176
  student achievement and, 465
Accreditation, 21–22
  of schools, 21–22
  of teacher education programs, 22
Acculturation, 49
Achieve, Inc., 360
Achievement gaps, 155, 386, 406
Active learning time (ALT), 415
Adaptation, change as, 345
Adequacy, in financing education, 166
Adequate yearly progress (AYP), 155, 156, 367
Adult education programs, 273–274
Advanced certification, 24
Advertising
  for the *New England Primer*, 249
  as source of school revenue, 171–172
Advisory role, of state boards of education, 150
Affective domain, 412–414
Affirmative action
  history of, 197
  legal basis for, 198
AFL-CIO, 470
African Americans
  computer access and, 449
  disproportionate placements in school and, 67–68
  dropping out and, 91
  early education programs for, 252–254, 257

equal educational opportunity and, 271
formation of racial identity, 98
postsecondary education and, 94–95
poverty among, 53–54
recognition of ethnic roots, 55
slavery and, 57, 242–243, 252, 257
in student and teacher populations, 16
in U.S. population, 56–57
violence and, 93–94
Afrocentric programs, 50, 122
After-school work, 95
Age of Pericles, 233
Age of Reason, 238–241
Aging population, 53–54, 80
Agostini v. Felton, 186, 188
Aguilar v. Felton, 186, 188
AIDS
  as disability, 199
  teenage sexuality and, 88
Aims
  defined, 408
  of education, 274–278
Alaskan Natives. *See* Native Americans
Alcohol use, 92–93
Alternative licensure, 35–36
AMD, 435
American Academy, 245–246, 280–281
American Association for Employment in Education, 36, 39
American Association of University Women (AAUW), 87, 103
American Bar Association, 225
American Educational Research Association (AERA), 383
American Educator (journal), 471
American Federation of Labor (AFL), 470
American Federation of Teachers (AFT), 205–207, 272, 469
American Indians. *See* Native Americans
American Journal of Education, 245
American Normal School Association, 470
American Psychological Association (APA), 331
American Sign Language (ASL), 59
American Spelling Book, 250–251
Americans with Disabilities Act (ADA), 225
Amidon, 283
Analysis of practice, 26
Analysis of teaching, 283–284
Analytic thinking, 296–298
  defined, 296
  logic, 297, 298

overview of, 298
Anti-Defamation League, 73, 135
Antiracist education, 132
Apple Classrooms of Tomorrow Project, 437
Apple I, 434–435
Application software, 436
Apprenticeships, teaching, 280
Arizona, property taxes for schools in, 170
ARPA-NET, 436
Asian Americans
  dropping out and, 91
  early education programs for, 254–255
  equal educational opportunity and, 271
  language diversity and, 126–129
  poverty among, 53–54
  in student and teacher populations, 16
  in U.S. population, 56–58
Assertive Discipline, 341–342
Assessment, 369–380. *See also* Account-ability; High-stakes assessment; Standard(s)
  authentic, 17, 27–29, 373–378
  defined, 359
  evolution of educational testing, 274
  global perspectives on, 385
  in licensure process, 23, 35
  nature of, 369–370
  objective forced-choice testing, 326
  performance, 19, 372–378
  philosophy of education and, 336
  professional aspects of, 378–380
  purposes for, 370–371
  standardized tests, 20, 23, 274, 357–358
  of teachers, 5
  teaching to the test, 20, 310–311, 382, 383–384
  technology in, 438–439
  traditional, 371–372
Assimilation
  defined, 49
  for English language learners (ELLs), 127–129
Assistant principals, 143–144
Association for Process Philosophy of Education (APPE), 317
Association for Supervision and Curricu-lum Development (ASCD), 471
Athenian education, 233–235
Athletic programs, student fees for, 171
Attestations, 27
Authentic assessment, 373–378

basing assessment on field of study, 375–376
context and, 374, 376
defined, 17
designing, 374
important elements in, 377–378
portfolios in, 27–29
questions in, 376–377, 378
reflective of instruction, 375
rubrics in, 369, 375, 377, 379, 457
standards in, 374
Authentic public space (Greene), 344
Automobile accidents, 94
Axiology
of idealism, 302
nature of, 296
of pragmatism, 306

Bake sales, 171
Bang Bang You're Dead, 75, 76
Bargaining rights, of teachers, 200, 205–207
Barre City Elementary and Middle School (Barre, Vermont), 347–348
BASIC, 434–435
Behavioral objectives, 411–412
Behavioral theory, 286
Behaviorism, 324–325, 334
defined, 324
focus of learning, 325
reinforcement, 325
Benchmarks, 365
Bethel School District No. 403 v. Fraser, 213, 216–217
Bidialectal, 59
Big ideas, 402
Bilingualism
bilingual education, 127–129, 418
need for student, 60–61
need for teacher, 15
Bits, 434
Blacks. *See* African Americans
Blackwell History of Education Museum and Research Collection, 263
Blogs, 438, 445
Bloom's Taxonomy, 285, 412, 413
Blue-Backed Speller, 250–251
Blue collar workers. *See* Working class
Board of Education, Island Trees Union Free District No. 26 v. Pico, 213
Board of Education of Kiryas Joel Village School District v. Grumet, 186, 187–188
Board of Education of Oklahoma City Public Schools v. Dowell, 195, 196
Board of Education of the Westside Community Schools v. Mergens, 191
Board of Regents of State Colleges v. Roth, 200, 205
Boards of education
local. *See* School boards
state, 150–152
BOCES (Boards of Cooperative Educational Services), 157
Book banning, 208–209
Boston Latin Grammar School, 247
Broad fields curriculum, 396
Brookside Elementary School (Nicholasville, Kentucky), 447–448
Brown v. Board of Education, 115, 194–195, 196, 229
Buckley Amendment, 209–210
Buddhists, 69
Building resource teachers, 474
Bullying, 75, 86–87
Bureau of Indian Affairs (BIA), 154

Burkey v. Marshall County Board of Education, 200
Busing, growth of, 267
Bytes, 434

California, reading standards, 356–357
Canada, social justice in schools, 132
Capstone/summative assessments, 372
Career development continuum, 468
Caring, 331
Carlsbad Unified School District (California), 139–140
Catechetical schools, 235
Catechumenal schools, 235
Categorical aid, 173, 174, 271
Cathedral (monastic) schools, 235
Catholics, 69
Cedarbrook Middle School (Wyncote, Pennsylvania), 89–90
Celebrationist historians, 227
Censorship
academic freedom and, 208–209
Internet filters in China, 443
Center for Educational Reform, 389
Center on Education Policy, 406
Centers for Disease Control (CDC), 199
Certification of teachers, 201–205
advanced, 24
state licensure, 22
Change
characteristics of, 462
educational, 462–463
paradigm, 358
teachers as change agents, 345–346
transformational, 462, 464–467
in the twenty-first century, 461–464
Change agents, 345–346, 474
Character Counts, 467
Character development, 467
Charter schools, 158, 467, 475–476
Chautauqua movement, 273
Cheating, 293–294, 383, 451–452
Chemical dependency, 92–93
Chief state school officers, 150–151
Child Abuse Prevention and Treatment Act (1974), 220
Child benefit theory, 188
Children
family life and, 77–79
poverty among, 53–54
Children's Defense Fund, 103
China
education in, 232–233
filtering of the Internet, 443
formal schools, 231
National College Entrance Examination, 385
philosophy of, 312
teaching Chinese to U.S. students, 17
Choice theory, 339–341
Church. *See also* Religion; Roman Catholic Church
education for African Americans and, 252
religion-affiliated schools, 159–161, 258, 259, 272
role of missionaries, 243, 252, 255
Citizenship, schools and, 109–110
Civil Rights Act (1964), 119, 195, 197–198, 205
Civil rights laws, 119
Civil rights movement, 257
Civil Rights Project, Harvard University, 91
Clark County School District (Las Vegas, Nevada), 32

Classroom(s). *See also* Instruction
authentic learning environments in, 464
classroom management and, 421
class size, 145
curriculum evaluation in, 405
curriculum implementation studies, 405
as dynamic centers of learning, 474
politics of, 164
technology use inside, 439–445
technology use outside, 437–439
Classroom climate, 343–344
defined, 343
space in, 344
voice in, 343–344
Classroom organization, 335–336
lesson planning, 335
physical setting, 335–336
student assessment and evaluation, 336
Class structure, 52–53. *See also* Socioeconomic status (SES)
Cleveland Board of Education v. LeFleur, 200
Coalition for Curriculum and Assessment (CCA), 389
Coalition of Essential Schools, 324, 425
Cocaine, 92
Cocurriculum, 397–398
Cognitive development theories, 286
Cognitive objectives, 412
Collaboration
professional learning communities, 472–473
among teachers, 468–469, 472–473
technology and, 438, 445
Colleges and universities
college preparation for all students, 277–278
colonial U.S., 244
early African American, 254, 257
early Spanish, 255
medieval universities, 236
postsecondary education of minorities, 94–95
state teachers colleges, 281–282
Colonial education, U.S., 242–244, 247–251, 278–279
Columbus, Ohio Public Schools, 43–44
Coming to Justice program, 99
Commission on Recognition of Secondary Education, *Cardinal Principles of Secondary Education*, 275
Commitments, professional, 25
Committee of Ten (NEA), 275
Common elementary schools, 244–245
Communication
email in, 438, 445
teacher–family, 128, 438
Community
community of inquiry (Peirce), 344
learning in groups, 473
professional learning communities, 472–473
promoting sense of, 420
Competition
equality in multicultural education versus, 118–120
schools and, 113, 467
Compulsory education, 245
Computers. *See* Technology
Concrete operations stage, 286
Confidential student information, 209–210

Conflict resolution, 342
Conflict theory, of schools, 108
Confucianism, 123, 312
Congress Middle School (Kansas City, Missouri), 277–278
Connecticut Common School Journal, 245
Connection, 299, 301
Constructivism, 331–333, 334
  curriculum, 331–332
    defined, 331
    problem-based learning, 332–333, 416–417
Consumers Union, 172
Content standards, 362–366, 375–376
Context
  in authentic assessment, 374, 376
  defined, 374
Continuing/adult education programs, 273–274
Continuing professional development, 37
Contract rights, of teachers, 200, 201–203
Control theory, 339–341
Cooperative learning, 417
Cooperative Research Program, 271
Coordinated service delivery, 466
Copyright, 452–453
Core curriculum, 396
Cornell Law School, 225
Corporal punishment, 217–219
Correspondence schools, 273, 283
Coteau-Bayou Blue School (Houma, Louisiana), 310–311
Council for American Private Education (CAPE), 159
Council for Exceptional Children, 73
Council of Chief State School Officers, 389
Council of the Great City Schools, 103
Course syllabi, 402
Criterion-referenced assessments, 372
Critical pedagogy, 329
Critical thinking
  educational critics, 286
  nature of, 129
Cultural choice, 50–51
Cultural relevance, 114, 120–123
  building on cultural context, 120–122
  centering cultures of students, 122
  teaching for social justice, 131–133
  validating student voices, 122–123
Cultural transmission, schools and, 111–112
Culture, 45–51. *See also* Multicultural education; Multicultural perspectives
  characteristics of, 46
  cultural relevance and, 114, 120–123
  defined, 45
  diversity, 45–51
  dominant, 47
  group identity and, 47–48
  religion and, 69–70
Curriculum. *See also* Curriculum development
  constructivist, 331–332
  defined, 393
  elements of, 392
  essentialist, 323–324
  evaluation of, 405–407
  global perspectives on, 401
  growth and changes in, 268
  hidden, 408–410
  humanistic, 330
  management of, 403–405
  selection of, 398–403
  standards for, 165, 397, 402

Curriculum development, 393–407. *See also* Curriculum
  cocurriculum, 397–398
  curriculum, defined, 393
  designs for, 396–397
  extra-curriculum, 397–398
  perspective and, 394
  questions in, 394–397
  resources and, 400–403
  steps in, 394, 395
Curriculum guides, 402
Curriculum specialists, 404

Dame schools, 244
Dark Ages, 235–236
Dartmouth College, 258–259
De facto segregation, 194
De jure segregation, 193
Del Oro High School (Loomis, California), 171
Democracy
  democratic schools, 130–131
  progressivism and, 328–329
  purposes of education in, 276
Department heads, 144
Departments of education, state, 151–152
Desegregation
  defined, 193
  release from court orders, 195–196
Diagnostic assessment, 370–371
Dialectic, change as, 346
Dialects, language diversity and, 59
Digital divide, 449–450
Direct instruction, 326–327, 415, 416
Dirksen Congressional Center, 225
Disability. *See also* Students with disabilities
  defined, 65
Disaggregated test scores, 155
Discernment, 299, 301
Discipline, 338–343
  Assertive Discipline, 341–342
  conflict resolution, 342
  Discipline with Dignity, 342
  in early elementary education, 245
  peer mediation, 342
  rules for, 342–343
  teacher behavior continuum and, 339, 340
Discipline-based standards, 362–366, 375–376
Discretionary duties, of school boards, 148
Discrimination, 97, 119
  against Asian Americans, 254–255
  based on sexual orientation, 65
  defined, 49, 197
  employment, 65
  peer sexual harassment, 222
  reverse, 198
  sex, 64, 197, 198, 218–219
  social justice versus, 132–133
  teachers' rights and, 200, 205
Disease
  AIDS, 88, 199
  homelessness and, 84–85
Dispositions, 18, 25, 365
Distance education
  correspondence courses, 273, 283
  defined, 445
  technology and, 445–446
Divergent thinking, progressivism and, 328
Diversity in society, 43–70. *See also* Multicultural education; Multicultural perspectives

acceptance of diverse groups, 48–51, 420
  community type and, 80–83
  cultural, 45–51
  diversity, defined, 44–45
  early education programs, 251–257
  exceptionalities, 65–68
  gender, 62–64, 124–126
  integration, 196–197
  language, 43–44, 58–61, 126–129
  No Child Left Behind (NCLB) and, 45
  racial and ethnic, 54–58
  religion, 68–70
  schools in teaching of tolerance, 116–117
  sexual orientation, 64–65
  socioeconomic status (SES), 44–45, 51–54
  teacher, 15–17
  as tenet of multicultural education, 115
Domestic violence, 85–86
Dominant culture, 47
Dress codes, 217
Dropout rates, 287
Dropping out, 90–91
Due process, 199, 215–217
  procedural, 199, 215–216
  student rights to, 215
  substantive, 199, 215, 216–217
  teacher rights to, 202

Eastern ways of knowing, 309–313
  Chinese thought, 312
  educational implications of, 313
  Indian thought, 312
  Japanese thought, 312–313
  non-Western education and, 231
Economic Opportunity Act (1964), 273–274
Edgewood Independent School District (San Antonio), 159
Edison School Corporation, 467
Educational Leadership, 428
Educational malpractice, 210–211
Educational Testing Service (ETS), 23, 274
Educational Theory, 353
Education Amendments Act (1972), Title IX, 64, 197, 198, 218–219
"Education for All American Youth" (NEA), 276
Education for All Handicapped Children Act (EAHCA), 198–199, 221–222, 270, 287
Education International (EI), 472, 479
Education Trust, 389
Education Week (newspaper), 179, 457
Edwards v. Aguillard, 190, 191, 193
Effective teaching, 121, 284
Egypt, education in, 233
Eighth Amendment, 217–218
Eight-Year Study (1932–1940; Progressive Education Association), 268, 275
Elderly
  aging population, 80
  poverty among, 53–54
Elementary and Secondary Education Act (ESEA; 1965), 19, 155, 166, 188, 271
Elementary schools
  academic freedom for teachers, 208
  distribution of expenditures for, 172
  European influences on U.S., 246
  universal elementary education, 244–245
Eleventh Amendment, 199

Email, 438, 445
Emergence of Common Man, 241–242
Émile (Rousseau), 241
Emotionally disabled label, 67
Employment
    adolescent, 94–95
    children alone and, 78–79
    continuing/adult education and, 273–274
    discrimination based on sexual orientation, 65
    in information technology, 449, 450
    teachers' rights in, 200, 201–210
    teaching job websites, 485–486
    workforce readiness purpose of schools and, 110
Empowerment, by teachers, 349
Enabling laws, 183
Enculturation, 46
Encyclopedias, 442–443
English as a second language (ESL)
    extent of teaching, 43–44
    need for bilingual teachers, 15
    newcomer programs and, 127–128
    programs in white schools, 56
    sheltered instruction and, 127–128
English Classical School, 246
English High School, 246
English language learners (ELLs)
    bilingualism and, 15, 60–61, 127–129, 418
    communicating with parents of, 128
    in curriculum selection, 399–400
    defined, 399
    guidelines for teaching English, 391–392
    student voice and, 123
    teaching strategies for, 127–129, 418–420
"English only" laws, 97
English Society for the Propagation of the Gospel in Foreign Parts, 243
Enrollment growth, 266
Epistemology
    of idealism, 302
    nature of, 295–296
    of pragmatism, 306
Epperson v. Arkansas, 193
Equal educational opportunity
    defined, 119
    as right of students, 214
    in school athletics, 64
    state responsibility for, 170–171
    struggle for, 271
Equality. *See also* Equity
    in access to technology, 444, 446–450
    as tenet of multicultural education, 118–120
Equal opportunity, 64, 197–199, 214. *See also* Equal educational opportunity
Equal Protection Clause, 197
Equity
    within accountability, 386–387
    defined, 114
    equality as tenet of multicultural education, 118–120
    equality in access to technology, 444, 446–450
    in financing education, 166, 168
    gender, 125
    modeling in the classroom, 129–130
    in multicultural education, 114
Essay Concerning Human Understanding (Locke), 238
Essentialism, 323–324, 334
    curriculum, 323–324

defined, 323
    Essential Schools movement, 324
    focus of learning, 323
Establishment clause, 185, 188, 189, 193, 194
Ethical codes, 25, 483–484
Ethnicity. *See also* Multicultural perspectives; Race and ethnicity
    ethnic groups, defined, 51
    as form of identity, 46
    nature of, 55–58
    of student and teacher populations, 16
Ethnocentrism, 96
Eugene, Oregon schools, 116–117
European Americans
    computer access and, 449
    dropping out and, 91
    formation of racial identity, 98
    poverty among, 53–54
    rural communities and, 80–81
    in student and teacher populations, 16
    suicide and, 94
    in U.S. population, 56–57
Everson v. Board of Education, 186–187, 188
Evolution, intelligent design versus, 190–193
Exceptionalities, 65–68. *See also* English language learners (ELLs); Students with disabilities
Existentialism, 308–309
    educational implications, 308–309
    humanism and, 329
    philosophers, 309
    in student-centered locus-of-control philosophies, 322
Experimentation, progressivism and, 328
Extracurricular activities
    extra-curriculum, 397–398
    liability insurance for, 212
    student fees for, 171

Face-to-face classroom meetings, 445
Fairmont Elementary School (St. Louis), 82
Fairness. *See also* Equity
    in assessment process, 379
Fair use guidelines, 453
Families, 77–79
    children alone, 78–79
    nature of, 77
    parenting and, 77–78
    socioeconomic status of. *See* Socioeconomic status (SES)
Family Educational Rights and Privacy Act (FERPA), 209–210
Fastback booklets, 471
Federal government. *See also* No Child Left Behind Act (NCLB)
    aid to education, 167, 174, 271
    in curriculum evaluation, 407
    in development of teaching profession, 270–272
    educational programs of, 154–155
    role in education, 152–157
Federalism
    defined, 152–153
    local control versus, 164–166
Feminist Majority, 73
Fields of study
    basing assessment on, 362–366, 375–376
    out-of-field teacher assignments, 15
    relative demand by, 14
Financing education, 166–177. *See also* Organization of education

accountability and, 175–176, 177
    early challenges of, 245
    educational spending and, 172–174
    entrepreneurial efforts in, 171–172
    federal aid, 167, 174, 271
    growth of school budgets, 268
    local property taxes in, 167–169, 170, 176
    state aid in, 169–171, 172–174, 185–187
First Amendment, U.S. Constitution, 184–185, 187, 188–189, 208, 216–217
Forest of Virtues, 467
Formative assessment, 370
Foundation for Critical Thinking, 354
Foundation programs, 173–174
Fourteenth Amendment, U.S. Constitution, 170, 185, 194, 208
Fourth Amendment, 222
Franklin v. Guinneth County Schools, 219
Free appropriate education (FAPE), 198–199, 221
Freeman v. Pitts, 195–196
Free speech
    First Amendment and, 184–185, 187, 188–189, 208, 216–217
    nature of, 185
    students' rights to, 216–217, 220–221
Frequently asked questions (FAQs), 438
Functionalist perspective, on schools, 108
Funderstanding, 353
Fund-raising efforts, 171–172
Future of education, 459–477
    accountability, 465
    change in profession of education, 468–472, 474
    change in the twenty-first century, 461–464
    character development, 467
    competition among schools, 467
    coordinated service delivery, 466
    futurism and transformational trends, 464–467
    safe schools, 465–466
    schools of twenty-first century, 472–476
    standards in, 368–369
    technology in, 453–454
Futurism, 464–467

Gambling, 169, 171
Gangs, 94
Gatekeeping, assessment and, 371
Gay, Lesbian, and Straight Education Network (GLSEN), 65, 73
Gender
    diversity based on, 62–64, 124–126
    as form of identity, 46
    graduation rates by, 91
    inclusion and, 66–67
    in multicultural education, 124–126
    parenting and, 77–78
    sex discrimination and, 64, 197, 198, 218–219
    sexism and, 99
    sexuality and, 87–88
    substance use and, 93
    Title IX and, 64, 197, 198, 218–219
General aid, 172–174
General Educational Development (GED) credential, 88
Generalists, 404
Generalization, 297, 298

Germany
  curricula in, 401
  religious instruction in schools, 206
GI Bill (1944), 270–271, 287
GI Bill (1966), 270–271
Gifted and talented programs, disproportionate placements in, 67
Giga-bytes (GB), 435
Global perspectives
  on assessment, 385
  cognitive development and, 286
  Coming to Justice program, 99
  on curriculum evaluation, 407
  on curriculum selection, 401
  on eastern ways of knowing, 313
  Education International (EI), 472, 479
  European influences on U.S.
    education, 246
  European origins of teacher training,
    279
  expenditures per student, 176, 177
  legal aspects of education in other
    countries, 206
  origins of educational ideas, 232
  political participation of women, 63
  social justice in Canada, 132
  teaching Chinese to U.S. students, 17
  on technology, 443, 449, 453
  on values, 113
  world as classroom, 350
Goals, defined, 408
God's Country, 75
Goss v. Lopez, 213, 215–216
Grades, rewarding with money and
  prizes, 363–364
Graduation rates, 90–91
Grand Rapids School District v. Ball,
  186, 188
Grant High School (Los Angeles),
  116–117
Gratz v. Bollinger, 197
Greece, education in, 233–235
Greely High School (Cumberland,
  Maine), 162–163
*Griffin v. County School Board of Prince
  Edward County*, 196
Grooming, student, 217
Group identity, 47–48
Grutter v. Bollinger, 197

Hall's Innovation Category Scale (HIC),
  463
Handheld devices, 431–432
Harassment, 75, 86–87
Hardware, 434–435
  defined, 434
  processing, 435
  storage, 435
Harvard College, 244
Harvard University, 274
Hazelwood School District v. Kuhlmeier,
  213, 221
Hebrew education, 231–232
*Helena Elementary School District v.
  State*, 170
Herbartian teaching method, 242
Heterogeneous grouping, 332, 417
Hidden curriculum, 110, 408–410
Higher Education Amendments (1972),
  Title IX, 64
Highly qualified teachers (HQT), 155,
  386–387
High schools
  in Coalition of Essential Schools, 324,
    425
  origins of, 246

school reform models for, 425
High-stakes assessment, 382–386
  cheating and, 293–294, 383
  defined, 382
  one-size-fits-all, 384
  preparing for, 382
  teacher burdens and, 386
  teaching to the test, 20, 310–311, 382,
    383–384
  threat of national exam, 384–386
Hindu education, 231
Hispanic Americans. *See* Latinos
Historical interpretation, 230
Historical perspectives, 227–290
  beginnings of education (to 476 CE),
    231–235
  changing aims of education,
    274–278
  development of teaching profession,
    270–274
  early education for diverse
    populations, 251–257
  educational awakening (1700),
    238–242
  evolution of U.S. education, 242–251
  growth of schools, 266–270
  key dates in Western education,
    487–490
  Middle Ages (476–1300), 235–236
  private education, 258–260
  recent trends, 283–287
  teacher preparation, 278–282
  transitional period (1300–1700),
    236–238
History of Education (journal), 263
Holmes v. Bush, 189
Holocaust, *Coming to Justice* program,
  99
Homelessness, 84–85, 103, 214
Home schooling, 272–273
  school choice and, 161
  values and, 112–113
Homework
  students with disabilities and, 269–270
  that requires technology access, 444
Homogeneous grouping, 332, 417
Homophobia, 65, 75, 86–87
Honig v. Doe, 213, 221
Hope, 300, 301
Hopi thought, 314
Hornbook, 247–248
*Hortonville Joint School District No. 1 v.
  Hortonville Education Association*,
  200, 207
Housing
  discrimination based on sexual
    orientation, 65
  shortage of, 84
Humanism, 236, 329–331, 334
  curriculum, 330
  defined, 329
  school environments, 330–331
Hypocrisy, tracking, 299–300, 301

IBM, 434–435
Idealism, 302–303
  educational implications, 302
  philosophers, 302–303
  realism versus, 305
  relationship to realism and
    pragmatism, 307
  in teacher-centered locus-of-control
    philosophies, 322
Illinois Mathematics and Science
  Academy Center, 353–354
Imaginative thinking, 297, 298

Immersion language programs, 128–129,
  418, 419
Immigration
  Asian, 254–255
  composition of U.S. population and,
    57–58
  language diversity and, 58–59,
    126–129
  religion and, 69–70
  rights of illegal alien students, 214
Incentive programs, 172
Inclusion, 66–67, 68
Inclusive curriculum, 122
Income, gender differences in, 63
Income taxes, 169
Indentured servitude, 243, 279–280
Independent School District v. Falvo, 210
Independent schools, school choice and,
  159–161
India
  Hindu education, 231
  Montessori education in, 113
  philosophy of, 312
Indirect instruction, 415–417
Individualism
  in existentialism, 309
  schools and, 113
Individualized education plans (IEPs),
  66–67, 68, 199, 371
Individuals with Disabilities Education
  Act (IDEA), 188, 199
Induction programs, teacher, 10–11
Infant mortality rates, 83
Informal note-taking, by teachers, 26
Information Age, 6
Information resources, technology and
  access to, 441–443
Information technology. *See also*
  Technology
  defined, 433
Ingraham v. Wright, 213, 217–218
In loco parentis, 215
Input statements, 410–411
Inquiry lessons, 416
Institute for Education Sciences (IES),
  418
Institute for Learning (IFL), 424
Institute for Learning Technologies, 479
Institutes of Oratory (Quintilian),
  234–235
Institutional discrimination, based on
  sexual orientation, 65
Instruction, 407–426
  kinds of instructional objectives,
    411–415
  models for school reform, 422–426
  nature of, 392–393
  objectives for student learning,
    408–411
  teaching strategies, 415–421
Integration
  achieving, 196–197
  defined, 194
  growth of busing, 267
Intel, 435
Interactionists, 339, 340
Inter-American Development Bank, 385
Intercultural Service Bureau, 115
Interest groups, in curriculum selection,
  398
Intermediate units, 157
International Baccalaureate (IB),
  140, 425
International Education Act (1966), 271
International Society for Technology in
  Education (ISTE), 433, 457

Internet, 436–437. *See also* World Wide Web
 distance education and, 445–446
 filtering of content in China, 443
 homework requiring access to, 444
 search engines, 442, 443
 socioeconomic status and access to, 449–450
 Web browsers, 436, 437
Internet Explorer, 436, 437
Interstate New Teacher Assessment and Support Consortium (INTASC), 22–23, 366
Interventionists, 339, 340
Iron Hill School, 263
Isolation, of lesbian, gay, bisexual, or transgender (LGBT) populations, 65
I–Thou relationships, 330–331

Japan, philosophy of, 312–313
Jehue Middle School (Rialto, California), 162–163
Jews, 69
 Hebrew education, 231–232
Job Search Handbook for Educators, 36
John Witherspoon Middle School (Princeton, New Jersey), 447–448
Jossey-Bass Reader on Gender in Education, 73
Journal writing
 reflective, 26
 systematic observation and, 26
 by teachers, 26
Judicial interpretive process, 183–184
Junior high school/middle school, origins of, 246

Kentucky Education Reform Act (KERA), 166, 170
Kindergarten, origins of, 242
Kiryas Joel v. Grumet, 186, 187–188
Kitzmiller v. Dover Area School District, 193
Knowledge, professional, 17–18
Korean War, 270–271

Labeling
 ability grouping and, 332
 of students with disabilities, 65–66, 67
Lakota thought, 314
Lamb's Chapel v. Center Moriches Union Free School District, 191
Language
 assimilation based on, 49
 bilingualism and, 15, 60–61, 127–129, 418
 communicating with parents of English language learners (ELLs), 128
 dialectical diversity, 59
 diversity of, 43–44, 58–61, 126–129
 "English only" laws, 97
 inclusion and, 66–67
 in multicultural education, 126–129
 teaching Chinese to U.S. students, 17
Laramie Project, The, 75
Latin grammar schools
 in colonies of U.S., 244, 247
 origins of, 234
Latinos
 computer access and, 449
 disproportionate placements in school and, 67
 dropping out and, 91
 early education programs, 255

equal educational opportunity and, 271
 formation of racial identity, 98
 postsecondary education and, 94–95
 poverty among, 53–54
 recognition of ethnic roots, 55
 in student and teacher populations, 16
 suicide and, 94
 in U.S. population, 56–57
 violence and, 93–94
Leadership
 at federal level, 153–154
 by school boards, 148
 at state level, 149–152
 by superintendent of schools, 148
 by teachers, 346–350, 468, 474
Learning focus, 344–345
 in behaviorism, 325
 in essentialism, 323
 in positivism, 326
Learning process, 284–285
Lee v. Weisman, 191
Legal perspectives, 181–223
 bases of, 182
 church and state, 181, 185–194
 copyright, 452–453
 education in other countries, 206
 equal opportunity, 64, 197–199, 214
 legal aspects of education, 183–185
 plagiarism, 293–294, 451–452
 religion and, 181, 185–194
 reporting requirements for abuse, 86, 220
 rights of students with disabilities, 198–199, 221–222
 segregation and desegregation, 193–197, 265
 students' rights and responsibilities, 212–223
 on taxation, 168–169
 teachers' rights and responsibilities, 199–212
 U.S. Constitution and education, 184–185
Legislatures, state, 152, 153
Lemon v. Kurtzman, 186, 187–188
Leonard and Gertrude (Pestalozzi), 241–242
Lesbian, gay, bisexual, or transgender (LGBT) populations, 64–65
Lesson planning
 in classroom organization, 335
 technology in, 439, 457
Lewiston High School (Lewiston, Maine), 239–240
Liability
 defined, 210
 government immunity from, 211
 insurance for, 212
 teacher, 210–212
Liberal Education of Boys, The (Erasmus), 237
Liberal historians, 227
Library of Congress Catalog, 225
Licensure, 22–23, 35–36, 201–205
 alternative, 35–36
 Interstate New Teacher Assessment and Support Consortium (INTASC), 22–23, 366
 praxis in, 23
 renewal of licenses, 37
 state teacher certification, 22
 tests for, 23, 35
Lincoln Elementary School (Atlanta), 82
Lincoln School (Brookline, Massachusetts), 310–311

Line relationships, 142
 school district, 149
 in schools, 146
 state education system, 151
Local Area Networks (LANs), 436
Local control
 defined, 164
 federalism versus, 164–166
 property tax funding of education and, 167–169, 170
Locker searches, 222
Locus of control. *See* Student-centered locus-of-control philosophies; Teacher-centered locus-of-control philosophies
Logic, 297, 298
Loneliness, of lesbian, gay, bisexual, or transgender (LGBT) populations, 65
Lotteries, 169, 171
Lutheran schools, 259

Magnet schools, 139–140, 157–158
Managerial workers, 52
Mandatory duties, of school boards, 148
Manpower Development and Training Act (1963), 271
Marijuana, 92
Marvin Ward Elementary School (Winston-Salem, North Carolina), 460
Massachusetts
 common elementary schools, 244–245
 early school laws, 243–244
Master teachers, 468, 474
Mastery curriculum, 396
McGuffey Readers, The, 250, 251
McKinney-Vento Homeless Assistance Act (1987), 85
Medieval universities, 236
Mentally retarded label, 67
Mentoring, teacher, 11
Meritocracy, 118–119
Metaphysics
 of idealism, 302
 nature of, 295
 of pragmatism, 306
Mexican Americans, 57. *See also* Latinos
Middle Ages, education in, 235–236
Middle class, 52, 83
 dropping out and, 91
 shrinking of, 119
Middle Colonies, U.S., 243
Middle school/junior high school, origins of, 246
Midwest Philosophy of Education Society (MPES), 317
Mira Mesa High School (San Diego), 60–61
Missionaries, 243, 252, 255
Missouri Synod Lutheran Church, 259
Model-centered instruction, 417
Modeling, by teachers, 349
Monitorial schools, 244
Montessori education, 113, 256, 283
Montwood High School (El Paso, Texas), 409–410
Morals education, 300, 319–320
Mormons, 69
Motivation, 336–338
 defined, 336
 rewarding grades with money and prizes, 363–364
Mozert v. Hawkins County Public Schools, 191
Mozilla Firefox, 436, 437

Multicultural education, 114–123. *See also* Multicultural perspectives
    challenges of, 123–129
    cultural relevance and, 114, 120–123
    defined, 114
    democratic schools and, 130–131
    equity and, 114, 129–130
    knowledge of history and, 285
    teachers as social activists, 129–133
    tenets of, 114–120, 129–133
Multicultural Pavilion, 135
Multicultural perspectives, 105–133. *See also* Diversity in society; Multicultural education
    acceptance and, 105–106
    multicultural education and, 114–133
    purposes of schools and, 109–112
    roles of schools and, 107–109
Multicultural Perspectives (magazine), 135
Multiple assessments, 380
Multiple intelligences (MI), 425–426
Muslims, 69

National Assessment of Educational Progress (NAEP), 357, 384–386, 389, 406, 407
National Association for Bilingual Education (NABE), 73
National Association for Multicultural Education, 135
National Association for the Education of Young Children (NAEYC), 135
National Association of Independent Schools (NAIS), 159
National Association of School Superintendents, 470
National Association of State Boards of Education, 179
National Association of State Directors of Teacher Education and Certification, 39
National Board for Professional Teaching Standards (NBPTS), 10, 24, 39, 366
National Center for Children in Poverty, 81
National Center for Education Statistics (NCES), 154, 179, 389
National Clearinghouse for English Language Acquisition, 418, 428
National Clearinghouse on Child Abuse and Neglect, 103
National Coalition for the Homeless, 103
National Commission on Teaching and America's Future, 15
National Conference of Community and Justice, 103
National Council for Accreditation of Teacher Education (NCATE), 22, 39, 366, 470
National Council of State Legislatures, 179
National Council of Teachers of Mathematics (NCTM), 365, 389, 403, 405
National Defense Education Act (NDEA; 1958), 268, 271
National Educational Technological Goals, 361–362
National Educational Technology Standards for Teachers (NETS-T), 433–434
National Education Association (NEA), 159, 225, 257, 272, 469–470
    bargaining rights of teachers and, 205–207
    Committee of Ten, 275

Educational Policies Commission, 276–278
    "Education for All American Youth," 276
    ethical codes, 25, 483–484
National Indian Education Association, 73
National Law Center on Homelessness and Poverty, 84
National origin, 55
National Science Foundation (NSF), 271
National Teacher Corps, 271
National Teachers' Association (NTA), 470
Nation at Risk, A, 108, 153, 286
Native Americans
    Bureau of Indian Affairs (BIA) and, 154
    computer access and, 449
    disproportionate placements in school and, 67–68
    dropping out and, 91
    equal educational opportunity and, 271
    Native North American ways of knowing, 313–315
    recognition of ethnic roots, 55
    rural communities and, 80–81
    in student and teacher populations, 16
    in U.S. population, 56–57
    violence and, 93–94
Native-centric programs, 50
Naturalism, 241
Nature, access to, 459–460
Navajo thought, 314
NEA Today (newsletter), 470
Neglect, 86, 220
Negligence
    defined, 210
    teacher, 211
Netscape Navigator, 436, 437
Networks, 436
Newark Memorial High School (California), 75
Newcomer programs, 127–128
New England Primer, 248–250, 251
New Jersey v. T.L.O., 213
News from the Stars Almanac, 248
New teachers
    becoming tenured, 202
    characteristics of, 11–12
    induction programs for, 10–11
    licensure and support for, 22–23, 35–36, 201–205
    location of school district and, 14
    recruitment incentives, 32, 33–34
    salaries and, 29–31
    searching for positions, 36
    standards for, 20, 22–23, 366
New York
    monitorial schools, 244
    school choice ventures, 467
Nineteenth Amendment, 257
No Child Left Behind Act (NCLB), 406, 407
    accountability and, 175–176, 380, 386–387
    adequate yearly progress (AYP), 155, 156, 367
    child benefit theory, 188
    diversity and, 45
    English proficiency requirement, 127
    federal government role in education and, 152, 154, 155–157, 164–166, 271–272
    highly qualified teachers (HQT), 155

    impact of, 156–157
    nature of, 19–20
    retention in grade and, 89–90
    schools in need of improvement (SINOI), 156
    standards and, 367
    teacher assignments out of field, 15
    teaching English language learners and, 418
Noncore subjects, student fees for, 171
Noninterventionists, 339, 340
Non-Western education, 231–233
Normal schools, 281
Norm-referenced assessments, 371–372
North Central Association of Schools and Colleges (NCA), 21
Northern Colonies, U.S., 243
North Haven Board of Education v. Bell, 200
Northwest Evaluation Association (NWEA), 438
Nuclear family, 78

Objective forced-choice testing, 326
Objectives
    behavioral, 411–412
    defined, 408
    hidden curriculum, 408–410
    instructional, 408–415
Observation, by teachers, 26
Office of Civil Rights, 154, 222
Office of Special Education and Rehabilitative Services, 154
Old Deluder Satan Act, 243–244
One-size-fits-all assessment, 384
Open adoption policy, 404
Operating system (OS) software, 436
Opportunity-to-learn standards, 366–367
Orbis Pictus (Comenius), 238
Organization charts
    defined, 146
    school, 146
    school district, 149
    state education system, 151
Organization for Economic Cooperation and Development (OECD), 176, 177, 179
Organization of education, 139–166. *See also* Financing education
    federal government and, 152–157
    line relationships, 142
    organization charts in, 146, 149, 151
    policy-to-practice continuum, 141–142
    politics and, 161–166
    school-based personnel, 143–147
    school choice and, 112–113, 139–140, 157–161, 189, 272–273, 467
    school district in, 147–149, 161–162
    staff relationships, 142
    at state level, 149–152
    typical design of schools, 142–143
Origin of the Species, The (Darwin), 190–191, 194
"Others," 96–97
Outlines of Educational Doctrine (Herbart), 242
Output statements, 410–411
Owens v. Colorado Congress of Parents, Teachers, and Students, 189
Oxy Contin, 92–93

Pablo Avila Junior High School (Camuy, Puerto Rico), 239–240
Palm Inc., 431–432
Panethnic membership, 54–55
    composition of U.S. population, 56–58

of student and teaching populations, 16
Paradigm change, 358
Parents
  booster groups, 171
  communicating with parents of English language learners (ELLs), 128
  family characteristics and, 77–79
  lack of involvement of, 476
  school involvement of, 82
  teacher–family communication, 128, 438
  values of, 112–113
Parochial schools, 159–161, 258, 259, 272
Paths of Learning Resource Center, 479
Patriotism, teaching, 229
PBS, 457
Peer mediation, 342
Perennialism, 334
Performance assessment, 19, 372–378
  authentic, 17, 27–29, 373–378
  performance, defined, 373
Performance-based licensing, 22
Peripherals, 434
Perry v. Sindermann, 200, 205
Persons of color. See also Ethnicity; Race and ethnicity; specific racial and ethnic groups
  poverty among, 53–54
Phi Delta Kappa/Gallup Poll, 7, 8, 92
Phi Delta Kappa International, 471, 479
Phi Delta Kappan (newsletter), 471
Philosophical perspectives, 291–354. See also Reflective approach
  applying philosophy of education beyond classroom, 345–350
  branches of philosophy, 295–296
  developing personal philosophy of education, 333–345
  relationship between philosophy and education, 321–322
  schools of philosophy, 302–315
  student-centered locus-of-control theories, 322, 327–333, 334
  teacher-centered locus-of-control theories, 322–327, 334
  teacher integrity and, 293–294
  thinking as a philosopher, 296–301
Philosophy Documentation Center (PDC), 317
Physical abuse, 86
Pickering v. Board of Education, 200, 208
Plagiarism, 293–294, 451–452
Plessy v. Ferguson, 194, 196
Pluralism, 49–50
Plyler v. Doe, 213
Podcasts, 438, 445
Police Department of the City of Chicago v. Mosley, 191
Policy-to-practice continuum, 141–142
Political action committees (PACs), 471
Politics in education, 161–166
Portfolios
  defined, 27
  in reflective approach, 27–29
  in teacher licensure process, 22–23
Positivism, 325–327, 334
  defined, 326
  direct instruction, 326–327, 415, 416
  focus of learning, 326
  objective forced-choice testing, 326
Postmodernist historians, 227
Poverty, 53–54
  extent of, 53–54

families and, 77
gap between wealth and, 119
homelessness and, 84–85, 103, 214
rural communities and, 80
in suburban communities, 81
teenage pregnancy and, 88
Title I teachers in religious schools, 188
urban communities and, 82–83
violence and, 94
Power, 95–99
  discrimination, 97
  ethnocentrism, 96
  motivation and, 338
  nature of, 95–96
  prejudice, 76, 96–97
  racism, 97
Power standards, curriculum and, 402
Pragmatism, 306–308
  educational implications, 306–307
  philosophers, 307–308
  progressivism and, 327
  relationship to realism and idealism, 307
  in student-centered locus-of-control philosophies, 322
Praxis Series (Educational Testing Service), 23
Prayer in school, 189–190, 192
Pregnancy, teenage, 88
Prejudice, 76, 96–97
Preoperational stage, 286
Princeton University, 274
Principals
  accountability and, 176
  role of, 143
Privacy
  student and locker searches, 222
  of student records, 209–210
Private schools, 258–260
  continued importance of, 272
  number of, 161
  parochial schools, 159–161, 258, 259, 272
  religious sponsorship, 185–186
  right to exist, 258–259
  role of, 259–260, 272
  school choice and, 159–161
  in urban areas, 83
  values and, 112–113
Privatization of schools, 467
Probationary period, 202
Problem-based curriculum, 396
Problem-based learning (PBL), 332–333, 416–417
Problem solving, 416
Procedural due process, 199, 215–216
Processing hardware, 435
Professional associations, 471–472, 491–492
Professional development
  continuing program of, 37
  teacher leadership in, 468, 474
Professional dilemmas
  adjusting attitudes of learners, 422
  authentic learning environments in classroom, 464
  communicating with parents of English language learners (ELLs), 128
  homework that requires technology access, 444
  homogeneous versus heterogeneous ability grouping, 332
  inclusion of students with disabilities, 68

keeping up with educational research, 258
knowledge of history and multicultural education, 285
nontraditional families, 78
preparation for standardized tests, 20, 382
religion in teaching about evolution, 194
teachers and politics, 165
teaching morals and values in public schools, 300
Professionalism, 17–29
  in assessment, 378–380
  changes in profession of education, 467–472
  development of teaching profession, 270–274
  knowledge in, 17–18
  most valuable professions, 7
  quality assurance in, 21–24
  reflective approach in, 25–29
  responsibilities in, 24–25
  skills in, 18–19
  standards in, 5, 10, 19, 20, 22–24
  teacher preparation and, 278–282
  of teaching, 272
Professional learning communities, 472–473
Professional workers, 52
Progressive Education Association, 283
  Eight-Year Study (1932–1940), 268, 275
Progressive taxes, 168
Progressivism, 327–329, 334
  critical pedagogy and, 329
  defined, 327–328
  democracy and, 328–329
Project-based activities, technology and, 444–445
Project Head Start, 271
Property taxes, 167–169, 170
  advantages and limitations of, 167
  defined, 167
  determining value of property for, 167–168
  as progressive versus regressive taxes, 168
  taxpayer revolt, 176
Prophetic thinking, 299–301
  defined, 296
  overview of, 301
Proposition 13 (California), 176
Protestants, 69, 237–238
Psychomotor domain, 414–415
Public Law 94-142, Education for All Handicapped Children Act (EAHCA), 198–199, 221–222, 270, 287
Public schools
  importance of, 259
  improving, 9
  long-term survival of, 475–476
  number of, 161
  privatization of, 467
  religious activities in, 188–190, 192, 193
  teaching morals and values in, 300, 319–320
Pupil–teacher ratios, 13–14, 15
Puritans, 243

Quality assurance, 21–24
  accreditation, 21–22
  advanced certification, 24
  licensure, 22–23
  professional standards, 24

Questions
    in authentic assessment, 376–377, 378
    in curriculum development, 394–397

Race and ethnicity, 54–58. *See also*
        Ethnicity; Multicultural perspectives;
        specific racial and ethnic groups
    discrimination based on, 97, 254–255
    ethnicity, defined, 55–58
    ethnocentrism and, 96
    graduation rates by, 91
    inclusion and, 66–67
    poverty and, 53–54
    race, defined, 55
    racism and, 97
    school characteristics and, 82
    of student and teacher populations, 16
Race-conscious assignment, 197
Racial identity, formation of, 97, 98
Racism, 97
RAM (random access memory), 435
Rationalism, 240–241
Rational process, change as, 345
Ratio Studiorum, 238
Realism, 304–306
    educational implications, 304–305
    idealism versus, 305
    philosophers, 305–306
    relationship to idealism and
        pragmatism, 307
    in teacher-centered locus-of-control
        philosophies, 322
Really Simple Syndication (RSS), 445
Real-world learning, 464
Real-world standards, 362
Reconstruction, change as, 345–346
Reconstructionalist role of schools,
        108–109, 334
Recruiting New Teachers, Inc., 7, 39
Recruitment of teachers, 32, 33–34
Reflective approach, 25–29
    analysis of practice in, 26
    journaling in, 26
    portfolios in, 27–29
    Socratic dialogue to enhance reflective
        learning, 304
    systematic observation in, 26
Reformation, 237–238
Regional accreditation, 21
Regional Service Centers, 157
Regressive taxes, 168
Regulatory role, of state boards of
        education, 150
Reinforcement, in behaviorism, 325
Relearning by Design, 389
Reliability, in assessment process, 380
Religion, 68–70. *See also* Church
    church and state, 181, 185–194
    education and, 252, 255, 258, 259
    education associations, 472
    evolution versus intelligent design,
        190–193
    as form of identity, 46
    inclusion and, 66–67
    instruction in German schools, 206
    parochial schools and school choice,
        159–161, 258, 259, 272
    public funds and religious education,
        185–188
    religious activities in public schools,
        188–190, 192, 193
Religion-affiliated schools, 258
Renaissance, 237
Reproduction role of schools, 108
Republic, The (Plato), 234
Research in education

on achievement gaps, 406
    class size, impact of, 145
    critique of relevant sources, 247
    ESL programs in white schools, 56
    gender in performance-based science,
        125
    homework and students with
        disabilities, 269–270
    keeping up with, 258
    learning in groups, 473
    Philosophy for Children, 337
    race in white schools, 82
    social context in computer use, 441
    Socratic dialogue to enhance reflective
        learning, 304
    teacher-guided research, 443
    teachers on rewarding aspects of
        work, 29
    variations in test results, 381
    vouchers, 189
Resegregation, defined, 194
Residence Park Latin Grammar Classical
        Studies Magnet School (Dayton,
        Ohio), 475–476
Resiliency, 100
Resistance theory, of schools, 108
Respect
    from adults, 84
    for cultural differences, 123
Results, equality of, 119–120
Retention in grade, 89–90
Rethinking Schools, 479
Rethinking Schools (journal), 135
Returning teachers, 12
Reverse discrimination, 198
Revisionist historians, 227
Ridgeview Elementary School (Olathe,
        Kansas), 431–432
Right Method of Instruction, The
        (Erasmus), 237
Riverside University High School
        (Milwaukee), 277–278
Roman Catholic Church
    doctrinal authority of, 236
    parochial school system, 259, 272
    Reformation and, 237–238
Roman education, 234
Romanticism, 329
*Rose v. The Council for Better Education
        Inc.*, 170
Routers, 436
Rubrics, 457
    in authentic assessment, 375, 377, 379
    defined, 369
Runaway youth, 86
Rural communities
    agricultural education programs, 273
    schools in, 80–81
Rutherford Institute, 210

Safe schools, 465–466
Salaries, 29–32
    differences in, 29–31
    supplements for teachers in nonpublic
        schools, 187
Salary schedules, 31
Sales taxes, 169
*San Antonio (Texas) Independent School
        District v. Rodriguez*, 168–169
*Santa Fe Independent School District, Pe-
        titioner v. Jane Doe*, 189–190, 191
Scholastic Instructor, 290
Scholasticism, 236
School(s). *See also* Instruction; Organiza-
        tion of education; Private schools;
        Public schools

accountability and, 175–176
    accreditation of, 21–22
    choice of, 112–113, 139–140, 157–161,
        189, 272–273, 467
    competition and, 113, 467
    coordinated service delivery through,
        466
    cultural transmission and, 111–112
    in curriculum management, 405
    in curriculum selection, 400
    democratic, 130–131
    disproportionate placements and,
        67–68
    future of, 465–466, 472–476
    growth of, 266–270
    inclusion and, 66–67
    labeling and, 65–66, 67
    lesbian, gay, bisexual, or transgender
        (LGBT) populations in, 65
    Montessori education, 113, 256, 283
    parent involvement in, 82
    personnel of, 143–147
    politics of, 163
    public views of, 6–9, 287
    purposes of, 109–112
    roles of, 107–109
    in rural communities, 80–81
    students with disabilities and, 66
    in suburban communities, 81
    in urban communities, 81–83
    values in, 112–113
    variations in testing across, 381
    violence in, 75–76, 86–87
School boards
    elections, 147
    leadership of, 148
    politics of, 147, 162
    powers and duties of, 147–148
    in school district organization, 147–149
    students' right to sue, 214
    teacher bargaining rights and, 200,
        205–207
    teacher employment contracts and,
        200, 201–203
School districts
    accountability and, 175–176
    consolidation of, 267
    in curriculum evaluation, 406
    in curriculum management, 404–405
    immunity from liability, 211, 212
    location of, 14, 80–83
    organization of, 147–149, 161–162
    politics of, 161–162
    searching for teaching positions, 36
School Improvement Process (SIP),
        398–399, 423–424
School Improvement Research Series,
        354
School reform, 422–426
    Accelerated Schools, 424, 428
    Coalition of Essential Schools, 324, 425
    defined, 422
    Institute for Learning (IFL), 424
    multiple intelligences approach,
        425–426
    School Improvement Process (SIP),
        398–399, 423–424
    Success for All (SFA), 424
Schools in need of improvement
        (SINOI), 156
School size, 158
Science
    gender in performance-based, 125
    research in, 271
    standards in, 407
Science of Education (Herbart), 242

"Scopes Monkey Trial," 192, 193, 194
Search engines, 442, 443
Secondary schools
    academic freedom for teachers, 208
    *Cardinal Principles of Secondary
        Education*, 275
    college preparation for all students,
        277–278
    distribution of expenditures for, 172
    dropout rates and, 287
    evolution of, 245–246
    high schools, 246, 324, 425
    junior high/middle schools, 246
Section 504, Rehabilitation Act, 198,
    221–222
Segregated schools, 193–197
    honorary diplomas for casualties of
        segregation, 265
    segregation, defined, 193
    "separate but equal" doctrine and,
        194–195
    types of segregation, 193–194
    values and, 112–113
Self-actualization, in existentialism,
    308–309
Self-contained classrooms, 143
Self-efficacy, 100
Self-esteem
    employment of youth and, 95
    respect from adults and, 84
Sensorimotor stage, 286
"Separate but equal" doctrine, 194–195
September 11, 2001, terrorist attacks, 229
Serrano v. Priest, 170
Seven liberal arts, 235–236
Sex discrimination, 64, 197, 198, 218–219
Sex education policy, 239–240
Sexism, 99
Sexual abuse, 86
Sexual harassment, 222
Sexual Harassment Task Force of the
    American Association of University
    Women (AAUW), 87
Sexuality, 87–88
Sexual orientation
    diversity based on, 64–65
    ethnocentrism and, 96
    family life and, 78
    as form of identity, 46
    homophobia and, 65, 75, 86–87
    violence in schools and, 75, 86–87
Sheldon High School (Sacramento), 75
Sheltered instruction, 127–128
Shinto, 312–313
Signing bonuses, 32, 33–34
Single-parent families, 77, 78–79
Site-based decision making (SBDM), 143
Site-based staff developers, 474
Skills, professional, 18–19
Skin color, race and, 55
Slates, 251
Slavery, 57, 242–243, 252, 257
Smart classrooms, 431–432
Smithsonian Institution, 290
Social activism, 129–133
    critical thinking in, 129
    modeling equity in, 129–130
Social Contract (Rousseau), 241
Social development, schools and, 111
Socialization, 96–97
Social justice, as tenet of multicultural
    education, 118, 131–133
Social mobility, 51–52
Social promotion, 89–90
Social stratification, 51–52
Society. *See also* Diversity in society

culture and, 45–51
defined, 45
importance of teachers in, 6
power in, 95–99
Society for the Propagation of the
    Gospel in Foreign Parts, 253
Society of Jesus (Jesuits), 238
Socioeconomic status (SES), 51–54
    class structure, 52–53
    computer access and, 448–450, 451
    defined, 44–45
    dropping out and, 51–54, 91
    as form of identity, 46
    inclusion and, 66–67, 68
    inequities of property tax in funding
        schools and, 168
    poverty and, 53–54
    social stratification, 51–52
    in urban areas, 82–83
    violence and, 94
Sociological perspectives, 41–135. *See
    also* Diversity in society; Multicul-
    tural perspectives
    abuse, 85–86
    challenges of childhood and youth,
        83–95
    community characteristics, 80–83
    dropping out of school, 89–91
    families and, 77–79
    harassment and bullying, 75–76, 86–87
    homelessness, 84–85
    power in society, 95–99
    resiliency, 100
    sexuality, 87–88
    substance use, 92–93
    teenage pregnancy, 88, 219–220
    violence, 75–76, 86–87, 93–95
Socratic method, 233–234, 303, 304
Software, 435–436
    application, 436
    defined, 434
    operating system (OS), 436
Some Thoughts on Education (Locke),
    238
Southern Colonies, U.S., 242–243
Southern Poverty Law Center, 135
Space, in classroom climate, 344
Spartan education, 233
Special education programs
    disproportionate placements in, 67–68
    growth of, 268–270
Spiral curriculum, 396
Spring Garden Middle School
    (St. Joseph, Missouri), 218–219
Staff relationships, 142
    school district, 149
    in schools, 146
    state education system, 151
Standard(s), 357–369. *See also* Assess-
    ment; Standards-based education
    in authentic assessment, 374
    common theme across, 367
    curriculum, 165, 397, 402
    defined, 358
    differences in, 367–368
    discipline-based/content, 362–366,
        375–376
    in future of education, 368–369
    for new teachers, 20, 22–23, 366
    professionalism and, 5, 10, 19, 20,
        22–24
    real world, 362
    for students, 20, 366–367, 403
    for teachers, 5, 10, 19, 20, 22–24,
        366–367
    technology, 433–434

world-class, 361–362
Standard English dialect, 59
Standardized tests, 20, 23, 274, 357–358
Standards-based curriculum, 397
Standards-based education, 358–369
    common theme across standards, 367
    curriculum and, 165, 397, 402
    defined, 358
    differences in standards, 367–368
    differing conceptions of standards,
        361–365
    future of, 368–369
    other uses of standards, 365–367
    traditional education versus, 358–361
State(s)
    board of education, 150–152
    certification and licensure offices,
        481–482
    in curriculum evaluation, 406
    in curriculum management, 403–404
    education and Tenth Amendment,
        184
    employment rights of nontenured
        teachers, 203–204
    equal educational opportunity and,
        170–171
    financing of education and, 169–171,
        172–174
    foundation programs, 173–174
    high-stakes tests and, 20, 310–311,
        357–358, 382–386
    immunity from liability, 211
    legislatures, 152, 153
    liability insurance for school districts,
        212
    licensure requirements, 39
    local control versus federalism in
        schools and, 164–166
    normal schools of, 281
    organization of education in, 149–152
    per-pupil expenditures, 173
    rewards for teachers, 465
    teacher certification, 22
    teacher salaries by, 30–31
    teachers colleges of, 281–282
    teaching job websites, 485–486
    transportation for church school
        students, 185–187
State adoption policy, 404
State aid
    challenges to school finance, 169–170
    defined, 169
    education spending and, 172–174
    gambling and lotteries, 169, 171
    income taxes, 169
    to private religious schools, 185–187
    sales taxes, 169
Stereotypes
    avoiding, 46
    defined, 45
Stewart B. McKinney Homeless
    Assistance Act, 214
Stone High School (Ann Arbor,
    Michigan), 409–410
Storage hardware, 435
Story Telling and Retelling (STaR), 424
Strikes, by teachers, 206–207
Student(s). *See also* Diversity in society;
    Student-centered locus-of-control
    philosophies; Students with
    disabilities
    adjusting attitudes of, 422
    bilingualism of, 60–61
    challenges of childhood and youth,
        83–95
    college preparation for all, 277–278

Student(s) (Continued)
confidential information concerning, 209–210
corporal punishment and, 217–219
dress codes and grooming, 217
enrollment growth of schools and, 266
fees as source of school revenue, 171
grouping of, 332, 417
growth in number of, 14
instructional objectives and, 408–415
marriage and pregnancy among, 88, 219–220
nature of communities and, 80–83
need for more schools, 267
Philosophy for Children, 337
racial and panethnic composition, 16
rights and responsibilities of, 212–223
sex discrimination and, 64, 197, 198, 218–219
standards for, 20, 366–367, 403
student-to-teacher ratios, 13, 15
technology use required of, 448, 450–451
testing focused on achievement of, 465
tracking student learning, 438–439
using of profanity in writing, 409–410
validating voice of, 122–123
voice of, 343
Student-centered locus-of-control philosophies, 327–333, 349
constructivism, 331–333, 334, 416–417
educational implications of, 322
humanism, 329–331, 334
progressivism, 327–329, 334
teacher-centered authority versus, 334
teacher–student control continuum, 339
Students with disabilities
ableism and, 99
disability, defined, 65
dispositions, 419–420
disproportionate placements and, 67–68
equal opportunity and, 198–199
homework and, 269–270
inclusion and, 66–67, 68
labeling and, 65–66
rights of, 198–199, 221–222
schools and, 66
special services for, 188
teaching strategies with, 418–420
violence and, 93–94
Subject-centered curriculum, 396
Substance use, 92–93
Substantive due process, 199, 215, 216–217
Suburban communities, 81
Success for All (SFA), 424
Suicide, 94
Summa Theologica (Aquinas), 236
Summative assessments, 370, 372
Summerhill, 283
Superintendent of schools
politics of, 163
role of, 148
Support staff
central office, 148–149
in schools, 145–146
Sylvan Learning Corporation, 467

Taoism, 312
Task analysis, 411–412
Tax credits, 467
Taxes
income, 169

property, 167–169, 170, 176
sales, 169
Taxonomy of Educational Objectives (Bloom), 285, 412, 413
Teachable moments, 284
Teacher(s), 3–37. See also Diversity in society; Instruction; New teachers; Professional dilemmas; Teacher-centered locus-of-control philosophies; Teacher perspectives; Teaching strategies
academic freedom of, 200, 207–210
accountability of, 175
behavior continuum of, 339, 340
bilingualism of, 15
certification and licensure of, 22–24, 35–36, 201–205
challenges affecting, 29–35
as change agents, 345–346
changing profession of education, 467–472
collaboration among, 468–469, 472–473
colonial, 278–279
conditions of employment, 200, 201–210
curriculum evaluation by, 405
demand by field of study, 14, 15
department heads, 144
development of teaching profession, 270–274
diversity of, 15–17
effective teaching, 284
future of education and, 468–472, 474
as heroes, 3–4
highly qualified teachers, 386–387
high-stakes assessment and, 385
importance to society, 6
individualized education plans (IEPs) and, 66–67, 68, 199
as leaders, 346–350, 468, 474
legal perspectives on education and, 183, 199–212
liabilities of, 210–212
need for more, 267
perspectives on work, 29
philosophy of education, 333–345
politics in education and, 164, 165
preparation of, 278–282
professional development and, 37, 468, 474
professional knowledge of, 17–18
professional responsibilities of, 24–25
professional skills of, 18–19
profile of U.S., 10
public views of, 6–9, 287
quality assurance and, 21–24
racial and panethnic composition of, 16
recruitment incentives, 32, 33–34
reflective approach of, 25–29
remaining in the profession, 10–11, 36–37
returning, 12
rewards by states, 465
rewards of work, 29
rights and responsibilities of, 199–212
salaries and benefits received by, 29–32
shortages of, 14, 15, 81
as social activists, 129–133
standards for, 5, 10, 19, 20, 22–24, 366–367
student-to-teacher ratios, 13, 15
supply versus demand for, 11–17, 32, 81

teaching as profession, 7, 17–29
team leaders, 144
technology use inside classrooms, 439–445
technology use outside classroom, 437–439
of today, 5
voice of, 344
working conditions of, 32–35
Teacher-centered locus-of-control philosophies, 322–327, 349
behaviorism, 324–325, 334
educational implications of, 322
essentialism, 323–324, 334
positivism, 325–327, 334
student-centered authority versus, 334
teacher-student control continuum, 339
Teacher development specialists, 404–405
Teacher-guided research, 443
Teacher perspectives
college preparation for all students, 277–278
on computer labs, 447–448
controversial discussions in classroom, 347–348
on corporal punishment, 218–219
length of school year, 162–163
retention versus social promotion, 89–90
rewarding good grades, 363–364
schools in teaching of tolerance, 116–117
sex education policy, 239–240
signing bonuses for new teachers, 33–34
student bilingualism, 60–61
student use of profanity in writing, 409–410
on survival of public education, 475–476
teaching to the test, 310–311
on work, 29
Teachers on special assignment (TOSAs), 404–405
Teacher unions, 469–471
Teaching materials
in curriculum selection, 400–402, 403–404
evolution of, 247–251
in Montessori schools, 256
Teaching strategies, 415–421
classroom management, 421
direct instruction, 326–327, 415, 416
for English language learners (ELLs), 127–129, 418–420
indirect instruction, 415–417
student grouping, 332, 417
for students with disabilities, 418–420
Teaching Tolerance (journal), 135
Team leaders, 144
Technology, 431–455
computer labs in schools, 447–448
copyright and, 452–453
defined, 433
distance education and, 445–446
equality in access, 444, 446–450
fundamental concepts, 434–436
future of educational use of, 453–454
global perspectives on, 443, 449, 453
Internet and, 436–437, 440
networks, 436
plagiarism and, 451–452
requiring student use of, 448, 450–451
social context in computer use, 441

standards for, 433–434
teacher uses of, 437–446
use inside the classroom, 439–445
use outside the classroom, 437–439
Technology Counts 2006, 457
Teenage pregnancy, 88, 219–220
Telephones, access to, 446–449
Tennessee STAR (Student/Teacher
  Achievement Ratio), 145
Tenth Amendment, U.S. Constitution,
  149–150, 152, 184
Tenure, 201–205
  becoming tenured, 202
  rights of nontenured teachers, 202–205
Testing, 380–386. *See also* Assessment
  curriculum and, 402–403
  for licensure, 23, 35
  objective forced-choice, 326
  standardized tests, 20, 23, 274,
    357–358
  student achievement and, 465
  teaching to the test, 20, 310–311, 382,
    383–384
  variations across nations, 385
  variations across schools, 381
Textbooks, in curriculum selection,
  400–402, 404
Thomas Edison Magnet Middle School
  (Meriden, Connecticut), 89–90
*Tinker v. Des Moines Independent
  Community School District*, 213,
  216, 220
Title I, teachers in religious schools,
  188
Title VI, Civil Rights Act (1964), 197, 198
Title VII, Civil Rights Act (1964), 197–198
Title IX, Education Amendments Act
  (1972), 64, 197, 198, 218–219
Tolerance, teaching of schools in,
  116–117
Torts, 210
Transformational change, 462, 464–467
Transitional bilingual education, 127,
  418, 419
Trends in International Mathematics and
  Science Study (TIMMS), 407
Tungston Learning, 438
Turnaround specialists, 474
Turn It In, 452
Two-parent families, 77, 78

Ubiquitous computing, 453–454
Unfunded mandates, in curriculum
  selection, 398
Unions, teacher, 469–471
United Federation of Teachers (UFT),
  205–206
United Nations, 257
  Children's Fund (UNICEF), 85–86
  Development Fund for Women
    (UNIFEM), 63

Educational, Scientific, and Cultural
    Organization (UNESCO), 385
  World Education Forum, 63
U.S. Agency for International Develop-
    ment (USAID), 385
U.S. Census Bureau, reporting by racial
    and ethnic group, 56
U.S. Constitution
  Eighth Amendment, 217–218
  Eleventh Amendment, 199
  First Amendment, 184–185, 187,
    188–189, 208, 216–217
  Fourteenth Amendment, 170, 185, 194,
    208
  Fourth Amendment, 222
  Nineteenth Amendment, 257
  Tenth Amendment, 149–150, 152, 184
U.S. Department of Defense (DOD), 154
U.S. Department of Education, 141, 154,
    179
  Institute for Education Sciences (IES),
    418
U.S. Department of the Interior, 154
Universal elementary education, 244–245
Universities. *See* Colleges and
    universities
University of California v. Bakke, 197
University of Oregon Clearinghouse on
    Educational Policy, 179
Unschooling, home schooling as, 273
Unz Initiatives, 127
Upper class, 52–53, 91
Upper middle class, 52, 83, 91
Upward Bound, 271
Urban communities, 81–83, 91
Urban Institute, 91

Validity, in assessment process, 379–380
Values, 112–113
  choice of, 112–113
  defined, 80
  global perspectives on, 113
  morals education public schools, 300,
    319–320
  nature of, 112
  rural versus urban, 80–81
  teaching in public schools, 300
  tolerance in schools, 116–117
Veterans, GI Bill and, 270–271
Vicodin, 92–93
Vietnam War, 270–271
Violence, 93–94
  domestic, 85–86
  in schools, 75–76, 86–87
Virtual schools, 446
Vision, of teachers, 348–349
Vocational Education Act (1963), 270, 271
Voice
  in classroom climate, 343–344
  defined, 122, 343
  validating student, 122

Voting rights, 257
Vouchers, 159, 160, 467
  school choice and, 189
  survival of public schools and, 475

Wallace v. Jaffree, 191
Web browsers, 436, 437
WebQuests, 443, 457
WestEd, 179
Whites. *See* European Americans
Wide Area Networks (WANs), 436
William D. Slider Middle School (El
    Paso, Texas), 218–219
William Nashold Elementary School
    (Rockford, Illinois), 60–61
Wolman v. Walter, 186
Women. *See also* Gender
  early education of, 253–254, 255–257
  equal educational opportunity and, 271
  voting rights and, 257
  women's rights, 257
Wood v. Strickland, 213, 214
Workforce readiness, schools and, 110
Working class, 52
  college preparation programs and,
    277–278
  dropping out and, 91
  overrepresentation in nonacademic
    tracks, 110
  postsecondary education and, 94–95
Working conditions, of teachers, 32–35
Working parents
  before- and after-school care for
    children, 79
  children alone and, 78–79
World Bank, 385
World-class standards, 361–362
World Confederation of Organizations of
    the Teaching Profession (WCOTP),
    472
World Declaration on Education for All,
    385
World War II
  discrimination against Asian
    Americans, 254–255
  GI Bill (1944), 270–271
  origins of existentialism in, 309
  testing of servicemen, 283
World Wide Web. *See also* Internet
  censorship and, 209
  classroom tools on, 440
  curriculum libraries, 400
  Web browsers, 436, 437

Yankton High School (South Dakota),
    431
Year-round schools, 158–159

Zelman v. Simmons-Harris, 189
*Zobrest v. Catalina Foothills School
    District*, 186, 187–188

This constitutes a continuation of the copyright page.

PHOTO CREDITS

Page 1: Jim Cummins/Corbis; **p. 2:** Jeff Greenberg/PhotoEdit; **p. 6:** Elizabeth Crews/The Image Works; **p. 9:** Laura Dwight Photography; **p. 11:** Jim Cummins/Corbis; **p. 12:** James Leynse/Corbis Sygma; **p. 13:** Bill Aron/Photo Edit; **p. 16:** Tom Lindfors Photography; **p. 18:** Frank Siteman Photography; **p. 20:** Tom Lindfors Photography; **p. 25:** Bob Daemmrich/PhotoEdit; **p. 41:** Lisette Le Bon/SuperStock; **p. 42:** Ellen B. Senisi/The Image Works; **p. 45:** Bluestone Productions/SuperStock; **p. 49:** Jim Cummins/Corbis; **p. 50:** Dennis MacDonald/PhotoEdit; **p. 59:** Spencer Grant/PhotoEdit; **p. 64:** Li-Hua Lan/The Image Works; **p. 67:** Ariel Skelley/Corbis; **p. 69:** Lon G. Diehl/PhotoEdit; **p. 74:** Kevin Radford/SuperStock; **p. 77:** Michael Newman/PhotoEdit; **p. 80:** Joe Bator/The Stock Market; **p. 84:** Rob Crandall/The Image Works; **p. 87:** Romeo Gacad/AFP/Getty Images; **p. 93:** David Young-Wolff/PhotoEdit; **p. 94:** David Young-Wolff/PhotoEdit; **p. 95:** Will and Deni McIntyre/Corbis; **p. 104:** Laura Dwight Photography; **p. 109:** Elyse Lewn/Getty Images; **p. 110:** Robert Harbison; **p. 112:** Pete Saloutos/Corbis; **p. 115:** Paul Chesley/Getty Images; **p. 118:** Bob Daemmrich/The Image Works; **p. 121:** Frank Siteman Photography; **p. 123:** Frank Siteman Photography; **p. 130:** Laura Dwight Photography; **p. 131:** Kateland Photography; **p. 137:** Bob Daemmrich/The Image Works; **p. 138:** Tom Lindfors Photography; **p. 144:** Jeff Greenberg/Alamy; **p. 148:** Bob Daemmrich/The Image Works; **p. 150:** Matthew McVay/Getty Images; **p. 154:** Najlan Feanny/Stock Boston; **p. 164:** Bob Daemmrich/The Image Works; **p. 171:** Brian Parker/Tom Stack & Associates; **p. 175:** Tom Lindfors Photography; **p. 180:** David Grossman/The Image Works; **p. 184:** North Wind Picture Archives; **p. 187:** Janine Wiedel Photolibrary/Alamy; **p. 190:** Annie Griffiths Belt/Corbis; **p. 201:** Jamea J. Bissell/SuperStock; **p. 207:** Bob Daemmrich/PhotoEdit; **p. 211:** Thinkstock/Jupiter Images; **p. 215:** Robin Nelson/PhotoEdit; **p. 217:** Gabe Palmer/Corbis; **p. 222:** Bob Daemmrich/Stock Boston; **p. 227:** Michael Krasowitz/Getty Images; **p. 228:** Genevieve Naylor/Corbis; **p. 231:** R.W. Jones/Corbis; **p. 233:** Araldo de Luca/Corbis; **p. 237,** both: North Wind Picture Archives; **p. 238:** North Wind Picture Archives; **p. 241,** top: Archivo Iconografico, S.A./Corbis; **p. 241,** bottom: North Wind Picture Archives; **p. 242,** top: Library of Congress; **p. 242,** bottom: Bettmann/Corbis; **p. 244:** Courtesy of the Blackwell Collection, Northern Illinois University; **p. 248:** North Wind Picture Archives; **p. 249:** North Wind Picture Archives; **p. 250:** North Wind Picture Archives; **p. 252:** Corbis; **p. 253:** Library of Congress; **p. 254,** top: North Wind Picture Archives; **p. 254,** bottom: Bonnie Kamin/PhotoEdit; **p. 255:** Corbis; **p. 256:** Courtesy of the Blackwell Collection, Northern Illinois University; **p. 257:** Library of Congress; **p. 264:** Kwame Zikomo/SuperStock; **p. 267:** Brown Brothers; **p. 271:** Culver Pictures; **p. 273,** top: James Marshall/The Image Works; **p. 273,** bottom: Photofusion Picture Library/Alamy; **p. 281:** Minnesota Historical Society/Corbis; **p. 286,** top: Corbis; **p. 286,** bottom: Lyrl Ahern; **p. 291:** Pierre Tremblay/Masterfile; **p. 292:** Charles Gupton/Corbis; **p. 299:** Gabe Palmer/Corbis; **p. 303,** top: Araldo de Luca/Corbis; **p. 303,** bottom: North Wind Picture Archives; **p. 305:** North Wind Picture Archives; **p. 306,** top: Courtesy of the Collections, Milbank Memorial Library; **p. 306,** bottom: Courtesy of the Blackwell Collection, Northern Illinois University; **p. 307:** Courtesy of the Blackwell Collection, Northern Illinois University; **p. 309:** Courtesy of the Collections, Milbank Memorial Library; **p. 312:** North Wind Picture Archives; **p. 314:** Lawrence Migdale/Stock Boston; **p. 318:** SuperStock/PictureQuest/Jupiter Images; **p. 324:** Mark Richards/PhotoEdit; **p. 326:** Thinkstock/SuperStock; **p. 327:** Courtesy of the Blackwell Collection, Northern Illinois University; **p. 329:** Archivo Iconografico, S.A./Corbis; **p. 330:** Laura Dwight Photography; **p. 333:** David Young-Wolff/PhotoEdit; **p. 335:** Richard Hutchings/PhotoEdit; **p. 336:** BananaStock/Super Stock; **p. 343:** Laura Dwight Photography; **p. 346:** Jeff Greenberg/PhotoEdit; **p. 355:** Stockbyte/SuperStock; **p. 358:** Steve Lyne, Rex Indexstock/Stock Connection/PictureQuest/Juniper Images; **p. 361:** Spencer Grant/PhotoEdit; **p. 362:** China Photos/Getty Images; **p. 364:** Charles Gupton/Corbis; **p. 366:** Laura Dwight Photography; **p. 369:** Charles Gupton/Corbis; **p. 370:** Jeff Greenberg/PhotoEdit; **p. 373:** FrankSiteman Photography; **p. 379:** Dennis MacDonald/PhotoEdit; **p. 384:** Olivier Ribardiere/Getty Images; **p. 390:** Tom Stewart/Corbis; **p. 394:** AP Images/Harry Cabluck; **p. 398:** Tom Stewart/Corbis; **p. 408:** Michelle D. Bridwell/PhotoEdit; **p. 410:** Tom Stewart/Corbis; **p. 421:** Jeff Greenberg/PhotoEdit; **p. 431:** photos_alyson/Getty Images; **p. 434:** Frank Siteman Photography; **p. 438:** Frank Siteman Photography; **p. 439:** Frank Siteman Photography; **p. 442:** Digital Vision/Getty Images; **p. 452:** Tom Lindfors Photography; **p. 454:** Frank Siteman Photography; **p. 458:** Mary Kate Denny/PhotoEdit; **p. 462:** Steven Begleiter/IndexStock; **p. 468:** Jeff Greenberg/Index Stock